U2 – A DIARY

By Matt McGee

Exclusive Distributors:
Music Sales Limited,
14/15 Berners Street,
London, W1T 3LJ

Music Sales Corporation,
257 Park Avenue South,
New York, NY 10010, USA

Macmillan Distribution Services,
53 Park West Drive,
Derrimut, Vic 3030,
Australia

Every effort has been made to
trace the copyright holders of the
photographs in this book but one
or two were unreachable. We would
be grateful if the photographers
concerned would contact us.

Printed in Thailand
A catalogue record for this book is
available from the British Library.

Visit Omnibus Press on the web
at www.omnibuspress.com

Contents

Photo credits

- Allied Pix Collection/Historical Society of Dauphin County, Harrisburg, PA: 141
- Amanda Gilligan: 317
- Anastasia Pantsois: 133
- Andre Csillag/Rex Features: 54
- Andrew Briscoe: 203, 204
- Armando Lopez: 307
- Bill Davila/Rex Features: 301
- Bjorn Lampe: 213 (top), 269
- Bleddyn Butcher/Rex Features: 99
- Bob Ferrell: 42
- Brendan Beirne/ Rex Features: 143
- Brian Rasic/Rex Features: 101, 164 (below), 165, 177, 283, 284
- Camilla Morandi/Rex Features: 213 (below)
- Ciara Evans/Mencap: 330
- Colin Tunnah: 71 (below), 86
- Colm O'Hare: 11
- Daniel Boud/Boudist.com: 296, 319, 320
- Dave Griffith: 128, 166
- Dave Lewis/Rex Features: 183
- David Corio/Michael Ochs Archives/Getty Images: 26, 27, 28, 29, 30
- David Klatt: 303
- David Pearson/Rex Features: 224, 236, 290
- Deanna Blazejewski: 245 (below)
- Donal Murphy: 89 (below)
- Donata Wenders, 2000: 217
- Eric Naulaerts: 49, 59 (below), 61 (top), 71 (top), 79, 88, 195 (below), 289 (top)
- Eric Vidal/Rex Features: 50, 275,
- Eva Van Der Valk: 292
- Gerard McNamara: 25
- Gosia Zawada: 197
- Greg Noakes/Retna: 126
- Greg Wigler: 62, 68, 69, 72
- Haydn West/Rex Features: 324
- Herbie Knott/Rex Features: 251
- Huw John/Rex Features: 291
- Ilpo Musto/Rex Features: 87
- Images/Rex Features: 95
- Insight/Visual UK/Rex Features: 267
- ITV/Rex Features: 59 (top), 64
- Jane Stephens: 318
- Jennifer Gokhman: 282
- Jim Rinaldi: 145, 147, 153, 155, 161, 187, 188, 206, 213 (middle), 219, 231, 239, 240
- John Harris: 289 (below)
- Kevin Mazur/Wireimage.com: 172, 242
- Kevin Wisniewski/Rex Features: 232
- Kim Haughton/Rex Features: 312
- LFI: 13, 19, 35, 39, 40, 41, 75, 80 (top), 89 (top), 92, 93, 102, 106, 110, 115, 117, 120, 151, 156, 157, 167, 168, 186, 189, 193, 194, 196, 202, 210, 212, 214, 215, 221 (top and below), 223, 226, 227, 228, 230 (top and below), 235, 238, 245 (top), 252, 254, 255, 256, 258 (top and below), 259, 260, 262, 263, 268, 272, 277, 278 (top and below), 279, 281, 287, 288, 309, 311, 316, 327, 329
- Linda Matlow/Rex Features: 65
- Mark Stevens: 66, 85, 104
- Marylinn Maoine: 270, 271
- Matt McGee: 195 (top), 229, 285
- Michele Coppola: 293
- Mike Laye: 31
- Niall Moran: 313
- Nils Jorgensen/Rex Features: 135
- Oliver Zimmer: 305
- Pascal Jacquemyn: 304
- Pat Maxwell/Rex Features: 179
- Pedro Costa: 58
- Peter Carrette/Rex Features: 77
- Peter Donnelly: 107 (top)
- Peter Stone/Rex Features: 160
- Phil Romans: 295
- Phil Romans: 302
- Philippe Carly/ newwavephotos.com: 61 (below)
- Rex Features: 82, 84, 94, 118, 158, 164 (top), 191, 207
- Rex USA Ltd/Rex Features: 144,
- Richard Johnson: 315
- Richard Young/Rex Features: 73, 116, 171, 175 (top and below), 176, 185, 216, 264
- Rob Wanenchak: 297
- Roman Gokhman: 298, 299, 306
- Sarah DeGrace: 294
- Sean O'Connor: 46
- Serena Campanini/Rex Features: 265
- Sheila Rock/Rex Features: 15
- Sipa Press/Rex Features: 78, 83, 181, 234, 244, 276
- Steve Callaghan/Rex Features: 131
- Steve Gillett/LIVE: 322, 333
- Sue Fell: 136, 208
- Susan Shoshinsky: 43, 51 (below)
- Theo Wargo/Wireimage.com: 246
- Today/Rex Features: 159
- Tom Sheehan: 31
- UrbanImage.tv/Adrian Boot: 12, 38, 44, 45, 47, 48, 51 (top), 52, 53, 57, 113, 122, 139, 140, 149, 154
- UrbanImage.tv/David Pearson: 225
- V Houten/Rex Features: 55
- Vera Anderson/Wireimage.com: 253
- Wanganui Chronicle: 97
- Xavi Balart: 199, 222, 233

Introduction

There's a diary entry in this book that I really love: May 21, 2007. U2 are in Cannes, France. Over the course of 24 hours, the band performs at the Cannes Film Festival and premieres their groundbreaking concert film, *U2 3D*, Bono parties on Kid Rock's yacht, and an Irish government official announces that Bono has joined an international Hunger Task Force.

In so many ways, that explains everything you need to know about U2.

But U2 is much more than that, too. To really understand U2, you have to understand Friendship, Faith, Heart and Soul, Heaven and Hell, Boyhood, Parenthood, Spirit, Death, Ambition, Contradiction, Irony, Ireland, Swagger and Style, Art and Fashion, Europe and America, Africa, Dublin, Punk Rock, Roots Rock, Grunge Rock, Opera, Rhythm & Blues, Elvis, Magic, Myth and Mystery, Dreaming Out Loud, and the decision to Reveal or Conceal. Oh, and some Bible knowledge would also go a long way.

How else to explain U2? Well, if you're inclined to believe in destiny and/or divine intervention, you can see some of both in the U2 story.

Four boys decide to form a band even though they can't play music very well. Luckily, this happens just as punk rock arrives and renders musical chops unnecessary. They live in a country with no rock and roll tradition, where there's no rock scene worth mentioning – nothing to help lift the band out of obscurity. But that's okay, because pirate rock radio begins to flourish at about the same time the band does, and a new rock magazine called *Hot Press* starts to capture the fancy of Ireland's youth.

The young band struggles to find a label willing to sign them internationally, and wouldn't you know it... while every other label has said no, Island Records just happens to be looking to add some rock bands to its stable. And unlike other labels, Island won't demand hit singles and Top 10 albums right from the start. (Good thing, too, since it takes a few years before U2 sniffs the Top Ten.)

As U2 develops, they're one of several hot, upcoming bands that gets tipped for major success. It looks like they'll have to compete for the world's attention with The Police, Talking Heads, The Pretenders, Big Country, The Alarm, The Clash, and others. But none of these bands survive the fashion-conscious '80s, and that clears the path for U2 to become rock royalty, the biggest rock band in the world.

What an odd title for U2 to claim! Here's a band with three members whose idea of fun was reading the Bible on the back of the bus in between shows. Here's a band whose most egregious behavior in 30+ years was when the bassist was arrested for having 19 *grams of marijuana* on him, and when a bad hangover forced him to miss a show four years later. That's a typical week for some rock bands. Sex, drugs, and rock and roll? Hardly. Even the *National Enquirer*, a US tabloid that loves to dig up celebrity dirt, gave up in 1988 and printed an article with this headline: "Surprise! Red-Hot Rockers U2 REALLY Are Squares". U2 must be the least "rock and roll" rock band ever.

Or maybe they're the *most* rock and roll band ever, because rock is all about rebellion, and U2 has been doing that since 1976. They did things on their own terms from the beginning. They rebelled against every rock cliché they encountered. They cared when indifference was cool. They went huge when rock wanted to be small. They openly flaunted ambition, said they expected to reach the top, and didn't stop taking care of business when they got there.

No one – including the band themselves – would be so naïve as to claim U2 have enjoyed a bump-free path from Dublin to the top of the music world. Faith almost destroyed U2 in 1981 after everyone but Adam got wrapped up in prayer meetings and the Shalom group. Some delicate and smart negotiating by manager Paul McGuinness helped U2 survive that period. Later in the 1980s, a dose of hubris led U2 to turn the ultra-successful *Joshua Tree* tour into a Hollywood film. Fans loved it, but a lot of US rock critics thought it was vanity run amok. In the mid-1990s, U2 misjudged the zeitgeist, and the irony of announcing a world tour in the lingerie department of a K-Mart store was lost on many fans. That, combined with an underwhelming opening night concert in Las Vegas that some media called a "flop", and an album that the band believes was never finished, produced an era that the band doesn't look back on fondly to this day.

But in each of those cases, and others, U2 has shown remarkable survival instincts. They have an uncanny ability to recover, regroup, and return even stronger and more popular than before. After three decades together, you'd think that a rock band – like a marriage – would settle into a routine. But U2 has avoided that trap so far.

U2 might be the last great rock band. We'll probably never see another band come along and do what U2 has done, and certainly not *the same way* U2 did it. The music industry is a different landscape today than in the 1980s. Bands aren't given years of financial support and allowed to grow an audience slowly. It's all about hit singles and album sales; one dud and you're done. If U2 were starting today, they wouldn't last past *October*.

In 1980, Bono told *Rolling Stone* magazine that he believed U2 would someday have a place in rock history alongside The Beatles, The Rolling Stones, and The Who. At the end of 2007, with 16 albums to their credit, 22 Grammys won, more than 30 years together, close to 200 million albums sold, countless lives touched, and at least one party on a yacht off the coast of France on the same day as an appointment to a hunger task force, we can say with certainty that Bono was right.

1950-1976

Though U2 is rightly known as an Irish band, Paul Hewson and Larry Mullen are the only two members who are natives of Ireland. Dave Evans and Adam Clayton are both born in England, but move to Dublin early in their childhood.

The four boys grow up separately, though for a brief period Dave and Adam attend the same school and see each other occasionally with their parents outside of school. While all four grow up enjoying music, only Dave and Larry show an early interest in playing. Adam comes to the bass guitar as a teenager, while Paul is more interested in pursuits such as chess, painting, and theater.

The signature event of this period occurs in 1974 when Paul's mother, Iris Rankin, dies just four days after the death of her father. The loss of his mom has a dramatic impact on Paul. Typical teenage pursuits are overshadowed by thoughts on life and death, and a developing interest in matters of faith. Faith, in fact, is one of the defining issues of Paul's childhood – thanks to his parents' bold marriage in 1950. And that's where we begin....

1950

August 19
Bob Hewson and Iris Rankin are married at St. John the Baptist Church of Ireland in Drumcondra, Dublin. Many view the wedding of a Catholic (Bob) and Protestant (Iris) as shameful, and Bob further defies the Catholic Church by being married in a Protestant church.

Bono on growing up in a religiously mixed family
"Both my mother and my father didn't take religion seriously, they saw the absurdity of the fuss made over their union, though my mother used to bring us to chapel on Sundays and my father would wait outside. I have to accept that one of the things I picked up from my father and my mother was the sense that religion often gets in the way of God."

1951

June 16
Paul McGuinness is born in Rinteln, West Germany, to Philip and Sheila McGuinness.

1960

March 13
Adam is born at his grandparent's house in Chinnor in Oxfordshire, England, to Brian and Jo Clayton. He has an older sister, Sarah Jane. A brother, Sebastian, will arrive later.

May 10
Paul David Hewson is born at the Rotunda Hospital in Dublin to Bob and Iris Hewson. He has a brother, Norman, who is seven years old.

June
The Hewson family moves from Dublin's south side to a home in the Ballymun area on the north side.

1961

March 23
Alison Stewart is born in Dublin to Terry and Joy Stewart.

August 8
David Evans is born in Barking Maternity Hospital, East London, to Garvin and Gwenda Evans. He has a brother, Dick, who is two years old. A sister, Gillian, will be born later.

September
Paul McGuinness begins attending Clongowes Wood College in County Kildare, Ireland, in the fall.

October 31
Larry Mullen, Jr., is born in Dublin, to Larry Sr. and Maureen Mullen. He has a sister, Cecilia, who is four years old. Another sister, Mary, is born in 1964, but dies in 1973.

1962

Early in the year, the Evans family moves from England to Dublin.

1963

Paul Hewson befriends Derek

Bono's Angry Childhood
"I can remember my first day in school. I was introduced to this guy, James Mahon, who, at age four, had the ambition of being a nuclear physicist, and one of the guys bit his ear. And I took that kid's head and banged it off the iron railing. It's terrible, but that's the sort of thing I remember. I remember the trees outside the back of the house where we lived, and them tearing those trees down to build an awful development. I remember real anger."

Rowen, a boy who lives across the street.

1964

The Clayton family relocates to Kenya where Adam's father works as an airline pilot for East African Airways.

1965

The Clayton family moves from Kenya to Dublin. Adam briefly attends St. Andrews Church of Ireland School, where Dave Evans is also a pupil. The Claytons and Evans get to know each other socially, but Adam and Dave are a year apart in school and don't forge a close friendship.

1967–68

Paul Hewson and Derek spend some of their free time together painting – a pastime that will continue throughout their friendship.

1968

Dave's mom buys him a small, toy-like Spanish guitar.

Paul McGuinness begins studying philosophy and psychology at Trinity College in Dublin. He makes friends with a music fan named Bill Graham.

1971

Having taken piano lessons at the College of Music for a year unsuccessfully, Larry tries the drums. "The [piano] teacher was a real nice lady, but one day she said, 'Larry, you're not going to make it.' I was delighted, because I had wanted to say the same thing to her." While leaving his last piano lesson, Larry hears someone drumming and tells his mom that's what he wants to do. Larry's parents, having spent enough money on piano lessons, tell Larry he'll have to pay his own way to learn the drums. He washes cars and cuts lawns and makes enough to become a student in a drum class taught by Joe Bonnie, a well-

Larry on why he wasn't the best drum student

"I wasn't very good at learning or technique; I didn't practice much, because I was far more interested in doing my own thing. I wanted to play along with records like Bowie and the Stones."

known Irish drummer.

Around this time, Dave gets his first real guitar, another gift from his mother, purchased for one pound at a swap meet. Dave plays it regularly during his free time at home.

Thanks to lessons from his father, Paul Hewson is an accomplished chess player who plays in major tournaments around this time.

The Young Chess Star… or not?

There are conflicting reports about Bono's talents as a chess player. Bono: "He [Bono's dad] taught me chess. That's something I've never admitted to because it was always so uncool to be a chess player. It's the most un-rock & roll thing you could do, so I never ever talked about it, but that was actually my obsession before rock & roll. When I was a kid, I played in adult tournaments and played internationally when I was ten or eleven. Things like that were important moments for me."

Bob Hewson: "I think that's been blown up. The press got it and blew it up. I taught him how to play chess…. He did join a chess club and he won a

couple of medals. He beat the chairman of the club and in order to maintain the chairman's reputation he more or less exaggerated Paul's prowess."

Bono: "Chess wasn't very good in the pursuit of women, so that went! Very quickly! As soon as I realized that that didn't ingratiate you in any way. That went about 14 [years old]!"

June 3
Paul Hewson watches the pop band Middle Of The Road perform their hit 'Chirpy Chirpy Cheep Cheep' on *Top of the Pops*. Ten years later, he tells *NME*'s Gavin Martin about the impact it had: "I must have been about 11 at the time, and I thought, *Wow!* This is what pop music is all about. You just sing like that and you get paid for it."

Fall
Paul Hewson reluctantly enters St. Patrick's Secondary School and has an unhappy year there. He's reportedly kicked out after throwing a bag filled with dog manure at a teacher.

1972

Dave begins taking piano lessons, but gives it up after two years.

September
Mount Temple School is established in Dublin. It's the first comprehensive, co-educational, multi-denominational school in the city. One of its students this first year is a 12-year-old Paul Hewson.

1973

Around this time, Paul Hewson and Derek Rowen meet Fionan Hanvey, a flashy dresser who also lives on Cedarwood Road and is a big music fan.

Dave enters Mount Temple in the fall and takes guitar lessons while at school.

Larry's first band, 1975-76

"I was 14 at the time and they asked me to get [my hair] cut. I did, but it wasn't quite short enough according to the Brother in charge. So I used an expletive, threw the drumsticks down, walked out and never went back."

1974

Fall

While a student at St. Columba's College boarding school in Dublin, Adam begins to show an interest in music. He buys an acoustic guitar in Dublin and tries learning some songs, even going so far as to take classical guitar lessons. John Leslie, a friend who also owns a guitar, tells Adam they could form a band if Adam had a bass guitar. Adam asks his parents to buy him one, and they do. "I'll play till I'm bigger than the Beatles!" he promises them. Also this year, Adam sees his first concert – a Rory Gallagher show at the Carlton Cinema in Dublin.

Larry enters Mount Temple School. Paul Hewson is interested in acting and the theater and creates the first student theater group at Mount Temple around this time. Larry becomes friends with a fellow student named Ann Acheson.

September 12

Paul Hewson's mother, Iris, dies just four days after her father, Alexander, died. She had collapsed and suffered a brain hemorrhage at the funeral.

At only 14 years old, Paul feels the loss tremendously, explaining in a 1987 interview with *Rolling Stone* magazine: "When it all went wrong, when my mother died, I felt a real resentment, because I had never got a chance to feel that unconditional love a mother has for a child. There was a feeling of that house pulled down on top of me, because after the death of my mother that house was no longer a home – it was just a house. That's what 'I Will Follow' is about."

After his mother's death, Paul struggles in school. He is unhappy and will later admit to thoughts of suicide. He has occasional violent outbursts at Mount Temple, but gets help from the school's guidance counselor, Jack Heaslip. Paul begins to ask questions about God and faith, life and death, trying to make sense of the world around him.

1975–76

Larry joins the Artane Boys Band, but his stint lasts only three days. The band demands Larry cut his long hair, which he does once. But when they tell him it isn't short enough, Larry quits the band.

Larry earns a spot in the Post Office Workers' Union Band. He remains with the group for two years.

Also around this time, Dave sees his first rock concert: a Horslips gig in the seaside town of Skerries. Horslips has a bassist Dave will get to know very well in the future: Barry Devlin.

1976

In Dublin, Paul McGuinness takes on the management of an Irish folk-rock band called Spud. Ireland doesn't have much of a "rock scene" and bands tend to move to London to progress their careers. Taste from Cork (featuring blues guitarist Rory Gallagher) leaves in 1970 and Thin Lizzy from Dublin (featuring Phil Lynott) leaves in 1971. The punkish Boomtown Rats, also from Dublin, would follow this year.

The four future members of U2 finally find themselves together this autumn at Mount Temple school, where creativity – whether it be in art, acting, or music – is much encouraged. Larry posts the famous note on a bulletin board at school this year, a drummer looking for guitarists to start a band. The group forms and quickly become friends. But their friendship is eclipsed, at least in the beginning, by a unique group formed by Paul Hewson and other kids in the Cedarwood Road area of northern Dublin – a group that would soon become the young band's first real supporters.

It's around this time, possibly earlier, that Paul Hewson and his friends in the Cedarwood Road area form a clique they call Lypton Village. They often meet at Paul's house after school. The group renames all its members; Paul Hewson becomes "Steinhegvanhuysenolegbangbang bangbang", then (thankfully) "Bonavox of O'Connell Street" – the name and location of a Dublin hearing aid store. It's later shortened to "Bonavox", then "Bono Vox". He's not too fond of the name – not until he realises it's almost Latin for "good voice". It is eventually shortened to "Bono". Bono renames Derek Rowen "Guggi", and the third founder of Lypton Village, Fionan Hanvey, becomes "Gavin Friday".

What was Lypton Village?
Bono explains.
"We used to put on arts installations, when we were sixteen, seventeen, with manic drills and stepladders. See, the alcohol level in our neighbourhood was so high, people going to the pubs a lot, and we were young, arrogant, and probably very annoying kids, but we didn't wanna go that route. The pub looked like a trapdoor to somewhere very predictable, so we wouldn't drink. We used to watch Monty Python. We invented our own language, gave each other names, and we'd dress differently. We would put on these performance art things, and in the end, we formed two bands, the Virgin Prunes and U2."

Other members of Lypton Village are "Strongman" (Trevor Rowen), "Day-vid" (David Watson), "Pod" (Anthony Murphy), "Bad Dog" (Reggie Manuel), "Clivejive", and "Guckpants Delaney". (When Feedback forms, Dave Evans, Adam Clayton, and Larry Mullen aren't formal members of Lypton Village, but each gets an unofficial nickname. The group calls Dave "Inchicore", which Bono later changes to "The Edge". Larry is "Jamjar" and Adam is "Sparky" and/or "Mrs. Burns". Even Paul McGuinness will eventually get a nickname: "The Goose").

Summer
Adam spends a month living with a friend in Pakistan. He starts smoking hash and discovers the music of Bob Marley.

September
With their son having struggled at St. Columba's, the Claytons decide to send Adam to Mount Temple. Having just spent a carefree month in Pakistan, Adam has little interest in school. He walks around wearing a long Afghan coat, mirrored sunglasses, carries a coffee flask into classes, and hangs out with a group of cigarette and dope smokers.

Also this month, Larry Mullen, Jr. posts a note on the bulletin board at Mount Temple seeking

Adam remembers his arrival at Mount Temple, September

"By the time I came to Mount Temple, the spirit of rebellion was upon me, and maybe I thought the best form of defense was attack: go in there with attitude and people wouldn't mess with you."

other musicians to start a band. Larry mentions in the note that he has "money wasted on a drum kit", and asks if there are "others out there who, perhaps, had done the same on guitars?"

September 25
Seven students respond to the note, meeting today at Larry's house. The entire group includes Larry, Dave and Dick Evans, Adam, Paul Hewson, Peter Martin and Ivan McCormick. Larry sets up his drums in the doorway between the family kitchen and a back porch. Adam brings his bass guitar – an Ibanez copy of a Gibson EB-3. Dick and Dave bring a homemade, yellow electric guitar that they've built themselves. Peter is there mostly as a bystander, and soon decides he wants to manage the group. Ivan, the youngest at 13-years-old, arrives with his Stratocaster-copy electric guitar – the best instrument of the bunch.

1976

U2 recalls its first day together, September 25

Larry: "During the course of the afternoon I saw that some people could play. The Edge could play. Adam just looked great. Big bushy hair, long kaftan coat, bass guitar and amp. He talked like he could play, used all the right words, like 'gig'. I thought, this guy must know how to play. Then Bono arrived, and he meant to play the guitar, but he couldn't play very well, so he started to sing. He couldn't do that either. But he was such a charismatic character that he was in the band anyway, as soon as he arrived. I was in charge for the first five minutes, but as soon as Bono got there, I was out of a job."

After discussing rock and roll and their plans to start a band, the boys agree it's time to start playing. They crowd the kitchen and start to jam, eventually trying the Rolling Stones' 'Brown Sugar' and 'Satisfaction'.

U2 recalls its first day together

Bono: "Larry is in this tiny kitchen, and he's got his drum kit set up. And there's a few other boys. There's Dave Evans – a kinda brainy-looking kid – who's fifteen. And his brother Dick – even brainier-looking – who's built his own guitar. He's a rocket scientist – a card-carrying genius.

"Larry starts playing the kit – it's an amazing sound, just hit the cymbal. Edge hit a guitar chord which I'd never heard on electric guitar. I mean, it is the open road. Kids started coming from all around the place – all girls. They know that Larry lives there. They're already screaming; they're already climbing up the door. He was completely used to this, we discover, and he's taking the hose to them already. Literally, the garden hose."

Adam: "We didn't have much equipment so we pooled what we had. There was Larry's first drum kit, which was kinda a toy thing, Edge and his brother Dick had made an electric guitar out of a piece of wood, and I had a bass and I think a speaker. And I had an amp. We plugged everything into the amp, we got an old microphone from a tape recorder and just made an awful noise. It was a random banging and clatter and strumming that bore no resemblance to anything else you've ever heard. But it was fun!"

Edge: "It wasn't a particularly auspicious beginning. There was a lot of talk, a lot of people playing songs they knew very badly trying to impress one another, trying to figure out if we had similar musical tastes…. I remember thinking that I liked everybody, which was the most important thing. Just a sense that actually these are cool people."

Before calling it quits for the day, the group agrees to get together again for another rehearsal. Donald Moxham and Albert Bradshaw, teachers at Mount Temple, take interest in the band and arrange for them to use a rehearsal room at the school to continue practicing. Away from school, the band practices at Adam's grandmother's house in Malahide. Dave continues to use Ivan's guitar during practices, at least until Ivan is weeded out of the lineup. The fledgling group decides to call itself "Feedback."

Around this time, Paul begins to date a fellow student at Mount Temple named Alison Stewart.

Autumn-Winter

Mount Temple School, Dublin. Feedback's first gig is at a talent contest in the school's cafeteria, quite possibly in November. They play as a four-piece without Dick, since he's not a Mount Temple student. Their nervous, brief set includes Peter Frampton's 'Show Me the Way', a Beach Boys cover, and the Bay City Roller's 'Bye Bye Baby'. The students love it, and yell for more. Unsure what to play, Feedback launches into a repeat of 'Bye Bye Baby'.

Bono remembers Feedback's first gig

"When I heard that D chord, I got some kick. It was like starting up a motorbike. And the audience went wild! That was a very special concert, that was one of the best concerts of our lives. I'll tell you, it was like four blind kids blustering away and there was the evidence of just a little light in the corner and we started to work towards that."

For Bono, Adam, and Dave, the 10-minute performance convinces them that being in a band is what they want to do. Larry, the youngest of the group, isn't ready to say the same thing.

The band reportedly plays a couple more small shows at Mount Temple before the end of 1976.

1977

Feedback continue to practice and develop their own songs, but also work on new covers including the Eagles' 'Witchy Woman', Neil Young's 'Heart Of Gold', and 'Nights In White Satin' by the Moody Blues. The latter proves difficult when Adam has trouble mastering an instrumental bass riff in the middle of the song. Meanwhile, punk music reaches Dublin and the lack of virtuosity appeals immediately to Feedback; by year's end, the band will be including a few punk covers in its shows.

Feedback take big steps this year, playing their first gigs for paying audiences. But it's important to note that Feedback is still a very loose group with varying levels of interest and commitment. Larry, Edge, and his brother Dick even play a few gigs this year with the Drifting Cowboys, a country band that tours across Ireland. Edge later recalls Larry falling asleep on the drums at a New Year's Eve gig with the Drifting Cowboys. One of the Cowboys suggests Edge and Larry become country artists: "There's no money in rock'n'roll, but if you get together a collection of country versions in your band I can set you up with as many shows as you can play."

Fortunately, Edge and Larry ignore that advice.

In school, Paul and Alison occasionally attend meetings of a group called the Christian Movement. Led by a Religious Education teacher named Sophie Shirley, the meetings offer students a chance to study the Bible and pray together.

April 7
Seeking their first real gig, Adam meets up with Colm O'Hare, a student at St. Fintan's High School in Dublin. O'Hare is organizing a concert the following week. After discussing Feedback's planned setlist, O'Hare agrees to have them open the show, but makes no guarantee of payment.

Edge: "Adam was our first manager"
"There was this undeniable belief that Adam instilled in us. We only wanted to play music, we didn't think about it in terms of making money or making records, but Adam always did."

April 11
St. Fintan's School, Dublin. This is Feedback's first show in front of a paying audience. They're the first act on the bill, playing before Rat Salad and the headlining Arthur Phybbes Band. Some friends from Mount Temple show up to support them, including Bono's girlfriend Alison and members of Lypton Village.

On the suggestion of friends, the band agree they need to spice up their line-up with female backup singers. Bono recruits two girls to join the band: Stella McCormick – sister of Ivan, who had shown up for the original meeting at Larry's house and practiced with Feedback

"It was all rather dull..." April 11
Orla Dunne remembers her brief time as part of Feedback.

"It was definitely the first proper gig we'd done and we were all pretty nervous. We practiced in Adam's house out in Malahide the week before the gig. But it was all rather dull as far as I was concerned. I'd been classically trained and I thought I'd go deaf with all the noise from the guitars and amplifiers!"

LIVE ROCK CONCERT

at

ST Fintans Assembly Hall

on

EASTER MONDAY 11th April

Commencing 8 pm till 12 Midnight

No admission guaranteed after 9.30 pm
Please come early

Adm 50p

in its earliest days – and Orla Dunne.

The group rehearse together at Adam's house because his parents are away. Bono starts writing his first song during rehearsals, and calls it 'What's Going On?' After rehearsing together for about a week, the girls suggest to Edge that he replace Bono as the singer.

Feedback only has time for a brief sound check, and it shows when they start performing. The 40-minute show is filled with mishaps. Stella's and Orla's microphones break down, leading Bono to hold his mic toward them so the crowd can hear Orla's flute solo during 'Nights In White Satin'. Other songs performed include 'Johnny B. Goode', 'Show Me The Way', and 'Peaceful Easy Feeling'.

U2 vs. Rat Salad

Jack Dublin, bassist with Rat Salad, remembers the show.

"There was a bit of a row between ourselves and Feedback over 'Johnny B. Goode'. We had planned to do it in our set but we heard them rehearsing it during soundcheck and we had discussions about who would do it. We felt a bit sorry for them and promised we wouldn't do it. But we did it anyway!"

As a whole, the concert is a success. The student organisers turn a small profit and are able to pay all three bands.

But for Feedback, the gig leads to changes. They agree that the experiment with Stella and Orla as back-up singers didn't work, and they return to a five-piece. They also decide Feedback is an inappropriate, unprofessional name. Adam suggests "The Hype", and all agree that's what they'll begin calling themselves.

Spring-Summer

The Hype continues to rehearse and play occasional gigs around Dublin, including one at a club on O'Connell Street called Slack Alice's. There's also a gig at a

Edge: "Not knowing how to play was not a problem" Spring-Summer

> "I suppose a watershed moment would have been seeing The Jam on *Top Of The Pops* and realizing that not knowing how to play was not a problem, in that music was more about energy and trying to say something and not necessarily about musicianship."

church hall in Raheny where their setlist includes a cover of Thin Lizzy's 'Don't Believe A Word'.

Meanwhile, punk rock starts to infiltrate Ireland. One of the Hype's first tastes of punk comes from the Irish band, the Radiators From Space. They also listen to singles by the Sex Pistols, Buzzcocks, and others. The Jam appears twice on *Top Of The Pops* – May 19th and June 21st – and make a big impression on The Hype.

Adam spends a couple months working at a fish market in London, forcing the band to take a break until he returns. Bono takes a job at a shoe store.

June 26

Edge catches a Rory Gallagher gig at the Mountain Dew Festival at Macroom Castle near Cork. At the festival, a new magazine being given out for free captures his attention: the first issue of *Hot Press*.

September

Bono enters University College, Dublin. Two weeks later the college discovers that he failed Irish (Gaelic) during his Leaving Certificate exams. They say it was a mistake to admit him to UCD, and send him back to Mount Temple

to complete the requirements for college entrance.

Back at Mount Temple, Bono shocks the school – staff and students – when he shows up for classes one day in full punk regalia: skin-tight, purple drainpipe pants, suit jacket, Cuban heels, and closely cropped hair. And to top it off, he wears a chain that hangs from an earring to a safety pin in his mouth. It's all a ruse, though: the "safety pin" is actually a clip-on, and the new look is just a one-day stunt designed (successfully!) to get a reaction.

October 7

Marine Hotel, Sutton. The Hype opens for a band called Albatross. Their set is still made up mostly of covers, but with a more punk influence now: 'Anarchy In The UK' (Sex Pistols), 'Gimme Gimme Shock Treatment' (The Ramones), and '2-4-6-8 Motorway' (Tom Robinson) all get played tonight. Gavin Friday joins them on stage to sing backup on a cover of David Bowie's 'Suffragette City'. They also perform 'What's Going On?', the country rock song Bono began writing earlier in the year.

After the gig, a presumably inebriated girl crashes through a window separating the bar and pool. Hotel management shuts down the bar and orders everyone to go home.

October 15

Suttonians Rugby Football Club, Sutton.

October 21

The Hype are spectators as The Clash brings their Get Out Of Control Tour to Trinity College in Dublin. Bono later recalls being awestruck at the energy and aggression of The Clash's performance, calling it "one of those nights that just turns your world upside down".

Bono recalls The Clash's influence on the young U2, 2003

"With U2, I always felt like we had a lot going

Above: Mick Jones, Paul Simonon, Joe Strummer and Topper Headon – The Clash.

Bono on The Clash, 2007

"Can't remember the set list, can't remember much about the music, to be honest. I just know that everything changed that night, and I'm sure it was not just for me.

"As I sat in the box room and stared out the window the next day, it was very clear. The world is more malleable than you think; reality is what you can get away with."

wrong, but ultimately, we had something special. Lots of bands around us were much better-looking, better players, better songwriters – they had everything. But we had the "it" – whatever "it" might be – and we built around that. That idea comes from the Clash – that you could come out of the audience, get up on stage, grab the microphone, and if you had something to say, then you had a valid reason for being there. That idea changed my life: It's the reason that U2 exists today.

"The Clash got terrible criticism for Sandinista! [1980]. But were it not for that record, I would have never heard about Nicaragua or ended up going there and meeting with Daniel Ortega, the leader of the revolution, and Ernesto Cardenal, a minister of culture, or ended up writing 'Bullet the Blue Sky', because my mind was blown by the experience. Those were the kinds of doors that the Clash – and Joe, in particular – opened up for me, and there were worlds behind them."

Winter, 1977-1978
The Hype play occasional gigs at Mount Temple. They continue working on original songs, including a rock tune called 'Street Missions' that Edge and Adam develop, and another track that Bono works on called 'The Fool'.

They also travel to Mullingar, Ireland, for a support slot in a small bar, where the locals are said to object to hearing them play so many covers (or perhaps to hearing them played so poorly).

December 17
Presbyterian Church, Howth.

1978

This is a monumental year for the band, a year in which the unstructured five-piece "The Hype" becomes the four-piece "U2" we know today. They win a talent contest, make their first TV appearances, get their first *Hot Press* coverage, have their first sessions in a recording studio, and find a manager. Adam is kicked out of school early in the year, giving him more time to focus on the band. But Larry remains unsure about committing full-time to U2; that changes late in the year when his mom dies in a car accident.

Early in the year, Bono learns that an RTE TV producer is coming to Mount Temple to see teacher Albert Bradshaw about having the school choir appear on the *Youngline* program. Bono asks to audition for the show, too, and Bradshaw brings the producer to a rehearsal expecting to hear The Hype play a couple

original songs. Instead, the band does two Ramones covers and the astonished producer asks if those are really original songs. "Yeah," Bono says. The Hype gets invited on the show.

Meanwhile, as the charismatic Christianity movement spreads through Ireland, Bono begins meeting with like minded friends to read the Bible and pray together. Edge accepts Bono's invitation to join the "Monday Night Group" – a small group of six or seven that meets at The Willows, a house Guggi and his brother are renting. Bono also invites Larry, who isn't interested at first, and Adam, who reacts negatively (and doesn't even want Edge getting involved). Thus are sown the seeds of an internal conflict that will weigh heavily on the band for several years.

January 14
Today's issue of *NME* includes a fake classified ad in which "Brian", a manager, "seeks the whereabouts of The Hype after amazing Howth gig". But there's really no "Brian" involved; Adam places the fake ad to drum up interest in the band.

February 10
Mount Temple School, Dublin. The Hype performs in the old school building at Mount Temple. Frankie Corpse and the Undertakers – which includes original Feedback member Ivan McCormick, his brother Neil, and future Cactus World News guitarist Frank Kearns in its line-up – provides support. The Hype's set includes original songs such as 'The Fool' and 'Street Missions'.

February/March
The Hype makes its first TV appearance, recording 'The Fool' on the RTE programme *Our Times*. Their performance is taped around the last week of February or first week of March, but doesn't air until later in the month after the band has changed its name to "U2".

March
Adam is kicked out of Mount Temple after running naked through the school's campus. Principal J.T. Medlycott gives Adam

the following reference letter:

"Adam Clayton, born 13.3.60, was a pupil of this school from September 1976 to March 1978. He has worked well when stimulated. He has shown considerable initiative and organizing ability, especially in relation to his music 'group', which has had considerable success. He is a pleasant, cheerful person, was popular and took part in the social life of the school. Because of his late arrival, he has not held a position of responsibility in the school, but I have found him to be a generally mature person. I believe him to be honest, truthful and reliable, and am sure that in a suitable position he will be both conscientious and committed."

With Adam out of school, he's able to spend much more time managing the band's affairs, and he continues to make valuable contacts with other musicians, industry insiders and media. He has cards printed saying, "Phone Adam Clayton to book U2".

One of his contacts is Steve Averill (stage name: Steve Rapid) of the band The Radiators from Space. Averill is an ad agency designer by day and very informed about marketing. Like Adam and Edge, Averill lives in Malahide, and the three have several discussions about the band. Averill declines when offered the chance to manage

The Hype, but he does help them find a new name. Averill gives Adam ten suggestions, and after careful review and discussion, the band chooses the last name on the list: U2.

Bono and Edge are soon seen wearing "U2" pins, and when asked what it means by friends, Bono says, "Whatever you want it to."

"It is not the most rock 'n' roll of names…"
Steve Averill recounts how he helped The Hype become U2.
"After several discussions with Adam on numerous music-related topics we talked about coming up with some potential names. We felt that The Hype was inappropriate. So Adam would say that the direction they were thinking was like this particular band or that particular band. He then said at one meeting that he would like a name like XTC. I thought about that and my suggestion was U2. As it had a graphic simplicity and strength and would be easily identifiable in a worldwide

"I just didn't fit in…"
Dick Evans explains that he left the band because it was getting too serious for him.

"They became very intense about it, and I wasn't, it was almost a generation gap type of gulf between us. I just didn't fit in, the attitude more than anything. Edge, for instance, really wanted a career… whereas I always thought of myself as going to college, getting a degree then doing something else. I was more interested in science.

   "I never at any stage thought, 'Yeah, I want to be in a band and that's all,' whereas everyone else was starting to feel that way."

context. It also comes from the frequently used expression 'you too', and it was the name of the Gary Powers spy plane as well as turning up in a lot of other places. For instance, my tape deck was a Sony U2."

March 16
Project Arts Centre, Dublin. The Hype – who have not yet publicly changed their name – are the headline act at a midnight show celebrating St. Patrick's Day.

March 17
Unknown venue, Limerick. The Hype – minus Dick Evans – enters the Limerick Civic Week Pop '78 competition, a two-day talent contest sponsored by the *Evening Press* and Harp Lager. Larry had read about the contest in the *Evening Press* and suggested they should enter. On arriving in Limerick, the band changes its name on the entry form from The Hype to U2.

Some 36 acts are entered. U2 play three songs in the preliminaries, which are held at several locations around Limerick. One of the songs is sung in Irish (possibly an early version of 'An Cat Dubh'). Their performance is strong enough to earn a spot in tomorrow's finals.

March 18
Savoy Cinema, Limerick. In the finals of the Limerick Civic Week Pop '78 competition, U2 compete against seven other acts. The finals take place in front of a live audience that includes Adam's father and a few of the band's Lypton Village and school friends. The band's set includes 'Street Missions' and 'Life On a Distant Planet', plus a track called 'The TV Song', so named because it was influenced by the band Television.

U2 wins the contest and receives a trophy, £500, and a demo session with CBS Ireland. Bono tells a local reporter how important it was for U2 to win: "This means we can solve our money problems in a big

"We were all dumbfounded when they won…" March 18

Fran Kennedy, guitarist with The Doves – one of the bands that U2 beat at the Limerick Civic Week talent contest – doesn't remember any of the songs U2 played at the finals, but does recall a few other things about the four kids from Dublin.

"To be honest, we were all dumbfounded when they won, because truly, they were awful! I remember Bono as being quite loud and brash. He wore a double-breasted jacket with brass buttons and epaulettes. We honestly thought that their [U2's] sound was absolutely awful! They were very basic musicians, not really in control of their instruments. They were little more than beginners at that time."

way, particularly with regard to equipment. Now we hope to be able to buy a van." In reality, the money is spent on the band's first formal photo shoot and some new clothes.

In congratulating the band afterward, CBS Ireland Marketing Manager Jackie Hayden expresses the hope that "maybe someday U2 might achieve the level of success enjoyed by the great Limerick band Reform."

Kennedy says that, while most of the bands competing hung out together, U2 kept to themselves away from the competition.

"U2 Malahide, as they were called, didn't mix with any of us. They were a little younger than all the others. I don't know why. I think it may be that up to then, they had not met any working musicians. I remember chatting with one of the Village group about U2, [and] we both agreed that they wouldn't be in the top three. They did seem to get sort of special treatment from the judges. Two of the judges, one from Hot Press magazine and a guy from RTE Radio chatted to U2 at the interval. They didn't speak to any of the others."

March 20
Presbyterian Church, Howth. The Hype plays a farewell gig with Dick Evans. At the end of their short set, as the band covers The Ramones' 'Glad To See You Go', Dick exits the stage and leaves the band. Bono announces that The Hype is no more, but that U2 will be back on stage later.

Adam and Edge remain on stage to play with the next band, the Virgin Prunes. It's the first gig ever for this band made up of members of Lypton Village. After that, Adam plays bass with Steve Averill's new band, the Modern Heirs. The night concludes with U2, as a four-piece band, performing a set of all original songs, including one of their newest creations, 'Shadows And Tall Trees'. At one point in U2's set, a fight breaks out on the floor, prompting Bono to leave the stage and join in ejecting the offenders from the building.

Late March
U2 perform 'Street Missions' on the RTE TV programme *Youngline*, an afternoon show aimed at school-aged music fans.

Also around this time, The Hype's earlier performance of 'The Fool' airs on RTE's *Our Times* program. As the band's performance is played back, three commentators

– Niall Stokes, Dave Heffernan, and Shay Healy – provide commentary. The band has changed its name since the performance, and the three commentators correctly refer to them as U2.

March 30
U2 gets its first mention in *Hot Press*, an influential Dublin-based rock magazine that will continue to support the band throughout its career. The brief mention reads: "Newly-formed Dublin new wave band U-2 scored a blow for rock'n'roll when they won the top prize of 500 pounds in a group contest co-sponsored by the *Evening Press* and Harp Lager held recently during the Civic Week in Limerick. That's what you call getting the breaks...."

April
Adam's persistent phone calls to Bill Graham's home finally pay off. The *Hot Press* writer agrees to meet U2 on a Saturday afternoon at the Green Dolphin bar in Dublin. The band invites him to their upcoming recording session.

U2 record their first demo session at Keystone Studios, a result of the March victory at the Limerick Civic Week talent contest. The session ends when Larry's dad arrives to demand his son return home because he has school the next day.

Graham writes the first feature about U2 in any media. The article titled "Yep! It's U2" appears in *Hot Press* on April 28. Of the demo, Graham writes, "It wasn't the happiest of sessions, the band's inexperience showing up on what was a rush job." But the band impresses him and the article is favourable. Perhaps more importantly, Graham shares his expert knowledge of the music business with U2, and tells them they need to find a manager. He contacts an acquaintance, Paul McGuinness, and suggests he see U2 in person.

The band, meanwhile, ask Jackie Hayden if he's willing to manage the band; he's not. Adam makes a few calls to McGuinness, and they eventually agree to meet, possibly late this month or in May. Adam brings a cassette for McGuinness to hear, but he doesn't have a tape player. They play the cassette on a telephone answering machine and McGuinness agrees to see them play live. Edge's dad, Garvin, has a meeting with McGuinness to make sure he's trustworthy and capable.

Around this time, Jackie Hayden offers U2 a standard CBS Ireland recording contract, which promises the band two or three singles while giving CBS world rights for potentially five years. After asking trusted friends and music associates, the band politely decline Hayden's offer, saying it's the wrong deal at the wrong time. Hayden isn't turned off by U2's decision; on the contrary, he's impressed by their sensible reasoning and begins to mention the band in his reports to CBS' London office.

Bill Graham explains why he suggested Paul McGuinness should manage U2, April

"[Paul] did talk about getting involved with a band from the start, rather than somebody who might be in their late 20's or 30's and who might have lost some of their enthusiasm.... Paul at least did have previous experience in media, in terms of the film business. He wasn't afraid of the media.... He wasn't somebody who was going to be intimidated by some A&R manager or some record company."

April 11
McGonagle's, Dublin, opening for Revolver.

Spring/Summer
Around this time, Bono and some of Lypton Village meet a man named Dennis Sheedy at a McDonald's restaurant on Grafton Street in Dublin. There's a ruckus in the restaurant when a patron objects to seeing Sheedy read his Bible. When the commotion settles, Bono and friends approach Sheedy and they talk about God and faith. Sheedy tells them about a gathering of Christians called Shalom, which is led by a charismatic preacher named Christopher Rowe. Like the Monday Night Group that Bono and Edge are in, Shalom shares a core belief in the surrender of the ego – the self – to God.

Bono recalls meeting Shalom
"We were doing street theater in Dublin, and we met some people who were madder than us. They were a kind of inner-city group living life like it was the first century A.D.

"They were expectant of signs and wonders; lived a kind of early-church religion. It was a commune. People who had cash shared it. They were passionate, and they were funny, and they seemed to have no material desires. Their teaching of the Scriptures reminded me of those people whom I'd heard as a youngster with Guggi. I realize now, looking back, that it was just insatiable intellectual curiosity."

Bono, Edge, and their Lypton Village friends explore Shalom, making new friends and associations outside their own fellowship. The Monday Night Group continues to grow, eventually moving out of the Willows house and meeting at Mount Temple.

May 10
Bono turns 18 and, according to a story he's told repeatedly, it's on this day that he writes 'Out Of Control'. But there's a problem with the story: the song begins with the line "Monday morning / 18 years of dawning", but May 10, 1978, is actually a Wednesday. Poetic license....

May 25
Project Arts Centre, Dublin, opening for The Gamblers. Paul McGuinness sees U2 perform for the first time, with The Gamblers, a band managed by McGuinness' younger sister. The young U2 impress McGuinness. "Edge's playing was quite unique," McGuinness says later. "And Bono, he just looked the audience in the eyes as if to say, 'I dare you to look back'. And all I had ever seen before were performers who looked out over the audience at some imaginary spot. There was something special about them."

After seeing the show, McGuinness invites the band to talk next door at the Granary bar. Everyone gets along well, and the band wants him to manage them, but McGuinness isn't quite ready to commit. It takes a few more meetings over the next couple months before McGuinness eventually agrees.

The Importance of Paul McGuinness
Edge: "We went after him in a very determined way. When he came on board it was very important. We didn't want to be a cult group, we wanted to be a big group and we thought that's where our talents lay, that's what we, as a group of guys together, that's what we had the potential to be. We needed Paul McGuinness to help us do that."

Bono: "More than anyone in my life, he is a person who believed in me and gave me the confidence to realize my potential as an artist. He has an enormous and sharp intellect, and mine was very unschooled and haphazard. On many occasions, he would sit me down and say: 'You have what it takes. You must have more confidence in yourself and continue to dig deeper. And don't be upset or surprised when you pull something out from the depth that's uncomfortable.'"

June
Mount Temple, Dublin, with Frankie Corpse and the Undertakers. U2 performs in the school parking lot on an Open Day shortly before the end of the school year. The band view it as their farewell to Mount Temple.

With all four members now out of school, U2 continue to rehearse and work on original songs during the summer. Many practice sessions take place in a shed behind the Edge's house. "They were all quite serious about music," Edge's mom Gwenda recalls later. "They would come here every morning at about ten and really work very hard. I used to make them lunch. I was amazed that they took it so seriously."

Edge's parents give him a year to devote to U2, telling him he'll have to enroll in college in fall, 1979, if things aren't working out with the band. Bono's dad also gives Bono a year to live at home. Larry joins the group after a day's work as a messenger for Seiscom Delta. He's the only one with a regular job at this point, and his late arrivals to rehearsals and sound checks are a problem. At one point, Larry gets hurt on the job and misses more time with U2. The band goes through a couple different stand-in drummers, and even has Guggi fill-in for Larry during photo shoots. Eric Briggs, a drummer who occasionally helps the band as a roadie, replaces Larry during a few rehearsals and gigs. The band

and Paul McGuinness question Larry's commitment and give brief thought to the idea of finding a new drummer.

Eric Briggs talks about replacing Larry ... or not
"There was never any real chance that U2 were going to kick Larry out of the band, it was really just a ploy to shake him out of his apathy."

June 11
Adam plans to see The Boomtown Rats at Dublin's Olympia Theatre, but instead trades his tickets for the phone number of Rats' guitarist Gerry Cott. Adam calls Cott and asks for advice about advancing U2's career. The conversation becomes a real morale booster for U2.

June 22
Paul McGuinness and Adam Clayton see Horslips and Thin Lizzy perform at Wembley Arena in London. Backstage, Horslips' bassist Barry Devlin accepts Paul's invitation to produce some demos for U2 later in the year.

July 31
McGonagle's, Dublin, opening for Modern Heirs and Revolver. Paul McGuinness refuses to allow U2 to take the stage before the crowd arrives, and requests to switch slots with Modern Heirs. McGonagle's manager won't let U2 go on second, but agrees to a later start time. Revolver remains in the prime time slot, with Modern Heirs going on last.

August
McGonagle's, Dublin, opening for Revolver and Advertising. Exact date is unknown. Bill Graham reviews the show in *Hot Press*: "Revolver recovered in time but they had better not stand still, U-2 are ready to pass everyone out. Oh, and both bands slew last week's British import, Advertising. Guaranteed Irish, guaranteed quality."

Liberty Hall, Dublin. U2 do a charity gig for the Contraception Action Campaign. Exact date is unknown.

August 16
On a family trip to New York City, Edge buys a used Gibson Explorer guitar for $248.40. Though he's concerned that the glam-rock look of the Explorer may not go over well in Dublin, the guitar becomes a signature part of U2's look and sound. "I didn't go with the intention of buying a Gibson Explorer," Edge recalls later. "A Rickenbacker six-string was what I was after. But when I picked up the Explorer it felt really, really good. I wasn't expecting it, but the guitar seemed to talk to me. There are some songs in this, I said to myself."

September
Crofton Airport Hotel, Dublin. Only six people attend. Exact date is unknown.

Also this month, Larry fills in as drummer for The Modulators, Ivan McCormick's current band, during a show at the Howth Community Centre.

September 9
Top Hat Ballroom, Dun Laoghaire, opening for the Stranglers. The crowd of 2,500 people is U2's biggest to date, but it's mostly made up of hostile Stranglers fans who throw lighted cigarettes on the stage while U2 perform. That's not the only challenge: lacking a dressing room, U2 have to dress and prepare behind the stage, and they don't get a soundcheck. Bono is furious at how the Stranglers treat U2, and confronts them about it in their dressing room. He swipes a bottle of wine from backstage and U2 drink it during the Stranglers' soundcheck. U2 survive the night and manage to win a few new fans. And they're paid £50.

September 18
Project Arts Centre, Dublin. U2 and their friends Virgin Prunes share the bill.

September 23

Arcadia Ballroom, Cork, opening for D.C. Nien. U2 are one of a handful of bands on the bill. They meet Cork native Joe O'Herlihy, who owns a local sound-hire company, at this show. Though U2 is only a supporting act, they're impressed by the attention O'Herlihy gives them and his efforts to make them sound good – a rare thing for supporting acts. O'Herlihy, though, is somewhat less impressed with U2.

Joe O'Herlihy meets U2 for the first time

"They barely knew how to turn on their own gear they were so inexperienced but we looked after them pretty well and they got a good sound. Things like that are noticed in this business…"

O'Herlihy works with U2 on a for-hire basis on and off over the next two years, sometimes renting gear for their use, and sometimes being their sound man. He doesn't join the tour crew on a full-time basis until spring, 1980.

September 24

Bono sees The Ramones play at the State Cinema in Dublin with his friend Regine Moylett (who would later become U2's public relations agent). Bono also meets local rock personality BP Fallon, who's touring with The Ramones, for the first time.

October

Magnet Bar, Dublin. U2 are the headline act at a benefit concert for Rock Against Sexism. Exact date is unknown.

October 20

Edge sees The Jam perform at the Top Hat Ballroom in Dun Laoghaire.

November 1

U2 records its second demo session at Keystone Studios. Barry Devlin oversees this session. They record 'Street Missions', 'The Dream Is

Bono on the impact of seeing The Ramones, September 24

"When I was standing in the State Cinema in Dublin listening to Joey sing and realizing that there was nothing else [that] mattered to him, pretty soon nothing else mattered to me. If they remind me of anything now, it's that singular idea."

Over', 'Shadows and Tall Trees' and 'The Fool'.

Above: Tommy, Johnny, Joey and Dee Dee – The Ramones.

November 16

Around this date, Larry's mother, Maureen, is killed in a car crash in Dublin. Her death affects Larry as deeply as the death of Bono's

mother affected Bono some four years earlier. Looking for comfort, Larry draws even closer to Bono, and starts to attend Bible study meetings with Bono and Edge. Larry quits his day job and throws all his energy into the band.

Larry: "Bono was the link"

"There was a connection there. There was an understanding. He understood a little of what I felt. I was younger than him. I didn't have any brothers. My father was out of whack anyway, so Bono was the link. He said, 'Look, I understand a bit what you're going through. Maybe I can help you.' And he did. Through thick and thin he's always been there for me. Always."

December 11

Stardust, Dublin, opening for the Greedy Bastards – a superstar band made up of members of Thin Lizzy and the Sex Pistols. Unable to soundcheck before the show, U2 slowly takes the stage one at a time, each member joining in a lengthy intro to 'Out Of Control' so the sound man has time to set levels for each instrument.

Late December

Around Christmas, Adam attends a Christmas party hosted by Charles O'Connor of Horslips. He's there to meet people, learn about the music business, and give out copies of U2's recent demo tape. One of the people he meets and gives a tape to is BP Fallon.

BP Fallon: "The singer was crap"

"On the demo, the singer was crap, the rhythm section was lumpy, but the guitarist had the magic with traces of Tom Verlaine's shimmer and – although he'd never heard of him – the fluid tones of Barry Melton from Country Joe & the Fish."

1979

U2's momentum continues throughout most of 1979. They write several new songs and spend more time in the studio. They sign a contract with CBS Ireland for local releases, but still lack an international contract with a major label. They play a series of now legendary summer concerts at the Dandelion Market in Dublin – U2's equivalent of The Beatles' shows at The Cavern. They gain support from a couple London music papers this year, which helps attract the attention of various record labels. But late in the year, a near-disastrous two-week tour of London clubs fails to land U2 a record contract, leaving them perilously close to breaking up.

Looking to improve his stage performance, Bono takes lessons this year from actors Mannix Flynn and Conal Kearney, a former student of Marcel Marceau. "[Flynn] had great energy, and his eyes were full of mischief and laughter," Bono recalls later. "He was talking about the theatre and how to use the space of being on a stage, how to move your body and make people believe you when you were pretending." The exact date(s) of these lessons is unknown.

Early this year (or possibly in late 1978), Edge meets Aislinn O'Sullivan, his future wife, at a Buzzcocks concert in Dublin.

Also this year, Bono takes a part-time job as a gas station attendant. The idea is that he'll use quiet time to write new songs. But the plan goes awry when an international oil crisis leads to long lines at the gas pump, forcing Bono to quit his job.

U2's Day Jobs, 1978-79

Here's how the band earned a day's wage before music started to fill their wallets.
Adam: Delivery van driver (handling fine china)
Bono: Gas station attendant, shoe store clerk
Larry: Messenger clerk (in 1978)
Edge: unknown

January 3
McGonagle's, Dublin. U2's growing reputation leads to a sellout show.

February
U2 come up short in the *Hot Press* poll's "Most Promising" category, losing to The Bogey Boys.

Also this month, U2 records new original songs at Eamon Andrews' studio in Dublin, a small facility typically used for radio voice work. Songs include 'Twilight', 'Alone In The Light', 'Another Time, Another Place', 'The Magic Carpet' (also known as 'Life On A Distant Planet') and 'I Realize'.

February-March
Bill Graham makes three visits to The Willows, a rented house in Dublin where Guggi and others from Lypton Village live. Graham is planning a lengthy interview about the Village, U2, and the Virgin Prunes, and wants to discuss each in separate interview sessions. In the first of the interviews, which is focused on Lypton Village, Bono blurts out, "One other thing you should know about the Village – we're all Christians." Graham leaves that revelation out of his *Hot Press* feature, which appears in the March 8 edition and is focused almost exclusively on U2.

U2 and The Virgin Prunes
Although the two bands could hardly be further apart in their approach to music, the connections between U2 and the Virgin Prunes run deep.

Lypton Village is the first and most obvious connection. The bands were friends, and their line-ups look almost like a family tree. Dick Evans played in both bands. Anthony Murphy (aka "Pod") was one of U2's roadies before he joined the Prunes. Peter Rowen, the boy who will appear on U2's first single and first and third albums, is the little brother of Derek (aka "Guggi") and Trevor (aka "Strongman").

The relationship also had a musical angle. In U2's early days, the Prunes were their default opening act; U2's early concert posters even had the Virgin Prunes name printed in small type at the bottom. Bono and Gavin Friday occasionally wrote different songs with the same title; 'Boy-Girl' and 'Exit' are two examples. They even wrote a song together called 'Sad'.

Membership in the two bands was quite fluid. Edge, Larry, and Adam would support the Prunes as needed. Guggi occasionally filled in for Larry at photo shoots and other duties when Larry's job or other commitments kept him away from U2.

February 3
McGonagle's, Dublin (afternoon). Trinity College, Dublin (evening). In an attempt to allow younger people to hear them play, U2 play twice on the same day. The first show is an all-ages afternoon gig at McGonagle's, which is followed by an evening show at Trinity College.

February 10
McGonagle's, Dublin.

February 17/18
Project Arts Centre, Dublin. U2 play the Dark Space Festival, a creation

of the Centre's director, Jim Sheridan – the same Jim Sheridan who will later work with U2 in the future as a major film director.

The Mekons are the headline act, and U2 is relegated to the 3:30 a.m. slot, playing after bands such as Protex and Rudi. Still, it's an important gig: U2 hopes to gain exposure in the UK thanks to the presence of famed DJ John Peel as well as a writer from *NME*.

U2's set includes originals such as 'Another Time, Another Place', 'Shadows And Tall Trees', 'Cartoon World', and 'Street Missions', along with a cover of the Ramones' 'Glad to See You Go'. But the show fails to push U2 along in cracking the UK; the *NME* article doesn't mention the band at all, and Peel is unimpressed.

March

Around this time, Paul McGuinness travels to London to pitch U2 to record labels there. He meets with Chas de Whalley of CBS Records and plays him the band's recent demos from Eamon Andrews' studio. De Whalley isn't an immediate convert, but says he'll try to see U2 perform in Dublin soon.

Chas de Whalley on hearing U2

"An awful lot of the bands I'd hear were very similar, very poor. The level of musicianship and imagination of most of the groups was not very good at all. And I don't remember that the early U2 tapes I'd heard stood out from that morass at all. What impressed me was the story that Paul McGuinness was telling, and obviously the fact that they'd won a CBS Ireland talent competition added to that story. I just felt there was a bit of a vibe. He also showed me some photos, some pop-art black and white photos, and it just felt that there was something

Remembering Dandelion Market, May

Hugo McGuinness, an early friend and photographer of many of the band's early promotional shots, remembers one of the Dandelion Market gigs.

"The band were playing in Dandelion Market on a Saturday afternoon and the place was always under one foot of water. Suddenly the PA went 'bang' and everything fused. Then this guy walked in screaming and shouting at Eric, their roadie. He lifted up a cable from an amp, ran a lighter under it, stuck it in his mouth, and bit the cable, exposing the wires. He plugged those directly into the amp and everything worked again. 'Who was that?' I said to Bono. 'That's Paul and he's our manager,' says Bono. 'Now you know why every band should have one.'"

happening with them, more than there was great music being made. And I think that's what I responded to."

March 8

U2 is profiled in *Hot Press* magazine. Bill Graham's article is full of praise, not to mention an eerily prophetic look at the band's future: "Somehow, I don't believe U-2's future will be among the more predictable. They have the originality and vivacity to make their especial contribution to Irish rock. But that lack of derivativeness means they could have translation problems in Britain.... Strangely, they may be more accessible to American ears...."

April

Not satisfied with Paul McGuinness' efforts to pitch U2 outside Ireland, Bono, girlfriend Ali, and Andrew Whiteway – a

friend who's become a trusted advisor – go to London to chat up record executives and music writers. Bono is broke, so Ali pays for the trip. It's Bono's first time in London. Bono impresses two of the writers they visit – Dave McCullough of *Sounds* magazine and Chris Westwood of *Record Mirror*.

May

Dandelion Market, Dublin. U2 play the first of six well received and increasingly popular shows at the Dandelion Market car park in the heart of Dublin. The shows draw healthy crowds, mostly teenagers who cannot see the band in clubs and bars. The exact dates of the six shows are the subject of debate, but they're spread out over the rest of spring and into summer. (Some sources suggest the first gig is May 5; others May 12.) Edge gets sick and misses one show, forcing Bono to try his hand at lead guitar and vocals.

Chas de Whalley on seeing U2 live, June 7-28

"Bono was phenomenal. The band was ordinary. They weren't great. But Bono was something very special. He reminded me of a young Ian McKellen, the actor. He [Bono] moved at three-quarters tempo, so he was measured the whole time, and he's throwing shapes… and I just thought, *Whooo, a bit of stagecraft*. I just remember him being absolutely riveting. And I said to Howard, this kid is either gonna be big and burn out quick, or he's gonna be the new David Bowie. He's got that kind of *thing*, which people are only born with, and never learn."

The first show is almost a disaster: early in their set, Adam's and Edge's sound dies. Rather than stop the show, Bono invites two members of the audience on stage and teaches them to hum the bass and guitar parts, which they do while Larry continues to drum and Bono sings.

As the summer progresses and the shows improve, Paul McGuinness realizes that performing live is the best way for U2 to build its fan base.

May 10
On Bono's 19th birthday, a few of his Lypton Village friends wallpaper Bono's car and break all its lights as a birthday surprise.

Also today, Alexander Sinclair of RSO Records in London writes Bono a brief letter:
Mr. P. Hewson,
10th May, 1979
Dear Mr. Hewson,
Thank you for submitting your tape of "U2" to RSO, but we feel it is not suitable for us at present. We wish you luck with your future career.
Alexander Sinclair

May 12
Trinity College, Dublin.

Summer
Paul McGuinness finds himself in the middle of a local controversy when the Dublin magazine, *Heat*, publishes an article under the headline "McGuinness (Isn't) Good For U2". The magazine alleges that McGuinness committed fraud in order to get U2 to replace another local band in the support slot for a big Dublin concert by Joe Jackson. *Heat* suggests that McGuinness made a fraudulent phone call pretending to be a London record executive who wanted to scout U2.

Infuriated, McGuinness takes action against the magazine, demanding withdrawal of all copies of the magazine. A benefit concert is planned in Dublin to raise money for *Heat* to defend itself. An all-star local band called The Defenders is formed just for the occasion, with help coming from none other than Steve Averill, U2's friend and consultant who also helped found *Heat*.

Though the concert was considered a success, McGuinness' legal action eventually leads to the closure of the magazine. He and U2 manage to stay on good terms with Averill.

June 7-14-21-28
McGonagle's, Dublin. U2 plays four consecutive Thursday night shows, promoting the series as "Christmas in June – The Jingle Balls". The stage is adorned with Santa Claus hats and other Christmas decorations. To help promote the shows, Edge shows up for a local radio interview in a Santa Claus suit.

Chas de Whalley and Howard Thompson of CBS Records come to Dublin to scout one of the McGonagle's shows.

De Whalley returns to London and suggests to his bosses that CBS sign U2 to an Ireland-only contract. The deal is signed quickly. It gives U2 freedom to negotiate additional contracts outside Ireland, and gives CBS time to decide how much of a commitment they want to make to U2. With a contract in place, plans are quickly made for de Whalley to produce a recording session at Windmill Lane Studios in Dublin.

Tom Nolan of EMI Records also shows up for one of the McGonagle's gigs, and stays an extra day to see U2 play at Dandelion Market. Nolan is thrilled with the shows, and drafts a contract in his hotel room with Paul McGuinness. Nolan returns to London to have his superiors approve the contract. "I went to Dublin to see them and decided there and then that this was the best new band around and must be signed immediately. Sadly I was alone in this opinion, and to my and the band's intense disappointment the deal was unceremoniously booted out."

July
U2 are mentioned briefly in a *Sounds* magazine article discussing various demo tapes the magazine has received. Writer Gary Bushell calls U2 "another great undiscovered Irish band" and alerts readers to a lengthier Dave McCullough feature coming later in the year.

July 11
Community Center, Howth. U2 perform for about 50 young kids. Chas de Whalley of CBS comes to see the show and discuss the upcoming recording session. "Because it was a community center," de Whalley recalls, "there were grannies sitting at tables around the edges, and little kids running about, as well as a gaggle of embarrassed-looking proto-punks

U2 remembers the Dandelion Market gigs, August 4

Bono: "It all started gelling. You could feel the energy, you knew something was going on. That was our Beatles-in-the-Cavern moment."

Larry: "People talk about these gigs as being legendary. They were. The Dandelion was where we really hit our stride."

down at the front of the stage. It was a very odd show, but the band was much better than the first time I saw them."

August 4

Dandelion Market, Dublin. U2 plays the last of its six free Saturday afternoon shows. The series of gigs establishes U2 as the band to beat in Dublin, and gives them new confidence and a passionate audience.

The shows also help get U2 more press support, both in print and on-the-air. RTE radio and Radio Dublin, a pirate radio station, help push the band along. In the August 31 issue of *Hot Press* magazine, Declan Lynch raves about the gig: "... obstacles mean nothing to these boys now, or so it seems. They're making everything into momentum, turning it into gravy, and they'll probably be in your town this week. U-2 have frankly gigged their butts off to be as tight and effective as their excellent set continues to indicate. No matter what band you play with south of the border, U-2 can piddle all over you, lucrative publishing deals or not."

After the show, the band heads to Windmill Lane Studios to begin work with producer Chas de Whalley. The studio is booked overnight, and the session lasts into tomorrow morning. U2 struggle to record three new tracks: 'Out Of Control', 'Boy-Girl', and 'Stories for Boys'. It's tense in the studio because de Whalley and Bono don't connect, and de Whalley is also unhappy with Larry and Adam's work.

Chas de Whalley in the studio with U2

"First, I have to presage everything by saying I was no producer. I really lacked the diplomatic skills and people skills and technical skills to do it. But yes, we had a difficult situation with 'Out Of Control'.

Three-quarters of the way through the song, there's a section where all the band drops out, and there's just drums before the band comes back in stages.

He [Larry] would go out of time, and because he went out of time, none of the band came back in properly. The track would fall apart. So I just kept saying, *'This isn't good enough, we have to do it again.'* I remember Bono saying, *'You can't be right. Larry's had lessons with the best drummer in Ireland, and he can't be playing it wrong!'* And I was going, *'He is!'*"

August 5

U2 and de Whalley are back in the studio to mix the three songs they recorded a night ago. De Whalley leaves Dublin feeling that the demos are a failure, and knows that his bosses in London won't like them. Paul McGuinness doesn't like them, either, and brings in Boomtown Rats soundman Robbie McGrath to do another mix of the songs prior to release. The studio work brings U2 no closer to a record deal.

Soon after, U2 appear nightly on Dave Fanning's RTE radio show – a different band member each night – where they play the three tracks and allow listeners to choose which one will be the A-side of their first single. Fanning's audience chooses 'Out Of Control'.

The single will be released on CBS in Ireland only. While CBS works on a promotional plan, U2 hires Steve Averill and photographer Hugo McGuinness to do the sleeve. Following Bono's belief that U2 represents the "primary colors" of rock and roll, everyone agrees to use black, white, and red on the first single's sleeve – a color scheme U2 will use quite often throughout its career.

August 11

Youth Club, Howth, with The Modulators. U2's set includes 'Cartoon World', 'The Magic Carpet', 'Stories For Boys', and 'Silver Lining'.

August 21

Baggot Inn, Dublin, with The Blades. Bono and Adam pick up writer Dave McCullough and photographer Paul Slattery early today at Dublin airport. They're planning a feature article in *Sounds* magazine; Paul McGuinness has agreed to split McCullough's and Slattery's costs with the magazine. They shoot promotional pictures with Slattery before the gig.

Dave McCullough reviews U2

In the first article about U2 outside Ireland, Dave McCullough reviews U2's Baggot Inn gig.

"Their set is quite brilliant. It's an often disarming experience traveling out of London and seeing relatively unknown bands taking on the prima donnas of the Hammersmith Odeon, Marquee and Nashville and wiping the proverbial floor with them (re: Tours and Undertones in the past) and this was yet another such occasion. U2 are total, solid music,

How 'U2-3' Earned U2 Another Chance, October
Chas de Whalley explains why CBS UK decided to take another look at U2.

"They put ['U2-3'] out in Ireland and it went gangbusters. So, quite clearly there was a demand for this group and there was something happening. And it was on the strength of that that Muff said he'd come over with me to see them again."

naturally intended for the head and for the feet, inculcating meaning and innovation, expressing enough power in communication to knock the unsuspecting listener on his back.
"Guitarist David Edge is the most flamboyant player I've seen since Stuart Adamson of the Skids (a major influence, as they say) creating a sizeable, unique niche sound that spreads across U2's music with scintillating effect, joining together with Adam Clayton's bass and Larry Mullin's (sic) drums to form what the band constantly seek, namely a wide sound and a big impression.
"Front man Bono is a new r'n'r performer. He takes the genre's tricks of the trade and tries them out on his audience, shifting their opinions and attitudes. In this sense U2 are unashamedly didactic; they attack their audience and hope maybe to leave

them at the end of the night feeling shifted or moved in their attitudes."

Legend has it that EMI and CBS records have scouts at this show, and that the EMI reps leave to watch another act on TV, but this actually happens at another Baggot Inn show in October.

August 29
Around this time, Dave McCullough gives U2 a plug in a *Sounds* Playlist article, where the magazine's writers list the bands and songs they're listening to currently. McCullough includes 'Out Of Control' and 'Shadows And Tall Trees'.

September
Making good on a promise to his mom and dad a year ago that he would resume school after a year devoted to U2, Edge briefly enrolls in the Natural Sciences course at the College of Technology, Bolton Street, in Dublin. His heart and mind, though, are devoted to U2 at this point, with the band just about to release its first single. Edge doesn't bother buying any textbooks, instead borrowing from classmates when he needs to read them.

Sometime this month, U2 plays two consecutive shows at the Project Arts Centre, opening up for Patrick Fitzgerald.

U2's first single, *U2-3*, is issued late this month on CBS Records in Ireland. With three tracks from U2's recording session with Chas de Whalley, the record is a first in Irish marketing, as CBS Ireland issues a 12-inch version that Jackie Hayden hand-numbers from 1 to 1,000, creating instant collectors' items. The 1,000 numbered copies sell out almost immediately. A 7-inch single is also released, and spends two weeks on the Irish singles chart, reaching number 19. A small quantity is imported into the UK, helping U2 get noticed by both fans and music critics.

Around this time, Bono appears on the Pat Kenny show on RTE radio during a programme about new Irish music. They play about 30 seconds of 'Out Of Control'.

September 15
Dave McCullough's feature on U2, titled "Coming Up For Eire", appears in *Sounds* magazine.

October
Baggot Inn, Dublin. Exact date is unknown. With 'U2-3' dominating the Irish charts, London record companies are again interested in seeing the band live – particularly Chas de Whalley and Muff Winwood from CBS UK, who are very familiar with U2's success on CBS Ireland.

CBS isn't alone; other labels also have scouts at the show. But the two reps from EMI, sent over by Tom Nolan, leave the gig early to watch The Specials on *The Old Grey Whistle Test*. De Whalley and Winwood show the most interest, taking Bono and Paul McGuinness out after the show to discuss a deal. Winwood offers U2 a singles contract, but with interest in the band growing, McGuinness wants more.

Chas de Whalley: "Paul wanted an albums deal"
"Paul wanted an albums deal, a deal like the Boomtown Rats had gotten a couple years earlier from Phonogram, which would have been able to fund the band to move into a house outside London and use that as a base to try to crack the UK. That might've been like a £300,000 deal, and Muff just wasn't that convinced about them."

Winwood also tells McGuinness he thinks Larry should be replaced. Ultimately, the sides are unable to agree on a contract.

Also this month, U2 perform 'Life On A Distant Planet' (also known as 'The Magic Carpet') on the RTE TV programme *Aspects of Rock*. The exact date of the performance is unknown.

October 5
Opera House, Cork. RTE TV airs the show live, the first full-length U2 gig on television.

October 26

U2 appear on the cover of *Hot Press* for the first time. The feature article, "Boys in Control", sees the magazine's editor Niall Stokes interviewing the whole band. Already facing questions about being too serious, Edge emphasizes that the band has a sense of humor: "It's comic strip. We might lack a bit of humour but we have enough humour in ourselves. I think that'll develop in the music. We're aware that we're not going to change the world or anything. But if we can reach *some* of the people...."

Bono and Edge go to the *Hot Press* office today to pick up a copy, and the sight of seeing himself on the cover has Bono feeling confident. "Looking good," he says. "We look like a rock band."

Also around this time, Dave McCullough gives U2 yet another plug in *Sounds*, listing the 'U2-3' single as one of his favourite new releases.

November 10

U2 is featured on the cover of *Record Mirror*, a British music magazine. It's their first cover story outside of Ireland. Bono tells Chris Westwood: "I want people in London to see and hear the band. I want to replace the bands in the charts now, because I think we're better."

Late November

U2 rehearse for their first shows in England, a visit that might be their last chance to nail down a UK recording contract. They've made a verbal agreement with Bryan Morrison, the former manager and publisher of Pink Floyd, who's paying U2 £3,000 for their song publishing rights. It's not much, but U2 need the money desperately to go to England and impress record executives.

November 28

Morrison halves his offer to U2 two days before the band is set to leave for England. Though they need the money badly, U2 reject Morrison's offer and borrow £3,000 from family and friends to pay their way to England.

Above: Rock Garden, supporting the Dolly Mixtures, December 5, 1979.

November 29

A day before U2 is due to leave for England, Adam and Edge are in a minor car accident on the way to rehearsals in Dublin. Edge's left hand goes through the window. The injury isn't serious, but it will impact his playing during the upcoming gigs.

November 30

U2 takes the ferry to England. Edge keeps his left hand in an ice bucket the whole way there, and he heads straight for the hospital when they reach Liverpool. Edge gets a plaster for his hand and morphine tablets to curb the pain.

Paul has rented an apartment for U2 to use for the next two weeks. In his room tonight, Edge takes out his guitar and works out how he'll play tomorrow's gig.

December 1

Moonlight Club, West Hampstead, opening for The Dolly Mixtures. The U2-3 Tour, U2's first club tour of London, begins. The band is billed as "Capital U2" on advertisements promoting the gig. Despite Edge's injury and difficulty playing the gig, Dave McCullough of *Sounds* magazine is impressed by what he sees: "... the most refreshing new pop music I've heard all year, powerfully pointing along a scintillating guitar sound, a flexible rhythm base, and Bono's ever-improving, identifying vocals. The effect is, three or four times in 20 minutes, having the hairs on the back of your neck stand on end...."

December 2

Nashville Rooms, London, opening for Back to Zero and Secret Affair.

December 3

100 Club, Clapham.

December 4

Hope & Anchor, Islington. Misnamed "The U2's", the band plays to only nine people. Several record company scouts are on hand, but Edge breaks a guitar string midway through the show and walks off the stage. With no guitarist, the band follows him and the show is over.

December 5

Rock Garden, Covent Garden, opening for The Dolly Mixtures. U2 are again misnamed in promotional announcements, this time as "V2". The show is a big hit, and Paul brings a couple of bottles of champagne to celebrate backstage afterward. The band visits *Record Mirror* before the show to thank them for last month's cover feature.

December 7-8

Electric Ballroom, Camden, opening both nights for Talking Heads and Orchestral Manoeuvres In The Dark.

December 10

Moonlight Club, West Hampstead, with Medium Medium.

December 11

Bridge House, Canning Town, with

Idiot Dancers. U2 is billed as "UR" before tonight's show.

December 12
U2 is due to open for The Photos at Brunel University in Uxbridge, but The Photos' singer's vocal problems force the gig to be cancelled days earlier.

Around this time, U2 open for Doll by Doll at The Venue in London's Victoria. The exact date is unknown, though it could be a replacement gig on this date. Chris Westwood reviews the concert in *Record Mirror*: "U2 are doing things within their chosen format – lyrically, idealistically, visually – that should be apparent to anyone with an imagination or, alternately, a disillusionment with the general bloated rock state-of-affairs; the blind and deaf are, of course, excused."

Adam: "We were ... in a state of shock." December 16

"We were coming home in a state of shock. Every record company came to see us and still we hadn't managed to set London on fire. We'd run out of money. I had two bass guitars and, at the end of that [trip], I had to sell my Rickenbacker bass to pay for our boat ticket back."

December 14
Dingwalls, Camden, with Straight 8. Photographer Paul Slattery – who first met the band in Dublin in August – bribes U2 into another photo shoot in exchange for a good meal. They shoot pictures at U2's rented flat, Slattery's house, and along the Thames River.

December 15
Windsor Castle, London. U2 wraps up its brief, inconsistent tour. Luck hasn't been on their side: U2 thinks they've played their worst shows with record executives in the crowd, and great shows when almost no one is watching. The band is unaware that Rob Partridge of Island Records caught one of the good shows, and is spreading the word to others at the label.

December 16
Before U2 returns to Dublin, CBS Records brings the band into the Whitfield Street studio to record two more tracks with Chas de Whalley: 'Another Day' and 'Pete The Chop'. They hope to use the new songs to impress the label's management and get U2 signed to a worldwide contract. Bono's voice is shot after doing 12 shows over the past 15 days, and he's forced to drink honey and lemon medication to soothe his vocal chords. The session is a struggle. De Whalley is certain that 'Pete The Chop' is the hit single that will persuade CBS officials to sign the band, but Bono calls to tell him the band doesn't like the song and wants it buried. CBS eventually passes on signing U2 outside Ireland.

Despite their failure to land a record deal, U2 head home with a plan to tout their tour of England as a big success. They'll play up the glowing reviews in *Sounds* and *Record Mirror* and plant the idea that U2 has made it in the UK.

December 19
A demo version of 'Stories For Boys' appears on *Just For Kicks*, a 12-song compilation album featuring Irish punk, pop, and rock bands. Edge also appears as guitarist on 'Something's Better Than Nothing', a track by Teen Commandments. It's the first recorded instance of any member of U2 appearing with another artist.

December 23
Dandelion Market, Dublin, with The Threat. U2 plays an afternoon gig that's billed as "A Christmas Spectacular".

Risk and breakthrough. With virtually no record label interest, U2 gambles on a tour of Ireland as a possible last-ditch effort to get a contract. It works, and U2 sign to Island Records. The game is on: U2 release their first international single and first album this year, and get their first airplay on US radio. They also tour mainland Europe and the US for the first time. The album and shows are widely praised and U2's fan base begins to grow.

Bono, Edge, and Larry strengthen their Christian commitment this year. They attend prayer group and Shalom meetings while in Dublin; while on tour, they pray and read the Bible together each morning. Bono talks about life being a "battle", and about using faith to resist the pressures of being in a rock band.

January
U2 wins five categories in the *Hot Press* readers' poll.

January 15
RTE Studios, Dublin. U2 performs 'Stories For Boys' on Ireland's long-running program, *The Late Late Show*, hosted by Gay Byrne. It's U2's first prime-time TV appearance.

February
Bridge House, Tullamore. Exact date is unknown.
Queen's University, Belfast. Exact date is unknown. In attendance are Annie Roseberry of Island Records and two reps from Blue Mountain Music, Island's publishing arm. The Blue Mountain duo aren't thrilled by U2's show, but Roseberry loves what she sees and visits with the band and Paul McGuinness after the show. They're all staying at the Europa Hotel, where U2 reportedly indulge in their only known bout of room trashing. It involves overturning furniture and spraying shaving cream all over the bathroom of what they thought was Paul McGuinness' room; it wasn't. In another incident, Adam tries to pour beer on someone else, but ends up drenching Roseberry instead.

Annie Roseberry recalls seeing U2 in Belfast
"They played a great show. They'd been playing together for a long time and they weren't all great players by any stretch of the imagination. The timing was pretty appalling, but it didn't matter. They just had something unique. Bono

Above: Backstage in Cork.

was already a star. He was running around and climbing on speaker stacks even then, like he was playing in a stadium. There was absolutely no doubt that he had something really special."

Island moves closer to signing U2 to a record deal thanks to Roseberry's recommendation.

February 26
National Boxing Stadium, Dublin. U2's Irish tour continues at the National Boxing Stadium, which is actually an arena that holds about 2,400 people. Only 1,000 people show up, many of whom are guests of the band. It's billed as a celebration concert, but is actually a big gamble on U2's part. They invite family and friends, media and pretty much everyone they can find. The idea is to fill this big venue with a U2-friendly crowd.

Most importantly, Nick Stewart of Island Records is in attendance and the band expect to get a contract offer from him. Bono hints about it during the concert. "This is our new single, it's out on the CBS label," he says, introducing the song 'Another Day'. "It won't be out on the CBS label for long, I can tell you that story there."

Thanks to Annie Roseberry's recent endorsement, U2's popularity in the *Hot Press* poll, and what he sees on stage today, Stewart offers U2 a recording contract after the show.

Nick Stewart: 'I've got to have this band"
"The band came on and played '11 O'Clock Tick Tock' and the stage was invaded. After about four numbers, I turned to Michael Deeny, who's the godfather of Irish music, and said, 'For fuck's sake! This is the Led Zeppelin of the 1980s!' I knew I was watching something special. Musically, I found them a little naive, but the way they got their own crowd going, the way Bono handled it ... I just thought, 'I've got to have this band.'"

Still, Stewart has to convince Island boss Chris Blackwell to sign U2. Blackwell isn't an easy sell, but eventually gives in after Stewart travels to Blackwell's home in the Bahamas.

Also today, U2 release the 'Another Day' single in Ireland, a song from U2's December session in London with Chas de Whalley, while the B-side 'Twilight' is from the Eamon Andrews session in February, 1979. Bono draws the sleeve artwork.

March 1

Country Club, Cork. Paul Morley of *NME* watches U2's gig tonight.

March 2

Garden of Eden, Tullamore, opening for the Tony Stevens Showband. Bono does an interview with Paul Morley of *NME* over breakfast at the Country Club Hotel in Cork. One of the main topics of conversation is the possibility of U2 relocating, temporarily, to London. Bono says the band may have to do it, but he's aware of the risk. "London is supposed to be freedom! London is traps," Bono says. "London is boxes. London is chained in bondage, in fact. And if a band coming from thick paddy land – and that is not true – comes along and tells these people what's up they might not be awfully pleased."

Morley joins the band for the four-hour bus ride to Tullamore. The show doesn't go well; Bono is unable to connect with the largely disinterested crowd.

March 9

Bono, Adam, and Larry make an appearance at a "National Milk Run" charity event, sponsored by Ireland's National Dairy Council.

March 19

Acklam Hall, London. U2 shares the bill with The Virgin Prunes and Berlin on the third night of the Sense Of Ireland festival. Several Island Records executives are in attendance for one last look before the two parties sign off on U2's record deal. Paul Rambali gives U2 high grades in *NME* a week later: "They're good tonight. Not yet totally sure and commanding, but committed and determined and eager to cut across – refreshingly eager to create a rapport and to communicate with the crowd more than merely to them. So eager they sometimes rush and stumble. U2 are on the up; not yet set on the course, not yet set in their ways. Now is the time to see them."

March 21

U2 sees The Cramps play the Electric Ballroom in London. What he perceives as a lifeless, goth-style

What if U2 had signed to a different label? March 23

Chas de Whalley: "[Island] allowed the band to work the US for about three years before they had a serious hit, and about four years before they made any serious money. They were subsidizing them for the better part of four years just because they recognized they were a great live act and they were getting better and better and better. They wouldn't have been allowed anything like that kind of leeway if they had signed to CBS."

crowd inspires Bono to write the lyrics for what will become their next single, '11 O'Clock Tick Tock'.

March 22
Paul Morley's feature, headlined "U2 Can Make It in the Rock Business", appears in *NME*.

March 23
Still in London, U2 signs its first international recording contract with Island Records in the ladies' room at the Lyceum. The money isn't great: a £50,000 advance plus another £50,000 in tour support. More importantly, the deal is for four years, covering four albums, with three singles to be released in the first year. The long-term commitment will allow U2 to develop at its own pace.

What if U2 had signed to a different label?
Tom Nolan: "I can say, having worked for both EMI and Island, that in my opinion Island were more geared up to work closely with such an individual young band, and eventually help bring out the best in them."

The contract calls for the band's debut album to be recorded in August for an October release. Island agrees to accept U2's material sight unseen and gives U2 control over album covers and other artwork. The deal is binding for all territories except Ireland. In the US, U2 will be distributed on the Warner label.

U2 don't have enough money to pay for their hotel and get home to Ireland, so they ask Nick Stewart for some cash; he delivers it to their hotel a couple hours later in a bag.

April
U2 spend about a week at Shepperton Studios outside London rehearsing for their upcoming tour. This likely happens late in the month.

April 5-6
U2 records its first single for Island

Records, '11 O'Clock Tick Tock', over the Easter weekend at Dublin's Windmill Lane studios. Joy Division producer Martin Hannett oversees the session. It's the first song the band records in the studio that will become their home for many years. Around this time, Dave McCullough and Paul Slattery from *Sounds* magazine visit the band in Dublin.

Shortly after these sessions, Edge buys an Electro Harmonix Memory Man Deluxe echo box, a purchase that will have a significant impact on his guitar style and U2's career.

Bono and Edge on the importance of Edge's echo unit
Edge: "We had a song we were working on called

Left: Bono and Edge backstage in Cork, March 1.
Below: Edge, with his Gibson Explorer, Acklam Hall, March 19.

'A Day Without Me' and Bono kept saying, 'I hear this echo thing, like the chord repeating.' He had this thing in his head so I said, 'I'd better get an echo unit for this single.'"

Bono: "I remember saying, 'Use this, because this will get us to another place.' This will get us outside of the concrete – into the abstract. I just knew that the echo unit would do that. Atmopsheres – we were very interested in atmospheric music. Punk started to look incredibly limited."

Edge: "It was like adding seasoning to the soup and suddenly we became aware of all these different flavours in our music we'd never known existed. The older songs took on a completely new life while, for about a month, we went through an intensely creative period when the echobox inspired us to write something like two new songs a day!"

May 1
Kris Needs, editor of the UK rock magazine *Zigzag*, arrives in Dublin today to interview U2. Bono and Paul McGuinness meet him at Dublin airport. They visit the *Hot Press* offices and then drive out to a place U2 calls the "Gingerbread House" – a small building the band is using for rehearsals. (It's located on the edge of Balgriffin Cemetery, where Bono's mom is buried.) Needs has never heard U2, so the band plays three songs for him, including the upcoming single, '11 O'Clock Tick Tock'. After the performance, they all go to a nearby pub for the interview. That night, U2 take Needs to see a local band called The Mystery Men perform. Near the end of their set, Bono joins them on a cover of Them's 'Gloria'.

May 10
Town Hall Theatre, Ballina, Ireland, with Mister Moon.

May 11
Garden of Eden, Tullamore.

May 22
Hope & Anchor, Islington, with Fashion. U2 opens its first tour since signing the Island Records contract in support of the '11 O'Clock Tick Tock' single. The band ask Joe O'Herlihy to be their sound engineer, but settle for a local sound crew when O'Herlihy passes.

Joe O'Herlihy recalls how he finally joined U2's tour crew
"I gave them a price for doing the tour and they wouldn't pay me the money. We had a fierce argument and I told them to fuck off – that was it. They basically had three and six to spend – I had a sound system worth thirteen and six and they wouldn't pay! In the course of the band doing the tour, they went through approximately five different engineers in the space of a ten-day tour, so I was called up to go and work somebody else's equipment. I went."

O'Herlihy and McGuinness talk more about a permanent position handling U2's sound. Confidently, McGuinness tells O'Herlihy "this thing's going to go big", and O'Herlihy eventually agrees to come along for the ride.

Around this time, U2 does an interview with French journalist Michka Assayas for *Le Monde de la musique* magazine.

May 23
Moonlight Club, London, with Fashion. *In Record Mirror*, Chris Westwood describes the show as "flawed and gorgeous".

U2 releases its first international single on Island Records, '11

O'Clock Tick Tock/Touch', produced by Martin Hannett. '11 O'Clock' is the song formerly called 'Silver Lining' and the B-side 'Touch' is previously known as 'Trevor'. The single fails to make the charts.

May 24
University, Sheffield, with Fashion.

May 26
New Regent, Brighton, with Fashion.

May 27
Rock Garden, London, with Fashion.

May 28
Trinity Hall, Bristol, with Fashion.

May 29
Cedar Ballroom, Birmingham, with Fashion.

May 30
Nashville, London, with Fashion.

May 31
Polytechnic, Manchester, with Fashion.

June 2
77 Club, Nuneaton, with Fashion.

June 3
Boat Club, Nottingham, with Fashion.

June 4
Beach Club, Manchester, with Fashion.

June 5
Fan Club, Leeds, with Fashion.

June 6
J.B.'s, Dudley, with Fashion.

June 7
Marquee, London, with Fashion.

June 8
Half Moon, London, with Fashion. The final show of U2's first full tour is a success. Peter Owens raves about it in *Hot Press*: "U-2 are like an imminent thunderstorm, inducing an electrostatic breathlessness, the prickling of the skin, the uncomfortable gnawing on the soles of the feet."

Steve Lillywhite remembers recording 'I Will Follow'

"Everyone was in such a good frame of mind, ideas would just flow. I had a bicycle turned upside down; Bono and I would spin the wheels and hit the spokes with a knife. There were also bottles smashing all over the place. We were having a great time – just like little kids."

July
Project Arts Centre, Dublin. U2 play a "secret" gig in Dublin this month. The exact date is unknown. It's possibly a warm-up for their four shows in London in the middle of the month, or for their show late in the month at the large Leixlip Castle festival.

July 10
Clarendon Hotel, London, with Midnight & The Lemon Boys, Medium Medium.

July 11
Half Moon, London. This show marks the first time U2 sells out a venue in the UK. After the show, U2 meet Chris Blackwell for the first time. Producer Steve Lillywhite is also at the show.

July 12
Moonlight Club, London. Another sellout, and 200 fans are left outside without tickets. Paul McGuinness buys a bottle of champagne to celebrate after the show.

Another sign of U2's rising popularity is today's feature article in *Sounds* magazine, in which Larry describes U2's developing audience: "... the guy that works from nine to five and just wants to go and see a band, and also the guy

who just goes out and buys the record. From them to hardcore punks. The type of people who just don't want rules and make up their own mind about a band. That's the way we'd like to keep it." The article also features photos of the band posing on construction equipment in front of a Heiton McFerran construction supply store.

July 13
Marquee, London, opening for The Photos.

With the 11 O'Clock Tick Tock Tour over, U2 returns to Dublin to begin work on its debut album. Martin Hannett had been scheduled to produce, but he cancelled after Joy Division vocalist Ian Curtis' suicide in May. U2 hire Steve Lillywhite to produce instead. Lillywhite's enthusiasm and sometimes-unconventional tactics bring out the best in U2.

At one point during the album sessions, Bono calls Sean O'Connor, guitarist with a Dublin band called The Lookalikes, and asks if U2 can borrow a couple guitars. Bono tells O'Connor that Steve Lillywhite wants some guitar sounds that are different from the Gibson Explorer that Edge is using.

While U2 work on the album, writer Paolo Hewitt and photographer Tom Sheehan visit for an upcoming feature in Melody Maker magazine. U2 decide to shoot a video for 'I Will Follow', and asks Meiert Avis to coordinate the project.

Meiert Avis: U2 "was always curious about video"
"We had just put Windmill together, built this beautiful recording studio downstairs, and U2 were in and out a lot trying to get together what would become the Boy album once they hooked up with Steve Lillywhite. They would wander around exploring the building late at night, escaping the studio. The band was always curious about

video even then, so we would hang out a bit while I was editing. It was far from what you would now think of as U2 Greatest Rock Band in the World, just a punk band trying to get their raw songs to sound good on tape."

July 27
Leixlip Castle, Leixlip. U2 play their first open-air show at the "Dublin Festival 1980" in front of 15,000 people.

July 29
Dalymount Park, Dublin. U2 perform at the Dalymount Festival.

U2 is one of the bands featured in *The Face*, a new style/music magazine making its debut today.

August
Late in the month, U2 release the single 'A Day Without Me'/'Things To Make And Do', produced by Steve Lillywhite. It fails to chart. The French single has the album version of 'I Will Follow' on the B-side, replacing 'Things To Make And Do'.

The single is also believed to be the first U2 song ever played on US radio, having been picked up this month by a DJ named Carter Alan and played on his WBCN-FM weekend radio show in Boston.

August 10
Paul McGuinness is in the US to meet with Frank Barsalona of Premier Talent, who is also the agent for the Who, Bruce Springsteen, and many others. However, the death of McGuinness' father, Philip, compels him to return to Dublin before the meeting happens. They'll eventually meet a couple weeks later.

August 13
U2 attend the funeral of Philip McGuinness at St. Fintan's Cemetery in Sutton.

September 6
General Woolfe, Coventry, England. U2 returns to England for the band's longest tour yet, the opening leg of the Boy Tour.

September 7

Lyceum, London. U2 are one of four opening acts for Echo & The Bunnymen. It's a frustrating show for Bono, who's unable to connect with the disinterested crowd. Reviewing the show for *NME*, Chris Salewicz says U2 "are basically little more than nonsense, or perhaps the new Boomtown Rats – one of the two, and they both amount to the same thing, anyway. This four-piece Irish group are nothing more than a very traditional hard rock outfit with a singer – one Bono by name – who'd love to be Rod Stewart, in imitation of whom he moves much of the time, when he isn't busy imitating the inevitable Iggy, of course... U2 are really quite awful, though the young people – particularly the mutant punks – at the pop concert seemed to enjoy their tired old fakery."

September 8

Marquee, London. U2 plays the first of four consecutive Monday night gigs at London's famous Marquee Club.

Below: U2 work the streets of Dublin, summer, 1980.

September 9

Berkeley, Bristol.

September 11

Wellington Club, Hull.

September 12

Taboo Club, Scarborough, with Midnight & The Lemon Boys.

September 13

Queen's Hall, Leeds. U2 plays at the Futurama Festival. Reviewing the gig in *Melody Maker*, Lynden Barber writes, "U2 play truly great rock music which inspires the heart. They make Echo & the Bunnymen sound as stupid as their name."

September 15

Marquee, London, with Vision Collision.

September 16

Fiesta Suite, Plymouth. U2 is billed as "The U2s" on posters promoting the show. A ticket costs £1.25.

September 17

Demelzas, Penzance.

September 18

Civic Hall, Totnes.

September 19

Marshall Rooms, Stroud, with Midnight & The Lemon Boys, Demob.

September 21

Nag's Head, Wollaston.

September 22

Marquee, London, with Jane Kennaway & Strange Behaviour and DJ Jerry Floyd. 'Boy-Girl' from this show will appear next year as a B-side when 'I Will Follow' is released in North America and Australasia. Before the show, U2 perform four songs at BBC radio for Mike Read's radio show: 'I Will Follow', 'Electric Co.', and 'An Cat Dubh-Into The Heart'. Read will play one song at a time on his show over the next several nights.

September 23

Limit Club, Sheffield.

September 24

Bogart's, Birmingham. Paul McGuinness is in the US putting together plans for U2's arrival later this year.

Bono's letter home to Dad

In his hotel room in Birmingham, Bono writes a letter to his dad, Bob, back home in Dublin. An excerpt:

"I'm looking forward to tonight's concert as the tour goes on. The band are getting tighter and tighter. The nights at the Marquee are very successful. Each Monday the crowd gets bigger and bigger, a situation that hasn't occurred at the Marquee on a Monday night for a long time. We did three encores last week. The single sold a thousand copies and for the first time we are getting daytime radio play on Radio One. We have

four DJs behind us now. It is only a matter of time....

"You should be aware that at the moment three of the group are committed Christians. That means offering each day up to God, meeting in the morning for prayers, readings, and letting God work in our lives. This gives us our strength and a joy that does not depend on drink or drugs. This strength will, I believe, be the quality that will take us to the top of the music business."

September 25
Brady's, Liverpool.

September 26
Cedar Ballroom, Birmingham.

September 27
Polytechnic, Coventry.

September 29
Marquee, London.

September 30
Polytechnic, Brighton.

October
'I Will Follow'/'Boy-Girl (live)' is released as the second single from Boy.

While in London, Bono meets again with writer Dave McCullough and photographer Paul Slattery from *Sounds* magazine. McCullough and Slattery are turned off when Bono talks about his Christian beliefs.

"Bono was becoming more theatrical and messianic in style," Slattery recalls later. "I just thought good luck to them but it ain't my cup of tea."

October 2
Fan Club, Leeds.

October 3
Porterhouse, Retford.

October 4
School of Economics, London.

October 5
Half Moon, London.

October 7
Boat Club, Nottingham.

October 9
Polytechnic, Manchester.

October 11
Kingston Polytechnic, London.

October 14
KRO Studios, Hilversum. U2 play their first show on mainland Europe. The show is for Dutch radio and a small studio audience is present.

October 15
Milkyway, Amsterdam.

October 16
Vera, Groningen.

October 17
Gigant, Apeldoorn. Prior to tonight's show, Island Records' Neil Storey arrives at the venue with copies of the *Boy* album. It's U2's first chance to see the finished product.

October 18
Klacik, Brussels. Before the show, U2 does a photo shoot with Virginia Turbett. After the show, the band

Bono, on *Boy*, October 20

"The tenderness, the spirituality, the real questions that are on real people's minds are rarely covered. There was a lot of posturing and posing. With that first record, I thought I would just let myself be that child, write about innocence as it's about to spoil."

does an interview with Mike Gardner of *Record Mirror* magazine.

October 19
Lyceum, London. U2 shares the bill with The Last Words, Discharge, and Slade.

October 20
U2's first album, *Boy*, is released in Europe. The cover features Bono's young neighbour, Peter Rowen, in a stark black and white photo; the band's name is almost hidden in his hair. It's a strong image, one that captures the album's power and innocence. Bono's lyrics tackle ideas and themes that are largely ignored in rock and roll – spirituality, youth, and growing from boys to men. Several songs are already familiar to U2's most ardent fans, having been part of the band's original repertoire for more than a year.

Boy peaks at number 52 in the British charts. Though it doesn't get much press attention, many of the reviewers are hooked. Declan Lynch grades the album an 11 out of 12 in *Hot Press*: "I find it almost impossible to react negatively to U2's music. It rushes your senses, it's so sharp, every song seems like it's been lying under the tree all year, and at Christmas it's taken out of its box and shown to everybody, open-mouthed." Paul Morley is equally effusive in *NME*: "I find *Boy* touching, precocious, full of archaic flourishes and modernist conviction, genuinely strange. It won't eradicate the grey feelings people have about U2, but it reinforces the affection I have for their character and emotionally forceful music." Tracks: 'I Will Follow', 'Twilight', 'An Cat Dubh', 'Into The Heart', 'Out Of Control', 'Stories For Boys', 'The Ocean', 'A Day Without Me', 'Another Time, Another Place', 'The Electric Co.', 'Shadows And Tall Trees'

November 7
University, Exeter. The Boy Tour resumes after a couple weeks off.

November 8
University, Southampton.

November 9
Moonlight Club, London.
Around this time, U2 perform
'I Will Follow' on the ITV
programme *Get It Together*, their
first TV appearance outside
Ireland.

November 11
Kent University, Canterbury.

November 12
University, Bradford.

November 13
Limit Club, Sheffield.

November 14
Town Hall, Kidderminster.

November 15
Polytechnic, Bristol.

November 18
University, Reading, with Medium
Medium.

November 19
Polytechnic, Wolverhampton, with
Medium Medium.

November 20
Polytechnic, Blackpool, with Medium
Medium.

November 21
Nite Club, Edinburgh. U2 plays its
first show in Scotland to a sellout
crowd of 400.

November 22
Brady's, Liverpool, with Medium
Medium.

November 23
Rolling Stone writer Jim Henke
arrives in London and meets the
band. He's working on an article
that will give U2 its biggest press
exposure in the US to date. They
invite Henke to attend tomorrow's
show in Coventry and their show
later in the week at the Marquee.

November 24
Polytechnic College, Coventry, with
Medium Medium. Jim Henke
interviews Bono while they drive
together by bus from London to

Coventry. During the drive, Bono gives Henke what would become a famous quote, especially coming from such a young, unknown band: "I don't mean to sound arrogant, but even at this stage, I do feel that we are meant to be one of the great groups. There's a certain spark, a certain chemistry, that was special about the Stones, the Who and the Beatles, and I think it's also special about U2."

November 26
Playhouse Theatre, Hulme. U2 are invited to perform on Peter Powell's afternoon BBC Radio 1 programme. They leave for London immediately after the taping.
Marquee, London, with DJ Jerry Floyd.

November 27
Marquee, London, with DJ Jerry Floyd. U2 invites Neil McCormick of *Hot Press*, an old friend from Mount Temple and brother of Ivan, to see the show. Afterward, McCormick interviews Bono, Edge, and Larry. Their conversation stretches well into the wee hours of the next morning. "We don't want to be the band that talks about God," Bono tells his friend. "Anything that has to be said is in the music or on stage and I don't want to go through the media. I'll talk to you personally about it but I don't want to talk to the world about it because we will face a situation where people will see us with a banner over our heads. This is not the way U2 is gonna work."

The lengthy conversation is heavy on faith and Christianity and the band's beliefs, but McCormick leaves most of it out of his article (which will appear in the December 17, 1980, issue) out of respect for his friends' wishes. McCormick will later print it in his 2004 book, *Killing Bono: I Was Bono's Doppelganger.*

Bono's missing quotes on U2's early spirituality
"When I was fourteen I called out and asked God to show me a direction, and I wondered whether there was any direction or not, and then I saw it happening. I saw the band taking shape and being pointed in that direction and it gave me an insight.

"Becoming a Christian you go into battle. Because of what this band stands for, 'cause of where we are in the business, you wouldn't believe the pressures we're under. I mean spiritually. We get up early in the morning and we work against it. Every day is a battle, every moment is a struggle....

"Look at Adam. He is as free as any individual. He honors our commitment. He realizes that it is a very important source of inspiration. But he rejects it himself. That's the way the world should be. I'm not going to hit somebody over the head if they don't believe."

November 28
Aston University, Birmingham.

November 29
Keele University, Stoke.

November 30
Jenkinson's, Brighton.

December
Hot Press prints a satirical article in their Christmas issue reporting that U2 is breaking up. UK papers don't get the joke, though, and run the story as if it's real.

December 1-2
Hammersmith Palais, London, opening both nights for Talking Heads.

December 3
Baltard Pavilion, Paris, opening for Talking Heads. U2 play their first show in France. They ask journalist Michka Assayas, who interviewed them in London during the spring,

Jim Henke on seeing U2 live, November 24

"The Coventry gig, at the Polytechnic, was akin to seeing a band in a high-school gymnasium: crappy acoustics, crummy environment. Even so, it immediately became clear that U2 was special. It didn't matter where the concert was taking place. Their sheer power and passion, coupled with Bono's ability to break down the barrier between the stage and the audience, completely knocked me out. I thought they were amazing."

to show them the Notre Dame Cathedral.

December 4
U2 fly to New York and get their first taste of America. After arriving at JFK airport, they ride to their hotel via limousine, a special treat from Paul McGuinness. While in the limousine, U2 hears a Billie Holiday song on WBLS, a famous soul music radio station. The whole episode is later captured in the lyrics to 'Angel Of Harlem'.

December 5
U2 are scheduled to open their first US tour out of the spotlight in Rochester, New York – a warm-up gig before the band's arrival in New York City the following day. Tonight's show is originally planned for a club called the Penny

Arcade, but the club owner decides he doesn't want a punk band playing and the gig is cancelled.

December 6
Ritz, New York. U2 bring the Boy Tour to New York for their first US show. Despite the pressure of playing the Big Apple, the band deliver a show that leads to two encores. Ellen Darst of Warner Brothers, Island's US distributor, sees her first U2 concert tonight. Her job is to assess the band and report back to Warner Brothers, who will be making key decisions about how much money and promotion to give to U2's tour. Darst will later be hired as a member of the Principle Management team and become a key member of the band's inner circle.

In attendance are writer Jim Henke and Frank Barsalona of Premier Talent, who has booked U2 for this tour without ever seeing them. He quickly realizes he has booked a winner.

Frank Barsalona on seeing U2 the first time
"The group comes in and I see them for the first time. And the only applause is from 100 people – the rest of the audience is either hostile or silent. And I go, 'Oh my God, I've made a major blunder.' But the group starts and there's no panic in their demeanor – as far as they're concerned those 2,200 people were their audience. And after that first number there's the stalwart 100 people and the rest do either nothing or boo.It was the most incredible way to have seen U2 for the first time, because it wasn't a pre-sold audience, it was an audience that was hostile, that they had to win and turn around. It was the most incredible thing, because with every song

Larry: "I was overwhelmed" December 4

"I was completely disoriented. For me, going to London felt strange, but New York was something else. I was overwhelmed. I wish I'd enjoyed my first time in New York City more."

a little bit more of the audience would start listening and getting involved. So as the show developed you would see this wave from that 100 all the way back. About 60 or 70 percent of the audience were now listening, because once they got about 70 percent then they were loud enough and everyone else said, 'Oh, hold it, what are we missing?' Then they got everybody, and from that point on it was a triumph – I think they got three or four encores, they probably could have done more, but they probably didn't have any. It was just so exciting, I was choked."

U2 are paid $2,300 for the gig.

December 7
Bayou Club, Washington, DC, with Slickee Boys.

December 8
Stage One, Buffalo, opening for Talas. U2 play a club owned by Harvey Weinstein, the future chief of Miramax Films. After the show, the band learns that John Lennon has been murdered in New York City.

December 9
El Mocambo, Toronto. U2 plays its

first show in Canada. Inspired and angered by the murder of John Lennon, U2 plays an emotional show that wins rave reviews in local media.

December 11
Mudd Club, New York.

December 12
Main Event, Providence.

December 13
The Paradise, Boston, opening for Barooga. U2 play their first show in Boston, a city that will soon become U2's unofficial US home. Most of the audience is there to see U2, thanks mainly to several months' airplay on Boston radio, and most leave after U2's set.

December 14
Toad's Place, New Haven.

December 15
Bijou Café, Philadelphia. Before the show, U2 does a shoot with photographer Lisa Haun.

December 17
Ulster Hall, Belfast.

December 18
Leisureland, Galway.

December 19
Baymount, Sligo.

December 20
Downtown Kampus, Cork.

December 22
TV Club, Dublin, with Microdisney.

Late December
Sometime near the Christmas holidays, Bono lends a hand to *Hot Press* magazine by doing a photo shoot for their upcoming launch in the UK. The photo shoot takes place in the home of photographer Colm Henry, and involves Bono holding an issue of the magazine that appears to be on fire. After the shoot, Henry agrees to shoot some private photos of Bono and Alison, who has come along. The day ends with Bono and Alison joining Neil McCormick for dinner at a Dublin restaurant.

1981

A year of contrasts for U2. The band continues to increase its fan base, thanks largely to an unforgiving tour schedule. They play new countries in Europe, and tour the US as if their lives depended on it; and in Paul McGuinness' view, their lives *do* depend on it. U2 gains welcome exposure with its first mention in *Rolling Stone*, and its first appearances on US TV and on *Top Of The Pops* in the UK.

But outside the public's eye, U2 is tearing apart at the seams. Differences over faith divide the band into two camps. Bono, Edge and Larry grow more zealous about U2's calling. But some of their Christian friends are pressuring the three to give up music, which makes the *October* recording sessions a tense struggle. In between tours of Europe and North America, they tell Paul McGuinness they want to quit. McGuinness persuades them to reconsider, and the tour goes on. Bono and Edge sort out their struggles, and eventually commit to U2 without compromising their faith.

January
U2 wins four categories in the 1980 *Hot Press* readers' poll: Best Single ('11 O'Clock Tick Tock', with 'A Day Without Me' finishing second), Best Group, Best Male Singer (Bono), and Best Album (*Boy*).

January 17
Bono, Edge, and Larry attend a weekend retreat for Christian musicians at the Gaines Christian Center in Worcester, England. Bono and Edge give a 45-minute presentation, talking about their faith, their struggles as Christians in the music industry, and U2's future. They read and comment on Bible verses that they they feel are important to U2's calling, with Bono choosing Isaiah 40:3 and describing it as "the Scripture that the Lord has basically shown us with regards to the band". Edge chooses Psalm 40, the same verses that will be used later as lyrics on the song '40'.

Bono explains U2's goals at the Christian musician's retreat
"I see our position as Christians as to make way, make straight a path for the Lord for a second time. In that sense we have to make the rough smooth and get involved in making the rough smooth. But before the Lord can use the band ... He has to sort of make our rough ends smooth and that's what the Lord had to do.

Above: *Top Of The Pops*, August 20.

"What we've got to do in the music business is destroy the image that has got through ... which has [given] God almighty and Jesus Christ ... an image of a weakling. A slightly effeminate image. A sort of Sunday image. A religious image. This is not the case. This is something we're trying in U2 to do something about.

January 23
Queen's University, Belfast. The 3rd leg of the Boy Tour – or, as Bono calls it in his journal, "The Battle of Britain" – begins tonight. U2's show is taped for the BBC TV programme, *Rock Goes To College*. A half-hour edit of the show airs months later.

January 24
Strathclyde University, Glasgow, with Altered Images. After the show, Gavin Martin of the NME rides back to the hotel with U2 and interviews them for an upcoming cover article.

January 25
Valentino's Club, Edinburgh, with Altered Images. After the show, U2 visits with Stuart Adamson, ex-guitarist and vocalist for the Skids and future guitarist and vocalist for Big Country.

Above: Boy Tour, London Lyceum, February 1.

January 26
University, York, with Altered Images.

January 27
Polytechnic, Manchester, with Altered Images.

January 28
University of East Anglia, Norwich, with Altered Images.

January 29
Iron Horse, Northampton, with Altered Images.

Around this time, Paul McGuinness meets with Chris Parkes, whose business involves selling U2 (and other bands') tour merchandise without permission. McGuinness and Parkes formalize an agreement in which Parkes will pay U2 for the right to sell merchandise with the band's name. Parkes is later hired to handle U2's merchandising officially.

January 30
University, Loughborough, with Altered Images.

January 31
City Hall, St. Albans, with Manic Jabs.

February
Boy makes it onto Melody Maker's list of the best albums of 1980.

February 1
Lyceum, London. Red Beat, Thompson Twins, and Delta 5 are also on the bill. U2 covers Bob Dylan's 'All Along The Watchtower' for the first time. Bono sings the song with help from Pete Wylie of a band called Wah! Heat.

February 9
Underground, Stockholm, with Chatterbox. Earlier in the day, U2 does two songs live on the Swedish TV show *Mandagsborsen*.

February 10
Beursschouwburg, Brussels. The show is recorded for TV with five songs airing on the *Rock Follies* programme on February 14.

February 11
Paradiso, Amsterdam, with Bugs. Earlier in the day, U2 do photo shoots at a local bar, where Bono plays a couple songs on piano, and outdoors in the city.

February 12
Paard Van Troje, The Hague.

Tonight's show is recorded for Dutch radio and TV.

February 13
De Lantaarn, Rotterdam.

February 14
Stadsschouwburg, Sittard.

February 15
Onkel Po's Carnegie Hall, Hamburg. U2's first show in Germany.

February 17
Kantkino, Berlin.

February 18
Sugar Shack, Munich. The combination of a very late show and some Bavarian Schnapps helps U2 fall asleep in their dressing room before the show. Paul McGuinness manages to wake them up in time for the 1:00 a.m. performance.

February 19
Salle Du Fauburg, Geneva, with Film de Guerre. U2's first show in Switzerland. The bus ride from Munich to Geneva is delayed at the border by Swiss customs officers, who let U2 bring only one guitar and one bass guitar into the country. The opening act offers U2 their equipment, but Larry refuses to use their drum set. The concert promoter has his own band, and loans U2 their drum set at the last minute.

U2 receives its first mention in *Rolling Stone* magazine in an article called "Here Comes The Next Big Thing" written by James Henke. Writes Henke: "*Boy*, scheduled for a late-January US release, does indicate that U2 is a band to be reckoned with. Their highly original sound can perhaps best be described as pop music with brains. It's accessible and melodic, combining the dreamy, atmospheric qualities of a band like Television with a hard-rock edge not unlike the Who's."

February 20
Ecole National Des Travaux, Paris.

February 21
Le Palace, Paris.

February 28

BBC Studios, London. U2 make their debut appearance on the venerable UK TV rock show, *The Old Grey Whistle Test*, with a three-song set.

March

'I Will Follow' is released in North America and Australasia. A live version of 'Out Of Control' is the North American B-side, while the Australasian release features the same live version of 'Boy-Girl' that was on last year's single in Europe. The vinyl reaches number one in New Zealand, giving U2 their first chart-topper outside Ireland.

March 3

Boy is released in North America. It enters the US charts at number 135 and climbs to number 94. The album cover shows silhouettes of the band, not the Peter Rowen photo used on the original release; record label officials changed it out of fear the original photo of a young boy, naked from the waist up, would associate U2 with paedophilia.

Bayou Club, Washington, DC. U2 begins its first major US tour with two shows at the Bayou Club. Ellen Darst of Warner Brothers is on hand again, but not just to observe. She's now actively handling promotion and media efforts.

March 4

Bijou Café, Philadelphia, with City Thrills.

March 5

J.B. Scott's, Albany, with Mission of Burma.

Below: On the street in Chicago, April.

March 6

The Paradise, Boston, with La Peste. U2 play two shows. The first is recorded and soon sent out to radio stations around the country under the name *Two Sides Live*. Several songs from the first show also appear as B-sides on future U2 singles.

March 7

The Ritz, New York, with Our Daughter's Wedding.

March 8

Bono and Edge go clothes shopping in New York and bump into a few fans they saw at last night's show. They decide to visit the World Trade Center together. At the top, Bono points out Ireland on a map and tells the fans that he misses his dad.

Edge on Touring Middle America

"One of the great things that Paul McGuinness figured out was that to break America you needed, more than anything, just to be there and go to these places. And so we did. We would go to parts of America that had never seen any European bands, certainly none of the bands from our set."

March 9
Le Club (now called Le Spectrum), Montreal.

March 10
Barrymore's, Ottawa. Motivated by the recent *Rolling Stone* article, 400 people show up for tonight's show in Ottawa. U2 agree to be paid the higher of $750 or 75% of the $5/each ticket sales; the band takes home $1,500.

March 11
Maple Leaf Ballroom, Toronto.

March 14
Globe Theater, San Diego.

March 15
Reseda Country Club, Reseda. U2 play their first Los Angeles-area show to a sellout audience of 600. Local radio station KROQ-FM has been playing U2 extensively for several weeks, and will become one of U2's friendliest radio stations in the US.

March 16
Woodstock, Anaheim. Only 12 people show up.

March 18
San Jose State College Auditorium, San Jose, with Romeo Void. 'The audience would have probably gotten them do the whole set over again,' writes a local reviewer.

March 19
The Old Waldorf, San Francisco, with Romeo Void.

March 20
The Old Waldorf, San Francisco, with Romeo Void.

March 22
Foghorn, Portland. After tonight's show in Portland, Bono leaves his briefcase behind in the band's dressing room. Denny Livingston, one of the sound crew, finds it, and plans to return it the next night in Seattle. When that doesn't happen, he and friend Steve Graeff try unsuccessfully to contact the band's promoter in the Northwest to return the briefcase, but his calls go unreturned. Graeff keeps the briefcase at his home in Tacoma.

For two decades, Bono will explain that two girls who visited the band backstage after tonight's show had stolen his briefcase. But, when he gets the material back in October, 2004, the truth is revealed: he left the briefcase behind himself.

March 23
Astor Park, Seattle.

March 24
Commodore Ballroom, Vancouver.

March 26
New Faces Club, Salt Lake City, with the Offenders.

March 28
Rainbow Music Hall, Denver, with the Offenders. Promoter Chuck Morris is so thrilled with the gig that he wakes up Frank Barsalona at 2:00 a.m. in New York to tell him how great the show was.

March 30
The Rox, Lubbock.

March 31
The Club Foot, Austin.

April 1
Cardi's, Houston.

April 2
Bijou, Dallas.

April 3
Quicksilver's, Oklahoma City.

April 4
Cain's Ballroom, Tulsa.

Right: The most unusual backstage pass in U2's history. April 20. Opposite page: Palladium, New York, May 29.

April 6
Uptown Theater, Kansas City, with Romeo Void.

April 7
Washington University, St. Louis. U2 play in a unique setting – inside Graham Chapel, with a giant stained-glass window serving as a backdrop. Before the show, the local promoter takes them out for drinks and to a local record shop.

April 9
Uncle Sam's, Minneapolis, with the Panic. Before the show, a local rock writer and photographer hang out with the band at their hotel and during soundcheck.

April 10
Fillmore, Ames.

April 11
University of Chicago, Chicago. U2's first show in Chicago. Tickets for the gig are only $1.

April 12
Park West, Chicago.

April 14
Merling's, Madison.

April 15
Palm's, Milwaukee.

April 17
Bogart's Club, Cincinnati. The three girlfriends – Ali, Aislinn, and Ann – arrive in Cincinnati and join Bono, Edge and Larry, respectively, during U2's first lengthy US tour.

April 18
Harpo's, Detroit.

April 19
The Agora, Columbus.

April 20
The Agora, Cleveland, with Bitch. The Agora has already booked an all-girl punk band called Bitch to perform, so when the chance to book U2 comes up, the club makes the girls U2's opening act. Bitch, as the story goes, aren't happy with the decision. After the soundcheck, Adam does a guest DJ stint at Cleveland State University's radio

station, WCSB, which is only two blocks from the Agora.

April 21
The Decade, Pittsburgh.

April 22
The U2 entourage take a vacation in Nassau, the Bahamas, during a break in the tour. They record 'Fire' with producer Steve Lillywhite at Nassau's Compass Point studios.

May
U2 is profiled in *New York Rocker* magazine. Bono tells Andy Schwartz that he's working on two new songs: 'Assaulted By Underpants', a song about Bono's reaction to underwear advertisements on the London tube, and 'Father Is An Elephant', a song about his dad, Bob.

May 12
Rathskeller Hall, Gainesville.

May 3
End Zone, Tampa.

May 4
The Agora, Hallendale.

May 6
The Agora, Atlanta.

May 8
Ol' Man River's, New Orleans. On their first visit to New Orleans, U2 go sightseeing in the French Quarter during the day.

May 9
Poets, Memphis.

May 11
Rainbow Music Hall, Denver, with Kamikaze Klones. Before tonight's show in Denver, U2 visits the Red Rocks Amphitheater for the first time. Concert promoter Chuck Morris tells the band, "You'll play here someday."

May 12
U2 arrive in Los Angeles, and Bono sees Ted Nugent perform at the Sports Arena.

May 13
Civic Center, Santa Monica, with the Suburban Lawns.

May 15
California Hall, San Francisco, with B Team and Romeo Void.

May 19
Ryerson Theater, Toronto.

May 20
A show planned tonight at the Red Creek in Rochester is cancelled. U2 arrive late and ask to have the facility cleared so they can do a sound check. About 100 guests are relocated to a different part of the facility, but two club regulars refuse to move. U2's crew tells the owner that the band won't play unless everyone is cleared out for soundcheck, and the dispute ends with the owner letting U2 pack up their gear and leave. U2 head back to the Holiday Inn Hotel, where Bono plays Pac-Man with two local radio personalities who have been supporting the band on-air and were planning to see tonight's show.

May 21
Uncle Sam's, Buffalo, with Pauline & the Perils.

May 22
City Limits, Syracuse.

May 23
J.B. Scott's, Albany.

May 24
Club Casino, Hampton Beach, with the Stompers.

May 25
Center Stage, Providence. U2 spend the day in Providence with writer Bill Flanagan who brings them to a lunch cookout at a friend's house, and interviews them for *Output* magazine. He later takes the band to a radio interview at Brown University and eventually to the Center Stage bar in time for tonight's gig.

May 27
Toad's Place, New Haven. U2 debuts 'Fire', which will be their next single.

May 28
The Metro, Boston. Prior to tonight's show, Bono, Edge, and Larry do an interview on WBCN-FM with DJ Ken Shelton.

Bono, Edge and Larry vs. Adam and Paul
You may have noticed that several entries for this time period involve Bono, Edge and Larry doing things together without Adam, or Adam doing things on his own separate from the rest of the band. This was the result of different values and beliefs, which Adam explained in U2 By U2 two decades later.

"I'd hang out with Paul quite a lot. He would always find something to go on to after the show. And maybe the guys were beginning to have prayer meetings on the bus and in their rooms. Paul and myself would be down the front of the bus; generally with loud music, people smoking drugs, having a couple of beers."

May 29
Palladium, New York, with the Teardrop Explodes. Busta Jones joins U2 on stage during the encore.

May 30
NBC Studios, New York. U2 make their first appearance on US television, taping *The Tomorrow Show* with host Tom Snyder. Bono and Edge sit down for a brief interview in between the band's performances of 'I Will Follow' and 'Twilight'. The programme airs across the US on June 4.

May 31
Fast Lane, Asbury Park. U2's first full-scale US tour comes to an end.

June
U2 win three catagories at the first Stag/*Hot Press* Irish Rock Awards in Dublin: Best Band, Best Live Band, and Best Album (*Boy*). Photographs show Bono holding an award, though it's unknown if the rest of the band is in attendance. The exact date is unknown.

June 4
University, Salford, with Altered Images.
U2 reportedly attend one of the six Bruce Springsteen concerts at Wembley Arena around this time. Bono says the experience had a big impact on U2: "He changed our life. He really communicated. For the first time, U2 realised that a bigger venue doesn't have to dilute the power of our music."

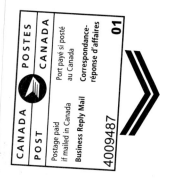

performed again. At Frank Barsalona's suggestion, Bruce Springsteen postpones his return home to stay in London to watch U2 tonight. During the show, a journalist asks Bruce what he thinks about U2. "I love 'em," Bruce gushes. Springsteen meets the band backstage after the gig. Barsalona hopes that a Springsteen-U2 association will help U2's growth in the US. Pete Townshend also visits the band backstage.

With the tour over, U2 heads back to Dublin and prepares to record a new album. To save money, they begin working by themselves at Mount Temple. Meanwhile, some of U2's Christian friends question Bono, Edge and Larry's involvement with a rock band.

U2 and Shalom grow apart

In Shalom, Bono, Edge and Larry took instruction from Chris Rowe, whom Bono called a "great teacher of the Scriptures". But the first signs of a separation occurred when Bono told Rowe that Shalom wouldn't have to worry about money because U2 would be able to support the group with its earnings.

"I remember [Rowe] said

Steve Lillywhite describes the October sessions, July

"They had about three weeks to rehearse, and they had about ten ideas for tracks. They didn't have any completed songs, put it that way – they were musical pieces. So we went in the studio and recorded these musical pieces, and then Bono was going in and singing his heart out without any lyrics."

to me: 'I wouldn't want money earned that way.' And I said: 'What do you mean by that?' He revealed to me that, even though he had known we were serious about being musicians, and being in a rock group, that he was only really tolerating it. He didn't really believe that our music was an integral part of who we were as religious people unless we used the music to evangelize. I knew then that he didn't really get it, and that indeed he was missing out on our blessing."

Larry is the first one to leave Shalom. "I got out before anybody else. I'd just had enough, it was bullshit. It was like joining the Moonies."

July

U2 begin recording *October* at Dublin's Windmill Lane studios, although at this point the record is tentatively named "Scarlet". They enter the studio largely unprepared. Between Bono's lyrics going missing in Portland, and not having enough time to write songs during the tour, U2 struggle to put the album together.

Ten songs from the two-month session make the new album, with the previously recorded 'Fire' also included.

U2 release the 'Fire' single, which climbs up the British charts, peaking at number 35. Various formats include the tracks 'J. Swallow', '11 O'Clock Tick Tock/The Ocean (live)', and 'Cry/The Electric Co. (live)'. It's released in Germany as a 12-inch single called 'U2 R.O.K.'. The single isn't released in North America.

August 1

MTV, a 24-hour music video channel, begins broadcasting in the US. One of the channel's popular early tracks is U2's upcoming single, 'Gloria'.

August 16

U2 play for the first time at Slane Castle outside Dublin, the band's only Irish show of 1981, supporting headliners Thin Lizzy at the annual Slane Festival. Despite their struggles in the studio, U2 decide to open their set with a handful of new songs from the forthcoming *October* album. None have lyrics that match what will eventually be released on the record.

August 20

U2 makes its debut on the long-running BBC chart show, *Top Of The Pops*, performing their current single, 'Fire'.

August 23

Paris Cinema Studio, London. U2 play a half-hour set for the BBC's *In Concert* radio programme. It airs on October 3.

August 24

Greenbelt Festival, Odell. U2 makes an unscheduled appearance at the Greenbelt Christian Arts & Music Festival, performing a seven-song set on borrowed instruments. Bono tells the crowd, "We've heard a lot of applause today for people on this stage. How about some applause for why we're here?" In the audience is Willie Williams, U2's future tour designer, who's seeing U2 perform for the first time.

How did U2 end up at the Greenbelt Festival?
John Cheek, a longtime Greenbelt Festival supporter, remembers U2's last-minute appearance in 1981.
"A call came through in the morning to the main Greenbelt site office: someone from the band U2 were ringing up to see if their group could play the Festival. Apparently, whilst praying in the early morning, Bono felt that God was 'telling him' to play at the Festival.

"Initially, a response came back from the venue

Above: On the streets of Atlanta, November 30. Left: Bono sings at Slane Castle, August 16.

Edge: "We were really a shambles" August 16

"That was one of the worst shows we'd ever played in our lives. We'd come out of the studio, one of the most traumatic recording experiences of our lives, straight into this show, without any time to rehearse. Some of the songs we'd never performed together, because Bono might have sung on top of something that we'd recorded as an instrumental, and no one had really figured out how they would translate live. So we were really a shambles."

47

manager of the mainstage: 'No, we've never heard of you, and we can't squeeze you in, anyway.' But soon, the Festival agreed to accommodate them and gave them a twenty-minute slot, shortly after 9:00 p.m. It seems that the Venue Manager, Geoff Boswell, had already been pestered [by one of the organizers] regarding this group, U2, and perhaps had wanted to check to see if the group he had waiting on the phone was indeed the same band."

Before their set, U2 visits backstage with other artists. Bono asks a couple of them why they call themselves "Christian bands", and suggests the label could limit their audience and cloud the way some people perceive them.

The band's appearance comes during a critical period of internal questioning for Bono, Edge and Larry, who have been spending the summer with Shalom members in a colony of mobile homes on the beach at Portrane, north of Dublin. "I think we have to own up to the fact that we really weren't that interested in being in a band after *Boy*," Bono recalls later. "We were, during *October*, interested in other things, really. We thought about giving up the band. And Adam's reaction to us thinking about giving up the band was he wanted to get out of the band. *October* we made with the attitude 'If people don't like it, hey, maybe that's better than if they do.' We were getting involved in reading books, the Big Book, meeting people who were more interestedin things spiritual, superspiritual characters that I can see now were possibly too far removed from reality. But we were *wrapped up* in that."

August 29
International Stadium, Gateshead.
U2 performs at the Rock On the Tyne Festival.

to tell the band the label wasn't happy with the album artwork they submitted. But when U2 objected to the interference, Island backed down and the album is released today as U2 designed it.

The songs reflect the difficulty U2 had in making it. Having lost his briefcase on tour in Portland, Bono makes up many lyrics as he sings the songs in the studio. Thematically, *October* is a deeply Christian album with lyrics that call out for and question God – just as three members of U2 have been dealing with their own spiritual questions.

The difficulties of the *October* era

Adam: "It was a case of, 'We'll make it up as we go along.' I think we probably would have pulled it together okay if, in the middle of it, we hadn't had Bono, Edge and Larry going, 'Maybe this isn't what we want to do.'"

Edge: "*October* was a struggle from beginning to end. It was an incredibly hard record to make for us because we had major problems with time. And I had been through this thing of really not knowing if I should be in the band or not. It was really difficult to pull all the things together and still maintain the focus to actually finish a record in the time that we had.

"At that stage we were going through our most out-there phase, spiritually. It was incredibly intense. We were just so involved with it. It was a time in our lives where we really concentrated on it more than on almost anything. Except Adam, who just wasn't interested."

Adam: "I didn't have a problem at *all* with

August 31
Coasters, Edinburgh, with Boots For Dancing.

September
Maida Vale Studios, London. Early in the month, U2 records four songs for Richard Skinner's BBC radio program. The performance airs on September 8.

October 1
University of East Anglia, Norwich, with Wall Of Voodoo.

October 2
Rock City, Nottingham, with Wall Of Voodoo.

October 3
University, Salford, with Wall Of Voodoo.

October 4
Tiffany's, Glasgow, with Comsat Angels.

October 5
U2 release the single 'Gloria'/'I Will Follow (live)' from the *October* album. It climbs to number 55 in the UK charts, and an import version reaches number 81 in the US.

Meiert Avis directs the promotional video for the track, which is shot along the Dublin docks.

October 6
Warwick University, Coventry, with Comsat Angels. Larry does an interview before tonight's show.

October 7
Polytechnic, Leicester, with Comsat Angels.

October 8
Lyceum, Sheffield.

October 9
Mayfair, Newcastle, with Comsat Angels.

October 10
Royal Court Theatre, Liverpool, with Comsat Angels.

October 12
Top Rank, Brighton, with Comsat Angels.

U2 releases its second album, *October*. The cover features an unflattering photo of the band at the Grand Canal Docks in Dublin. As the story goes, Island Records had reportedly sent a rep to Dublin

spirituality and identity.

I just had a problem with the disruptiveness that it brought to the band's activities. And then later, as we got into the *October* album, and the others were considering whether rock'n'roll was the right form of expression – I never wanted to go to those meetings. I didn't like the tone of what was going on. It was another band. It was an exclusivity that I didn't buy into."

The album enters the British charts at number 11, and peaks there. It climbs no higher than 104 in the US.

Reviews are mostly positive. In *Hot Press*, Neil McCormick says: "*October* is a musical and spiritual growth for U2, a passionate and moving LP for me. U2 have

evolved constantly, songs changing and growing over a period of time." Dave McCullough raves about the album in *Sounds*: "It all breathes fire, recovering too from the pair of standouts appearing at the start of each side – 'Gloria' being possibly Their Finest Moment and 'Tomorrow', low and muted, gently oozing emotion. This *October* will last forever." Writing in *Rolling Stone*, Jon Pareles calls the album "barely coherent" and dismisses Bono's lyrics as cliché: "... the way to enjoy U2 is to consider the vocals as sound effects and concentrate, as the band does, on the sound of the guitar."

Tracks: 'Gloria', 'I Fall Down', 'I Threw a Brick Through A Window', 'Rejoice', 'Fire', 'Tomorrow', 'October', 'With A Shout (Jerusalem)', 'Stranger In A Strange Land', 'Scarlet', 'Is That All?'

October 13
Locarno, Portsmouth, with Comsat Angels.

October 14
BBC Radio Studios, London. U2 perform 'Scarlet' for the first and only time on Kid Jensen's radio show. The performance is taped early in the day for airing tonight. *Top Rank, Cardiff*, with Comsat Angels.

October 16
King's Hall, Stoke, with Comsat Angels.

October 17
Sports Centre, Bracknell, with Comsat Angels.

October 18
Locarno, Bristol, with Comsat Angels.

October 19
Locarno, Birmingham, with Comsat Angels.

October 20
Tiffany's, Leeds, with Comsat Angels.

October 21
Pavilion, Hemel Hempstead.

October 23
Ancienne Belgique, Brussels.

October 24
Brielpoort, Deinze. A live version of 'An Cat Dubh' appears on an *NME* compilation tape, *Dancin'* Master.

October 25
Zaal Lux, Herenthout. Earlier in the day, U2 lip-sync two songs on *Generation 80*, a live TV show on RTBF 1.

October 26
Elysee Montmartre, Paris.

October 28
Stadsgehoorzaal, Leiden.

October 29
De Harmonie, Tilburg.

October 30
Paradiso, Amsterdam, with Phantom Limb. U2 are still on stage at midnight, prompting Bono to lead the crowd in singing 'Happy Birthday' for Larry.

October 31
Stokvishal, Arnhem.

November 1
De Lantaarn, Rotterdam.

November 3
Fabrik, Hamburg. U2 play to a hostile crowd expecting to also see The Psychedelic Furs, but the Furs choose not to play.

November 4
Metropol, Berlin. The last show of the European tour is taped for the Rockpalast TV series, but doesn't air for several months.

Having completed the European tour, Bono and Edge tell Paul McGuinness they will not tour North America for *October*, and are ready to quit U2 and the music business altogether. McGuinness asks them to come back in a couple of hours after he's had time to think about their decision.

When they resume, Paul explains that U2 has legal and moral commitments to their crew, the record company, tour promoters and many others who have helped the band get to where they are now. He tells them if they want to quit, the proper way would

commit to this band or whether at this point I just have to back out.'"

Bono and Edge eventually decide that it's okay to accept the contradictions between the Christian and rock'n'roll lifestyles. The band goes on tour in North America, and a major crisis – perhaps the end of the band – is barely averted.

Also this month, U2 publishes the first issue of *U2 Magazine*, a small print periodical that helps cultivate and unite U2's fans around the world. Geoff Parkyn is the editor. The premiere issue includes an update on the *October* album and tour, lyrics for a few songs from the *Boy* album, and a reprint of Jim Henke's February *Rolling Stone* article, "Here Comes the Next Big Thing."

Introducing *U2 Magazine*
Editor Geoff Parkyn explains U2 Magazine *in the first issue.*
"Welcome to the first issue of the U2 mag, which will come out four times a year from now on. The basic purpose will be to provide details and keep you up to date on all the news from the group, but we are also keen to include your contributions – so if you feel like sending in a

be to do so after they've fulfilled their current commitments. The band agrees it wouldn't be right to quit so suddenly, and prepares for an upcoming North American tour. Bono and Edge use the time off between tours to consider their future. The decision is especially difficult for Edge.

U2's Crisis of Faith
Bono: "There was a moment where myself and Edge sat around and we thought: 'Well, maybe we should knock this group on the head. Maybe it is frivolous, maybe these people are right, maybe this is just bollocks, this being in a band....' For a couple of weeks, we were at that place. Then we came to a realisation:

'Hold on a second. Where are these gifts coming from? This is how we worship God, even though we don't write religious songs....' We ended up at a place where we thought: 'The music isn't bollocks. This kind of fundamentalism is what's bollocks.'"
Edge: "I didn't actually leave the band, but there was a two-week period where I put everything on hold and I said, 'Look, I can't continue in my conscience in this band at the moment. So hold everything. I want to go away and think about this. I just need a couple of weeks to reassess where I'm headed here and whether I can really

Above: Bono kicks up his heels in Atlanta, November 30.
Below: Bono with fans, Asbury Park, New Jersey, November 25.

gig review, record review, or even some sketches, please do so! There will also be a letters section from the next issue for you to air your comments and suggestions. I also hope to include some of the lyrics to U2's songs in each issue."

November 7
October enters the US album charts at number 181 and eventually peaks at number 104.

November 12
U2 arrive in New York and watches a Rolling Stones gig at Madison Square Garden. Bono, exhausted, dozes off briefly during their set.

November 13
J.B. Scott's, Albany.

November 14
Orpheum, Boston, with David Johansen. The show airs live on WBCN-FM and is syndicated nationally via ABC Radio and the King Biscuit Flower Hour.

November 15
Toad's Place, New Haven. Bono reacts angrily when Larry struggles with his drum kit and misses the start of '11 O'Clock Tick Tock'. Thinking Larry is hiding behind his drum kit, Bono picks up the drums and tosses them toward the audience, then chases after Larry. Edge catches Bono from behind and throws a punch at him.

Bono will refer to this event at U2's Rock and Roll Hall of Fame induction in 2005: "A fight breaks out. It's between the band. It's very, very messy. Now you look at this guitar genius, you look at this Zen-like master that is the Edge, and you hear those brittle icy notes and you might be forgiven for forgetting that you cannot play like that unless you have a rage inside you. In fact, I had forgotten that on that particular night, and he tried to break my nose."

November 17
Center Stage, Providence.

November 18
Ripley's Music Hall, Philadelphia.

November 20-21-22
The Ritz, New York. A sign of their growing popularity: U2 sell out three consecutive shows in New York City.

Prior to the November 22 show, U2 spend a full day at Kingdom Sound, a 24-track recording studio on Long Island. They're working with Sandy Pearlman, who has previously produced for The Clash and Blue Oyster Cult. It's a test-run of sorts, since Steve Lillywhite has told U2 he won't produce more than two albums in a row with one band. U2 appear tired at the concert, and during the encore Bono tells the crowd, "This is far too late for everybody to be up."

November 23
U2 spends another day at Kingdom Sound working on new material with Sandy Pearlman.

November 24
Hitsville North, Passaic, with the Nitecaps. Having completed the recording session yesterday, U2 spend the morning back at Kingdom Sound mixing their work. Bono tells *Trouser Press* magazine that they're working on one three-minute track: "We don't know how it's going to turn out; it'll either be brilliant or an absolute failure. If I played it for you you'd say 'What the hell is that?' It's sort of a psychotic rockabilly song, with a drum figure that runs from beginning to end."

U2 are apparently not pleased with the Sandy Pearlman experiment and the material is never released. After their studio work is done, U2 heads to Passaic for tonight's gig, which starts at midnight.

November 25
Hitsville South, Asbury Park. Early in the day, U2 does a shoot on the Jersey shore with photographer Lisa Haun. Three fans who've been

Above: U2 attend to promotional duties in Atlanta.

to several shows on this tour are also there. Despite the cold, Bono walks around in barefeet and even goes into the cold water for a quick swim in his underwear. U2 and the three fans all go see a movie – *Time Bandits*. Afterward, Bono, Larry, and Adam go back to their hotel to rest before the gig, while Edge and the fans go bowling.

November 28
Hollywood Palladium, Los Angeles, with Romeo Void.

November 29
Warfield Theater, San Francisco, with Garland Jeffreys.

November 30
After arriving in Atlanta, U2 do a series of photo shoots with Adrian Boot.

December 1
The Agora, Atlanta.

December 2
Vanderbilt University, Nashville. While in Nashville, Edge buys an Epiphone lap steel guitar.

December 4
Royal Oak Music Theater, Detroit.

December 5
Fountain Street Church, Grand

Rapids. Bono isn't feeling well, so the band cut the show short with three songs left to play. But the local paper still raves about U2's performance: "[Their] sermon of rock tunes with religious overtones won over new followers. U2 could be the band of tomorrow."

December 6
Park West, Chicago.

December 7
Dooley's, East Lansing, with the Producers.

December 8
The Agora, Cleveland. U2 plays two shows today at The Agora: the first is a free lunchtime show sponsored by local radio station, WMMS. That's followed by their regularly scheduled show in the evening.

December 9
Bono has breakfast with local college DJs from radio stations WUJC, WCSB and WRUW before leaving for Pittsburgh.

December 10
Uncle Sam's, Buffalo.

December 11
Ontario Theater, Washington, with Bow Wow Wow.

December 12
Stage West, Hartford.

December 13
Malibu Night Club, Lido Beach.

December 20-21
Lyceum, London, with the Alarm. U2 returns from the US tour to play two sold out shows at the Lyceum, earning tremendous critical praise in the process. The shows are described in *Record Mirror* as "the gig of 1981". After the first show, Neil Storey of Island Records presents the band with a Gold Disc for the *October* album.

With a full year of touring complete, U2 plan a couple of weeks off. But their so-called "vacation" includes time in the studio recording a new song, 'A Celebration'.

1982

With U2 growing and in need of a more structured support organisation, Paul McGuinness creates Principle Management this year. The band continues to tour relentlessly, including a rewarding stint playing support to the J. Geils Band in US arenas.

With a major crisis averted late last year, Bono and Edge grow more comfortable as active Christians in a rock band. Their faith is as strong as ever – perhaps even stronger – and they'll continue to meet with Christian friends for prayer meetings and Bible reading during the year. Perhaps emboldened by their decision to continue in U2, Bono and Edge do interviews with Christian magazines and talk more openly about their faith.

Bono and Ali get married in the summer, and the band begin work on their third album, *War*. By year's end, U2 are touring in support of the new album, fully committed to seeing how high they can climb in the music business.

January
U2 wins seven awards in the annual *Hot Press* readers' poll.

January 23
Leisureland, Galway. The October Tour restarts with three Irish shows.

January 24
City Hall, Cork.

January 26
Royal Dublin Society Hall, Dublin. U2 play the first rock concert at Dublin's RDS Hall. A show planned in Belfast around this time is cancelled due to structural problems at the concert hall.

February
The second issue of *U2 Magazine* is published this month.

U2 makes a respectable showing in the annual *NME* poll: number five for Best Group; number four for Best Album (*October*); number six for Best Male Singer (Bono), and number three Best Guitarist (Edge).

Before leaving for the US tour, Bono and friends spend a day helping in a Dublin centre for the homeless.

February 8
U2 leaves for the US, where the *October* tour is due to continue in a few days.

February 11
S.S. President Riverboat, New Orleans, with RZA. The second half of U2's US tour begins with a show on a five-deck riverboat, the S.S. President, as it sails up the Mississippi River. The crowd

Left: Torhout Festival, Belgium, July 3.

is a bit rough, but the only incident is when a couple of fans toss ice cubes at Bono; Bono retaliates by pouring beer on them.

Boston DJ Carter Alan is on hand, and interviews the band before the gig. *NME* writer Richard Cook attends the show to report on U2's progress, and brings with him Dutch photographer Anton Corbijn, who meets the band for the first time and begins a working friendship that lasts to this day.

Island Records' Rob Partridge introduced U2 to Anton Corbijn
"The link with Anton was absolutely instant – the band is very shrewd and they'd noticed his pictures in the *NME*; they had an aesthetic about them, which appealed to U2. And that progressed to Anton doing every picture since then, doing their videos,

and essentially becoming cultural advisor to the band."

Anton Corbijn remembers meeting U2
"I didn't like their music much. I listened to it for the first time on the plane on the way to New Orleans to photograph them. They'd just released *October*. They were going to be playing on a boat in the Mississippi, and I thought, 'Okay, I'll stay for just a few songs and then I'll leave.' But when I got there the boat took off. I didn't realise it was actually going to go out on the water. So I couldn't leave."

February 12
Richard Cook joins U2 on the bus ride from New Orleans to Austin, and interviews them for an upcoming *NME* feature. Cook asks about U2's lack of chart success. "My attitude is 'so what?'" Bono says. "We've still sold more records than most 'hit single' bands. We've excited audiences more. But the time may have come for us to sharpen our singles outlook."

February 13
Opry House, Austin. After tonight's concert, a group of fans invite Bono, Edge and Larry to Sunday church services tomorrow morning. They accept.

February 14
Cardi's, San Antonio. Bono, Edge and Larry go to morning services at Westlake Bible Church, which has its services in an Austin schoolhouse. On the drive from Austin to San Antonio, U2 stops to visit a small zoo which Adam Clayton, in his *Hot Press* tour diary, calls "very depressing".

Adam writes about U2's odd visit to the zoo
"The high point was a mad monkey which had

Edge: "It's time we get into line" February 23

"We realize the band ... is at a crossing point. For a long time we haven't talked with interviewers about the fact we're Christians, because it's so easy for people to misunderstand. It's easy for people who are not Christians, especially writers who do not understand, to take what we say and misinterpret it.

"I really believe Christ is like a sword that divides the world, and it's time we get into line and let people know where we stand. You know, to much of the world, even the mention of the name of Jesus Christ is like someone scratching their nails across a chalkboard."

epileptic fits accompanied by blood-chilling shrieks. It was really quite a scream because Bono started singing. This infuriated the creature even further – its shrieks grew louder. Bono matched its volume until the deranged creature started to beat his head against the wall."

February 15
Cardi's, Houston.

February 16
Cardi's, Dallas.

February 17
Jammie's, Oklahoma City.

February 19
Night Moves, St. Louis.

February 21
First Avenue, Minneapolis.

February 22
Headliners, Madison, with the Vers.

February 23
University Of Illinois Auditorium, Champaign, with Combo Audio. After tonight's show, U2 are interviewed by Terry Mattingly for CCM, a Christian music magazine. Although the band have gone out of its way to avoid talking about their faith up to this point, they speak candidly now. "It's time to talk about it," Edge says. One of the revelations in the article, which appears in the magazine's August issue, is that Edge, Larry and Bono use Bible study and prayer to help them "wind down" after concerts. Bono says U2 doesn't want to be stereotyped as a "religious band", but is confident that most fans understand the messages in many U2 songs.

February 25
Uptown Theater, Kansas City.

February 26
U2 arrive in Denver and the band members escape to a ski resort about an hour outside the city. They don't tell anyone where they're going, figuring a ski trip won't be approved. When they get back to Denver, the band goes to a local movie theater to see *Reds*.

February 27
Rainbow Music Hall, Denver. Tickets for the show are $4.

February 28
Colorado State University, Fort Collins.

March
U2 spend time in the studio this month with Blondie's Jimmy Destri producing. In this session, U2 finish a rarity called 'Be There', which is never released. They also develop ideas that will eventually become 'Endless Deep', a future B-side, and 'The Unforgettable Fire'.

March 3
Lee County Arena, Fort Meyers, opening for the J. Geils Band. U2 plays the first of 14 support dates with the J. Geils Band, a stint arranged by Premier Talent as a way to get U2 extra exposure while sales of the *October* album are slowing down dramatically. It also introduces them to the experience

Below: Backstage at the Ritz, March 17, U2 and Paul McGuiness (third right) with friends.

of playing large arenas, and helps them pocket some much-needed extra cash. "We're nearly always close to break even on the road," Adam says early in the tour, "but this time we were going to lose too much. Then we found out that we were going to do a couple of weeks with the J. Geils Band."

March 4
Civic Auditorium, West Palm Beach, opening for the J. Geils Band. After tonight's show, local DJ MC Kostek invites the band back to the WCEZ studios. Adam and Edge accept, and serve as guest DJs on Kostek's overnight show, choosing songs and introducing them on air.

March 5
Curtis Hixon Convention Hall, Tampa, opening for the J. Geils Band.

March 6
Leon County Arena, Tallahassee, opening for the J. Geils Band.

March 10
University Of Tennessee, Knoxville, opening for the J. Geils Band. After the show, U2 catch the end of a Rod Stewart concert.

March 11
Civic Center, Atlanta, opening for the J. Geils Band.

March 12
North Hall Auditorium, Memphis, opening for the J. Geils Band. *Miller's Cave, Memphis*. After tonight's show at the North Hall Auditorium, U2 celebrates Adam's birthday at a club called Miller's Cave, and play a couple songs to mark the occasion.

March 13
Gardens, Louisville, opening for the J. Geils Band.

March 14
Indiana Convention Center, Indianapolis, opening for the J. Geils Band.

March 16
University Of Massachusetts, Amherst. With a week off before the J. Geils tour resumes, U2 play a few extra shows on their own.

March 17
On break from the J. Geils support slot, U2 plans to take part in the annual St. Patrick's Day parade in New York City by playing a live show on a large float. Paul McGuinness came up with the idea as a promotional gimmick – putting an Irish band in an Irish parade.

The plan falls apart when McGuinness learns that the organisers of the parade are considering naming Irish hunger

1982

Lynn Goldsmith: "Get in the street! Now!" March 17

"When I took them out on the street to make some pictures, I thought, 'Oh my God, I'm so lucky it's St. Patrick's Day, put them in the street, in the parade.' And Bono stood there and said, 'We can't just get in the middle of the street!' And I stood there, screaming at U2, *'Get in the street! Now!'*"

striker Bobby Sands honorary Grand Marshall. McGuinness discusses the situation with parade officials, and ends up in a heated debate about the Irish Republican Army (IRA). U2 pull out of the parade, not wanting to take part in something that could be construed as showing support for the IRA. This experience – going face-to-face with IRA supporters in New York – will have a noticeable impact on the band's musical direction.

While not officially part of the parade, the band does a photo shoot on the parade route, walking together in the rain with umbrellas while Lynn Goldsmith takes photos.

Parade organizers are upset with the band's unauthorised walk along the route, and nearly have U2 arrested.

Concerts tonight and tomorrow at The Ritz are hastily arranged so that the band's time in New York isn't wasted.

March 17-18
The Ritz, New York.

March 19
Nassau Community College, Garden City.

March 20
Brown University, Providence.

Below: U2's first show in Portugal, August 3.

March 21
Nightclub, Phoenix. Still on break from the J. Geils tour, U2 jam with a local artist.

March 22
U2 releases single 'A Celebration'/ 'Trash, Trampoline, And The Party Girl', which reaches number 47 on the UK charts. 'Fire' is the B-side on the Japanese release.

March 25
Coliseum, Phoenix, opening for the J. Geils Band.

March 26
San Diego Sports Arena, San Diego, opening for the J. Geils Band.

March 27
Sports Arena, Los Angeles, opening for the J. Geils Band.

March 29-30
Civic Center, San Francisco, opening for the J. Geils Band. U2 plays its final support shows with the J. Geils Band. The supporting slot is beneficial for U2, as they manage to win over new fans and even earn a few encores – very rare for

supporting acts on a major tour. Peter Wolf, lead singer for J. Geils, later refutes reports that his band resented U2's success: "There was never any feeling of being threatened, even if U2 got nine encores! We felt great that there was a band that we thought had a certain integrity; we respected them."

U2 cancel plans to continue touring in Canada, Australia, Japan and even India, so they can take their first real break in almost two years. They return to Ireland and rent a small house in Howth to use as rehearsal space over the summer.

April
U2 shoot a video for 'A Celebration' at Kilmainham Jail in Dublin with Meiert Avis directing.

Bono and Edge speak openly about their faith during an interview in Dublin with Derek Poole, a writer from *Streams*, a Belfast-based Christian magazine.

May
The third issue of *U2 Magazine* is

published this month. It includes excerpts from an interview Bono did in the US earlier in the year: "We may well be the future of rock'n'roll, but so what? When I go back to Dublin to my girlfriend it's more of a distraction that I'm in a band than any big deal, and my old man still shouts at me for not doing the dishes before I go to bed."

May 1
U2 performs three songs for a UK TV special called *Get Set For Summer*.

May 14
'T Heem, Hattem, with Powerplay. U2 performs for a Dutch TV programme that airs on July 7. Trying to capitalize on the success of this appearance, Island Records releases the live version of 'I Will Follow' from this show as a single in The Netherlands and Germany. It reaches number 12 in the local charts, and becomes a highly sought-after collector's item. 'Gloria' is the B-side.

May 15
London. U2 performs three tracks for the TV show, *Something Else*, which air a week later.

July 1
Groenoordhallen, Leiden, opening for Tom Tom Club and Talking Heads.

July 2
Festival Grounds, Roskilde, Copenhagen.

July 3
Festival Grounds, Torhout. With U2 playing several large festivals this summer, Bono looks for new ways to connect with the crowd on these vast grounds. In Torhout, he stumbles on two ways that will become staples at future shows: Bono climbs to the top of the stage rigging so fans far away can see him, and also calls for a large, white flag to be passed up to the stage where he carries it around and waves it to the crowd.

July 4
Festival Grounds, Werchter.

July 17
Sheriff Street, Dublin. U2 perform a free, rooftop gig at the *Inner City Looking On* festival on Sheriff Street in Dublin. It's a dangerous neighbourhood that's known for crime and unemployment. While U2 play on the roof to a crowd below, about 30 people climb the only stepladder to the roof and join U2 on stage, standing in front of the band as they play. One boy joins Larry behind the drum kit, and a young girl jumps into Bono's arms as he sings. An older man takes the mic away from Bono, and sings for so long that Bono has to unplug that mic and use another.

"I just stopped the show and started to sing…"
Bono remembers one of the dangerous moments of U2's rooftop gig on Sheriff Street.
"This guy who looked six feet wide, a docker, just walked on stage and stood in front of me. 'Let's twist again like we did last summer', he said. 'Play it.'
   "The whole crowd quieted – this was the confrontation: were we chicken or not? I must admit, I was chicken. I just stopped the show and started to sing, no accompaniment, 'Let's twist again, like we did last summer…' And I looked at the crowd, and all the kids, the mothers, fathers, the wine and whiskey bottles in their hands, started singing and dancing. And the guy smiled."

July 18
Punchestown Racecourse, Dublin. U2 plays a *Hot Press* rock festival. During the show, Bono brings his fiancée Alison on stage, and also introduces Dublin well known rock biz personality BP Fallon on stage during '11 O'Clock Tick Tock'.

Above: Gateshead Festival, July 31.

July 31
International Stadium, Gateshead.

August
The fourth issue of *U2 Magazine* is published this month.

August 3
Festival Grounds, Vilar De Mouros. U2 plays its first show in Portugal, at the Festival of Vilar de Mouros.

August 7
Ruisrock Festival, Turku. On the way back to Dublin after this show, Bono meets Irish politician Garret Fitzgerald at Heathrow Airport, and sits next to him on the flight to Dublin.

August 8
On Edge's 21st birthday, U2 begin work on the *War* album at Windmill Lane Studios in Dublin. Though they had considered other producers, Steve Lillywhite joins them to produce his third straight U2 album. Unlike their first two albums, U2 are more prepared and have a plan as they enter the studio.

Steve Lillywhite: "Don't be like The Edge! Be like Mick Jones!" August 8

"I think it was a case of, 'OK, guys, we need to be The Clash'. I always have these memories of Bono saying to Edge, 'Don't do that! Don't be like The Edge! Be like Mick Jones!' – trying to push Edge into a more aggressive guitar playing. Edge is a very whimsical, ethereal sort of person, and I think Bono was trying to get him to be more pointed and more sharp. He had his echo box, and you play around with the sound you make, so Bono was pushing him to be more aggressive. I seem to remember the words 'The Clash' came out more than once in the sessions."

Adam explains U2's approach to recording the *War* album

"In the past, when we went in the studio, we simply didn't know our craft well enough. On *War* you can hear more of the arrangements coming from a bass-and-drum thing; the rhythm section's standing up. That means Edge doesn't have to play as much. On the first two albums, knowingly or not, he was covering up for a rhythm section that wasn't quite mature. We're a much tougher band now."

Recording lasts for about three months, with an interruption for Bono's wedding. The final track, '40', is recorded on U2's last day of work, while the next band is waiting to use the studio. Adam isn't there, so Edge plays both the guitar and bass.

August 21
Bono marries his high-school sweetheart, Alison Stewart, at a ceremony in Raheny, Dublin. The wedding is officiated by Reverend Jack Heaslip, who first met Bono and Ali while serving as a guidance counselor at Mount Temple. Chris Rowe of Shalom, with whom Bono has remained close, gives the sermon. Bono chooses Adam to be his best man, another sign that the band is moving past the spiritual conflicts that separated them in recent years.

The ceremony is held at the Guinness Church of Ireland church and the reception takes place at Sutton Castle. A group called The Cyclones perform, but during the party U2 take over their instruments and joins Paul Brady in a performance of 'Tutti Frutti'. The party is so wild that it knocks out electricity in the castle.

Barry Devlin remembers Bono's wedding
"I just remember that the wedding was tremendous fun. There was a lot of dancing, there was a lot of people bumping into each other. There was a lot of high spirits. And it was a kid's wedding, you know. But it was a great day."

Bono and Ali spend their two-week honeymoon at Chris Blackwell's "Goldeneye" property in Jamaica, the former home of James Bond creator Ian Fleming. Bono continues working on lyrics for U2's next album. While Larry and Adam also take a couple weeks off, Edge continues working on new music; he comes up with 'Sunday Bloody Sunday' and 'Seconds' during this time.

November
The fifth issue of *U2 Magazine* is published this month. It contains the news that U2's next album is likely to be called *War*.

Responding to an invitation from Bono, Garret Fitzgerald, head of the Fine Gael political party, and his wife, Joan, visit U2 in the recording studio during the *War* sessions for a photo opportunity in the final days of a political campaign. Fitzgerald's photo in U2's studio is all over the papers. He'll go on to win the race for Taoiseach.

December 1
Tiffany's, Glasgow. U2 begin a four-week European tour designed to introduce new songs from the *War* album prior to the record's release in the new year. 'Surrender', 'Sunday, Bloody Sunday' and 'New Year's Day' are all premiered tonight.

December 2
Apollo Theater, Manchester, with the Alarm. It's cold in Manchester today, so Bono invites a group of fans into the Apollo to thaw out while they listen to U2's soundcheck.

December 3
De Montfort Hall, Leicester, with the Set. Bono invites about 30 people inside to hear today's soundcheck.

December 4
Odeon, Birmingham, with the Alarm. Another show, another free soundcheck performance for a couple dozen fans that are allowed inside before the show.

December 5
Lyceum, London, with the Alarm.

December 6
Hammersmith Palais, London, with Zerra One and the Alarm. Bono joins the Alarm on stage for 'Knocking On Heaven's Door'. During U2's set, Bono dedicates 'I Fall Down' to a U2 fan named Duncan who was supposed to be at the show, but was hospitalised in a serious car accident. Bono isn't aware that Duncan dies in a Dublin hospital tonight. The show is recorded by BBC Radio.

December 8
Muziekcentrum Vredenburg, Utrecht, with Zerra One.

December 9
Martinihal, Groningen.

December 10
Volksbelang, Mechelen, with Angry Voices.

December 11
Brielpoort, Deinze, with Angry Voices.

December 12
Limburghal, Genk.

December 14
Falkoner Teatret, Copenhagen. Steve Wickham joins the band on stage to play violin during 'Into The Heart' and 'Sunday Bloody Sunday'. Wickham had also contributed to the upcoming *War* album. During '11 O'Clock Tick Tock', Bono invites fans to join the band on stage. Several dozen fans, mostly girls, take him up on the offer, dancing or sitting around the band members as the show continues.

December 15
Konserthuset, Stockholm. While in Scandinavia for a few shows, U2 shoots a music video for 'New Year's Day' at the Salen ski resort.

VOLKSBELANG MECHELEN
Vrijdag 10 december 1982 te 20 uur
U 2
Angry Voices
Tickets: 320 Fr.
No 20961

They travel by plane from Stockholm to Salen, and then fly by helicopter to the video shoot location. Paul McGuinness and Anton Corbijn arrive hours later on the helicopter's second trip.

U2 stand in fairly deep snow as the crew films them miming the song. The group moves to another location in the late afternoon, when it's already dark in Sweden, and the shoot continues as the band plays around a campfire. They finally head back to Stockholm for tonight's show.

December 16
Unknown, Oslo. The video shoot for 'New Year's Day' continues today. Female stand-ins are used for shots of four people riding horses through the deep snow, because U2's insurance wouldn't cover any injuries. Since Anton Corbijn arrived so late yesterday, U2 agree to do a photo shoot near Stockholm before traveling to Oslo for tonight's show.

December 18
City Hall, Cork.

December 19
Leisureland, Galway, with Blue In Heaven.

December 20
Maysfield Leisure Center, Belfast. U2 fans in Belfast hear 'Sunday, Bloody Sunday' for the first time. Introducing the song, Bono tells the audience it's not a rebel song, and recites some of the lyrics to make sure the audience understands the song's intent. He promises that if

Below: Bono on stage at Mechelen, Belgium, December 10.

the crowd doesn't like it, they'll never play the song in Belfast again. The crowd roars with approval when the song ends. "It was very emotional," Larry says later. "It's a very special song, because it's the first time that we ever really made a statement."

December 22-23-24
S.F.X. Center, Dublin, with Big Thorp (Dec. 22), Zerra One (Dec. 23), and Blue In Heaven (Dec. 24). U2's brief pre-*War* tour ends with three shows in Dublin.

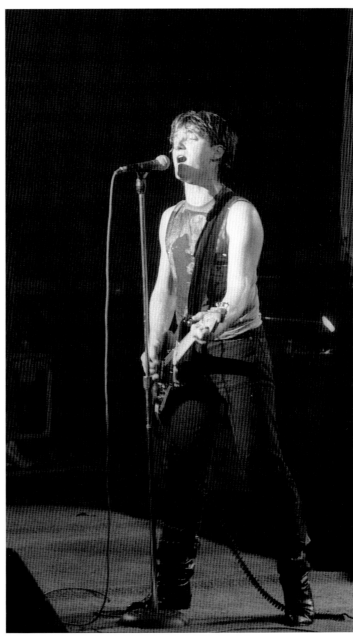

1983

U2 issues its third album, *War*, and cracks the UK Top 10 with 'New Year's Day'. The song doesn't reach the Top 50 in the US, but gets substantial airplay on radio and helps expose U2 to more new fans. Still, U2's plan to play anywhere and everywhere they can has the greatest impact on the band's success. They play a high-profile US Festival in California, and days later play what will become the most important gig of their early career: Red Rocks Amphitheatre near Denver. The show is recorded and gets heavy TV airplay. Some songs are included on *Under A Blood Red Sky*, U2's first live release. The show and album cement U2's status as a must-see live act.

Despite the band's development, they're deep in debt to Island Records. An Island executive writes a note to Chris Blackwell explaining the situation: "We're too much in debt with this band, we must drop them." Blackwell simply writes "No" on the note, underlines it, and sends it back. U2 is building a dedicated fan base via touring, and Blackwell is willing to wait for that success to translate to album and single sales that make the label money.

Edge steps outside of U2 this year for some solo work. Paul McGuinness also expands his outside interests, launching McGuinness/Whelan Music Publishing with composer Bill Whelan. The venture operates out of the Principle Management offices.

January
U2 releases the 'New Year's Day' single in Europe, with various formats including remixes of the song and additional tracks 'Treasure (Whatever Happened to Pete the Chop)', 'Fire (live)', 'I Threw a Brick Through a Window / A Day Without Me (live)', and 'Two Hearts Beat As One (US remix)'. The single reaches number 10 in the UK – U2's first UK Top 10 single. Late in the month, they play over a pre-recorded performance of the song on the BBC's *Top Of The Pops*.

U2 wins four awards this month in the annual *Hot Press* readers' poll: Best Polling Act, Best Group, Best Live Band, and Best Video ('A Celebration').

February
The sixth issue of *U2 Magazine* is published.

Also this month, 'New Year's Day' is released in North America. The song will rise as high as number 53 on the *Billboard* Hot 100 Singles chart, and number two on the *Radio and Records* AOR chart.

In an interview with *NME*'s Adrian Thrills, U2 reveal they're working on a score for the Royal Dublin Ballet.

February 14
U2 and Anton Corbijn do a photo shoot in the Dublin countryside for an upcoming edition of *NME*. Peter Rowen, the child featured on the *Boy* and upcoming *War* albums, is also part of the photo shoot.

February 16
U2 earns its first major award: They're named Best Live Act at the Brit Awards ceremony in London.

February 23
Boy and *October* are certified Silver by the British Phonographic Industry (BPI), with sales of more than 60,000 for each album.

February 26
Caird Hall, Dundee, with the Nightcaps. U2 kicks off the *War* Tour with a sold-out show. During 'Electric Co.', Bono climbs up to the balcony and walks precariously along the thin railing to the back of the hall. Edge makes his debut on lead vocals when the band plays 'Seconds'. Tonight is also the start of a long U2 concert tradition: closing a show with '40'.

February 27
Capitol Theatre, Aberdeen, with the Nightcaps.

February 28
Playhouse Theatre, Edinburgh, with the Nightcaps.

U2 releases its third studio album, *War*, produced by Steve Lillywhite. It features Peter Rowen on the cover, reprising his role from the *Boy* album. But the innocence of the first cover is replaced on *War* with a photo that shows the child scarred and afraid. The music is louder and more aggressive than the band's first two albums, and sounds nothing like the smooth pop

Left: U2's historic concert at Red Rocks, June 5.

and synthesizer artists that are taking over the charts. *War* sees U2 addressing the world around them more directly than ever. In addition to 'Sunday Bloody Sunday', songs like 'Seconds', 'New Year's Day' and 'The Refugee' are grounded in Cold War and conflict, hardly the subject matter of most songs on the radio at the time.

Bono explains the "uncool" *War*
"It was incredibly uncool to make this record, and it completely freaked out most people – Geldof being one of them. I remember Geldof saying, *'What are you at? I mean, this is pop music we're talking about, and you're taking on these ideas.'* All these people – Sting. They were doing the do-do-do-do/de-da-da-das! So this was a break, this was not cool – for a band to take this position."

War debuts at number one in the UK, U2's first chart-topping album. It debuts at number 91 in the US, and eventually climbs as high as number 12.

Reviews for the album are very positive. "U2 may not be great intellectuals," writes J.D. Considine in his four-star *Rolling* Stone album review, "and *War* may sound more profound than it really is. But the

Above: U2 perform before the *War* backdrop on The Tube, Newcastle, March 16.

songs here stand up against anything on The Clash's *London Calling* in terms of sheer impact, and the fact that U2 can sweep the listener up in the same sort of enthusiastic romanticism that fuels the band's grand gestures is an impressive feat."

"It is a major leap forward," says Liam Mackey in *Hot Press*, "conceptually and technically, quickly persuading this listener to the view that it totally eclipses their previous two albums. I'll even go a step further and proclaim *War*, among the major albums of the last few years."

But *Sounds* magazine isn't convinced: "*War* suggests a tired U2, a U2 that perhaps hasn't quite sorted out the variances between live and recorded rock music." Tracks: 'Sunday Bloody Sunday', 'Seconds', 'New Year's Day', 'Like A Song', 'Drowning Man', 'The Refugee', 'Two Hearts Beat As One', 'Red Light', 'Surrender', '40'

March

U2 issue two singles this month: 'Two Hearts Beat As One' is released in Ireland, the UK, France, Australia, Japan, and the US The single has many formats, with 'Fire', 'New Year's Day (US remix)', and several remixes of the main track as B-sides. It climbs to number 18 in the UK. 'Sunday Bloody Sunday' is released in other European countries and Japan at the same time, with 'Endless Deep', 'Two Hearts Beat As One (US remix)', 'New Year's Day (US remix)', and 'Red Light' as B-sides on its various formats, and reaches number seven in the UK as an import.

U2 makes their first movie contribution, as two versions of 'October' appear on the soundtrack to *They Call It An Accident*.

March 1
City Hall, Newcastle, with the Nightcaps.

March 2
Lancaster University, with the Nightcaps.

March 3
Royal Court Theater, Liverpool, with the Nightcaps.

March 4
Victoria Hall, Hanley, with the Nightcaps.

March 6
Guildhall, Portsmouth, with the Nightcaps.

March 7
Colston Hall, Bristol, with the Nightcaps.

March 8
University, Exeter, with the Nightcaps.

March 9
Arts Centre, Poole, with the Nightcaps.

March 10
Odeon, Birmingham, with the Nightcaps.

U2 play over a pre-recorded version of 'Two Hearts Beat As One', which airs tonight on the BBC's *The Kenny Everett Show*. The taping date is unknown.

March 11
St. David's Hall, Cardiff, with the Nightcaps.

March 12
War debuts at number one on the UK album chart, replacing Michael Jackson's *Thriller*.

March 13
Top Rank, Brighton. Adam gets champagne, cake, and gifts brought to him on stage to celebrate his 23rd birthday. Mike Peters of the Alarm joins Bono to sing 'Knocking On Heaven's Door'.

March 14
Hammersmith Odeon, London, with the Nightcaps.

March 15
Gaumont Theatre, Ipswich, with the Nightcaps.

March 17
City Hall, Sheffield, with the Nightcaps.

March 18
Tune Tees TV Studios, Newcastle.
Leeds University, Leeds, with the Nightcaps. U2 does two performances. First is a five-song set for *The Tube* television show. When that ends, U2 drives to Leeds, arriving late for an 8:30 p.m. show.

March 19
Apollo Theater, Manchester, with the Nightcaps.

March 20
Assembly Rooms, Derby, with the Nightcaps.

March 21
Hammersmith Odeon, London.

Below: On stage at the US Festival, California, May 30.

March 22
Hammersmith Palais, London, with the Alarm.

March 23
U2 take a quick flight from London to Glasgow for a concert tomorrow night. On the plane with them is writer Jim Henke, who's working on a lengthy feature article that will appear a couple months later while U2 are touring the US.

March 24
Tiffany's, Glasgow, with the Alarm. Jim Henke interviews the band in the hotel restaurant in Glasgow shortly before tonight's show. The band shares some of their most overt statements on faith yet. "Three of us are committed Christians," Bono says. "We refute the belief that man is just a higher stage of animal, that he has no spirit. I think that when people start believing that, the real respect for humanity is gone."

March 25
Royal Court Theater, Liverpool, with the Alarm.

March 26
City Hall, Newcastle, with the Alarm.

March 27
Odeon, Birmingham, with Big Country.

March 28
Royal Centre, Nottingham, with the Perfect Crime and Big Country.

March 29
Hammersmith Palais, London, with Big Country. Mike Peters of the

Alarm and Big Country's Stuart Adamson join the band to sing 'Knocking On Heaven's Door'.

March 30
BBC TV Studios, London. U2 tapes 'Two Hearts Beat As One' for *Top Of The Pops* for airing a day later. The appearance backfires, and the song makes an unheard of drop in the charts the week after U2's appearance.

"We're not going to do *Top Of The Pops* anymore," Edge says in a 1984 interview with *Jamming!* magazine. "It just doesn't work for us, it's not the right arena for this group. I don't think the people who buy U2 records want to see us on *Top Of The Pops* – I don't think they're particularly interested in what's happening on *Top Of The Pops*."

April
Around this time, Edge records some songs with Jah Wobble at the Fallout Shelter recording studio in London.

April 3
Festival De Printemps, Bourges. While in France, U2 spend a day in the Sacré Coeur Basilica in Montmartre, Paris, shooting a music video for 'Two Hearts Beat As One'. The clip is directed by Meiert Avis. Anton Corbijn also does a photo shoot while the band is in Paris; one of the photos from this shoot is later used on the cover of the 'Pride (In the Name of Love)' single.

April 5
War is certified Gold by the BPI, with sales of more than 100,000 in the UK.

April 21
U2 arrive in New York two days ahead of a tour that will begin in North Carolina.

April 22
Bono does an interview with Scott Isler of *Trouser Press* magazine in his hotel room. He tells Isler that the band plans to go see the movie *Tootsie* while in New York.

April 23
Kenan Stadium, Chapel Hill. U2 open a North American tour supporting the *War* album. They're the third of four acts on the bill for this "Carolina Concert for Children" benefit gig, and play after sets from Grand Master Flash and the Producers, and before Todd Rundgren. The crowd is far back from the stage, but there's a walkway that runs about 75 feet out toward the audience. Bono uses the walkway to get closer to the crowd, and will request similar staging at future shows. Though it's raining during the show, Bono dangerously climbs up the slippery scaffolding with a white flag. He reaches the top of the stage some 30 feet up and continues to sing while the band looks on very concerned. This will become an ongoing routine throughout this tour – Bono climbing to the highest point he can reach, with no regard for the risks involved, in an effort to reach out and connect with everyone in the growing audiences that are coming to U2's concerts.

Before the show, Bono and Edge do interviews with D.D. Thornton of WKZL radio. Bono, Edge, and Adam do interviews with WQDR.

April 24
Chrysler Hall, Norfolk, with Pylon.

April 25
Ritchie Stadium, College Park, with Pylon.

April 27
Cayhuga County Communty College Gym, Auburn, with Robert Ellis Orrall. Some fans track down the band at the local Holiday Inn and get autographs after the show.

April 28
Rochester Institute Of Technology Ice Rink, Rochester.

April 29
State University Of New York, Delhi. U2's bus breaks down on the road after the show. They continue on in taxis and then find a pilot to fly them to Providence.

April 30
Brown University, Providence, with NRBQ. After their overnight travel problems, U2 arrives about two hours before their 12:00 p.m. concert.

May
The seventh issue of *U2 Magazine* is published.

May 1
University, Stony Brook.

May 3
Fulton Theater, Pittsburgh.

May 4
Adam, Edge and Larry join Carter Alan for an interview at Boston's WBCN-FM during Alan's evening program. They take phone calls and play Guest DJ for a couple hours. That night, Edge and Alan take in a Jah Wobble gig at a local club. Backstage after the show, Wobble plays Edge the completed version of his upcoming *Snake Charmer* EP, which isn't due for release for several months. Edge contributed to the recording session at the Fallout Shelter in London a month ago and is now hearing the results for the first time.

After saying goodbye to Wobble, Edge returns to U2's hotel where Adam and Larry are hanging out with Cars' guitarist Elliot Easton. Edge and Easton stay up talking into the wee hours of the morning.

May 5-6
Orpheum Theater, Boston. The May 6 show is recorded for radio, and the version of '11 O'Clock Tick Tock' from this show will appear on *U2 Live – Under A Blood Red Sky*.

May 7
State University Of New York, Albany, with Robert Hazard and David Johansen.

May 8
Trinity College, Hartford, with Our Daughter's Wedding. U2 perform during a student festival at Trinity College. Wanting to keep the concert a students-only event, college officials tell outside callers U2 is not playing there that day.

May 10
Yale University, New Haven, with Dream Syndicate. At Bono's request, a smaller stage is set out into the crowd away from the main stage, allowing Bono closer interaction with the audience, and previewing future tours like Zoo TV, PopMart, and Elevation.

Also today, tickets go on sale for U2's June 28 show at the Centrum, U2's first arena show in the Boston area. They sell all but a couple of hundred of the 11,000 available tickets.

May 11
Palladium, New York, with Dream Syndicate.

May 12
Capitol Theater, Passaic, with Dream Syndicate. After the show, guests backstage include The Who's John Entwistle and Sting of The Police. The two bass players enjoy a spirited conversation with Adam.

May 13-14
Tower Theater, Philadelphia, with Dream Syndicate. The first show is recorded for radio distribution. Bruce Springsteen is at the second show, and Bono dedicates a song to Steel Mill, one of Bruce's first bands. After the show, Springsteen joins U2 backstage.

May 16
Shea Center, Buffalo, with Dream Syndicate.

May 17
Massey Hall, Toronto, with Dream Syndicate.

May 19
Music Hall, Cleveland, with Dream Syndicate. Before tonight's show, Bono, Edge and Adam do an interview with DJ Kid Leo of WMMS-FM.

May 20
Grand Circus Theater, Detroit, with Dream Syndicate. In between soundcheck and the gig, Adam and Bono do an interview with Kevin Knapp for *Creem* magazine.

Terri Hemmert remembers meeting U2, May 21

"[U2] were exhausted because they were touring the Midwest by bus and weren't even staying overnight in Chicago. They were due to play the Aragon later that evening but took the time to hear what we had to say. Marianne brought catalogues of past exhibits including *The Unforgettable Fire*, an exhibit about the atomic bombings of Japan at the end of World War II and *Martin Luther King Jr, Peacemaker*. Bono and the lads were so interested in the concept of a museum for peace. We had a wonderful meeting and they promised to deliver. Did they ever!!! They donated their stage backdrop from the tour, one of the white flags Bono used on stage and the manuscript I requested at the very beginning of this process. So we were thrilled that they were so generous. Give Peace A Chance was an enormous success!"

May 21
Aragon Ballroom, Chicago, with Dream Syndicate.

Early in the day, U2 meets at their hotel's café with Marianne Philbin and Terri Hemmert of the Chicago Peace Museum. The museum is exhibiting a series of paintings and drawings made by survivors of the Hiroshima and Nagasaki nuclear bombings called *The Unforgettable Fire*. U2 is inspired by what they learn about the exhibit and the museum's message of non-violence. They agree to contribute some of the stage set from the *War* tour as well as Bono's handwritten lyrics to 'New Year's Day' for inclusion in the museum's Give Peace A Chance exhibit, which is due to open September 11, 1983.

U2's relationship with the Peace Museum will continue well after this initial meeting. In later years, the band will help pay for the museum to send travelling versions of its exhibits around the US and to Dublin. In 1987, Bono will write a poem about the Chicago Peace Museum, *Dreams In a Box*, which will be used in many of the museum's displays and exhibits.

May 22
Northrop Auditorium, Minneapolis, with Dream Syndicate.

May 25
Queen Elizabeth Theater, Vancouver, with Dream Syndicate.

May 26
Paramount Theater, Seattle. Bono bodysurfs on top of the audience, which passes him all the way to the back of the theater.

May 27
Paramount Theatre, Portland, with Dream Syndicate.

May 30
Glen Helen Regional Park, Devore. U2 play at the massive outdoor US Festival. During 'The Electric Co.', Bono gets a white flag and, with it, climbs 100-foot-high scaffolding to the highest point of the stage, where he continues singing the song. He crosses the scaffolding and climbs down the other side. The U2 crew tells Bono after the show that they don't approve of the risks he's taking on stage. Edge phones Carter Alan at Boston's WBCN-FM and discusses U2's performance, and Bono's stage antics, in an impromptu, on-air phone interview.

June 1
Civic Auditorium, San Francisco, with Romeo Void.

June 2
The crew bus breaks down in Nevada early today, and they're stranded overnight until the band's bus finds them.

June 3
Salt Palace Assembly Hall, Salt Lake City, with the Alarm. The Alarm borrow U2's gear for their set because their own gear is on the crew bus that broke down in Nevada yesterday.

Above: In the rain and mist at Red Rocks, June 5.

Bono remembers Red Rocks, June 5

"We had all the camera people over here. We'd paid all their wages, we'd paid their flights over. We had to go on with the concert. We heard that Barry Fey was coming into town … very, very cross that this concert couldn't take place at Red Rocks. We had to explain to him there was no way we could afford for it not to take place."

Above: "We had to go on." Bono at Red Rocks, June 5.

June 5

Red Rocks Amphitheatre, Denver. With U2's live shows becoming the band's calling card on this successful tour, they decide it's time to capture a U2 performance on video. Having seen Red Rocks in 1981, the band decides it's the perfect spot for filming. Paul McGuinness hires a film crew from the popular British TV program, *The Tube*, and brings an audio crew out from Boston (Randy Ezratty's Effanel Music, the same crew that recorded the band a month ago at The Orpheum) to record the show. Radio broadcast rights are sold to NBC, and US TV rights are divided up between cable networks Showtime and MTV. The gig becomes a Big Production.

But problems abound, largely due to poor weather that begins several days before the show.

Concert promoter Chuck Morris remembers Red Rocks

"Barry [Fey] and I were flying back from the US Festival that day. Horrible weather. We were flying back at 1 o'clock in the afternoon and we saw snow in the mountains. It was scary."

The poor conditions make it difficult to get the band's gear and the video equipment up the mountains to the amphitheatre. There's great concern about safety with so much rain falling on the electrical wiring and equipment. Many people, from promoters to crew, encourage U2 to cancel the show. But with so much money invested in bringing over the video crew from England, and with a last-minute assurance that the band, crew, and fans will be safe, U2 plays on.

The band promises a free indoor show the following night in Denver for those unable to make it to Red Rocks; Bono, Edge and Adam personally call local radio stations to spread the word. But despite the cold temperature, rain and the promise of a free show the following night, an estimated 5,000 fans still make the trek to see U2 perform. As the fans stay dry in their cars, Bono goes out to bring them coffee and tell them the band is planning to do the show. He also tells them the show will be general admission; everyone should come up close to the stage no matter what seat is printed on their ticket.

Promoter Barry Fey introduces the band, and U2 starts the show with a burst of energy, winning the crowd immediately. The fans witness a magical show in which U2, as they often do, delivers one of their best performances when up against the most challenging odds.

Barry Fey remembers Red Rocks

"I had Neil Diamond in town that night at McNichols Arena. I was gonna do both shows – Neil's a friend. I did the opening announcement for U2. I stood there and every number got stronger and stronger. I know that magic is an overused phrase, but if there was ever magic at a show, it was there."

"I stood by the stage and didn't move. I couldn't move. It didn't even occur to me to go to Neil Diamond. It was the biggest show in town that night, but not as far as importance."

The concert airs later in the US on the Showtime cable network, but at a dozen songs, it's not the full show. MTV later airs a nine-song version of the show, but with a different mix of songs from the Showtime program. The audio is also distributed via NBC Radio under the title, *War Is Declared*.

The band is so pleased with the performance they also decide to issue a live mini-LP, *U2 Live – Under A Blood Red Sky*. In the end they elect to use only two songs from Red Rocks: 'Gloria' and 'Party Girl'. The other six songs come from concerts in Boston and West Germany.

June 6
University of Colorado, Boulder, with the Divinyls and the Alarm. U2 offer free admission to tonight's show. The Alarm joins U2 on stage to do 'A Hard Rain's Gonna Fall'.

June 7
A show planned for Wichita, Kansas, is cancelled because of the late addition of last night's show in Boulder. U2 arrive in Kansas City tonight and watch *Star Wars: Return Of The Jedi* at a local movie theater.

June 8
Memorial Hall, Kansas City, with the Shapes.

June 9
Brady Theater, Tulsa, with the Alarm.

June 10
Lloyd Noble Center, Norman.

June 11
South Park Meadows, Austin, with the Alarm.

June 13
Bronco Bowl, Dallas, with the Alarm.

June 14
Music Hall, Houston, with the Alarm.

June 17
Sports Arena, Los Angeles, with the Alarm. Bono takes off into the crowd during 'Electric Co.', but this time, real trouble ensues. He's mobbed by fans grabbing for him and can't get back to the stage. Panicking, Bono jumps 20 feet down from the balcony to the main floor where he's caught by fans below. Other fans in the balcony follow his lead, jumping dangerously to the floor below. Luckily, no one is seriously hurt.

While trying to return to the stage, Bono pushes a fan; the fan pushes back and nearly starts a fistfight. Tour Manager Dennis Sheehan eventually rescues Bono and gets him back to the main stage. The incident forces U2 to confront Bono about leaving the stage, and demand that he won't do it again.

Watching all this happen somewhere in the Sports Arena tonight is a U2 fan named Phil Joanou.

June 18
U2 sees The Alarm play at Club Lingerie in Hollywood. Edge has trouble getting in because he doesn't have ID. Bono is there with Ali. Adam leaves early, presumably to enjoy the LA nightlife. Also on hand is Ethlie Ann Vare, who interviews Bono for *ROCK!* magazine.

June 21
Jai Alai Fronton Hall, Orlando, with the Alarm.
The Tube broadcasts footage from U2's recent Red Rocks concert.

June 22
Curtis Hixon Convention Hall, Tampa, with the Alarm.

June 23
Sunrise Musical Theater, Miami, with the Alarm.

June 24
Civic Auditorium, Jacksonville, with the Alarm.

June 25
Civic Center, Atlanta, with the Alarm.

June 27
Coliseum, New Haven, with Marshall Crenshaw and the Alarm.

June 28
The Centrum, Worcester, with the Alarm. U2 nearly sells out this 11,000-seat arena, and earns its biggest payday yet.

June 29
Pier 84, New York, with the Alarm. U2 finishes the US leg of its War tour. The tour grosses nearly $2 million and marks the first time U2 makes money while touring.

July
At a Dublin pub this month, Bono gives advice to a 17-year-old Canadian tourist who tells him she's thinking about studying at Dublin's Trinity College to become a teacher, but is concerned about not having respect from students. "Respect is something you have to fight for," Bono says. "You have to be true to yourself, and you have to have the craic." The girl doesn't know she's talking to Bono until her cousin tells her later. For the record, she does become a teacher and in telling the story to local press years later, credits Bono's inspiration for her career decision.

Bono talks about the L.A. Sports Arena stage jumping incident, June 17

"I lost my senses completely. I was trying to get the crowd to trust us. I went into the crowd with a flag, but I ended up standing on the balcony of the Sports Center [sic]. I threatened to jump off if they didn't back off. And, in fact, I did jump. The crowd caught me – but what about the others who followed me? Somebody could've died at that concert, and it was a real sickener for me. It's meant a total reevaluation of what we are about live. We don't need to use a battering ram. It has to be down to the music."

July 2
Festival Grounds, Torhout.

July 3
Festival Grounds, Werchter. Simple Minds singer Jim Kerr joins Bono on stage during U2's set, and Annie Lennox and Dave Stewart of Eurhythmics help out on a lengthy version of '40'.

July 8
NBC radio stations in the US begin airing *War Is Declared*, the two-record audio recording of U2's recent concert at Red Rocks. The programme is syndicated as part of the NBC Radio's *The Source* music series.

July 12
Edge marries girlfriend Aislinn O'Sullivan at a Catholic mass in Enniskerry. Since Edge is Protestant, he and Aislinn are required to complete Catholic education/counseling before the wedding. Bono serves as best man, and wedding guests include Steve Lillywhite and the Virgin Prunes. The newlyweds honeymoon in Sri Lanka, but struggle to get home after civil war breaks out there.

July 15
U2 receives their first Recording Industry Association of America (RIAA) certification when *War* reaches gold status with sales eclipsing 500,000 units.

August
The eighth issue of *U2 Magazine* is published.

Irish Prime Minister Garrett Fitzgerald asks Bono to join the Select Government Action Committee on Unemployment. Bono accepts, but his tenure is short-lived.

Bono recalls his time on the unemployment committee
"They had another language, committee-speak, and it wasn't mine. They did some very good work but I have to say my own contribution wasn't

as vital as it could have been. I just felt that if they were going to talk about unmarried mothers, I wanted an unmarried mother to be there and to talk. I wanted to put flesh and blood on statistics."

Also this month, US-based funk band War – playing off the idea that U2 borrowed their name for the War album – includes a track called 'U-2 Medley' on its new album, *Life* (*Is So Strange*).

August 14
Phoenix Park Racecourse, Dublin. U2 headline the "A Day at the Races" concert. It's the first of what will become a recurring theme when U2 plays Ireland: "Conquering heroes return home!" Bono's dad, Bob, makes his first appearance at a U2 show when Bono pulls him on stage. Annie Lennox helps Bono sing '40'.

August 20
Lorelei Amphitheater, St. Goarshausen. The Lorelei Festival airs live on German TV and radio. Though U2 play a tentative show, the German crowd is won over and U2's albums sell well after the gig. Five songs from this show are included on *U2 Live – Under A Blood Red Sky.*

U2's success at Lorelei prompts Island Records to rush '40' as a single to the German market, with 'Two Hearts Beat As One' on the B-side. The single's sleeve crows that U2 were "the discovery of Loreley '83".

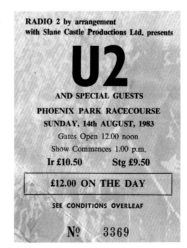

August 21
Kalvoya Festival, Oslo. After their final show of the summer, U2 answer media questions and Bono addresses the band's future: "We feel that U2 are to disband. Today was the last U2 gig. I'm not talking about the end of U2 – I'm talking about the start of U2. U2 is just beginning. This is the end of a cycle."

September 23
Bono joins the Alarm on stage at The Ritz in New York to sing a cover of 'Knocking On Heaven's Door'.

October
U2 release 'I Will Follow (live)' in the US only to help promote the upcoming *Under A Blood Red Sky* mini-LP. A remix of 'Two Hearts Beat As One' is the B-side. The single only reaches number 81 on the charts.

Edge appears on Jah Wobble's *Snake Charmer* EP. The set had been recorded earlier this year in London. Edge appears on three of the EP's five tracks: 'Snake Charmer', 'Hold On To Your Dreams', and 'Snake Charmer (reprise)'.

October 23
Bono joins the Alarm on stage again, this time in Dublin. He and Alarm singer Mike Peters sing 'Knocking On Heaven's Door', improvising lyrics and extending the song substantially.

November
The ninth issue of *U2 Magazine* is published.

November 13
U2 leaves Dublin for the next leg of the *War* tour, which will start with a date in Hawaii before moving on to Japan.

November 15
Bono and Edge do an interview with Honolulu radio station KPOI, and mention that they enjoyed a boat ride earlier today with Oingo Boingo.

November 16
NBC Arena, Honolulu, with Oingo

Boingo. During soundcheck, U2 try out new ideas for the next album and discover the guitar riff that will become 'Pride (In the Name of Love)'.

November 21

U2 releases *U2 Live – Under A Blood Red Sky*, a live mini-album produced by Jimmy Iovine. The cover has a photo of Bono taken at the June 5 Red Rocks concert, but only two of the eight songs come from that show. Five tracks are taken from the Lorelei Festival gig on August 20, and one from May 6 in Boston. The idea behind *Under A Blood Red Sky* is to capture the magic of a U2 live performance and document what the band feels is the end of its current phase.

The mini-album enters the UK charts at number nine and climbs as high as number two. It reaches number 28 in the US. In the *New Zealand Herald*, Darrell Giles sums up the feeling of many U2 fans when his review calls *Under A Blood Red Sky* "superb, but too short".

'Electric Co.' includes a costly oversight: Bono sings a bit of Stephen Sondheim's 'Send In The Clowns' during the song, but since U2 never obtained approval to include it on the release, they're

forced to settle a legal dispute by paying $50,000 and agreeing to remove the song snippet from future pressings.
Tracks: 'Gloria', '11 O'Clock Tick Tock', 'I Will Follow', 'Party Girl', 'Sunday Bloody Sunday', 'The Electric Co.', 'New Year's Day', '40'

November 22

Festival Hall, Osaka. U2 plays its first live show ever in Japan, the first of six shows in the country over eight days.

While in Japan, the band visits with their Japanese publisher, Tatsui Nagashima. He tells the band stories about the nuclear bombings of 1945.

November 23

Seto Bunka Centre, Nagoya. While in Japan, U2 appears on a TV show for an interview and a live performance of 'New Year's Day'. The hosts speak Japanese, so a translator is on camera helping with the conversation. The band brings its own still and video cameras on the set and takes pictures during the interview. Edge's guitar is DOA during the performance, making for a unique version of 'New Year's Day' with only drums, bass, and piano. The TV appearance likely takes place November 25, but the exact date is unknown.

November 26-27

Shibuya Kokaido, Tokyo.

November 29

Kosei Nenkin Hall, Tokyo.

November 30

Sun Plaza Hall, Tokyo.

December

U2 are voted Band of the Year in *Rolling Stone*'s writers' poll.

December 1

Before leaving Tokyo, U2 does an interview on Japanese TV with an English-speaking host. When they return home, U2 get together at Bono's house to work on ideas for their next album.

December 7

Under A Blood Red Sky is certified Gold by the BPI, with sales of more than 100,000 in the UK.

December 18

Victoria Apollo, London. U2 does a short set at "The Big One", a charity show for the Campaign for Nuclear Disarmament in London. Organizers plan to release an album and video from this show, but it never happens.

Larry explains the impact of visiting Japan on U2, November 22

"In *The Unforgettable Fire*, there are many Oriental touches, even in the design of the album cover, with the rich purpley colour and the calligraphy. When we went to Japan, we avoided all the 'touristy' trappings. Most bands stay in rock'n'roll hotels there; we stayed in traditional Japanese hotels and ate at traditional Japanese restaurants. Everywhere we went, we heard the traditional music, and it was fantastic. Obviously, we were all influenced by it."

1984

With U2's record contract close to expiring, Paul McGuinness successfully negotiates a new deal with Island founder Chris Blackwell. Other labels have approached the band, but McGuinness wants what only Island can give U2: the return of the band's copyrights. Terms of the new contract reportedly call for U2 to get $2 million per album for the next four albums and double their previous royalties; freedom to choose their album producers; Island to pay $75,000 per video and produce three videos per album; and, as McGuinness wants most, for U2 to get all their publishing rights back.

"I don't know. I don't have a million dollars in my pocket or in my bank account," Bono later says about the band's new contract. "I don't want to say that money is not important to me, because it is disgusting for me to say that at a time when a lot of people don't have money. So I'm thankful that I don't have to worry about my next meal. It is a threat to the band, because I don't want anything to take away from our focus."

U2 issues its fourth studio album this year, *The Unforgettable Fire*, with Brian Eno the surprising choice of producer. Bono meets Bob Dylan for the first time – an event that will have a huge impact on U2's direction for the rest of this decade. U2's reputation as a band that cares takes shape this year, with shows for Amnesty International and Bono's and Adam's involvement with Band Aid.

U2 tours Australia for the first time, and at year's end, a brief North American tour introduces the band to a level of fan frenzy they haven't experienced before.

Above: Adam and Bono arrive at Island Studios in London Notting Hill Gate to take part in the recording of 'Do They Know It's Christmas', November 25.

1984

January

U2 dominate the *Hot Press* readers' poll, with eight number ones: Best Polling Act, Best Group, Best Male Vocalist (Bono), Best Album (*War*), Best Live Band, Best Irish-based Act, Best Instrumentalist (The Edge), and Best LP Sleeve (*War*). They also claim six number twos.

Edge is named Best Guitarist in *NME*'s annual poll. And, although U2 have yet to visit New Zealand, the band scores highly there in a poll by *Rip It Up* magazine: Best Group of 1983, Best Album (*War*), and Best Vocalist (Bono).

January 25

Under A Blood Red Sky is certified Platinum by the BPI, with sales of more than 300,000 in the UK.

February

The 10th issue of *U2 Magazine* is published this month. In it, Bono hints at the radical changes U2 in mind for the next album: "I can't tell you where we're about to go but I know that I can't sleep at night with the thought of it all. I'm so excited about this idea that we've just begun – the way I feel is that we're undertaking a real departure. I can't stop talking about it. It would take about ten men to hold me down at the moment."

February 18

Adam travels to Galway to see Simple Minds perform.

February 27

Under a Blood Red Sky is certified as a Gold album by the RIAA.

March

Around this time, U2 shoots a "Happy Saint Patrick's Day from U2" video for MTV. They walk happily around the Dublin docklands near Windmill Lane, kick a soccer ball around, and talk with a mom and her kids about St. Patrick. BP Fallon is with the band, and shoots photos as they walk around the area.

March 2/3

Adam is arrested in Dublin and charged with dangerous driving and driving with excess alcohol

Nick Stewart of Island Records reacts to U2's choice of Brian Eno, April

"I thought: Brian Eno? Are they mad? But they wanted someone to stretch them musically, and that decision was the turning point in heir career. Because Brian Eno and Trevor Horn are unquestionably the two really outstanding rock producers of the Eighties and Nineties. U2 saw something in Brian Eno and Daniel Lanois which would give them an extra dimension."

after failing to stop at a police checkpoint overnight. After ignoring the checkpoint, an officer follows him on motorcycle until Adam finally stops the car. When questioned, Adam tells the officer that he's a celebrity and asks how he's supposed to know it was a police checkpoint.

April

U2 make the surprising announcement that Brian Eno will produce the band's next studio album. Coming off the success of the *War* album and tour, the choice of Eno – known for his love of atmospheric sounds – is a signal that U2 isn't interested in the safe choice. The band sends a clear message: U2 will not give in to public expectation from album to album.

U2 had considered working again with Jimmy Iovine, the producer of *Under A Blood Red Sky*, but decided the early material they

had was more European; they felt an American producer wouldn't fit their new direction. They also considered German producer Conny Plank, whose previous credits included the likes of Kraftwerk and Echo & the Bunnymen, and Roxy Music producer Rhett Davies.

Ultimately, the band chooses Eno, who is hesitant about working with a rock and roll band. But after meeting U2 in person, Eno accepts their invitation. "We decided that the music should decide," Bono says. "And we made some music, and we could see that it was a more abstract – dare I say it, *ambient* – record that we were going to make. And who better?"

When the news of Eno's hiring reaches Chris Blackwell, he tries to talk U2 out of it.

Brian Eno on why he agreed to work with U2

U2 first contacted Eno in 1983, but he rejected them. Meeting Bono finally convinced him to say "yes".

"Once I'd met Bono I knew I had to work with him. I thought there was something about him – something that made the idea of spending time in a studio with him very interesting. His attitude struck me as very intelligent and inspiring. He talked about how they work as a band, not in terms of playing and so forth, but in terms of contribution, what contributed to the identity of the band as a whole. I hadn't heard anyone talking about a band like that in a long time – and so, on that basis, out of curiosity, I agreed to work with them."

May

U2 Live At Red Rocks – Under A Blood Red Sky is released on video.

May 7

U2 begin recording *The Unforgettable Fire* album at Slane Castle. Located about an hour north of Dublin, the castle is close enough to have the conveniences of home, but gives the band some needed breathing room at the same time.

The band choose Slane after seeing the magnificent ballroom, and they hope the non-traditional setting of recording in a castle will inspire them. Randy Ezratty, who had recorded U2 live in Boston and at Red Rocks last year, arrives with his 24-track recording studio and sets up in the castle's library. Cables are run into the adjacent ballroom, where the band will do much of its playing.

Adam explains the decision to record at Slane Castle instead of Windmill Lane

"First of all, Windmill isn't conducive to live recording, they don't have a live room, it's very much a controlled studio atmosphere. And our plan has been progressively over the albums that we've done, that we want to get back to doing live takes rather than the usual way of recording from the bass drum up. So we needed a place where we could do that, we needed a place that sounded good. Slane we could play live and the rooms sounded good. Also, we've done three records here (Windmill Lane) and to be perfectly honest it was nice to have a different environment."

Barry Devlin, the producer of U2's second demo session back in 1978, visits the castle with a film crew. He's making a documentary for RTE-TV about the band's recording sessions, *The Making of the Unforgettable Fire*. The 30-minute programme will also be released in 1985 on VHS as part of the *The*

Unforgettable Fire Collection and on DVD as a bonus feature on *U2 Go Home: Live from Slane Castle* in 2002.

Chrissie Hynde of the Pretenders joins U2 in the studio one night to sing backing vocals on the new song, 'Pride (In the Name of Love)'.

June

The 11th issue of *U2 Magazine* is published this month.

June 5

U2 wrap up a month-long stay at Slane Castle and relocate to Dublin. They'll continue work on the new album tomorrow at Windmill Lane studios.

Summer

U2 meets with an Island Records art director who is keen to do the cover for the band's upcoming

album. Steve Averill, who's designed all of U2's cover art since day one, sits in to offer guidance. At one point, Paul McGuinness calls Averill out of the meeting and asks how soon he can come up with an idea for the record sleeve.

July

With their biggest tour yet just around the corner, U2 realise they have no clothes to wear and don't have time to sort out a concert wardrobe. Adam contacts a friend in the fashion industry, Marian Smyth, who agrees to help. She shops in London, Paris, and Florence, and brings her finds back to Slane Castle. When Larry asks Marian to suggest someone who can go on tour with them to handle wardrobe duties, Marian nominates herself.

July 4

Edge and Aislinn give birth to their first child, a girl named Hollie.

July 8

Bob Dylan is in Dublin for a concert at Slane Castle. Sensing a grand opportunity, *Hot Press* magazine arranges for Bono to interview Dylan for the magazine. Irish legend Van Morrison joins them for what becomes a wide-ranging conversation about the roots of rock and roll. Bono admits that he has little knowledge in this area. "There is no particular musical roots or heritage that we plug into. In Ireland there is a tradition, but I've never plugged into it. It's like as if we're caught in space."

Dylan chastises him: "You have to reach back. You have to reach!" Dylan goes on to lecture Bono about a great Irish traditional group called The McPeake Family, which Bono admits he's never heard. The conversation has a dramatic impact on Bono, and on U2's direction.

Bono on Dylan's influence

"Bob Dylan... made us reassess a lot of things. He was the one that sent us on this journey in the past that ended up with *Rattle And Hum*. He did that to

us! Blame him! It was that conversation with Dylan and later, another with Keith Richards about the blues [*Ed. Note: see October, 1985*], that allowed U2 to rediscover our past."

At the end of their conversation, Dylan asks Bono to perform with him on stage. After Bono admits to not knowing songs like 'It Takes A Lot To Laugh, It Takes A Train To Cry' and 'Stuck Inside of Mobile With The Memphis Blues Again', they settle on 'Leopard-Skin Pill-Box Hat', which Bono bluffs about knowing. Bono ends up making up new lyrics on stage, but Dylan isn't bothered too much, because he invites Bono back on stage to sing 'Blowin' In The Wind', the final song of the show. Unfortunately, Dylan ends up singing the only verses Bono knows, so Bono again makes up new lyrics on the spot.

July 29
Adam does an interview with Island Records PR man Neil Storey at Windmill Lane. The interview is for an upcoming edition of *U2 Magazine*.

Is That a Keyboard We Hear?
Neil Storey asked Adam about U2's use of a Fairlight, the first time U2 has used keyboards on an album.
"In a funny way we haven't ended up using as much keyboards as we thought we might. We had done some demos in a studio with a Fairlight, we had Brian who obviously knows about synthesizers, and we've just filled out the textures of the songs with instruments and sounds. In fact we've only really used the Fairlight on one track, and in fact we've added to that with real orchestration. We used the Fairlight just for

Left: U2 below the Sydney Harbor Bridge, September.

convenience to put down some string ideas, and came back to it later with an arranger and put down real strings as well. So I think the Fairlight was only really used as a means to an end, to see if an idea worked."

August
U2 grant an exclusive interview to *Jamming!*, a UK music fanzine which is making the jump to monthly magazine. Early this month, editor Tony Fletcher flies to Dublin for a one-on-one interview with Edge. Edge is tired from a late night in the studio, but speaks with Fletcher for two hours. They talk at length about the new album, about U2's decision to play large arenas, and about the band's spiritual side.

The interview is filmed for possible use in a documentary about the making of U2's new album. Fletcher also speaks briefly with Adam and Bono, who gives Fletcher a tour of Windmill Lane Studios and lets him listen to 'Pride (In The Name of Love)'.

Also this month, U2 shoots a video in Dublin for 'Pride' with director Donald Cammell. The band isn't satisfied with Cammell's video, so they agree to Anton Corbijn shooting an alternative. U2 is set to leave for their Australian tour, so Corbijn films them in a basement near London's Heathrow Airport. It's a "one-take" video that features U2 standing sternly in front of a wall with poor lighting conditions. The U2 camp is unimpressed with this video too, and it is decided to compile a third video from footage shot at Slane Castle during the album sessions.

August 1
U2 launches its own label, Mother Records, with a debut single from In Tua Nua, 'Coming Thru'. In Tua Nua's line-up includes Vinnie Kilduff, who had contributed Uileann pipes on the U2 song 'Tomorrow', and Steve Wickham, who had played electric violin on U2's 'Sunday Bloody Sunday' and 'Drowning Man'.

August 5
U2 finish recording *The Unforgettable Fire*, less than a month before the tour is set to begin.

With the album sessions complete, U2 spends a few days traveling across Ireland with Anton Corbijn. They do several photo shoots, often in front of castle ruins. The photos will be used for artwork and publicity on the new album campaign. The cover photo from *The Unforgettable Fire* comes from a shoot at Moydrum Castle in the heart of Ireland; photos taken at a castle called Carrickgogunnel are used on the back cover and the vinyl labels. The front cover photo is almost a direct copy of a photo on the front of a book, *In Ruins: The Once Great Houses of Ireland*. U2 later pays a small fee for unknowingly copying the other book's cover.

After the promotional duties are over, U2 begin rehearsing for the upcoming tour. Edge, however, can't remember how to play many of the band's old songs. A staffer buys all of U2's previous albums so Edge can listen and re-learn the songs.

August 29
Town Hall, Christchurch. U2 open the Under Australian Skies Tour with their first show in New Zealand. The timing is odd: The Red Rocks video has already wrapped up one era of U2's career, but the new era is still two months away with the release of *The Unforgettable Fire*. The early shows are called a "disaster" because the band's new music doesn't translate easily to the live setting. At first, U2 decide to play the same set from the *War* tour, and gradually work in new songs when they're ready. After the tour, the band return to Dublin, canceling some shows in Europe to sort out problems.

August 31
Show Building, Wellington.

September
The 12th issue of *U2 Magazine* is published this month. It includes Adam's recent interview with Neil Storey.

Bono introduces U2 to the people of Australia, September 4-9

"We want to do this interview because, we felt, we haven't been here before and people don't know us. And we're scared about the interviews they may have heard or the impression they may have of us. I suppose the reason we agreed to do this interview – and we don't do many interviews – is to show people how … un-anything we are. We're just jerks like anybody else. No manifesto, nothing to lay on people other than the music. That's what it's all about."

U2 releases 'Pride (In The Name Of Love)', with various formats including the tracks 'Boomerang I', 'Boomerang II', '4th Of July', '11 O'Clock Tick Tock', 'Touch', and 'A Celebration'. The single reaches number one in Australia and number three in the UK, but only climbs to number 33 in the US after a 15-week run on the charts.

Also this month, the video shot last month in Dublin by Donald Cammell makes its debut on MTV.

September 1-2
Logan Campbell Centre, Auckland. While in Auckland for two concerts, U2 hires local staff to assist its regular crew. One of the locals they hire is a Maori named Greg Carroll. The band is immediately impressed with Carroll, and Paul McGuinness offers him a permanent job on the tour, which he accepts. After the show, Carroll takes Bono to see a local landmark called One Tree Hill.

September 4-5-6-8-9
Entertainment Center, Sydney, with Matt Finish. U2 plays their first Australian concerts. While in Sydney, Bono, Edge, and Adam are interviewed by Ian "Molly" Meldrum for the *Countdown Saturday Special* TV show.

September 11
Festival Hall, Brisbane, with Matt Finish.

September 13-14-15-17-18
Sports And Entertainment Centre, Melbourne, with Matt Finish. Around this time, U2 meets the Reverend John Smith, a Methodist minister who's considered the most respected religious figure in Australia.

September 20-21
Apollo Entertainment Centre, Adelaide, with Matt Finish.

September 23-24
Entertainment Center, Perth, with Matt Finish. U2 wrap up the Australian tour in Perth. The band and crew have an end-of-tour party with the guys from supporting act, Matt Finish. U2 return to Dublin

1984

and use a three-week break in the schedule to rethink the stage show and continue practicing the new songs.

October 1

U2 releases *The Unforgettable Fire*, their fourth studio album, and the first produced by Brian Eno and Daniel Lanois. The album cover features a cinematic shot of Bono and Edge in front of the ruins of Castle Moydrum near Athlone, Ireland. Musically, *The Unforgettable Fire* finds U2 taking a more subdued approach, shedding the anthemic sounds of *War* and allowing the production to almost obscure the "U2 sound".

Edge on the old and new "U2 sound"

"As far back as the War album, we'd become quite aware of having a very defined sound. We were becoming more of a sound than a band; those echoey guitars and that ethereal vocal sound. For War we decided to get back to something a bit more abrasive and raw, and for the next studio record we wanted to take a really radical step. In order to do that, we had to change our methods, our approach and some of the influences on our work – in other words, the producer and the studio."

The album reaches number one in the UK and number 12 in the US. Despite the commercial success, critical reaction is mixed. In *Rolling Stone*, Kurt Loder pans the album: "Unfortunately, with *The Unforgettable Fire*, U2 flickers and nearly fades, its fire banked by a misconceived production strategy and occasional interludes of soggy, songless self-indulgence.... The album sounds formless and uninhabited." Even *Los Angeles Times* critic Robert Hilburn, a big supporter of the band, has problems with the album: "Unfortunately, many of Hewson's

lyrics – especially on 'Elvis Presley And America' - are unnecessarily ethereal and vague." In the *NME*, Paul Du Noyer shares a more realistic outlook: "In *The Unforgettable Fire* I think they've made the record they needed to make. Set against *Boy*, I don't say it's their best album yet, but it sounds like music worth spending some months getting to know." Liam Mackey rates the album 12 out of 12 in *Hot Press*: "This then, is the beginning of the new chapter of U2. With an album as rich and rewarding as *The Unforgettable Fire* as an introduction, the possibilities for the future seem limitless." Tracks: 'A Sort Of Homecoming', 'Pride (In The Name Of Love)', 'Wire', 'The Unforgettable Fire', 'Promenade', '4th Of July', 'Bad', 'Indian Summer Sky', 'Elvis Presley And America', 'MLK'

October 13

After a week of tour rehearsals at the Oscar Theatre in suburban Dublin, U2 fly to mainland Europe where the tour will start in a matter of days.

The Unforgettable Fire begins a two-week run at the top of the UK album chart.

October 18

Espace Tony Garnier, Lyon, with Big Audio Dynamite. U2 perform 'Bad' live for the first time.

October 19

Marseilles Stadium, Marseilles, with Big Audio Dynamite.

October 20

Palais De Sports, Toulouse, with Big Audio Dynamite. Still trying to learn new songs, and where each fits in the live set, U2 plays a short, 15-song show in Toulouse that runs only 70 minutes. American journalist Bill Flanagan interviews the band after the show in which, as the band do in many interviews around this time, Bono sings the praises of Bruce Springsteen: "I'm in awe of the way Bruce Springsteen can communicate directly with people."

October 21

On a night off, U2 rides the ferris wheel at a fair in Bordeaux. They try to stay incognito, but Bono blows their cover at a shooting gallery when he shouts encouragement as Edge plays, "Yeah, Edge! Go, Edge!" Whoops. As they try to evade the growing crowd coming toward them, Bono escapes into the freak

show tent and his face goes pale at the sight of animal and human fetuses in jars, Siamese twins, and the like. As the band leaves the carnival, an announcer is shouting over the PA, "U Deux! U Deux!"

October 22
Pattinoire, Bordeaux, with Big Audio Dynamite.

October 23
St. Herblain, Nantes, with Big Audio Dynamite.

October 25
Espace Ballard, Paris, with the Alarm. After the show, Chris Blackwell introduces U2 to Jean-Paul Goude, a designer/director who has worked with Grace Jones. Blackwell thinks Goude might help dress up U2's stage set. Bill Graham is at the show, and will travel with U2 for the next week for an upcoming feature in *Hot Press*.

October 26
Journalist Lisa Robinson interviews Bono at the Warwick Hotel in Paris. Robinson forgets to bring a tape recorder, so they borrow one from Edge and record the interview over a tape of the previous night's sound check. Robinson, who was at the concert a night earlier, tells Bono he seems to be doing less stage-climbing on the current tour. Bono agrees: "If things go bad, everyone will be silent on the way back to the hotel and then there'll be a phone call from Adam, he's the diplomat,

and he'll say, 'Can we have a word with you?' I'll have to go down there and face the firing squad. They'll just say, 'Come on – you don't have to do this; you must keep control of this thing.' It's supportive; they know that if I fall off the stage I'll break some bones. They tell me the music should speak for itself."

October 27-28
Vorst National, Brussels, with the Alarm. Ali, Aislinn, and Adam's girlfriend, Sheila, arrive to see the shows in Brussels. Before the first show, Ariola Records, Island's local distributor, presents U2 with two golds discs at a dinner party. The sound level during the first show leads local seismological officials to declare that a series of small tremors has hit the area.

October 30-31
Sport Paleis Ahoy, Rotterdam, with the Alarm. At the second show, Bono sprays champagne on Larry and leads the audience in singing 'Happy Birthday' to the now 23-year-old.

November
T-Bone Burnett's *Behind The Trap Door* is released, and includes a track co-written with Bono: 'Having A Wonderful Time, Wish You Were Her'.

November 2-3
Brixton Academy, London, with the Waterboys. U2 return to London for the first time in a long while with two shows at Brixton Academy. The crowd is rowdy both nights, and Bono is affected to the point of rambling during his speeches between songs. The *NME* is unimpressed with the shows, saying this about U2: "The most boring band in the world. There may be groups equally as dull, but I fail to see how any of them can be worse."

November 5
Edinburgh Playhouse, Edinburgh, with the Waterboys.

November 6-7
Barrowlands, Glasgow, with the Waterboys. Simple Minds guitarist

Charlie Burchill joins U2 for '40'. *Kerrang!* magazine, which is known more for coverage of hard rock and heavy metal, gives the second show a glowing review: "We may strive, we may struggle to cling to the belief that somewhere out there in the garish land of Heavy Metal there is someone who will be able to match the awesome challenge laid down by this band but in reality, or course, there is no one to touch U2. The future of rock is firmly grasped in their hands and everything else must follow in their wake."

November 9-10
Apollo Theater, Manchester, with the Waterboys. Producer Tony Visconti is on the road with U2 as the band performs in Manchester. He's there to help U2 record a new, live version of 'A Sort Of Homecoming' for future release.

Visconti's involvement comes about after a recent phone call from Bono, who explained that Brian Eno and Daniel Lanois were struggling to edit the song into a shorter single version. Bono asked Visconti to listen to the song and invited him to either try editing the album version, or record a live version. Visconti accepted Bono's offer, and suggested they record a new version.

Tony Visconti on his brief work with U2
"We had a meeting in a London rehearsal studio to work on the ideas for a single format arrangement of the song I had written out; the band tried my suggestions.... After a couple of plays they agreed that they loved the new version.

"A few days later I was on the tour bus with U2, catching their shows in Manchester and Birmingham. We recorded the shows every night with a mobile recording studio with their trusted engineer Kevin Killen. We didn't get a satisfactory, steadily played version in Manchester or Birmingham and I was a little worried. I suggested that we record a backing track right on the stage at Wembley Arena prior to the show and then, if we didn't get a better version that night, we would take the backing track, plus the enormous reverb of the arena, into the recording studio and overdub from there.

"I was able to overdub the audience from that evening – the recording studio is a magical place. Bono thanked me and told me that I had given him a great lesson in song writing, which I found hard to believe, but he was sincere. I had hoped to work with them again, but it never happened."

November 12
NEC, Birmingham, with the Waterboys. The version of 'Bad' from this show is used on the *Wide Awake In America* EP.

November 14-15
Wembley Arena, London, with the Waterboys. During soundcheck before the second show, U2 records 'A Sort Of Homecoming' for use on the *Wide Awake In America* EP. They weren't pleased with performances of the song during recent concerts.

November 16
U2 and producer Tony Visconti are at Good Earth Studios in London, working on the live versions of 'Bad' and 'A Sort Of Homecoming' that will appear on the *Wide Awake In America* EP and 'The Unforgettable Fire' single in 1985.

While in London, U2 meet up with writer Christopher Connelly, who follows the band for a few days for an upcoming feature in *Rolling Stone* magazine.

November 21
Westfalenhalle, Dortmund. Still

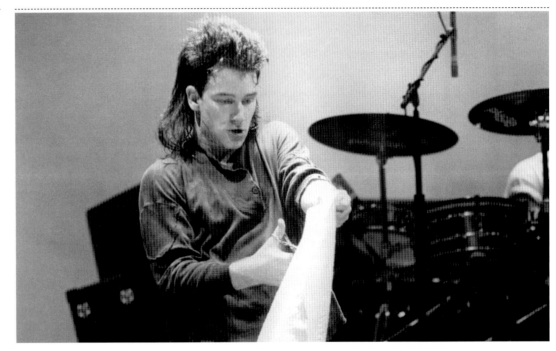

trying to break through in West Germany, U2 plays the Rock Pop festival, which is filmed and airs on German TV on January 12, 1985.

The band stays in Dusseldorf, and are surprised to encounter Ronnie Drew, the singer of the legendary Irish band, The Dubliners, at their hotel. "You're a great band," Drew tells Larry. "My kids just think you're the greatest, have all your records, listen to them all the time. The kids love ya."

U2 are interviewed by *Rolling Stone*'s Christopher Connelly over the three days the band is in Germany, and he returns to Dublin with them, too. Connelly spends time with Bono at the Dockers Pub, before the two go for a drive

Above: Bono cuts a white towel, Cleveland, December 9.

around Dublin. Bono tells Connelly he's just finished writing a song called 'I Don't Live in Irishtown'. "It's about a man who isn't Protestant or Catholic, English or Irish," Bono says.

While in Germany, Boomtown Rats singer Bob Geldof calls Bono and asks him to come to London in a few days to be part of an all-star charity recording to raise money for Ethiopian famine victims.

November 25
Bono and Adam take part in recording the charity single 'Do They Know It's Christmas?' in London, as part of an all-star line-up calling itself Band Aid. The effort is to relieve the famine

in Ethiopia and is organized by Geldof and Ultravox front man Midge Ure.

November 29
U2 arrive in New York to prepare for a brief US tour. As word spreads that the band is in town, a crowd of fans gather outside their hotel for a chance to meet them. Bono calls Carter Alan at WBCN-FM in Boston and does a short phone interview on-air, telling Alan – and all his listeners – that he's stuck inside the Parker Meridien hotel. The revelation leads U2 fans in Boston to call the New York hotel hoping to speak to Bono, and they jam the hotel's phone system in the process.

Jack Healey on his first U2 concert, December 3

"Behind the band were slides of Dr. Martin Luther King, Jr., and the American Indian, and to my mind, these are two causes that the United States must understand and come to grips with. You know, the taking of the land and the issue of slavery and racism in the United States. And I just said to myself, 'This is my band. This is it.' And of course, the talent on the stage, you know, the fire they had. I thought, 'This band could carry the message of human rights.'"

December
The 13th issue of *U2 Magazine* is published this month.

December 1
Tower Theater, Philadelphia, with the Waterboys. U2 open this short US tour which is designed to whet appetites for a longer tour next year. An unwanted sign of U2's burgeoning popularity is the presence of ticket scalpers outside the theater. Before the show, tickets are selling for $150 each. During afternoon soundcheck, a few dozen fans get inside the building. When security tries to remove them, Bono asks the guards to let the fans stay in the theatre lobby with doors open so they can at least hear the rest of soundcheck.

December 2
The Centrum, Worcester, with the Waterboys. U2 sell out a US arena for the first time. The show is a big success and the band will later say this gig gave them the confidence to play larger arenas.

December 3
Radio City Music Hall, New York, with the Waterboys. The show is a fundraiser for Amnesty International's "Stop Torture Week" but, ironically, the show is notable for crowd violence. When fans begin leaving their seats and rushing forward, security men panic. One guard clashes with a fan during 'I Will Follow', forcing Larry to leave the drum-kit and the show to stop. Edge throws his guitar down, breaking it in two, and tries to stop the fight.

The show resumes, but is stopped twice during the encore while fans climb on stage to avoid the crush. The hall manager stops the show temporarily and security guards come on stage before Bono convinces everyone to move back. U2 finish the show with a quick version of '40' and leave the stage.

In attendance is Amnesty International USA's Executive Director, Jack Healey, who is developing an idea for a series of concerts to celebrate Amnesty's 25th anniversary in 1986. It's the first time Healey has seen U2 play, and he's thrilled by the experience.

Also today, *The Unforgettable Fire* is certified Gold by the RIAA, and 'Do They Know It's Christmas?' is released. The song immediately tops the charts in the UK and 12 other countries, and raises £8 million for Ethiopian famine relief.

December 5
Constitution Hall, Washington, with the Waterboys.

December 7
Massey Hall, Toronto, with the Waterboys. Brian Eno is at this show.

December 8
Fox Theater, Detroit, with the Waterboys. U2 are faced with an intense, aggressive audience throughout this show, so bad that they consider not playing an encore. They do, but the crowd continues to push and fight with each other for space. After the show, guests are told U2 are too upset to entertain any visitors.

December 9
Music Hall, Cleveland, with the Waterboys. U2 arrive in Cleveland and find their hotel (the Boncourt) overrun with fans. Hotel security eventually clears them out and locks two entrances while police handle crowd control outside. Before the show, Adam and Edge do an interview with Carter Alan that will be distributed to college radio stations across the country.

December 11
Aragon Ballroom, Chicago, with the Waterboys.

December 12
While in Chicago, U2 visit the Peace Museum. They make plans to bring the *Unforgettable Fire* exhibit and a Martin Luther King, Jr., exhibit to Dublin in 1985.

December 15
Civic Auditorium, San Francisco, with the Waterboys.

December 16
Long Beach Arena, Long Beach, with the Waterboys.

December 31
U2 are featured in a *Newsweek* magazine article, "Stop in the Name of Love" by Jim Miller. "From the outset," Miller writes, "the group's atmospheric style – one of the few truly original styles to appear in the '80s – represented an odd but effective fusion of two rival rock archetypes: the didactic grandeur of The Who playing *Tommy* and the sleekly modernist David Bowie of *Heroes*."

Rolling Stone magazine's final issue of the year includes its Top 100 Albums of 1984 chart, which has three U2 albums: *Under A Blood Red Sky* (48), *War* (56), and *The Unforgettable Fire* (68).

1985

A string of successes this year land U2 on the brink of major international stardom. *The Unforgettable Fire* tour sees U2 playing the legendary Madison Square Garden for the first time. *Rolling Stone* declares U2 is the "Band of the 80s" and they head home as heroes to play Dublin's enormous Croke Park. Bigger than that is Live Aid, a performance that U2 thought was a failure but was considered by many to be one of the best sets of the day. The event inspires Bono and Ali to do humanitarian work in Ethiopia, the beginning of what will become a lifetime quest for both to make a difference there.

Larry is named the no. 1 "Up and Coming" drummer in the *Modern Drummer* magazine readers poll this year. Bono appears on the *Sun* City album and sings with Clannad, while Edge composes his first film soundtrack.

January 5
Bono shows up at a Simple Minds concert in Glasgow, and joins them on stage to sing 'New Gold Dream'.

January 11
Adam pleads guilty in a Dublin court to dangerous driving and driving with excess alcohol after his arrest last March. He's fined £225 and his license is revoked for two years. The incident makes headlines in Irish newspapers. "I was an asshole," Adam tells *Hot Press* a few years later. "I was drunk. But it was pretty embarrassing to see it spread all over the papers."

January 12
U2's November 21 performance at the Rock Pop festival in Dortmund airs on German TV.

January 23
Drammenshale, Drammen. The Unforgettable Fire Tour resumes in Norway. After the show, fans bump into the band at the Oslo train station, waiting for a train to Stockholm.

January 25
Ice Stadium, Stockholm. While in Sweden, U2 take care of promotional duties for the upcoming 'The Unforgettable Fire' single: Anton Corbijn does an outdoor photo shoot with U2 in snowy landscapes, and Meiert Avis shoots a music video.

January 26
Scandinavium, Gothenburg.

January 27
On a night off in Hamburg, U2 hang out in the city's red light district, the area of town where the Beatles

Left: Live Aid, Wembley Stadium, London, July 13.

developed their skills before fame beckoned.

January 28
Congress Center, Hamburg, with Belfegore. Bono dedicates 'Bad' to the "pretty girls" he met last night.

January 29
Stadthalle, Offenbach, with Belfegore.

January 31
Sporthalle, Cologne, with Belfegore.

February
The Unforgettable Fire and 'Pride (In The Name of Love)' are included on *Melody Maker*'s lists of the best albums and singles, respectively, of 1984 published this month.

February 1
Musensaal, Mannheim, with Belfegore.

February 2
Rudi-Sedlmayerhalle, Munich, with Belfegore.

February 4
Teatro Tenda, Milan. U2 play their first show in Italy. The gig is originally planned for the Palazzetto Dello Sport, but the building's roof collapsed a couple weeks before the gig under the weight of heavy snow.

February 5-6
Teatro Tenda, Bologna.

February 7
US sales of *The Unforgettable Fire* pass the one million mark, giving U2 its first Platinum album in America.

February 8
Hallenstadion, Zurich, with Belfegore. Bono's voice becomes so bad that the band leaves the stage for 20 minutes. His voice is not much better when they return.

February 10
Palais Omnisports De Paris Bercy, Paris, with Belfegore.

February 25
Reunion Arena, Dallas, with Red Rockers. U2 return to the US for the fourth leg of *The Unforgettable Fire* Tour. The show is briefly interrupted when a fan in the front row screams and points an object at Bono – it appears to be a gun and security quickly apprehend the man, but the incident leaves Bono feeling angry.

War is certified Platinum with sales of one million records.

February 26
Frank Erwin Center, Austin, with Red Rockers.

February 27
The Summit, Houston, with Red Rockers.

Above: Bono contemplates his leap into the audience at Live Aid, July 13.

March 1
Compton Terrace, Phoenix, with Red Rockers. U2 play to 23,000 fans at an outdoor amphitheater on an Indian reservation near Phoenix. It's the largest crowd the band has drawn on its own to date.

March 2-4-5
Sports Arena, Los Angeles, with Red Rockers. At the March 4 show, Bono brings a guitarist on stage to play 'Knockin' On Heaven's Door'. One by one, the band leaves the stage and the audience cheers wildly as the fan continues to play. The crowd finally erupts when U2 return to the stage. A new tradition is born, as U2 will repeat this on many shows later

Larry learns from Max Weinberg, March 7-8

"He'd had eight operations on each finger in his hands. He'd had a problem for years and he hadn't taken care of his hands – he was in serious pain. So he said to me, 'Don't be a martyr.' Having seen the damage that had been done in his case I was aware of the need to take care of my hands."

during this tour. While in LA, U2 does an interview with Robert Hilburn of the *Los Angeles Times*.

March 7-8
Cow Palace, Daly City, with Red Rockers. Prior to the second show in San Francisco, Larry is rushed to a hospital with severe pain in his left hand. A doctor orders him to take two weeks off to rest the hand, but the band explains that is not an option. Larry gets a plaster for his hand that he can remove before each concert. He's also prescribed painkillers to carry him through the end of the tour when he can get proper treatment. Larry gets in touch with Max Weinberg, Bruce Springsteen's drummer, who's also had hand problems during his career.

March 11
Neal Blaisdell Center Arena, Honolulu, with Red Rockers.

March 14
Rolling Stone magazine puts U2 on its cover with the caption: 'Our Choice: Band of the '80s'. It's arguably the biggest honour the band has received to date in the US. The accompanying article explains that for many fans, U2 has become "The Only Band That Matters".

March 17
McNichols Sports Arena, Denver, with Red Rockers.

March 19
Minneapolis Auditorium, Minneapolis, with Red Rockers.

March 21-22
University Of Illinois Pavillion, Chicago, with Red Rockers (March 21) and Lone Justice (March 22).

March 23
Joe Louis Arena, Detroit, with Lone Justice.

March 24
Bono and Adam do an interview in their Detroit hotel room with Pam Lambert of the *Wall Street Journal*. The article is being prepared for U2's upcoming visit to New York.

Also today, U2 rents a small, passenger plane to make travel easier for the rest of the tour.

March 25
Richfield Coliseum, Cleveland, with

Lone Justice. Before tonight's show in Cleveland, Edge does an interview with DJ Kid Leo of WMMS-FM. After the show, Bono tries to cheer up Lone Justice singer Maria McKee, who is depressed by the reaction, or lack thereof, her band is getting from the crowd as U2's opening act.

March 27
The Forum, Montreal, with Lone Justice.

March 28
Maple Leaf Gardens, Toronto, with Lone Justice.

March 30
Civic Center, Ottawa, with Lone Justice.

April
The 14th issue of *U2 Magazine* is published.

April 1
Madison Square Garden, New York, with Lone Justice. U2 plays the renowned Madison Square Garden for the first time. Anticipating the importance of this show, U2 brings the band's family and friends, as well as many Irish journalists and celebrities, over from Ireland to witness the occasion.

While in New York, Joe O'Herlihy, Dave Fanning, and tour promoter Ian Wilson strike up a conversation about the Lark By The Lee festival this summer in Cork, O'Herlihy's hometown. Joe tells the band about the festival, and they're keen to play it.

April 2
Civic Center, Providence, with Lone Justice. In the morning, U2 does a news conference in New York with a mostly Irish press contingent, and announces a homecoming show in Dublin in June.

The *Wall Street Journal* features U2 in an article by Pam Lambert headlined "U2: Keeping the Rock Faith with Unforgettable Fire". Having seen a recent U2 concert in Detroit, Lambert paints a picture somewhat similar to Beatles' performances twenty years earlier: "When Bono, Clayton, drummer

Larry Mullen Jr. and guitarist and keyboard player Dave 'the Edge' Evans took the stage, the vast maw of the Joe Louis Arena crackled with electricity. Fans rose to their feet with a roar and surged toward the small figures bathed in the spotlights. They held aloft matches, banners, the Irish colors and white flags of peace. They stamped, they cheered, they danced. A few wept hysterically."

With the tour going well and U2 getting key publicity from mainstream media, Island Records issues 'Wire' as a promo-only single, i.e. – not released to stores. Radio picks up the song only briefly and it fails to add to U2's momentum. Island tries the same approach with 'A Sort Of Homecoming', but again fails to find success on radio.

April 3
Nassau Coliseum, Uniondale, with Lone Justice.

April 8
Capitol Centre, Landover, with Lone Justice. Fire officials ask the band not to call fans out of their seats, but Bono ignores them, inviting the audience to the stage, and forcing the show to be stopped for a time. After the show, police arrive backstage and try to arrest Bono, Paul McGuinness and Production Manager Steve Iredale.

Steve Iredale: "That was a close one."
"I pointed out that they couldn't arrest all of us, because only I had signed the paper – so they promptly arrested me! About half an hour later they took me down to the police station to book me. They slapped me up against a wall, gave me a number, took my photo and fingerprints, read me my rights and asked me for a statement. Hours later I was bailed out for $500, and carried on with the tour. Fortunately though, after months of arguing, U2's attorney in America

managed to get the charges dropped. That was a close one."

April 9
Civic Arena, Pittsburgh.

April 10
Coliseum, Hampton, with Lone Justice.

April 12-14-15
Brenden Byrne Arena, East Rutherford, with Lone Justice. While in New Jersey, Bono and Edge do an interview after one show with the BBC's *Old Grey Whistle Test* programme. It airs on April 23, along with the performance of 'Wire' from the first concert.

April 16-18-19
The Centrum, Worcester, with Lone Justice. Near-disaster as U2 plays the first of three shows at The Centrum. During the show, Adam notices that a lighting rig is slipping from its position above the audience. He whispers this to Bono and the band stops playing. Bono asks the crowd to move away from underneath the rig while crew climb up to fix it. Twenty minutes later, all is fixed and the show goes on.

Adam and Edge tape an interview with WBCN's Carter Alan on April 18 at the Bostonian Hotel. After that night's show, a fan gives Ellen Darst some brochures about the Martin Luther King Center in Atlanta and suggests the band visit while they're in Atlanta later this month.

Around this time, Bob Geldof asks U2 to perform at Live Aid, a daylong charity concert he's planning this summer. They agree to do it.

April 20
Civic Center, Hartford, with Lone Justice.

April 22
The Spectrum, Philadelphia, with Lone Justice.

U2 release 'The Unforgettable Fire' single in several formats with extra tracks including 'A Sort of

Homecoming (live)', 'The Three Sunrises', 'Love Comes Tumbling', 'Bass Trap', 'Sixty Seconds In Kingdom Come', and 'MLK'. It enters the UK charts a week later at number eight, and climbs to number six.

April 23
Civic Center, Hartford, with Lone Justice.

April 24
The Spectrum, Philadelphia, with Lone Justice.

April 25
Anton Corbijn does a photo shoot with U2 for *NME*.

April 29
The Omni, Atlanta. Before the show, U2 visit the Martin Luther King Center at the invitation of Coretta Scott King, Dr. King's widow. Bono's Dad is flown over to watch the band tonight. Bono has pre-arranged with lighting technicians to shine a spotlight on his Dad when Bono introduces him to the crowd. When it happens, Bono's Dad stands up and gives Bono the finger!

April 30
Memorial Coliseum, Jacksonville.

May
U2 release the four-track *Wide Awake In America* EP. It features two live songs and two new studio tracks, none of which, ironically, are recorded in America. 'A Sort Of Homecoming' was recorded live during a London sound check last November 15, and the crowd applause was added in during mixing. 'Bad' is from a Birmingham gig three days prior to that, but since Edge misplayed the last note of the song, that had to be fixed during mixing.

Originally intended just for North America and Japan, the EP is so popular in the UK as an import that it reaches number 11 in the charts there. In the US, it climbs as high as number 37, and the eight-minute long live version of 'Bad' becomes a popular track on album radio (AOR) stations like WMMR-FM in Philadelphia and WBCN-FM in Boston. Demand for the song increases when U2 performs it at Live Aid.
Tracks: 'Bad (live)', 'A Sort of Homecoming (live)', 'The Three Sunrises', 'Love Comes Tumbling'

May 2
Sun Dome, Tampa, with Red Rockers.

May 3-4
Hollywood Sportatorium, Fort Lauderdale, with Red Rockers. The US tour ends in Fort Lauderdale. The band head back to Dublin for a two week break, and the first thing on Larry's priority list is a series of appointments with top hand surgeons in the UK and Europe. An Irish doctor prescribes an anti-inflammatory pill that helps control the pain and swelling in his left hand. "I don't know how it works," Larry says later, "but it reduces the swelling and there's less of a problem now. It's a question of knowing how far I can push my hand, and then taking care of it, bathing it in cold water and resting it as much as possible."

May 25
Nurburgring Racecourse, Adenau/Koblenz. Bono brings back an old trick when he climbs the

scaffolding during 'Electric Co.' so people in the back of the park can see him.

May 26
Neckarstadion, Stuttgart.

May 27
Freigelande Halle Munsterland, Munster.

June
Edge is profiled in this month's edition of *Guitar Player* magazine. He tells the magazine about a new guitar he's excited about trying out: "It's a guitar that plays itself [*laughs*]. You just depress the string, pluck it once and get infinite sustain." He's referring to the Infinite Guitar, which is being developed by musician Michael Brook.

Also this month, U2 publishes *The U2 Portfolio*, their first official songbook. It features photographs by Anton Corbijn.

June 1
St. Jakob's Stadion, Basel.

June 22
Milton Keynes Bowl, Milton Keynes. U2 headline "The Longest Day" festival. Technical problems cut off the start of 'Bad', and leave Bono telling jokes while the problem is fixed. He even brings a fan on stage to tell a joke and help kill time. Still, the show is a grand success and U2 get rave reviews. U2 meet R.E.M., who are also on the bill, for the first time.

June 27
All four band members visit RTE for an interview with Dave Fanning.

Around this time, the band also pays a visit to Dublin's Lord Mayor Michael O'Halloran.

Below: On stage at Milton Keynes, June 22.

June 28
While rehearsing for their homecoming show the following day, U2 are forced to stop when they learn their volume is so loud at Croke Park that they have disturbed students taking exams at the Rosmini Community School a half-mile away.

Also tonight, U2 attend the Dublin opening of two exhibits on loan from the Chicago Peace Museum – the *Unforgettable Fire* exhibit of drawings and paintings by Japan's nuclear war survivors, and the *Martin Luther King – Peacemaker* exhibit. U2 has helped organize and finance the exhibits' temporary move to Dublin.

June 29
Croke Park, Dublin. U2 play what is billed as their "Homecoming Concert" before 57,000 people at Croke Park, the sight of 1920's

original Bloody Sunday. This is U2's first headlining show at a football stadium, and the crowd's euphoria lasts the entire show as they welcome their world-conquering heroes back home. More than 200 people are injured, including six police officers, and stores are looted when windows are broken during rioting as the massive crowd spills into the city after the show. U2 donate the proceeds from this show to the building of a music rehearsal center for young bands without equipment and a place to practice called The City Centre, which will open in June, 1989.

July
The 15th issue of *U2 Magazine* is published.

July 6
Festival Grounds, Torhout.

July 7
Festival Grounds, Werchter. U2 end *The Unforgettable Fire* Tour at the Rock Werchter Festival in Belgium. As U2, R.E.M., and other bands drive back to their hotel, it's time to celebrate. Bono and Edge lead the others through a selection of corny ballads and '70s pop songs.

July 12
U2 phone Bob Geldof the night before Live Aid and tell him they don't want to perform. They're concerned about not having a soundcheck. Geldof brushes their request aside.

July 13
Wembley Stadium, London. Live Aid: London and Philadelphia. Boomtown Rats frontman Bob Geldof's concert to raise money for famine victims in Ethiopia becomes the concert of the century, broadcast worldwide and watched by over a billion. U2 are set to play at Wembley Stadium in London, about halfway through the day's line-up. Tickets are sold for £25, but £20 of that is advertised as a donation to the Live Aid charity. Touts outside the stadium are getting as much as £80 for a ticket. Official souvenir stands offer Band Aid videos, Live Aid posters, programs, and shirts – all of which include the line, "This Saves Lives".

At about 5:20 p.m. London time, Jack Nicholson stands on stage at JFK Stadium in Philadelphia and introduces U2 at Wembley Stadium. The crowd roars and what seem like dozens of U2 flags are waving in the air. The band's planned set is 'Sunday, Bloody Sunday', 'Bad' and 'Pride (In The Name Of Love)', but U2 only manage to play the first two in their allotted 20 minutes.

After a tight version of 'Sunday, Bloody Sunday', U2 deliver an epic version of 'Bad' that lasts an astonishing 14 minutes. During the song, Bono breaks one of Geldof's rules – *don't leave the stage* – when he climbs down to ground level to dance with a girl in front of the crowd. It's one of the most memorable moments of the entire two-continent event, but it leaves the rest of U2 angry with Bono; they never had a chance to play 'Pride', the hit single that many of the billions watching on TV might know.

Bono: "Larry told me he was going to stop playing"
"I was trying to find an image that would be remembered for the day. I was not happy with just playing our songs and getting out of there. I wanted to find that moment. Of course, afterwards, I got a terrible

time from the band. I was almost fired. Because I had climbed on roofs, I had left stages before, I had climbed on PA stacks, I had jumped into the crowds, I had physical confrontations in crowds, but this was the worst one for them, to leave them for what felt like hours, apparently. Larry told me he was going to stop playing. This was a big show for our band, there were a billion people watching, and we didn't do our big song. Everyone was very annoyed with me, I mean, very annoyed."

Bono is so depressed that he reportedly thinks about leaving U2. He decides to take some personal time to sort through his feelings and emotions. He escapes to the Irish country, to a small town where Ali has family. There, Bono meets a sculptor who is working on a statue called *The Leap*, inspired by Bono's dance with the young girl at Live Aid. Bono rethinks the idea that he made a mistake.

An estimated 1.5 billion TV viewers around the globe see U2's performance. Many journalists pick U2 and Queen as the top performances of the day. The band's album sales rise worldwide after Live Aid, and U2 later wins *Rolling Stone* magazine's Readers' Poll award for Best Performance at Live Aid.

At the request of the UK press, the band issues the following statement about their participation at Live Aid: "U2 are involved in Live Aid because it's more than money, it's music... but it is also a demonstration to the politicians and the policy-makers that men, women and children will not walk by other men, women and children as they lie, bellies swollen, starving to death for the sake of a cup of grain and water. For the price of Star Wars, the MX missile offensive-defense budgets, the desert of Africa could be turned

vocals at Windmill Lane Studios. In the studio with Bono is a group of Dublin teenagers who are protesting because their employer sells South African produce.

August 1

Boy is certified Gold by the BPI, with sales of more than 100,000 in the UK.

August 25

Lark By The Lee Festival, Cork. U2 play at the first Lark By The Lee Festival in Cork. Organisers keep U2's appearance a secret to avoid extra security and insurance costs, which would've likely forced them to charge an admission fee. U2 play a nine-song set from the back of a truck. A local singer named Freddie White introduces U2 after his set finishes, and then White returns to perform 'All Along The Watchtower' with U2. About two-dozen fans close to the stage pass out during U2's set and have to be taken to a nearby hospital. After the gig, U2 relax at a club called Sir Henry's in the Grand Parade Hotel.

August 29

The BPI certifies *October* as Gold (100,000 sold) and *War* as Platinum (300,000 sold).

September

Around this time, Bono's exploration of "roots music" continues when he visits a man named Bob Quinn in the

into fertile lands. The technology is with us. The technocrats are not. Are we part of a civilization that protects itself by investing in life... or investing in death?" Hoping for something more quotable, many in the media ignore the band's statement.

July 18

Under A Blood Red Sky is certified Platinum by the RIAA.

Summer

With U2's commitments over for the summer, Adam takes time off in Australia visiting an old school friend. Edge spends time in London writing new material, but not for U2. It's more ambient music, and includes Edge's first attempts at playing the Infinite Guitar developed by Michael Brook.

August

On his way to Finland for a meeting of Amnesty International leadership, Amnesty USA Executive Director Jack Healey stops in

Dublin for a quick visit with Paul McGuinness at U2's Windmill Lane headquarters. He asks the band to take part in a concert tour the following year to raise awareness of human right violations around the world and about Amnesty's efforts to stop them. The band knows they'll be interrupting work on a new album, but agree to give Amnesty a week of their time. Paul McGuinness writes a note giving confirmation of U2's involvement.

"I knew the human rights movement really changed that day," Healey says. "It really did. No question. I knew what was coming. I knew what was gonna happen. I knew we were gonna grow. I knew we were gonna go into colleges, and high schools, and grade schools. I knew we were gonna be able to get it done."

Also this month, Bono records vocals for an upcoming project being organized by "Little" Steven Van Zandt called Artists United Against Apartheid. Van Zandt sends tapes to Dublin, and Bono adds

Above: Bono on stage with George Michael, Bob Geldof, Freddie Mercury and many others at the climax to the London Live Aid concert, July 13.

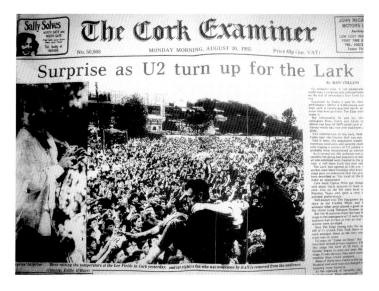

Bono talks about working in Ethiopia, September

"I got more than I ever gave to Ethiopia. My head was in the clouds, and my feet were not on the ground. Spending time in Africa and seeing people in the pits of poverty, I still saw a very strong spirit in the people, a richness of spirit I didn't see when I came home. I had no culture shock going, but I had culture shock coming home. I saw the spoiled child of the Western world. I started thinking, 'They may have a physical desert, but we've got other kinds of deserts.' And that's what attracted me to the desert as a symbol of some sort."

Connemara region near Ireland's west coast. Quinn is a filmmaker and TV producer who believes that Irish art and music can be traced back to North Africa and the Middle East, not elsewhere in Europe as is commonly believed. Quinn gives Bono a list of contacts in Africa, where he and Ali are headed soon to do relief work.

Bono's and Ali's first stop is in Cairo, Egypt. They visit one of Cairo's "cities of the dead" – a community of millions of citizens living in the massive cemeteries around the city because of Cairo's ongoing housing crisis.

From there, they fly to Ethiopia. On the plane, they sit next to Sue Germein, a nurse working with a World Vision emergency medical team. She tells the Hewsons about the severity of the situation on the ground. "She was the woman that got me fired up about these issues," Bono says later. "She had a huge impact on me. Her passion changed my life."

Bono and Ali meet with Steve Reynolds of World Vision at the Ethiopia Hotel to discuss their assignment. A couple days later,

when all the permits and clearances are in place, Reynolds puts the Hewsons on a plane bound for a feeding center in Ajibar, Ethiopia.

Steve Reynolds remembers Bono's and Ali's work in Ethiopia

"I remember thinking something like 'they won't last a week.' But they did. In fact it was almost exactly one month later that Bono and Ali came back, having spent the entire time in Ajibar, working with our staff, helping develop music and drama programmes for the children who were in the centre all day. The staff were full of stories about the man that the children had named 'The Girl with the Beard' – a reference to the mop-type, 'mullet' hairdo that Bono was sporting at the time... and the beard he had grown while in the camp.

"The staff praised his

energy, his spirit, and his creativity in helping write songs about eating healthy vegetables, washing your hands before you eat, etc. Bono and Ali had truly endeared themselves to the staff and to the children and families in the centre. They were sad to see him go.

In later years, Bono will recount the story of an Ethiopian man who brought his son to see Bono and Ali, telling them to take the son "because if he stays with me, he will surely die." Bono had to say no, but the moment would fuel his passion for Africa deep into U2's career.

Also during the time in Ajibar, a Communist leader takes Bono and Ali to a monastery where they see royal and religious jewels and artifacts that belonged to Emperor Menelik II, Ethiopia's ruler from 1889 to 1913. After spending about a month at the camp in Ajibar, Steve Reynolds takes Bono and Ali on a tour to see camps and compounds in other parts of the country. "It seemed that he wanted to hold every child in Ethiopia just once, and comfort every mother," Reynolds recalls.

Meanwhile, work on Edge's solo material continues. Believing the material is better suited for a film soundtrack, Edge asks Anne-Louise Kelly of Principle Management to contact film directors to let them know about the new material. They eventually connect with Don Boyd, who's producing a film called *Heroine*, which will later be renamed *Captive*. Edge goes to Paris to see early clips of the film, and they all agree to move forward with the soundtrack project.

September 4
Wide Awake In America is certified Silver by the BPI, with sales of more than 60,000 in the UK.

September 13
Under A Blood Red Sky is certified Multi-Platinum by the BPI, with sales of more than 600,000 in the UK.

October

The 16th and final issue of *U2 Magazine* is published.

A day after returning from Africa, Bono flies to New York for additional work on Little Steven's Artists United Against Apartheid (AUAA) project. He takes part in a video shoot in Washington Square with dozens of other artists who have joined the cause, where he meets Lou Reed for the first time. Also there is Peter Wolf of the J. Geils Band, whom Bono hasn't seen since U2 opened for them in 1982. Bono tells Wolf that he'd like to meet Keith Richards, so Wolf takes him to the recording studio where the Rolling Stones are recording their *Dirty Work* album (which, coincidentally, is being produced by Steve Lillywhite).

The musicians end up hanging out long into the night, singing old country and blues songs. When the others ask Bono to do a song, he's unable to do so.

Bono on the inspiration for 'Silver And Gold'

"I was very down about the fact that I couldn't contribute. Even though I have such a background of Irish music, at age 15 I didn't want any part of that background.... I was completely uneducated and I decided after spending a night with these old timeless delta blues songs, that as I couldn't contribute one, I'd write one.

I went away and wrote it, very quickly."

Frustrated and inspired, he returns to his hotel and writes 'Silver And Gold', a song written from the point of view of a prisoner in South Africa. Bono brings the song back to the Stones' studio, where Keith Richards and Ron Wood agree to record it with Bono. They play it for Little Steven, who likes the song and agrees to add it to the *Sun City* album at the last minute. Since the album cover is already complete, a sticker will be added to every copy

announcing the additional song.

In addition to 'Silver And Gold', Bono's contributions to *Sun City* include his vocals on the title track and an interview appearance on the accompanying video, *Voices Of Sun City*.

The 'Sun City' single struggles to get airtime on US radio, but the project ultimately raises more than a million dollars for anti-apartheid education and projects.

Also this month, U2 convenes in Dublin to begin plans for their next album. It's just the four of them for now, and they plan to bring Brian Eno and Danny Lanois on board later.

October 15

Edge and Aislinn give birth to their second daughter, Arran.

November

The Bridge by Cactus World News is released on Mother Records. Bono produces three tracks on the album.

Principle Management issues a statement saying that an impostor is doing radio interviews, pretending to be Larry Mullen, Jr.

December

U2 releases *The Unforgettable Fire Collection* home video.

Two U2 releases appear in *Rolling Stone*'s list of the *Top 100 Albums of 1985*: *The Unforgettable Fire* (54) and *Wide Awake In America* (59).

December 11

Bono and Adam arrive in Gweedore, a small town in the far northwest corner of Ireland, after a seven-hour bus ride from Dublin. Bono is there to shoot a video for the Clannad song, 'In A Lifetime', on which he provides vocals; Adam is just tagging along. Artist Charlie Whisker, a friend of Bono's, is there, too – he'll drive the hearse that's used in the video. Part of the shoot takes place at the Poison Glen, a stream where British soldiers died after drinking poison water. The setting inspires Bono to start writing a song called 'The Poison Glen'. (No song with that title has appeared on a U2 release, but Clannad has a song with that name on their 1990 album, *Anam*.)

Bono and Edge develop the video's concept, and Meiert Avis handles the on-site directing. The video production crew is so large that a local hotel, normally closed at this time of year, has to open up so everyone has a place to stay.

For Bono, working with Clannad is another step in the musical education that Bob Dylan encouraged in July, 1984, and continued just a couple months ago with his recording work with Keith Richards and Ron Wood. Bono and Clannad's Maire Ni Bhraonain met at Windmill Lane earlier this year, when Bono wanted to know more about Clannad's song, 'Harry's Game', which U2 used as the exit music after gigs on *The Unforgettable Fire* Tour. His recent work with both Irish and American music legends will have interesting implications for U2's next album.

Bono: "I'm torn between two continents"

"I'm torn between two continents, whereas The Edge has a more European sensibility. I think the justification for that combination is that U2's music has both. It can reach into Europe and reach into America."

December 13

Still in Gweedore, Bono and Maire play bartender at a local pub, as the artists and video crew enjoy a night of music and fun there.

December 15

RTE TV airs *Wide Awake In America*, a documentary that includes footage of U2's gigs earlier this year at Croke Park and Madison Square Garden.

Late December

After Christmas, Edge's *Captive* soundtrack project wraps up. Edge and Michael Brook write, produce, and play all instruments on the soundtrack, with the exception of the theme song, 'Heroine'. Larry does the drumming on that song, and a promising, young female singer named Sinead O'Connor handles vocals.

1986

After an ultra-successful 1985, U2 enters 1986 in pole position to claim the mantle of Best Band in the World. They begin the year in the recording studio, with plans to release a new album by year's end. Edge wants to steer U2 further down the atmospheric, European trail they began on *The Unforgettable Fire*. Bono, still inspired by Dylan's command to "go back", wants to explore a more American, bluesy sound. The band works past its deadlines and the album gets pushed into 1987.

1986 is a year marked by dramatic ups and downs.

U2 headline a two-week tour for Amnesty International, playing to adoring fans across America. But back in Ireland, a headlining spot at Self Aid brings stinging criticism on U2. Perhaps the most important events of the year happen back-to-back in July, when Bono's personal assistant Greg Carroll dies in Dublin just before Bono is due to spend a couple weeks exploring Central America. It's an intense period that has a dramatic impact on U2's music, and the personal struggles lead Bono to call 1986 "an incredibly bad year for me".

January

U2 relocate to Danesmoate House, a Georgian mansion south of Dublin to continue work on their next album. (Adam will later buy the house.) The setting is similar to the arrangement U2 used at Slane Castle in 1984, and the goal is the same: to use new spaces or places to create a new atmosphere and new inspiration. The recording desk is set up in the dining room, and other rooms are used for recording and performing. Brian Eno and Daniel Lanois are on hand for production duties, while Mark Ellis – a newcomer to the team who, in true U2 style, goes by a one-word nickname: Flood – handles the recording. One of the first songs the band works on is 'Heartland', a song they started during *The Unforgettable Fire* sessions; it won't appear on record until *Rattle And Hum* in 1988. Another early song is 'Desert Of Our Love', which goes through several incarnations and eventually becomes 'I Still Haven't Found What I'm Looking For'.

While the band records mainly downstairs, their friends Guggi and Gavin Friday are upstairs painting. Bono regularly joins the pair for weekly trips into Dublin to work with artist Charlie Whisker. (Some of the work the group creates during this time will be shown at an exhibition in Dublin in January 1988).

Recording lasts throughout the year with a few interruptions. Later recording takes place at Edge's house as well as S.T.S. studio and Windmill Lane.

Also this month, Clannad releases its new single, 'In A

Above: Bono on stage during the 'Self Aid' concert, Dublin, May 17.

Lifetime', featuring Bono on vocals.

January 11

Bono attends the funeral of Phil Lynott in the Dublin suburb of Howth. Lynott, the former lead singer of Irish band Thin Lizzy, died January 4 of pneumonia and heart failure after a heroin overdose.

January 30

RTE Studios, Dublin. U2 appear on an Irish TV programme called *TV Gaga*. Bono and Larry do an interview before the band performs three songs. The first song is called 'Womanfish', which Bono says is

"about this mermaid we met in America". It's the only time the song has ever been played. They also perform a very early version of 'Trip Through Your Wires' and a cover of 'Knocking On Heaven's Door'. U2 agree to do the performance only on the condition that RTE never re-run the program.

February

The debut issue of *Propaganda*, U2's new fanclub magazine, is published.

February 27

U2 dominate the voting in the 1985 Music Awards issue of *Rolling Stone*.

They're named "Band Of The Year" by both fans and critics. Fans also name U2's Live Aid performance the best one of that historic concert, and include each member of the band in his respective "Best" category.

Bono also shares his favourite music of 1985 with the magazine:
Macalla, Clannad
Ordinary Man, Christy Moore
The Bridge, Cactus World News
Anthem, De Danann
The Storm, Moving Hearts
Full Moon, Paul Brady
Gunpowders, Light A Big Fire
Four Green Fields, Makem And Clancy
Rain Dogs, Tom Waits
'The Banks Of The Royal Canal', Bob Dylan

February 28
Bono and Ali attend a gig by Shook Up!, Neil McCormick's current band, at Trinity College in Dublin.

April
Larry appears on Paul Brady's album, *Back To The Centre,* playing drums on the track 'Airwaves'.

April 15
In Dublin, the Self Aid organization announces plans for a benefit concert next month intended to help the country's unemployment crisis by raising money and creating new jobs. U2 are announced as headliners of the 27-act concert, the largest ever in Ireland. Criticism of the Self Aid concept begins almost immediately, and culminates in the days before the show when *In Dublin* magazine runs a cover story called "Rock Against the People: The Great Self-Aid Farce". The magazine puts Bono on the cover, and calls out U2 as hypocrites. Critics say Self Aid will only take pressure off the Irish government to do its part to solve the unemployment crisis. They also question the plan to invite businesses to "pledge" job openings during the concert, and the need for citizens to pledge money when tax dollars already go to government job creation programs.

Larry plays drums on 'Make It Work', the theme song of the Self Aid concert, which is sung by Christy Moore.

Above: Two fans join Bono on stage during the Amnesty International Concert, Los Angeles, June 6. Right: Bono with Sting at the press conference preceding the Amnesty International Concert, New York, June 14.

May 17
U2 headlines the Self Aid benefit for the unemployed at RDS stadium in Dublin. U2's short set is half-original material, and half covers of songs by Eddie Cochran, Bob Dylan and John Lennon – another sign of U2's ongoing interest in exploring the roots of rock and roll. The highlight is a sinister version of 'Maggie's Farm', which tackles the issue of Irish emigrants going to work in Margaret Thatcher's Great Britain and even finds Bono ranting about the Sellafield nuclear plant in England. He takes a shot at the press criticism of Self Aid during 'Bad', singing "… they crawled out of the woodwork / onto pages of cheap Dublin magazines." *Hot Press* later calls U2's performance "the blackest and most ferocious set of their entire career."

The concert airs live on RTE television and radio. More than 1,200 jobs are pledged during the concert, and TV viewers donate more than £500,000 toward unemployment relief. Later in the year, Edge tells *Hot Press* that the band's involvement in Self Aid was more about the idea than the statistics. "We concurred with the sentiment behind it. And we just knew we couldn't turn our backs on it. It was a gestural thing that was all about hopes and aspirations and very little about real answers."

June
Issue 2 of *Propaganda* is published this month.

June 1
The Unforgettable Fire is certified Gold by the BPI, with sales of more than 100,000 in the UK.

June 3
All four members of U2 attend a news conference at the Cow Palace in San Francisco with other artists involved in Amnesty International's "Conspiracy of Hope" tour, which will begin here tomorrow. Stage crews are busy setting up, but soundcheck has to be delayed so everyone can hear what's being said during the Q&A session with several dozen reporters.

"We're here," Bono says,

Edge explains U2's involvement with Conspiracy of Hope, June 3

"We've been supporters of Amnesty for a couple years now. One of the founders of Amnesty is an Irishman, Sean McBride, whose involvement with human rights goes back to the early part of Irish history – to our country's founding in 1916. The Irish in general are very much involved in campaigning for human rights around the world. When Live Aid started, the Irish gave more money per capita than any country in the world, about 3 million pounds, almost a pound per person in Ireland."

"because we very much want to be and because Jack Healey is a hard man to argue with." The artists are seated in front of the portraits of six prisoners of conscience who are "adopted" for the tour. "Many of these prisoners are artists and poets in their own right," Edge says, "arrested for exactly that power to influence and change society."

Bono lightens the mood a bit when he announces that U2 will sing 'Yummy, Yummy, Yummy, I've Got Love In My Tummy' during tomorrow's concert.

Edge explains U2's involvement with Conspiracy of Hope

"I think we're more aware, due to our situation in Ireland. The civil rights in our area of the country could be improved upon. Ireland has been struggling for some time to extricate itself from a system of colonialism that is less than ideal. And that is something America hasn't really experienced, so the profile of an organization like Amnesty is lower as a result.

"I think Amnesty sees America as territory they really haven't opened up yet; really, I think the bottom line is to make some more friends."

June 4

Cow Palace, San Francisco. Amnesty International's Conspiracy of Hope Tour kicks off with the first of six shows in 11 days. U2 takes the stage last, and opens its short set with a cover of Eddie Cochran's 'C'mon Everybody'. When U2 finishes, all of the artists take the stage to end the show with a group performance of Bob Dylan's 'I Shall Be Released'.

While in San Francisco, Bono meets Dave Batstone from Central American Mission Partners, a Latin American relief organization. Batstone takes Bono and Edge to meet Chilean artist Rene Castro at the Mission Cultural Center for

Latino Arts. Bono is interested in Castro's silkscreen print of Martin Luther King, Jr., which hangs on a wall next to a print of Chilean singer/activist Victor Jara. They also visit one of Castro's murals at Balmy Alley, a few blocks away.

June 5

The artists and crew travel to Los Angeles. U2 and others give a news conference when they reach LA.

June 6

The Forum, Los Angeles. The celebrities come out for tonight's Amnesty concert. Special guests include Bob Dylan, Tom Petty, Bob Geldof and Dave Stewart. Madonna and husband Sean Penn are also in attendance.

June 7

The artists and crew fly to Denver.

June 8

McNichols Sports Arena, Denver. Tonight's Conspiracy of Hope gig is the only one on the short tour that doesn't sell out. "It was an empty arena," Bryan Adams says later. "Unbelievable. I think it was because it was Amnesty. The promoter was afraid it was some sort of real conspiracy. He was so afraid to promote the show, he forgot to promote it."

June 10

While in Atlanta on a day off, most of the Conspiracy of Hope artists gather in the cocktail lounge at the Ramada Renaissance Hotel where they're staying. Two of the musicians ask the local band playing that night if they can borrow their instruments to play a few songs. They can, and Bono joins them to sing Lou Reed's 'Sweet Jane'. He sings to a girl at the bar, who tells him her name is Rose, so he changes the lyrics to "...sweet Rose". The rest of the group, Larry and Adam included, continue jamming into the wee hours of the morning, until the show is brought to a halt by a bartender who wants to go home. Edge and Lou Reed find out about it the next day and regret having gone to bed too early.

June 11

The Omni, Atlanta. The Police reunite for tonight's show, and will do the same at the final two shows of the tour. After the show, many of the artists gather in the hotel bar for another jam session. Edge and Lou Reed are on hand for this one.

June 12

The artists and crew fly to Chicago.

June 13

Rosemont Horizon, Chicago. Bono joins The Police for 'Invisible Sun'.

June 14

A massive pillow fight – involving even the flight attendants – breaks out during today's flight from Chicago to New York. On arrival in New York, U2 attend an anti-apartheid rally in the city where Peter Gabriel and Little Steven, among others, are performing. They get on stage to sing 'Sun City' with Little Steven and other artists.

June 15

Giants Stadium, East Rutherford. The Conspiracy of Hope Tour ends with a daylong concert that draws 55,000 fans. The 11-hour show airs live on MTV and the Westwood One radio network, and an edited version is shown later on Fox TV. A number of additional performers are drawn by the scope of the event, including Joni Mitchell, Yoko Ono, Peter, Paul & Mary, The Hooters, and more. Pete Townshend plans to perform, but returns to London when he learns that his father has died.

U2 rise to the occasion with a set that includes blistering versions of 'Pride', 'Sunday, Bloody Sunday', and 'Maggie's Farm'. Bono returns to the stage to join The Police on the last song of their set, 'Invisible Sun'. In the middle of the song, the members of U2 take the stage one-by-one and The Police give U2 their instruments – a symbolic passing of the torch. U2 ends the show with 'I Shall Be Released', which includes all the performers singing together, as well as actual prisoners of conscience who have been freed thanks to Amnesty International.

The tour is a grand success. Amnesty International pockets $3 million and nearly triples its US membership.

Jack Healey remembers the Conspiracy of Hope Tour, June 15

"I think in Giants Stadium [U2] were probably the best band in the world at that moment, when they came out on that stage that day. They were still raw and rough, but it was a raw roughness that I don't think had ever been seen before. I don't know, but I was awed by their talent that day, and it was truly amazing."

Healey's favourite memory about that final show at Giants Stadium is what it did for Amnesty International USA.

"It changed everything. Amnesty was branded – it became a household name that day. There were 45,000 new members, and it just shot up – just kept going. The 45,000 new members were all under 40. When you change the demography of an organization, and you make it young – you have a mailing base forever. [Amnesty's] future was guaranteed."

June 28

Bono joins The Simple Minds on stage at their Croke Park show. With Jim Kerr, Bono sings a medley of 'Lovesong', 'Sun City', and 'Dance To The Music'.

Bono remembers Greg Carroll, July 3

"It was a devastating blow. He was doing me a favour, he was taking my bike home. Greg used to look after Ali. They would go out dancing together. He was a best friend. I've already had it once, with my mother, and now I've had it twice. The worst part was the fear, and fear is the opposite of faith. After that, when the phone rang, my heart stopped every time. Now when I go away I wonder, 'Will these people be here when I get back?' You start thinking in those terms."

July 3
Bono arrives in Texas for an appearance at tomorrow's Farm Aid II concert. Shortly after landing, he gets a phone call telling him that his personal assistant, Greg Carroll, has died in a motorcycle accident in Dublin, while running an errand for Bono at the time. Bono hops back on a plane and flies to Dublin to join the rest of U2. "I had been in my hotel one hour after a 13-hour flight. I caught the next plane back to Dublin," Bono says later.

The U2 organization is overwhelmed by the tragedy. "What happened was this avalanche of questions," The Edge recalls later. "Is it a question of destiny? Is chance a power? How does belief in God come into that?"

July 9
Bono and Larry, with other members of the U2 organization, arrive in Wanganui, New Zealand, for the three-day funeral of Greg Carroll.

July 10
Bono reads a poem and delivers a short eulogy during the main funeral ceremony for Greg Carroll. Later during a supper, he sings 'Let It Be' and 'Knockin' On Heaven's Door' with help from violinist Gavin Buxton of a local band, The Ponsonby DC's. After the funeral, Bono and Larry also visit the Ratana church temple where Carroll was a member.

The experience inspires Bono to write the song 'One Tree Hill',

Above: Bono and his wife Ali at Greg Carroll's funeral at Wanganui, New Zealand, July 10.

named after the highest of the volcanic hills that overlook Auckland, the city where U2 and Carroll first met.

Mid-July
Bono and Ali fly from New Zealand to Nicaragua for a visit organized by Central American Mission Partners (CAMP), an organization dedicated to human rights and economic development in Latin America. Three members of CAMP – Dave Batstone, Wendy Brown, and Harold Hoyle – meet Bono and Ali at the airport in Managua.

The group spends almost a week in Nicaragua. They meet with Ernesto Cardenal, a Roman Catholic priest who is also the Minister of Culture in the

Sandinista regime, and with musician Luis Mejia Godoy, who works under Cardenal in the Department of Music. They also pay a visit to the crumbling palace of former president Anastasio Somoza.

On July 19, the group hears President Daniel Ortega give a lengthy speech on the country's Revolution Day. (Unbeknownst to anyone, Salman Rushdie is at the same speech.) On another day, possibly July 20, Bono goes to mass and is moved by the sight of churchgoers standing up and calling out the names of loved ones who have died fighting the *contras*.

From Nicaragua, the group flies to El Salvador where they stay for another 4-5 days. They visit the US Embassy there, and meet a group called COMADRES – the Mothers of the Disappeared – a group of women whose children have disappeared or been killed at the hands of the government. One day, Bono, Ali, and Hoyle set out to deliver aid to farmers at a co-operative that Bono has supported financially. As they walk through a remote area about 100 miles north of San Salvador, government troops fire bullets in their direction, but miss purposely.

Bono: "Why have I brought Ali here?"

"We just freeze on the road. We don't know what's gonna happen, whether we should take for cover or we should stand still. There's silence, big silence … We can hear each other's hearts beating, then laughing from the government troops who were just letting us know that they don't like us and they could take our life if they really wanted to.

"If I'm honest, I was at that time thinking seriously that maybe we should have stayed in the Sunset Marquis at Los Angeles and gone to the beach. [*laughs*] There was

no heroism present at this point, just: 'Oh, shit … why have I brought Ali here?'"

Bono's experiences on this visit will form the basis for several songs on *The Joshua Tree* album, including 'Bullet The Blue Sky' and 'Mothers Of The Disappeared'.

Late July
U2 holds a memorial service for Greg Carroll in Dublin.

August 1
U2 regroups at Windmill Lane studios in Dublin to resume work on the new album.

August 26
Robbie Robertson arrives in Dublin to record two songs with U2 for his upcoming solo album. They get the work done in two days.

September
The *Captive* soundtrack, which Edge recorded with Michael Brook, is released in the UK.

Issue 3 of *Propaganda* is published.

Also this month, an article in the UK tabloid, *Daily Mirror*, causes a stir when it claims that Larry is in a New York hospital about to undergo hand surgery. A Dublin DJ picks up the story and announces it on Radio 2. The Irish Independent and *Evening Herald* also run the story without checking. *Hot Press* calls U2's office and eventually talks to Larry, who is not in New York, but in Dublin working on U2's next album. "We're recording the new album at the moment and I'm having very few problems with my hand," Larry says.

October
U2 continue working on *The Joshua Tree* album. Though it's late in the game, the band has a creative spurt that produces several good song ideas. Brian Eno cautions them about pursuing the new material too earnestly, because it will surely keep them in the studio well beyond schedule and delay the album.

Also this month, U2 sees blues legend B.B. King perform in Dublin.

B.B. King remembers meeting U2, October

"When I go to the dressing room, I'm told U2 is here. 'Oh, God, they were here.' They seemed to be kind of in awe of me, and I was just as nervous, meeting them. We had a nice chat, and I said to Bono, 'Sometime when you're writing a song, will you think of me?'"

They visit King in his dressing room after the show.

November 14
Bono sees The Damned play a gig at the Top Hat Ballroom in Dub Laoghaire.

December
Issue 4 of *Propaganda* is published. It includes an update on the hand problems that have bothered Larry since March, 1985.

December 14-16
Around this time, U2 spends three days traveling in and around the California desert with Anton Corbijn and Steve Averill, shooting pictures in the stark, desert landscape. The shoot begins in Bodie, a ghost town in the upper Sierra Nevada near Yosemite National Park. The album cover photo is taken at Zabriskie Point in Death Valley. Photos of U2 and the real Joshua tree are taken just outside of Death Valley National Park.

Late December
Just before Christmas, U2 call old friend Steve Lillywhite and ask him to come to Dublin to remix a few of the new songs. He works at Windmill Lane over the turn of the year.

1987

Breakthrough. After four albums and seven years of almost non-stop touring, U2's slow ascent to the top of the rock'n'roll tree is over. With memories of Live Aid and the Conspiracy of Hope tour still fresh, music fans worldwide are anxious for U2's next step. *The Joshua Tree* album and tour don't disappoint; both are enormously successful, and propel U2 to heights no Irish band has reached before. With a number one album and several number one singles, U2 gains attention beyond the world of rock music; *Time* magazine puts them on the cover with the headline, "Rock's Hottest Ticket". There's no doubt U2 has become the biggest the band in the world. It's an amazing year, and in what is perhaps a momentary flash of hubris, U2 decide to capture it all on film.

January

With the new album finished, U2 turn their attention to the B-sides that are needed to fill out an ambitious singles release plan. The band revisits several of the song ideas that formed late in the album recording. Tracks like 'Walk To The Water', 'Luminous Times (Hold On To Love)', and 'Spanish Eyes' are completed around this time. There's also a tune called 'Birdland' that U2 agree is too strong for a B-side; they decide to hold it for a future album release.

January 9

Adam attends a convention in Amsterdam hosted by the Dutch U2 fan club. He accepts a gold album award and joins the band Tuesday Blue on stage for a cover of Them's 'Gloria'.

February

U2 meets Anthony DeCurtis, who is in Dublin preparing a feature for an upcoming issue of *Rolling Stone* magazine. DeCurtis interviews Bono and Larry at Larry's house in Howth, and elsewhere in and around Dublin. DeCurtis also interviews The Edge while the band are in London shooting a video for 'Red Hill Mining Town' with director Neil Jordan.

Anthony DeCurtis recalls the 'Red Hill Mining Town' video shoot

"We were on the set of the video shoot which was, like, 9,000 hours long. I don't remember much of the set – it was pretty dark. It seemed like a performance piece. It was just the band on a sound stage pretending to play. It was interesting to see Bono hanging out for about two hours or so and then it would be, 'Okay Bono, get up and do your thing!' And you'd see this total commitment. That complete ability to perform."

U2 shoots another video this month in Dublin, for 'With Or Without You'. Meiert Avis and Matt Mahurin co-direct the clip, which includes abstract shots of dancer Morleigh Steinberg edited in between shots of U2 performing the song.

February 27
Dave Fanning interviews Larry on RTE.

March
Issue 5 of *Propaganda* is published.

March 4
At 11:30 a.m., US radio stations are finally allowed to begin playing U2's new single, 'With Or Without You'. In an attempt to coordinate airplay and maximise impact, Island Records has distributed the single with a strong warning for any station tempted to play it earlier.

The single includes 'Luminous Times (Hold On To Love)', 'Walk To The Water', and 'Mothers Of The Disappeared' as B-sides on its various formats. It debuts at number 64 on the *Billboard* Hot 100 and reaches number one in early May. It climbs to number four in the UK.

March 8
U2 perform a six-song set in Belfast for broadcast on *The Old Grey Whistle Test* TV programme. The band's performance airs three days later. Immediately after the taping, U2 head to a local record store to meet fans who are buying U2's new album.

March 9
U2 releases *The Joshua Tree*, their fifth studio album. The cover features another cinematic Anton Corbijn photo, this time showing the band in black-and-white in the California desert. The album is

dedicated to Bono's assistant, Greg Carroll, who died July 3, 1986. With U2's stature at an all-time high after Live Aid and the Conspiracy of Hope Tour, anticipation for *The Joshua Tree* is sky-high. U2 delivers a tour de force that tops the charts, produces number one singles, earns U2's first Grammy awards, and vaults the band into the stratosphere. Brian Eno and Daniel Lanois produce again, but *The Joshua Tree* has little of the ambience and lack of focus of *The Unforgettable Fire*. On the contrary, U2 tries and succeeds in crafting a thematic album with tight, direct lyrics and the best songwriting of their career.

The Joshua Tree becomes the fastest selling album in British music history, selling 300,000 copies in its first two days and reaching number one. It enters the US chart at number seven, U2's best debut yet and first Top 10 album, and quickly climbs to number one.

Sensing that U2 is about to reach superstar status, Island Records throws all of its marketing muscle behind the album. Island president Lou Maglia calls it "the most complete merchandising effort ever assembled" in his career. $100,000 is spent on store displays alone. It's the first album to be shipped on vinyl, cassette, and CD simultaneously. (Typically, CDs hit stores several weeks later than records and cassettes.) It's also the first album to sell one million CDs in the US.

Album reviews are almost universally positive. In the *Boston Globe*, Steve Morse describes *The Joshua Tree* as U2's "most challenging work to date. It's another spiritual progress report, enwrapped in music that strikes a healthy balance between the lushness of their last album, 1984's *The Unforgettable Fire*, and the more volcanic rock of their early years."

Says *Los Angeles Times'* critic Robert Hilburn: "*The Joshua Tree* finally confirms on record what this band has been slowly asserting for three years now on stage: U2 is what the Rolling Stones ceased being years ago – the greatest rock'n'roll band in the world. In this

Edge explains U2's plan for *The Joshua Tree*, March 9

"We felt on this record that maybe, options were not such a good thing, that limitation might be very positive. So we decided to work within the limitations of the song as a starting-point. Let's actually write songs. We just wanted to leave the record less vague, open-ended, atmospheric and impressionistic. Make it more straightforward, focused and concise."

Above: Wembley Stadium.

album, the band wears that mantle securely."

In *Hot Press*, longtime supporter Bill Graham writes: *"The Joshua Tree* rescues rock from its decay, bravely and unashamedly basing itself in the mainstream before very cleverly lifting off into several higher dimensions. They've been misunderstood occasionally, even by their committed supporters – but after *The Joshua Tree*, with its skill, and the diversity of issues it touches, one thing is absolutely clear: U2 can no longer be patronised with faint and glib praise. They must be taken very seriously indeed after this revaluation of rock."

Jon McCready of NME says the album is "a better and braver record than anything else that's likely to appear in 1987."

Tracks: 'Where The Streets Have No Name', 'I Still Haven't Found What I'm Looking For', 'With Or Without You', 'Bullet The Blue Sky', 'Running To Stand Still', 'Red Hill Mining Town', 'In God's Country', 'Trip Through Your Wires', 'One Tree Hill', 'Exit', 'Mothers Of The Disappeared'

After their TV taping last night, U2 appears at the Makin' Tracks record store in Belfast at midnight, signing autographs and speaking with about 200 fans who are there to buy *The Joshua Tree* on its first day of release. (The crowd would likely have been bigger if not for a local radio DJ mistakenly announcing that the album release had been delayed a week). In London, more than a thousand fans line up at midnight outside a record store to buy the record as early as possible – one of the fans in line is singer Elvis Costello.

March 12
Robert Hilburn of the *Los Angeles Times* is in Dublin to interview U2 for an upcoming feature. He spends several days with the band, gets a tour of the city from Bono, and watches them rehearse for the tour.

The Joshua Tree is certified Platinum by the BPI, with sales of more than 300,000 in the UK.

March 13
U2 invite a country band to come perform at Boland's Mill, where the band has been rehearsing for the tour, in honour of Adam's birthday. U2 takes over and performs 'People Get Ready' at around midnight.

March 16
U2 appear on RTE's *The Late Late Show* as part of a tribute to the Irish folk band, The Dubliners. They sing 'Springhill Mining Disaster', a song The Dubliners performed regularly, and take part in a finale at the end of the show with The Dubliners and The Pogues.

March 21
The Joshua Tree begins a two-week run atop the UK album chart.

March 26
U2 shoots promotional photos with Anton Corbijn on the roof of the Million Dollar Hotel in Los Angeles.

March 27
U2 attracts a crowd of 1,000+ while recording the video for 'Where The Streets Have No Name' atop the Republic Liquor Store at 7th and Main in downtown Los Angeles. In addition to recording the video, U2 play a few songs for the crowd, which gets so big that police have to pull the plug on U2's performance.

Bono begins work on a new song, 'Wild Irish Rose'. The name is inspired by the sight of empty bottles of Wild Irish Rose wine in this part of downtown.

March 28
Tickets for some of U2's upcoming shows go on sale today. In New Jersey, the crush of fans trying to get inside a ticket outlet breaks a plate glass window. No one is hurt.

April
While U2 is in Arizona early in the month, director Barry Devlin shoots footage for a documentary, *Outside It's America*, which airs later in the year on MTV. The documentary includes music videos for 'In God's Country' and 'Spanish Eyes', an upcoming B-side.

The overwhelming success of *The Joshua Tree* has several ripple effects this month. *The Unforgettable Fire* is certified Platinum by the BPI on April 1, and then Multi-Platinum just five days later, on April 6. *Under A Blood Red Sky* is certified Multi-Platinum on April 13, with sales exceeding 900,000 in the UK. In North

America, Virgin Records finally releases Edge's solo album, the *Captive* soundtrack, which was recorded in 1985 and released in the UK in 1986.

April 1

U2's final rehearsal before the start of *The Joshua Tree* Tour includes covers of 'People Get Ready' and a medley of 'I Walk The Line' and 'Folsom Prison Blues'. But as the band goes through its planned set, a near-disaster happens during 'Bullet The Blue Sky': Bono falls while walking up a ramp with a spotlight in his hand. He falls on the spotlight, cuts his chin, and requires stitches at a local hospital. The injury will be concealed beneath makeup during tomorrow's show.

April 2

Arizona State University Activity Center, Tempe, with Lone Justice. U2 opens *The Joshua Tree* Tour. Arizona has rescinded a holiday honouring Martin Luther King, prompting many artists to refuse performing there. After talking with fans and members of a statewide campaign to recall Arizona Governor Evan Mecham, Paul McGuinness says the band will proceed with the concert as a way of dramatizing opposition to the governor's action.

Prior to the show, U2 makes a "sizable financial contribution" to the Mecham Watchdog Committee, which is trying to recall the governor. Before U2 take the stage, concert promoter Barry Fey reads a statement explaining why U2 has decided to play in Arizona despite the Mecham controversy.

Below: Shooting the 'I Still Haven't Found...' video in Las Vegas, April 12.

U2's opening statement

An excerpt from U2's statement about Arizona Governor Evan Mecham. "We were outraged when we arrived in Arizona last weekend and discovered the climate created by Governor Mecham's rescission of the holiday honouring Dr. Martin Luther King, Jr. Governor Mecham is an embarrassment to the people of Arizona. We condemn his actions and views as an insult to a great spiritual leader. We urge all forward thinking Arizonans to support the campaign to recall Governor Mecham."

The show itself is a solid, but somewhat shaky beginning to U2's biggest tour yet. Bono is struck with opening night vocal problems and is unable to sing parts of many songs, likely due to the band's extensive rehearsals in the hot, dry desert air. On several occasions, he holds the microphone out and lets the crowd sing for him, which they do eagerly, even on new tracks from *The Joshua Tree*.

Most critics give the show positive reviews despite Bono's vocal problems. In the *Arizona Republic*, Andrew Means says, "Thursday's show was an auspicious start. The power of this music surged across the audience, not only in terms of volume but conviction as well." Linda Romine of the *East Valley Tribune* is less enthusiastic: "Last night's concert was not a dismal disappointment; neither was it the cathartic experience it could have been."

April 3
Today's concert is postponed a day because of Bono's vocal problems.

April 4
Arizona State University Activity Center, Tempe, with Lone Justice. Bono tells the audience that *Time* magazine is preparing a cover story on the band, and brings the photographer on stage to take pictures of the band with the audience as a background. Those photos are not used, however; the magazine instead chooses a portrait photo taken backstage prior to the concert.

April 5
Community Center, Tucson, with Lone Justice.

April 6
On a night off, U2 are in Las Vegas to attend the Sugar Ray Leonard vs. Marvin Hagler fight at Caesar's Palace. After the boxing match, they see Frank Sinatra perform at The Golden Nugget at 1:00 a.m. Sinatra announces that U2 are in attendance and the band stands up to a round of applause, while Frank makes fun of the way the band is dressed. They visit Sinatra in his dressing room after the show, talking with him at length about music.

April 7-8
The Summit, Houston, with Lone Justice. Before the second concert in Houston, Bono and Edge do an interview with Carter Alan for Island Records. Writer Steve Pond is also with the band, working on an article for *Rolling Stone*.

After the gig, U2 and friends go to a local bar called the LA Club. Paul McGuinness pays to have the club closed for the remainder of the night. U2 borrow instruments from a country-rock group that had been performing, and plays a short acoustic set with the bar band providing some support. U2's performance is relaxed and fun and the small crowd in the bar shout encouragement as they plays mostly old-time country classics. The set list includes Johnny Cash's 'I Walk The Line' and 'Folsom Prison Blues', Hank Williams Sr.'s 'Lost Highway', and even a couple of U2 songs – 'Lucille' and 'I Still Haven't Found What I'm Looking For'.

April 10
Pan American Center, Las Cruces, with Lone Justice.

April 12
Thomas And Mack Arena, Las Vegas, with Lone Justice. After their first concert in Las Vegas, U2 take to the streets to film the video for 'I Still Haven't Found What I'm Looking For', a late choice to be the second single from *The Joshua Tree*. The original plan was to use 'Red Hill Mining Town', but U2 is unhappy with the video shot three months earlier and Bono was unable to sing the song during pre-tour rehearsals, so it's dropped as a single.

April 13-14
Sports Arena, San Diego, with Lone Justice. Before the second show, U2 learns that *The Joshua Tree* has reached number one in the US after three weeks on the charts. After the show, Bono sings a couple songs on acoustic guitar for fans outside their hotel. U2 videotape a special

Edge on U2's visit to Las Vegas, April 12

"To see all the gambling, to see all the strangeness of the American people coming with their savings for the year to Las Vegas generally to lose it all. We found that fascinating and that's why we went there. The 'Still Haven't Found What I'm Looking For' video was perfect in that location. It was a real laugh doing that."

message in their hotel room for the popular UK rock programme, *The Tube*. Bono sings the Hank Williams country hit, 'Lost Highway' while Edge plays acoustic guitar. This airs on April 24 during *The Tube*'s final episode.

On April 13, *The Joshua Tree* is certified Multi-Platinum by the BPI, with UK sales surpassing the 600,000 mark.

April 17-18-20-21-22
Sports Arena, Los Angeles, with Lone Justice. On April 20, U2 is featured in a *Newsweek* magazine article, "An Irish Pied Piper of Rock", written by Cathleen McGuigan and Frank Gibney, Jr. "U2 is turning itself into the rock phenomenon of 1987," they write. "Concert tickets on the current 13-city US tour are as hard to come by as a suntan in Dublin."

At the April 20 show, Bob Dylan joins U2 on stage to sing 'I Shall Be Released' and 'Knockin' On Heaven's Door'. "As we were leaving the stage," Bono recalls later, "I said, 'Those songs are gonna last forever, Bob.' And he said, 'Your songs are gonna last forever, too – the only thing is, no one's gonna be able to play them.' They're hard to figure out, you know?"

An excerpt from *Time*, April 27

"Their concerts are as revivifying as anything in rock, with a strong undertow of something not often found this side of Bruce Springsteen: moral passion. U2's songs speak equally to the Selma of two decades ago and the Nicaragua of tomorrow. They are about spiritual search, and conscience and commitment, and it follows that some of the band's most memorable performances – and, not incidentally, the ones that have helped U2 break through to an even wider audience – have been in the service of a good cause, at Live Aid or during last summer's tour for Amnesty International. This is not, then, just a band for partying down."

After the show, Dylan and T-Bone Burnett join Bono and Edge at the Sunset Marquis Hotel. Burnett suggests they write a song together, and Edge plays an unfinished song called 'We Almost Made It This Time'. Dylan comes up with lyrics almost immediately, leaving Bono and Edge feeling inferior and unable to finish the song.

April 24-25
Cow Palace, Daly City, with Lone Justice.

April 26
Adam does an interview in his San Francisco hotel suite with Steve Morse of the *Boston Globe*.

April 27
U2 appear on the cover of *Time* magazine with the headline "U2: Rock's Hottest Ticket". The lengthy article opens up U2 to a whole new audience, and includes praise from

the likes of Lou Reed and musician/ producer T-Bone Burnett.

There's a possibly telling quote elsewhere in the article, as Edge shares a confession: "My life revolves around the music, the keyboard. My family should make a difference, but I am not able to spend enough time with them."

U2 is also on the cover of *Rolling Stone* magazine this week, marking the first time any band has been on both covers at the same time.

April 29
Rosemont Horizon, Chicago, with Lone Justice.

April 30
Pontiac Silverdome, Detroit, with Lone Justice. U2 sell all 51,000+ tickets at their first headlining stadium show in the US. Media reviews are favourable following the show, but they also say a video screen is a must so people at the

other end of the stadium can see the band.

Willie Williams on the video screen question
"There was much debate over the use of video screens for camera close-ups. Touring video systems were just becoming available but there was concern that there would be a danger of dividing the audience's attention between the stage and the video screen."

May
U2 releases 'I Still Haven't Found What I'm Looking For' with 'Spanish Eyes' and 'Deep In The Heart' as B-sides. It reaches number one in the US and number six in the UK.

Island Records has also commissioned New York choir director Dennis Bell to record a gospel version of the single, and the label plans to release that version shortly after U2's. But Island chief Chris Blackwell vetoes the idea of a second single, believing it would look like a money grab. Bell, believing his choir's version is too good not to be heard, forms his own label, lines up a distributor, and records a demo.

May 2-3-4
The Centrum, Worcester, with Lone Justice. A crew from the Irish TV show *Today Tonight* tapes during the second show.

May 5-6
On the invitation of Boston Garden President Larry Moulter, U2 attend a Boston Celtics playoff game on one of these dates. After the game, the band is allowed to shoot baskets on the famed parquet floor of Boston's oldest arena. Moulter's generosity is part of a pitch to convince U2 to play the Garden.

May 7-8-9
Civic Center, Hartford, with Lone Justice. After the first show, Bono retires to his hotel room with J.

Geils Band singer Peter Wolf and writer Lisa Robinson, who interviews Bono. Wolf gives Bono a compilation tape of country songs that Bono had asked him to make. After the third show, DJ Carter Alan gives Bono an Atlantic Records box set of vintage blues cassettes.

While in Hartford, U2 meet 25-year-old film director Phil Joanou for the first time. Joanou has arrived to make an unsolicited pitch to direct a feature-length documentary about the *Joshua Tree* Tour. One of U2's first questions to Joanou is about what kind of movie he would make. He replies with a question, asking U2 what kind of movie do they want to make?

Phil Joanou on meeting U2
"I think the reason that we got along was that I wanted to find out what kind of movie they wanted to make, instead of coming in and telling them how it should be done."

After speaking with U2 about their plans, Joanou suggests they hire Martin Scorsese, Jonathan Demme, or George Miller to direct the film – all are much more experienced than Joanou. But U2 invites him to Dublin during an upcoming break in the tour, and they all get along famously. Although U2 has yet to commit to doing the movie, they ask Joanou to spend the summer developing the idea further.

Paul McGuinness: Why make a movie?
"I was very keen on the idea of going wide at a time like that, just seeing how big this thing could get. I had always admired Colonel Parker and Brian Epstein for realizing that music could capture the imagination of the whole world."

May 8
'With or Without You' reaches number one on the *Billboard* singles chart.

May 10
U2 gives a press conference at Tommy Makem's Pavilion in New York. More than a dozen European journalists make the trip over to hear them discuss the upcoming European tour, including plans for two shows at Dublin's Croke Park. They get that news, and also get unexpected comedy from the usually reticent Larry. A reporter asks the band if Larry's status as a sex symbol in Japan has spread elsewhere. Larry raises his head, leans forward and says, "Not yet, but we're hopeful." It's also Bono's birthday, and a reporter asks what his plans are. "I'm feeling well on the way to having the best birthday I've ever had," Bono says. "Number one single, number one LP, what more can you say?"

May 11-12-13-15-16
Brenden Byrne Arena, East Rutherford, with Lone Justice. U2 concludes the first leg of their North American tour to support The Joshua Tree with five shows at the Meadowlands. At the May 12 show, Bono tells the audience that Edge's daughter, Hollie, is attending her first U2 concert.

The tour is a huge success. The first leg is a 99 percent sellout, with only Las Vegas (April 12) not selling out. All seven of U2's albums are on the *Billboard* Top 200 Albums chart. U2 have conquered North America.

With the North American tour over, U2 heads back to Dublin and spends five days with Phil Joanou making plans for what will become the *Rattle And Hum* film. While in Dublin, they also record a full-band version of 'Silver And Gold'. The track will appear as a B-side on the 'Where The Streets Have No Name' single.

May 13
The Joshua Tree is certified as Multi-Platinum by the RIAA, with US sales already above the two million mark.

May 18
U2 are the special guests of Ireland's Taoiseach Charles Haughey at an event in Dublin to celebrate the success of *The Joshua Tree* and the start of the world tour.

May 26
U2 rehearse at Stadio Flaminio in Rome. During a break, the band does a rambling cover of 'My Girl'. Sean O'Hagan interviews U2 for an upcoming *NME* article. Larry talks about dealing with fame: "You begin to feel like a fish in a bowl. You get some girls who just stare, never come near, never speak. Today, at the pool, there were four or five who stared down from the balcony for about two hours. Weird."

May 27
Stadio Flaminio, Rome, with Lone Justice, Big Audio Dynamite, the Pretenders. U2 opens the European tour in Rome. The band is so loud that hundreds of local residents flee their homes thinking there's an earthquake. Ron Wood, Brian Eno, and Little Steven are at the show. Back at the hotel afterward, Sean O'Hagan continues to interview the band. At one point, they sing 'Lucille' while Bono strums an acoustic guitar.

May 28
Ron Wood interviews Bono in Rome for an Italian TV special.

May 29-30
Stadio Comunale Braglia, Modena, with Lone Justice, Big Audio Dynamite, the Pretenders.

June 2
Wembley Arena, London, with Hurrah!. During a restless night of sleep in London, Bono listens repeatedly to Roy Orbison's 'In Dreams'. When he wakes up today, he decides to start writing a song for Orbison called 'She's A Mystery To Me'. He sings bits of the unfinished song to the band when they arrive at Wembley Arena for tonight's show.

After the gig, there's a knock on U2's dressing room door: Security announces that Roy Orbison is here and would like to meet the band. Everyone is understandably shocked by the strange twist of fate. Bono sings 'She's A Mystery To Me'

for Orbison, too. They agree to meet again later in the year.

June 3
National Exhibition Centre, Birmingham, with Hurrah!.

June 6
Eriksberg Shipyard Docks, Gothenburg, with Lone Justice, Big Audio Dynamite, the Pretenders.

June 12-13
Wembley Stadium, London, with World Party, Spear of Destiny, The Pretenders (June 12); with Lone Justice, The Pogues, Lou Reed (June 13).

June 15
The Zenith, Paris, with Lone Justice. Lone Justice open for U2 for the last time this tour. During U2's soundcheck, the band spots Lone Justice guitarist Shane Fontayne watching, and call him up to the stage with an idea: U2 wants Lone Justice to join them on stage for a special performance.

"I was touched and elated"
Lone Justice guitarist Shane Fontayne remembers playing with U2.
"I saw Larry beckon in my direction. It was one of those moments where you look around to see who else they could be talking to, but I was the only one there. I went to the stage and when I got there, Bono said that they wanted Maria McKee (Lone Justice's singer) and myself to join them on stage that night – our last show of the tour, suggesting that we play 'Sweet Jane', the Lou Reed/Velvet Underground song that was part of the Lone Justice repertoire. I was understandably touched and elated at this invitation.
"After their sound-
check, I went to their dressing room to run through the chord changes with the band. We played the song that night – I played acoustic guitar, standing next to Edge. One of the great professional honours of my career and life."

June 17
Mungersdorfer Stadion, Cologne, with Big Audio Dynamite, Lou Reed, the Pretenders.

June 21
St. Jakob's Stadion, Basel, with the Pretenders, Lou Reed.

June 24
King's Hall, Belfast, with Lou Reed. U2 plays Belfast for the first time since 1982.

June 25
In the morning, Bono visits On The Wall art gallery in Belfast to see an exhibit by artist Anthony Davies. *World In Action* films the visit for an upcoming documentary. Later, Bono attends another Davies exhibition – this one in Dublin at the Hendricks Art Gallery, and Edge is there, too.

U2 appears on RTE radio with longtime friend and supporter Dave Fanning. Early in the programme, Iggy Pop's 'Lust For Life' is played and the band react to the song's lyrics by undressing and doing the entire interview in the nude.

June 27-28
Croke Park, Dublin, with Light A Big Fire, the Dubliners, the Pogues, Lou Reed (June 27); with Christy Moore, the Pretenders, Lou Reed, Hothouse Flowers (June 28). On the first night, Dave Fanning introduces the band and says "they have their clothes on now," a reference to the "naked interview" a couple days earlier. One fan manages to climb to the top of the Cusack Stands to dance, prompting Bono to urge him to get back down to safety. Ali brings a bottle of champagne on stage during 'Party Girl'.

Above: Bono and Edge in Belfast, June 24.

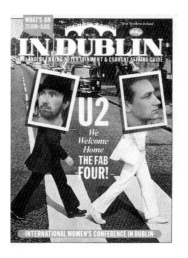

During the second show, Lou Reed joins U2 on stage to sing 'Bad'.

For Edge in particular, returning home is a challenge. He has two young children to care for and the switch back to home life is difficult.

Edge on the challenge to balance U2 and family
"Aislinn and I were trying to keep our family together. We had two daughters during a period when U2 had recorded two albums and embarked on two world tours. It was tough on Aislinn and I really found myself desperately trying to keep band and family working in parallel."

The shows are filmed for use in an upcoming *World in Action* documentary.

July 1
Elland Roads Stadium, Leeds, with the Fall, the Mission, the Pretenders.

July 2
Bono hangs out at a local club in Paris with David Bowie.

July 3
All four members of the band see Bowie's concert at the Hippodrome in Paris and visit with him backstage after the show.

July 4

The Hippodrome, Paris, with the Pogues, UB40. Several songs from tonight's gig are shown via satellite on British TV during a live programme celebrating Island Records' 25th Anniversary. Near the end of the show, a tear gas bomb explodes close to the stage. Bono is angered and forces the band stop during 'With Or Without You'. No one is hurt.

Before the band goes on stage, Bono is on the phone with New Zealand DJ Scott Cleaver, who records a message from Bono to be played next week at the dedication of Carroll's headstone in New Zealand. Bono recites two Bible verses: Isaiah 40: 27-31, which inspired the lyrics of U2's song, 'Drowning Man', and Psalm 40, which inspired the lyrics of U2's '40'. Of the former, Bono says, "This piece of Scripture has given me a lot of strength over the past few years, particularly in the aftermath of Greg's death. There's great life in these words, and that's why I've chosen that piece of Scripture today." At the end of the call, Bono expresses his regret about not being able to attend the ceremony next week, and thanks Cleaver for the opportunity to record a message.

July 7

The Joshua Tree is certified Multi-Platinum by the BPI, with UK sales surpassing the 900,000 mark.

July 8

Vorst National, Brussels, with In Tua Nua. Bono dedicates 'Bad' to Greg Carroll, whose funeral was held one year ago.

July 10-11

Feyenoord Stadium, Rotterdam, with In Tua Nua, the Pretenders (July 10); with In Tua Nua, Big Audio Dynamite, the Pretenders (July 11). Bono and Adam do an interview for Dutch TV shortly before the first show starts.

July 11

About 300 people attend the unveiling of a headstone in New Zealand for Greg Carroll, U2's former employee who died a little

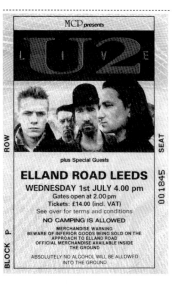

more than a year ago in Dublin. Bono's four-minute memorial message, which was recorded last week in Paris, is played during the ceremony and also airs on many New Zealand radio stations. U2 sends flowers for the headstone ceremony, and sends three platinum album awards as gifts for Carroll's family.

July 15

Estadio Santiago Bernabeu, Madrid, with Big Audio Dynamite, UB40, the Pretenders. U2 plays its first show in Spain, attracting 115,000 people – the largest crowd of the year. To reach all the people, Bono again climbs the scaffolding during 'Electric Co.'

July 18

Espace Richter, Montpellier, with World Party, UB40, the Pretenders.

July 21-22

Olympiahalle, Munich, with the Pretenders (July 21); with In Tua Nua (July 22). While in Munich, Edge does an interview for *Propaganda* magazine and talks about playing in stadiums. "A lot of the outdoor shows I've seen recently have had video screens, and I think that although they can be good for the people at the very, very back, I think it's a real distraction."

July 25

Arms Park, Cardiff, with the Silencers, the Alarm, the Pretenders. U2 play Cardiff thanks to a female fan who had gathered 10,000 signatures on a petition requesting the show. While in Cardiff, Bono meets with writer David Breskin, who is preparing a major interview for *Rolling Stone.* Breskin follows Bono to Dublin after the show where they spend two days talking. Bono reveals that he's writing a play called *Melt Head* with Gavin Friday.

July 29-30

Scottish Exhibition Centre, Glasgow, with Hoodoo Gurus (July 29); with Hue & Cry (July 30). During the first show, Bono receives the news (and tells the audience) that 'I Still

Haven't Found What I'm Looking For' is the number one single in the US. During sound check before the second show, U2 records their version of Phil Spector's 'Christmas (Baby, Please Come Home)', which will appear on the *A Very Special Christmas* benefit album later in the year.

While in Glasgow, Island Records' Rob Partridge plays for U2 a tape of the New Voices of Freedom's gospel version of 'I Still Haven't Found What I'm Looking For'. They're impressed with the song and give thought to working with the choir when U2 is back in the US.

August

Around this time, U2 learn that Island Records is in serious financial trouble and cannot pay the $5 million the label owes the band from *The Joshua Tree* royalties. Island has branched out into film distribution and financing, and after some early successes (*Kiss Of The Spider Woman, The Trip To Bountiful*), the film venture is now eating away at U2's share of the album's profits.

Marc Marot: "We started investing our cash flow into movies"

Marc Marot, former Managing Director at Island Records, explains how the label went into debt to U2.

"Island invested in a number of movies. [We] won Oscars in our first year of trading as a film company. And all of a sudden Island Records thought it was in the film industry. And so, the following year, when *The Joshua Tree* royalties started flowing, what happened was that we started investing money that wasn't – we started investing our cash flow into movies. And the problem with that is that all you need is two dud

movies at $6 million a piece for production, and you've eaten up U2's royalties."

Acting quickly, Paul McGuinness strikes a new deal: U2 invests the unpaid $5 million back into Island Records in exchange for a stake in the company. Subsequent negotiations would finalise the deal at an estimated 10% stake.

U2 releases the 'Where The Streets Have No Name' single, with three additional tracks on its various formats: 'Silver and Gold', 'Sweetest Thing', and 'Race Against Time'. The single reaches number four in the UK and number 13 in the US.

Also this month, *Playgirl* magazine includes Bono on its list of the 10 Sexiest Men in America, calling him "beautiful to gaze upon". He's joined on the list by Australian publisher Rupert Murdoch, basketball star Michael Jordan, and fictional TV star Max Headroom.

August 1
Murryfield Stadium, Edinburgh, with Run Rig, Love & Money, the Mission, the Pogues.

August 3-4
National Exhibition Centre, Birmingham, with Hoodoo Gurus.

August 5
Back in Dublin, U2 spends time at Windmill Lane listening to three new tracks that will appear on their next single – 'Race Against Time', 'Silver And Gold', and 'Sweetest Thing'. The band also gives an interview to John Hutchinson for a feature that will appear in the October issue of *Musician* magazine.

August 8
Pairc Ui Chaoimh, Cork, with the Dubliners, the Subterraneans, UB40. The European leg of *The Joshua Tree* tour ends with a celebration of Edge's birthday. During 'Party Girl', a huge birthday cake is brought on stage and Edge's wife Aislinn jumps out of it with a bottle of champagne.

August 14
U2 announce the itinerary for its fall tour of the US in a nationally syndicated broadcast from New York City.

August 28-29
Bono and Ali attend the Greenbelt Arts & Music Festival at Castle Ashby in Northamptonshire. It's the same Christian festival U2 played in 1981, but this year Bono and Ali dress as stewards to avoid drawing attention.

On the first night, Bono spends time with Martin Wroe, Australian minister John Smith (whom U2 met in 1984 in Melbourne), Canadian singer Bruce Cockburn, and Gustavo Parajon, a Nicaraguan minister. Reverend Smith is launching his autobiography at the festival, *On The Side Of The Angels,* which includes a quote from Bono on the cover: "Truly a preacher to the convertible. John Smith's message is for those who want to do more than just listen."

On the second day, Bono and Ali attend seminars given by Smith and Parajon, and attend a fund raising concert that night where Cockburn performs.

September
Issue 6 of *Propaganda* is published.

Early in the month, Phil Joanou visits U2 in France for final negotiations on *Rattle And Hum*. Though they've met several times over the summer to discuss the film, U2 has yet to give Joanou their full stamp of approval. They meet with him for a day, then head back to Dublin to make a decision: Joanou is their man.

Though we know it now as *Rattle And Hum*, the movie's original title is "U2 In The Americas", and plans are to film the band in Chicago and Buenos Aires, Argentina, before the end of the year.

September 4
U2 contacts Phil Joanou in London to give him the green light to direct *Rattle And Hum*. He flies to New York a day later.

September 8
U2 is in New York to be interviewed on a live radio call-in programme called "Trip Through Your Wires", with hosts Carter Alan of WBCN, Boston, Norm Winer of WXRT, Chicago, and Linda Ryan of KUSF, San Francisco. Cognisant of their growing image as a "serious" band, U2 takes a relaxed and humorous approach to this interview. Bono, Edge, and Adam tell drummer jokes, and all four often give lighthearted answers to serious questions from their fans.

One of Edge's cracks during the show is that U2 plans to quit rock and roll and form a country band called the Dalton Brothers. To illustrate the point, he and Bono sing their country song, 'Lucille'. Later in the show, they cover Hank Williams Sr.'s 'Lost Highway'.

Phil Joanou's film crew is in the studio to record the event, but none of the footage is used in *Rattle And Hum*. It's Joanou's first day of filming for the movie.

September 10-11
Nassau Coliseum, Uniondale, with Mason Ruffner. The third leg of *The Joshua Tree* tour opens with two shows in New York.

On September 11, 'With Or Without You' wins the Viewer's Choice Award at the MTV Video Music Awards.

September 12
The Spectrum, Philadelphia, with Mason Ruffner.

September 14
Giants Stadium, East Rutherford, with the BoDeans, Little Steven & the Disciples of Soul.

September 17-18
Boston Garden, Boston, with Little Steven & The Disciples of Soul (September 17); with Mason Ruffner (September 18). During the first show, U2's lighting system breaks down and the band plays for a full hour with the house lights on in the arena. "Rock and roll doesn't need all these expensive lights and smoke bombs," Bono tells the crowd. "We have the spirit of Larry Bird with us tonight!" Bird is the star of the Boston Celtics basketball team, and the crowd erupts at the

mention of his name. Bono returns for the encore in a Celtics jersey.

Before the second show, Boston Mayor Raymond Flynn grants U2 honorary citizenship in the city.

While in Boston, U2 contacts WBCN-FM to request a copy of the song 'Jesus Christ' by Woody Guthrie, which they're planning to record. They also get in touch with Dennis Bell, a choir director in New York, about recording with his gospel choir when the band gets to the city later in the month. U2 has heard his choir's vesion of 'I Still Haven't Found What I'm Looking For', and wants to collaborate.

September 20

Robert F. Kennedy Stadium, Washington, DC, with Little Steven & the Disciples of Soul. Bono sprains his left shoulder while falling on the slippery stage during tonight's rain-soaked show.

A video screen is installed behind the lighting tower so fans in the back half of the stadium can see the band, a move that will continue at most stadium shows throughout the tour. For U2 – a band that's always preferred stripped-down productions that invite fans to focus on the band members and the music – this is the first clue that they realize stadium shows demand a stronger visual element.

"It probably became unraveled to some degree…."
Willie Williams, U2's longtime lighting director and tour designer, talks about the band's early struggles with stadium-sized productions.
"We used to agonise over how to play bigger and bigger venues whilst maintaining the club atmosphere and stripped down production value. Up to arena-size places (20,000 people indoors) I think we did incredibly well. They were electric shows with no gimmicks, carried purely by the

relationship between U2 and their audience. When it came to stadiums (up to 70,000 outdoors) it probably came unraveled to some degree – I recall doing Wembley Stadium in 1987 without even a backdrop, never mind video. The only saving grace would have been that most of our audience wouldn't have expected a great deal more at the time, but it is a little toe curling to think of it now.

"Having said that, from the earliest days the seeds of what was to come were already present. The first year I knew him, Bono

mentioned to me that at some future point in their career he could envisage wanting to do 'Pink Floyd-size shows'. We had talked about a stunt for the US Festival – a modest event in California with an audience of 400,000 at which U2 were about 30th on the bill – where we would launch an inflatable cruise missile over the crowd and then explode it. It escapes me now quite why we wanted to do this, but it serves to show that U2's minimal phase was due to intention rather than lack of imagination."

September 21

U2 gives a press conference for US fanzine editors at The Paradise in Boston. Bono arrives 45 minutes late and in a lot of pain. He's been at a local hospital getting shoulder treatment.

September 22

Sullivan Stadium, Foxboro, with the Pogues, Little Steven & the Disciples of Soul. This is the first of a dozen shows in which Bono wears his arm in a sling. A roadie fills in for him, shining a spotlight on Edge during the guitar solo in 'Bullet The Blue Sky'.

September 23

Coliseum, New Haven, with Mason Ruffner. The crowd of about 10,500 is the smallest of the fall tour.

September 25

John F. Kennedy Stadium, Philadelphia, with Little Steven & the Disciples of Soul. Bruce Springsteen joins U2 to sing 'Stand By Me'. With more than 86,000 people at the show, it's the biggest crowd of the fall tour.

September 26

U2 visits Greater Calvary Baptist Church in Harlem, accompanied by Phil Joanou and his film crew, for a rehearsal with the New Voices of Freedom gospel choir. Choir director Dennis Bell is surprised by the presence of a film crew and cameras, and almost balks when asked to sign release sheets to appear in *Rattle And Hum*. Bell says he was only expecting the band to show up to rehearse, and was never told about the film U2 are working on.

Before the rehearsal begins, several choir members take photos with Bono. The band talks with Bell about the live performance at Madison Square Garden in two days. Bell plays the choir's version of 'I Still Haven't Found What I'm Looking For' on a small portable stereo, and everyone confers on who'll be singing which parts of the song. Edge brings his guitar to the rehearsal, but that's the only piece of equipment U2 has; Larry borrows a conga drum, Adam sits and watches, and the rehearsal is done with the church's audio system. Several performances are done with a piano player, but the one that makes the movie is just Bono, Edge, and Larry with the choir belting out the song, too.

After the rehearsal, U2 are told by locals to be very careful and avoid dangerous areas as they walk around Harlem. The band stops at a nearby diner and chats with locals who don't know who they are, but talk with them about Martin Luther King, Jr., civil rights, and the role of the church in the African-American community. Back on the streets, U2 come upon a pair of street buskers, Adam Gussow and Sterling Magee, and watch as they perform a song called 'Freedom For My People'. The song will be included in *Rattle And Hum*.

After the filming ends, Bono, Joanou and Jimmy Iovine stay out eating and talking until about 4:00 a.m.

September 28–29
Madison Square Garden, New York, with Little Steven & the Disciples of Soul (September 28); with the Pogues (September 29). During the first show, U2 is joined on stage by the New Voices of Freedom choir for a performance of 'I Still Haven't Found What I'm Looking For'. The song will later appear on the *Rattle And Hum* album, but film footage

Paul McGuinness reacts in *Propaganda* magazine to Dunphy's book, October

"The coverage of people's personal lives and family lives is something I think that none of us anticipated.... It is a pity that Eamon Dunphy reneged on his promise to let us correct errors, I suppose he was pressured by his publisher."

doesn't make it into the movie.

After the show, Bono asks Dennis Bell to have his choir record a version of 'Sweetest Thing'. They do, and it appears in 1989 on the *Scrooged* soundtrack album.

September 30
The Joshua Tree is certified Multi-Platinum, with US sales of more than three million.

October
Eamon Dunphy's *Unforgettable Fire: The Definitive Biography of U2* is published around this time. It's the first book authorized by the band, and earns some favourable reviews. But critics close to the band decry its inaccuracies. Larry Mullen, Sr., sends seven pages of corrections to Dunphy and the book's publishers. The band are upset by Dunphy's digging into their childhoods and pre-U2 lives, and a verbal war erupts in the press. At one point, Dunphy calls Bono a "pompous git".

October 1
Olympic Stadium, Montreal, with Little Steven & the Disciples of Soul, Los Lobos. Bono brings over a few family members and friends from Ireland to see tonight's gig. After the show, Anton Corbijn photographs Bono and his dad, Bob, backstage.

October 3
Canadian National Exhibition Stadium, Toronto, with Little Steven & the Disciples of Soul, Los Lobos.

October 6
Municipal Stadium, Cleveland, with Little Steven & the Disciples of Soul, Los Lobos.

October 7
Memorial Auditorium, Buffalo, with Little Steven & the Disciples of Soul. Bono's voice snaps during a cover of the Beatles' 'Help'. He struggles to sing the rest of the night, and verbally snaps at a female fan who runs on-stage at him during 'Bullet The Blue Sky'.

October 9
Carrier Dome, Syracuse, with Little Steven & the Disciples of Soul, Los Lobos.

October 11
Silver Stadium, Rochester, with Little Steven & the Disciples of Soul, Los Lobos.

October 12
U2 appears on the charity album, *A Very Special Christmas*, the first in a series of albums designed to raise funds for Special Olympics, the organization started in the 1960s by Eunice Kennedy Shriver. U2 contributes a cover of 'Christmas (Baby, Please Come Home)', with Darlene Love – who sang the Phil Spector original in 1963 – providing backing vocals. Jimmy Iovine, who produced *Under A Blood Red Sky*, organizes the project and produces the album.

A Very Special Christmas includes appearances by Bruce Springsteen and the E Street Band, Sting, the Pretenders, and Run DMC among others. It's a big success, selling millions of copies and raising millions of dollars for Special Olympics.

October 13
Three Rivers Stadium, Pittsburgh, with Little Steven & the Disciples of Soul, Los Lobos.

Bono: "Anything else would be less", November 8

"It's almost like that song was made real on the day. It was made real for the moment, in a way that it's never going to be again. I think that that was the ultimate performance of the song and anything else would be less than that."

October 19
Island Records releases the *Wide Awake In America* EP in the UK, two years after its North American release.

October 20
Carver-Hawkeye Arena, Iowa City, with the BoDeans. Bono is finally able to perform without the sling on his arm.

October 22
Assembly Hall, Champaign, with the BoDeans.

October 23
Rupp Arena, Lexington, with the BoDeans.

October 25
St. Louis Arena, St. Louis, with the BoDeans. Bono takes the stage in a St. Louis Cardinals jacket and baseball cap in honour of the team, which is playing a World Series game this same night in Minnesota.

October 26
Kemper Arena, Kansas City, with the BoDeans.

October 28-29-30
Rosemont Horizon, Chicago, with the BoDeans. U2 plans to film the indoor portions of *Rattle And Hum* during this series of shows, but they decide the venue isn't suitable for a film production, and prefer Denver a week from now. After one of the Chicago concerts, U2 go to a local blues club and perform while Phil Joanou's cameras are rolling. But the footage never appears in *Rattle And Hum*. "We got up on stage after a few too many tequilas," Edge explains later. "We had a great time, but when we looked at the footage afterwards, it was just so embarrassing. We were so gone, we knew it was wrong."

November
U2 release 'In God's Country' as a single in North America only. 'Bullet The Blue Sky' and 'Running To Stand Still' are the B-sides. Island Records does little to promote it and, although a music video is available, it's not released to MTV and other outlets. Not surprisingly, the single fails to connect with radio and only climbs to number 44 on the *Billboard* singles chart. It reaches number 48 as an import in the UK.

November 1
Hoosier Dome, Indianapolis, with the BoDeans, the Dalton Brothers, Los Lobos. In between sets by support acts the Bodeans and Los Lobos, U2 finally delivers on an idea they first discussed on the September 8 "Trip Through Your Wires" radio interview – performing as their own support act, The Dalton Brothers. All four are dressed in Western outfits and wigs, and Bono speaks with a twangy southern accent. They play 'Lucille' and 'Lost Highway' to a crowd who fail to recognise them. Later, during U2's set, the band plays 'Lucille' again right before '40', and the crowd realizes they had been fooled by the Dalton Brothers earlier.

November 3-4
Civic Center, St. Paul, with the BoDeans.

November 6
U2's stage equipment arrives in Denver along with eight film cameras and Phil Joanou's entire production crew. They'd like to begin setting up for tomorrow's show, but a pro basketball game keeps them out of the building until midnight.

November 7
McNichols Sports Arena, Denver, with the BoDeans. Tonight's show is filmed for the *Rattle And Hum* project. U2 hopes to capture the magic they enjoyed in this city four years earlier at Red Rocks. "We decided to shoot the Denver concerts because we thought lightning might strike twice," Edge says. But tonight's show is a wreck. Cameras follow Bono everywhere, and frustrate his ability to play to the crowd.

November 8
McNichols Sports Arena, Denver, with the BoDeans. Tonight's film shoot is much better. The band play a tight show, inspired in part by the news today of an IRA bombing which kills 11 people at a Remembrance Sunday service in Enniskillen, County Fermanagh. Bono jumps into the crowd during 'Bad', and fans hold him up as he screams the song. Bono delivers a fiery speech during 'Sunday, Bloody Sunday', and makes the performance a highlight of *Rattle And Hum*. The performance caught on tape is so powerful that U2 isn't sure it belongs in the movie. After seeing the movie, the band even considers the possibility of never performing the song again on future tours.
After the show, U2 meet with concert promoter Barry Fey to ask advice. Production problems – not to mention a $1.2 million price tag – will keep the band from playing South America next month, and U2 isn't sure where to shoot the outdoor film segments. Fey suggests Sun Devil Stadium in Tempe, Arizona, the same city where the tour began seven months ago.

November 11
Justin Herman Plaza, San Francisco. In the morning, U2 tell a couple San Francisco radio stations that they're planning to do a free concert at the Embarcadero Center. The news spreads quickly, guaranteeing them a big audience. With their gear and crew already in Vancouver, U2 play with equipment borrowed from the Grateful Dead.

Bono calls it a "Save the Yuppies" benefit in reference to the stock market crash the day before. During 'Pride', Bono spray paints "Rock and Roll" and "Stop the Traffic" on a nearby piece of modern sculpture, prompting the city to issue a warrant for his arrest for vandalism to city property. Bono writes a letter of apology to local officials, saying, "I hope that the real street artists of San Francisco will not suffer because of a scrawler like me."

November 12
B.C. Place Stadium, Vancouver, with the BoDeans, Los Lobos.

The Joshua Tree is certified Multi-Platinum by the BPI, with UK sales surpassing the 1,200,000 mark.

November 13
Bono sees R.E.M. play at the Oakland-Alameda County Coliseum Arena.

November 14-15
Oakland-Alameda County Stadium, Oakland, with the BoDeans, the Pretenders. U2 invites Armand Vaillancourt to come from his home in Quebec to the first show. It is Vaillancourt's statue that Bono spray-painted three days earlier in San Francisco, and after apologising to the sculptor, Bono allows him to spray-paint on U2's set. He writes "STOP THE MADNESS!"

During the second show, Bono brings mural artist Rene Castro on stage and invites him and a group of community artists to spray-paint the stage backdrop.

November 17-18
Memorial Coliseum, Los Angeles, with Steve Jones, the Pretenders (November 17); with the BoDeans, the Dalton Brothers, the Pretenders (November 18). U2 meet Elvis Presley's daughter, Lisa Marie, after the first show.

Before the second show, Paul McGuinness does an interview with *Propaganda* magazine. The Dalton Brothers make another appearance in between the support acts. The Olympic Torch at the Coliseum is lit before the encore, marking only the fourth time the torch burns – it had burned twice for the Olympics and once for a visit by the Pope.

While in Los Angeles, Bono meets with Bob Dylan and they write a song called 'Prisoner Of Love' that will eventually become

1987

'Love Rescue Me' on *Rattle And Hum*. Dylan sings lead vocals on the original recording, but will later ask U2 not to use it, citing his involvement with The Traveling Wilburys. Bono called Dylan's version "astonishing".

Bono also meets up again with Roy Orbison while in Los Angeles. They begin working together on 'She's A Mystery To Me'.

November 19
U2 gives a press conference in Los Angeles. A brief segment is included in *Rattle And Hum*.

November 20
U2 are the guests of honour at a party hosted by Jane Fonda and her husband Tom Hayden. Guests include Eddie Van Halen and Valerie Bertinelli, David Crosby, Graham Nash, Quincy Jones, and others from the music and film industries. "We wanted to give them an opportunity to make some new friends and meet some new people," Hayden says.

November 22
Frank Erwin Center, Austin, with the BoDeans. After the show, the band goes to a blues club where Bono and Edge jam with Stevie Ray Vaughn, T-Bone Burnett, and Dr. John.

November 23-24
Tarrant County Convention Center, Fort Worth, with the BoDeans (November 23); with B.B. King (November 24). Before the first show, U2 do a photo shoot in Dallas with photographer Tom Sheehan. B.B. King supports U2 at the second show. Together, they perform 'When Love Comes To Town', which had been rehearsed earlier in the day and filmed for the *Rattle and Hum* movie.

November 26
Assembly Center, Baton Rouge, with the BoDeans. Prior to tonight's show, U2 film a video for 'Christmas (Baby, Please Come Home)'.

November 27
On a free day in Nashville, Bono and Edge talk with Bill Graham for an upcoming *Hot Press* feature. (Graham had arrived a day earlier for U2's Baton Rouge gig.) Talking about next year's concert film and double album, Bono tells Graham, "You may not like it, U2 fans may not like it – but we need it."

November 28
Charles M. Murphy Athletic Center, Murfreesboro, with the BoDeans.

November 29
U2 visit Graceland this morning. Phil Joanou's film cameras roll, and much of the visit is included in the *Rattle And Hum* film. The visit leaves a lasting impression on U2: "I saw more of a sense of humor than bad taste," Edge says. "What struck me again is that Elvis was so outrageous for his time. I think he knew that, and his house was put together with that in mind."

While in Memphis, U2 also have secret plans to visit and record at the legendary Sun Studio, where all-time greats like Elvis Presley, Johnny Cash, Roy Orbison and Jerry Lee Lewis recorded in the studio's heyday. Sun has been closed for more than two decades, however, and only re-opened earlier this year.

While the band tour Graceland, last-minute details are still being arranged at the studio. Jimmy Iovine calls and asks for three female backup singers to be ready. The band has no instruments with them, so Sun owner Gary Hardy calls around to local stores and buys the best gear he can find. It's all for naught; when U2 arrives at around 7:30 p.m., they immediately head for the vintage instruments already in the studio.

U2 works on a half-dozen songs: 'Angel Of Harlem', 'Jesus Christ', 'Love Rescue Me', 'Can't Help Falling In Love', 'When Love Comes to Town', and 'She's A Mystery to Me'. The recording session lasts until 3:00 a.m.

Gary Hardy remembers U2's visit to Sun Studio
"[U2] loved it. They loved everything. I mean they are very, very real people, no pretensions about themselves or others. They're artists. And for them and for all of us, this was a true historic happening. This room brings it out in people. No one can take credit for it. It's just here."

After their visit to Memphis, U2 still have a few days off until their next concert. Bono and Adam have a moment of clarity while hitchhiking in Tennessee. A young kid picks them up; on his car stereo is the new Def Leppard album turned up to high volume. When the driver recognizes his passengers, he quickly pulls Def Leppard off and puts in *The Joshua Tree*. The difference in volume stuns Bono and Adam.

Bono: "We had never heard anything so loud"
"It [Def Leppard] sounded like the end of the world, it sounded like Godzilla was stomping along beside the car. There was the most incredible bass drum and snare sound I'd ever heard.... I looked at Adam, and Adam looked at me. We had never heard anything so loud. It was Def Leppard's 'Pour Some Sugar On Me' and it sounded about twice as loud as 'Where The Streets Have No Name.' We took note! I think we both made a mental note that next time we had better go after a more sonic experience on our records."

December 3
Orange Bowl, Miami, with Buckwheat Zydeco, Los Lobos.

December 5
Tampa Stadium, Tampa, with Buckwheat Zydeco, Los Lobos.

December 8-9
The Omni, Atlanta, with the BoDeans.

December 11-12

Coliseum, Hampton, with the BoDeans. For the last scheduled show of the tour, the Dalton Brothers make one more appearance but this time it's in the middle of U2's set and it's actually U2's crew dressed up as the band's alter ego.

Meanwhile, in Arizona, installation of the outdoor stage is already underway for next week's film shoot at Sun Devil Stadium.

December 13

U2's production crew relocates to Arizona and begins setting up for the final two shows of the tour.

December 14

It's raining in Arizona as production continues for U2's upcoming outdoor shows. Film crews are busy scoping out angles and lighting with four stand-ins on stage for U2.

December 17

U2 do a full rehearsal of their upcoming film shoot in a powerful thunderstorm at Sun Devil Stadium.

December 18

Rehearsals continue for the band's movie shoot. Tonight, the only staged part of the movie is filmed: U2's entrance on stage during 'Where The Streets Have No Name'. The process is slow and difficult, but the band tries to keep itself entertained between takes – Edge plays 'Stairway To Heaven' at one point, while Bono sings 'Dear Prudence' another time. The band even plays a rough version of 'Walk To The Water', a B-side that has never been played live in concert.

Rehearsals are interrupted for a live interview on local radio station, KUPO. Edge again plays a bit of 'Stairway To Heaven', and does a full version of 'Lost Highway'. Bono explains that 'Mothers Of The Disappeared' will be the last song of the upcoming concerts, and that he hopes it will replace '40' as U2's standard show closer. Thousands of fans show up outside to stadium to listen, prompting local police to clear the area.

December 19-20

Sun Devil Stadium, Tempe, with B.B. King. U2 return to Sun Devil Stadium for two concerts that will be used in the *Rattle And Hum* movie. The band's original plans were to film two shows in Buenos Aires, Argentina, but costs and complications force a change of plans. The Tempe shows are organised quickly. Tickets are sold for only $5 each to these shows and fans are told in advance that camera crews will be very active and potentially disrupt the concerts.

It rains lightly during the first show, and the shoot doesn't go well. Bono reacts against the rigidity of being filmed for a motion picture, which doesn't allow room for spontaneity of words or action. He mixes up the setlist and spends much of time out on a camera ramp that extends into the crowd. Says director Phil Joanou after the show: "We can't have this happen again, guys, or we will not get the concert. We did not get it tonight. In my opinion, we got three songs. To me, it was an utter fucking disaster."

The weather is better for the second show. The band and film crew are in sync, and the shoot is a great success. Most of the color portion of *Rattle And Hum* comes from this show. Phil Joanou is in a much better mood afterward: "I am so hyped and so pumped, because it was a great show and we nailed it visually and they nailed it musically and the crowd was great." Adds Bono: "We had problems with this movie, but tonight I think we did it right." The band parties afterward with family members who traveled to Arizona, plus Island Records founder Chris Blackwell, representatives from Paramount Pictures, and even a general manager from Kodak Film.

December 21

With *The Joshua Tree* tour now complete, U2 heads home for the holidays and a short break. Phil Joanou travels to Los Angeles where he will begin sifting through the film he's shot over the past three-plus months.

Also today, *Rolling Stone*'s list of the Top Albums of 1987 includes *The Joshua Tree* at number three.

December 22

The Joshua Tree is certified Multi-Platinum, with US sales of more than four million.

December 28

People magazine names Bono one of its "Most Intriguing People of 1987."

1988

After a whirlwind year, U2 postpones tour dates in Australia and tries to stay out of the public eye while working on the *Rattle And Hum* project. Laying low proves difficult thanks to a stream of awards this year, including U2's first Grammys. Plus, it's an election year in the US, and given the band's political leanings, some wonder which candidate they support. Jesse Jackson asks for an official endorsement, but U2 turns him down on the grounds that an Irish band shouldn't stick its noses into a US presidential race.

Bono takes on a couple of non-music side projects, including an essay called "The White Nigger", which appears in a book published this year, *Across the Frontiers:* *Ireland in the 1990s*. The book talks about Irish roots and what it means to be Irish. Bono writes: "I was called a 'White Nigger' once by a black musician, and I took it as he meant it, as a compliment. The Irish, like the blacks, feel like outsiders. There's a feeling of being homeless, migrant, but I suppose that's what all art is – a search for identity." He also appears on T-Bone Burnett's new album, *The Talking Animals*.

By year's end, U2 are back in the spotlight: *Rattle and Hum* is released with an over-the-top Hollywood promotional push. Critics push back even harder with some of the most scathing reviews U2's ever received; the inevitable backlash has begun.

January
Issue 7 of *Propaganda* is published.

Having postponed an Australian tour that was due to begin this month, U2 begin work on new tracks for the upcoming *Rattle And Hum* album at STS Studios in Dublin. 'Desire' is one of the first songs recorded.

In mid-January, writer Jim Henke visits Edge in and around Dublin for a feature-length interview, which will appear in *Rolling Stone* in March.

Early in the year, U2 wins a *Sunday Independent*/Irish Life Arts award.

January 14
Bono takes part in the opening of the *Four Artists – Many Wednesdays* exhibition at Hendricks Gallery in Dublin. His friends Charlie Whisker, Gavin Friday and Guggi show original paintings, while Bono shows a collection of photographs from his 1985 work in Ethiopia.

Bono: "I couldn't even take my camera out"
"At first, as we walked through the camp, we kept our eyes down and were so overpowered by the suffering we saw around us that I couldn't even take my camera out of its case. Weeks later, a different but more lasting impression set in of the beauty and strength of spirit of the Ethiopian people. It was then that I started taking photographs, not to deny the waste of human life that was and still is Ethiopia, but to make the people and therefore the tragedy real by bringing their sense of dignity back into the picture."

Bono's photos are offered at £1,000 each and are also compiled in a book, *A String of Pearls*. All money from photo and book sales is targeted for Ethiopia via Concern/World Vision, the organisation that made his work in Ethiopia possible.

The exhibition, originally scheduled to end January 30, is successful enough to continue into February.

Below: U2 at the Brit Awards at London's Royal Albert Hall, February 8.

February
U2 relocate to Los Angeles to work on the *Rattle And Hum* movie and album. Edge and his family stay in the Hollywood Hills, while the rest of the band share a house in Bel Air. While in LA, U2 works on the new songs 'Hawkmoon 269', 'God Part II' and 'All I Want Is You'.

February 8
U2 wins *Best International Group* at the Brit Awards. Bono tells reporters he's only at the ceremony to see The Who, who win this year's *Outstanding Contribution* Award. Bono also says he and Edge have just spent a week in western Ireland writing songs, fishing and visiting local pubs.

March
U2 issues 'One Tree Hill' as a single in Australia and New Zealand only, where it reaches number one. The single features the same artwork that was used in North America on the 'In God's Country' single last fall, and the same B-sides: 'Bullet The Blue Sky' and 'Running To Stand Still'.

Also this month, U2 dominates the *Rolling Stone* 1987 Music Awards. Readers and critics name U2 *Artist of the Year* and *Best Band*. Readers also give the band the nod for *Best Live Performance*. *The Joshua Tree* is named *Best Album* by readers, and U2 takes the top three *Best Single* spots with 'With Or Without You', 'Where The Streets Have No Name', and 'I Still Haven't

Above: U2 backstage at the Grammy Awards, March 10.

Found What I'm Looking For'. The individual band members also dominate their respective categories, including *Best Male Singer*, *Best Guitarist*, *Best Bass Player*, and *Best Drummer*.

Larry also shares his favourite music of 1987 with the magazine:
Bring The Family, John Hiatt
Poetic Champions Compose, Van Morrison
T Bone Burnett, T Bone Burnett
Introducing The Hardline According To Terence Trent D'Arby, Terence Trent D'Arby
Lord Of The Highway, Joe Ely
Out Of Our Idiot, Elvis Costello
Hillbilly Deluxe, Dwight Yoakam
Sign o'The Times, Prince
Document, R.E.M.
Lyle Lovett, Lyle Lovett

March 2
U2 collect their first two Grammy Awards: Best Rock Performance by a Group or Duo for 'I Still Haven't Found What I'm Looking For' and Album of the Year for *The Joshua Tree*. Adam is missing when U2 take the stage for its first acceptance speech of the night. Edge explains that he's gone to the bathroom and motions Adam to the stage when he re-enters the room. Contradicting their austere image, both Edge and Bono deliver comical speeches.

U2 accepts its first Grammy Awards
The Edge: "Well, uh, we seem to have lost our bass player. He went to the loo a couple of minutes ago and he's still in the back. [*laughter*] [*Edge sees Adam approaching*] Oh, Adam, this way. Here he comes. I don't know about you, but I'm still recovering after Whitney Houston. Um. Okay. I have a bit of a list here I want to read out. It's just a few people we thought we should thank. Um, I've got to be careful of this list 'cause it's got the lad's votes and, uh, stuff on the back. Okay. Uh, first I'd like to thank our lawyer and friend, Owen Epstein, who couldn't be with you, us tonight. Um, thanks go to Paul McGuiness our

manager for the loan of yet another suit. Uh, our management team in New York and Dublin, Ellen and Anne Louise, Island Records, Atlantic Records and WEA, Frank Barsalona and Premier Talent, everybody in college radio – I don't know where we'd be without them. I'd also like to thank, uh, I'd like to thank Jack Healey and Amnesty International for all their work, Desmond Tutu for his courage, Martin Luther King. [*occasional laughter during rest of Edge's speech*] I'd like to thank, uh, Bob Dylan for 'Tangled Up In Blue', Flannery O'Connor, Jimi Hendrix, Walt Disney, John The Baptist, Georgie Best, Gregory Peck, James T. Kirk, Morris Pratt, Dr. Ruth, Fawn Hall, Batman and Robin, Lucky the Dog, Pee Wee Herman, the YMCA, Eddie the Eagle, sumo wrestlers around the world, and, of course, Ronald Reagan."

Bono: "Well, this is all very Celtic. We appreciate it. It's actually, um, it really is hard, um, carrying the weight of the world on your shoulders, and, uh, saving the whale, and, uh, organising summits between world leaders and that sort of thing. [*laughter*] But, we enjoy our work. And, um, uh, it's hard when there's fifty million people or so watching not to take the opportunity to talk about things like South Africa and what's happening there and remarkable people like Bishop Tutu and what they have to put up with. [*mild applause*] But, tonight is maybe not the night for me to do that, so, uh, instead just, uh, I'd like to talk about the music, uh, as we set out to make music, soul music. Uh, that's what U2 wanted to make. It was soul music. It's not about being black or white, or the instruments you play, or whether you use a drum machine or not. It's a, it's a decision to reveal or conceal. And, uh, without it, uh, people like Prince would be nothing more than a brilliant song-and-dance man. That he is, but he's much more than that. People like Bruce Springsteen would be nothing more than a, he would be nothing more than a great storyteller. But he's much more than that. Um, without it, U2 would probably be getting better reviews in the *Village Voice*, but, um, that, that's a joke. [*laughter*] Sometimes they don't understand. Uh, without it, U2 certainly wouldn't be here and we are here and I wouldn't want to be anywhere else than New York City tonight. [*applause*] Thank you. And, I'd also like to thank Daniel Lanois and Brian Eno without which we couldn't have made that record. Thank you very much."

During the post-Grammy parties, Roy Orbison lets it slip that he's working on a new song with Bono and Edge.

March 3-4-5
While playing at Madison Square Garden, Michael Jackson invites U2 to come to see a show and meet him afterwards. U2 accepts the invite, but when Jackson has a videocamera record their backstage conversation, the band decides to leave as quickly as possible.

May
U2 uses Dublin's Point Depot theatre to record more songs and scenes for *Rattle And Hum*. Phil Joanou flies in from Los Angeles and films interview sessions and many scenes in and around Dublin that will appear in the movie. He also films U2 as they perform 'Desire', one of the new songs that will appear on the album and in the film. 'Van Diemen's Land', which features Edge on lead vocals, is recorded during this period.

June
U2 is back in Los Angeles to finish the *Rattle And Hum* soundtrack album. Adam and Bono quickly immerse themselves in the LA scene, Bono hanging out regularly at an avant-garde club called The Flaming Colossus and Adam attending a party at the Playboy Mansion with Jimmy Iovine's wife, Vicky.

Edge: "I was going under, personally"
"I was holding on to the record as a kind of lifeline. I was going under, personally, and my marriage was disappearing up in smoke very fast. I think I was probably the only one, although maybe Larry as well, who wasn't really going for it in a party sense."

Sometime this summer, Bono and Edge (along with Maria McKee) attend the wedding of David Batstone at Pacific Lutheran Theological Seminary in Berkeley, California. Batstone has become a friend since he accompanied Bono into Central America in 1986.

July 12
The Joshua Tree is certified Multi-Platinum by the BPI, with UK sales surpassing the 1.5 million mark.

July 18
Edge watches a Depeche Mode concert at the Rose Bowl in Pasadena, California.

August
Issue 8 of *Propaganda* is published.

The band throws Edge a poolside toga party for his 27th birthday on August 8. Around this time, U2 shoot a music video for 'Desire' with director Richard Lowenstein, and get their first look at a rough cut of the *Rattle And Hum* film.

September
U2 appear on the Woody Guthrie/Leadbelly tribute album, *Folkways: A Vision Shared*. Their contribution is a cover of Guthrie's 'Jesus Christ', which U2 recorded at Sun Studios last year. The album is a fund raiser commissioned by the Smithsonian Institution, and the proceeds are used to purchase the historical folk and blues recordings of Folkways Records.

Bono: "U2 has to sing it"

"'Jesus Christ' is a song that has to be sung [and] U2 has to sing it. It's more relevant today than it was even when he wrote it. We decided to do that because of the line, 'the bankers and the preachers they nailed him in the air'. I've said it before, but these people we see on our television sets, TV evangelists, literally are stealing money from the sick and the old."

September 8
'Pride (In The Name Of Love)' is ranked 46th in a *Rolling Stone* list of the *Top 100 Singles of the Last 25 Years*.

September 10-11
Edge meets blues legend John Lee Hooker at the San Francisco Blues Festival. "Everybody says he's hot – everybody couldn't be wrong," Hooker says of Edge. "I know one thing: he's a nice person."

September 19
U2 release 'Desire' as the first single from *Rattle And Hum*, with 'Hallelujah (Here She Comes)' and 'Desire (Hollywood Remix)' as B-sides on various formats. It is U2's first number one UK single, and reaches number three in the US.

September 21
Bono makes a guest appearance at the "Human Rights Now!" concert at the Los Angeles Coliseum to benefit Amnesty International. He joins an all-star lineup performing Bob Dylan's 'Chimes Of Freedom'.

October 3
'Desire' reaches the top of the UK charts.

October 5
Rattle And Hum arrives at North American radio stations.

October 6
The Joshua Tree is certified Multi-Platinum, with US sales of more than five million.

October 10/11
U2 releases the *Rattle And Hum* album. The band, minus Larry but including Paul McGuinness, show up unexpectedly at midnight at the HMV store in Dublin to mingle with fans and sign autographs.

Rattle And Hum is released as a double-LP, single CD, and single cassette, with Jimmy Iovine producing. The 17 tracks are a mixture of live cuts from *The Joshua Tree* tour and nine new studio songs, and even a couple non-U2 songs. *Rattle And Hum* is, in many ways, the culmination of a journey to explore the roots of rock and roll that Bob Dylan kick started in July, 1984, when he and Bono met and spoke for the first time. The album includes a Dylan appearance (on 'Love Rescue Me') and a cover of his song, 'All Along The Watchtower'. U2 also covers The Beatles, sings with B.B. King, dedicates a song to John Lennon ('God Part II'), sings about Billie Holiday, and includes Jimi Hendrix's famous version of 'The Star Spangled Banner'.

U2's intention is to show themselves as fans of these rock and blues legends, but many critics take it differently, and assume U2 are aligning themselves with the all-time greats. Reviews of the album are mixed, but it's the negative reviews that shout the loudest and get the most attention.

In the *New York Times*, Jon Pareles blasts U2 and the album in a review headlined "When Self-Importance Interferes with the Music." Pareles calls the album a "mess", and slams Bono's lyrics and vocals, as well as U2's overall musicianship. "Mass popularity can be hard on performers," he writes, "particularly a band like U2, which has always tried to make the sincerest statements possible. From the beginning, U2 has had an unguarded quality, a sense of urgency and vulnerability that it maintained even as its audience grew into the millions. But that urgency has curdled on *Rattle And Hum*, where U2 insists that clumsy attempts at interpreting other people's music are as important as the real thing. What comes across

Bono defends *Rattle And Hum*, October 10/11

"This was a record made by fans – we wanted to own up to being fans. And we thought rock and roll bands just don't do that – we all know they are [fans], but they don't do it…. We thought of it as: 'We have this thing, U2; now let's just put it aside almost and let's just get lost in this music.'

"I still think it was the right thing to do. We were in there as apprentices – it was quite obvious."

in song after song is sincere egomania."

Pareles' review is the first of several from key media sources to paint an unflattering picture of the *Rattle And Hum* project. In the *Village Voice*, Tom Carson writes, "By almost any rock and roll fan's standards, U2's *Rattle And Hum* is an awful record. But the chasm between what it thinks it is and the half-baked, overweening reality doesn't sound attributable to pretension so much as to monumental know-nothingism."

It's not all bad, though. In the *Los Angeles Times*, critic Robert Hilburn gives the album four stars (out of five). He says it's a "frequently remarkable album – a work that not only lives up to the standards of the Grammy-winning *The Joshua Tree*, but also places U2 more convincingly than ever among rock's all-time greatest groups."

In the *Boston Globe*, Jim Sullivan calls *Rattle And Hum* "forceful" and "hard-edged", but tempers his praise: "The weakness of the record are the covers – the Beatles' 'Helter Skelter' (which Bono claims to steal back from Charles Manson) and Dylan's 'All Along The Watchtower'. When approaching covers, U2 is often too studied and too easily crosses the righteous/self-righteous line."

The backlash doesn't seem to bother U2 fans. The album sells nearly three million copies in its first month and reaches number one in the US, UK, Australia, Canada and several more countries. It's the first double album to top the US charts since Bruce Springsteen's *The River* in 1980. It's certified Double-Platinum by the BPI almost immediately, with UK sales quickly passing the 600,000 mark.
Tracks: 'Helter Skelter (live)', 'Van Diemen's Land', 'Desire', 'Hawkmoon 269', 'All Along The Watchtower (live)', 'I Still Haven't Found What I'm Looking For (live)', 'Freedom For My People', 'Silver And Gold (live)', 'Pride (In The Name Of Love) (live)', 'Angel Of Harlem', 'Love Rescue Me', 'When Love Comes To Town', 'Heartland', 'God Part II', 'Bullet The Blue Sky (live)', 'All I Want Is You'

Also around this time, reports surface that U2 may not be done with movie work. Phil Joanou tells reporters that Bono is working on a movie script about a New Orleans blues singer who's involved in a sexually abusive relationship.

October 16

Dominion Theatre, London. U2 participates in the first of two "Smile Jamaica" benefit concerts to raise money for victims of Hurricane Gilbert. Their 20-minute set is played before a crowd of only 2,500 at the Dominion Theatre, and is simulcast on UK radio and TV. The live version of 'Love Rescue Me' from this show, with Keith Richards on guitar and Ziggy Marley singing a verse, will later appear as a b-side on the 'Angel Of Harlem' single.

October 22

Rattle and Hum reaches number one on the UK album chart. It'll be replaced next week by a Dire Straits greatest hits album.

October 23

MTV airs *U2 And Friends: Smile Jamaica*, a two-hour recap of last week's charity concert in London.

October 27

Rattle And Hum has its world premiere at the Savoy Cinema on O'Connell Street in Dublin. U2 play a short acoustic set before the movie, and return for two more songs when the movie ends. U2 donate proceeds from the screening to the "People In Need" fund. After the premiere, U2 hosts a party at the Gresham Hotel while fans pack the five Savoy movie screens to see the film. "The kids are going absolutely berserk in there," says Anne-Louise Kelly of Principle Management. "I was almost in tears just looking at their reaction."

October 29

U2 attend the Spanish premiere of *Rattle And Hum* at Cine Gran Via in Madrid. U2 talk about the film from the theater's stage and Bono and Edge sing a bit of 'I Still Haven't Found What I'm Looking For'.

October 31

U2 attend the London premiere of *Rattle And Hum* at the Empire Theatre, but are not allowed to play live as police fear a riot would break out. After the movie, there's a party in the nearby National Space Centre.

November 1

Rattle And Hum premieres in the US with a showing at the Astor Plaza Theater in New York. U2 cracks jokes during a news conference before the film. When asked what they thought of the film, Bono says, "We've never been to a U2 concert before," while Edge adds, "I thought I was much taller."

U2's plans to perform before the premiere are derailed by steady rain all day long. The band enter the

theatre quietly after the film has begun, but the audience quickly discovers them and many leave their seats to get autographs and be closer to the band. U2 leave the film early and head off to a party in their honor.

While in New York, U2 shoots a video for 'Angel Of Harlem' with Richard Lowenstein directing.

November 3

U2 appear at the Los Angeles premiere of *Rattle And Hum* and play a brief acoustic set before the show in front of Mann's Chinese Theatre.

November 4

Rattle And Hum opens around the world. The film earns $3.8 million in its first weekend of US release, making it the number two movie of the week (behind the horror film, *They Live*). Three weeks later, the film has earned a total of $8.3 million and is pulled from theaters in favour of Christmas releases.

Much like the reaction to the album, critics are mixed in their response to the film, often in the same review. Cary Darling offers this praise in the *Orange County Register*: "Intelligently crafted and impeccably shot, this concert documentary revolving around one of the world's most invigorating mainstream rock bands – U2 – is suffused with the same energy and joy that is at the heart of the best rock'n'roll." But Darling later tempers that thought: "Yet U2 can be overly melodramatic at times. At the end of 'Bullet The Blue Sky', Bono and bassist Adam Clayton are posed in such a way as if they expect the audience to fall down in immediate genuflection."

In addition to the film, ABC-TV is set to air a documentary, *The Making Of Rattle And Hum*, but it never comes to fruition. Phil Joanou says the programme was completed too late for the network to air.

Also this week, 'Desire' peaks at number three on the *Billboard* singles chart. The song does better on the *Radio And Records* AOR chart, hitting the number one spot.

With the pomp and

circumstance of movie premieres over, Bono and Adam rent a car and spend 2-3 weeks driving from Los Angeles to New Orleans via Memphis. Before leaving LA, they sneak in to watch *Rattle And Hum* in the back of a theater and aren't noticed. In Memphis, they connect with a friend, Lian Lunson, and everyone visits with *New York Times* writer Robert Palmer. Palmer takes them to a local juke joint to hear some authentic blues music. Bono and Adam meet up again with Cowboy Jack Clement, who takes them to see Johnny Cash and John Prine. One night, Bono and Adam play a few songs – including 'Love Rescue Me' – in front about 15 people in a local bar who have no idea who they are. The trip ends in New Orleans, where Bono and Adam visit with Danny Lanois and the Neville Brothers.

December

U2 do a photo shoot with Anton Corbijn for *Rolling Stone* magazine. The images are black-and-white portraits, and a shot of Bono makes the cover of the magazine's March 9, 1989, issue.

Rattle And Hum lands at number 29 on *Rolling Stone*'s list of the *Top 100 Albums of 1988*. *The Joshua Tree* is ranked number 57.

Bono contributes to *Hungry for Heaven: Rock'n'Roll And The Search For Redemption*, a new book by Steve Turner.

December 6

Rattle And Hum is certified Multi-Platinum, with US sales already eclipsing the two million mark.

Legendary singer Roy Orbison dies of a heart attack in Tennessee before the release of his *Mystery Girl* album, which will feature a track written for him by Bono and Edge, 'She's A Mystery To Me'.

December 8

U2 release 'Angel Of Harlem', with various formats including additional tracks 'A Room At The Heartbreak Hotel' and 'Love Rescue Me (live)'. It reaches number nine in the UK and number 14 in the US. It fares better on US radio, hitting number one on the *Radio And Records* AOR chart.

December 13

Edge makes a guest appearance at Bryan Ferry's gig tonight at the Royal Dublin Showground. They perform the traditional Irish ballad 'Carrickfergus'.

December 16

U2 are interviewed on the RTE-TV programme *The Late Late Show*, and also perform an acoustic version of John Lennon's 'Happy Christmas (War Is Over)'.

While in Dublin, Bono does an interview for *Propaganda* magazine. He reveals that he's written a poem titled 'Elvis is alive, We're dead', as well as two new songs: 'One Love' for the Neville Brothers, and 'Love Is Blindness But I Don't Want To See' for Nina Simone.

1989

After three years of work on *The Joshua Tree* and *Rattle And Hum*, U2 decide to take some time off early in the year – again postponing plans to tour Australia. The band make news for personal reasons: Bono and Edge have children, while Adam has a couple of run-ins with the law. U2 also has a chance encounter this year with Richard Lang, the founder of a company called Explore Technologies, which is developing technology to stream video to computers via the Internet. Although the World Wide Web is still a couple years away from being invented, U2 is fascinated by the idea. They invest $2 million in Lang's company, buying a 44% ownership stake. The company will change its name in later years to Instant Video Technologies, and eventually to Burst.com.

The band continue to release singles from *Rattle And Hum* throughout the year. The tracks chart highly in the UK but are mostly ignored in the US. That, combined with the negative critical reaction to *Rattle And Hum*, leads U2 to stay away from North America on the Lovetown Tour. The tour goes to Australia, New Zealand, Japan, and a few European countries. Poor scheduling and Bono's ongoing voice problems make for a frustrating four months on the road. By the end of the tour, Bono announces that it's time for U2 to "dream it all up again".

January
Issue 9 of *Propaganda* is published.

Also this month, U2 does an interview with Steve Pond for an upcoming cover story in *Rolling Stone*. The interview takes place in a cramped, private booth inside a Dublin pub and the setting gets the band talking about privacy. It's clear U2 are struggling with their current position. "We now drink in little boxes like this," Edge says. "Our world gets smaller the bigger the band get," Adam adds. Bono explains it best: "We would be lying, I think, if we said that everything is okay these days. Everything's *not okay*, you know? Even talking about U2, we really don't know how to talk about U2 anymore."

Bono also does an interview this month in Los Angeles with Adam Block for *Mother Jones* magazine.

Around this time, possibly earlier, Bono and Edge write a song, 'Conversation On A Barstool', for Marianne Faithfull. The track is expected to appear on her *Blazing Away* album this year, but doesn't make the cut. The song resurfaces in 1993 on the *Short Cuts* movie soundtrack, with vocals by Annie Ross. Faithfull's version doesn't appear until her 1998 album, *A Perfect Stranger*.

Paul McGuinness is appointed to the Arts Council of Ireland.

Late this month, U2 get together in the studio to work on upcoming B-sides. They decide to record several covers, including 'Dancing Barefoot', 'Fortunate Son', 'Unchained Melody', 'If I Had A Rocket Launcher', and 'Everlasting Love'.

January 10
'Desire' is certified as Gold by the RIAA with sales of more than 500,000. It's U2's first Gold single in the US.

January 17
Rattle And Hum is certified Multi-Platinum by the RIAA, with US sales of more than three million.

January 25
Rattle And Hum is certified Multi-Platinum by the BPI, with UK sales surpassing the 900,000 mark.

February
Early in the month, Academy Awards organisers notify U2 that original songs from *Rattle And Hum* will not be eligible to win an award in the Best Original Song category. U2 had hoped the movie performances of 'Desire', 'Angel Of Harlem', or 'When Love Comes To Town' would be nominated. Says U2 attorney Mike Adler: "We were told the music did not contribute to the film's drama."

Island Records releases 'God Part II' as a radio-only single in the US. The song eventually climbs to number seven on the *Radio and Records* AOR chart.

February 1
Roy Orbison's *Mystery Girl* album is released. It includes 'She's A

Mystery To Me,' the song Bono and Edge co-wrote for Orbison. Bono also produces and plays guitar on the song.

February 13
U2 take home an award for Best International Group at the Brit Awards.

February 19
Rock and roll legend Little Richard records vocals that will be used on the upcoming 'When Love Comes To Town' single. His contribution is included in the 'Live From The Kingdom' mix of the song.

February 22
U2 win two more Grammy Awards: Best Rock Performance by a Duo or Group with Vocal for 'Desire', and Best Performance Music Video for 'Where The Streets Have No Name'.

Also today, *Rattle And Hum* is released on home video. Director Phil Joanou has told reporters there would "most likely" be extra tracks on the home video, but those plans never materialise. The movie debuts at number 26 on *Billboard*'s Top VHS Sales chart, and eventually climbs to number one.

February 25
Bono, Edge and Adam attend the premiere of *My Left Foot* tonight in Dublin. It's a chance to renew acquaintances with director Jim Sheridan, who founded The Project Arts Center in Dublin many years

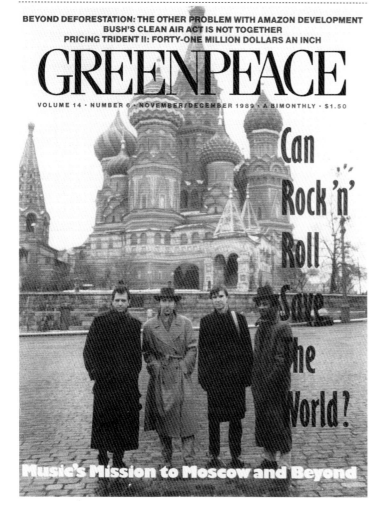

BEYOND DEFORESTATION: THE OTHER PROBLEM WITH AMAZON DEVELOPMENT
BUSH'S CLEAN AIR ACT IS NOT TOGETHER
PRICING TRIDENT II: FORTY-ONE MILLION DOLLARS AN INCH

GREENPEACE

VOLUME 14 · NUMBER 6 · NOVEMBER/DECEMBER 1989 · A BIMONTHLY · $1.50

Can Rock 'n' Roll Save The World?

Music's Mission to Moscow and Beyond

Above: Edge and friends on the cover of *Greenpeace* magazine.

ago. Sheridan asks Bono to do the music for his next film (*In The Name Of The Father*).

March 6

Edge is in Moscow to help Greenpeace launch their new fund raising album featuring popular songs by 24 artists. U2 contribute 'Pride (In The Name of Love)', making it the first U2 song to be released officially in Russia. The album is known as *Breakthrough* in the Soviet Union, but will be called *Rainbow Warriors* everywhere else. Edge joins Annie Lennox, Peter Gabriel and others to autograph copies of the album at the Melodia record shop. While in the USSR, many of the artists are rushed into a TV studio for an informal live broadcast to promote the album release. The host asks Edge to sing a song from *Rattle And Hum*. Stunned

---

Would U2 ever play Russia? March 6
While in Moscow, Bill Graham asked Edge if U2 would consider playing gigs in Russia.

"Whether a tour is possible, let alone practical, remains to be seen. For my part, and I think for the rest of the band, we'd love to do some shows. But getting things done in Russia can be very difficult. Even getting around. Like I wanted to go to Leningrad and couldn't because of visa problems. And rock 'n' roll bands, groups of Western musicians, chasing around the USSR will not be an easy thing to organise."

momentarily, and not having an instrument to play, Edge instead leads a sing-along of the old war song, 'It's A Long Way To Tipperary'. While in Moscow, Edge and Peter Gabriel visit a monastery and spend time with Russian writer Artemy Troitsky. The album sells 500,000 copies in its first day of release in the USSR.

Also this month, U2 again dominates the *Rolling Stone* Music Awards. Readers hand U2 the nod for Artist of the Year, Best Band, Best Album (*Rattle And Hum*), Best Single ('Desire'), Best Male Singer, Best Drummer, and Best Bass Player.

Edge shares his favourite music of 1988 with the magazine:
Fisherman's Blues, The Waterboys
Lovesexy, Prince
Irish Heartbeat, Van Morrison & The Chieftains

Our Beloved Revolutionary Sweetheart, Camper Van Beethoven
Green, R.E.M.
Dream Of Life, Patti Smith
Tender Prey, Nick Cave and the Bad Seeds
16 Lovers Lane, The Go-Betweens
Flag, Yello
Miss America, Mary Margaret O'Hara

March 10
U2 wins Best International Group at the Irish Recorded Music Awards in Dublin.

March 11
Bono and Edge join B.B. King on stage in Dublin to perform 'When Love Comes To Town' and a cover of Little Richard's 'Lucille'.

March 12
U2 are named International

Entertainer of the Year at the Juno Awards in Toronto.

Spring
Ron Daniels, director of the Royal Shakespeare Company, approaches Bono and Edge with an idea to have them compose music for an upcoming production of *A Clockwork Orange*.

April
U2 releases 'When Love Comes To Town' as the third single from *Rattle And Hum*. B-sides include 'When Love Comes To Town (Live from the Kingdom Mix)' and 'God Part II (Hard Metal Dance Mix)'. It only gets as high as number 68 on the *Billboard* singles chart, but climbs to number six in the UK. US radio likes the song, and it tops out at number three on the *Radio And Records* AOR chart.

Issue 10 of *Propaganda* is published.

April 18
U2 shoot a video for 'All I Want Is You' in Rome. The shoot likely lasts more than this one day, though the exact starting and finishing dates are unknown.

April 24
The Greenpeace fund raising album, *Rainbow Warriors*, is released worldwide. The opening track is the live version of 'Pride (In The Name Of Love)' from *Rattle And Hum*, though the track features an edited beginning for this release.

April 27
Bono joins best friend Gavin Friday on stage in Dublin to perform 'We Are The Champions' and 'My Way'.

April 30
Bono makes his first solo live appearance when he sings two adaptations of William Butler Yeats' poems ('September 1913' and 'Mad As The Mist And Snow') at a fund raising event in the Abbey Theatre in Dublin.

May
Adam joins a recording session at Winkles Bar & Hotel in Kinvara, Ireland, for newcomer Sharon

Shannon, who's working on her debut album. He plays on the track, 'The Marguerita Suite'. The album isn't released until 1991.

Nicaraguan President Daniel Ortega visits Ireland as part of a tour of several European countries. While in Ireland, he meets U2 in a private, unpublicized visit.

May 4-5
U2 attend at one of the two Lansdowne Road concerts featuring Frank Sinatra, Liza Minnelli, and Sammy Davis, Jr.

May 10
On Bono's 29th birthday, he and Ali become parents for the first time as daughter Jordan is born today. Bono describes watching the birth as "really psychedelic".

May 16
Irish media are waiting outside Mount Carmel Hospital as Bono and Ali take daughter Jordan home. When asked why they chose the name Jordan, Bono tells the line of journalists, "Because we will be running after her for the rest of our lives."

June
U2 release 'All I Want Is You' as the fourth and final single from *Rattle And Hum*, with 'Unchained Melody' and 'Everlasting Love' as B-sides on its various formats. The song does well on US radio, reaching number 13 on the *Radio And Records* AOR chart, but barely makes a ripple commercially, debuting at number 93 on the *Billboard* singles chart and peaking at number 83. But much like the previous singles from this album, it fares better in the UK, going as high as number four on the singles chart.

Also this month, Edge and Adam appear on the Greenpeace flagship in Dublin Harbour for the Irish launch of Greenpeace's *Rainbow Warriors* album.

June 2
Bono visits with Ireland's Taoiseach, Charles Haughey, in Dublin's city centre arts complex.

June 4
Bono joins Bob Dylan on stage in Dublin for performances of 'Knocking On Heaven's Door' and 'Maggie's Farm'.

June 16
Adam is arrested at around 3:00 a.m. in the Rathmines section of Dublin on suspicion of drunken driving.

June 18
Adam attends the Glastonbury Festival, and joins Hothouse Flowers on stage for one song.

Around this time, Adam spends three days playing music in Galway with fellow musicians including Sharon Shannon and Philip King.

June 23
Adam joins Maria McKee on stage at Mother Redcaps in Dublin and plays a few songs with her band.

June 26
Edge and Aislinn give birth to their third daughter, Blue Angel.

July
While the rest of the band is on vacation, Adam does an interview in Dublin with *Propaganda* magazine.

Below: Irish media cover the birth of Bono and Ali's first child, Jordan.

No rattle or hum from 'quiet' baby

By PADDY CLANCY

PROUD dad Bono spoke yesterday of the greatest experience of his life — watching his baby daughter being born. "It was really psychedelic," said the U2 singer. "To have seen birth at first hand was amazing.

"The job the midwife and the nurses did was terrific. It doesn't really compare to anything else in my experience. Everything else seems insignificant in comparison to it. I've always had the utmost respect for women. But after this my admiration for them is boundless."

The bouncing baby, still unnamed, was born to wife Alison in Dublin's exclusive Mount Carmel Hospital last Wednesday — Bono's 29th birthday. She is their first child and arrived a little earlier than expected. Alison had thought she might have to sit her university finals in hospital if the baby didn't arrive until the end of the month.

The couple marked the double event — the birth and Bono's birthday — with a private champagne celebration in the hospital room shortly after becoming a family of U3.

After visiting Alison yesterday Bono said: "She's a truly beautiful baby. Just like her beautiful mother. And she has her mother's outlook. She is a really quiet child. She looked incredibly bored when she was born. She yawned as if to say 'What's all this about?'

"Ali is just incredible. It's been quite a year for her. We moved house. She is doing her finals. And we had a baby. I wanted a daughter and it's a great birthday present. The greatest compliment I can pay a child of mine now is to continue to make the noisiest rock 'n' roll music I can."

Would he like the baby to be a musician? "She'll probably be something like a rocket scientist, a politician or a removal truck driver." He added: "I'm very proud of Ali and the baby."

■ Finally found what he's looking for . . . 'Amazed' Bono sits on the steps of Mount Carmel yesterday after visiting his wife Ali and baby daughter.

B.B. King remembers his birthday bash on Sydney Harbor, September 16

"Once we started to leave the dock, then they started letting out balloons and singing happy birthday. They hired a band to play for me, and we jammed and sang and had a lot of fun. And Bono sang a song he wrote for me, 'Happy Birthday B.B. King,' and it was so good, I cried. I couldn't hold back the tears.

"We came back in at sunset, and I thought it was all over. We'd had such a wonderful time. Then I saw one of the greatest fireworks displays I've ever seen, and it was in my honour, so I cried some more."

August
U2 begin rehearsals for the upcoming Lovetown Tour.

Bono and Edge visit London this month to see the Royal Shakespeare Company's production of *MacBeth*. They agree to write music for the RSC's *A Clockwork Orange* production next year.

August 1
Island Records founder Chris Blackwell announces his intention to sell the record label to Polygram International for $300 million.

August 6
Adam Clayton is arrested at the Blue Light Pub in Glencullen when police officers Michael Moody and Sean Campbell approach a group of people surrounding Adam's Aston Martin. Officers find 19 grams of marijuana in the car, and a pocketknife with traces of marijuana. They charge Adam with possession and intent to supply.

August 13
The whole band shows up for Gavin Friday's gig tonight at the Tivoli Theatre, but they arrive late and cause a ruckus during the first song.

September
Melissa Etheridge releases *Brave And Crazy*. Bono plays harmonica on the track 'Royal Station 4/16'.

While U2 are rehearsing for the upcoming Lovetown Tour, Bono and Edge are also busy in the studio working on new songs for *A Clockwork Orange*.

September 1
With Paul McGuinness and Larry at his side, Adam appears today in a Dublin court to answer charges related to his arrest three weeks ago. Adam agrees to plead guilty to marijuana possession, and the intent to supply charge is dropped. Adam's lawyers plead for leniency, saying a conviction could affect Adam's ability to travel. The district judge scolds Adam – "Taking into account the particular influence people like Mr. Clayton have on small children, it's a dreadful example to them to find one of their heroes caught in this situation" –

but admits that this case is of "low importance" on the scale of drug offenses. The judge invokes Ireland's Probation of Offender's Act, which allows Adam to make a charitable contribution in exchange for dismissal of the charge against him. The judge suggests a £25,000 contribution to the Women's Aid and Refuge Centre, which Adam's attorney indicates can be paid immediately. There is no mention of the arrest or conviction on his police record. About two-dozen U2 fans and many reporters are waiting outside the courthouse. "Nothing to say," is Paul McGuinness' only comment as he and Adam get in their car and drive away. By keeping the offense off Adam's permanent record, the band avoids a major disaster: had the conviction stood, Adam might have encountered problems obtaining a US visa, in which case U2's upcoming tour – which starts in just three

Left: BB King joins U2 on stage. Below: Paul McGuinness reacts to press criticism over the price of tickets for U2's concert at The Point, Dublin.

U2 boss gets 'sour grapes' rap

By KEN WHELAN

THE decision by U2 to reduce ticket prices for their series of Christmas concerts in Dublin was welcomed today by the National Youth Council of Ireland — but it said remarks made by the band's manager Paul McGuinness smacked of "sour grapes".

Mr. McGuinness asked if critics of prices for the U2 concerts in the Point Depot would be using their influence on other issues.

The cost of the U2 tickets was first highlighted in the EVENING PRESS last month, when youth leaders said the £20 and £25 prices would be beyond many fans who were on unemployment benefit.

The prices have now been reduced to £16 and £18.

But Mr. McGuinness said he hoped the "coalition of priests and commentators" who raised the question in the first place would now bring their influence to bear on other financial issues facing youth, like interest rates, the cost of travel and the price of butter and coal.

National Youth Council director, Mr. Tom Curran, said he resented the "disparaging" remarks made by the U2 manager. His council was continously highlighting numerous issues affecting youth with the authorities.

Mr. Curran said the remarks smacked of "sour grapes" and U2 had now admitted a mistake in pitching the concert prices too high.

He added: "There was widespread dismay at the prices being charged for the concerts and we were entitled to raise the question.

"We don't tell U2 how to play their music and Mr. McGuinness should not be telling us how to run our affairs.

"U2 are a group who claim to be responsive to Irish youth and also claim a social message. It would be totally contradictory to their image to charge the prices they were asking for."

Mr. McGuinness, in his statement last night, said the band recognised that the prices were too high

● **U2's manager Paul McGuinness**

U2 ticket prices 'are excessive'

By Ken Whelan

THE price of tickets for the series of concerts at the Point Depot this Christmas was today described as "excessive".

The Evening Press exclusive on September 15 highlighting the ticket prices for the U2 Christmas concerts in the Point Depot.

weeks – would have to be cancelled.

September 7
'When Loves Comes To Town' wins the Best Video from a Film award at the MTV Video Music Awards.

September 14
After months of rumours, U2 confirm a series of five concerts in Dublin at the end of the year. The announced dates are December 26, 27, 29, 30, and 31 at the Point Depot. The December 29 show will be dropped shortly before tickets go on sale in November.

September 15
In today's *Evening Press*, the National Youth Council of Ireland says ticket prices for U2's upcoming shows at the Point Depot in late December "are excessive". The Council says the £20 and £25 tickets are beyond the means of many young fans who are unemployed. Paul McGuinness fires back weeks later, asking if the Youth Council would also protest interest rates or the cost of butter. In the end, U2 bows to pressure and lowers the tickets to £16 and £18. The price drop scotches U2's plan to donate its profits from the shows to local charities. "There may be no net profit to speak of on these shows," Paul McGuinness says.

Meanwhile, in Sydney, U2 and B.B. King meet the media to talk about the upcoming Lovetown Tour.

September 16
B.B. King turns 64 today, and U2 throws him a surprise birthday party on a luxury yacht in Sydney Harbor. King's manager tells B.B. that he's going fishing with U2, and asks if B.B. would like to go. B.B. gets on the yacht, and even though there are about 50 people on board, he still thinks it's a fishing trip.

B.B. plays a few songs on the boat, with Bono and others joining in.

September 17
U2 arrive quietly in Perth in preparation for the Lovetown Tour opener later in the week. The band holes up at the Observation City

Hotel and does its best to avoid the media.

September 20
Daniel Lanois' first solo album, *Acadie*, is released today. Larry and Adam perform on two tracks: 'Still Water' and 'Jolie Louise'.

September 21-22-23
Entertainment Center, Perth, with Weddings Parties Anything, B.B. King. U2 kicks off the Lovetown Tour. Bono's friend Rene Castro, the mural artist, designs the stage backdrop for this tour. U2 is making good on a promise from the end of *The Joshua Tree* tour, when Australian dates were first cancelled.

Press reports suggest the band plans to write new material and record demos in a Sydney studio in preparation for their next studio album.

September 27-28-29
Entertainment Center, Sydney, with Weddings Parties Anything, B.B. King. During the third show, Bono pulls Larry to the front of the stage to sing part of 'Stand By Me', then takes Larry's spot at the drum kit. Bono tries a drum solo at the end of the song, but one drumstick flies out of his hand.

October
Issue 11 of *Propaganda* is published.

October 2-3-4
Entertainment Center, Brisbane, with Weddings Parties Anything, B.B. King. During the second show, Bono brings his four-month old daughter, Jordan, on stage and tells the crowd it is her first time at a U2 concert.

October 7-8-9-12-13-14-16
National Tennis Center, Melbourne, with Weddings Parties Anything, B.B. King. U2 play a stretch of seven shows in 10 days in one venue. It's a schedule the band feels obligated to play because demand is so high to see them, and indoor venues in Australia are so small. Though fans may not notice a difference, such a long stay in one city leaves the band somewhat uninspired.

Paul McGuinness: "The shows deteriorated."
"Playing multiple dates in Sydney and Melbourne ... wasn't very good. The shows deteriorated. They probably weren't dull, but the band just felt that [the concerts] were turning into a chore, like going to work. The sense of event that is very important for their performance was missing."

U2 realizes they can't schedule a tour like this again, and future indoor tours will be very heavy with one night stands.

Before the last show in Melbourne, the band invite a small group of fans inside to listen to soundcheck. They hear U2 do a cover of Patti Smith's 'Dancing Barefoot'. Bono complains about a sore throat before the show begins.

While in Melbourne, U2 and Willie Williams pay a visit to their friend, the Reverend John Smith. Bono and Edge also record with a local band called Ecco Homo. Edge plays guitar and Bono sings backing vocals on their song, 'New York New York', which will be released in 1990.

October 20-21
Entertainment Center, Sydney, with Weddings Parties Anything, B.B. King. After the second show, U2 appear on Triple M radio. Bono performs the first verse of 'Slow Dancing', a song he says he wrote for Willie Nelson. Nelson will eventually record it with U2 eight years later in Dublin.

October 22
After complaining of throat pain for several days, Bono is diagnosed with laryngitis and three shows in Sydney are postponed until mid-November.

October 27-28
Memorial Drive Stadium, Adelaide, with Weddings Parties Anything, B.B. King.

November 3
U2 arrive in Auckland today and give a news conference for local media. With so many free days in between the four New Zealand gigs, U2 has time for extra-curricular activities like water rafting and bungee jumping on the South Island.

November 4
Lancaster Park, Christchurch, with B.B. King.

November 8
Athletic Park, Wellington, with B.B. King.

November 9
U2 spend a day visiting the grave of Greg Carroll and visiting his family in Wanganui.

November 10-11
Western Springs Stadium, Auckland, with B.B. King. During a soundcheck, U2 come up with a new song that eventually becomes 'Acrobat' on the *Achtung Baby* album.

November 16
The Joshua Tree lands at number three in *Rolling Stone*'s list of the *Top 100 Albums of the Eighties*. War is ranked number 40.

November 17
Tickets for U2's shows in Dublin next month go on sale tonight at 11 locations across Ireland. In Dublin, 4,000 fans try to score tickets at the

Point Depot, but many go home empty-handed when the 10,000 tickets sell out quickly. Although the sale isn't supposed to begin until midnight, it starts three hours early due to the growing crowd at the Point Depot.

November 17-18-19
Entertainment Center, Sydney, with Weddings Parties Anything, B.B. King. Australian Richard Lowenstein films all three shows for an upcoming documentary about the Lovetown Tour. Shortly before the second show is about to begin, an anonymous bomb threat is phoned in to the venue. All 12,500 in the crowd are asked to leave, but no explanation is given. They are promised U2 will play a concert. After a 90-minute search, no bombs are found and the concert proceeds.

At this point, U2 have spent the past two months in just two countries. They've played multi-night stands in only a handful of cities, and the tour has been a challenge. Frustration continues to mount in the U2 camp. The band realise this tour will be the end of their exploration of the roots of rock and roll.

November 20
The 747 jet that's flying U2's gear to Japan is hit in midair by a flock of seagulls and grounded for a couple days. The gear doesn't get to Yokohama until the afternoon of the next show.

November 23
Sports Arena, Yokohama.

November 25-26
Tokyo Dome, Tokyo. While in Tokyo, U2 give a news conference at the Irish Ambassador's home.

November 28-29, December 1
Castle Hall, Osaka. Gavin Martin of *NME* is in Osaka for all three shows, and interviews the band after the final show for an upcoming feature. But exhaustion sends Adam, Larry, and Edge to an early bed, leaving Martin to chat with Bono into the early morning hours. The band spend their November 30 day off visiting Buddhist temples in Kyoto.

December

Rattle And Hum is ranked number 32 on *Rolling Stone*'s list of the *Top 100 Albums of 1989*.

December 6

The BBC announce that U2's New Year's Eve concert in Dublin will be broadcast on radio to millions of music fans in Eastern Europe and the Soviet Union. Paul McGuinness says the broadcast is a tribute to democratic reforms in those areas.

December 11-12

Palais Omnisports De Paris Bercy, Paris, with B.B. King. Prior to the first show in Paris, part of U2's lighting grid falls during installation and takes one of the crew 40-feet down to the floor below. The rigger, Steve Witmer, suffers a fractured pelvis.

December 14-15-16

Westfalenhalle, Dortmund, with B.B. King. Bono cuts the third show short when he has trouble singing during 'Love Rescue Me'. The show lasts only 75 minutes, and many in the crowd voice their anger through jeers and whistles.

December 18

Rai Europa Hal, Amsterdam, with B.B. King. Another show is cut short when Bono's voice hurts again. The band decides to refund each ticket for this show, and fans are advised to wait for an announcement about the shows planned for the next two nights.

December 19

A doctor tells Bono to rest his voice for a week, or risk permanent damage to his vocal cords. Concert promoters go on local radio to announce that tonight's and tomorrow's shows in Amsterdam are cancelled, and that U2 will make it up with four new shows after the new year in Rotterdam.

Newspapers in Dublin report the news of U2's cancelled shows and fuel speculation that one or more of the upcoming Point Depot shows may also need to be cancelled.

December 26

Point Depot, Dublin, with B.B. King.

Bono at the Point Depot, December 30

"We've had a lot of fun over the last few months, just getting to know some of the music which we didn't know so much about – and still don't know very much about, but it was fun! (*pause*) Anyway, thanks for coming along. It wouldn't have been the same without you. (*applause*) Some people have traveled a long way to come here tonight. (*applause*) This – I was explaining to people the other night, but I might've got it a bit wrong – this is just the end of something for U2. And that's what we're playing these concerts – and we're throwing a party for ourselves and you. It's no big deal, it's just – we have to go away and… and dream it all up again."

U2 play the first of four end-of-the-decade shows at Dublin's Point Depot. It's their first indoor show in Dublin since 1982, and should be a time for celebration. But U2 are criticized roundly for playing such a small venue – only 5,000 tickets are available for each show, far less than the demand. Scalpers are selling the £16 and £18 tickets for as much as £350.

December 27

Point Depot, Dublin, with B.B. King. At the second Dublin show, Bono alarms the crowd with a brief speech before 'Love Rescue Me': "I suppose this is a kind of going away party, because I think that's what we gotta do. We've had a great ten years…. We gotta do something else the next while, just gotta go away for a little bit." Though Bono is saying U2 needs to take a break, newspapers misinterpret his remarks and report that U2 are splitting up. Doctors advise Bono to rest his still-troubled throat after tonight's show.

December 30

Point Depot, Dublin, with B.B. King. Bono delivers the now famous "dream it all up again" speech during the beginning of 'Love Rescue Me'.

December 31

Point Depot, Dublin, with B.B. King. U2 ends the 1980s and begins the 1990s with the last of four shows at the Point Depot in Dublin. At the start of 'Where The Streets Have No Name', the crowd counts down the final 15 seconds of the 1980s, and before returning to 'Streets', Bono sings a few lines from 'Auld Lang Syne'. The show airs live on radio throughout Europe. U2 places ads in several music magazines on the continent encouraging fans to tape the show.

1990

This is a transition year for U2. The band finishes the Lovetown Tour at the start of the year, and everyone realises it's time for change.

Changes occur first on the business side, as Polygram Records assumes control of Island Records. The sale is a financial windfall for U2, whose $5 million investment several years ago for 10% of Island Records is now worth $30 million. As part of the buyout, U2 also gains the right to buy shares in Polygram in the future at their market value at the time of the takeover.

U2 takes most of the year off. The process of musical change starts late in the year, when the band arrives in Berlin to begin work on a new album. In Berlin, they find that "dreaming it all up again" isn't as easy as it sounds.

January 5-6-9-10
Sport Paleis Ahoy, Rotterdam, with B.B. King. The Lovetown tour ends with four make-up dates for the Amsterdam shows that were cancelled a month earlier. The rescheduled shows cut into Bono and Edge's plans to finish the music for *A Clockwork Orange*, which will premiere next month in London.

With the tour complete, it's a time of reassessment for U2. The long trek that began in late 1985 with *The Joshua Tree* recording sessions and continued through two tours and the *Rattle And Hum* project is now finally over. It's time, as Bono said a couple weeks earlier in Dublin, to "dream it all up again".

Larry: "I can't do this anymore"
"It had become very serious, very had work. And just no fun. It was nothing to do with the music. It was to do with getting up and going to work. Because we take care of a lot of our own business, we spend a lot of time in meetings. We've always done that. On the stage it was good but it was very intense and was very hard work. You were *grimacing* because you were stressed. I remember coming off that tour [Lovetown] and feeling, 'If this is what it is, I really don't want to do it any more. I *can't* do this any more.'"

Bono: "This is not enough"
"I had a terrible time at Christmas, a very convenient end-of-decade depression. I looked back and said, 'OK, it was wonderful and a lot of good work was done,' but I felt very unhappy. I said, 'If this is it, this is not enough.'"

January 17
With all of U2 in attendance, Bono inducts The Who into the Rock and Roll Hall of Fame at a ceremony in New York City. During his speech, Bono jokingly says the key to great rock'n'roll bands is "a great nose". The reference to Pete Townshend's profile draws big laughs from the crowd.

January 25
Today's issues of *Hot Press* and *Q* contain pre-printed cassette inlay covers for fans to use with their radio recordings of U2's New Year's Eve show in Dublin.

February 6
A Clockwork Orange 2004, produced by the Royal Shakespeare Company, debuts at the Barbican, a multi-arts centre in London. It's an updated version of Anthony Burgess' 1962 classic, co-written by Burgess and Ron Daniels. Bono and Edge provide the musical score, which is used in place of Beethoven's Ninth Symphony from the book. Burgess isn't impressed; he dismisses Bono and Edge's musical contribution as "neo-wallpaper".

As part of his research for the project, Edge listens to industrial bands like KMFDM, and Einsturzende Neubaten. Though it won't be obvious until later, the "abrasive" and experimental nature of the *Clockwork Orange* songs is a

Edge explains the *Clockwork Orange* score, February 6

"There are some very abrasive tracks in there. I wouldn't expect a U2 fan to recognise this music as that of Edge and Bono, except on a couple of tracks. It is not really to do with U2, it's a different attitude. In fact, not only is it not U2 music, it's not really Bono and Edge music either – if we have a style, we definitely laid it aside for this project."

clear indicator of a new direction for U2's own music.

February 18
U2 is named Best International Group at the Brit Awards.

March
Issue 12 of *Propaganda* is published.

Around this time, Bono and his family rent a van and drive across the US. They stay two weeks in New Orleans, where Bono writes two songs with the Neville Brothers: 'Jah Love' and 'Kingdom Come'. When they get to Los Angeles, Bono continues to work on his *Million Dollar Hotel* screenplay. And in San Francisco he works on a poem called 'Ballad of New Orleans'. By April, they are back home in Dublin.

March 8
Though U2 didn't put out an album or tour in the US, *Rolling Stone* readers name Bono Best Songwriter in the 1989 Music Awards.

April
Larry writes and plays drums on 'Put 'Em Under Pressure', the official anthem of Ireland's 1990 World Cup soccer team. The song is released on Son Records, a branch of U2's Mother Records label, and reaches number one on the Irish singles chart. Though he's not credited on the release, popular London DJ Howie B meets with Larry in London and helps with the track.

April 5
Edge and his brother, Dick, see

Gavin Friday perform tonight at the Electric Cinema in London.

April 10
The Edge joins a collection of Irish musicians at Ringsend Road Studios in Dublin to record a song called 'April The Third', which will appear in the upcoming BBC/RTE series, *Bringing It All Back Home*. The song title is a reference to the day Donal Lunny wrote the song.

June
U2 gathers in Edge's basement to record a cover of Cole Porter's 'Night And Day' for inclusion on an upcoming fund raising album. Paul Barrett plays keyboards and Noel Eccles plays congas.

June 16
Bono and Adam see Depeche

Mode play at Giants Stadium in New Jersey. During the show, they meet up with Mark "Flood" Ellis, who had engineered *The Joshua Tree*. They invite him to come to Germany later this year and engineer help on their new album.

June 20
Bono joins David Bowie on stage in Cleveland at a show which Adam also attends, and which U2's longtime lighting designer Peter "Willie" Williams is working. Bono sings Them's 'Gloria' to great applause. The Bowie tour uses a new, thin video screen to illustrate some songs with pre-recorded images. A local newspaper claims Bono and Adam are at the show to see this technology and may use it on U2's next world tour.

June 30

The whole band travels to Rome to watch today's Ireland vs. Italy World Cup Quarterfinals match. Italy escapes with a 1-0 win.

Summer

U2 gather at STS Studio in Dublin to begin work on new material for their next album. They manage to record some rough demos, with Bono and Edge apparently delegated to continue working on lyrics and melodies before the formal recording sessions begin in a couple months.

Adam spends a month in New York, hanging out with Catherine Owens and other friends.

July 28

Paul McGuinness and U2 fly to Turin to watch the Rolling Stones play a show on their Urban Jungle tour.

August 7

The Neville Brothers release *Brother's Keeper*, which features one of the songs Bono wrote for them: 'Jah Love'. Bono also appears on The Call's *Red Moon* album, singing backing vocals on 'What's Happened To You?'.

August 9

U2 see David Bowie perform tonight at the Point Depot. While Bowie is in Dublin, Bono hosts a dinner with plenty of music industry guests joining the fun.

September

Issue 13 of *Propaganda* magazine is published around this time. In it, Bono talks about a couple of new songs the band are working on, provisionally titled 'Ultraviolet' and 'Sick Puppy'.

October 3

U2 travel to Germany to begin work on their next album. They arrive in Berlin just as the city is celebrating its Liberation Day and reunification. Soon after their plane lands, the band mistakenly joins a parade of hard-core Communists marching in opposition to reunification. They quickly leave to join the revelry of supporters elsewhere in the city, walking back and forth between what used to be the east and west sides of the city. At one point, they pass the Zoo Station subway terminal.

That night, the band head home to their temporary headquarters – a house that had previously belonged to the East German government, and had been used by former Soviet premier Leonid Brezhnev. Early the next morning, a naked Bono goes downstairs when he hears strange voices. He's greeted by a German family demanding he leave because the house had been theirs before the government seized it. The band relocate to a hotel on the east side of the city.

Prior to recording, the first order of business is shooting a music video for 'Night And Day' at director Wim Wenders' home in Berlin. The song appears later this month on the *Red, Hot & Blue* album, a compilation of Cole Porter songs to heighten awareness and raise money for AIDS charities.

After the video shoot, U2 move into Studio Two at the famous Hansa Ton Studios, the same studio where David Bowie recorded his *Low* and *Heroes* albums in the mid-1970s. Hansa isn't in good shape. The facilities have been neglected for years, forcing producers Brian Eno and Daniel Lanois to bring in their own recording equipment.

The early recording sessions are heavy going as the band struggle to agree on what direction they should take after Bono's promise to "dream it all up again". Edge and Bono have been listening to more experimental, electronic music. Adam and Larry feel that their bandmates didn't come to Berlin prepared, that Bono and Edge never finished developing the demos recorded in Dublin in the summer.

What happened in Berlin? U2 tells U

Edge: "Berlin was difficult. I had quite a strong feel where I thought it should go. Bono was with me. Adam and Larry were a little unsure. It took time for them to see how they fit into this.

"I also think Danny [producer Daniel Lanois] didn't fully understand where we were headed, because we were working on more of the throwaway, trashy kinds of things. The U2 that he loved was the U2 of *The Joshua Tree* and *The Unforgettable Fire*, the textural and emotional and cinematic U2. By the time we finished with the lyrics and the mixes, it came back a bit toward more usual U2 terrain. But for a while, I think Danny was at sea."

Larry: "Some people were quicker at finding the route than others, and it caused immense strain within the band. Because for the first time in the band there was no consensus musically. Whereas in the past, although everyone might not agree, there was some sort of understanding of what was going on. This time there was no understanding. No one knew what the fuck anyone else was talking about."

Bono: "There was a lot of tension between us during the making of that album, with Edge and

---

Keeping Up with the Stones, July 28
Paul McGuinness and Mick Jagger spoke about the "arms race" in concert staging after U2's August 28, 1993, show in Dublin. McGuinness told Jagger about seeing the Stones show in Turin in 1990.

"We realized you had raised the stakes of stadium shows forever. If U2 were going to play football stadiums, we had to try and match it."

myself wanting to chop down *The Joshua Tree*, and Adam and Larry wanting to put a glass house around it and play to our strength. Because Larry and Adam have that humility, but Edge and myself had the arrogance that it wasn't the sound of the guitar, it wasn't a collision of notes that made up a melody, or a particular bass and drums approach that made U2. We believed that what made U2 was the spark, and that you could destroy all the outward manifestation, and it would still be there … you could just deface all that was recognizable in the band, and it still would come through."

Adam: "There was a general problem with communication between everyone. There was a misunderstanding about the amount of effort and cohesion needed to see the project through…. We had time and that was a two-edged sword. It enabled us to not face the problem, to just continue to be frustrated…. I felt it was there if we could only let it happen. I didn't feel we were as far away from it as Bono felt. It just lacked a few ballsy decisions made with everyone contributing to the consensus."

October 21

Bono appears on the long-running UK arts magazine programme, *The South Bank Show*. The episode, "Cool, Clear Crystal Streams", is a documentary about Irish music made by Bob Geldof's TV production company. Bono talks about songwriting and what it means to be an Irish songwriter.

December

U2 and Anton Corbijn do several photo shoots in Berlin this month around their hotel and at Hansa Studios. The pictures will be used on the album artwork and as publicity shots.

Meanwhile, the recording sessions are still a struggle. The band is working on plenty of material, but very little of the material has progressed into songs. It's cold and rainy outside, but inside the studio the band's tempers are flaring up. On one occasion, after Bono is critical of Adam's playing, Adam takes off his bass and holds it out for Bono. "You tell me what to play and I'll play it. You want to play it yourself? Go ahead." Edge starts to wonder if the band should break up.

The band calls Brian Eno – who has been away from the sessions – back to Berlin to help move things along. Eno listens to the new material and tells the band they're doing better than they think.

One night, while working on 'Ultraviolet', Edge comes up with a new guitar part and plays it in the studio. Adam and Larry start playing along to Edge's lead, and Bono joins the jam session, making up words on the microphone: "We're one, but we're not the same. We get to carry each other." After jamming for about 10 minutes, they listen to a playback and immediately know they have something special. 'One' is recorded by the next morning. Everyone is relieved to have made real progress, and more importantly, to be functioning as a unit again. The band agree they'll leave Berlin soon and continue recording the new album in Dublin.

Over Christmas, the band get together in Dublin not to record, but to talk. Larry wants to address the bigger issues that came out of their time in Berlin and make sure each band member wants to continue. It's agreed they all do.

Also this month, U2 releases 'Night And Day' as a 12-inch promo-only single. The song's video is featured in *Red, Hot & Blue*, an ABC-TV special hosted by Whoopi Goldberg.

"I thought this might be the end. We had been through tough circumstances before and found our way out, but it was always outside influences that we were fighting against. For the first time ever it felt like the cracks were within. And that was a much more difficult situation to negotiate."

December 12

U2 are named Best Act in the World Today at the inaugural Q Magazine Awards in London. With the band busy in Berlin, Paul McGuinness accepts the award for them: "It's a little bit embarrassing, as you might expect, to get an award like this when they haven't made a record for two years. They hope the record they're working on at the moment will be sufficient to justify this in retrospect."

Below: Bono joins David Bowie on stage at Cleveland, June 20.

1991

This is a year of focus and reinvention. After struggling in Berlin at the start of the recording sessions in late 1990, U2 spends much of this year in Dublin, locked in on the new sound they're chasing. Minor distractions will crop up in the form of stolen album session tapes, and a copyright dispute involving an unknown band and the well-known radio host Casey Kasem.

But all the while, U2 is undergoing a major reinvention. The band's internal struggles are out of the way, and they're working together to steer U2 in new directions. They'll continue to react to the world around them; the Persian Gulf War will light U2's way for the next world tour, while trips to Morocco and Tenerife will help paint U2's new image. The band's new attitude is summed up in a quote Bono lifts from Irish poet Brendan Kennelly: "The best way to serve the age is to betray it." By year's end, U2 releases *Achtung Baby* and is set to launch their longest and most ambitious tour yet.

January
U2 return to Berlin to wrap up some recording work before all the equipment is sent back to Dublin.

January 16
U2 are in Berlin as the Persian Gulf War begins (early morning January 17 in Baghdad). The band watches CNN's live coverage of the bombing on TV, aware of how easily they can flip back and forth between channels during commercials. Bono and Edge are amazed by the video game-like technology being used, and at hearing US pilots describe a bombing mission as "so realistic". The experience plants several ideas in Bono's head about how to reflect this on the next U2 tour.

Bono on "war in the comfort of your own home"
"I found the Gulf War thing completely absurd. I actually couldn't believe what I was seeing or hearing. I couldn't believe that I would change channels back and forth from watching cartoons to John Simpson [a BBC reporter] describing a Cruise missile turning left on Main Street. I couldn't believe that I was part of this Pythonesque scenario, this madness. War in the comfort of your own home. Even better than the real thing."

February 9
U2 arrive in the warmer climate of Tenerife, one of the Canary Islands off the western coast of Africa, for almost two weeks of photo and video shoots that the band hope will help change their image. They feel the recent shoots in the cold Berlin winter aren't reflective of the spirit of their new material and the new impression they want to get across.

Their visit coincides with the annual festival in the capital of Santa Cruz, and the band ask their staff to bring costumes and masks so they can get lost in the crowds and show a different, more fun side of the band. It's during this visit that many of the well-known photos showing U2 in drag are taken. (Some also come from a photo shoot later in the year in Morocco.) The band's presence is supposed to be a secret, but fans begin to congregate outside the Mencey Hotel as word spreads that U2 is staying there. A local radio station even catches on to U2's presence, and tracks Bono down for an interview during one video shoot.

Willie Williams talks about the birth of Zoo TV in Tenerife
"Each time we regroup after an absence, I bring with me a whole agenda of my own in terms of things I want to do, developments that have happened since the last tour, new technology & new ideas. All of the

Eno describes the making of *Achtung Baby* in two sentences, February 9

"Buzzwords on this record were *trashy, throwaway, dark, sexy* and *industrial* (all good) and *earnest, polite, sweet, righteous, rockist* and *linear* (all bad). It was good if a song took you on a journey or made you think your hi-fi was broken, bad if it reminded you of recording studios or U2."

members of U2 do the same – not to mention that they'll be in the middle of making a new album – so we inevitably begin the process with plenty of different concepts to toy with. It usually starts with an incredibly long phone call between Bono & I where he'll call to fill me in on the previous two years and tell me what he has in his head for the tour to come and vice versa. This stream of conscious dialogue is invariably the most revealing part of the whole process and no matter how many ideas we explore subsequently, the key principles are almost always unearthed at this early stage.

"In [early] 1991, Bono called me having just got home from U2's exile in Berlin. He asked me to come and join them in Tenerife where they were going to see the carnival. He told me they were making the most exciting album of their career and that it would demand a live show unlike any they'd done before. He had a phrase in his head – 'Zoo TV' – which he felt was a key to something, oh, and an absurd pair of oversized sunglasses which he felt were important, too.

"In Tenerife we talked for hours as Anton photographed the band on various beaches, in bars, dressing up in women's clothing, etc. They had also air freighted a small German car – called a Trabant, I was informed – to the island, so I knew something was up. I'd just done David Bowie's Sound & Vision tour, which utilised film projection to fantastic effect and had

some video content too – mainly of the side-screen camera close-ups variety. It was the first time I had toured with a full scale video package and it was very clear to me that there was potential to take rock show video to a level as yet undreamed of."

After Tenerife, U2 relocate back to Ireland to continue work on the Achtung Baby album. They've rented out Elsinore House in Dalkey through July at a cost of £10,000 per month. Big Bear Sound, a Dublin audio services company,

Above: The Trabant featured in the adverts for U2's forthcoming album, Achtung Baby.

installs a recording studio at the five-bedroom Victorian manor. Separate recording rooms are set up on the main floor and upstairs, and the band use video cameras and TV monitors to see what is happening in both places. U2 name the studio "Dogtown", a reference to a pair of large, empty kennels next to the house. 'So Cruel' is one of the tracks written and recorded in this period. Fintan Fitzgerald, U2's wardrobe guru, brings Bono a pair of large, black sunglasses that Bono puts on to keep the mood light at Dogtown. He starts developing a character while wearing the shades.

U2 works at Dogtown for a couple months before wrapping up in the familiar surroundings of Windmill Lane Studios. Throughout the recording process, U2 remains out of the public eye – a reaction to the backlash they felt after the publicity overload of the Rattle And Hum period. When it comes time later in the year to do an article with Rolling Stone about the new album, U2 asks Brian Eno to write it.

Also this month, U2 pay a £500 fine on behalf of the Irish Family Planning Association, which has been found guilty of selling condoms at the Virgin Megastore in Dublin.

March 17
Willie Williams visits U2 in Dublin to hear the band's new songs and continue the discussion on plans for a tour.

Late March
Sometime around Easter (March 31), Edge and his wife, Aislinn, separate. Edge moves into Adam's house for a few weeks, then into a small house near Adam's place.

Edge's separation and its impact on Achtung Baby
"It was a grim period for me, finally looking failure in the face and seeing this was something that could not be redeemed. We tried. We went to counseling. I think it had gone too far.

So making the record was a welcome distraction but inevitably it started to reflect what was going on in my life, partly because my own creative instincts were overwhelmed by it, but I think it also infused Bono's contribution."

Above: Edge in Dublin, November.

April
News spreads that bootleggers have obtained high-quality, digital audio tapes (DATs) of U2's recording sessions in Berlin, and fans around the world quickly share copies. Though never confirmed, the tapes are reportedly taken from a trashcan in one of the band's hotel rooms. A U2 spokesperson casts doubt on that version of events: "It's impossible to fathom the band leaving these tapes in the hotel trash. They would always be under lock and key." Another theory arises in Dublin, where observers report seeing band members casually leaving tapes in their unlocked cars.

Paul McGuinness issues a statement: "There is always a strong demand for U2 material, but these tapes are very early recordings and I don't like to see

people being ripped off." Bono calls the bootlegs "gobbledygook", and adds, "I don't know why anyone would be interested in them."

Edge: "It was like being violated"
"It was like being violated. People are listening to very private things, stolen things. Most of it is just mumbo-jumbo crap, but it's made significant by becoming a U2 artifact. Even U2 goofing around becomes an artifact!"

The tapes are quickly pressed for distribution and a double vinyl bootleg hits the market first. After correcting some duplication errors, the final vinyl version of the bootleg is distributed in November, 1991. It includes nearly three-and-a-half hours of U2's unfinished studio work. Titled *The New U2: Rehearsals and Full Versions*, the nearly 30-songs are pressed on a five-LP set. In February, 1992, the full set finally makes its way to a three-CD set titled *Salome: The [Axtung Beibi] Outtakes*.

Around this time, Bono takes writer Steve Turner on a tour of U2-related sites in Dublin for an upcoming travel article in *The Independent*.

April 7
RTE airs the first of a five-part television documentary, *Bringing It All Back Home*, which celebrates the history of Irish music and its influence on other musical forms, particularly American folk and blues. A CD album of songs from the documentary accompanies the series. Bono is interviewed for the TV program, and appears with Edge performing a new song called 'Wild Irish Rose'. The album that accompanies the TV series is already complete, so this song isn't included. There are, however, two U2 appearances on the album: The Edge performs on the song 'April The Third' (credited as "A.N. O'Ther" in some pressings) and Adam Clayton performs on the song 'The Bucks Of Oranmore'

as part of The Hughes Band.

May
U2 file a lawsuit against *The Sunday Independent* over an article that appeared in the paper's October 7, 1990, edition. The article, titled "It Could Happen To U Too" and written by Hugh Leonard, recounts a third-hand story about U2 behaving arrogantly in a Dublin restaurant. The lawsuit says the article hurt U2's "standing, credit, and reputation". The matter is settled out of court, and the paper prints an apology to U2, admitting, "there was no foundation in fact" in the original article's references to U2.

May 6
Bringing It All Back Home premieres on BBC Northern Ireland.

Mid-May
Island Records places ads in music magazines warning record store owners that legal action will be taken against anyone found to be selling the recently bootlegged U2 studio tapes. Record shops in London and Germany are caught selling the bootleg and given substantial fines. In late May, authorities trace the distribution to a printing press in Germany. The original DAT tapes are found there, and the factory is shut down.

June
Still not fully satisfied that the various photo shoots of the past eight months have produced an image suitable for the cover of their new album, U2 summon Anton Corbijn to Dublin for still more time in front of the camera. It's during this shoot that the famous shot of a nude Adam is taken. Though the photo isn't used on the front cover of *Achtung Baby*, it does make the CD sleeve. But not in North America, where Adam's privates are covered up with a shamrock or a black "X".

June 14
U2 meets with Willie Williams, Catherine Owens, and others, to discuss plans for the next tour. Two ideas are born: placing TV monitors

Unsettling settlement with Bono and the boys

By GENE KERRIGAN

ONO, Adam, Larry and he Edge have settled their rst-ever libel action, gainst *The Sunday Independent*. Within hours of the ttlement a new row had oken out, following the lease of an account of the ise by a London public lations firm on behalf of e band and a counter statement by the newspaper.

The affair began in Octor 1990, when Hugh Leond wrote a column in *The unday Independent* in which he described dining in a Monkstown restaurant and recounted a number of anecdotes about dining in general and that restaurant in particular. The piece was accompanied by a cartoon in which Bono and The Edge were portrayed.

One of the anecdotes, which had been told to Hugh Leonard by the restaurant owner, mentioned U2. The story was third-hand, the owner had taken it up wrong, and the anecdote was untrue. This reference, which involved the four members of the band expecting special treatment at the restaurant because of their celebrity, totalled four sentences in a 1,200-word piece.

Bono, Adam, Larry and The Edge decided that the anecdote suggested they had, in the words of their PR statement, "abused the position their fans had put them in." They had their lawyers state that the anecdote was "a gross libel" which had caused "grave embarrassment" and that they had "been injured in their personal and professional reputations."

The band's lawyers drafted two apologies, both of which they wanted printed in *The Sunday Independent*. One said that the newspaper "wished to state categorically that we are absolutely satisfied that U2 did not at any stage make a reservation for dinner" at the restaurant. The paper was to apologise for the "grave embarrassment" it caused the band. Two weeks later the band's lawyers instituted proceedings.

The newspaper's inquiries determined that U2 had not been at the restaurant, although David Evans, the U2 member who trades under the name The Edge, had been there among a party of eight. He had behaved entirely properly. The paper informed the band's lawyers that it was "anxious to deal in a reasonable way with any concern your clients might have" and was "prepared to publish an appropriate statement."

Bono, Adam, Larry and

APOLOGY U2

THE *Sunday Independent* and Hugh Leonard unreservedly withdraw the statements made in an article entitled "It Could Happen To U Too" written by Hugh Leonard in the *Sunday Independent* of October 7, 1990, referring to U2 and an alleged incident in Mr Hung's restaurant in Monkstown, Co Dublin.

The *Sunday Independent* and Hugh Leonard unreservedly accept that there was no foundation in fact to the article insofar as it referred to the members of U2 and very deeply regret the contrary impression and the implications as contained in the said article.

The *Sunday Independent* and Hugh Leonard unreservedly apologise to Adam Clayton, The Edge, Bono and Larry Mullen in their capacity as members of U2 and in their personal capacity for the hurt and embarrassment caused to them and their families. — THE EDITOR

● Continued on page two

all over the stage, and using Trabants as light sources above the stage.

July
Issue 14 of *Propaganda* magazine is published around this time.

U2 join Anton Corbijn, Steve Averill, and others in Morocco for a four-day photo shoot.

July 7
Bono and Ali become parents for the second time when their daughter Eve is born today.

July 26
Bringing It All Back Home premieres on BBC 2 in the UK.

August 20
Electronic band Negativland releases a single called 'U2' on the SST record label. The song is a collage that includes unauthorized samples of U2's 'I Still Haven't Found What I'm Looking For' song from 1987, plus outtakes of radio host Casey Kasem trying to introduce the song on his *American Top 40* programme. The Negativland track catches the attention of Island Records

in North America, however, more for its packaging – the letter "U" and the numeral "2" appear in large type, while "Negativland" appears in small print at the bottom.

September 5
Island Records/Warner-Chappell Music sue SST Records and Negativland, and successfully obtain an injunction against the sale and promotion of Negativland's 'U2' single, which was released two weeks ago.

September 13
Directors Jon Klein and Ritchie Smyth shoot portions of a music video for 'The Fly' in Dublin. They'll finish the video shoot on the streets of London in a couple weeks. "The last three albums have been of a piece in some ways," Klein explains. "What we want to do here is start a new chapter. 'The Fly' feels different to me."

September 21
It's the final night of work on *Achtung Baby*, and as usual, U2 are pushing hard against the deadline to finish the record. Edge is due to fly the final album to the US in the

Marc Marot: "Nobody cared in U2's camp" August 20

"Negativland made *absolutely* the most massive capital they possibly could out of every legal letter. The reality of it is nobody cared. Nobody cared in U2's camp. Nobody cared within Island Records' camp. The only people that cared were people in Negativland's camp. It got turned into this, kind of, monster with three heads, but you know what? Nobody cared. I don't remember ever having discussed it – and I was the president of the label – ever with the band or with Paul McGuinness. It was not on our agenda."

Above: *The Sunday Independent* says they're sorry, May.

morning. Chris Blackwell arrives in Dublin expecting a celebration, but U2 works into the wee hours of the morning. They choose the final mixes of several songs and then decide the album's final running order.

September 22
After breakfast with the band, Edge takes the tapes of U2's new album on a flight to Los Angeles for final mastering. The long, difficult journey to produce this album is finally over. "There were black days when I thought it would never be finished," says Paul McGuinness.

October

U2 shoots a music video for 'Mysterious Ways' in Fez, Morocco, with director Stephane Sednaoui. Photographer Anton Corbijn is also on hand to shoot photos during the two-day video shoot.

Adam appears on Sharon Shannon's self-titled debut album, which is released around this time. He plays on the track, 'The Marguerita Suite'.

October 9

'The Fly' arrives at radio stations in North America. It debuts at number three on the *Radio And Records AOR* chart, and climbs to number one two weeks later.

October 15

Island Records and SST Records agree on a settlement of Island's copyright infringement suit regarding the Negativland 'U2' single. SST agrees to stop all production related to the single and to recall all existing copies (estimated at 13,000) and forward those to Island Records. SST also agrees to immediately pay Island/Warner-Chappell $29,292.25 in damages, and additional future payments of approximately $15,000. The settlement also transfers copyright ownership of the single from SST Records to Island.

October 16

Larry and Joe O'Herlihy attend Ireland's European Championship qualifier football match in Poznan, Poland.

October 21/22

U2 release 'The Fly' as the first single from their upcoming studio album, *Achtung Baby*. Bono describes the song as "the sound of four men chopping down *The Joshua Tree*". The single includes 'Alex Descends Into Hell For A Bottle of Milk / Korova 1' and 'The Lounge Fly Mix' as B-sides.

U2 announce that the single will only be sold for three weeks. Critics call that an "underhanded tactic" that will virtually guarantee strong sales. A U2 spokesman denies the charge, saying, "They only did it

because they want to release two singles and their new album before Christmas." Sure enough, the song debuts at number one in the UK, ending the 16-week reign of 'Everything I Do' by Bryan Adams. The song doesn't fare as well on the *Billboard* singles chart, peaking at number 61.

October 28

Paul McGuinness is in San Francisco to attend the funeral of legendary rock promoter Bill Graham who died in a helecotpter crash three days earlier.

November

U2 shoot a music video for 'Until The End Of The World' in Dublin with Richie Smith directing.

U2 and R.E.M. share the Best Act in the World honour at the Q Awards in London. (This is possibly a December event.)

November 6

Although 'The Fly' is still fresh on the singles charts, U2 releases 'Mysterious Ways' to radio stations.

November 13

After a couple months of meetings, U2 makes some decisions today about the upcoming tour: It will be called the Zoo TV Tour, and they'll use both of Willie Williams' ideas

Bono explains U2's new direction, November 18/19

"We've always had this idea that what was special about U2 was the spirit, that you could tear away at the flesh of the group but the spirit would remain intact. With *Achtung Baby*, we wanted to see just how far we could go in defacing the idea of U2 that had grown around us."

that were discussed in the summer – TVs placed all over the stage, and Trabants as part of the lighting system.

November 18/19

U2 release *Achtung Baby* worldwide. The album cover features a colorful collage of 16 small photos, a vivid change from the black and white imagery that distinguished *The Joshua Tree* and *Rattle And Hum* albums. The inner sleeve includes a small photo of a naked Adam Clayton, prompting many stores in North America to threaten not selling the album because of the full-frontal nudity. Island Records quickly covers Adam, adding a black 'X' or green shamrock over the picture on the CD and cassette version of *Achtung Baby*. The small amount of vinyl that is printed in North America retains the original, uncensored photo.

Achtung Baby is a dramatic shift from all of the band's previous work, fulfilling Bono's promise from late 1989 that U2 would "dream it all up again". The album begins with the industrial guitar sounds of 'Zoo Station', which also features heavy treatmeants on Bono's vocals. The lyrics are some of the most personal and introspective Bono's ever written, dealing mostly with love and relationships. It is, in short, U2 as we've never heard them before; a complete departure in sound and style from almost everything they've done to date.

Despite the change in musical direction, the album is an instant success. It debuts at number one in the US and number two in the UK (behind Michael Jackson's *Dangerous*). The album spends nearly 30 weeks on the *Billboard* Top 20 albums chart; in the UK, it's immediately certified Platinum (300,000+ sold). Critics respond to the album with universal praise. Writing in *Hot Press*, Niall Stokes says, "*Achtung Baby* plunges into the rich complexity of adult experience, the spiritual, the cerebral and the sensual all clashing in a cauldron of ambition, insecurity and desire. Ostensibly decadent, sensual and dark, it is a record of, and for, these times." In *Time* magazine, Jay Cocks writes, "The album is full of major-league guitar crunching and mysterious, spacy chords. Evanescent melodies float seamlessly between songs of love, temptation, loose political parable and tight personal confession. There's a lot indeed to be cheered on *Achtung Baby*. And celebrated. It's a monster."

Achtung Baby is an album of firsts for U2. It's their first album since Island Records was sold to Polygram. From a marketing perspective, being with Polygram is easier because of the company's size and international reach. It's also the first U2 album the band allows to be sold in South Africa, which happens only after a UN clarification on its cultural boycott in the country. U2 agrees to give proceeds from South African sales of *Achtung Baby* and all its albums to anti-apartheid musicians groups.

With *Achtung Baby*, U2 also makes a quiet decision to fight the US retail industry's preference for releasing CDs inside a cardboard "long box". Retailers like the long box because it's more difficult to shoplift, but the music industry and others consider the packaging environmentally wasteful. The *Achtung Baby* CD is released in the long box and standard jewel case formats, but retailers are given substantial discounts on their orders of the jewel case version. Tracks: 'Zoo Station', 'Even Better Than The Real Thing', 'One', 'Until The End Of The World', 'Who's Gonna Ride Your Wild Horses', 'So Cruel', 'The Fly', 'Mysterious Ways', 'Tryin' to Throw Your Arms Around The World', 'Ultraviolet (Light My Way)', 'Acrobat', 'Love Is Blindness'.

November 24/25

U2 releases 'Mysterious Ways' as the second single from *Achtung Baby*, with varying formats also including one or more of seven different remixes of the song. The single climbs to number one on the *Radio And Records* AOR chart and holds the spot for seven weeks. Commercially, it reaches number nine on *Billboard*'s chart and number 13 in the UK.

Adam explains the influence of Archaos, December 10

"We've seen Archaos a few times, the French circus, and we realized that, you know, concerts have kind of become very boring, because people come to them and there's a stage at one end and they know what's gonna happen. And we said well, we wanna surprise people, we want to give them something to think about."

December

Issue 15 of *Propaganda* magazine is published around this time.

U2 rehearse for the Zoo TV Tour at The Factory in Dublin.

A different version of 'Until The End Of The World' appears on the soundtrack to the film of the same name, U2's first collaboration with director Wim Wenders.

December 1

Achtung Baby is certified Multi-Platinum by the BPI, with UK sales surpassing the 600,000 mark.

Below: Island Record's boss Chris Blackwell and Bono.

December 10

Adam and Edge join U2's stage designer Willie Williams in London to watch a performance by Archaos, an avant-garde French circus that features acts that juggle unusual artefacts like chainsaws instead of animals that perform tricks. Williams suggests that the band invite Archaos to become involved in the outdoor version of Zoo TV next year, and the madness of the circus makes an impression on the band.

Welcome to Zoo TV, y'all! With *Achtung Baby* selling millions of copies worldwide, U2 are once again on top of the music world. The Zoo TV Tour opens in North America with a string of one-night stands that don't come close to meeting the demand to see U2 live. Ticket sales are, pardon the expression, a zoo – the phone-only sales format brings telecommunications systems to their knees.

Where past tours were about convictions and honesty, Zoo TV deals in media manipulation and insincerity. Style kicks substance's arse, or so it seems. Despite the glitter and glamour that surrounds them, U2 still finds time to storm the coast of England for Greenpeace and insert itself into the US elections. Old habits die hard.

The tour consumes U2's year, but they still find time to make a couple real world investments this year: The band buys Dublin's Clarence Hotel, while Bono and Edge buy property on the coast of Eze-Sur-Mer in the south of France. There are two houses on the property and they agree to share the space. Bono also finds time to co-write 'Miserere' with Italian rock star Zucchero.

January 3
Bono calls BP Fallon and invites him to write the Zoo TV Tour Program. Fallon accepts.

January 13
In Dublin, Willie Williams and others who will be working on the video elements for Zoo TV do a shoot with Bono as 'The Fly'. Williams and his crew will stay in Dublin working on other video pieces, including a rapid-fire text barrage to be used during 'The Fly' and burning crosses for 'Bullet The Blue Sky'.

January 14
Writer Bill Flanagan arrives to watch U2 rehearse at The Factory in Dublin. The band is struggling to replicate all the sounds of *Achtung Baby* in a live setting. "We can do it if Edge plays something different with every one of his appendages," Bono cracks. Edge tells Flanagan that the band has considered bringing along an extra musician to help. "I can't say I have any major reservations against it, other than an almost sentimental attachment to the concept of the four-piece."

After rehearsals, Bono, Edge, and Adam help Flanagan celebrate his birthday at Kitty O'Shea's pub. After the pub closes, Bono finds a guitar and plays 'Slow Dancing' for Flanagan.

Rolling Stones' guitarist Ron Wood visits U2 around this time while they rehearse.

January 15
Edge catches an early morning flight to New York, where he

Left: U2 set to storm Sellafield, June 20. Above: Zoo TV rehearsals, Hershey, Pennsylvania, August.

inducts the Sixties British R&B band The Yardbirds into the Rock and Roll Hall of Fame. He writes his speech during the flight. Adam is supposed to be in New York, too, but has trouble clearing immigration because of his marijuana arrest in 1989.

At the end of the ceremony, Edge joins in the traditional jam session, performing with Neil Young, Johnny Cash, Keith Richards, Jimmy Page and others. Afterward, he heads back to Dublin to rejoin the band's tour rehearsals.

January 16
BP Fallon is in Dublin showing the band some early work for the Zoo TV Tour Program. He records a series of interviews, asking each band member the same set of questions. The Q&A will be included in the tour program. Bono asks BP to come on the road with them to spin records and warm up the crowd in between the opening band and U2's set. Fallon's official title will be "Guru, Viber, and DJ".

January 21
Achtung Baby is certified Multi-

Bono explains the decision to put Anton Corbijn's 'One' video on the shelf temporarily, February

"When we put the film together, it looked extraordinary. But there was one problem: We had dedicated the single to David Wojnarowicz, who died of AIDS – a great New York painter. It had become an anthem for people in the United States and elsewhere who were suffering from AIDS, and here we were with a load of Irish boys in drag. It did seem a little insensitive, stereotyping AIDS sufferers as gay, which is also dangerous."

Platinum, with US sales of more than two million in barely two months.

February
U2 returns to Berlin where Anton Corbijn directs a video for 'One'. The video features Bono's dad, Bob, in a starring role, along with the members of U2 dressed in drag and several Trabants driving around the streets of Berlin. Performance sequences are shot at Hansa Studios, while other scenes are shot in a former brothel.

Corbijn's video is held back for several months, and is only distributed to music video outlets after the song has run its course as a single.

While in Berlin, U2 does an interview with writer Sean O'Hagan. The interview continues in the middle of the month while the band is in London, with Bono undressing during the interview at Nikita's restaurant. "I did it," Bono tells O'Hagan later, "to try and snip in the bud any possibility of another serious, in-depth U2 inquisition."

February 10
U2 are at work in Dublin's STS Studios on 'Salomé', an unreleased song that will later appear as a B-side on the 'Even Better Than The Real Thing' single.

February 13
U2 spend a few days in London shooting a video for 'Even Better Than The Real Thing' with director Kevin Godley. The band performs the song inside the window of *Zoo*, a clothing store on Carnaby Street, while a crowd of fans watch through the glass. Also performing in the clothes shop is a lookalike U2 band, The Dopplegangers. When the final video is edited together, it features some shots of the real U2 and some of The Dopplegangers. Two days later, the shoot moves inside to Pinewood Studios, where many James Bond movies were filmed.

After today's shoot, the band does an interview with Mark Goodier at BBC Radio in the evening. Several clips from the interview will appear on the upcoming *Achtung Baby* home video.

February 15
Tickets go on sale for some of the upcoming Zoo TV concerts in North America. The opening show at the 7,000-seat Arena in Lakeland, Florida, sells out in only four minutes. Tickets for the March 1 show in Miami sell out in 12 minutes.

February 18
Adam leaves Dublin a day earlier than everyone else. He wants to visit AIDS activist and artist David Wojnarowicz in New York City.

February 19
The rest of U2 depart Dublin for the US, where they'll start the Zoo TV tour in 10 days. Dublin media are at the airport as the band leaves, and press the band about rumours they almost split up while recording *Achtung Baby*. "We split up every week," Bono says. "It's just four guys really into what they are doing. As a result, there are differences. Every album, including *Achtung Baby*, has been a difficult one to get together."

February 21
Tickets go on sale for U2's upcoming concert at the Providence Civic Center. Problems come up at the arena's box office, where an extra 115 tickets are sold to unauthorised buyers – people without wristbands. Three days later, box office manager Joe Joel is suspended for a month without pay.

February 23
Zoo TV ticket sales continue today. To counter ticket scalpers, U2 demand that tickets be sold only via telephone and limit sales to two per person. In the first hour that lines are open for next month's Boston concert, ticket buyers jam the phone system with close to a half-million calls. The show eventually sells out – several hours and a couple of million phone calls later. A spokesperson for New England Telephone tells the *Boston Globe*: "It was complete gridlock. I don't know how else to describe it. They bombed us right out of the water. We expected a lot of calls, but this was unbelievable."

February 24
U2 rehearse at Lakeland Civic Center in Florida.

February 25
About 150 fans waiting in the rain outside the Lakeland Civic Center are invited inside to hear tonight's rehearsal. Bono leaves early, concerned that he may be losing his voice. The band continues without him.

February 26
In the morning, U2 shoots new video footage with director Mark Pellington for his 'One' music video. In the end, the material is left

Gone are the austere, almost minimalist productions of U2's tours in the 1980s. During 'The Fly', words and slogans flash on the vidiwalls and TV screens in rapid-fire succession, many too fast to be read, but the effect is real: Zoo TV is sensory overload.

Bono opens the show in full leather and dons "Fly" shades, a pair of oversized black sunglasses that will become a symbol of Zoo TV. He play-acts at living up and loving the rock-and-roll lifestyle, preening for the media photographers assembled in front of the stage while the phrase "Photo Opportunity" appears on the video screens. Bono is all swagger and style, not the earnest lead-singer-cum-preacher he was before. For the encore, he becomes the Mirrorball Man, dressed head-to-toe in a silver suit. "He believes in ratings," Bono says to describe the character, "that's really all he believes in and…he'll say anything that anybody wants to hear. That's kinda like religion is getting these days."

U2 rip through eight songs from the *Achtung Baby* album to start the show, yet another clear sign that this is not the U2 fans came to know and love in the 1980s. "We had to get through to the MTV generation," Adam says later. "From here on in, U2 is an audio-visual idea."

Willie Williams: "This was the only place to be"
"My goal was to create a giant video installation that was part of the physical staging – to use cameras as props, use television images, static interference, all the mad stuff you can imagine…. It was Bono who came back with the final piece of the puzzle. He said we should put out a press release saying that U2 were taking a TV station on tour. We should not only bring live satellite images into the stage screens but also send out live broadcasts

out, and Pellington's video consists mostly of footage of buffalo in motion and flowers. MTV will air the video for a while, but believing that it's too "arty", they refuse to put it in heavy rotation. U2 will have to shoot yet another video if they want MTV's support.

In the afternoon, U2 tape a live performance of 'One' for airing on BBC's *Top Of The Pops* programme tomorrow. It's a difficult performance, because the BBC has given U2 a 4:40 hole in the show to fill – not a second more or less. The band performs, Dreamchaser edits, and the clip is sent by satellite to the BBC.

Tonight's rehearsals include work on a routine that Bono calls "Dead Cowboy". It involves him being lifted up by a hoist above the stage at the end of 'Running To Stand Still'. The image doesn't work and the idea is quickly dropped. Also dropped is a plan for Bono to call a phone sex hotline during the show and let the audience listen in to the call. The problem? It would take too long to provide a credit card number after the call is picked up, and no one wants their credit card account being broadcasted to an arena full of people. For the second straight night, Bono leaves rehearsals early to rest his voice.

The band continues without him, and Edge handles lead vocals.

February 27
Tonight's rehearsal is U2's first full run-through of the planned Zoo TV set. Yesterday's rehearsal performance of 'One' is shown on *Top Of The Pops*.

February 28
Photographer Annie Leibowitz arrives to start three days of shooting the band.

Before tonight's final dress rehearsal, a young Florida woman, Christina Petro, introduces herself to tour production manager Jake Kennedy. She's a belly dancer, and Kennedy asks her to come to the rehearsal to surprise Bono during 'Mysterious Ways'. Her appearance is a hit.

February 29
Lakeland Arena, Lakeland, with the Pixies. U2 opens up the Zoo TV tour with an indoor show at the 7,000-seat Lakeland Arena near Miami. Like the album it promotes, the Zoo TV tour is a dramatic shift for U2: the band play in front of dozens of TV screens which reflect their own images, pre-recorded video images, and even live satellite transmissions during the concert.

from every show – to individual homes, to space stations, TV channels, you name it. One thing I have noticed about good ideas is that they get bigger by themselves. Once Zoo TV was up and running the ideas just kept coming – everybody had ideas and for once we found ourselves able to put them into practice. More and more video sequences were made, the legendary 'Video Confessional' appeared, the on-stage telephone call became a daily feature, the stage got bigger & bigger and so did the venues.

"Frankly we were giddy with the success and excitement of it all and in the most glorious way the whole thing spiraled out of control. The tour riggers took charge of the party calendar and would mount incredible spectacles of their own; there were enough crew to spawn at least five 11-a-side football teams; the band decided they were having such a good time that they'd record another album right there and then; and we did daily live link-ups to the war in Sarajevo. The tour was extended to nearly two years duration and everyone but everyone in the music industry knew that this was the only place to be."

Media reaction to the show is overwhelmingly positive, and many fans are quick to embrace U2's new image and direction. But Zoo TV leaves other fans less certain at first, wondering what happened to the band they've followed for years.

March

U2 release 'One' as the third single from *Achtung Baby*, with additional tracks 'Lady With The Spinning

Above: U2 shooting the video for 'One' in Times Square, New York, March 11.

Head (UV1)', 'Satellite Of Love', and 'Night And Day (Steel String Remix)' included on its varying formats. The single is a big hit all over the world. It reaches number seven in the UK and number 10 in the US. The front cover is a David Wojnarowicz photo showing buffalo being herded by Indians off a high cliff to their death. In the liner notes, U2 explain that Wojnarowicz "identifies himself and ourselves with the buffalo, pushed into the unknown by forces we cannot control or even understand". U2 donates its royalties from the single to AIDS research.

March 1

Miami Arena, Miami, with the Pixies. Bono calls Christina Petro – the belly dancer from rehearsals – today and invites her to dance during tonight's show. She accepts, and becomes a regular on the tour a couple of weeks later when Zoo TV reaches Boston.

The Joshua Tree is certified Multi-Platinum by the BPI, with UK sales surpassing the 1.8 million mark. *October* is certified Platinum,

and *War* is certified Double Platinum.

March 3

Veterans Memorial Coliseum, Charlotte, with The Pixies.

Achtung Baby is certified Multi-Platinum, with US sales of more than three million.

March 4

It's an off day in Atlanta and Edge spends the day out on the town. He shops with BP Fallon at a local landmark shop called Junkman's Daughter. Afterward, they walk around the (Jimmy) Carter Center where Edge chats with a small group of U2 fans. Finally, they catch blues guitarist Jimmy Rogers at a local club.

March 5

The Omni, Atlanta, with The Pixies. After the show, Bono does an interview backstage with CNN news anchor Bobbie Battista. In their review of the show, the *Atlanta Journal-Constitution* claims that the barrage of words shown during 'The Fly' includes the phrase "Bomb Japan Now". As other outlets pick up the story, U2 is forced to issue a statement: "At no time do the words 'Bomb Japan Now' appear together... U2 have no wish to offend the people of Japan, where they have many fans."

Paul McGuinness calls Phil Joanou today and asks him to fly to Atlanta right away to talk about shooting a new video for 'One'. He arrives in time to see the show, then everyone heads for a local bar to talk about the video. The setting provides Joanou with his idea: He'll shoot Bono and U2 in a bar.

Rolling Stone writers award U2 with *Comeback of the Year* in the magazine's 1992 Music Awards. Bono later tells the magazine he found the "Comeback" award funny. An upset Larry, however, reportedly hangs the clipping in his house for motivation. (Voting for the awards took place before *Achtung Baby*'s release, so U2 doesn't appear in the readers' poll.)

Edge also shares his favourite music of 1992 with the magazine:
Weld, Neil Young
Nevermind, Nirvana
Road To Freedom, The Young Disciples
Stress, Isekt
Diamonds And Pearls, Prince
Blue Lines, Massive Attack
Trompe le Monde, Pixies
The Evolution Of Gospel, Sounds of Blackness
Sharon Shannon, Sharon Shannon
Out Of Time, R.E.M.

March 7
Hampton Coliseum, Hampton, with the Pixies.

March 9
Nassau Coliseum, Uniondale, with the Pixies.

March 10
The Spectrum, Philadelphia, with the Pixies. U2 heads to New York immediately after the gig to shoot a new video for 'One'.

March 11
It's just after midnight when U2 shoots a new video for 'One' with director Phil Joanou. The band walks around Times Square in the cold and rain, before heading inside

a nightclub called Nell's, which has been closed for the video shoot. Bono lip-synchs for a few hours while sitting at a table in the bar.

March 12
Civic Center, Hartford, with the Pixies.

March 13
The Centrum, Worcester, with the Pixies. U2 is back at The Centrum, the first arena the band ever headlined in the US (in 1983). Before tonight's show, they receive a plaque in memory of the occasion.

For Adam's 32nd birthday, U2 bring a "Bunnygram" on-stage – a woman dressed scantily, like a Playboy Bunny, who delivers a bouquet of balloons to Adam and places a feather boa around his neck. It's an election year in the US, and Bono mentions it while introducing 'I Still Haven't Found What I'm Looking For': "Who you vote President of the United States is everybody's business. I hope you find what you're looking for."

March 14
On an off day in Boston, the band and Paul McGuinness meet with Phil Joanou in Adam's hotel room to watch an early edit of Joanou's 'One' music video. Larry suggests that the video is "too male-female", and doesn't represent the song's appeal to the gay community.

March 15
Civic Center, Providence, with the Pixies.

March 16
While in Boston, Edge sneaks off for a visit to the Boston Public Library. Later tonight, the band and some crew gather in Bono's suite at the Four Seasons Hotel to watch the Oscar Awards. BP Fallon is there, and plays a new song he likes for the band: 'Television, The Drug Of The Nation' by the Disposable Heroes of Hiphoprisy. The song will later become the theme song of Zoo TV.

March 17
Boston Garden, Boston, with the Pixies. Before the show, Larry and Edge visit an Irish pub in town and join a local band playing U2 songs. Boston radio station WZLX offers 25 free pairs of tickets to people wearing clothing or costumes promoting their radio station. Several thousand hopefuls show up outside the arena, bringing downtown traffic to standstill. Manager Paul McGuinness has trouble convincing local police he needs to get through, but eventually succeeds. In addition to Boston band the Pixies, U2 invites the Greater Boston Pipe Band to perform as an opening act and help set the mood on St. Patrick's Day in Boston. The show itself is loose and festive, with Larry singing made-up lyrics during 'Tryin' To Throw Your Arms Around The World' and then soloing on a cover of 'Dirty Old Town'. Neil Young and Peter Wolf are at the show.

March 18
Brenden Byrne Arena, East Rutherford, with the Pixies. Bono sings "Let's go to Vegas and get married, for a while..." at the start of 'With Or Without You'. Perhaps inspired by the idea, Phil Joanou does just that the next day with Kate Hyman, a woman he meets backstage after tonight's show. Also in attendance tonight: artist David Wojnarowicz, sex therapist Dr. Ruth Westheimer, Tatum O'Neal and John McEnroe, and Little Steven.

March 19
Bono and Ali attend a preview performance of *A Streetcar Named*

Desire in New York. Adam tours the city with Christina Petro.

March 20
Madison Square Garden, New York, with the Pixies. Celebrities including Peter Gabriel, Mike Scott, John McEnroe and Gary Oldman are at the show. Bono spends most of his time backstage after the show talking with Bruce Springsteen.

March 21
Knickerbocker Arena, Albany, with the Pixies.

March 23
The Forum, Montreal, with the Pixies.

March 24
Maple Leaf Gardens, Toronto, with the Pixies.

March 26
Richfield Coliseum, Cleveland, with the Pixies.

March 27
Palace Of Auburn Hills, Detroit, with the Pixies. Bono orders 10,000 pizzas during tonight's Zoo TV show in Detroit. The local pizza parlor eventually sends 100 to the arena and a delivery boy brings them into the arena on a trolley with the Zoo TV camera showing him on the vidiwalls. The scene quickly deteriorates into a hysterical mess of pizza box Frisbees.

March 28
Edge, BP Fallon, and Christina

Petro watch Pearl Jam play at the Cabaret Metro in Chicago tonight, and visit with the band backstage afterward. From there, the whole group goes to see R&B legend Albert King, who's playing at a local blues club.

March 29
U2 meets today with Willie Williams and Mark Fisher's design team. It's just a month into the tour, but already time to start planning the outdoor version of Zoo TV.

March 30
Target Center, Minneapolis, with the Pixies.

U2 fans trying to buy tickets for the upcoming shows at the Los Angeles Sports Arena make 54 million calls, bringing the GTE phone service to its knees. "As a result of the U2 rush," a GTE spokesperson says, "many customers experienced interruptions in their phone service. Many got no dial tone at all."

March 31
Rosemont Horizon, Chicago, with the Pixies.

April 2
Edge and BP Fallon go for a boat ride in the Louisiana swamps.

April 5
Reunion Arena, Dallas, with the Pixies.

April 6
The Summit, Houston, with the Pixies.

April 7
Frank Erwin Center, Austin, with the Pixies. Axl Rose, the lead singer of Guns N' Roses who has spoken publicly of his love for U2's song 'One', is at tonight's show and visits U2 backstage afterward.

April 10
Activity Center, Tempe, with the Pixies.

April 12-13
Sports Arena, Los Angeles, with the Pixies. Jack Nicholson, Dennis

Hopper, Robert De Niro and Julia Roberts are among the Hollywood celebrities who catch the first show show in Los Angeles. Bruce Springsteen, L.L. Cool J, Billy Idol, and Axl Rose represent the music industry.

After the second show, U2 attend a party in Hollywood where they hang out with Springsteen and Patti Scialfa, Axl Rose, and assorted Hollywood bigwigs.

April 15
Sports Arena, San Diego, with the Pixies.

April 16
Bono writes the foreword for *The King Of Twist*, a book of Christian poetry by Steve Turner that's published today.

April 17
Arco Arena, Sacramento, with the Pixies.

April 18
Oakland Coliseum Arena, Oakland, with the Pixies. Tonight's show is taped so that a segment can be used in the tribute to the late Queen singer Freddie Mercury at Wembley Stadium two days later, and 'Until The End Of The World' is shown on video screens during the tribute.

April 19
Bono attends Easter Sunday services at Glide Memorial Church in San Francisco. Later in the day, he and Edge go sightseeing north of the city.

April 20-21
Tacoma Dome, Tacoma, with the Pixies.

April 22
With the North American tour almost over, U2 and crew celebrate today with a boat ride around Vancouver Harbour.

April 23
P.N.E. Coliseum, Vancouver, with the Pixies.

April 3
U2 announces four UK dates for the upcoming leg of the Zoo TV Tour.

Fans begin lining up immediately even though tickets won't go on sale for 48 hours.

Above: U2 on the B-stage, New York, March 20.

May
Issue 16 of *Propaganda* magazine is published around this time.

May 7
Palais Omnisports De Paris Bercy, Paris, with Fatima Mansions. Zoo TV arrives in Europe, where anticipation has grown after the rave reviews U2 received in North America. Edge does an interview with MTV before the show.

May 9
Flanders Expo Hall, Gent, with Fatima Mansions.

May 11
Espace Tony Garnier, Lyon, with Fatima Mansions.

May 12
Patinoire De Malley, Lausanne, with Fatima Mansions.

May 14
Velodrome Anoeta, San Sebastian, with Fatima Mansions.

May 16-18
Palau Sant Jordi, Barcelona, with Fatima Mansions. Many of the text images shown during 'The Fly' are translated into Spanish. Translations will also be done for upcoming shows in Italy and Germany.

May 20
A crowd of 12,500 shows up in Milan, Italy, for their first Zoo TV experience, but go home unhappy because the show is postponed. One of U2's trucks broke down on the road from Barcelona two days ago. The driver, who didn't notify the band quickly enough that he was having a problem, is fired.

While in Milan, U2 do interviews with Irish journalist John Waters, who's writing a book about U2 and the band's place in Irish culture.

May 21-22
Forum Di Assago, Milan, with Fatima Mansions.

May 22/23
MTV Europe programmes a "U2 Weekend."

May 23
U2 watches Guns N' Roses play on Danube Island in Vienna and the two bands hang out together afterwards.

May 24
Donau Insel, Vienna, with Fatima Mansions. This is U2's first show in Austria, and their first open-air show since 1989. For the first time, BP Fallon plays 'Television: The Drug Of The Nation' as the last song before U2 enters the stage – a tradition that will continue for the rest of the tour. Axl Rose of Guns N' Roses joins the band on stage to duet with Bono on 'Knocking On Heaven's Door'.

May 25
Olympiahalle, Munich, with Fatima Mansions. Before the show, Bono introduces the idea of Public Enemy as a future opening act to the rest of the band. All seem agreeable to the idea, but Edge is the hardest to convince.

May 27
Hallenstadion, Zurich, with Fatima Mansions. Bill Graham of *Hot Press* is at the show, and is mesmerized by what he sees – particularly Bono's performance: "Bono's great asset is that he's dared to make more mistakes than 50 other frontmen have had ideas and now he's reaping the harvest."

May 28
On a day off, U2 and crew take a boat ride across Lake Zurich and have dinner in the city of Stafa. On the way back after dinner, Bono undresses and dives in the lake. Paul McGuinness dives in, too, and the boat's captain frantically turns around to pick them up.

May 29
Festhalle, Frankfurt, with Fatima Mansions. The members of Kraftwerk are at the show.

May 31
Earl's Court Arena, London, with Fatima Mansions. Bono and Sinead O'Connor have a lengthy conversation in the dressing room before the show. It's the first time they've spoken since O'Connor attacked the band in Dublin papers in 1988. (She said U2 were hypocritical and patronising, that they stifled anyone who spoke negatively about the band, and that they were not really interested in helping the Irish music scene.)

At the end of 'The Fly', the standard WATCH MORE TV message is replaced on the video screens with BE AT SELLAFIELD 11 AM JUNE 20. It's the first publicity for U2's plan to protest the Sellafield 2 nuclear plant in England. Celebrities in attendance tonight include Elvis Costello,

Chrissie Hynde and author Salman Rushdie. After the show, Bono meets Rushdie for the first time. The two speak briefly about politics, particularly Nicaragua – Rushdie was in Nicaragua at the same time as Bono in 1986 researching his book, *The Jaguar Smile*, which Bono later read. It's the first seed of a friendship between Bono and Rushdie that will grow in years to come.

June 1
National Exhibition Centre, Birmingham, with Fatima Mansions.

June 4
The "breaking news" in Dublin papers is that Bono is replacing the wooden gates at his Killiney home with 12-foot high iron gates.

June 4-5
Westfalenhalle, Dortmund, with Fatima Mansions. A group of fans are let in to watch U2 soundcheck before the first show.

June 6
Bono attends the wedding of David Bowie and Iman in Florence, Italy.

June 7-8
'Even Better Than the Real Thing' is released as the fourth single from *Achtung Baby*, with its varying formats including the tracks 'Salome', 'Where Did It All Go Wrong?', 'Lady With The Spinning Head (Extended Dance Remix)', and up to six remixes of the main track as B-sides. The single reaches number 32 in the US and number 12 in the UK. U2 also release a remix version of 'Even Better Than The Real Thing', which climbs even higher, reaching number eight in the UK.

June 8
Scandinavium, Gothenburg, with Fatima Mansions.

June 10
Globen, Stockholm, with Fatima Mansions. During an interview at a Stockholm bar after the show, a young female fan begs Bono for a dance at the disco next door. Bono offers several excuses, but goes along when she refuses to take "no" for an answer.

June 11
Globen, Stockholm, with Fatima Mansions. In the afternoon, manager Paul McGuinness does a lengthy interview with Pimm Jal, a fan who publishes the *U2 Collectormania* magazine. The interview goes so well that McGuinness suggests Pimm also interview the band, and promises to ask them.

Tonight's show in Stockholm is one of the most memorable nights of the tour. Bjorn Ulvaeus and Benny Andersson of ABBA – who haven't been on stage together in many years – join U2 for a performance of their 1977 hit 'Dancing Queen'. The collaboration is a smash with ABBA's hometown fans.

The show is beamed live to the home of John Harris of Nottinghamshire, England, who won an MTV Europe contest by sending in dozens of postcards with the answers to a five-question U2 quiz. U2 and MTV spend the day installing a large video screen and several smaller TVs in Harris' living room. Special t-shirts and "stage" passes are printed ("All Access – John's Living Room"). One of the Trabants U2 has used is brought to John's house, though he's not allowed to keep it.

John and his friends are shown throughout the show on the Zoo TV screens in Stockholm. Bono chats with John and his girlfriend, Dawn Evans, on several occasions, and invites them both to see U2 play in the US later in the year. After the show, MTV's Ray Cokes presents John with an autographed photo from the band, and an invitation to meet the band when the tour visits Sheffield.

June 13
Ostseehalle, Kiel, with Fatima Mansions.

June 14
On a night off in Hamburg, Bono, Edge, and others end up in a club where the entertainment is an adult

Right: Landing at Sellafield, June 20.

version of *Phantom Of The Opera*. Larry, meanwhile, is at a pool hall next door.

June 15
Sport Paleis Ahoy, Rotterdam, with Fatima Mansions. Before tonight's show, Adam is interviewed by Pimm Jal of *U2 Collectormania* magazine, an interview that Paul McGuinness had suggested only four days earlier.

June 17
Indoor Sports Arena, Sheffield, with Fatima Mansions. U2 meets during the day with lawyers and other authorities to talk about the band's plans to visit the Sellafield nuclear plant in a couple days. U2 fans John Harris and Dawn Evans – who had last week's Stockholm concert beamed into their living room – meet U2 backstage before tonight's show. Phil Joanou and Simon Le Bono are also in attendance.

June 18
Scottish Exhibition Centre, Glasgow, with Fatima Mansions.

June 19
G-Mex Center, Manchester. U2 headline the Stop Sellafield show, with Big Audio Dynamite II, Public Enemy, and Kraftwerk also on the bill. The show is designed to protest the plan to operate a second nuclear facility, which has already been built on the northwest coast of England. Lou Reed joins Bono on stage to sing 'Satellite Of Love'. The flashing messages seen during 'The Fly' are rewritten to fit the occasion, and include messages such as LEUKEMIA … CHILD … PLUTONIUM … STOP SELLAFIELD NOW. Greenpeace later issues a 40-minute video featuring highlights from the concert, which includes U2's performances of 'The Fly' and 'Even Better Than The Real Thing', along with interview comments from Bono and Edge. In attendance is future Oasis guitarist Noel Gallagher.

Immediately after the concert, U2 depart for a small port and boards the Greenpeace ship *Solo*,

Larry talks about working for Greenpeace in the middle of Zoo TV, June 20

"After we did Amnesty International and Live Aid and a lot of benefit concerts, Bono and I sat down and talked about how we were going to approach the future. We came to the conclusion that maybe the best thing to do was leave Amnesty – continue to support them, obviously, but doing more concerts may be a mistake for now – and let's do something for Greenpeace. We've donated to them for a long time, we've done gigs with them, but we've never actually been involved in an action. When this came up, it was an opportunity."

which is bound for the Sellafield nuclear plant. The decision to approach the plant by water is triggered by legal requirements: a High Court has recently approved British Nuclear Fuels' (BNFL) request to block any demonstration from happening on their property. The ruling prompts Greenpeace and U2 to state publicly that there will be no protest at all. But behind the scenes, they've decided to approach by water and go no further ashore than the high water mark of the Irish Sea – the line where BNFL property legally begins.

In the days leading up to tonight's show and the on-site protest, BNFL invites U2 to visit Sellafield to "get our side of the story". A U2 spokesperson rejects the idea: "They are inviting [U2] to go on a perfectly constructed public relations tour of the plant and [U2] are not going to do it."

June 20

U2 takes part in a Greenpeace protest at the Sellafield nuclear plant. About 60 demonstrators approach in rubber dinghies and go onshore at 7:00 a.m., creating a three-kilometer long line of 700 placards that says, "React – Stop Sellafield." Wearing white radiation suits (and Fly Shades, in Bono's case), U2 brings drums of Irish dirt said to be contaminated by the power plant and deposits them back on Sellafield grounds. Standing on the beach, the band semaphores HELP (just as The Beatles had done on their album of the same name). The demonstration lasts about three hours.

Despite U2's recent denials that anything is planned today, the press is quietly notified of what's going to take place and the event becomes a media circus. U2 conducts a press conference before leaving the beach, speaking out against both BNFL's plans for Sellafield 2 and the Irish government's inaction against BNFL. As they leave by bus, Bono sees a young boy trying to swipe Bono's irradiated boots from a Greenpeace bag. They stop the bus, but the boy doesn't give back the boots until he gets autographs from the whole band.

Photos and articles about the demonstration are carried worldwide. Nonetheless, Sellafield 2 – the Thermal Oxide Reprocessing Plant (THORP) – begins operating in March, 1994.

With the second leg of Zoo TV over, U2 returns to Dublin.

June 25

U2's publicity team arranges for Edge to do a phone interview from Dublin today with *Mondo 2000* magazine. Without Edge's knowledge, the magazine invites two members of Negativland to join the interview. Early on, the interviewers question Edge about U2's use of copyrighted TV programs during Zoo TV concerts, putting him on the defensive about U2 sampling the work of others after Island sued Negativland less than a year ago. It's a difficult interview, but Edge even calls them back after the phone disconnects. By the end of the interview, the Negativland members praise Edge for his "amazing good humor" about the interview, and even ask for a loan to help them put out more records.

June 29

Bono tucks himself away in the STS Studios for the night to record his solo version of 'Can't Help Falling In Love' for the upcoming *Honeymoon In Vegas* movie soundtrack.

June 30

Bono, Gavin and BP Fallon have breakfast at a small café in Dublin before the band flies to New York.

Mid-July

U2's tour crew arrives in Hershey, Pennsylvania, to begin setting up the stage for U2's upcoming Zoo TV Outside Broadcast rehearsals. On seeing the massive stage and lighting rig that Willie Williams has created, Joe O'Herlihy notes: "You'd be afraid to get a hard-on in this place in case Willie'd put a light on it!"

July 23

A windstorm in central Pennsylvania destroys the largest of the video screens being installed at Hershey Stadium.

August

'Who's Gonna Ride Your Wild Horses' is released with varying formats including the tracks 'Paint It Black', 'Fortunate Son', 'Who's Gonna Ride Your Wild Horses (The Temple Bar Remix)', 'Salome (Zooromancer Remix)', and 'Can't Help Falling In Love (Triple Peaks Remix)'.

August 1

U2 arrive in Harrisburg, Pennsylvania, to begin a week of rehearsals in nearby Hershey for the Zoo TV Outside Broadcast tour.

August 2

U2 do their first rehearsal at Hersheypark Stadium. Afterwards, Bono stops briefly to meet fans waiting for the band outside the Hilton and Towers Hotel.

August 3

On the way to tonight's rehearsal, U2 greet fans outside their hotel wanting autographs.

August 4

With fans listening to tonight's rehearsal outside Hersheypark Stadium, Bono apologizes from the stage for not being able to let them in, and says "we'll see what we can do by the end of the week".

August 5

U2 confirm rumours that they'll play a dress rehearsal show in Hershey in two days. Tickets go on sale immediately at $15 each, and the band announce it will identify local charities to receive proceeds from the surprise show. On the way to the stadium, Bono takes the band on a detour for lunch through the drive-thru of a McDonald's restaurant. During a break in tonight's rehearsal, Bono and Adam do a quick interview with the local newspaper.

August 7

Hershey Park Stadium, Hershey, with WNOC. U2 wrap up a week of rehearsal in Hershey with a public

Edge talks to Negativland, June 25

After learning he was speaking to members of Negativland, Edge explains U2's side of the incident.

"I can't remember the exact sequence of events, but as it was presented to us, you know, 'Here's the record, here's the album sleeve, Island are already on the case here, and they've objected because they feel it's, because of the artwork, this is at a time when a lot of people are expecting a new U2 record,' and they felt that, from their own point of view, in a pure business sense, nothing about art, I just think they felt there was a chance that people would pick up the record in a record shop and think, 'Oh, this is the new U2 album.'"

'run-through' show. Since it's Edge's birthday tomorrow, Bono brings out a cake during the show. Morleigh Steinberg makes her debut as the belly dancer during 'Mysterious Ways'. Proceeds from the show are donated to five local charities. While many in the small city are glad to have had U2 in town, some are not. Police say they received about 200 calls complaining about the loud noise and late rehearsals; one man goes a step beyond, filing a noise complaint against Hershey

Entertainment and Resort Company.

August 11
A new idea is born one day before the outdoor tour is to begin: the video confessional. The band wants to put a photo booth inside the stadium and videotape fans saying whatever they want on camera before the show begins. U2's video crew will edit the tapes while U2 is on stage, and the best fan clips will be shown during intermission.

The Honeymoon In Vegas soundtrack album is released. Bono's solo version of 'Can't Help Falling In Love' is the last track.

August 12-13
Giants Stadium, East Rutherford, with Primus, Disposable Heroes Of Hiphoprosy. U2 launch the Outside Broadcast version of Zoo TV. At the first show, Lou Reed joins the band on stage for a live version of 'Satellite Of Love'. After the show, Adam meets supermodel Naomi Campbell for the first time but alhough he declares Campbell is the object of his desires, the pair don't hit it off. (In the Zoo TV tour book, Adam gave her name when asked, "What would you like to have that you don't?") Bono, meanwhile, stays up until 4 a.m. for an interview with Lisa Robinson in the bar at the Rihga Royal Hotel in New York.

Before the second show, Lou Reed is taped singing along in duet-style to 'Satellite Of Love', and this taped performance will be used throughout the tour as a virtual

Below: Flying Trabants on the Zoo TV tour.

duet between Reed and Bono.

August 15-16
Robert F. Kennedy Stadium, Washington, DC, with Primus, Disposable Heroes Of Hiphoprosy. While channel surfing early in the first show, Bono comes upon a station showing old concert footage of Elvis on the eve of the 15th anniversary of Presley's death. At the second show, Bono sings 'Can't Help Falling In Love' for the first time on the US tour.

August 17
Bono, Adam and Edge meet with Ned O'Hanlon and Maurice Linnane in Edge's hotel room to watch an early cut of the *Achtung Baby: The Videos, The Cameos, And A Whole Lot Of Interference* home video.

August 18
Saratoga Raceway, Saratoga Springs, with Primus, Disposable Heroes Of Hiphoprosy.

August 20-22-23
Foxboro Stadium, Foxboro, with Primus, Disposable Heroes Of Hiphoprosy. During the day of the second show, U2 go for a swim at nearby Hyannisport. After the third show, Edge leaves his hotel room at about 4 a.m. to visit with a small group of fans waiting outside the Four Seasons Hotel. He brings a tray of food from U2's hospitality suite.

August 25
Three Rivers Stadium, Pittsburgh, with Primus, Disposable Heroes Of Hiphoprosy.

August 26
On an off day in Montreal, Bono and Larry help TV producer Philip King, who's shooting *Rocky World*, a documentary about Daniel Lanois. They head to La Ronde amusement park and board the giant "Le Monstre" roller coaster and get stuck in the air during the ride. Later, the production moves to a local pool hall.

August 27
Olympic Stadium, Montreal, with

Primus, Disposable Heroes Of Hiphoprosy. Daniel Lanois joins U2 on stage to sing an acoustic version of 'I Still Haven't Found What I'm Looking For'. His appearance is filmed for the *Rocky World* documentary.

U2 are scheduled to fly to New York immediately after tonight's show, but the primary Zoo plane is grounded for repairs and a replacement doesn't have the necessary authorisation to take off. Larry, Adam and Paul are stuck on the runway while the situation is sorted out. Bono, Edge, and Lanois kill some time in a nightclub before leaving for New York on a small jet at about 4 a.m. (August 28).

August 28
U2 visit the studios of New York radio station WXRK tonight for an appearance on the national call-in radio show, *Rockline*. U2 take an expected call from US Presidential candidate Bill Clinton, who's introduced as "Bill from Little Rock". U2 and Clinton hit it off quite well. "I want to say, as a middle-aged man, I appreciate the fact that you made *The Joshua Tree* and that record, 'Angel Of Harlem' in Sun Studios," Clinton says. "You made me feel like I had a place in rock music even at 46." Says Bono: "Well, Bill, if we got you into it we must have got something wrong."

August 29-30
Yankee Stadium, New York, with Primus, Disposable Heroes Of Hiphoprosy. U2 becomes only the second rock artist to play in "The House That Ruth Built." (Billy Joel was the first.) After the first show, they meet legendary producer Phil Spector, who later says Bono is the only musician he's met who compares to John Lennon. Peter Gabriel and Lenny Kravitz are also on the celebrity guest list. U2 fans John Harris and Dawn Evans are flown in by U2 for the first show, fulfilling the promise Bono made in Stockholm in June.

September 2-3
Veteran's Stadium, Philadelphia, with Primus, Disposable Heroes Of Hiphoprosy.

September 5-6
Canadian National Exhibition Stadium, Toronto, with Primus, Disposable Heroes Of Hiphoprosy.

September 8
Rolling Stone guitarist Ron Wood releases a solo album, *Slide On This*, which includes Edge playing guitar on several tracks.

Bono and Edge take Willie Williams out for dinner to celebrate Willie's birthday.

September 9
Pontiac Silverdome, Detroit, with Primus, Disposable Heroes Of Hiphoprosy. U2 connects via satellite to Los Angeles where MTV's Video Music Awards are taking place. Dana Carvey, dressed as "Garth" of *Wayne's World* hosts the show and introduces U2 when their satellite transmission is picked up. After a brief conversation, Bono invites "Garth" to play drums during 'Even Better Than The Real Thing'. Later, that song wins an MTV award for Best Group Video, and MTV goes live to U2's post-show dressing room where the band collects its trophy, and Bono sprays champagne at the camera as they say goodbye.

September 10
Edge and Larry return from a trip to a local shooting range to find Bono in the lobby of the Ritz-Carlton Hotel outside Detroit. They get mobbed by fans on the way into the hotel, which sets Bono off on a rant. "These kind of rich girls, they've got *nothing* to do with rock and roll. This is celebrity. It's getting harder and harder to meet the people who actually *listen* to the records."

September 11
Cyclone Stadium, Ames, with Primus, Disposable Heroes Of Hiphoprosy.

September 13
Camp Randall Stadium, Madison, with Big Audio Dynamite II, Public Enemy.

September 14
U2 arrive at the Ritz Carlton Hotel in Chicago at around 3 a.m. and learn that they are staying at the

Bono recalls U2's day with candidate Bill Clinton, September 14

"We talked about everything from the troubles in Ireland to the place of the saxophone in rock and roll. He is very easy with people and has enormous curiosity for what could make the world a better place.

A new kind of politician had entered the world stage, the first of our kind, meaning someone who grew up listening to rock and roll rather than Mantovani…. It's fair to say that though we had the bigger suite in the Ritz Carlton, he had the bigger motorcade."

same hotel as Arkansas governor, and Democratic Presidential hopeful, Bill Clinton. Bono jokes that he wants someone to bring Clinton to see the band. One of U2's crew thinks it's a serious request, but the governor's security team refuses to wake him. Bono and Edge, meanwhile, spend the wee hours of the morning working on a new song for Frank Sinatra called 'Two Shots Of Happy, One Shot Of Sad'.

Clinton learns about the band's invitation later in the morning and a meeting is quickly arranged in Bono's room. The U2 crew scrambles to find Bono, who's fallen asleep in Edge's room. The band eventually arrive to greet a waiting Clinton, who gets a laugh at the "morning after" condition the band is in. They talk for more than an hour, and though it's more than a month until Election Day, Clinton invites the band to play at his inauguration.

After the governor leaves, Anton Corbijn does a photo shoot that shows Bono in his suite, dressed in a white, terry cloth bathrobe, holding a guitar and sitting at a grand piano. Later, U2 and Clinton share a police escort as they head to

Soldier Field to watch the Chicago Bears play on *Monday Night Football*. Also today, U2 makes *Forbes* magazine's annual list of the highest paid entertainers for the first time. The magazine ranks U2 in 16th place.

September 15-16-18
World Music Amphitheater, Chicago, with Big Audio Dynamite II, Public Enemy. After the second show, the mayor of a nearby town goes to court to get the sound lowered at the third show. He loses the case.

While in Chicago, U2 shoot a music video for 'Who's Gonna Ride Your Wild Horses' with Phil Joanou directing.

September 16
Achtung Baby is certified Multi-Platinum, with US sales of more than four million.

September 20
Busch Memorial Stadium, St. Louis, with Big Audio Dynamite II, Public Enemy.

September 23
Williams-Brice Stadium, Columbia, with Big Audio Dynamite II, Public Enemy. As a gesture of thanks for

handling Bono's phone calls, U2 invites the White House operators' staff to tonight's show in Columbia, South Carolina. They refuse the invitation. Two nights later in Atlanta, Bono reiterates the invitation during that night's phone call to the White House.

Larry talks about calling President Bush

"I wasn't sure if it was something we should be involved with. There were differing opinions in the band about using George Bush. I was a little concerned about that. I'm naturally cautious. I'm still unsure whether it was the right thing to do."

September 25

Georgia Dome, Atlanta, with Big Audio Dynamite II, Public Enemy. Before today's show, the band decides against playing Australia at the end of the year. They postpone the dates until 1993.

September 26

With a short break in the tour, U2 takes a break at Chris Blackwell's home in Jamaica.

October

Around this time, Rob Bakie, a U2 fan at the University of Washington in Seattle, establishes *u2-list*, the first known international Internet mailing list for U2 fans. Commonly known as "Wire", the list eventually grows to several thousand fans in the late 1990s. It becomes the most important online gathering place for U2 fans, but starts to fade away as many fans decide to create smaller lists of their own.

"Ginormous!"

Sebastian Clayton, Adam's brother and the original developer of U2.com, talks about getting inspiration from the "Wire" mailing list in the mid- and late-1990s.

"There was a ginormous U2 community online before we ever launched an official site. There was a mailing list called 'Wire' – they used to e-mail each other all the time – just a ginormous mailing list where all the fans used to keep in touch with each other. The band and I joined up to it just to see what was going on and how it worked and what happened and what people were saying. And once we saw that there were so many people involved and inspired by this mailing list we decided that it would be a good idea to put together an official site for them."

October 3

Joe Robbie Stadium, Miami, with Big Audio Dynamite II, Public Enemy.

October 7

Legion Field, Birmingham, with Big Audio Dynamite II, Public Enemy.

October 10

Tampa Stadium, Tampa, with Big Audio Dynamite II, Public Enemy.

A fan gets on stage and speaks with Bono, who tells the crowd the fan is also a songwriter. Bono asks if the crowd wants to hear one of his songs. The fan gets a guitar from Edge and introduces his own song, 'An Eye For An Eye Makes The Whole World Blind'. It's the first time a stranger is allowed to perform his own material on a U2 stage. His song lasts six minutes, and U2 leaves the stage to change and prepare for the encore.

October 11

Edge and Dennis Sheehan play tennis at Don Cesar Beach Resort in St. Petersburg, where the band is staying. Adam and BP Fallon hang out at a nightclub called The Bridge Club.

October 14

Astrodome, Houston, with Big Audio Dynamite II, Public Enemy.

October 16

Texas Stadium, Dallas, with Sugarcubes, Public Enemy.

October 18

Arrowhead Stadium, Kansas City, with Sugarcubes, Disposable Heroes Of Hiphophrosy. While in

Kansas City, author William Burroughs visits U2 at their hotel to videotape a reading of his 'Thanksgiving Prayer' poem for use on an upcoming TV special. After the show, U2 fly to Los Angeles and sets up camp there for its next series of shows.

October 21
Mile High Stadium, Denver, with Sugarcubes, Public Enemy.

October 24
Sun Devil Stadium, Tempe, with Sugarcubes, Public Enemy.

October 27
Sun Bowl, El Paso, with Sugarcubes, Public Enemy. U2 play the first stadium show in El Paso since 1972. The show is beamed via satellite to a fan named Sherry in California, who won an MTV contest.

October 30-31
Dodger Stadium, Los Angeles, with Sugarcubes, Public Enemy.

Celebrating Larry's birthday, TV vampiress Elvira appears on the video screens to lead the crowd in singing 'Happy Birthday' during the second show.

November
U2 and Point Depot owner Harry Crosbie purchase the famed Clarence Hotel in Dublin this month for a reported £2 million. The new owners say they want to renovate the building, and add a nightclub on the premises. (In the future, Adam and Larry will sell their stake in the hotel. Crosbie will also leave the hotel ownership group later, being replaced by Irish investors Paddy McKillen and Derek Quinlan.)

Also this month, U2 are named Best Act in the World Today at the Q Awards. They accept the award via a pre-recorded video they made with R.E.M., who win for Best Album.

November 3-4
B.C. Place Stadium, Vancouver, with Sugarcubes, Public Enemy. U2 watch US election results on TV before the first show. The crew cheers each time the news

announces another state has elected Bill Clinton. Before the second show, Bono, Edge, and Larry speak with Paul Du Noyer of *Q* magazine in Bono's hotel room for an upcoming feature on the band.

November 7
Oakland-Alameda County Stadium, Oakland, with Sugarcubes, Public Enemy. Before tonight's show, U2 meet with Richard Lang of Instant Video Technologies, the company U2 invested in three years ago. Lang demonstrates a new system for delivering video over the Internet. The Edge, Lang will say later, was particularly interested in the idea. "He was very excited. They all kept asking questions. They saw the possibilities, both educational and as a way to deliver music on demand. They were also interested that there wouldn't be tapes, there'd be no waste, it'd be environmentally friendly." Lang and his team tell U2 the technology to make this idea work won't be ready for five years.

During the show, Bono dedicates 'I Still Haven't Found What I'm Looking For' to legendary local concert promoter Bill Graham, who died last year. Graham promoted all of U2's show in the Bay Area since the earliest days, was a major force in the Conspiracy of Hope tour in 1986, and made it possible for U2's free show in San Francisco in 1987 to happen on just 24 hours' notice.

November 8
Bono attends church services at Glide Memorial United Methodist Church in San Francisco, where the congregation is celebrating Bill Clinton's election win.

November 9
There's trouble today when Bono, Larry, Paul and others cross the border into Tijuana, Mexico. They're drinking beer while walking around town, and a police car shows up just as Larry tries to relieve himself on the side of the road. The Mexican police find a Swiss Army Knife on Larry, making the situation worse. Paul steps in and offers the officer tickets for tomorrow's concert in San Diego

in exchange for letting everyone go free. It works.

November 10
Jack Murphy Stadium, San Diego, with Sugarcubes, Public Enemy. Tonight's show is recorded using a Greenpeace-owned, solar-powered studio that the organisation is using to record a fund raising album. U2 donates tonight's version of 'Until The End Of The World' to the *Alternative NRG* album, which is released in February, 1994.

November 12
Sam Boyd Stadium, Las Vegas, with Sugarcubes, Public Enemy.

November 14
Anaheim Stadium, Anaheim, with Sugarcubes, Public Enemy. U2 wraps up Zoo TV's North American run with a terrific show that's helped along by a loud, enthusiastic crowd. During 'Where The Streets Have No Name', the upper level of the stadium is clearly moving up and down a foot as people bounce and jump to the song. Anaheim and stadium officials will have to repair and strengthen the stadium before other concerts can be held.

With a week off before the next show, U2 stay busy in Los Angeles working on their Zoo TV Thanksgiving television show. Bono is also busy trying to finalize a deal to get his screenplay, *The Million Dollar Hotel*, made. He meets during the week with the likes of Mel Gibson, Winona Ryder, Gary Oldman, and Phil Joanou. He has lunch one day with T-Bone Burnett and Bill Flanagan at the Beverly Hills Hotel.

November 20
While the tour crew leaves for Mexico, U2 stay behind because there's still work to be done on their upcoming Zoo TV television program.

November 21
U2 finally finishes up their TV work at 4 a.m. and catch a few hours sleep before flying to Mexico City. The band sit inside the Sunset Marquis Hotel waiting to be told it's time to leave, while their driver and

car sit outside waiting for them. They nearly miss the last flight that can get them to Mexico City on time.

U2 land and heads immediately to the show, arriving while opening act B.A.D. II is already on stage.

November 21-22-24-25
Palacio De Los Deportes, Mexico City, with Big Audio Dynamite II. U2 play its first shows in Central America. As a birthday present, the band fly in longtime friend Barry Devlin from Dublin to see the end of the tour. The band and crew gather at a swanky restaurant/disco after the first show.

Disaster almost strikes on November 22 when a small fire breaks out in the back of the arena early in the show. Jerry Mele, U2's security chief, rushes to the scene and gets the situation – and the fire – under control as the show goes on. After the show, everyone returns to the same restaurant as last night and the party later moves to another bar across town.

While in Mexico City, Bono, Larry, Paul McGuinness and others visit the ancient city of Teotihuacan, possibly on their off day (November 23). The band also begins discussions about next year: The plan is to bring the outdoor show to Europe and call the tour Zooropa.

November 27
U2 return home from Mexico City.

November 28
U2's *Zoo TV* documentary is broadcast tonight in 32 countries around the world. The documentary runs an hour in the US, and 90 minutes in most other countries. To mark the programme's premiere, U2 themselves appear on the *Kenny Live* talk show on RTE. A Zoo TV-style viewing room is set up at RTE headquarters for media and friends to watch the program. Kenny introduces a surprise live performance by U2, but it's actually a performance by The Dopplegangers, the lookalike band U2 hired earlier in the year for the 'Even Better Than The Real Thing' music video.

Above: Bono as Mirrorball Man, Anaheim, November 14.

The real U2 sit with Kenny for an interview, then speak to the press after the show before hitting the Dublin party circuit to celebrate the show and their return home.

Late November
Tickets go on sale for many of U2's European stadium shows next summer. Most shows sell out quickly.

December
Bono appears on the cover of the British *Vogue* magazine with supermodel Christy Turlington. It's the first time they've met, and their friendship lasts to this day. Decked out in full Zoo TV / Fly regalia, Bono is the first male on the magazine's cover in more than 25 years. "I thought doing the cover of *Vogue* was a very funny thing to do," Bono says. "Any U2 fan would find it funny. Every big group collects celebrity-hunter, rock'n'roll part-timers, but we have an audience to whom our music means a lot, and they know we're not a regular rock band."

Also this month, Adam performs as part of an all-star band on *The Late Late Show* for a tribute to Irish singer Sharon Shannon.

Although the tour has barely ended for the year, Bono and Edge spend time this month working on new material at The Factory in Dublin.

December 9
U2 capture five awards at the *Billboard* Music Awards, including Number One Album Rock Track for 'Mysterious Ways', Number One Modern Rock Track for 'One', Number One Album Rock Artist, Number One Modern Rock Artist, and Number One Concert Tour. Bono, Adam, and Edge accept the awards via a live satellite hook-up from Docker's Pub in Dublin. It's 1:30 a.m. there (Dec. 10) and the band is drinking Guinness and in a mood to mess with host Phil Collins. After Bono makes a quip about drummers who sing, as Collins does, Adam says that the bartender and U2's parents are fans of Collins' music. The bartender can be heard saying, "I'm not *that* old." It's an awkward scene, though perhaps exactly what U2 wanted – another public turn away from the earnest, do-good image of their pre-Zoo TV days.

1993

In a word? Madness. U2 spends the early part of the year holed up in the studio, trying desperately to record a full album faster than they have in a decade. They don't finish before the Zooropa Tour begins in May, so they're forced to fly back to Dublin after their gigs to get the work done. They make a variety of public appearances in the first half of the year, but none create a scene like the news that Adam and supermodel Naomi Campbell are engaged. That brings a whole new level of attention on U2's activities, and when Adam goes on a bender in August and misses a gig in November, there's no playing down what happened. Even without those issues, the Zooropa Tour is mad enough: Satellite links into war-torn Sarajevo, Salman Rushdie on stage, and Tokyo, the perfect place to wrap up two years of Zoo TV. Madness, indeed.

January
Issue 17 of *Propaganda* magazine is published around this time.

January 19
Adam, Larry, Paul McGuinness, and Paul's wife, Kathy, are in Washington, DC, for tomorrow's inauguration of President-elect Bill Clinton. The McGuinnesses, however, head back to Ireland tonight after Paul gets news that his younger brother, Niall, has died of a heart attack.

Adam and Larry meet Michael Stipe and Mike Mills of R.E.M. at a club tonight. Stipe and Mills invite Adam and Larry to perform U2's 'One' tomorrow night at MTV's inaugural ball, and after a while to think about it, the two U2ers accept. After working out the logistics, they agree to get together and rehearse tomorrow afternoon. Mills, a bassist, will play guitar; Larry only wants to use congas, not a full drum kit. "There's a large chance we could come across badly, whereas if I have the congas there it won't be too loud, we could get a good mix on the TV," he says.

January 20
In the morning, Adam and Larry attend the inauguration ceremony in Washington, DC.

Larry talks about attending the inauguration
"There was a real sense of change. I noticed a lot of older people were incredibly emotional, there were tears. I'm not used to it. I know nothing about how the systems work. But from an observer's point of view it was something I won't forget."

Later tonight, as planned, Adam and Larry join forces with R.E.M.'s Michael Stipe and Mike Mills to perform 'One' at MTV's 1993 Rock-N-Roll Inaugural Ball. The musicians name themselves "Automatic Baby" for the night, using their own band's recent releases as inspiration (*Automatic For The People* and *Achtung Baby*).

January 30
On the invitation of actress Vanessa Redgrave, Bono and Edge attend the two-day Festival Against Racism at the Thalia Theatre in Hamburg. Bono is one of a few artists invited to speak, and his five-minute-plus comments include: "We started the century with so many competing ideas as to how we should live together. We ended with so few." After the event, Bono walks around the Reeperbahn – Hamburg's nightlife hub and also its red-light district.

January 31
On the final day of the Festival Against Racism, Bono and Edge perform 'One' with Jo Shankar on violin and a drummer from a local German band.

While in Hamburg, Bono and Edge attend a performance of *The Black Rider*, a theatrical collaboration between writer William S. Burroughs, musician Tom Waits, and director Robert Wilson. Bono's MacPhisto character is essentially born here,

When Johnny Came to Town, February 11

"I couldn't sing it. For whatever reason, it didn't sit well. But it is a complete cop-out. And Brian Eno worked very hard to try to get me to sing that song. But I wanted Johnny Cash to sing it. It was his voice that I heard in my head. So I didn't argue with my own instincts."

gaining inspiration from one of the characters in the play. "Bono and I saw the show in Hamburg," Edge reveals later, "and I thought there was a certain license in that figure that would be interesting for Bono. It wasn't the other three members of the band going, 'Oh, my God, he's wearing devil's horns! How embarrassing!' We were into it."

February
During a break in the Zoo TV/Zooropa tour, U2 begin recording new material at three studios in Dublin: The Factory, Westland Studios, and the new Windmill Lane Studios. At first planned to be an EP, the effort eventually produces the full-length *Zooropa* album.

Adam attends the *Hot Press* Awards and picks up U2's trophy as Best Irish Band.

Meanwhile, on the business side, Paul McGuinness goes to court to challenge the British Performing Rights Society, the organisation charged with collecting rights payments for U2 (and most other artists). McGuinness wants U2 and its agents to handle that collection directly.

Also this month, Alan Light visits U2 in Dublin for a feature-length interview with Bono that will appear in the March 4 issue of *Rolling Stone*. Bono reveals that he and Edge are working on two songs for legendary soul singer Al Green (one is later revealed to be called 'Revolution Of The Heart'), and that the band is working with Sega on a Zoo TV interactive CD. Bono explains that the CD will allow fans to remix U2 songs as they wish, and make their own U2 music videos from a library of images on the CD. The project never becomes reality.

February 5
Bono and Paul McGuinness watch Bob Dylan's show tonight at the Point Depot in Dublin. After the show, they join Dylan and others, including Elvis Costello, Nanci Griffith, and Chrissie Hynde at Tosca, the Dublin restaurant owned by Bono's brother, Norman.

February 6
Tonight it's Van Morrison playing the Point Depot, and Bono is part of a star-studded encore that includes some of last night's entourage – Bob Dylan, Elvis Costello and Chrissie Hynde – along with Steve Winwood and Kris Kristofferson. Together they sing Morrison's 'Gloria' and Dylan's 'It's All Over Now, Baby Blue'.

February 11
Bono, Larry and Edge perform with Johnny Cash during Cash's show at the Olympia Theatre in Dublin. The show is filmed for Irish TV, and is released on DVD in 2006, but without the U2 appearance. While Cash is in Dublin, he visits U2 in the studio and records his vocals for a new song that's tentatively called 'Wandering'.

Bono and Cash had previously worked together on a song titled 'Ellis Island'.

February 17
U2 are in London to pick up a surprise Brit Award for Most Successful Live Act. The band and friends gather at Paul McGuinness' London apartment after the ceremony. Adam meets his longtime crush, supermodel Naomi Campbell, for the second time, but there are no sparks between the two.

February 18
U2 cancels plans for a free concert this summer at Phoenix Park in Dublin. At a news conference in Dublin, Paul McGuinness says it will be "impossible" to meet the comfort and safety requirements for such a concert. The band came under fire for first announcing the show would be free, then saying there'd be a £10 charge to pay for security and infrastructure costs. McGuinness says the Phoenix Park show will be replaced by three Zooropa Tour shows in Ireland in late August.

February 23
Much of the U2 organization is in New York for a farewell dinner honoring Ellen Darst, the longtime director of Principle Management's US office. She's leaving to take a position with Elektra Records.

Bono is a late arrival at the Waterclub restaurant, but finally arrives with a surprise guest: Naomi Campbell. (They were on the same flight into New York, and Bono convinced her to come to the party.) Seats are re-arranged so Adam and Naomi can sit together, and they eventually leave the party early together.

Notably missing from the festivities is Edge, who's deep in recording work in Dublin.

February 24

Adam and Larry travel to Los Angeles for tonight's Grammy Awards. When Naomi Campbell misses her flight, she ends up on the same plane as the U2ers. Campbell asks the flight crew to make sure Adam sits next to her on the flight, and the two hold hands, kiss for the first time, and fall asleep next to one another.

The ceremony itself is a mixed bag for U2. *Achtung Baby* wins Best Rock Vocal Performance by a Duo or Group, but loses the Album of the Year vote to Eric Clapton's *Unplugged*. Adam's attention this night, however, is on Clapton's date: Naomi Campbell.

Late February/Early March

Around this time, Bono attends a birthday party for the painter Balthus, who's turning 85. The two have become friends since Louis Le Brocquy introduced them. Though there are many guests at the costume ball, Bono and Balthus eat dinner and spend time alone. Balthus invites Bono into his studio and reveals that, while he can still paint, he's unable to draw.

March

Anton Corbijn does a photo shoot at Bono's house for *Details* magazine.

Early in the month, U2 reach consensus on their new material: they're going to go for a full album, not an EP. They continue to work at The Factory.

Around this time, Adam attends the IRMA Awards in Dublin and presents an award to the night's big winners, R.E.M.

March 4

U2 are back atop the annual *Rolling Stone* magazine polls. Readers name U2 Best Band, Artist of the Year, and Comeback of the Year. Zoo TV wins Best Tour and *Achtung Baby* wins Best Album and Best Album Cover. 'One' is named Best Single. Bono is the readers' choice for Best Male Singer, Best Songwriter, and Sexiest Male Artist. Larry Mullen is name Best Drummer. Edge and Adam take second in their respective musical categories. Critics are slightly less enthusiastic. They name U2 and R.E.M. co-winners of Best Band. Zoo TV manages to win both Best Tour and Worst Tour.

March 21

U2 are named International Entertainers of the Year at the Juno Awards in Toronto.

March 22

Adam's relationship with Naomi Campbell becomes public knowledge when they show up together at a Duran Duran concert in Dublin.

March 23

All four band members and their wives and girlfriends help Ali Hewson celebrate her birthday with dinner at Tosca restaurant and a party at Lillie's Bordello in Dublin.

April

U2 continue recording new material and preparing for the upcoming Zooropa Tour of Europe. They have meetings to review video footage with Maurice Linnane and Ned O'Hanlon from Dreamchaser Productions, and have to take care of mundane details like the tour wardrobe and what aliases they'll use while on the road.

Around this time, Adam makes an appearance on Irish radio in support of an Amnesty International effort to drive food and medical supplies into Bosnia, past a Serbian blockade. Bono does an interview with *Hot Press* magazine's Joe Jackson, and plays him several tracks from U2's upcoming album.

Supermodel Naomi to wed U2's Adam

By BARRY O'KELLY

SUPERMODEL Naomi Campbell is to wed U2 star Adam Clayton. Only months after they started going out together, he proposed to her last Tuesday night.

Asked on the Kenny Live television show last night if she would ever marry an Irishman, she broke the news, saying that she was already engaged to the U2 bassist.

It is believed the marriage will take place at the end of this year at the earliest because of Adam's commitments to performing on U2's European tour.

Naomi, whose raunchy pose in a Falmers jeans advertisement caused a stir recently, has been a regular visitor to Ireland since she began going out with Adam last Christmas.

Showing off a sparkling diamond engagement ring on TV last night, she explained that "Adam was straight forward about it" when he proposed to her over the phone. There was "a trust" between them, she said, "and that's what I've always wanted."

Naomi told of how their relationship began, some months after the pair first met at a concert. "Then I missed a flight from New York to the Grammy's. We sat together on the next flight...I kissed him on the plane," she recalled.

The London-born model said while "we don't have a date set yet", she expected to link up with her fiance as they both may be working at the same time in their respective jobs in Amsterdam, Madrid, Paris, German and London later this year.

Naomi, who will be 23 on May 23 next, said she is

■ the controversial Falmers Jeans poster.

"absolutely" sure that she wants to start a family at some stage, "but not right now".

She presently lives in New York, but has frequently visited the U2 star's georgian home in Rathfarnham in recent months.

The hugely successful £10,000-a-day model said that her mother "very unhappy" about her appearances in Madonna's book, "Sex", and she regretted her involvement in the project.

She revealed that she has just signed a record deal with Sony Music. "At least I will be able to say that I tried," she remarked on her plans to make a bid for pop stardom.

But she discounted the idea that she might record music at some stage with her fiance.

Her last boyfriend was screen star Robert De Niro.

Right: Adam and Bono at the Brit Award, London, February 17. Above and below: Adam and Naomi Campbell announce their engagement.

April 3-4

Larry and soundman Joe O'Herlihy travel to Derry, Northern Ireland, at the invite of former Undertone Billy Doherty, who wants them to see the new Big River recording studio there. While in Derry, Larry catches a live show by an up-and-coming local band, Schtum.

April 13

Larry and Paul McGuinness help open the Rock Class of '93 music seminar in Dublin, at a "rock school" which Larry helped establish months earlier with a donation of £10,000 of musical equipment.

Shortly before Larry opens the seminar, Paul does an impromptu Q&A session about band management and the music industry. The seminar features 70 speakers and showcases 35 bands. "To be told to go back and remix your single, redo your album, or that they don't like your art work is something that U2 would never have tolerated – and never did. I hear so much now that I really wonder whether there hasn't been a general weakening of the resolve of the creative side of the business. I would certainly recommend to groups that they should stick to their guns," McGuinness says.

Above: Bono as Mr. MacPhisto, Rotterdam, May 10.

April 19
Bono's wife, Ali, and a team from Dreamchaser Productions leave on a trip to Chernobyl, Russia, to shoot *Black Wind, White Land*, a documentary about the effects of the nuclear disaster there in 1986. They'll be gone until May 10.

April 27
Adam proposes over the phone to girlfriend Naomi Campbell, who says yes. He also calls Naomi's mother, Valerie, and gets permission to marry her daughter.

May 1
British supermodel Naomi Campbell announces on Pat Kenny's RTE TV talk show that she and Adam are engaged. "There are things we don't have to discuss," Campbell tells Kenny.

"If I'm working late, or he is, there's an understanding. There's a lot of trust. That's always the way I wanted it." She says Adam proposed over the phone while he was in London and she was in New York.

Achtung Baby is certified Multi-Platinum by the BPI, with UK sales surpassing the 900,000 mark.

May 2
Dublin media track down Adam and Naomi at Adam's home south of the city, and chat with the couple as they stroll around the grounds. "I just knew from the very first moment that this was it," Adam says. Media follow the couple closely, and soon report Campbell's announcement that the couple will marry September 14 in Dublin.

May 6
U2 fly to the Netherlands to prepare for the start of the *Zooropa* Tour in a few days.

May 7
U2 perform a dress rehearsal for the upcoming European tour in front of a small group of fans in Rotterdam. Bono adds a sartorial twist to his "Fly" character tonight, wearing a red version of the standard black, leather outfit.

May 8
For the last dress rehearsal before opening night, Bono introduces a completely new alter ego: a devil-like character who wears a glittering gold suit from head to toe. He's first called "Mr. Gold" but Bono renames him "Mr. MacPhisto"

before tomorrow's opener and wears red horns on his head.

May 9
Feyenoord Stadium, Rotterdam, with Utah Saints, Claw Boys Claw. The *Zooropa* Tour kicks off in Rotterdam. Macnas, a theatre group from Galway is invited to perform a sketch prior to the support acts taking the stage. Other aspects of Zoo TV are changed to fit the European audience: images from Leni Reifenstahl's Nazi-propaganda film *Triumph of the Will* immediately precede the beginning of 'Zoo Station'; as the show begins, the Zoo TV colour bars that were used on video walls elsewhere in the world are now replaced by the 12-star blue logo used by the European Community – one star eventually falls off, and the entire logo collapses on screen; during 'Bullet The Blue Sky', the flaming crosses seen on screen now turn into swastikas, prompting Bono to remind the audience, "We must never let it happen again"; perhaps the biggest change is the introduction of MacPhisto, Bono's character who replaces the Mirrorball Man and is dressed in a gold lamé suit and wears platform shoes with red horns on his head. Bono will later reveal in interviews that MacPhisto is The Fly "when he's old and fat and playing in Las Vegas".

Edge causes a small stir after the first show when he tells *NME*, "I've been doing this for 10 years and I've enjoyed it, but I don't think I'll want to do it for another 10. It's no job for a grown-up." U2's publicity team is called on to quell rumours that the band is thinking about calling it quits.

May 10
Feyenoord Stadium, Rotterdam, with Einsturzende Neubauten, Claw Boys Claw. Supporting act Einsturzende Neubaten is tossed off stage and off the tour when one of the band members throws an iron bar into the sea of booing fans, hitting a girl who has to go to the hospital. One of Bono's most memorable telephone calls occurs tonight when he rings a

local travel agent looking for a flight out of town, anywhere "as long as it's sunny". After the show, management will contact the agent again to explain Bono's call and offer her two complimentary tickets to the show the following night.

There's a party in Rotterdam to celebrate Bono's 33rd birthday. When Bono gets back to his hotel room in the morning (May 11), he finds a gift from Gavin Friday on the bed: an eight-foot-tall cross, painted blue, with "Hail Bono, King of the Zoos" inscribed on the top. Bono has the cross blessed and flown back to Dublin.

May 11
Feyenoord Stadium, Rotterdam, with Claw Boys Claw.

May 15
Estadio Jose Alvalade, Lisbon, with Utah Saints. U2 regularly fly back to Dublin after this month's shows to work on the *Zooropa* album.

May 19
Estadio Carlos Tartier, Oviedo, with Utah Saints, the Ramones.

May 22
Estadio Vincente Calderon, Madrid, with Utah Saints, the Ramones.

Above: The official currency of Zoo TV. Below: Bono signs a soccer ball, Rotterdam, May 8.

May 26
Stade De La Beaujoire, Nantes, with Urban Dance Squad, Utah Saints.

May 29
Festival Grounds, Werchter, with Stereo MC's, Urban Dance Squad.

June
U2 releases 'Numb' as a video single this month. The VHS release includes two extra videos: 'Numb (Video Remix)' and 'Love Is Blindness'.

June 2
Waldstadion, Frankfurt, with Stereo MC's, Die Toten Hosen. During tonight's show, Bono makes repeated references to the latest in a stream of racist incidents in Germany, where a firebomb was thrown into a house owned by a Turkish family in the town of Solingen. The first Zooropa show in Germany is also noteworthy because U2 continue to display burning swastikas on screen during 'Bullet The Blue Sky', even though it is illegal to display the image of the swastika publicly in the newly united Germany.

Before the show, U2 and Island Records announce an extension of the band's current record contract. The agreement gives Island the rights to U2's next six albums. The deal reportedly pays the band $60 million, a $10 million-plus advance per album, and an incredible 25 percent royalty rate on every album sold. According to published reports, U2 are now the highest-paid rock act in music history. "Island Records and their owner Chris Blackwell have stood behind U2 since the second he heard them," says Paul McGuinness. "We are extremely pleased to stay with a company that believes in us. Couldn't be happier." The contract also includes provisions for what's expected to be a major change in how music is delivered via the Internet in future years.

Also today, *Hot Press* magazines publishes 'In Cold Blood', a poem by Bono that describes in graphic detail the atrocities of violence – on the war front and home front. Bono had thought about reciting the words over a drumbeat on the *Zooropa* album, or during the band's live shows. Neither comes to fruition.

June 3
In Miami today, Chris Blackwell and other Island/Polygram executives get an advance listen of U2's new album, *Zooropa*. But in two other locations, police are looking for stolen copies of the album. Dublin police are investigating a break-in at Gavin Friday's home in which the thieves stole several tapes, including a copy of *Zooropa*. And another copy of the album is missing in Los Angeles, after a courier was mugged. Paul McGuinness tells reporters the band is aware of the situation: "We're working as fast as we can. Why would anyone buy an expensive, bad-quality bootleg when the real thing will be out in a month?"

June 4
Olympiastadion, Munich, with Stereo MC's, Die Toten Hosen.

June 6
Cannstatter Wasen, Stuttgart, with Stereo MC's, Die Toten Hosen.

June 9
Weserstadion, Bremen, with Stereo MC's, Die Toten Hosen.

June 12
Muengersdorfer Stadion, Cologne, with Stereo MC's, Die Toten Hosen. Adam and Larry do an interview with local TV before tonight's show. Cyndi Lauper joins the after-show party in Bono's hotel suite.

June 13
U2 head to Berlin, the next stop on the *Zooropa* Tour. Paul McGuinness decides to drive alone to Berlin, and takes a detour to Rinteln, the town where he was born. Larry, Morleigh and Bill Flanagan visit the site of the Berlin Wall. When they come upon one section still standing, Larry gets out of the car and uses a chunk of concrete to smash the wall some more. Later, the band and crew gather at their hotel with Kevin Godley, who's been called in

to shoot a music video tomorrow for 'Numb', the first single from the upcoming *Zooropa* album.

June 14
U2 shoot the music video for 'Numb' today at a studio in Berlin. It's one of U2's most memorable and comic videos, and features Edge sitting directly in front of the camera reciting lyrics as a variety of people push and poke him, blow smoke in his face, wrap string around his head, and perform other acts of minor torture. After a full day's work, the shoot ends at about 1:15 a.m.

June 15
Olympiastadion, Berlin, with Stereo MC's, Die Toten Hosen. U2 play Berlin's famous Olympic Stadium for the first time. Before the show, the band and crew walk around the stadium, taking in the Nazi sculptures and architecture that Adolf Hitler built for the 1936 Olympics. The show is one of the tour's best, with the band inspired by what they call the "ghosts" inside the stadium. From day one, the *Zooropa* Tour has taken mocking aim at some elements of Nazi Germany, with the use of Leni Riefenstahl documentary footage at the start of each show, and the use of swastikas on the video walls during 'Bullet The Blue Sky'.

Edge talks about playing the house that Hitler built
"I think we all were very aware of the ghosts running around that building tonight. And with the Leni Riefenstahl opening, you know those drums are summoning up some demons, some spirits, and you'd just better make sure it's the right spirit or it could have been a very different show.... It's a fairly heavy presence that you're mocking. I was a bit intimidated by that tonight. The only way to deal with being intimidated it to launch

at it full force, and I think that's why there was such energy."

After the show, local police arrive to arrest Joe O'Herlihy for violating local sound limits. But by the time the stadium lights come on, Joe is already on a plane back to Dublin.

With more than a week until the next show, Bono leaves for his house in Eze, France, immediately after tonight's show. He'll join his family for some downtime together and to reconnect. The rest of the crew celebrate Paul McGuinness' birthday on the Zoo airplane as they fly back home for a short break.

June 23
Stade De La Meinau, Strasbourg, with Stereo MC's, Velvet Underground.

June 26
The Hippodrome, Paris, with Belly, Velvet Underground. While in Paris, Bono does an interview with US writer Lisa Robinson.

June 28
Stade De La Pontaise, Lausanne, with Velvet Underground.

June 30
St. Jakob's Stadion, Basel, with Velvet Underground.

July
With a £15,000 bid at a charity auction in London this month, Paul McGuinness wins Bono a chess match against world champion Garry Kasparov. Bono announces he'll give £10,000 to charity if he loses. Reports suggest the two will square off in September, but it's not known if the match ever happened.

July 2-3
Stadio Bentegodi, Verona, with An Emotional Fish, Pearl Jam. U2 meet Bill Carter before the second show. Carter is an American documentary filmmaker who is working in a relief camp in the besieged city of Sarajevo. He's made the dangerous, two-day trek out of Sarajevo with two friends, Jason Aplon and Ivana Sirovic, and some TV gear. Carter interviews Bono before the show, asking him about Zoo TV and the

war in Bosnia. As they talk, Bono ends up asking Carter what it's like in Sarajevo. At the end of the interview, Carter suggests Bono should come visit the city. Bono is visibly shaken by the experience, and is in tears in the dressing room before the show starts. During the show, Bono dedicates 'One' to the people of Sarajevo.

Carter also spends time with Bono and Edge after the show, and the seeds are planted for U2 to do something that will shine a light on what's happening in Sarajevo. Bono is eager to bring the band into the city one week from now, after U2 plays a pair of shows in Rome. He gets quick approvals from his band mates, but Paul McGuinness doesn't like the idea. He calls it "foolhardy" and "vain". Bono continues to press the idea.

Bill Carter Talks About Meeting U2
"I had a real serious conversation with Bono and Edge about what was going on. They said, 'Well, what can we do?' That hit me with a huge trip – the largest rock band in the world is asking me what can they do. They wanted to play – Bono and Edge, all of them, really – wanted to come play in the disco in Sarajevo. But it was a difficult time then: a lot of shelling. I went back to Sarajevo and thought about it.

"A few days later, someone in their office called me and said, 'They really want to come – bad.' I wrote a long fax explaining why that shouldn't happen, but what about linking up to the show? They said, 'Let's do it.'"

Also after the second show, Bono and Edge do an interview at the hotel pool with Carter Alan for the Westwood One radio network.

With a couple days off between shows, U2 take separate routes from Verona to Rome. Bono drives through the Italian countryside, bumping into Robert Plant in Florence. Larry and Ann ride their motorcycle. Adam travels with Naomi Campbell and Christy Turlington. Edge flies on the Zoo Plane and meets up with Aislinn, his kids, and his parents in Rome.

July 5/6
U2 releases *Zooropa* worldwide. Originally planned as an EP, U2's studio time over the past few months is productive enough to produce a full album. The band finished recording in Dublin even while the *Zooropa* Tour was moving through Europe, often flying back to Dublin immediately after shows to work on the album. Flood, Brian Eno and Edge are credited as producers. *Zooropa* expands on the European vibe and experimental nature of *Achtung Baby*. The title track addresses European unification, while tracks like 'Numb' and 'Daddy's Gonna Pay For Your Crashed Car' push U2's sound even further away from what fans are used to.

Zooropa hits number one in the US and UK, and several other countries, but it gets mixed reviews in the press. Mark Brown of the *Orange County Register* raves that it's U2's "best album since *The Joshua Tree*". In the *Chicago Sun-Times*, Jim DeRogatis says the album is "inconsistent", but admits, "it's satisfying and surprising to hear a band of U2's status being so playful, experimental and downright weird".

Paul McGuinness is critical of the Irish media for being consistently negative in its reviews of the album. George Byrne's review in the *Irish Independent* is particularly scathing: "The songs sound like they were knocked up in double-quick time and with about as much thought put into the lyrics as goes into a DJ's timecheck.... For all the bleeps and squiggles courtesy of The Edge, the nagging feeling is that *Zooropa* is merely a lot of mickey-taking over a variety of drum patterns. Lyrics have never been one of U2's strong points, but at least here Bono has shifted from

Edge explains *Zooropa*, July 5/6

"One of the central ideas of *Zooropa* is that it is of the moment, it's catching the stuff that's in the ether at that time. We went into the recording studio with that in mind. And looking back now, I'm delighted that it became an album because it has captured the moment, for me at any rate. Of all our records it probably is the most vital and current. It's like a Polaroid of what was happening to us and what was happening around Europe at that time."

nicking chunks of the Bible and the long-range weather forecast and taken to lifting advertising slogans ... wow, the great leap forward!" Tracks: 'Zooropa', 'Babyface', 'Numb', 'Lemon', 'Stay (Faraway, So Close!)', 'Daddy's Gonna Pay For Your Crashed Car', 'Some Days Are Better Than Others', 'The First Time', 'Dirty Day', 'The Wanderer'

July 6
Stadio Flaminio, Rome, with An Emotional Fish, Pearl Jam. As U2 prepares for tonight's show, the Sarajevo issue is finally resolved. Paul McGuinness is adamant that there will be no concert in Sarajevo – it won't be safe for the band, crew, and U2's audience. Bill Carter sends a three-page fax telling the band it's too risky. Carter instead suggests

live satellite linkups between Sarajevo and the Zooropa concerts as the tour moves across Europe.

An Excerpt of Bill Carter's Fax to U2 Suggesting Satellite Linkups

"The idea is to show the insanity, the surrealness, the survival. The audience, if anything, would realize, Jesus, lucky I'm here enjoying the concert and not in Sarajevo. Maybe they will think about not letting it happen in their country, their city, their house…"

After the show, Paul McGuinness speaks with MTV boss Tom Freston about turning the Zoo TV concept into a television network.

July 7
Stadio Flaminio, Rome, with An Emotional Fish, Pearl Jam. With *Zooropa* just released, new songs from the album begin working their way into the set list. Tonight, Edge performs 'Numb' for the first time, reading the lyrics from a stand.

After the show, U2 and friends – Eddie Vedder and Jeff Ament of Pearl Jam, Naomi Campbell and Christy Turlington – party into the wee hours of the morning at a beachfront club. On the way back to the hotel, Bono stops for a visit at the top of the Victor Emmanuel monument.

July 8
Bono dresses as MacPhisto for a photo shoot with Kevin Davies at the Hotel Majestic in Rome. Ned O'Hanlon and Maurice Linnane also videotape MacPhisto.

July 9
Stadio San Paolo, Naples, with Velvet Underground. Kevin Davies is behind the camera again before tonight's show, capturing MacPhisto prancing around the Vatican as tourists look on curiously.

July 12
Stadio Delle Alpi, Turino, with An Emotional Fish, Ligabue.

July 13
A live version of 'Satellite Of Love' with Lou Reed appears on the *Peace*

Above: U2 rehearse at Wembley Stadium before there two August concerts. Below: Galway's Macnas Theatre Group warms up the Wembley crowd in their outsize U2 masks.

Together charity album to benefit youth in Northern Ireland.

July 14
Stade Velodrome, Marseille, with An Emotional Fish. Bono calls Bill Carter in Sarajevo on the telephone and asks Carter to explain to the concert audience what is happening there. After hearing Carter's account, Bono ends the call by saying, "We are ashamed tonight to be Europeans and to turn our backs on you and your people."

July 17-18
Stadio Comunale, Bologna, with An Emotional Fish, Galliano. The first show includes the first satellite linkup with Bill Carter in Sarajevo. Carter and two Bosnian friends get safely to the TV station building in Sarajevo, and use portable batteries to power their camera gear and a satellite dish that U2 sent. To make the satellite hook-ups possible, U2 has paid £100,000 to join the European Broadcasting Union. Carter tells the audience that two bombs have killed a child and injured five others within the hour. He says the violence is happening close enough to the concert grounds that if he left Sarajevo by plane, he could be at the concert before it was over. It's an incredibly powerful moment, and after the show the band agrees it came too early in the show – it ruined the mood of the show before the mood had been established.

Also at the first show is director Jim Sheridan, who talks with Bono about scheduling his work on the *In*

The Name Of The Father soundtrack. With U2 as busy as they are, Bono suggests Sheridan also get Gavin Friday involved.

Zooropa debuts at number one on the UK album charts – it's U2's fifth UK number one album.

July 23
Népstadion, Budapest, with Akos. U2 plays their first show in a former Eastern Bloc country.

July 27
Gentofte Stadion, Copenhagen, with PJ Harvey, Stereo MC's. Before tonight's show, Paul McGuinness does an interview with the *Irish Times*, which focuses mostly on the band's finances. McGuinness allows writer Paddy Woodworth to see the tour budget, saying, "I'm breaking the habit of a lifetime in revealing this budget." The spreadsheet shows U2 expects to make a pre-tax profit of £2.2 million, not including an estimated £2.3 million in merchandise sales.

July 29
Valle Hovin Stadion, Oslo, with PJ Harvey, Stereo MC's.

July 31
Stockholms Stadion, Stockholm, with PJ Harvey, Stereo MC's. While in Stockholm, Edge does an online interview with the *Irish Times*. He's connected on a computer underneath the Zoo TV stage (with help from chief video engineer Dave Lemmink), while an *Irish Times* writer and a 14-year-old U2 fan are online from Dublin. "I have left a few messages on InterNet," Edge says, "but as yet I haven't formally joined any of the networks." During the chat, Edge admits to being a fan of computer games and says he's aware of the U2 Bulletin Board for fans using the CompuServe access service.

August 3
Goffert Park, Nijmegen, with PJ Harvey, Stereo MC's.

August 7-8
Celtic Park, Glasgow, with Utah Saints, PJ Harvey (August 7); with Utah Saints, Stereo MC's (August 8).

The satellite linkup with Sarajevo during the first show in Glasgow is difficult for the band to bear. Bill Carter invites a Bosnian woman to speak, and she tells the concert audience, "We would like to hear the music, too, but we only hear the screams of wounded and tortured people and raped women." After the show, the band decides they'll put an end to the satellite link-ups after two upcoming shows at Wembley Stadium in London.

Larry explains his struggles with the Sarajevo link-ups
"We were playing a rock and roll show… then suddenly seeing video footage of people being bombed and a satellite link-up with people in Sarajevo saying, 'We're being killed, please come and help us.' That was really hard to watch and hard to listen to. I was worried we would be accused of exploiting these people. I remember saying to Bono, 'I don't know if I can handle this anymore, it's really hard up there.' He just pushed through. He said, 'I want to do this and I'm going to do it.'"

August 11
Wembley Stadium, London, with PJ Harvey, Big Audio Dynamite II. U2 play the first of four shows in 10 days at Wembley Stadium. During his nightly telephone call, Bono tries to reach author Salman Rushdie, who's been in hiding for four years because of a fatwa issued against him by Iranian leader Ayatollah Khomeini over Rushdie's book, *The Satanic Verses*. Not only does Rushdie answer the phone call, but he also walks onto the stage waving a finger in MacPhisto's face: "I'm not afraid of you," he says. "Real devils don't wear horns." Fans cheer Rushdie's appearance wildly and media around the world picks up the story. In later

Bono on Salman Rushdie's appearance in the Zoo, August 11

"I think he has behaved with enormous grace under pressure and with humour. It must have scared the shit out of him to be on stage at Wembley Stadium with the Devil [MacPhisto]. But I like it when it's mixed up."

Above: Bono with Salman Rushdie on stage at Wembley, August 11.

interviews, Rushdie thanks U2 for their "gesture of solidarity and friendship". He also admits to being a music lover and says that standing in front of a crowd of 72,000 people was an extraordinary occasion for a writer. Roger Daltrey and the Pet Shop Boys are among the backstage guests after the show.

Around this time, U2 shoot a music video for 'Lemon' in a London studio. Mark Neale is the director. Anton Corbijn also does a photo shoot at the same time.

August 12
Wembley Stadium, London, with PJ Harvey, Big Audio Dynamite II. Tonight's show marks the last time U2 will do a satellite link-up with

Bill Carter in Sarajevo. The band feel the situation in Bosnia is now getting enough press attention. Boy George, who's made no secret of his affection for Larry, is one of the guests backstage. Larry manages to slip away when George tries to say hello.

August 14

Roundhay Park, Leeds, with Marxman, Stereo MC's.

Around this time, Adam has what is later described in the press as a "three-day sex and drink binge" at the Regent Hotel in London. According to a British newspaper, Adam spends more than £1,500 on several escorts, specifically requesting that the girls be "young, beautiful, and black". When the story goes public in October, U2 spokeswoman Regine Moylett says, "Adam was in a fine mess at the time. He thought it was all over with Naomi. He went completely off the rails." British tabloids track down one of the prostitutes, who says, "We shared drugs, then had sex." Newspapers report that Adam "made a full and frank confession" to Naomi shortly after the incident, and that the couple has patched up their relationship.

August 15

On a day off, the band and friends visit Chris Blackwell at his estate south of London.

August 18

Arms Park, Cardiff, with Utah Saints, Stereo MC's.

August 20-21

Wembley Stadium, London, with Utah Saints, Stereo MC's (August 20); with Bjork, Stereo MC's (August 21). U2 plays their third and fourth shows of the tour at Wembley Stadium in London, becoming only the fourth act to play four or more shows in this historic stadium. (The others are Michael Jackson, Rolling Stones, and Genesis.) Eric Clapton and Robbie Robertson are among the special guests at the show. The U2 crew throw a party after the show at the Regent Hotel, which lasts until early the next morning. The UK

tour is such a success that five U2 albums crack the UK album chart's Top 40: *Zooropa*, *Achtung Baby*, *Rattle And Hum*, *The Joshua Tree*, and *War*.

August 24

Pairc Ui Chaoimh, Cork, with Engine Alley, Utah Saints. The *Irish Times* celebrates the arrival of Zoo TV in Ireland with a 24-page supplement called *Zoo Times*. Prior to tonight's show, a local governing body bans the sale of U2 condoms at the concert. Manager Paul McGuinness reacts by handing out condoms personally to fans at the show, prompting criticism from the city's mayor. There's no criticism from seven charities, who are set to benefit from U2's three shows in Ireland: Dublin Simon Community, Dublin Rape Crisis Centre, Focus Point, Cork Simon, Alone, the Irish Hospice Foundation, and Dublin Aids Alliance. The seven charities come forward today to thank the band publicly.

U2 fly into Cork a few hours before the show and are greeted by VIPs at the airport. A police motorcade helps them avoid traffic problems on the way to the stadium. U2 are everywhere in Cork – on the radio, TV, and the newspaper. The celebrity scene is wearing on Larry, in particular, who is talking about moving to New York next year to escape the increased attention U2 is getting in Ireland and to spend time studying music and improving as a drummer.

After the show, a last-minute plan to fly the Zoo Plane to Paris falls apart because only a few crew members have passports with them. Instead, the band and crew return to Dublin and party at Lillie's Bordello, a nightclub in Dublin.

August 25

U2 have a band meeting at the Clarence Hotel in Dublin. Later, Bono has dinner at Tosca's, the restaurant owned by his brother, Norman.

August 26

Bono records his vocals for 'I've Got You Under My Skin' at STS Studios in Dublin with producer

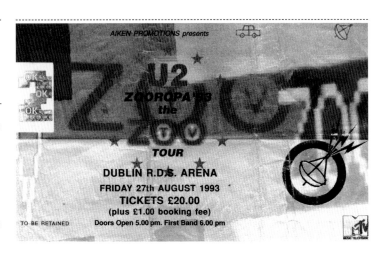

Phil Ramone. The song is a duet with Frank Sinatra that will appear on his *Duets* album, but the two singers record their vocals separately. Bono sings the song five different ways before the session breaks. Bono and Paul McGuinness go to lunch with writer Bill Flanagan while Ramone works on the track at STS. The recording session resumes in the afternoon and is over by dinner. Bono and Flanagan eat with EMI Records executive Don Rubin and his wife, and later watch a Katell Keineg concert at Whelan's with Gavin Friday.

Achtung Baby is certified Multi-Platinum, with US sales of more than five million.

August 27

Royal Dublin Showgrounds, Dublin, with Marxman, The Golden Horde. As U2 prepare to play the first of two Dublin shows, airlines announce a brisk uptake in business thanks to an influx of U2 fans flying to Dublin for these homecoming shows. Icelandair even charters a special flight to Dublin for U2 fans.

35,000 fans pack RDS for U2's first show in Dublin since the end of 1989. Celebrities turn out in droves for the gig, including Michael Hutchence, Bob Geldof, Liam Neeson and Wim Wenders. Adam's fiancée Naomi Campbell is here with her supermodel friends Helena Christensen and Christy Turlington. During the show, MacPhisto calls home, where Bono's four-year-old daughter Jordan has left a message on the answering machine explaining that the family is on vacation, and saying, "We're not coming home until you take the horns off."

August 28

Royal Dublin Showgrounds, Dublin, with Scary Eire, Stereo MC's. U2's second show in Dublin and the final show of the European Tour is a celebrity-studded affair. On hand are Bob Geldof, Mick Jagger, Salman Rushdie, Wim Wenders, MTV executive Tom Freston, *Rolling Stone* publisher Jann Wenner, and dozens more. Adam's parents and Edge's parents are there, as is Bono's dad.

The show is broadcast live on radio to countries around the world, but several Islamic nations drop plans to air it because of Salman Rushdie's recent on stage appearance in London. During the show, Naomi Campbell comes on stage during 'Trying To Throw Your Arms The World'. Rumours now have Naomi and Adam getting married next May.

After the show, the party starts at a hotel bar, moves to the POD nightclub, and continues into the early morning.

U2 donate the proceeds from both Dublin shows – more than £300,000 – to a handful of local charities.

August 29

Bono and Ali host an end-of-tour party at their house in Killiney. 140 guests are there, and crowds of U2 fans hang out just beyond Bono's front gates. Director Jim Sheridan speaks with Larry about doing some acting. "I'd like to try it," Larry says, "because it's so unlike me. I'm not an extrovert at all. So I think it would be good for me. But it would have to be the right very small role, so if I was shite the director could say, 'You're shite,' and I could say, 'Oh, okay, thanks,' and that would be it." Inside, party guests notice Edge and Morleigh Steinberg spending time together in close quarters.

Late in the evening, Bono gets a call at home from Willie Williams, who left Dublin to head to the Greenbelt Christian Arts & Music Festival in Northamptonshire, England. Willie is standing on the main stage when Bono comes to the phone. Willie explains where he is, and asks Bono if he has a message for the 18,000-strong crowd. Bono: "Oh... um... tell them... everything you know, is *right*."

August 30

Edge flies from Dublin to Los Angeles, where he'll perform later in the week at the MTV Music Awards.

September

'Lemon' is released as a single, with varying formats including up to six different remixes of the song as additional tracks. Oddly, there's no commercial release in Europe, and only a limited release in the US, Australia, and Japan. The single does reach number six on the Australian charts.

September 1

Edge hangs out with Peter Buck and Michael Stipe of R.E.M., Peter Gabriel and Sinead O'Connor in the Bel Air Hotel bar, before joining several friends and crew at a Japanese restaurant in Los Angeles. There, they find Morleigh Steinberg, who's returned to L.A. after the tour to tell her boyfriend about the relationship that's developing with Edge.

September 2

Edge makes his first solo live appearance with an intentionally strange performance of 'Numb' at the MTV Music Awards in Los Angeles. He walks on stage solemnly, wearing U2's blue, military-style *Zooropa* Tour uniform and sits down facing the audience. He delivers the lyrics while the rest of the band appear in pre-taped footage on a bank of TVs behind him.

Later, Bono is watching the programme back in Dublin while talking to Edge on the phone. They hear Eddie Vedder hold up the MTV trophy and say, "It looks like Bono!" Concerned that he may have screwed up, Vedder finds Edge to apologize.

After the awards, Edge goes to a party that R.E.M. is hosting, and hangs out with old friend Anton Corbijn and Zoo TV contributor Mark Pellington.

September 3

Edge and Morleigh have breakfast together at the Sunset Marquis

Hotel, and make plans to spend more time together.

September 8
Zooropa is certified Multi-Platinum, with US sales of more than two million.

September 24
The *Short Cuts* movie soundtrack is released, and includes 'Conversation On A Barstool', a song co-written by Bono and Edge in 1989.

October
U2 rehearse for the upcoming Pacific tour at the Factory in Dublin. When his work with the band is done, Bono often joins Gavin Friday at STS Studio to work on the *In The Name Of The Father* soundtrack. Sinead O'Connor joins them briefly to record her vocals for 'You Made Me The Thief Of Your Heart'. Allen Ginsberg and William Gibson make separate visits to U2's studio. They both record video segments that the band expects to use in the Triplecast, an ambitious plan to put Zoo TV content on three TV channels simultaneously.

Edge explains the Triplecast
"We're going to try to present the viewer with a series of choices as they watch any of the three channels, which will all start to change into one another as they go along, so they'll kind of blend and switch around. Say you're watching a concert and Bono takes off his sunglasses and puts them down in the middle of the show; you zoom out and suddenly we're in the middle of a large studio and we're selling the glasses. And if you want to follow the concert, you'll be going from one channel to the next and back again."

After taping his Triplecast segment, Gibson interviews Bono and Edge

for *Details* magazine.
Early in the month, UK tabloids break the news of Adam's "sex binge" in London back in August. In a show of support, Bono and Ali, Larry and Ann, all join Adam at a fashion show in Paris where Naomi is modeling this month.
U2 shoot a music video for 'Stay (Faraway, So Close!)' in Berlin. Wim Wenders directs the video, which features U2 as guardian angels who come to earth to help a band performing the U2 song. The song will be included on the soundtrack to Wenders' upcoming film, *Faraway, So Close!*
Also this month, U2 is named Best Act in the World Today at the Q Awards. Flood, Brian Eno, and Edge also win the Best Producer award for *Zooropa*.

October 1
U2 and friends help Gavin Friday celebrate his wedding with a reception at the Clarence Hotel. Down in The Kitchen nightclub, the party is filled with karaoke. Larry

leads U2 through 'The Boys Are Back In Town', with Bono, Adam, and Edge on backing vocals. Edge does a solo rendition of the Monkees' 'Daydream Believer', a preview of things to come on 1997's PopMart Tour.

October 8
As rumours continue to spread that Adam and Naomi Campbell are no longer together, Campbell talks about the postponed nuptials in today's issue of *Entertainment Weekly*: "It's safe to say [we'll marry] sometime in the new year. We've not had time to think because Adam's on tour and I'm working." The engagement will eventually break off before the two are married.

October 13
Achtung Baby: The Videos, The Cameos, And A Whole Lot of Interference is certified Platinum by the RIAA, with more than one million copies of the video sold.

October 14
In a special issue, *Rolling Stone* magazine includes two U2 videos in its list of the Top 100 Music Videos: 'Mysterious Ways' at number 76, and 'One' (the buffaloes version) at number 99.

October 19
Ali Hewson narrates *Black Wind, White Land*, a documentary about the effects of the Chernobyl nuclear disaster, which premieres on RTE-TV.

November
Issue 18 of *Propaganda* magazine is published around this time.

November 5
On the way to Australia, Bono stops to shoot the music video for 'I've Got You Under My Skin' with Frank Sinatra in Palm Springs, California. Edge is there to watch and help as needed. Martin Scorsese was the first choice to direct, but he turns the idea down at the last minute, so Bono asks Kevin Godley to do it.
Bono meets Sinatra and his wife, Barbara, outside a children's center bearing her name. Bono and Frank hop into a limousine with a film

The Night Adam Missed a U2 Gig, November 26

Bono: "We went ahead with the show out of respect for the people who turned up and the size of the bills we were going to have to pay if we didn't roll cameras. Adam's bass tech, Stuart Morgan, understudied that night, it was a heroic performance from him, and in fairness a performance deserving to be lit, which he wasn't. He was left in the shadows.... I felt an enormous void that night and I felt I was falling down it. I felt we all were."

crew and the shoot is underway. They head to a local bar owned by a friend of Sinatra's, where the film crew has been told to stay out of sight. When it's time to re-shoot their entrance, Frank gets edgy and acts like he doesn't know what's happening. Bono and others try to calm him down, but Sinatra rushes out the door.

Later, Barbara calls Bono to apologise and invite him to their house. Sinatra and several friends are there, drinking and telling stories. Bono toasts Sinatra and sings him 'Two Shots Of Happy, One Shot Of Sad'. Bono later falls asleep as everyone starts to watch a movie, and wakes up later with wet pants. He's afraid he had an accident, but it turns out he only spilled his drink while sleeping.

November 12-13
Cricket Ground, Melbourne, with Kim Salmon and the Surrealists, Big Audio Dynamite II. The final leg of what has become a nearly two-year long Zoo TV tour begins in Melbourne and is dubbed the Zoomerang tour. More songs from the *Zooropa* album are worked into the set list, but the title track and 'Babyface' are left out after the band struggled to play them during the Zooropa summer tour.

November 16
Football Park, Adelaide, with Kim Salmon and the Surrealists, Big Audio Dynamite II. An MTV Australia contest winner appears on the vidiwalls to talk to Bono after 'The Fly'.

November 18
Larry and the other football fans on tour wake up at 5 a.m. and head to an Irish pub in Brisbane to watch Ireland battle Northern Ireland to a 1-1 draw at a World Cup qualifying match in Belfast. The tie puts Ireland into the World Cup, and prompts RTE to call Larry to get his reaction on-air.

November 20
ANZ Stadium, Brisbane, with Kim Salmon and the Surrealists, Big Audio Dynamite II.

November 22/23
U2 release 'Stay (Faraway, So Close!)' as the third single from *Zooropa*. Additional tracks on the varying formats are 'I've Got You Under My Skin', 'Lemon (Bad Yard Club Edit)', 'Lemon (The Perfecto Mix)', 'Slow Dancing', 'Bullet The Blue Sky (live)', and 'Love Is Blindness (live)'. The single reaches number four in both the UK and US.

November 26
Aussie Stadium, Sydney, with Kim Salmon and the Surrealists, Big Audio Dynamite II. As they prepare to play two shows in Sydney, U2 cancel plans for the Zoo TV Triplecast, losing a big paycheck from MTV in the process. They had planned to film the Sydney shows for the Triplecast, but decide they're not ready to pull it off.

The news gets much worse: as show time approaches, Adam Clayton is nowhere to be found. The band attempts to reach him, and finds him hung-over in his hotel room. He had been avoiding alcohol since the Pacific tour began, but went on a drinking binge last night.

Shortly before the show starts, U2 meet in their dressing room. They tell Dallas Schoo, Edge's guitar tech, that Adam won't be playing, and ask his opinion on the situation. Canceling the show isn't an option because tonight's show is a dry run for tomorrow's worldwide pay-per-view broadcast. Edge suggests he play bass while Dallas plays guitar, but that idea is quickly dismissed. Paul McGuinness asks Dallas if Stuart Morgan, Adam's bass technician, can fill in. "Stuart can do it," Dallas says. "He knows

those songs. But you gotta keep eye contact with him, let him know when a bridge is coming up."

Morgan fills in admirably; it's the first time since the band's earliest days that they've played a show with someone missing. Bono tells the crowd that Adam is ill, but Adam reveals in later interviews that he was unable to perform because of a severe hangover.

The Night Adam Missed a U2 Gig
Adam: "I remember the night before thinking, 'Mmm, it might be nice to have a glass of wine.' The next thing I remember it was about 7 o'clock in the evening of the next day and people were trying to wake me up and see if I could go down and do the gig. I don't really know what happened in the intervening time, other than that I'd been out for a bit and I'd gone through the mini bar in the room. I was so wobbly and shaky and emotionally all over the place, just in complete meltdown, there was no way I could stand on stage for two hours."

The incident isn't taken lightly within the U2 camp; other members of the band and management impress upon Adam that his lifestyle is jeopardizing the band's future. They all agree to finish the tour and discuss the future afterward. "It's something that we have to think a lot about next year," Paul McGuinness says a week later. "I don't know what's going to happen. It's not up to *him* anymore."

Adam & alcohol: "It's over."
A week after the Sydney incident, Bill Flanagan asked Adam about what happened.

"I'm empty..." December 2
Excerpts from Bill Flanagan's interview of Adam Clayton.

"I'm empty, completely empty. We really need to take time off, to go live without thinking about music.

"I feel like we have really got something out of our system. I think that we have become the group that we always wanted to become.... We've got to the point where we may well be the greatest group in the world. Now what do you do with it?

"I don't know if we will feel the necessity for live work. We might just want to get the records out and enjoy time with our families and creative time.... I personally feel it would be very hard to beat Zoo TV, and I wouldn't want to do another two-year tour."

"It was a moment where I had to face a lot of things I hadn't really been facing and realise that if I was going to be able to go on and be a useful member of this band – and indeed a husband – I had to beat alcohol. I had to realise that every fuckup of mine, every problem over the last ten years that hasn't been quite so serious as that night, has been related to alcohol abuse. So I'm kind of glad I finally had to confront it... I feel it's a life-changing decision. And maybe I'll slip up. But I think for me and the bottle – it's over."

After the show, McGuinness, Ned O'Hanlon, Maurice Linnane and others gather backstage to watch the videotape of tonight's show and plan tomorrow's shoot down to the smallest detail.

November 27
Aussie Stadium, Sydney, with Kim Salmon and the Surrealists, Big Audio Dynamite II. Adam returns to the stage for tonight's show, which is shown live via pay-per-view in the US. A technical problem leaves some fans disappointed: the first half hour of the show is broadcast in mono, not stereo. The show airs later in 46 more countries, and is eventually released on home video.

November 28-29
Officials from Polygram Australia take U2 and a couple of dozen family, friends and crew on a four-hour tour of Sydney Harbor. As he is wont to do when near water, Bono jumps off the yacht and tries to steal a boat from the waterfront homes nearby. He fails to start a motorboat, and settles for a small rowboat, taking it from one home to another before swimming back to the Polygram yacht.

Later, Bono, Edge, Morleigh and a couple friends eat dinner at a Thai restaurant before spending the night going from club to club. At their last stop, somewhere around 4 a.m. (Nov. 29), Bono decides to celebrate wardrobe guru Fintan Fitzgerald's birthday with a swim at Bondi Beach. Bono drags along a waitress from the bar, and has to explain to her boss afterward where she went so she doesn't get fired.

November 30
U2 – minus Larry – spends a day at a winery in the New Zealand countryside outside Christchurch. Edge and Morleigh go horseback riding while others relax and enjoy a day away from the tour machine. After the winery, the group head to Akoroa Harbour for coffee and then to Mount Cavendish for dinner – taking a ski-lift ride to a restaurant up on the mountain. Arriving back in Christchurch, they meet up with Larry and others at a bar, where Bono is corralled into fulfilling a World AIDS Day interview request with a Dublin radio station.

Around this time, Bono turns down an invitation from Roger Daltrey to sing at the "Daltrey Sings Townshend" concerts planned for February, 1994, at Carnegie Hall.

December 1
Lancaster Park, Christchurch, with Big Audio Dynamite II. After tonight's show, Bono, Larry and others end up at a club called Wonderbar. A young woman invites Bono to come visit her paint studio nearby, but it's 3:30 a.m. (Dec. 2) and Bono has a flight to Auckland in the morning so he invites her to drop off photocopies of her work at the hotel. She does, and in the morning Bono buys two of her paintings and has them shipped to Dublin.

December 2
As the band settle in their Auckland hotel, writer Bill Flanagan – still following the band for his book, *U2 At The End Of The World* – visits privately with Adam to talk about how he's doing.

December 4
Western Springs Stadium, Auckland, with Three D's, Big Audio Dynamite II. After tonight's show, Bono leads a group out for a night on the town that goes until early morning. At about 5 a.m. (Dec. 5), they all go to One Tree Hill, jump the fences and climb to the top of the hill to watch the sunrise. It's Sunday morning, and on the way back into Auckland, the group goes to Mass.

December 5
U2 fly to Japan for the final two shows of the tour. As if jet lag from the long flight isn't enough, they

have a long drive from Narita Airport into Tokyo that takes them through the surreal, neon-lit skyscrapers that the band later says looked like a scene out of *Blade Runner*. After settling in at the Four Seasons Hotel, the tired group heads off in search of a highly recommended fish market restaurant. Local guides provided by the concert promoter follow behind in a separate car. Record producer Hal Willner joins them at the restaurant. After dinner, most of the U2 crew explores the parlors and clubs in the area into the early morning, landing at a disco where David Morales is DJing. Bono stays out with Fintan Fitzgerald, finally ending up at an apartment that belongs to some young Japanese girls. He refuses their offers of drugs and sex, and falls asleep. He's soon awakened by the feeling of a python crawling on his leg. Fintan manages to get the snake off him, and the two leave quickly to get back to U2's hotel.

Bono Recalls Strange Days at the End of Zoo TV

"I went to bed hardly at all. I just couldn't sleep, there was just so much going on outside. We spent a lot of time in this area called Shinjuku and Electric City, where you have these 25-50 foot neon signs in blue gold, flashing messages and huge hoarding advertising manga movies and cartoons.

"We had to keep escaping our minders – because the promoter wants to take care of you – to get into the dodgy areas of town. So we'd slip out of the back door and disappear into the night just to meet people."

Later during the week, Bono, Edge and Paul McGuinness do some of their Christmas shopping in Tokyo. Anton Corbijn arrives for a photo shoot with the band that takes them around the city. Photos are

shot in front of adult shops, at a Communist rally in Alta Square, and at the Shinjuku train station. The band also attend a banquet hosted by the Phonogram Nippon record label.

Above: Naomi Campbell and Adam at the premiere of the movie *In The Name Of The Father*, London, December 12.

December 9
Egg Dome, Tokyo, with Big Audio Dynamite II. In the morning, Bono and writer Bill Flanagan take a walk around Tokyo and have lunch at an Italian restaurant. They get back to the hotel only to find everyone gone; the shows in Japan start an hour earlier. He arrives at the Tokyo Dome with little time to spare before tonight's concert. The band is rusty after five days off, there are technical problems, and the crowd is typically reserved – it all adds up to a bland show. U2 are running on fumes. Even the soundchecks – U2's favourite time to jam and try out new material – are uninspiring. "The ideas have really dried up lately," Edge says.

December 10
Egg Dome, Tokyo, with Big Audio Dynamite II. U2 plays the final show of its Zoo TV/Zooropa/ Zoomerang tour. The band is inspired by the final show vibe, and tonight's show is much better than last night. Bono jumps into the crowd and runs around the arena during 'Where The Streets Have No Name'. Madonna, Simon Le Bon, Terence Trent D'Arby and even the members of Deep Purple watch the show from the

sound desk.

After the show, a fan gets under the security rope and makes a dash toward Bono. A security man knocks the fan to the ground but Bono helps him up, talks to him and signs his tourbook.

After nearly two years of touring, the Zoo TV tour barely makes a profit: $30 million in merchandise sales is what keeps the band from ending up in the red.

Larry: "We've all made enough money…"
"By putting on a show like this, we're not making any money, but that's irrelevant. It broadens our base so next time round we can do what we want, we can make more music. In the end, it's investing in our future. Not in our future financially, in our future musically – 'cause at the end of the day that's what it's all about. We've all made enough money to live for the rest of our lives quite comfortably. That's enough money."

The long *Achtung Baby/Zoo* TV campaign may be over, but Larry has important plans for his time off. "After ten years of being on the road, it's time now to advance a bit musically," he tells *Rolling Stone*. "I really want to learn how to explain myself in musical terms, the basics of music theory."

December 11
Bono and Edge do an interview with Canada's Much Music.

December 12
Bono, Ali, Adam and Naomi Campbell attend the Dublin premiere of Jim Sheridan's film, *In The Name Of The Father*.

December 31
Bono, Ali, and a few friends end the year with a Japanese ritual on the beach near their home: they light a bonfire, make a list of everything they want to let go of, and throw it into the fire.

With the Zoo TV era behind them, U2 goes its separate ways for a much-needed vacation and break from one another. Adam and Larry spend much of the year in New York City, both devoting themselves to learning new techniques about the bass and drums, respectively. Bono spends time with his family at their home in France, while Edge's relationship with Morleigh Steinberg continues to develop in Los Angeles and France. Bono and Edge are also heavily involved this year in plans to renovate The Clarence, U2's hotel in Dublin.

U2 and Paul McGuinness get into the merchandising business with the launch of Ultra Violet, a joint venture with the Winterland Productions merchandising company. It lasts until 1996, when Winterland bows out.

U2 eventually regroup late in the year to work with Brian Eno on a new project that's unlike any U2 has done before.

January 1
'Stay (Faraway, So Close!)' is certified Silver in the UK, with sales surpassing the 200,000 level.

January 19
Bono inducts Bob Marley into the Rock and Roll Hall of Fame at a ceremony in New York.

Bono inducts Bob Marley
An excerpt of Bono's speech inducting Bob Marley into the Rock and Roll Hall of Fame. **"Bob Marley didn't choose or walk down the middle. He raced to the edges, embracing all extremes, creating a oneness. His oneness. One love. He wanted everything at the same time. Prophet. Soul rebel. Rastaman. Herbsman. Wildman. A natural, mystic man. Lady's man. Island man. Family man. Rita's man. Soccer man. Showman. Shaman. Human. Jamaican!"**

January 22
Bono, Ali, Edge and Paul attend the Golden Globe Awards in Los Angeles, where Bono is competing against himself (and U2) with two nominations in the Best Song category: U2 is nominated for 'Stay (Faraway, So Close!)' from Wim Wenders' film *Faraway, So Close*, while Bono, Gavin Friday, and Maurice Seezer are nominated for 'You Made Me The Thief Of Your Heart' from Jim Sheridan's *In The Name Of The Father*. Both songs come up short as Bruce Springsteen's 'Streets Of Philadelphia' wins the award.

On the way into the show, Bono mistakenly assumes he has to stop and do interviews with every TV crew lined up along the red carpet. Told that he missed a crew from Argentina at the beginning of the line, he returns and speaks with them, too.

While in Los Angeles, Bono, Ali and Paul pay a visit to Bill Carter, who's now living in Santa Monica.

January 25
The *In The Name Of The Father* soundtrack is released. Bono co-writes and performs on the title track and 'Billy Boola', and co-writes 'You Made Me The Thief Of You Heart', which Sinead O'Connor performs.

New versions of 'Stay (Faraway, So Close!)' and 'The Wanderer' appear on the *Faraway, So Close!* soundtrack, which is released today in North America.

February
U2 and the British Performing Rights Society are still battling over the collection of rights payments, a fight that began one year ago (see February, 1993). Since the two sides have been unable to reach agreement, U2 brings an action against the BPRS to the High Court of Justice this month. The case will drag on for more than two years. The court rules in U2's favour in 1996, and the two sides eventually settle their differences.

Also this month, Paul McGuinness speaks at the annual MIDEM music business conference in Cannes, France. He says radio station representatives around the

Above: Bono with Frank Sinatra, March 1

world should play more local music and nurture new talent, "otherwise you'll have nothing to listen to in 10 years' time but U2 records".

February 1
U2 appears on the *Alternative NRG* Greenpeace benefit album, which is released today. The band contributes a live version of 'Until The End Of The World' recorded in San Diego on the Zoo TV Tour.

February 14
U2 formally opens The Kitchen, a new Dublin nightclub they've developed beneath the Clarence Hotel. Local media are impressed with the club itself – it represents "a brave new era in Dublin nightlife", says one – but disappointed by the lack of star power on opening night. "Stars fail to shine" says the *Irish Independent*, noting that the biggest celebrities aside from U2 who show up are Dolores O'Riordan of The Cranberries, Def Leppard's Joe Elliott and veteran rocker Jerry Lee Lewis.

February 28
Bono, Ali and Paul attend the first annual Rock the Vote Patrick Lippert Awards in New York, which honour R.E.M. this year for their contributions to Rock the Vote. During the show, President Clinton's advisor, George Stephanopoulos gives a speech that makes repeated references to the "young people". On his way out of the awards, Bono tells a TV reporter that he's turned off by the phrase "the young people" and how it was used tonight.

March 1
Bono is at Radio City Music Hall in

"I'm not gonna mess with him, are you?" March 1

Full text of Bono's introduction for Frank Sinatra at the 1994 Grammy Awards.

Frank never did like rock and roll
And he's not crazy about guys wearing earrings either
But he doesn't hold it against me
And anyway, the feeling is not mutual

Rock and roll people love Frank Sinatra because Frank
    has got what we want: swagger and attitude; he's
    big on attitude
Serious attitude, bad attitude
Frank's the Chairman of the Bad
Rock and roll plays at being tough but this guy, well,
    he's The Boss
The Boss of Bosses
The Man
The Big Bang of Pop
I'm not gonna mess with him, are you?

Who's this guy that every city in America wants to
    claim as their own?
This painter who lives in the desert, this first-rate,
    first-take actor
This singer who makes other men poets
Boxing clever with every word
Talking like America
Tough, straight-up, in headlines
Comin' through with the big stick, the aside, the
    quiet compliment
Good cop, bad cop, all in the same breath
You know his story 'cause it's your story
Frank walks like America – cock-sure
It's 1945 and the US Cavalry are trying to get their
    asses out of Europe, but they never really do
They're part of another kind of invasion AFR –
    American Forces Radio [sic]
Broadcasting a music that'll curl the stiff upper-lip
    of England and the rest of the world
Paving the way for Duke Ellington, the big band,
    Tommy Dorsey
And right out in front – Frank Sinatra
His voice as tight as a fist
Opening at the end of a bar
Not on the beat, over it, playing with it, splitting it
    like a jazz man, like Miles Davis
Turning on the right phrase and the right song

Which is where he lives, where he lets go, where he
    reveals himself
His songs are his home and he lets you in
But you know that to sing like that you've gotta have
    lost a couple of fights
To know tenderness and romance you've gotta have
    had your heart broken

People say that Frank hasn't talked to the press, they
    wanna know how he is, what's on his mind
But you know Sinatra's out there more nights than
    most punk bands
Selling his story through the songs
Telling and articulate in the choice of those songs
Private thoughts on a public address system
Generous

This is the conundrum of Frank Sinatra
Left and right brain hardly talking
Boxer and painter, actor and singer, lover and father,
    bandman and loner
Troubleshooter and troublemaker
The champ who would rather show you his scars than
    his medals
He may be putty in Barbara's hands
But I'm not gonna mess with him, are you?

Ladies and gentlemen, are you ready to welcome a
    man heavier than the Empire State, more connected
    than the Twin Towers, as recognizable as the Statue
    of Liberty, and living proof that God is a Catholic!

Will you welcome the King of New York City, Francis
    Albert Sinatra!

173

Patrick Pfeiffer shares his favourite story from a summer of giving bass lessons to Adam, May 11

"One day there was a monsoon-like thunderstorm in New York City, right around Adam's lesson time. I thought for sure he'd call and tell me to reschedule the lesson. The weather really was ridiculous. Instead, the doorbell rings at his regular time, and as I open the door he stands there, drenched to the bone. I mean soaked. He just looks at me as I stare at him incredulously, and says – in his Irish accent – 'Couldn't get a cab, didn't want to miss my lesson...can I hang my shirt somewhere?' That just floored me! He would simply let nothing come between him and what he's determined to do."

New York City for tonight's Grammy Awards. Arriving in the afternoon, Bono visits and drinks whiskey with Frank Sinatra in Sinatra's dressing room.

During the show U2 wins its fifth Grammy Award: Best Alternative Album, for *Zooropa*. Bono accepts the award by thanking the college radio scene and makes a sarcastic comment about U2 being considered an "alternative" band. He stammers a bit, and then likely remembering last night's Rock the Vote event, he offers a message to *the young people*: "I'd like to give a message to the young people of America. That is, we shall continue to abuse our position and fuck up the mainstream." TV censors, along with a good portion of the US viewing audience, are shocked by Bono's word choice on live TV. But Bono comes back on stage later to deliver the night's true highlight: an introduction of Frank

Sinatra, who's picking up a Living Legend award.

Sinatra, clearly moved by Bono's words, says Bono's introduction is "maybe the best I've ever had". Sinatra rambles a bit while accepting the award, and organizers want Bono to go out and lead him off-stage. When Bono refuses, the orchestra begins playing and the TV production cuts to a commercial. At that point, Bono goes on stage and says, "Time to go, Frank." In the aftermath of the Sinatra controversy, his handlers say they called for the speech to be cut because they were afraid "he would have talked for about an hour".

After the Grammys, Bono and Ali attend a post-show party at the Rainbow Room. Paul McGuinness collects them and takes them to a different party, where Sinatra gives Bono a wristwatch inscribed, "To Bono – Thanks – Frank A. Sinatra."

March 2
Still in New York City, Bono and Ali have dinner with writer Bill Flanagan.

April
Around this time, Adam and Larry record four tracks in New York City with Nanci Griffith for her upcoming *Flyer* album.

April 4
U2's *Zoo TV: Live From Sydney* is released on video today in the UK and Europe. 'Trying To Throw Your Arms Around the World' is edited out without explanation, prompting great speculation. Fans suggest the edit allows the concert to fit on one 2-hour VHS tape, or that the female dancer didn't agree to appear in the home release, or that she was underage and drank champagne on stage with Bono.

May
While in New York, Adam helps Little Steven Van Zandt record his *Born Again Savage* album, playing bass on every track. Due to record label issues, the album won't be released until 1999. During a conversation about singing, Little Steven suggests Adam see a teacher named Katie Agresta for lessons.

Issue 19 of *Propaganda* magazine is published around this time.

Mexican music magazine *La Mosca en la Pared* (The Fly on the Wall) publishes a set of photos from U2's visit to Teotihuacan in November, 1992. A couple of photos show Bono and Larry posing shirtless with friends in front of the pyramids. The magazine reports that these photos were stolen from a room at U2's hotel, and then delivered anonymously to the magazine's offices.

Early this month, Bono and Ali attend the 21st anniversary celebration for Mount Temple Comprehensive School at the Grand Hotel Malahide. "I would love to send my own kids there, or somewhere with a similarly progressive attitude," Bono tells reporters. "Mount Temple had a knack of discovering what you were good at and steering you in that direction."

Around this time, Bono records a solo cover version of 'Hallelujah' at STS Studios in Dublin. The track will appear on a Leonard Cohen tribute album in 1995.

May 2
Paul McGuinness attends the annual TJ Martell Foundation dinner in New York City, which honors MTV chief Tom Freston this year. While in New York, McGuinness also spends a week negotiating with Freston and MTV about details of a proposed Zoo TV network.

May 11
Adam has his first singing lesson today with Katie Agresta. Agresta also introduces Adam to bass instructor Patrick Pfeiffer, and after they talk a while, Adam agrees to work with Pfeiffer after the vocal lessons are finished.

During the summer, Pfeiffer takes Adam to Sadowsky Guitars, where Adam buys a Sadowsky bass.

After his singing lesson, Adam meets Bill Flanagan for dinner in New York City, in part wanting to clarify some of the things they discussed during the Zoo TV tour that Flanagan might write about in his upcoming book. After dinner, they catch a show by Gil Scott-Heron at a club called S.O.B.'s.

During their time together, Adam tells Flanagan that he and Naomi Campbell have split up. Adam also says he's been hanging out at The Cooler, a blues/soul club, listening to artists like Me'shell Ndegeocello, and sending tapes of the new artists he discovers to Bono.

Larry is also taking lessons this summer. His teachers include David Beal in New York, who teaches Larry about studio operations, drum machines, and the like. Larry also visits Gary Schaffe, a "drum doctor" in Boston who helps teach Larry about form and technique, so he can play better and with less pain.

May 17
U2's *Zoo TV: Live From Sydney* is released on video in North America.

May 23
Seveal U2 releases are certified today by the RIAA: *Wide Awake In America* and *The Unforgettable Fire* (Multi-Platinum, two million sold); *Under A Blood Red Sky* (Multi-Platinum, three million sold); *October and Boy* (Gold, 500,000 sold).

May 25
Bono and Edge attend the Ivor Novello Awards in London tonight, where U2 earns an Award for International Achievement.

June 16
U2 and friends throw a birthday party in New York City for Paul McGuinness, who's 43 today.

June 18
Many in the U2 organization are in attendance today as Ireland stuns Italy, 1-0, in a first round World Cup

Bono with Ali (above) and Edge (below) at the Ivor Novello Awards, Grosvenor House Hotel, London, May 25.

soccer match at Giants Stadium in East Rutherford, New Jersey. Edge, Paul McGuinness and a couple of dozen friends watch from a luxury box high above the field. Larry Mullen and Joe O'Herlihy skip the skybox and watch the match from seats close to the field. (Bono is in London.)

The party begins as soon as the match ends, and the U2ers decide to celebrate the win over Italy at Carmine's Italian restaurant. From there, Edge and a couple friends head to the Irish pub, Sin-é, and later settle at another pub in the city.

June 28
Larry attends the Ireland v. Norway World Cup match at Giants Stadium, which ends in a 0-0 draw. Afterward, Larry takes many of the Irish players on a tour of New York City and hosts a party in his apartment.

June 29
After many months of pestering from Negativland, Paul McGuinness signs a letter okaying the return of the 1991 'U2' parody single – which is legally owned by Island Records – back to Negativland, and giving them

permission to re-release the single on two conditions: 1) that it has new artwork, and 2) that Casey Kasem agrees to having the song re-released. Polygram and Island Records sign similar letters in September of this year.

Summer
Bono and Larry attend an inter-church youth event in Dublin organised by a Church of Ireland officer named Steve Stockman. Australian minister John Smith is speaking at the event.

August 20
Bono contributes an original drawing to an auction that benefits the AIDS Drop-In Centre in Dublin.

September
Issue 20 of *Propaganda* magazine is published around this time.

French environmentalists publicly criticise Bono and Edge for uprooting several centuries-old trees in order to build a road leading toward their villa in the south of France.

September 13
Larry and Adam appear on Nanci

Griffith's *Flyer* album, which is released today.

September 14
At a Sotheby's auction in London, Bono pays £35,000 for Charlie Chaplin's uniform from the 1940 film, *The Great Dictator*. He plans to display it at Mr. Pussy's Café Deluxe in Dublin. Meanwhile, in Dublin tonight, Ali bids £200 and wins a vasectomy during a charity auction for the Dublin AIDS Alliance. Bono never uses the voucher, instead donating it to a local woman whose husband can't afford the operation. Edge is also at the auction, and wins a signed Allen Ginsberg photo and artwork by Brian Eno.

September 15
BP Fallon throws a party at Mr. Pussy's Café in Dublin to celebrate the release of his book, *U2 Faraway So Close*. None of the band members attend, but Bono, Edge and Adam (with Naomi Campbell) are spotted tonight at the Clarence Hotel.

September 28
Edge attends the opening of *Little Pieces From Big Stars*, an art exhibit in London benefiting the War Child

organization. Bono's contribution to the exhibit is a music box containing Fly glasses, a cigar and a gold American Express card. The items will be auctioned off on October 4.

October
Sometime this month, Edge takes part in an anti-Sellafield protest march in Dublin. The march ends with a short concert at St. Stephen's Green. Edge doesn't perform, but he does say a few remarks to the crowd.

October 1
U2's Clarence Hotel closes temporarily for refurbishing.

October 4-5-6-7
Nanci Griffith plays four shows in four nights at the Point Theatre in Dublin. Larry reportedly shows up at one of the shows and plays drums.

November
U2 spends two weeks recording at Westside Studios in London with Brian Eno – their first time playing together since the end of the Zoo TV tour 11 months ago. Eno's influence is obvious: he decorates

Below: Bono and UK Labour Party leader Tony Blair at the Q magazine awards, Park Lane Hilton Hotel, London, November 9.

the studio walls with rare cloths from India, Africa, and the Arab world in an attempt to add ambience; he sets up a giant TV/movie screen and uses it to show a variety of video clips while the band is recording; and he keeps the band alert by having them switch instruments during some sessions. Anton Corbijn is there to document the unusual sessions on film. Bono says the vibe reminds him of being back in Tokyo at the end of Zoo TV: "I thought we'd have to go back to Japan to get that spirit, but it's with us."

U2 aren't sure these sessions are the start of the next U2 album, and have given Eno more creative control than normal over the studio and the music. At dinner one night, Edge says the work feels like a new, five-man group and suggests they give themselves a new name. Singer Neneh Cherry is at the restaurant, too, and the band invite her to their table and talk about having her join them in the studio. Bono convinces the restaurant to play a tape of one of the songs they're working on, and Cherry and a friend sing improvised lyrics as they listen at the table.

November 9
U2 win a Merit Award at the Q Awards at the Park Lane Hilton Hotel in London. Bono addresses the guest of honor, Labour Party leader Tony Blair, saying "que cojones hombre" ... or, "what balls, mate." This is the first occasion that the two men meet.

November 24
Bono accepts the Free Your Mind award on behalf of Amnesty International at the MTV European Music Awards in Germany. He tells the crowd, "Free your mind and your ass will follow."

December 1
Paul McGuinness speaks today at a conference on the economy and arts in Dublin. He defends U2's record on creating jobs and bringing revenue into Ireland, and calls for arts minister Michael D. Higgins to be restored to office as soon as possible.

After an extremely quiet 1994, U2 are only slightly more visible this year. The band shows up on a few soundtrack albums, do a few collaborations with other artists, and Bono records a couple of solo songs. Early in the year, U2 show up in a US TV documentary, *The History Of Rock & Roll*. Bono is interviewed about U2's early days, and about the impact of Elvis Presley, The Clash, Jimi Hendrix and others.

U2's main project is a partnership with Brian Eno that results in The U2 Album That Shall Not Be Called a U2 Album: *Original Soundtracks I* by Passengers. The album sees U2 taking its experimental tendencies to the extreme. Shortly after the Passengers album hits stores, U2 returns to being U2. But Larry has back surgery and misses the first couple months of work on the next proper U2 album.

January

Issue 21 of *Propaganda* magazine is published around this time. It includes *Melon: Remixes For Propaganda*, a fanclub-only CD featuring nine remixes of U2 songs. The CD becomes an instant collectors' item, and is widely bootlegged.
Tracks: 'Lemon – (Perfecto mix)', 'Salome – (Zooromancer mix)', 'Numb – (Gimme Some More Dignity mix)', 'Mysterious Ways – (Perfecto mix)', 'Stay (Faraway, So Close!) – (Underdog mix)', 'Numb – (Soul Assassins mix)', 'Mysterious Ways – (Massive Attack mix)', 'Even Better Than The Real Thing – (Perfecto mix)', 'Lemon – (Bad Yard Club mix)'

Bono and Ali take a vacation in Jamaica, spending time with Island Records founder Chris Blackwell at his home in Strawberry Hill. Anton Corbijn happens to be on the island, too, and shoots some pictures.

January 6

Zoo TV – Live From Sydney is nominated for a Grammy Award: Best Music Video, Longform.

January 16

Edge attends the Dublin premiere of Neil Jordan's *Interview With The Vampire*.

January 24

The Chieftains' release a new album, *The Long Black Veil*.

Below: Brian Eno, Bono, Edge and operatic tenor Luciano Pavarotti at the Children of Bosnia charity concert, Modena, Italy, September 12.

Although he's not credited in the album notes, Bono is believed to sing on the title track.

February 6
U2 settles a $38,000 lawsuit brought against them by a US-based interior decorator that worked on the Clarence Hotel in 1993. O'Brien and Associates Design claimed that U2 failed to pay for work the firm completed before their contract was cancelled.

February 15
Zoo TV – Live From Sydney is certified Gold by the RIAA, with video sales eclipsing 500,000 in the US.

February 28
Bono and Edge join forces with Irish singing legend Christy Moore to record a song entitled 'North And South Of The River' in Windmill Lane Studios. The track will appear on Moore's *Graffiti Tongue* album in 1996, and U2 will re-record it as a B-side on the 'Staring At The Sun' single in 1997.

Also today, Paul McGuinness' new venture, the Celtic Heartbeat music label, issues its first seven releases. McGuinness forms Celtic Heartbeat with former Clannad manager David Kavanagh and Barbara Galavan of Principle Management. The intention of the label is to bring non-rock Irish artists to an international audience, but the venture folds in 2000 due to poor sales.

March
No one is particularly happy with a cover of 'Hallelujah' that Bono is recording, prompting Island Records' Nick Angel to call DJ Howie B and ask him to listen to the track. Within a couple hours, Howie remixes the song and everyone is happy. It's the first time the well-known DJ has worked with U2, but it won't be the last.

March 1
U2 wins the Best Music Video, Longform Grammy award for *Zoo TV – Live From Sydney*.

March 17
Bono and Edge watch Simple Minds play tonight at the Point Depot in Dublin.

March 30
Bono joins Prince on stage at The Pod nightclub in Dublin to perform parts of Prince's song, 'The Cross'.

April
Early in the month, Bono brings a cassette tape of U2's new song, 'Hold Me, Thrill Me, Kiss Me, Kill Me', and asks a DJ at the Pod nightclub to play it for the crowd.

May
Issue 22 of *Propaganda* magazine is published around this time.

May 24
Brian Eno joins U2 in Dublin to continue work on their new project together. They're working on a song currently called 'Tenterhook', which is set around the Miss Sarajevo Beauty Pageant and features Bono repeating lyrics that begin with "Is there a time...".

Meanwhile, opera star Luciano Pavarotti is calling Bono almost every day. When Bono refuses to take his calls, Pavarotti leaves a message: "Tell God to call me back!" The tenor wants Bono to write him a song and perform at his charity concert in September. Bono repeatedly refuses both requests, but Pavarotti refuses to take no for an answer and continues phoning.

Simultaneous to this project, Bono and Edge are writing the theme song for *Goldeneye*, the next James Bond film.

June
Bono contributes a poem titled *Elvis: American David* to a special edition of *Q* magazine, which has asked various musicians to contribute to a feature called "The Record That Changed My Life." The poem is a longer version of the lyrics to 'Elvis Ate America', one of the new U2-Eno tracks.

June 1
At 6:30 a.m., directors Kevin Godley and Maurice Linnane wrap up the last-minute production on an animated music video for U2's new single, 'Hold Me, Thrill Me, Kiss Me, Kill Me'. The song – an unfinished track from the *Zooropa* sessions – is the lead single for the film, *Batman Forever*. The video is delivered to MTV in New York for its world premiere tonight.

Ned O'Hanlon describes the frantic final day
"When the video was so late, I literally ran out of an edit suite in London and jumped on the Concorde, as you do [*laughs*], to deliver the tape to MTV in New York for its world premiere the same day. And I had to bring it down for their legal people to look at it. And in one of the animated shots, there's a pan down from a shop sign which, in America, says 'Mr. Swampy's'. In the original it says 'Mr. Pussy's'. There was a drag artist here in Dublin, and Bono and – it might've been the whole band – and Bono's brother, Norman Hewson, were responsible for running a place called Mr. Pussy's. So that was sort of an homage to Mr. Pussy, but it wouldn't pass the censors in New York. So I had to go into an edit suite there and just change that to 'Mr. Swampy'. Swampy was the name of a dog that Kevin Godley owned, a three-legged dog that had died about three weeks beforehand."

June 5/6
'Hold Me, Thrill Me, Kiss Me, Kill Me' is released, with varying formats including the additional tracks 'Themes from *Batman Forever*' by Elliot Goldenthal and 'Tell Me Now' by Mazzy Star. It hits number one in Australia and Ireland, number two in the UK, number 11 in Canada, and number 16 in the US charts. Had the film's producers gotten their way, the

song wouldn't have been U2's only contribution to the film: they offered Bono $5 million to play MacPhisto, his Zoo TV alter-ego, as a bad guy in the film alongside Jim Carrey's Riddler.

June 12/13
The *Batman Forever* soundtrack is released. On June 12, the RIAA certifies *War* (three million sold) and *The Joshua Tree* (six million sold) as Multi-Platinum.

June 14
Legendary Irish guitarist Rory Gallagher dies in London. "A beautiful man and an amazing guitar player. He was a very sensitive man and a great musician," says Edge.

June 18
The Xpress, a small, underground Irish newspaper publishes an exclusive interview with Bono and Adam, in which they reveal that the band is working on two albums simultaneously: one, a soundtrack album with Brian Eno, and two, a "rock and roll album". It's U2's first interview in two years. U2 talks to *The Xpress* because it's made up of some of their journalist friends who recently lost their jobs when several newspapers shut down.

Meanwhile, today's plans originally call for Bono to speak at the UK Year of Literature and Writing in Swansea, but the event is postponed at the last minute until later in the year.

July
U2 and Brian Eno continue work on their upcoming album in Dublin. They've set the end of July as the deadline to have the album completed. Howie B is in Dublin to DJ at The Kitchen, so U2 ask him to come listen to their new material.

July 6
Bono and Ali are on hand for an invitation-only Gavin Friday show at the Pod nightclub, where Friday is previewing material from his upcoming album. After the gig, it's on to U2's own club, The Kitchen, where Bono, Edge, and Larry help Amnesty International's Irish

Below: During 1996 Bono and Adam supported the Divorce Referendum in Eire which achieved a yes vote in November.

branch celebrate winning MTV's Free Your Mind Award late last year.

July 7
As he's been doing regularly since May, Italian tenor Luciano Pavarotti calls Bono again today – twice. He's still asking U2 to perform at his charity concert in September. Bono and Edge are more open to the idea, but Paul, Larry, and Adam aren't interested.

July 9
Bono, Brian Eno, and others – including Elvis Costello – have dinner at Adam's house tonight.

July 10
Undaunted by continued rejection, Luciano Pavarotti shows up with a camera crew at U2's Dublin studio to continue pressing his case for a collaboration. Pavarotti, Bono, Edge and Brian Eno do an interview for the camera crew, prompting Bono to say, "We have to do Modena." The band is still split on the idea of going to Italy. They eventually reach an agreement: Pavarotti will sing on one of U2's new songs, 'Miss Sarajevo', and Bono, Edge, and Brian Eno will perform the song with him at the charity concert.

July 11
Carole King visits Bono at the

studio and the two begin writing a song together.

July 12
Bono and others see Howie B do a DJ set at The Kitchen tonight, and hang out with Bjork.

July 26
While U2 and Brian Eno are trying to make final decisions before the deadline to finish their new album, Anton Corbijn is with them in Dublin to shoot more promotional photos. All five pose in chefs' costumes; for other photos, Larry dresses as a biker, Bono wears Hawaiian clothes, and Edge dresses as a 1940s-era golfer.

July 29
U2 and Eno put the final touches on their new album. With the recording done, the members of U2 take a month-long vacation during August.

August
Bono and Edge appear on Gavin Friday's album, *Shag Tobacco*, which is released this month in Europe. They sing backing vocals on 'Little Black Dress'. The album will be released in the US in January, 1996.

Around the middle of the month, Willie Williams travels to Cleveland to install a Zoo TV exhibit at the Rock and Roll Hall of Fame, which is due to open in early September.

August 1
Rattle And Hum is certified Multi-Platinum, with US sales of more than four million. In the UK, 'Hold Me, Thrill Me, Kiss Me, Kill Me' is certified Gold, with sales of more than 400,000.

August 10
Having heard the finished U2/Brian Eno album, Island Records tells Eno they're nervous about releasing it under U2's name. They're afraid that fans will be confused by the collaboration, and that it might undo some of U2's success to date. "Isn't this the sort of liberty that that kind of success is meant to earn you," Eno asks. Together, Eno and the label come up with the "Passengers" name.

1995

Island Records' Marc Marot on why it couldn't be a "U2 record"

"I was very, very, very strict on trying to stop this from being perceived by everybody as a U2 record, for a number of reasons. *Zooropa* had not been particularly critically well received, and it hadn't done particularly well commercially. And what I didn't want was there being another – the perception of there being another U2 record that didn't do well critically, and didn't do well commercially."

August 11
Eno discusses the Passengers concept with U2, and agree that confusion might occur in music stores if U2's name is put on the album. They expand the Passengers idea into something that can include other artists in the future.

August 16
More than 100 people are evacuated from The Kitchen when a fire is spotted on the Clarence Hotel's roof. No one is inside the hotel itself, which is undergoing renovations.

September 1
The Rock and Roll Hall Of Fame and Museum opens in Cleveland. The Zoo TV exhibit includes four Trabants that hang from the ceiling of the main lobby, and the "Zoo TV" neon sign hangs nearby. The exhibit is the first thing visitors will see when they enter the museum.

September 2
Bono, Edge and Paul McGuinness attend the formal Rock and Roll Hall Of Fame dinner and concert. Despite rumours to the contrary, Bono and Edge don't perform at the concert.

September 6
Achtung Baby is certified Multi-Platinum, with US sales of more than seven million.

September 7
'Hold Me, Thrill Me, Kiss Me, Kill Me' wins the International Viewer's Choice: MTV Europe award at the MTV Video Music Awards.

September 10
Bono, Edge and Brian Eno arrive in Modena, Italy, today for the first day of rehearsals before a benefit concert that opera star Luciano Pavarotti is hosting in two days.

September 11
The Passengers rehearse again today, then have a late dinner at a restaurant Pavarotti owns. US sales of *The Joshua Tree* pass the 10 million mark, just one of several RIAA certifications today: *Rattle And Hum* (Multi-Platinum, five million sold); *War* (Multi-Platinum, four million sold); *The Unforgettable Fire* (three million sold); *Boy and October* (Platinum, one million sold).

September 12
Parco Novi Sad, Modena. Bono, Edge and Brian Eno perform at the annual Pavarotti and Friends charity concert. They premiere a new song, 'Miss Sarajevo', featuring vocals in Italian by Pavarotti, do an acoustic version of 'One' backed by a classical orchestra, and are part of the closing ensemble performance of 'Nessun Dorma'. After each song, Bono calls home to ask Ali how they did; she's watching on satellite TV.

Backstage after the concert, Pavarotti joins Bono's dad, Bob, and Edge's dad, Garvin, in singing 'Happy Birthday' to Eno's wife, Anthea. Later, all the artists attend a formal dinner where Princess Diana, who had attended the show, is the guest of honor.

September 13
After widespread rumor and several title changes, Island Records announces the formation of Passengers, the collaboration of U2 and Brian Eno. The new album is titled *Original Soundtracks I*, and is slated for release on November 7.

September 26
Bono sings 'Hallelujah' on *Tower of Song: The Songs Of Leonard Cohen*, a

Bono and Adam explain Passengers, September 13

Adam: "For us, this is an opportunity to get all this stuff out that there isn't really room for on our own records."
Bono: "We've always wanted to make what you might describe as a blue record, an ambient record, an atmospheric record. U2 hasn't yet made an *After Midnight* record. We want to make music that you can have sex to."

tribute album that's released today. Also out today is *Wrecking Ball* by Emmylou Harris, which includes Larry's drum and percussion work on nine of the album's 12 songs.

October
Larry and his longtime girlfriend, Ann Acheson, give birth to a son, Aaron Elvis.

October 1
Bono appears at London's Swansea Grand Theater to participate in the UK Year Of Literature and Writing series. BBC *Newsnight* journalist and *Guardian* music writer Robin Denselow handles the relaxed interview, which includes a fair amount of talk about the upcoming Passengers album. Bono also explains why the band has become less outspoken about its politics, explaining that they didn't want to bore people with its personal tirades: "The first responsibility of someone in a rock band is to be interesting," Bono says.

After the show, Bono bumps into a small group of fans outside the Marriott Hotel. He asks them if they enjoyed the interview, and

agrees to a couple photographs before leaving for the airport.

Rattle And Hum is certifiedMulti-Platinum by the BPI, with UK sales surpassing the 1.2 million mark.

October 15
Bono, Adam, and Edge show up for Gavin Friday's gig at the Tivoli Theatre in Dublin.

October 17
Bono sings 'Save The Children' on the Marvin Gaye tribute album, *Inner City Blues*, which is released today.

October 18
Bono and Brian Eno discuss plans for the next U2 album. Bono tells Eno that Larry is about to have back surgery and will be in New York City recovering until Christmas, and will miss the early recording sessions.

November
Issue 23 of *Propaganda* magazine is published around this time.

U2 reassembles in Dublin this month to start making plans for a new album. Paramount Pictures invite them to do theme song for their upcoming blockbuster, *Mission: Impossible*. At first, no one thinks it's a good idea. Adam, however, decides he and Larry can work on the song during down times after U2 starts recording. "*Mission: Impossible* is such a great tune that we thought we'd try to do an updated version, and think of it more as something that would work in clubs rather than something that would promote a movie," Adam says.

November 6-7
Original Soundtracks 1 is released worldwide under the name Passengers. With the project guided more strongly by Brian Eno than a traditional U2 album, the band avoids heavy promotion fearing fans will mistake it for a new U2 release. But when the CD arrives in music stores, it carries a sticker on the front: "File under U2." The album is a mix of instrumentals and vocal songs, only one or two of which are even recognizable as U2 songs. Though some song titles have changed since the summer recording sessions, several early titles – 'Tokyo Drift', 'Tokyo Glacier (Fact)', and 'Ito Okashi' – make reference to U2's mindbending stay in Japan two years ago at the end of the Zoo TV tour.

Bono: "Tokyo seems to be the home of this record."
"For whatever reason, Tokyo seems to be the home of this record. Arriving there at the end of the Zoo TV tour, it became clear to us that this was actually the capital of Zoo TV. In Tokyo, you don't feel you are in the present tense. You feel as if you have stepped into the future."

Reviews are a mixed bag. Tom Moon of Knight-Ridder likes it: "Anybody with a synthesizer can generate drone music. On Original Soundtracks I, U2 argues that it takes skill, and heart, to make such austerity meaningful." The

Below: Bono in Sarajevo for New Year's Eve.

Washington Post's Mark Jenkins says, "... 'Soundtracks' is seldom anything more than high-tech slug music."
Tracks: 'United Colours', 'Slug', 'Your Blue Room', 'Always Forever Now', 'A Different Kind Of Blue', 'Beach Sequence', 'Miss Sarajevo', 'Ito Okashi', 'One Minute Warning', 'Corpse (These Chains Are Way Too Long)', 'Elvis Ate America', 'Plot 180', 'Theme From The Swan', 'Theme 'From Let's Go Native'

'Goldeneye', the James Bond soundtrack song written by Bono and Edge and recorded by Tina Turner, is released today as a single. And Bono sings on 'Let The Good Times Roll', a track from Quincy Jones new album, Q's Jook Joint, which is also out today.

November 12
Bono writes a poem for the people of East Timor, who are fighting for freedom while under Indonesian rule. Some East Timorese living in Australia hear Bono's poem and set it to music. The song is called 'Love From A Short Distance', which is how Bono signed off the written poem. The song inspires other artists to write or donate songs, all of which appear on a late 1996 compilation album in Australia also called Love From A Short Distance.

November 20/21
'Miss Sarajevo' is released, with varying formats including the tracks 'One (live)', 'Bottoms (Watashitachi No Ookina Yume)',

and 'Viva Davidoff'. It reaches number six on the UK charts. U2 and Brian Eno donate all proceeds from the single to War Child.

November 22
Bono attends the London premiere of *Goldeneye*.

November 23
U2 appears at the MTV Europe Music Awards in Paris to accept the award for Best Group, as voted by MTV Europe viewers. U2 is one of many artists who use the show to criticize French President Jacques Chirac for recent nuclear tests conducted underwater in the Pacific Ocean.

December 5
Ronnie Drew releases a new album, *Dirty Rotten Shame*. Bono co-writes the track 'Drinkin' In The Day'.

December 14
Bono and Edge appear via tape from London on a US television birthday tribute for 80-year-old Frank Sinatra, performing 'Two Shots Of Happy, One Shot Of Sad'. The ceremony was recorded November 19th, so U2's segment was likely taped in the days shortly before this recording date.

December 19
The Passengers track 'Always Forever Now' appears on the *Heat* film soundtrack, which is released today. The version on the soundtrack is about 30 seconds longer than the original.

December 30
Bono and Ali fly to Sarajevo, where they'll spend a highly publicized few days celebrating the New Year holiday in the city that has been ravaged by ethnic war. Cameras follow the pair everywhere they go, and Bono often provides great photo opportunities for the media. They meet with city officials, socialize at a Sarajevo dance club, and Bono sits down for a press conference in which he discusses his visit, the 1993 live satellite reports from Bill Carter, and the story behind the song 'Miss Sarajevo', among other things.

1996

With the Passengers project now in their rear view mirror, U2 devotes its attention to the next proper U2 album. They start early in the year without Larry, who's still recovering from back surgery. U2's nightclub and the presence of people like Howie B and Nellee Hooper gives the band lots of reasons to spend time away from the studio. "We went out a lot during the making of *Pop*," Bono says later. "There was a lot of music in that period coming from the dance end of things. We were just loving it – loving being alive and 'living it large' I think is the expression."

U2's original plan calls for recording to end in July with a September/October release. But the band misses that deadline and pushes the release back to November. Polygram pressures the band to have the album on shelves in time for the holiday shopping season. But U2 is still unhappy with the work they've done and misses the second deadline, too. They go back into the studio in September, making a release this year impossible. The album release is delayed until early 1997 – shortly before a world tour is due to start.

January
U2 wins six honors in the *Hot Press* 1995 readers poll: Irish Group, Irish Single ('Miss Sarajevo'), Irish Live Act, Irish Songwriter (Bono), Irish Musician (Edge), and Music Video ('Miss Sarajevo').

U2 begin recording their new album this month in Dublin.

January 16
Bono and his family are on the receiving end of police gunfire as their plane lands in Negril, Jamaica, where they plan to meet up with Adam. Local police had been tipped that a plane loaded with drugs would be landing in Negril around the same time and open fire – but not until after the Hewsons, Chris Blackwell and Jimmy Buffett had all gotten off the plane. The police apologize for firing at the wrong plane.

February
Finally recovered from back surgery, Larry rejoins the band in the studio this month.

February 1
U2 meet with Willie Williams for their initial discussion about the next world tour. One of Williams' early ideas is for U2 to play in the round, with video screens and smaller stages mounted on vehicles moving around the venue. Another idea is a nightly party called U2000 that includes a giant clock ticking down to midnight, December 31, 1999, and a plan for U2 to play 'New Year's Day' as 1999 becomes 2000. "Bear in mind," Williams says later, "there was no title for the album, no lyrics. So I was going on instinct." The band passes on both ideas. They also pass on one of Bono's early ideas, which involves giant lotto balls with mini-projectors inside being distributed at each show, and Bono's image being shown on the lotto balls during the song 'Playboy Mansion'.

February 3
Bono attends the Brown Thomas charity fashion show – organised by his wife, Ali – at Dublin's Point Theatre. Adam and Naomi Campbell hang out at a party at The Kitchen afterward; it's reportedly the first time they've seen each other since their engagement broke off 18 months ago.

March 5
U2 misses out on the Best Band award at tonight's *Hot Press/Heineken Music Awards*, but Edge wins the first annual Rory Gallagher Rock Musician Award.

Edge accepts the Rory Gallagher Rock Musician Award
"I want to accept the award on behalf of all the young men and women in bedsits and bedrooms all over the country trying to work out how to do that first Bar A chord, and dreaming of being in a rock'n'roll band, up there on stage making a lot of noise. In 1966, that would have been Rory at home in Cork, and about ten years later that would have been me in Malahide doing exactly the same thing."

March 13
U2 throw a surprise birthday party for Adam in their Dublin studios.

March 22
Bono sees Oasis play at the Point Depot.

March 24
The Sunday Independent publishes a photograph of Bono and Oasis' lead singer Liam Gallagher exchanging an open-mouth kiss. The photo was taken after Oasis' show at the Point Depot two nights earlier. Similar photos from a slightly different angle are also published in other UK media outlets. In a 1999 article in *Rolling Stone*, Bono explains the photo: "Actually, what happened was he had a guitar pick in his mouth, and he dared me to take it off him while the paparazzi were standing around. I couldn't resist. I can't say his breath smelled sweetly – let me put it that way. I, however, look like I've just come from the local boxing club."

Late March
Near the end of the month, Irish police arrest a Canadian U2 fan who has been stalking U2 with repeated phone calls and letters. The man is arrested while lurking on Adam's property south of Dublin. Police escort him to Dublin Airport and send him home.

March 30
Bono and Larry watch Irish boxer

Wayne McCullough fight Jose Luis Bueno at The Point in Dublin.

April 2
Bono and Edge appear on *Together For The Children Of Bosnia*, a compilation album that includes all three songs they performed at the Pavarotti & Friends concert last September 12.

April 24
Willie Nelson visits U2's studios in Dublin to record a version of 'Slow Dancing', the song Bono had written for him years earlier.

April 25
Bono joins Willie Nelson on stage for a couple songs at the Point Depot.

Late April
After considering a visit to Cuba, U2 instead travel to Miami in search of inspiration, hoping a change of scenery will stimulate their songwriting and push the recording in a new direction. They spend about three weeks in Miami and manage to write one new song, 'Miami', a travelogue of their time in the city. Anton Corbijn comes over to do publicity photos. Morleigh Steinberg shoots video footage, some of which will become an alternate music video for 'Staring At The Sun'.

Above: Larry at the premiere of the movie *Mission Impossible*, Los Angeles, May 22.

Adam explains the move to Miami, Late April

"We'd been in the studio for a while, slugging it out with the direction of the record. And it's a very nice place to be stuck for six months or so – but I think at that stage we all needed a bit of fresh air. So we went to Miami and we had a very good time!"

May 11
Irish rock journalist Bill Graham dies of a heart attack at the home he shares with his mother, Eileen, in Howth. It was Graham who first championed the band in Dublin media and who suggested to both the band members and Paul McGuinness that McGuinness manage their career. Bono and Adam contribute recollections to special editions of *Hot Press* magazine. "I can't imagine how the people in *Hot Press* are feeling right now," Bono writes. "From the beginning there were four or five in there who were like a band – losing Bill, for them, must be like how I'd feel if something happened to Edge or Adam or Larry. He was like a brother to his colleagues and a cousin to us."

May 14
The *Mission: Impossible* soundtrack is released. Larry and Adam perform the theme song, which is released as a single on June 4 and reaches the Top 10 in the US, UK, and elsewhere around the world.

May 15
U2 take part in the funeral of Bill Graham at Church of the Assumption in Howth. Paul McGuinness is one of several people who bring offertory gifts to the church altar. During communion, Bono sings Leonard Cohen's 'Tower Of Song' with musical backing that includes Edge, accordionist Martin Hayes and other members of Altan. Bono and Edge are also pallbearers.

After the funeral Mass, Bono, Edge, Ali and many others retreat to a wake at the Royal Hotel in Howth.

May 22
The *Mission: Impossible* film opens in the US Adam and Larry attend the Los Angeles premiere party.

May 28
Bono and Adam appear on *Common Ground*, an album released today that features new versions of traditional Irish songs. Bono is originally asked to record a traditional Irish song called 'The Yellow Bittern', but with deadlines

looming he decides he can't give the track proper attention. Instead, Bono and Adam rework U2's 1982 song 'Tomorrow' for this compilation.

July
Issue 24 of *Propaganda* magazine is published around this time.

August
Spin magazine sends Ann Powers to Dublin to profile U2 in advance of the new album they're finishing this month. Her article, though, won't see the light of day until next March because U2 is far behind schedule. Powers is in the studio as the band works on 'Discotheque' with producer Howie B, but it's one of only five songs the band has finished by now. "We're trying to find the access points connecting lots of different music," Adam tells Powers, explaining the struggles the band is having in the studio. Adds Bono: "We're actually trying to make a kind of music that doesn't exist yet. That is a terrifying place to be."

'Discotheque' is completed and delivered to Island Records this month, but will sit around for months as U2 continue working on the new album. Having already missed the first deadline (July) to have the album released in September or October, U2 tell Paul McGuinness they're also going to miss another deadline and won't be finished in time to release the album before Christmas. The band takes a short break and agrees to return to the studio next month.

August 8
Edge's mom, Gwenda, visits her son in the studio on his birthday.

August 13
Bono is one of several rock artists to contribute to a new album, *Exile On Classical Street*. Each artist selects a favourite piece of classical music, and the choices make up the album. Bono's selection is 'String Quartet No. 8 in C Minor'.

August 27
The *Los Angeles Times* reports that U2 will miss its deadline to release

Edge: "We missed the personality of the band"
September

"When the songs started to emerge from the mist, we missed the personality of the band. The songs were resting on drum machine beats and sequenced bass and had a little bit of a sterile quality. What makes a great U2 record is the sense of four personalities working in accord, in a particular moment in time. So during the course of recording, we tried to change direction."

a new album in November. Island Records, though, is either unaware of the latest delay or in denial. An Island spokesperson says, "As far as we're concerned, we still have a U2 record this year."

September
U2 resume work on their new album at Hanover Quay studios, delaying its release into 1997, several months later than first planned.

The band's slow embrace of Internet technology moves forward when they create a Web page that displays a live image of the recording sessions via a studio cam. The band occasionally have fun with fans viewing the Web page, leaving somewhat cryptic notes on a marker board for the world to see.

Bono contributes a recipe for Smoked Haddock Hash Browns and Poached Eggs to *The Sinatra Celebrity Cookbook*, a new compilation published this month

benefitting Barbara Sinatra's children's charity.

October
Media reports hint at growing tensions between U2 and Polygram Records over the delays in completing the new album. Without a U2 album this year, Polygram's corporate sales will fall millions short of estimates. Paul McGuinness tells *The Guardian*, "I believe PolyGram respect the creativity of the band. The problem with the delay in the album is that forecasts are made and expectations generated. PolyGram have to acknowledge that the creative process is imprecise."

Marc Marot on the repeated *Pop* album delays
"It was an absolute nightmare for us. Chris Blackwell's philosophy had always been, 'Worry about the music first, and then the money will sort itself out.' So that was all very well and good when you're running an independent label, but very difficult when you've got shareholders that own a company like Polygram or Universal. And so I couldn't just worry about the music by that stage because I was under *enormous* pressure to deliver the record because, obviously, any U2 record that could sell anywhere between 4 and 10 million units for a company like Polygram and Universal is a *huge* record and a very, very important thing for their shareholders.

"I was under enormous pressure from above to get the record out. And there was nothing that I could do about it. There was nothing I could do without damaging my relationship with U2, and I felt that my relationship with U2 was much, much more

important than, frankly, meeting fiscal year-end requirements for that particular year. And I also felt that I was protecting Polygram in protecting U2. So, I lied through my teeth and told my bosses it was coming, it was coming … 'Mañana, mañana, mañana' … and kept the pressure away from U2 the best that I could."

U2's Clarence Hotel re-opens after an 18-month, $8 million renovation.

Bono gets in trouble this month with the Irish National Parents' Council when he donates a sketch of his penis to a fundraising auction for Romanian orphans. He had been asked to donate his "favourite childhood toy", and drew the sketch and captioned it, "Me Rattler". The Council calls his donation "tasteless."

October 15
Carl Perkins releases *Go Cat Go*. Bono joins Johnny Cash, Willie Nelson, and Tom Petty in singing backing vocals on 'Give Me Back My Job'.

October 31
U2 manager Paul McGuinness receives third degree burns and serious injuries when a firework explodes in his hands during a party at his home in Wicklow. "We're all worried about him," Bono tells reporters. "He's conscious and trying to play the whole thing down. But he will be all right. He looks as though he's been blown up." McGuinness gets treatment at the Blackrock Clinic in Dublin and is back at work three weeks later. Fireworks are illegal in the Republic of Ireland.

November
A U2 fan in Hungary makes two 30-second audio clips of new U2 music available on his Web page. 'Discotheque', the first single from the upcoming album, is one of the clips, and a song called 'Wake Up, Dead Man' is the other. As word of these clips spreads, radio stations begin to play the clips on-air as a

taste of the new U2 sound. Island/Polygram steps in to block access to the Hungarian web site, but the clips are quickly shared among other U2 fans on the Internet. Though some U2 fans suspect the clips to be spread purposely by Island/Polygram records, the source is traced back to a recent meeting of Island's worldwide executives. The label had given each executive a VHS tape with previews of the U2 tracks. An Island executive in Hungary gave the tape to his marketing manager, who gave it to a friend – the fan who posted the clips.

November 8

U2 win the Inspiration Award at the Q Awards in London. Bono gives a long and funny acceptance speech. Dermot Morgan of *Father Ted* fame does a Riverdance routine for U2. When asked about the next album, Edge says there's "six weeks work to be done in a week".

November 10

Edge attends a benefit concert in Dublin for martyred Nigerian writer Ken Saro-Wiwa, who was executed by the Nigerian military a year ago to the day after campaigning for human rights and environmental causes in Nigeria.

November 14

Larry and Adam present the Breakthrough Award to Garbage at the MTV Europe Music Awards in

Above: U2 accept their Inspiration Award from *Q* Magazine, London, November 8.

London. When they get back to Dublin, Robert Hilburn of the *Los Angeles Times* is waiting to interview the whole band and spend time with them in the studio.

November 20

After two delays, U2 finish recording its new album. The band's studio-cam closes down with a shot of a markerboard that reads, "Elvis Has Hacked His Way Out Of The Building". They relocate to New York for final

mastering of the album, but even that is no easy task. Bono tells a flabbergasted Howie B that he wants a new intro to 'Discotheque'.

With the album work complete, the band turns its attention to upcoming B-sides – recording a cover of the Beatles' 'Happiness Is A Warm Gun' – and the tour.

December

U2 begin their media duties to promote *Pop*. They spend a few days in New York shooting photos and doing an interview with Tom Doyle for Q magazine.

Edge plays guitar on *Undark 3396*, an ambient music album by Russell Mills. Brian Eno and Michael Brook also appear on the album.

December 1

Robert Hilburn's *Los Angeles Times* article chronicling U2's final days of recording the new album also offers the first official announcement on the album's title: *Pop*.

December 31

Billy Corgan is one of the guests at a New Year's Eve party at Bono's house.

Howie B: "It was outrageous", November 20

"It was outrageous. Like, we were in the middle of mastering an album and they wanted to change the intro! It was like, 'any ideas?' And swirl was the idea. That was what they came up with, a 'swirl' sound. For fuck's sake!"

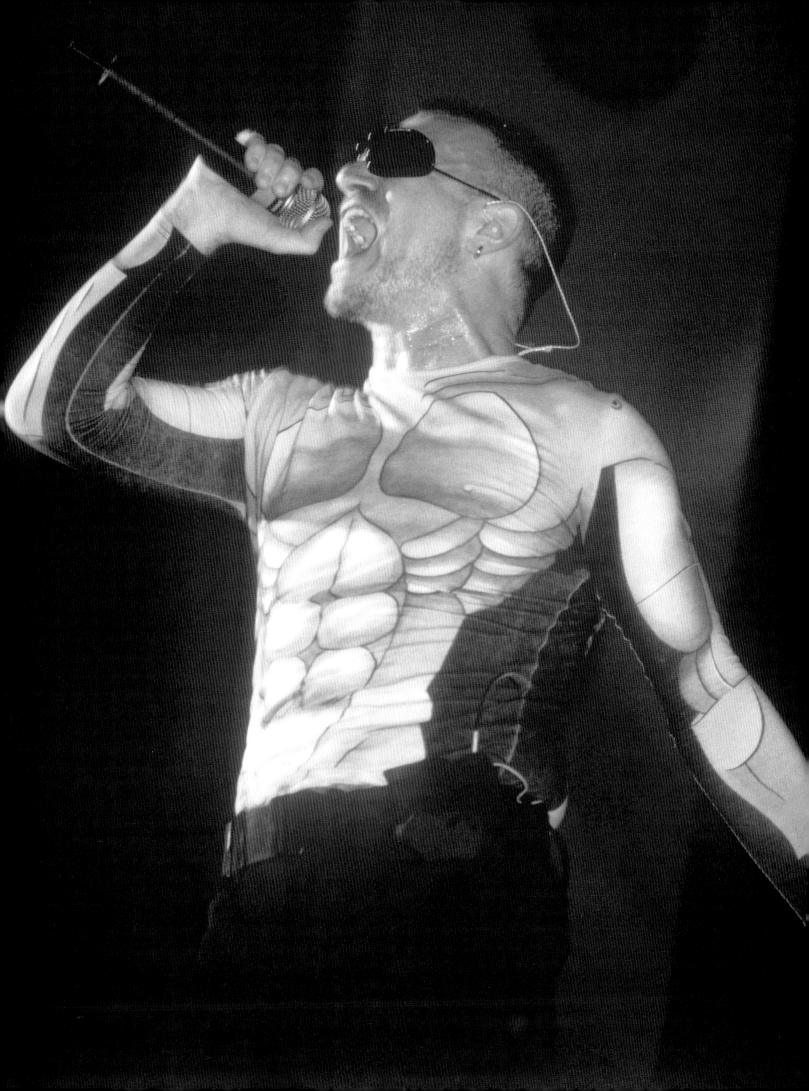

1997

A year of struggle. Having promised to top the *Achtung Baby*/Zoo TV era, U2 re-introduces themselves with a campy music video ('Discotheque') and a tour announcement inside a K-Mart department store. The *Pop* album is a huge hit when released, but drops quickly off the US charts. Most of the U2 audience is glad to have U2 back again in any form after a three-plus year absence, but many react to the album and tour with a collective "What?"

A trio of factors add up to a lukewarm response to PopMart: tickets cost more than $50, ticket sales start before *Pop* is released, and there's little urgency among fans because U2 are playing stadiums. The band is nervous and underprepared as the tour begins in Las Vegas, and the early shows suffer. An ABC-TV special becomes the lowest-rated programme in US television history. Though U2 eventually hits its stride on stage, few of the US shows sell out.

The tour – and the fans' response – improves dramatically in the summer when PopMart arrives in Europe. U2 are in a groove, playing great shows in front of many more sell out crowds. The highlight is a historic concert in Sarajevo that's broadcast live on radio around the world. But when PopMart returns to North America in the fall, U2 again plays to several half-empty (or worse) stadiums. The death of close friend Michael Hutchence and the near-loss of U2 security chief Jerry Mele in December make an already-difficult year worse.

January
Issue 25 of *Propaganda* magazine is published around this time. It's a special issue devoted to the upcoming *Pop* album and, reflecting the band's uncertainty over tour plans, it incorrectly announces that the tour will begin in May.

January 1
A nearly full-length version of 'Discotheque' appears on the Internet after being recorded from radio several weeks before radio was allowed to air the song. Radio stations are quickly told – by U2 – to stop playing the song illegally.

January 7
Paul McGuinness hand-delivers 'Discotheque' to Dublin radio personality and longtime U2 friend, Dave Fanning, for its first "official" airplay on Ireland's 2FM. "I'm very superstitious. You have to be the first to play it," McGuinness tells Fanning.

Also today, Adam and Larry's version of the *Mission: Impossible* theme is nominated for a Grammy Award in the Pop Instrumental Performance for an Orchestra, Group Or Soloist category.

January 8
U2 officially releases 'Discotheque' to radio stations worldwide. The release is earlier than originally planned due to Internet and previous radio airplay. The song sets a record for most new airplay

Above: U2 at the K-Mart store in New York to announce the dates on their forthcoming PopMart tour, February 12.

in a seven-day period on the *Billboard* Modern Rock chart.

Also today, Bono appears via telephone on BBC's Radio One to wish David Bowie a happy 50th birthday.

January 9
MTV premieres the video for 'Discotheque', which features U2 dressed up as the Village People.

February 3/4
With radio recordings of the song

spreading online, 'Discotheque' is released commercially today, a week earlier than planned. The single comes in multiple formats, and extra tracks include two versions of 'Holy Joe' and 11 versions of 'Discotheque'. The song hits number one in the UK, Japan, and Canada. In the US, it debuts at number 10 but drops off the charts after a month.

February 6
Bono contributes to *Milestones*, an

As part of the new touring system, U2 also cuts ties with its longtime agents, Ian Flooks and Frank Barsalona, both of whom have handled U2's tours since the band's earliest days and are considered friends as much as business partners.

Paul McGuinness: "It was a question of financial efficiency"

"It was a question of financial efficiency really. Doing an enormous tour like this requires an enormous investment by the band and on our last tour we made that investment. But we were effectively at risk until the last few shows of the tour, and if anything had gone wrong with them we wouldn't have broken even. I was determined on this occasion to get someone else to take the financial risk for the tour."

art exhibit opening today in London to benefit War Child.

February 10

U2 fly from Dublin to New York in preparation for this week's tour announcement. Photographers take pictures as the band leaves Dublin Airport.

February 12

U2 appear at a Manhattan K-Mart store to announce tour dates for their upcoming PopMart world tour. The band answers questions from the media and performs the B-side track, 'Holy Joe', live on a makeshift stage in the lingerie section of the store. A store sign that says POP GROUP hangs over them, and a blue light – K-Mart's trademark – flashes in the background. The event is broadcast live on MTV and VH-1 in the US, on MuchMusic in Canada, and elsewhere around the world on TV and radio.

As part of MTV's coverage, Kurt Loder interviews U2 on a hotel balcony overlooking the city. MTV also shows poet Allen Ginsberg doing a dramatic reading of the lyrics of 'Miami', one of the new songs on *Pop*. Ginsberg's appearance is taped for an ABC-TV

special that will air on April 26. It's the poet's last public appearance before his April 5 death.

The PopMart Tour marks a major change in how U2 handles the business aspects of touring. Rather than work with local promoters in each city, U2 sells the right to promote the tour to Michael Cohl's Concert Productions International for a reported $100 million. The local promoters – many of whom have worked with U2 since the band's early days – are upset at U2's decision.

Michael Cohl: "Some promoters think I'm a scoundrel"

"I've heard through the grapevine that some promoters think I'm a scoundrel undermining their business. And I'm sure they'd all rather have a system in play where they could make more money. But what we offer the band is consistency, so that instead of having to deal with 50 different promoters and explain what they want to

Above: Bono meets the press, February 12.

February 14

Although *Pop* won't be in stores for almost three more weeks, concert tickets for selected PopMart shows go on-sale via an MTV/VH-1 programme called "Tickets First." This will be done each Friday for the next four weeks.

February 20

2FM DJ Dave Fanning gives the *Pop* album its official world premiere and interviews Bono live in the studio. The event is also broadcast on the Internet from 2FM's web site with audio and video feeds available. Afterward, Bono and Edge catch Propellerhead's DJ set at The Kitchen.

Also tonight, Larry Mullen, Jr. wins the Rory Gallagher Musician Award at the *Hot Press*/Heineken Music Awards show in Belfast. Edge won this same award last year, the first time it had been given out.

March

U2 shoots a video for 'Staring At The Sun' in New York with Jake Scott directing.

March 1

Dave Fanning interviews U2 for a joint RTE/BBC Radio presentation broadcast promoting the *Pop* album. They also do an interview with Jo Whiley of the BBC that is syndicated worldwide to help promote *Pop*.

March 3/4

The *Pop* album is released worldwide. The Virgin Megastore in London opens at midnight, anticipating a big crowd of U2 fans ready to buy the album as early as possible. But few fans are in line when the doors open. Says Virgin spokesperson Anne Morgan, "We had the store open for over an hour, but hardly anybody turned up. It would've been better if we'd had a signing or some special event to tie in with, but as it was, it was pretty disappointing."

With the exception of *Rattle And Hum*, *Pop* is the first record U2 has made without Brian Eno's

Below: U2 greet their audience in front of the Popmart light show.

involvement since *War*. Although hyped in the media as U2's attempt to make so-called "techno" music, many fans feel the album includes sounds that represent a wide variety of U2's career. Despite a difficult recording process, U2 is confident they've succeeded in bringing in elements of dance culture into rock and roll.

Critical reaction to *Pop* is mixed. *Rolling Stone* gives the album four stars (out of five): "What we can say immediately is that *Pop* sounds absolutely magnificent. Working with Flood, who engineered *Achtung Baby* and co-produced *Zooropa*, the group has pieced together a record whose rhythms, textures and visceral guitar mayhem make for a thrilling roller-coaster ride." John Bitzer of *Allstar* magazine says, "It's a rich, delicious meal, one that takes multiple listens to digest, and leaves a ghost of a sense memory." Somewhat less enthused is Jim Sullivan of the *Boston Globe*: "Pop is a moving record, but it is not a thrilling record. While not quite up to *Zooropa* or *The Joshua Tree*, it is by no means the misguided stretch of *Rattle And Hum*."

On the JAM Showbiz web site, John Sakamoto writes, "As with so many elements of the ephemeral culture it both disparages and celebrates, [*Pop*] ends up being something considerably less than has been advertised."

Pop debuts at number one on the charts in more than 30 countries, a record for U2, but quickly drops out

of several major sales charts. It stays in the *Billboard* Top 10 for only three weeks. Marketing the album is somewhat problematic in the US, where retailers are demanding "price and positioning" fees from record labels in order to guarantee prominent placement in record stores. Island Records, however, refuses to pay these fees, a stand that U2 supports, even though it's likely to hurt their record sales.

One of the tracks on the album is called 'The Playboy Mansion', a title that prompts *Playboy* magazine founder Hugh Hefner to invite U2 to visit the actual Playboy mansion. He also requests an interview with Bono for his magazine.
Tracks: 'Discotheque', 'Do You Feel Loved', 'Mofo',' If God Will Send His Angels', 'Staring At The Sun', 'Last Night On Earth', 'Gone', 'Miami', 'The Playboy Mansion', 'If You Wear That Velvet Dress', 'Please', 'Wake Up Dead Man'

March 15

Pop debuts at number one on the UK album chart, but is replaced a week later by the *Spice* Girls' Spice album.

Late March

U2 continue with tour rehearsals at The Factory in Dublin. Old songs are being re-worked into newer versions, and the band is trying to figure out nearly all of the songs on *Pop*. One surprising song being rehearsed is 'Miss Sarajevo', which never makes it into a PopMart Tour set list.

Edge explains the mix that makes up Pop, March 3/4

"With this record, there was a lot that we were trying to take on. We wanted it to be a record with some real songs, some discipline and some focus in the material. We also wanted to take in some new ideas from the world of dance music and hip hop, because we felt strongly that that's where music is at its most interesting at the moment."

Rolling Stone's David Fricke is with the band for an upcoming cover story about the tour. Larry comes clean about the struggles to get ready for PopMart: "I'm scared shitless, to be honest with you. Every night I wake up with this nightmare of getting up on stage and nothing working." Bono is also having doubts. When asked five years later if he ever felt "maybe this won't work out, maybe this band will fail", Bono tells Michka Assayas he had those thoughts "Maybe before PopMart. That's the only time I actually thought about failure. I never thought about it up to that."

March 30
The 'Staring At The Sun' video premieres on MTV. It casts U2 in a much more traditional look, especially compared to the earlier video for 'Discotheque', but the video is a straight performance video – and a bland one, at that.

Paul: "We made a crap video"
"We all believed that 'Staring At The Sun' was a solid-gold hit and all we had to do was release it and it would go to number one everywhere and it didn't. We were so wrong. We made a crap video for it. And you know you can't really argue with the public."

April
U2 begins an assault of television airwaves as MTV airs *Zoo TV*, a three-part television show inspired by U2. The programme airs as part of MTV's *10 Spot* show on April 13, 20, and 27. Additional TV promotion will be coming soon, mainly via tie-ins with the ABC television network.

April 7
'Discotheque' is certified as a Gold single by the RIAA, with US sales of more than 500,000.

April 12
U2's US TV invasion continues as ABC premieres a new series called *Gun*. The show's theme song is U2's cover of The Beatles' 'Happiness Is A Warm Gun'. The programme lasts only six episodes before ABC cancels it.

April 14/15
'Staring At The Sun' is released as the second single off the *Pop* album, with 'North And South Of The River', 'Your Blue Room', and three remixes of the main track included on various formats. It climbs to the number three spot in the UK, but only reaches number 26 in the US. Paul McGuinness and Island Records disagree publicly on the reason for the song's struggles. McGuinness tells *Music Business International*, "The research response hoped for by Island's promotional people didn't occur until about 16 weeks in. Unfortunately they took their foot off the pedal at around 13 weeks and lost the opportunity to cross over." Island's Hooman Majd counters by saying, "I deny vehemently that this has been due to Island. 'Staring At The Sun' got as much exposure as possible, including incredible coverage on MTV, but it failed to strike a chord."

April 16
U2 begin rehearsing at Sam Boyd Stadium in Las Vegas for its upcoming PopMart Tour, which will begin April 25. During eight days of rehearsals, U2 reportedly write three new songs. That might include 'I'm Not Your Baby', a duet between Bono and Sinead O'Connor which will feature in Wim Wenders' film, *The End of Violence*, later this year. Bono finishes writing the lyrics and records his vocals while in Las Vegas.

Around this time, U2 visit the Fox TV studios in Los Angeles to record their voices for an upcoming episode of the super-popular animated comedy, *The Simpsons*.

April 25
Sam Boyd Stadium, Las Vegas, with Rage Against The Machine. U2 open its PopMart Tour with a good, but flawed, performance in front of

Edge: "It's trying to be humorous…", April 25

"PopMart is just our way of making sense of playing in big, open air stadiums. It's a big show and it's really a setting as much as it is a theme for the concert. It's trying to be humorous about the position we find ourselves in as a big band playing big stadiums…. We're able to laugh at the sheer commercial size of what we're undertaking."

38,000 people at a sold-out Sam Boyd Stadium. The band enters the stage like boxers, walking through the crowd with a security contingent escorting them to the B-stage while the 1970s hit 'Pop Muzik' plays on the PA system. Bono wears a boxer's satin robe on-stage, and shadow boxes as the band members take their positions.

Bono again fights opening-night vocal problems, Edge suffers through several guitar difficulties, and the band is forced to stop and restart 'Staring At The Sun' after beginning it off-key. "Talk amongst yourselves, we're just having a little family row," Bono tells the crowd. Due to the opening night flaws, the show gets mixed reviews from critics. USA Today says the show "outshines Vegas glitz", but the NME review carries the headline, "FLOPMART."

Bono: "No problem" with the press reaction
"We had a bit of bad press in the UK for the Las Vegas show. A load of people came over and they

thought we hadn't got our act together and that we were a big band and so they gave us a clip around the ear. I have no problem with that."

The stage is the star of the first show, almost overshadowing the band. It features the largest single video screen on the planet, a 40-foot mirror ball lemon which the band uses as it enters the stage for the encore, and a 100-foot tall toothpick with an olive on top. The centerpiece of the stage is a single, golden arch under which the band plays. All of this technology and staging will cost U2 $250,000 per day to operate.

The PopMart tour lacks the cerebral sophistication of Zoo TV, but aims to hit the audience's emotions and funny bone more so than that tour.

In justifying another massive stadium spectacle to media before the tour starts, Paul McGuinness says, "The competition these days isn't just other bands, but the big production values in movies and other forms of entertainment. Mick Jagger came to [U2's flashy 1993] Zoo TV tour in Dublin and he said rock 'n' roll had entered the era of *Star Wars* – and I think he's right. I don't think audiences can be expected to go to football stadiums for concerts if they are not going to see something that is very spectacular as well as hearing something great."

Dozens of celebrities are at the show, including Dennis Hopper, Robert De Niro, Sigourney Weaver, several members of the *Friends* cast, Michael Stipe and Mike Mills from R.E.M., Trent Reznor, Kylie Minogue, and Helena Christensen.

Edge gives the weather forecast today on ABC's *Good Morning, America* programme.

Below: U2 emerge from their mirrorball lemon on the second night of their ambitious Popmart tour, San Diego, April 28.

April 26
U2 heads to San Diego. They've booked four days at the Signature Sound Studio where they work on two projects: a new version of 'Last Night On Earth' that will be released soon as a single, and the mixing of 'I'm Not Your Baby', a Bono-Sinead O'Connor duet that will appear in Wim Wenders' upcoming movie, *The End of Violence*.

U2: A Year In Pop airs nationwide on ABC-TV. The hour-long programme includes a look at the band's history, the recording of the *Pop* album, and highlights from the PopMart Tour opener just 24 hours earlier. To make the quick turnaround possible, a video-editing suite has been built in The Luxor Hotel, where U2 and crew have been staying while in Vegas. The final programme is sent to ABC headquarters via satellite.

Ratings for the programme are

the worst-ever for a non-political show on the Big Three networks (ABC, NBC, CBS). (The record has since been broken.) The band intends to include its latest single, 'Staring At The Sun', during the programme, but instead uses 'Do You Feel Loved' after the difficulties playing the former song.

April 28
Jack Murphy Stadium, San Diego, with Rage Against The Machine.

May
Issue 26 of *Propaganda* magazine – renamed *Popaganda* just this once in honour of the album and tour – is published around this time.

It's "sweeps" month for US TV networks, and ABC ties its month-long promotions to U2's *Pop* album and PopMart Tour. The network airs brief promos that use U2 songs including 'Discotheque', 'Mofo', and 'Staring At The Sun'. The promos also include images from the latter's music video, along with album and tour icons and logos.

May 1
Mile High Stadium, Denver, with Rage Against The Machine. With snow in the forecast and very cold temperatures in the high altitude of Denver, less than 30,000 fans show up for the show.

May 3
Rice Stadium, Salt Lake City, with Rage Against The Machine. U2 return to Salt Lake City for the first time since 1983. They fly to San Francisco right after the show.

May 4-5
U2 spends two off days at Fantasy Studios in Berkeley, California, working on the live set and trying new ideas for upcoming shows.

May 6
Autzen Stadium, Eugene, with Rage Against The Machine. A couple hundred residents complain about how loud the show is, and city officials confirm that U2 has broken noise laws. But they decide not to pursue the band because the fines are less than the cost of prosecuting the case.

Bono remembers his final visit with William S. Burroughs, May 21
Burroughs chased U2 around the video set in Kansas City, waving his cane and its three-foot-long, attached sword at the band.

"His last words to us on camera, which we didn't actually use in the finished video, he starts mumbling, wagging this [cane] around, then he says: 'I came not to bring peace but a sword.' He had a big smile on his face and we should have looped it in. That would have been amazing: William Burroughs, the devil's best advertisement, quotes Christ."

May 7
Pop is certified Platinum by the RIAA.

May 9
Sun Devil Stadium, Tempe, with Rage Against The Machine.

May 12
Cotton Bowl, Dallas, with Rage Against The Machine.

May 14
Liberty Bowl, Memphis, with Rage Against The Machine. U2 continues to have trouble playing their current single, 'Staring At The Sun'. Bono begins singing off-key and immediately stops the song, grabs an acoustic guitar, and after he finds the right key, the band begins the song again. "It's not a Broadway show," Bono tells the crowd. "We can stop if we want to." Ex-Big

Country vocalist Stuart Adamson is at the show.

May 15
U2 hangs out at B.B. King's Blues Club in Memphis. Bono leaves early due to pain from a sore throat, but Edge sticks around and sings 'Stand By Me' with the house band. Earlier in the day, Bono records the narration to an hour-long documentary called *Elvis: From The Waist Up*, which will air at a later date on the VH1 cable channel in the US.

May 16
Memorial Stadium, Clemson, with Rage Against The Machine. R.E.M. attends the show.

May 19
Arrowhead Stadium, Kansas City, with Fun Lovin' Criminals. Fun Lovin' Criminals joins the tour for tonight's show in Kansas City.

U2 welcomes the Fun Lovin' Criminals
Steve Borgovini, former drummer with Fun Lovin' Criminals, remembers their first day on the PopMart Tour.
"We weren't sure if we'd ever meet the guys. Just because we were touring with them didn't mean they would make themselves accessible. We were backstage in an R.V. in the parking lot. About an hour before we went on, each of the guys [in U2], one by one, came out to the R.V. to introduce themselves and welcome us to the tour. They hung out with us, had a drink and told us they were excited to have us. We were floored… now that's class!"

May 20
U2 brings traffic to a crawl in Kansas City, as busy highways are shut down so the band can shoot a video for their next single, 'Last

Night On Earth'. Local residents are angered by the delays and the fact the road closures were announced with less than 24 hours notice. "I can't believe the stupidity of it," says Mike Right, vice president of public affairs for the AAA Auto Club of Missouri. "They're going to close down an interstate highway that serves downtown Kansas City for a… music video?"

May 21
U2 wraps up filming of the 'Last Night on Earth' video, forcing the closure today of several downtown Kansas City streets. City officials receive dozens of complaints about the inconvenience. "I'd never heard of U2," says Mayor Emanuel Cleaver, "though I now know they're one of the most popular bands on the planet."

The video is a send-up of 1950s and 1960s sci-fi movies. Beatnik poet William S. Burroughs appears at the end of the video pushing a shopping cart with a spotlight in the basket.

May 22
Three Rivers Stadium, Pittsburgh, with Fun Lovin' Criminals.

May 23
On a day off, U2 visits the Andy Warhol Museum in Pittsburgh. Edge also does an interview with *Guitar World* magazine while in Pittsburgh.

May 24
Ohio Stadium, Columbus, with Fun Lovin' Criminals.

May 25
U2 visits US President Bill Clinton at the White House.

May 26
Robert F. Kennedy Stadium, Washington, DC, with Fun Lovin' Criminals. Heavy rains a night earlier hamper U2's show tonight. A large section of the PopMart video screen remains blank throughout the whole show, and other sections flash and blink random colors. Fans are able to see U2's crew on scaffolding behind the

Below: Bono greets fans at the Tibetan Freedom show, New York, June 7.

screen trying to fix the problems during the show.

The screen problems lead U2 to cancel a show three nights later in Raleigh, North Carolina. Fans in North Carolina are understandably upset, and media suggest the real reason for the cancellation is light ticket sales in Raleigh.

May 31, June 1-3
Giants Stadium, East Rutherford, with Fun Lovin' Criminals (all three shows), Longpigs (May 31 & June 1). Among the countless celebrities at the first New York-area show are artists Roy Liechtenstein and Run Wrake, who are seeing their own work used in the show for the first time.

During the second show, Bono sings a brief portion of 'Hallelujah', in memory of folk-singer Jeff Buckley, who has drowned recently in Memphis. Tonight's is the first show in which Bono and Edge perform an acoustic version of 'Staring At The Sun' on the b-stage, the song that has given the band trouble since the tour's opening night in Las Vegas. After the gig, U2 does a TV shoot on the PopMart stage for Channel 4 and popular

presenter Chris Evans.

While in New York, Bono records his vocal contribution for 'Perfect Day', an all-star charity single recorded for the BBC Children in Need Appeal.

June 7
Tibet Freedom Festival, Randall's Island. U2 plays a five-song set at the Tibetan Freedom Concert.

June 8
Franklin Field, Philadelphia, with Fun Lovin' Criminals. Prior to the show, fans outside the stadium are polled about whether or not they've purchased the *Pop* album, if they've seen U2's TV commercials, and if they understand the concept behind PopMart. It's unclear who is responsible for arranging the polling. Radiohead are in attendance at tonight's gig.

June 9
Bono, Edge, and Adam see Radiohead play at Irving Plaza in New York City. Madonna, R.E.M., Marilyn Manson, and basketball star Michael Jordan are also at the show.

June 10
Bono and Larry appear together on *The Late Show with David Letterman*. They're interviewed for nearly 10 minutes, but don't perform.

June 12
Winnipeg Stadium, Winnipeg, with Fun Lovin' Criminals. After tonight's show in Winnipeg, U2 does an interview with MuchMusic's Kim Clarke Champniss at Winnipeg Arena.

June 13
U2 arrives in Edmonton. Local TV cameras are there to greet the band and get quick sound bites for the local news. Bono visits and signs autographs for fans at the airport.

June 14-15
Commonwealth Stadium, Edmonton, with Fun Lovin' Criminals. After the first show, U2 stays at the venue into the wee hours of the morning. Finally leaving at about 5 a.m. (June 15), Bono and Edge visit with a group of about 20 fans. Bono signs one fan's acoustic guitar and then uses it to sing a song for the dedicated fans.

U2 fly to San Francisco immediately after the second gig, barely making it out of Edmonton before a major thunderstorm.

June 18-19
Oakland-Alameda County Stadium, Oakland, with Oasis. On the first night, U2 wears various disguises so they can watch Oasis' set without being noticed. Backstage after the first show, Oasis' singer Liam Gallagher plays his band's new album, singing along with occasional help from Bono.

The two bands spend the early morning hours at Tosca Cafe, which is held open by U2's private reservation. On the way there, 'One' is played over the radio in their minibus, prompting Noel Gallagher to yell, "This is the greatest song ever written!" The Gallagher brothers sing along loudly with help from Bono and Edge. After much imbibing at the bar, Bono serenades his mates with a solo version of Caruso's 'O Sole Mio'. The morning festivities end

when Bono, Edge and some friends go watch the sun rise over the Golden Gate Bridge.

While in the Bay Area, Anton Corbijn does a photo shoot that involves the band walking around in public while wearing their PopMart concert clothing.

June 20
The first official U2 web site opens at http://U2popmart.msn.com, and is done in conjunction with Pop Invasion, an event billed as "U2 Takes Over a Radio Station." It all happens today at the KROQ-FM studios in Burbank, California, and is simulcast on stations around the US and on the official web site.

June 21
Los Angeles Coliseum, Los Angeles, with Rage Against The Machine. Former Monkee Davy Jones joins Edge on-stage and leads the crowd in a karaoke rendition of the Monkees' classic 'Daydream Believer', which has been a staple of early PopMart shows.

June 25
Camp Randall Stadium, Madison, with Fun Lovin' Criminals.

June 27-28-29
Soldier Field, Chicago, with Fun Lovin' Criminals. After the first show, everyone stays at the stadium to work on new video and lighting pieces for the show.

Bono and Gavin Friday are out bicycling on the morning of the third show, and somehow join Chicago's Gay Pride parade. After the show, the band and some of the crew party in Bono's hotel room until the wee hours of the morning.

July 1-2
Foxboro Stadium, Foxboro, with Fun Lovin' Criminals. Bono does a live interview with Carter Alan on WBCN before the first show. The final night of the tour sees the band sipping champagne as they descend from the lemon. During Edge's karaoke version of 'Suspicious Minds', the guys from Fun Lovin' Criminals come on stage to sing and stalk Edge, who laughs heartily at their efforts.

July 14/15
U2 release 'Last Night On Earth', with varying formats also including the tracks 'Pop Muzik', 'Numb (Soul Assassins Mix)', two versions of 'Happiness Is A Warm Gun', and a remix of the main track. The single reaches number 10 in the UK and number 57 in the US.

July 17
U2 does a full dress rehearsal tonight in Rotterdam. Afterward, the band performs 'Please' a couple more times so that video crews can get close-ups that aren't possible during a real gig.

July 18-19
Feyenoord Stadium, Rotterdam, with

Skunk Anansie. U2 open the European leg of the PopMart Tour with two shows at Feyenoord Stadium. 30 minutes of the first show is aired live over the Internet from U2's official web site and the same 30 minutes airs on MTV Europe. 'Please', 'Where The Streets Have No Name', and 'Staring At The Sun' will later appear on the *Popheart* live EP.

July 25
Festival Grounds, Werchter, with Skunk Anansie.

July 27
Butzweiler Hof, Cologne, with Die Fantastischen Vier. Tennis star Steffi Graf and Luciano Pavarotti are at the show.

Around this time, U2 record a new version of 'Please' at Wisseloord Studios in Hilversum, The Netherlands for the upcoming single release.

July 29
Festwiese, Leipzig, with Die Fantastischen Vier.

July 31
Maimarktgelaende, Mannheim, with Die Fantastischen Vier.

August 1
After much debate and political posturing in Ireland, the Irish Supreme Court rules that two U2 shows planned this month at the Lansdowne Road Rugby Stadium in Dublin may proceed. Three local residents had challenged the band's plans, saying the concerts would be too loud and that 40,000 fans in their neighbourhood on

consecutive nights would damage the area. The entire episode draws attention to what many consider "ridiculous" planning rules regarding outdoor concerts in Ireland. U2 manager Paul McGuinness is quoted before the decision as saying, "We can take PopMart anywhere on Earth, but we can't play our own hometown."

August 2
Ullevi Stadion, Gothenburg, with Audioweb. After the show, Polygram hosts a party for the band that lasts into the wee hours of tomorrow morning.

Author William S. Burroughs dies at age 83. "I thought he might have had another few centuries left in him," Bono says. "He was a great advertisement for doing everything you shouldn't do."

August 3
Bono and a few friends are out in Gothenburg this afternoon when they get in a car chase with paparazzi. It ends with Bono drawing the photographers out of their cars while Howie B steals the keys and leaves the paparazzi stranded. The photographers get their keys back a day later at U2's hotel.

August 4
Parken Stadium, Copenhagen, with Audioweb. Supermodel Helena Christensen is at tonight's show and hosts a party for the band afterward.

August 6
Valle Hovin Stadion, Oslo, with Audioweb. From the It-Had-to-

Above: The unmistakable red wave of 'Streets', Los Angeles, June 21.

Happen-Sooner-or-Later department, U2's mirrorball lemon shuts down while transporting the band to the B-stage to start the encore.

Fintan Fitzgerald: "Inside it was pandemonium"
U2's wardrobe coordinator, Fintan Fitzgerald, rode inside the lemon with U2 at every show. He was hidden from public view, and had access to a big, red emergency button. This is his account of what happened in Oslo.
"The machinery broke and the lemon only opened about a foot and a half. I've been told it looked quite funny from outside because all you could see were the band's legs. Inside it was pandemonium! Edge was trying to look out of the base, and the others were saying, 'Don't do that, Edge!' And they were shouting, 'Hit the red button', which I was, but nothing was happening. Eventually it had to be opened manually and the band had to exit out the back down a ladder."

August 7
U2 announce plans to play at Botanic Gardens in Belfast on August 26. Almost immediately, the extremist Loyalist Volunteer Force issues a warning that it will try to disrupt the concert. Northern Irish police take the terrorist threat seriously: "We are taking no chances. Intelligence sources report that this is exactly the sort of event the LVF will try to target and we are pulling out all the stops."

August 8
U2 celebrates Edge's birthday on land and sea. The band and crew goes to the small city of Porvoo, Finland, and rents a yacht for a couple hours. When they're back on land, everyone has dinner at the Wanha Laamanni restaurant, where a large Stetson-shaped birthday

Below: Edge, the techno cowboy at work.

cake is served for dessert. The party continues as U2 takes over the entire second floor of the nightclub Helmi back in Helsinki.

August 9
Olympic Stadium, Helsinki, with Audioweb. Edge's birthday celebration continues on stage tonight. Edge's girlfriend, a noticeably pregnant Morleigh Steinberg, reprises her Zoo TV role when she belly dances during 'Mysterious Ways'.

August 10
Edge takes part in an online chat hosted by the U2 PopMart site on MSN.

August 12
Horse Track, Warsaw, with Audioweb. U2 plays its first show in Poland. The concert is marred by poor crowd-control. Lines begin forming in the early afternoon and reach nearly a mile-long before the gates open. With only a few entry gates, an estimated 200 people are injured as the crowd pushes to get into the stadium. Many climb over fences, never having their tickets checked. U2 waits an extra 20 minutes before taking the stage to allow more people to get settled inside. The show itself is marked by a tribute to Polish Solidarity leader Lech Walesa during 'New Year's Day', the song Bono wrote about Walesa's movement in the early eighties. Bono tells the crowd, "This is your song," and images of Walesa appear on the video screen to great applause and emotion.

August 14
Strahov Stadium, Prague, with Audioweb. U2 play in the Czech Republic for the first time. Before the show, Paul McGuinness does an interview with *Music Business International* magazine.

Bono contributes to Lian Lunson's *Willie Nelson: Down Home*, a documentary that premieres today in the US.

August 15
U2 collect the Best International Act award at the Viva! Awards in Cologne.

August 16
Airfield, Wiener Neustadt, with Paradise Now. On the 20th anniversary of the death of Elvis Presley, tonight's show is filled with tributes and references to the King. Liam Fay reviews the show for *Hot Press*: "That any rock band could deliver a show like PopMart is astonishing. They they could deliver a show like PopMart that has a heart should numb even our faculty for astonishment. Already, I want to see it again."

August 17
A story in today's *Sunday Times* says U2 will stop touring after PopMart. The article quotes Bono: "I can't imagine us playing live again. I don't think we would be stupid enough to take this on again. I think it is as big as a live show can go. It's a shame but I can't imagine how we could advance a live show beyond PopMart. We will not bring another show the same size on the road again."

August 18
Zeppelinfeld, Nuremberg, with Die Fantastischen Vier. Tonight's show is at the Zeppelinfield in Nuremberg, a stadium that was the site of Nazi rallies during the Third Reich. Although other big rock concerts have been played there in years past, there's some controversy about U2 doing a concert at this site.

Bono says Howie B chased the devil away
"I remember thinking: *No, we should never be afraid of a building. And if people are so scared of it, paint it pink or something like that.* Howie B, my great friend, was deejaying. He has produced U2 and was on tour with us. Jewish. He was very unnerved by playing there. He said to me: 'I'm not sure if I want to do this.' I said: 'Well, you don't have to if you don't want.' But he went on and started his set by playing the Third Degree's

'When Will I See You Again?' It was just the most remarkable thing to see this joyous jazzman with tears down his face, decades later, mourning people of his own ethnic group that he'd never met, but feeling it. I really felt this song just chase the devil away."

Above: U2's tribute to Solidarity leader Lech Walesa, Warsaw, August 12.

August 19

Island Records issues a press release refuting a recent report in the *Sunday Times* newspaper that PopMart will be U2's last world tour. Says Bono: "Of course this is not U2's last tour. The next tour will be different but there certainly will be more U2 tours." Paul McGuinness is more succinct: "This story was crap."

A tribute album, *The Songs of Jimmie Rodgers*, is released. Bono and Larry perform on a cover of 'Dreaming With Tears In My Eyes'.

August 20

Expo Gelaende, Hannover, with Die Fantastischen Vier. U2 christens the site in Hannover, Germany, where Expo 2000 will begin a little less than three years away, on June 1, 2000. The band leaves for London right after the show.

August 22-23

Wembley Stadium, London, with Audioweb, Longpigs. While in London, U2 also shoots a music video for 'Please'. This version is directed by Anton Corbijn and filmed in a local studio.

August 26

Botanic Gardens, Belfast, with Ash. U2 passes on a week's vacation and plays a hastily scheduled show at the Botanical Gardens – their first show in Belfast in 10 years. The concert goes on in peace, despite threats of violence in recent weeks from an extreme loyalist faction.

August 28

Roundhay Park, Leeds, with Cast. The morning papers include an unexpected attack on U2 from ex-Beatle George Harrison: "You know what irritates me about modern music, it's all based on ego. Look at a group like U2. Bono and his band are so egocentric – the more you jump around, the bigger your hat is, the more people listen to your music. The only important thing is to sell and make money. It's nothing to do with talent. Today there are groups who sell lots of records and then disappear. Will we remember U2 in 30 years? Or the Spice Girls? I doubt it."

The band is baffled by Harrison's comments. In response, Bono sings bits of 'Something' and 'My Sweet Lord' during tonight's show.

August 30

Lansdowne Road Stadium, Dublin, with Ash. U2 return home for the first of two shows at Dublin's Lansdowne Road Stadium – shows which were in jeopardy for months while local residents protested the use of the stadium, and only approved by the Irish Supreme four weeks earlier. U2 pay for many local residents to vacation out of Dublin for the weekend, and those who choose to stay home are given free tickets to see the shows. During the show, Bono jokes about the legal fight: "I wouldn't have you in my back yard, either!"

August 31

Lansdowne Road Stadium, Dublin, with Ash. As U2 gets set to play its second show in Dublin, the world is stunned by the overnight death of Princess Diana in a car crash in Paris. The crowd is somewhat subdued as they enter the stadium in the rain, but U2 plays a fireball of a show that gets everyone's heart racing. It's a more personal show than the night before, as several songs are dedicated to the band's families and friends. As 'Gone' begins, Bono sings, "She's gone... she's gone...", the first of many references to Diana. During 'Last Night On Earth', the ad-libbed bridge includes lyrics like "Beautiful girl, big black car...." After 'Mysterious Ways', Bono is walking back to the main stage with his head down and appears to be crying. He begins to sing 'MLK', and just as he hits the second "sleep tonight" lyric, a Warholian-like image of Diana appears on the screen. It remains there through the song, and as the song closes Bono says, "I was stunned to hear the news today." As Edge starts into 'One', Bono continues that thought: "I really think we all were," he says, then sings: "Is it getting better...."

Before the show, Adam takes part in an online chat hosted by the U2 PopMart site on MSN.

September 2

Murryfield Stadium, Edinburgh, with Seahorses. Immediately after the show, U2 fly to New York to get ready for a performance at the MTV Video Music Awards.

September 3

U2 rehearse tonight at Radio City Music Hall.

September 4

Radio City Music Hall, New York. U2 perform a live version of 'Please' during the MTV Video Music Awards. The band leave for Paris immediately after their performance.

September 5

After stopping to refuel in Canada and Iceland, U2 finally arrives in Paris today. Bono and Edge do an interview on NRJ radio.

September 6

Parc des Princes, Paris, with Placebo.

Before tonight's show, some of the U2 crew visit Pont de l'Alma, the site where Princess Diana died a week ago, and join the crowd paying their respects.

September 8/9
U2 releases the *PopHeart* EP, which features four live tracks recorded earlier in the PopMart Tour, in Europe, Japan, and Australia, but not in the US. It reaches number four in Canada and number seven in the UK.
Tracks: 'Please (Live from Rotterdam)', 'Where The Streets Have No Name (Live from Rotterdam)', 'With Or Without You (Live from Edmonton)', 'Staring At The Sun (Live from Rotterdam)'

September 9
Estadio Vincente Calderon, Madrid, with Placebo.
   'I'm Not Your Baby', U2's collaboration with Sinead O'Connor, appears on the soundtrack to *The End of Violence*, which is released today.

September 11
Estadio Jose Alvalade, Lisbon, with Placebo.

September 13
Estadi Olimpic de Montjuich, Barcelona, with Placebo. Edge sings a karaoke version of 'Macarena', a song that most people in this part of Spain find offensive. Rather than singing along, the crowd boos so loudly that Edge chooses not to finish the entire song. In later interviews, manager Paul McGuinness would call the choice of 'Macarena' one of the biggest mistakes of the entire tour.

September 15
Espace Grammont, Montpelier, with Placebo.

September 18
Aerporte Del-Urbe, Rome, with Prozac, Casino Royale. U2's show in Rome is marred by the death of a 28-year-old fan, caused by a brain aneurysm during the massive crush of fans as U2 enters the stadium.

September 19
A French court awards the equivalent of $34,000 to a U2 fan who claims he lost most of his hearing at U2's July 14, 1993, concert in Marseilles.

September 20
Festival Site, Reggio Emilia, with Prozac, Casino Royale. An enormous crowd fills this wide-open festival site; an estimated 150,000 to 175,000 fans are at the show. As U2 flies in at about 4:00 p.m., they get permission to fly over the concert site to see the massive crowd gathering; they give the horde of fans a thrill by making three circles at about 900 feet altitude. The gig is said to be the largest paying crowd at a one-act concert in rock history. At the end of the show, Bono tells the audience, "You gave four Irish boys an evening they'll never forget."

September 23
Kosevo Stadium, Sarajevo, with Gazi-Husruf Beg choir, Protest, Sikter. U2 brings PopMart to Sarajevo, fulfilling a desire Bono first expressed in 1993 during the *Zooropa* Tour. It's a historic and monumental day for the city – one that locals view as an important step back toward normalcy after the war. The first passenger trains to operate since the end of the war bring fans in from Mostar and Maglaj. Travel restrictions in the country are lifted so people can attend from all directions. The arena next door to the stadium is used as a dormitory for about 3,000 fans who won't be able to make it home immediately after the show. The concert even attracts large contingents of uniformed NATO soldiers who are here for fun, not to provide security.
   Bono's voice suffers through the entire show, but the crowd eagerly sings what he cannot. Bono mumbles the verses during 'Pride', while Edge takes over during the chorus. Before 'I Still Haven't Found What I'm Looking For', Bono begs the crowd to help him sing. Edge performs an acoustic, solo version of 'Sunday, Bloody Sunday' on the B-stage,

starting a change in the set list that will continue for the rest of the tour. During the encore, U2 play 'Miss Sarajevo' with Brian Eno – it's the first time U2 has ever performed this song as a full band. As fans leave at the end of the night, they begin to applaud the soldiers still waiting in the grandstands; the soldiers quickly return the applause.
   The show is broadcast live on radio all around the world and garners great publicity for U2, the PopMart Tour, and most importantly the people of Sarajevo who are trying to reconstruct their city and their lives. In coming weeks, there are reports that U2's concert has raised only $13,500 for the people of Bosnia, a figure U2 defends by explaining that the show wasn't designed to raise money, and that Bono's offer to bring a stripped-down – and less-expensive – concert to the city was refused in favour of the full PopMart production.

September 24
The band spends part of the day touring Sarajevo, seeing first hand the devastation they'd only seen before on news reports about the war. From there, U2 and some of the crew head to a coastal resort on the island of Crete. This will serve as headquarters until they travel to Israel in six days.

September 25
Edge hosts a birthday party in Crete tonight for one of the Principle Management ladies.

September 26
Harbour Yard, Thessaloniki, with Echo Tattoo, Nikos Portokaloglou. U2 plays its first show in Greece.

September 30
Hayarkon Park, Tel Aviv, with Apollo 440. U2 plays its first show in Israel. Bono dedicates 'One' to the late Prime Minister of Israel, Itzhak Rabin, who was murdered two years ago. He also stirs controversy by appealing for the release of nuclear secrets traitor Mordechai Vanunu – an appeal that generates little

response from the audience. Local radio reports that 34 fans require medical treatment due to the crush of the crowd as U2 enters the stadium. With many international acts avoiding Israel after recent bomb attacks in Jerusalem, U2's appearance is politically sensitive and the band announce publicly they will spend as little time there as possible.

October 1
Edge and Morleigh Steinberg have their first child, a girl named Sian, who arrives earlier than anticipated. Edge is still on a plane from Israel when Sian is born in Los Angeles. He arrives a few hours after his daughter.

October 4
Bono appears in a BBC2 documentary, *The Great Hunger – The Life and Songs of Shane MacGowan*. Bono calls the former Pogues' frontman "the greatest songwriter Ireland has ever produced". Others singing MacGowan's praises include Sinead O'Connor and Christy Moore.

October 20/21
'Please' is released as a single, with varying formats also including the tracks 'I'm Not Your Baby', two versions of 'Dirty Day', and the four live tracks that appeared a month ago on the *Popheart* EP: 'Please (Live from Rotterdam)', 'Where The Streets Have No Name (Live from Rotterdam)', 'With Or Without You (Live from Edmonton)', and 'Staring At The Sun (Live from Rotterdam)'. The cover features four politicians who have been involved in the Irish peace process: Gerry Adams, David Trimble, Ian Paisley, and John Hume. It fails to chart in the US, but reaches number seven in the UK.

October 24
Bono attends the VH1 Vogue Fashion Awards in New York.
Achtung Baby is certified Multi-Platinum, with US sales of more than eight million.

October 25
U2 are unable to rehears tonight because some stage equipment is late arriving from Europe.

Below: Bono amidst the audience at Montpelier, September 15.

October 26-27
Skydome, Toronto, with Third Eye Blind. U2 begins the third leg of the PopMart tour – and second in North America – with two shows in Toronto. As he did for the last few shows of the European tour, Edge continues to sing a solo, acoustic version of 'Sunday, Bloody Sunday' from the B-stage, replacing the nightly karaoke sing-along that he sang the first time through North America in the spring.
Before the second show, police arrest a Toronto man who's been stalking U2 for three years. It's the same man who was caught outside Adam's home in Dublin in March, 1996. Police say he's been calling Adam as much as 200 times per day.

October 29
Hubert H. Humphrey Metrodome, Minneapolis, with Smashmouth. Bono and others check out a Keith Haring exhibit at the art museum in Toronto this morning before leaving for Minneapolis. Howie B doesn't spin records before the show for the first time on the tour – he's caught with a small amount of marijuana in his pocket while trying to pass through customs between Toronto and Minneapolis, his work visa is cancelled, and he is immediately kicked off the tour. After the show, the band leaves for Detroit.

October 31
Pontiac Silverdome, Detroit, with Smashmouth. As the band exits the lemon to begin 'Discotheque', Bono sings 'Happy Birthday' to Larry for the second time tonight. As Larry gets to the B-stage, longtime girlfriend Ann Acheson is waiting for him with a birthday cake and a kiss.

November 1
With Phil Joanou directing, U2 shoots a music video tonight for 'If God Will Send His Angels' at a restaurant in Detroit. They don't wrap up until almost breakfast time the following morning.

November 2
Olympic Stadium, Montreal, with Third Eye Blind. After tonight's

show in Montreal, the band boards a 747 and flies to Rotterdam for the MTV Awards show in a couple days.

November 4
U2 rehearse at the Ahoy in Rotterdam. Their June 7 performance of 'One' at the Tibetan Freedom Concert appears today on a compilation album from the concert. The CD also includes a brief video interview with Bono.

November 5
Anton Corbijn introduces Bono to the Dutch singer and painter Herman Brood at Brood's studio.

November 6
Sport Paleis Ahoy, Rotterdam. U2 perform 'Mofo' at the MTV European Music Awards and win the award for Best Live Act. While accepting the award, Bono sings Jacques Brel's 'Port Of Amsterdam' – he changes the lyric to 'Rotterdam' and dedicates the song to Herman Brood. After the ceremony, U2 fly to St. Louis to resume the PopMart Tour.

November 8
Trans World Dome, St. Louis, with Third Eye Blind.

November 10
Houlihans Stadium, Tampa, with Third Eye Blind. A crowd of only 20,232 turns out tonight.

November 12
Municipal Stadium, Jacksonville, with Third Eye Blind. The crowd for the show is estimated at 20,000. Bono jokes about the meager attendance: "Those of you in the back, can you hear us? Both of you?"

November 14
Pro Player Stadium, Miami, with Smashmouth. Tonight's concert had been targeted earlier in the year for a live TV broadcast in the US. But those plans eventually change, and an upcoming show in Mexico City is chosen instead. After the gig, the band and crew enjoy a party at Chris Blackwell's Marlin Hotel.

November 17
Bono appears on 'Perfect Day', an all-star charity single organized by Lou Reed for the BBC.

November 21
Superdome, New Orleans, with Third Eye Blind.

November 23
Alamodome, San Antonio, with Third Eye Blind. Tonight's show is a somber one – it's the first since the death of INXS lead singer Michael Hutchence two days earlier. Bono discusses his close friend during the opening strains of 'I Still Haven't Found What I'm Looking For', saying, "He was a good friend, and he was one of us. We're thinking about him today." Hutchence's image appears on the video screen as Bono and Edge perform an acoustic duet on 'Staring At The Sun'. INXS' classic 'Never Tear Us Apart' is played over the PA system as the fans exit the stadium.

November 26
Georgia Dome, Atlanta, with Smashmouth. Michael Stipe hosts an aftershow party for the band.

November 27
Though the tour crew is a mix of nationalities, everyone celebrates Thanksgiving with a turkey dinner tonight.

November 28
Astrodome, Houston, with Smashmouth. U2 flies from Atlanta to Houston for tonight's show, then leaves for Mexico City immediately after the gig. Though they arrive in Mexico City in the middle of the night, fans are waiting at the airport for the band's arrival.

December
U2's first official foray onto the Internet, the MSN PopMart site, closes down. Issue 27 of *Propaganda* magazine is published around this time.

December 1
In Mexico City, U2 does a lengthy rehearsal to allow the video and audio crews time to prepare for the upcoming TV broadcast.

December 2
Foro Sol, Mexico City, with Control Machete. U2's first show in Mexico City is marred by an off-stage incident: the three sons of Mexico's president show up unannounced at the concert with their bodyguards. The group leaves early, driving an unmarked, all-black vehicle through a restricted security zone being used for the TV crew's heavy machinery. Two camera operators try to stop the mysterious car, but are confronted by the sons' bodyguards, who draw their guns.

Jerry Meltzer, one of U2's security crew, sees this happening and tries to intervene. One of the bodyguards pistol-whips Meltzer, knocking him to the ground unconscious. He's bleeding heavily from the forehead. U2's security chief, Jerry Mele, arrives as the president's sons' car is starting to leave. He sees Meltzer on the ground and believes he's been shot. Mele tries to stop the president's sons' car, but is hit and grabs on to the front grill to keep from being run over as the car drives slowly away. Mele is dragged for a short while until another crew member, Steve Iredale, grabs him and pulls him away. Mele is hit by a second car belonging to the president's sons while they leave the area.

Both Meltzer and Mele are taken

Bono: "I let Michael down" November 23

"I felt I had let Michael down because I was lost to my own busyness and hadn't called as much as I would have liked. In fact, Ali had spent some time with him and she'd said he looked a bit shaky to her. I just wished I'd been around a bit more. He would confide in me and I in him."

to a nearby hospital. Meltzer receives five stitches and returns home a day later to recover. Mele suffers spinal and other injuries, but returns to work the final three shows of the North American tour despite the severe pain. He'll travel to South America in the new year, planning to work the next leg of the PopMart Tour, but the pain is too much. He collapses before the first show in Brazil, is hospitalized, and eventually returns home for treatment. The upcoming Seattle PopMart show will be the final show of his career.

Also today, 'Miss Sarajevo' appears on the *Diana, Princess of Wales Tribute* album.

December 3
Foro Sol, Mexico City, with Control Machete. Before tonight's show, U2 visits Mexican President Ernesto Zedillo, who has asked the band not to publicize last night's incident. When the band arrives, the President's sons are there and have albums to be signed. Bono and Zedillo exchange angry words, and the President refuses U2's demand for a public apology. Zedillo, believing his sons' version of the story, tells U2 that the band's security roughed up his sons. He finds out shortly thereafter that his sons lied about the night's events. Mele sues the concert promoter and the Mexican government, and wins his case in 1999.

Meanwhile, tonight's show is broadcast live on TV in the US – the first hour is shown on MTV while the entire concert shows on cable channel Showtime. After the show, the band and crew watch a tape playback of the broadcast and celebrate their success with a party.

U2 heads to Los Cabos immediately after the show. With almost a week off until the next show in Vancouver, they take a short break. While in Mexico, Anton Corbijn does a photo shoot with Bono in a Mohawk haircut and occasionally wearing a sombrero.

December 4
Bono does an interview via phone from Los Cabos with Mark Blake of Q magazine.

Jerry Mele: "The life I loved was over" December 2

"I've been hurt and worked in pain so many times I just figured this was another episode. Now I realize the Universe was sending me a message but I didn't want to hear it. So I worked the next night's show, also in Mexico City, and then went on to Vancouver and Seattle. We (U2) were in South America six weeks later when I collapsed. My body finally forced my mind to accept how hurt I was. And that was it. The life I loved was over."

December 8/9
U2 releases two singles: 'If God Will Send His Angels' is the primary single, with varying formats including the tracks 'Slow Dancing', 'Two Shots Of Happy, One Shot Of Sad', 'Sunday Bloody Sunday (Live from Sarajevo)', and 'MOFO (Romin Remix)'. The song is being used in the film, *City Of Angels*, and some singles feature stills from the movie on the sleeve. The version of 'Slow Dancing' on this release is U2's collaboration with Willie Nelson. 'Mofo' is also released in varying formats including five remixes of the main track and a remix of 'If God Will Send His Angels'.

December 9
B.C. Place Stadium, Vancouver, with Smashmouth.

December 12
Kingdome, Seattle, with Smashmouth. U2 plays its final US PopMart show. Like most final shows, it's a special night. The 100-foot arch is adorned with a Christmas tree, whose lights will go on and off in tune with various songs, and Bono's boxer's cape on this night is red-and-white – the boxing Santa! During 'Even Better Than The Real Thing', a handful of crew comes on stage behind Edge and Bono, all wearing the same muscle-man shirt Bono has worn throughout the tour. During 'If You Wear That Velvet Dress', the girl Bono dances with is actually bass technician Stuart Morgan, who promptly grabs Bono's arse before leaving the stage. As the band heads to the main stage after 'With or Without You', Bono brings two fans – two "Wire" mailing list members – on stage, and thanks all the fans on "Wire", many of whom have come to Seattle and crowded around the catwalk and B-stage for tonight's show.

December 21
Bono appears with Luciano Pavarotti at the opening of the Music Therapy Center for children in Mostar, Bosnia-Herzegovina. The facility is funded in part by proceeds from the 'Miss Sarajevo' single. Bono and Pavarotti also attend a children's choir concert, which goes ahead despite heavy rain. "I will be in a rock band one day," says one of the children. "Just like Bono."

December 24
Bono does a phone interview with Jo Whiley during her BBC radio show.

1998

After a short break, the PopMart Tour continues early this year. U2 visit cities and countries that they've never played before, and is energised by the rapturous response from fans who have, until now, only dreamed of having a U2 concert close to home. But still, by the time the tour ends in mid-March, the band is understandably glad it's over and ready to move on to something new.

Back home, U2 throws its considerable weight into the debate over a peace agreement for Northern Ireland. Their YES concert performance is believed to sway the vote in favour of the peace plan.

Later in the year, U2 starts some preliminary work on its next studio album, then decides instead to shock fans by doing something they said they'd never do: release a *Best Of* album.

January 26
U2 do a full rehearsal in Rio de Janeiro tonight.

While in Rio this week, Mayor Luis Paolo Conde gives U2 the keys to the city in a ceremony at the Mayor's Palace.

January 27
Nelson Piquet Autodrome, Rio de Janeiro, with Bootnafat & Gabriel. U2 opens the fourth and final leg of the PopMart Tour in Rio de Janeiro – the first time the band has ever played in South America. The concert is originally planned for Maracana Stadium, the largest stadium in the world. At the last minute, the promoter moves the concert to the smaller Autodrome, claiming that some construction equipment couldn't fit inside Maracana; McGuinness doubts that explanation and is upset U2 weren't told about the change sooner. He's also upset with the use of a U2 cover band in recent commercials promoting Skol, a beer company that is sponsoring U2's visit to Brazil.

Bono, Edge, and Willie Williams arrive at the venue by helicopter, but not before circling several times in front of the famous Christ the Redeemer statue that overlooks the city. Many fans miss the early parts of the show while stuck in an enormous traffic jam heading to the stadium. During an acoustic version of 'Desire', drummers from a samba school that Bono visited earlier in the week join him and Edge on stage.

January 29
U2 attend a birthday party for Brazilian soccer star Romario. U2 join the birthday boy and many of his Brazilian teammates in a

friendly match in Romario's back garden.

January 30-31
Morumbi Stadium, Sao Paulo, with Bootnafat & Gabriel. During an appearance in Brazil in November, 2000, Bono says these shows in Sao Paolo helped U2 regain its confidence and appreciation for playing together.

February
U2 announce it will start Kitchen Records, an underground dance label named after their own nightclub at Dublin's Clarence Hotel. Bono and longtime friend Reggie Manuel will handle A&R duties with the label, which will reportedly specialize in vinyl releases for club DJs.

U2 win five honors in the *Hot Press* 1997 Readers' Poll: Irish Group, Irish Album (*Pop*), Irish Live Act, Irish Songwriter (Bono/U2), and Best Album Sleeve (*Pop*).

February 4
While in Buenos Aires, U2 meet with the famous "Mothers de Plaza de Mayo" human rights group. The mothers have made regular marches around the Plaza de Mayo in front of the Argentine Presidential Palace since the darkest days of that country's 1976-1983 military dictatorship to demand justice for their missing children. This Argentine group is similar to the El Salvador-based group Bono wrote about in the 1987 song 'Mothers Of The Disappeared'. After today's

meeting, Bono records the Yeats poem 'Mother of God' for use on a Mothers' CD, *Ni un Paso Atras*, which will be released later this year.

February 5-6-7
River Plate Stadium, Buenos Aires, with Babasonicos & Illa Kuriaki & The Balderramas. At the first of three shows in Buenos Aires – the band's first shows in Argentina – U2 bring a large group of the Mothers de Plaza de Mayo on stage as the band sings 'One'. The show ends with 'Mothers of the Disappeared', during which most of the Mothers are brought to Bono's microphone to share the name of their missing children. As the show closes, the audience begins to jump up and down, chanting an anti-army slogan: "El que no saltar, es military." ("If you don't jump, you're military.")

February 9
U2 win a Brit Award for Best International Group. Bono gives an acceptance speech from inside the band's mirrorball lemon, which was videotaped days earlier during one of the shows in Buenos Aires.

February 11
Estadio Nacional, Santiago, with Santa Locura. U2 continue to visit cities that have had some importance in their 20-year history, stopping tonight for a single performance in Santiago. Tonight, there are two connections: Victor Jara – Bono dedicates a song to the Chilean poet who was first mentioned 11 years ago in the song 'One Tree Hill'; and the Mothers of the Disappeared, a group who, like their counterparts in Argentina, continue to protest the disappearance of their children during the military rule of Augusto Pinochet.

It's U2's first show in Chile, and it's being shown live on national TV. A group of mothers are brought on stage at the end of the show, and Bono makes an emotional plea to Pinochet to "give the dead back to the living". Crowd reaction to the scene is mixed.

Bono gets mixed reaction in Santiago, February 11

"I spoke to Pinochet as if he was there, as if he was watching television, which I'm sure he wasn't. I just said: 'Mr. Pinochet, God will be your judge, but at the very least, tell these women where the bones of their children are buried....' And this crowd divided quickly into two halves. One half cheered, and one half booed, because there are still mixed feelings about what went on."

February 12
Bono visits a cemetery in Santiago with several dozen Mothers of the Disappeared, and continues the message he spoke about during last night's show. He calls on former dictator Augusto Pinochet to tell the women what happened to their husbands, brothers, and sons. "Our hope and our prayer is that the weight that these women carry will be lifted by someone who still has a heart and soul (and) who would tell them where are the bones of their children," Bono says.

Bono's message reaches some in the Chilean government. Today, members of the opposition party bring in photos and names of the missing and stage a protest in Parliament.

February 15
On the way to Australia, U2's plane makes a surprise stop in Johannesburg, South Africa. Edge, Adam, Larry, and a couple dozen

crewmembers arrive at about 2 am and go to ESP, a hip nightclub in the city, before getting some rest at a Hyatt Hotel. They board the PopMart plane at about 8 p.m. for the flight to Australia. Bono is not with the band, having flown from South America to Germany on his own, before heading to Australia.

February 16
U2 arrives in Perth today and goes to the movies together.

February 17
Burswood Dome, Perth, with Sidewinder. The smallest PopMart show of the tour. The arena is so small, the toothpick and olive are missing, and the arch nearly scrapes the dome's ceiling. Now that PopMart has arrived in Australia, Bono resumes his tributes to the late INXS singer Michael Hutchence. The band is upset when they learn that the Burswood Casino sold prime tickets to its hotel guests at 2x and 3x face value, leaving U2's most avid fans several rows away from the stage. "Somebody sold tickets in the front row for 300 bucks, blocks of them, in a deal with the casino. That stinks," says Paul McGuinness after the show.

February 21
Waverley Park, Melbourne, with Sidewinder. U2 do an extensive soundcheck prior to tonight's show in Melbourne. One of the more developed songs the band seems to

Below: Bono arrives at Waverley Park, February 21.

be trying out includes a chorus that repeats the phrase, "I don't know the way."

February 22

U2 takes part in the Sea of Hands campaign at Treasury Gardens in Melbourne. They appear at the request of the Australians for Native Title Group, which is fighting for Aboriginal reconciliation and native land rights. Bono gives a short speech at the event, but admits to not knowing all the complexities of the situation. "It's a big deal but we don't want to make a big deal of it because we are Irish and we are pop stars. We come from a naive point of view."

February 23

U2 causes a stir in Noosa when they get kicked out of the Rolling Rock nightclub due to inappropriate footwear. Two members of the band – who were never identified – are asked to leave because their sandals don't meet the club's dress code. "They were daggy old things that presented a potential danger to them if there was an accident or something like that," says the club's owner. The incident makes the front page of the local newspaper.

Below: Bono lets the crowd do the strumming, Melbourne, February 21.

February 25

ANZ Stadium, Brisbane, with Sidewinder. At tonight's show in Brisbane, Bono jokes about the sandal incident in Noosa two nights ago. During 'Mofo', he sings, "Brisbane, I've got the right shoes on tonight!"

February 27

Football Stadium, Sydney, with Sidewinder. As PopMart arrives in Sydney, rumours abound that the remaining members of INXS will join U2 on stage to play a tribute to Michael Hutchence in his hometown. INXS are at the show (as are Hutchence's parents and

brother), but the collaboration never materializes. Instead, Bono sings 'MLK' for his close friend. At one point in the show, a fan climbs some 100 feet up a lighting tower in the middle of the stadium to watch the show, but is quickly brought back down by security. The lemon breaks down and isn't used before the encore. A lightning storm begins just as the concert ends with 'One', and Bono calls for all the PopMart lights to be turned off – the final song is performed in complete darkness, save for Mother Nature's display above and a crowd full of lighters below. Kylie Minogue, Helena Christensen, Keanu Reeves and Samuel Jackson are among the celebrities in attendance.

February 28
U2 and some of the crew, along with friend/model Helena Christensen, attend the Gay and Lesbian Mardi Gras in Sydney today.

March 3
U2 loans its PopMart cargo plane to the city of Auckland, which uses it to deliver power generators to help relieve to the city's 12-day power outage.

March 5
Tokyo Dome, Tokyo.

March 11
Osaka Dome, Osaka.

March 13
U2 arrives in Cape Town, South Africa, after a 21-hour flight that began in Osaka and stopped in Singapore and Johannesburg before reaching Cape Town. Fans and media are waiting when the band gets off their plane.

While in Cape Town, U2 meets Archbishop Desmond Tutu for the first time. They visit his Truth and Reconciliation Commission, and when asked to play a song for several hundred people there, the band sings *a cappella* versions of 'Amazing Grace' and 'I Still Haven't Found What I'm Looking For'. U2 also visits Robben Island, where Nelson Mandela was kept prisoner for two decades.

March 16
Greenpoint Stadium, Cape Town, with Just Jinger. U2 plays its first show in South Africa. Edge's parents are in attendance. During 'Mysterious Ways', images of a wedding appear on the videoscreen, leaving fans confused; the concert is being filmed by Phil Joanou for his next movie, *Entropy*, and the unusual footage is actually part of a scene in the movie about a man who's directing a documentary about U2 while his personal life falls apart.

March 20
U2 arrives in Johannesburg. One of their first stops is Downtown Studios, where the band reportedly works on a new song.

March 21
Johannesburg Stadium, Johannesburg, with Bayete. U2 wraps up its 11-month long PopMart Tour with an emotional show in Johannesburg. Before the show, a Chilean ambassador shows U2 photos of the anti-Pinochet protest that took place in Parliament the day after U2's concert in Santiago.

Tonight's show airs on TV throughout South Africa in honour of Human Rights Day. As he did to the people of Sarajevo, Bono tells the South Africans, "To be united – to be one – is a great thing. But to be tolerant, to respect differences maybe even a greater thing." As the mirrorball lemon opens up at the start of the encore, balloons and streamers surround the band and they're drinking champagne to celebrate the tour's last show.

After nearly a year on the road, U2 are relieved the tour is over. Having staged two of the biggest tours in music history over the past six years, the band is ready to do something different next time. Both Edge and Larry drop hints in coming months that U2's next tour will be smaller.

Although PopMart is a financial success with gross revenue of more than $170 million, and although U2 sells nearly 4 million tickets, the band and crew head home well aware of the mistakes they made.

U2 on PopMart's problems, March 21

Paul: "There was this notion that the irony, with which the project was supposedly imbued, would translate. But it didn't. No matter how many times we tried to explain, there were still plenty of people who thought the tour was sponsored by K-Mart and McDonald's. I don't think people were stupid, they just didn't want irony in rock'n'roll and they certainly didn't want it from U2. It was a campaign that took a lot out of everyone and doesn't have a lot of happy memories."

U2 on PopMart's problems
Larry: "I have moments of rage when I think about how stupid we were to allow ourselves to be talked into booking a tour before *Pop* was finished. Sometimes you can get caught up in a certain madness, where you believe you can do anything. We were wrong."

April 7
Author Salman Rushdie reveals on British TV that U2 are the inspiration for a novel he's writing about rock'n'roll.

April 9

U2 wins two awards – Best Band and Best Live Performance – at the annual *Hot Press* Rock Awards, held in Belfast. Bono and Adam are on hand to collect the awards.

April 26

An animated U2 guest stars on the US comedy TV series, *The Simpsons*. It's the show's 200th episode, and also features comedian Steve Martin. In the episode, titled 'Trash of the Titans', Homer Simpson calls upon U2 to help his campaign for Springfield Sanitation Director. Homer joins U2 on stage at a PopMart concert in Springfield, and the band later sings a song, 'The Garbage Man Can', to the tune of 'The Candy Man'. The programme airs on various stations around the world. The show's producers explain later that U2's staff contacted them to suggest the band make an appearance.

Executive Producer Mike Scully explains how U2 got involved with The Simpsons

"We have a hit-list of people who have made it clear that they would like to be on the show if we can find them the right part. In the case of U2, they were just starting their PopMart

Above: Bono and Adam at the Hot Press Awards, April 9.

tour, and we'd already heard from them that they wanted to do the show someday. We had a story [the 200th episode 'Homerpalooza' (sic)] that called for a big stadium concert which had a big political theme, because Homer is running for political office. Since U2 are a politically conscious band, it seemed like the perfect chance to get Homer on stage with Bono – you know, talking politics."

May

With musical ideas that developed on tour still fresh, U2 quietly enters their Dublin studios to continue working on the new material.

Also this month, rumours spread that U2 will split with longtime accountant Ossie Kilkenny.

May 6

Larry attends the opening of a Michael Stipe photo exhibit at the Robert Miller Gallery in New York.

May 8

It's almost Mother's Day, and Bono does an interview on Atlanta radio station 99X with Adora Mills, the mother of R.E.M.'s Mike Mills. Bono's daughter Eve gets on the phone quickly to wish Adora a Happy Mother's Day. Bono, who's at home in Dublin, is fulfilling a promise he made when U2 played Atlanta last November to call Adora for Mother's Day.

May 19

Waterfront Hall, Belfast, with Ash. U2 performs at a Yes Campaign concert in Belfast to draw support for the national vote on the Good Friday/Northern Ireland Peace Agreement. U2 brings on stage David Trimble and John Hume, leaders of the traditionally opposing Ulster Unionist Party and Social Democratic and Labour Party, respectively. Both leaders support the Yes vote, but have never appeared together before.

The political leaders stand on each side of Bono as he raises their arms together in a show of unity. Photographs appear in all the papers in the morning. Three days later, voters in both the North and South approve the Peace Agreement overwhelmingly. "People tell me that rock concert and that staged photograph pushed the people into ratifying the peace agreement. I'd like to think that's true," Bono says.

May 24

U2 earns two spots in a *Sunday Times* list of the Top Ten Irish Rock Albums. *The Joshua Tree* comes in at number two, and *Achtung Baby* is number six on the list. (Number one is The Undertones' self-titled debut album from 1979.)

May 31

U2 deny recent reports that they're being courted to purchase the Glasgow Celtic football club.

July

Issue 28/29 of *Propaganda* magazine, a double issue on the PopMart Tour, is published around this time.

July 17

Edge signs autographs for a group of fans in Dublin and tells them the band is writing new songs.

July 19

Paul McGuinness confirms that Ossie Kilkenny will no longer handle U2's accounting. Sources tell the media the dispute stems from several bad investments during the band's 20-year history.

August

While vacationing in France, Bono enjoys a few jam sessions on the beach with Sinead O'Connor and former Eurhythmic Dave Stewart.

August 9

A 20-minute film called the *PopMart Movie* debuts at the Festival Revue in Edinburgh, Scotland. The movie is presented by Catherine Owens, who organized the video presentations used on the PopMart Tour.

August 2
'Trash of the Titans', the *Simpsons* TV episode starring U2 and Steve Martin wins an Emmy Award for Outstanding Animated Program.

September
Irish tabloid, *The Star*, publishes photos of Bono's naked backside as he changes clothes while on vacation at an Italian beach. Bono and Ali sue the paper for invasion of privacy and defamation of character.

September 5
US President Bill Clinton meets with U2 at the end of a three-day visit to Ireland. Clinton tells reporters: "They're nice people. He's a smart man…" in reference to the band, and Bono in particular.

London's *Financial Times* newspaper reports that U2 will soon sign a new, $50 million record deal with Polygram that calls for the band to release three *Best Of* records. The first of the three, the article says, will cover the 1980-1990 period and will be released this November.

September 9
Island/Polygram confirm the release of *U2 The Best of 1980-1990*, the first of three compilations to be released under a new record deal. The album is due for release on November 2/3, and will include a bonus CD compilation of previously released B-sides. The bonus CD will only be available for one week, and then will be pulled from store shelves.

September 12
U2 meets with Brian Eno and Daniel Lanois to discuss collaborating again on the band's next studio album. But the decision to release a *Best Of* album – along with a new single and a music video – means U2 has to stop working on new songs for a few weeks.

September 20
U2 shoots the video for the remake of its upcoming single, 'Sweetest Thing', on the streets of Dublin. The video features Bono

singing to Ali as they ride around Fitzwilliam Square in a horse-drawn carriage. It includes guest appearances from a host of Irish celebrities, including the Riverdance dancers and members of pop band Boyzone (who appeared at Ali's request). Kevin Godley – who also directed the video for 'Even Better Than the Real Thing' – directs today's shoot. Bono does a local TV interview during the day, and chats with fans in the early evening after the shoot finishes.

September 29
Kirk Franklin releases *The Nu Nation Project*. Bono sings on 'Lean On Me'.

Fall
Health concerns become a major issue for Bono, as his dad is diagnosed with cancer around this time. As if that's not enough, Bono's throat problems get worse and doctors are unable to control a swelling of his vocal cords. One specialist thinks it might be cancer, prompting Bono to question his own mortality. A biopsy proves it's not cancer, and he's able to continue singing.

Bono on the impact of real life on U2's plans, Fall

"Ali was pregnant again not long after that, so whether it was my dad having cancer, or Michael [Hutchence]'s untimely death or whether it was a fresh image of a new life and how vulnerable that child is when you first hold it in your arms, it seemed like the moment to make an album about the essential things."

Below: Bono on the video shoot for 'Sweetest Thing', Dublin, September 20.

October
U2 donates the track 'If God Will Send His Angels' to a charity CD titled *Forgotten Angels*, which will raise money for Temple Street Children's Hospital in Dublin. They also donate 'Please' to an all-star

album, *Across The Bridge Of Hope*, that raises money for the Omagh Memorial Fund.

Above: The 'Sweetest Thing' video shoot.

October 5
U2 regroups at Hanover Quay to work on ideas for new material.

The video for the new version of 'Sweetest Thing' makes its US debut on MTV and VH1.

October 11
The *Sunday Independent* publishes a story that claims controversial author Salman Rushdie has made Bono and Ali's house his "regular home since 1993" while trying to hide from Islamic fundamentalists. U2 moves quickly to refute the story, and the paper prints a retraction on October 18.

October 15
Edge presents B.B. King with a Lifetime Achievement award at the third annual MOBO (Music Of Black Origin) Awards at London. Of King's music, Edge says: "It's just always fresh, eternally fresh. It eternally inspires every new generation of musicians and music friends, because it's just so authentic, and you listen to any of his recordings, B.B.'s stuff still shines. It doesn't date."

October 16
Bono phones the Irish TV programme *The Late Late Show* to congratulate guest John Hume, who along with David Trimble was named a co-winner of the 1998 Nobel Peace Prize earlier in the day for their efforts towards bringing peace to Northern Ireland.

October 18
Bono hosts a dinner at his home for Nobel Peace Prize winner John Hume, who attends with his wife. Also present are many Irish entertainment celebrities, along with Adam, Edge and Paul McGuinness.

October 19/20
A re-recorded version of 'Sweetest Thing' is released. The two-CD single includes several extra live tracks: 'Twilight' (1983), 'An Cat Dubh / Into The Heart' (1983), 'Stories For Boys' (1981), 'Out Of Control' (1981). The 1983 live tracks are from Red Rocks; the 1981 tracks are from Boston. The single tops the charts in Ireland and Canada, and reaches number three in the UK and number six in Australia. There's no commercial release in the US, but the song reaches number 63 on the strength of radio airplay alone.

Bono, Edge and Adam kick-off an Amnesty International campaign in Ireland with a public appearance on O'Connell Street in Dublin. The band signs a petition in support of the Universal Declaration of Human Rights. Amnesty hopes to get one million Irish signatures on the petition before it's presented to the United Nations in December. Bono tells the gathered crowd,

"One of the greatest problems in the world is the cynical idea that the world can't be changed and that politics and economics are too complicated to deal with. But with Amnesty it's simple; you can write a postcard and make a gigantic difference to the life of someone who is in jail or suffering human rights abuses."

October 24
Canongate Publishing confirms that Bono is writing an introduction to the Book of Psalms for their upcoming Bible series. The publishers say Bono will be paid $1,440 for a 1,500-word essay.

October 27
Marianne Faithfull's *A Perfect Stranger* is released. It includes 'Conversation On A Barstool', the song Bono and Edge wrote for her in 1989.

October 30
Island Records opens up a website at http://www.island.co.uk/u2/ to promote the *Best Of 1980-1990* album coming out in the next week. The web site features a contest giveaway, archive pictures, and an interactive game in which contestants try to maneuver U2 through the streets of Dublin away from their "admirers".

November
Author Salman Rushdie denies reports that he spent five years living at Bono's house while hiding from Islamic fundamentalists. He tells SonicNet that he's spent "three or four days" with Bono over the years since they became friends.

November 2/3
U2 releases its first retrospective album, *U2 The Best Of 1980-1990*. The album is released in two versions: a "limited edition" 2-CD set which is released today, and a single, 15-track CD released one week later. Although Island Records originally announces that the 2-CD version will only be sold for a week and then pulled, it's later re-issued and is available in stores for years.

The album is a worldwide success, debuting at number one on

Adam explains U2's first *Best Of* album, November 2/3

"This is sort of a case of us clearing out the cupboard.... We weren't really sure about [it] to begin with. But there's never really a right time to do something like this. But it seemed like a good time to do it now."

the sales charts in Ireland, the UK, Australia, and Canada among others. Although it debuts at number two in the US, behind a new album from Alanis Morrisette, the album has the highest first-week sales of any greatest hits album. In the *Ottawa Sun*, Joshua Ostroff says the album is "a nice reminder of a time when U2 meant aching sincerity, swooning romanticism and epic swagger instead of really big lemons." Tracks, Disc 1: 'Pride (In The Name Of Love)', 'New Year's Day', 'With Or Without You', 'I Still Haven't Found What I'm Looking For', 'Sunday Bloody Sunday', 'Bad', 'Where The Streets Have No Name', 'I Will Follow', 'The Unforgettable Fire', 'Sweetest Thing', 'Desire', 'When Love Comes To Town', 'Angel Of Harlem', 'All I Want Is You', 'October' (hidden track), 'One Tree Hill' (bonus track in Japan)
Tracks, Disc 2: 'The Three Sunrises', 'Spanish Eyes', 'Sweetest Thing', 'Love Comes Tumbling', 'Bass Trap', 'Dancing Barefoot', 'Everlasting Love', 'Unchained Melody', 'Walk To The Water', 'Luminous Times (Hold On To Love)', 'Hallelujah Here She Comes', 'Silver And Gold', 'Endless Deep', 'A Room At The Heartbreak Hotel', 'Trash, Trampoline And The Party Girl'

November 4
U2 take part in a two-hour interview special to be syndicated on worldwide radio. The band speak with fans who submitted questions on the Internet. The radio programme will air in most countries within the next week.

November 5
The *Los Angeles Times* publishes a recent interview with Edge, ostensibly to promote the *Best Of* album, but writer Robert Hilburn peppers Edge with questions about U2's next album and tour. Edge timidly refuses to talk about what the new songs sound like: "I'm nervous about that – after what happened with *Pop*... the way people started making judgments even before they ever heard it." He does admit that U2 will likely move back to arenas on their next tour.

November 6
'Sweetest Thing' is certified Silver by the BPI, with UK sales of more than 200,000. The BPI also certifies *The Best Of 1980-1990* as Platinum, with sales surpassing 300,000.

November 9/10
The single CD version of *The Best Of 1980-1990* is released.

November 12
U2 launches Kitchen Records, its new dance record label, with a party at The Kitchen nightclub.

November 13
Billboard reports that U2 are about to leave Island Records and make Interscope Records their North American label.

Zucchero's *Blue Sugar* album is released. Bono writes English lyrics for the song 'Blue'.

November 14
The Best Of 1980-1990 & B-Sides debuts at number one on the UK album chart, but is replaced a week later by a George Michael greatest hits album.

November 20
RTE Studios, Dublin. U2 appears on a special edition of Irish TV programme *The Late Late Show* dedicated to the victims of the Omagh bombing on August 15, which killed 29 people and injured more than 200 others. U2 opens the show with 'North and South of the River', their first live performance of the song, and close the show with 'All I Want Is You'.

December 4
The two-disc version of *The Best Of 1980-1990/B-Sides* is certified Multi-Platinum, with US sales of more than two million.

December 10
Paul McGuinness and The Edge attend the Nobel Peace Prize ceremony in Oslo in Norway. Bono appears in a taped, greeting congratulating Irish peace brokers David Trimble and John Hume.

The single-disc version of *The Best Of 1980-1990* is certified Gold by the RIAA.

December 11
VH1 premieres *U2 Legends*, an hourlong documentary with new interviews and rare footage of U2's early days.

December 23
Larry becomes a father for the second time. He and longtime girlfriend Ann Acheson give birth to a baby girl, Ava.

Late December
Bono spends the New Year's holiday in Gstaad, Switzerland.

U2 spend much of the year working on new material, but they're in no rush and have no deadline. Their work is interrupted by Bono's growing involvement in debt relief work around the world on behalf of the Jubilee 2000 organization. In the latter part of the year, Bono gets involved with the NetAid concert, speaks at the United Nations, and visits the Pope.

His outside work leads to tension inside the band and at Principle Management, which has taken on the responsibility of scheduling Bono's political appearances and meetings. "He was sometimes a little careless of other people's time and there were certainly strains on Principle Management and strains on the band," says Paul McGuinness. Although the situation affects how U2 operates, it has little impact on the music the band is making.

U2 renegotiates its contract with Island/Polygram this year, replacing both the 1998 agreement that covered the *Best Of* albums and the main album contract U2 signed in 1993.

Adam and Larry buy homes this year in the south of France near where Edge and Bono have had homes since 1992. As the saying goes ... the band that vacations together, stays together.

January

U2 continue working on a new album this month in Dublin. Larry advocates a change of direction away from the experimentation of recent albums.

Larry introduces the idea of "four people working in a room"

"There was a sense that Pop was us experimenting beyond our means. A certain amount of panic set in. Where should we be as a band? What is it that makes U2 'U2'? And I said, 'What makes U2 'U2' is the idea of four people working in a room. We haven't done that for a while – maybe we should look at that again."

Early this month, Paul McGuinness miraculously escapes serious injury when he's involved in a serious car accident while driving to his home in the Irish country. McGuinness' only injury is a bruised finger, yet his luxury Jaguar XJ6 is totaled in the wreck. "It was totally amazing all he had was aches and pains," says a Garda spokesperson. The driver of the other vehicle also escapes without serious injury.

January 8

The Best Of 1980-1990 is certified Double Platinum by the BPI, with UK sales surpassing the 600,000 mark.

Above: Bono addresses the United Nations on world poverty, New York, September 9.

January 12

Bono sings vocals on a live version of 'Sweet Jane', one of the tracks on a new Lone Justice album, *This World Is Not My Home*. The performance is taken from one of Lone Justice's opening slots during *The Joshua Tree* Tour.

January 22

Island Records announces that U2 and author Salman Rushdie have collaborated on a new song with lyrics taken from Rushdie's upcoming novel, *The Ground Beneath Her Feet*.

February

U2 cleans up in the latest *Hot Press* magazine readers' poll, taking first in eight categories: Irish Group, Irish Male Singer, Irish Single ('Sweetest Thing'), Irish Album (*Best Of 1980-1990*), Irish Live Act, Irish Album Sleeve (*Best Of 1980-1990*), Irish Video ('Sweetest Thing'), and Best Overall Polling Act.

Meanwhile, as the band continues working on new material, 'Kite' is one of the first songs they come up with. It includes a vocal from Bono that leaves the rest of the band delighted. "I don't think we had heard that voice for a long time," Adam says later.

February 2
Film crews begin shooting *The Million Dollar Hotel* in downtown Los Angeles. The script is based on a story by Bono. The movie is being directed by the band's longtime friend, Wim Wenders, and will star the likes of Mel Gibson, Milla Jovovich, and others. Bono has a cameo appearance in the movie, too.

February 7
Around this time, Bono undergoes surgery for a sinus problem at the exclusive Blackrock Clinic in Dublin. Clinic staff confirm Bono's surgery a week later, and Ali tells Irish media that Bono is "absolutely fine now".

February 10
Just out of the hospital, Bono appears at the Dublin launch of portrait photographer Perry Ogden's collection of young horse owners, *Pony Kids*. He speaks to the city's young horseowners – telling them he rode horses while growing up – and criticizes the recent legal clampdown on urban horses.

February 16
Bono helps launch the Jubilee 2000 campaign, first with an editorial he writes for *The Guardian*.

Later, Bono accepts a Brit Award in London on behalf of Jubilee 2000. He enters the audience to present the award to boxing legend Muhammad Ali, an international ambassador for Jubilee 2000. The campaign, which aims to eliminate the debt owed by Third World nations, is immediately criticised in the press. In *The Sunday Times*, Michael Rose says, "Bono might have picked the wrong cause this time…. The consensus appears to be that it is a waste of time."

February 23
Bono appears the Grammy Awards in Los Angeles to sing 'Lean On Me' with Kirk Franklin, Mary J. Blige and others. Bono's performance marks the first time any member of U2 has sung at the Grammys.

March 2
Bono joins Bob Dylan on stage in Las Vegas at a new House of Blues inside the Mandalay Bay hotel. They sing 'Knockin' On Heaven's Door' and Bono makes up lyrics about Dylan's birthday, though Dylan won't celebrate that until late May.

March 5
Bono is one of many celebrities who show up at the Universal Amphitheater in Los Angeles to take in the first of three sold-out shows by Lauryn Hill, who recently cleaned up at the Grammy Awards. Bono has expressed his admiration for Hill during interviews in the last year.

March 12
Bono, dressed in drag as a supermodel, appears on British television during the Comic Relief charity telethon to urge people to donate to the relief effort for the underprivileged in Africa and the UK. The appearance has presumably been taped in advance, as Bono is believed to be still in the US preparing for other upcoming appearances.

March 15
Bono inducts Bruce Springsteen into the Rock and Roll Hall of Fame at a ceremony in New York City. It's Bono's third induction, having previously done the same for The Who in 1990 and Bob Marley in 1994.

An excerpt from Bono's induction speech for the Boss
"He was the first whiff of Scorsese, the first hint of Patti Smith, Elvis Costello and The Clash. He was the end of long hair, brown rice and bell-bottoms. He was the end of the 20-minute drum solo. It was good night, Haight-Ashbury; hello, Asbury Park.

"They call him the Boss. Well that's a bunch of crap. He's not the boss. He works *for* us. More than a boss, he's the owner, because more than anyone else, Bruce Springsteen owns America's heart."

In addition to his speech, Bono joins the all-star jam session at the end of the night, and helps sing a rendition of Curtis Mayfield's 'People Get Ready'.

U2's *The Joshua Tree* receives the newly-created "Diamond"

Bono introduces Jubilee 2000 to the masses, February 16

"People don't want crumbs from the table. They don't want charity. They want to be at the table…. There's been a mix of bad lending, bad borrowing, bad economics and bad luck. Jubilee 2000 says, write off those unpayable debts in the year 2000, under an open, fair and transparent process. Put in place a new discipline for lending and borrowing to stop the debts building up again. I'm with Jubilee 2000."

certification from the RIAA. The certification is for releases that have sold 10 million units in the US.

April 6

U2 pays tribute to country legend Johnny Cash with a performance of 'Don't Take Your Guns To Town' during a made-for-TV concert taping in New York City. The band's performance is pre-taped at their Dublin studios. The TV tribute airs for the first time April 18 on the US cable network TNT.

April 13

Bono and Edge appear on the *Cookie's Fortune* soundtrack, which is released today.

April 15

Entropy, the latest film by Phil Joanou, makes its premiere at the Los Angeles Independent Film Festival. The film is semi-autobiographical, as it tracks the story of a film director who's shooting a U2 video while his personal life is falling apart. All four members of U2 appear in the film, which is partially shot at the PopMart concert March 16, 1998, in Cape Town, South Africa. Bono and Larry are the only band members with speaking parts. U2's support for the movie includes a very generous offer to use the band's music. "U2 gave us [five songs] for $1,000," Joanou tells *Stumped* magazine. "Normally, one of their songs costs about $250,000 to use in a movie." The film gets some interest from major Hollywood distributors, but is never released to theaters; it lands on video store shelves in February, 2000.

April 22

Bono and Edge appear on BBC television performing an early version of 'The Ground Beneath Her Feet', the track composed from lyrics written by Salman Rushdie for his novel of the same name.

May

US magazine *Entertainment Weekly* announces its 100 Greatest Moments in Rock and U2's June 5, 1983, concert at the Red Rocks

Above: Bono on stage with Bruce Springsteen after he'd inducted The Boss into the Rock'n Roll Hall of Fame, New York, March 15. **Right top:** Bono at the G8 summit, Cologne, June 19. **Centre:** With Wyclef Jean and George Clinton, New York, September 8. **Bottom:** With Pope John Paul II, Rome, September 23.

Amphitheater near Denver is number 40.

May 4

U2 allows 'With Or Without You' to be used in a TV commercial aimed at world leaders attending the State of the World Forum, which starts today in Belfast.

May 21

Bono and Larry appear live on RTE's *The Late Late Show* to present longtime host Gay Byrne with a black Harley Davidson as a going away present. Byrne is retiring after 37 years hosting the show, which is listed in the *Guinness Book of World Records* as the World's Longest Running TV Talk Show. Byrne asks Bono and Larry to sing, but all he gets is Bono quickly humming the show's theme song.

June

Paul McGuinness tells Irish media that U2 are considering legal action against an Italian political party that's using the cover image from *The Best Of 1980-1990* in its political ads. The Alleanza Nazionale party is using the image of a young boy wearing a soldier's helmet on posters around Rome, urging Italians to vote for them in forthcoming elections. "The misrepresentation of U2 and the illegal use of U2 album artwork in this way is outrageous," McGuinness says.

June 10

Bono takes part in his first online Internet chat during a session hosted by Jubilee 2000 to promote their Drop the Debt campaign. Microsoft officials soon say that the chat is one of the most popular they have ever hosted.

June 19

Bono appears at the G8 Summit in Cologne, Germany, to present a petition with 17 million signatures supporting Third World debt relief to world leaders. With Ali and Edge, Bono then takes part in a human chain around the G8 Summit facility. More than 20,000 people are said to take part in the demonstration. From there, the group heads to a news conference but gets stopped by local security who don't know who they are. The only way to get to the news conference is to walk through Cologne's underground transportation system. After the day's events, Bono has dinner with Tony Blair.

July

Bono writes and sings additional lyrics on 'Slide Away', a song Michael Hutchence began writing before his death in 1997. The song will appear later this year on Hutchence's self-titled posthumous album.

July 5

Bono records a new song, 'New Day', with Wyclef Jean at Jean's basement studio in New Jersey. The track will become the theme song

for the NetAid charity concert event in the fall.

July 16
Bono joins Van Morrison on stage at the Nice (France) Jazz Festival to sing a duet on Van's 'Gloria'.

Late July
While vacationing at the family home in the south of France, Bono helps Mick Jagger celebrate his 56th birthday by joining Elton John and Ron Wood, among others, in a jam session at Jagger's home.

August
Bono returns from vacation and joins U2 in the studio to work on new U2 material.

August 17
Bono and Ali give birth to their third child, a son named Elijah Bob Patricius Guggi Q Hewson. They already have two daughters, Jordan and Eve.

September 2
Bono and Edge are in attendance at the first annual Hall of Fame induction at the Irish Music Hall of Fame in Dublin. Van Morrison is the first inductee, and the only inductee honored on this night.

September 7
Bono and Wyclef Jean perform 'New Day' live for the first time during a taping of VH1 *Storytellers* starring Jean.

September 8
Bono and Wyclef Jean appear together to sing 'New Day' at the Wyclef Jean Foundation's Caribbean Soiree at the Copacabana in New York City. George Clinton and Joan Osborne join them to sing the Parliament song, 'Give Up The Funk'.

September 9
Bono helps launch the NetAid campaign with a speech in front of the general assembly of the United Nations, and later at a news conference in New York City. After the speech, Bono and Wyclef Jean sing 'New Day' outside the UN. NetAid aims to use the Internet to increase awareness of global poverty, and centers on the launch of www.netaid.org, which is touted as "the world's most powerful web site to fight extreme poverty." But Bono is more guarded in his remarks today: "I'm kind of suspicious of the warm, fuzzy feeling aspect of what we're doing. To be honest with you, it's a really hard sell." The news conference also includes the world premiere of the 'New Day' music video, and includes details of three NetAid concerts next month. Bono and Jean will perform together at Giants Stadium in East Rutherford, New Jersey. Other shows will take place in London and Geneva.

September 14
The 'New Day' single is released. Proceeds are slated for Kosovo relief efforts and the Wyclef Jean Foundation.

September 23
Bono, Bob Geldof, and other supporters of Jubilee 2000 visit Pope John Paul II at his summer home in the Alban Hills outside Rome. During the 25-minute meeting, Bono gives the Pope a book of poetry by Irish poet Seamus Heaney. But headlines are made when Bono hands the Pope his sunglasses and the Pope puts them on, prompting Bono to tell the world's media that John Paul II is the world's "first funky Pontiff".

Bono spends much of the day, both before and after meeting the Pope, doing media interviews with the likes of CNN television, *Newsweek* magazine, and Radio Four, and the hundreds of media gathered for the event today.

After a very late dinner and early-morning drinks at a Rome nightclub, Bono catches a 6 a.m. flight to Washington, DC, where he'll continue the campaign for debt relief.

September 27
Christy Moore releases a new album, *Traveller*. Edge plays guitar on the final track, 'What's The Story Git?'.

Bono on recording the *MDH* soundtrack, November

"Recording the soundtrack was a piece of piss. We did it in ten days. It was effortless, we just put up the pictures, we got three giant monitors in the studio, and everyone just kind of responded to the picture. It was a thrill."

October

Early in the month, Bono vacations in France with his family. While there, he does a phone interview with BBC Radio 1, saying that U2 is "a couple songs" away from finishing its new album.

U2 is listed twice in the newly released Millennium edition of the *Guinness Book of World Records*: (1) Largest Audience for a rock tour: playing to over 3.9 million people in 93 shows on the PopMart tour, and (2) Largest Video Screen: the screen on the PopMart tour.

October 7

'Sweetest Thing' wins the award for Best Single at the 1999 *Hot Press* Rock Awards in Dublin.

October 8

Bono appears on Michael Hutchence's self-titled posthumous album, which is released today in Australia and Europe. Bono sings the lyrics he wrote earlier this year on the track, 'Slide Away'. The album will be released February 22, 2000, in North America.

October 9

Bono helps launch the US portion of the NetAid concert at Giants Stadium in New Jersey. As the London – and Geneva – based NetAid shows near an end, the three venues are linked together for a worldwide "Moment of Unity", which includes a brief speech from

UN Secretary General Kofi Annan. Following Annan's comments, Wyclef Jean and Bono lead a stageful of artists in singing 'New Day', the NetAid theme song written specifically for this event. Bono stays on stage to sing 'One' with Quincy Jones conducting a 30-piece orchestra from Julliard and Italian rocker Zucchero on guitar. Bono returns to the stage later during Jean's set for another go at 'New Day'. Despite an impressive lineup of artists, NetAid is sparsely attended and critics suggest "compassion fatigue" has hit the public. The *New York Post* reports that "nearly three quarters of the stadium was empty".

October 25

Edge and Morleigh Steinberg give birth in Los Angeles to their second child, a boy named Levi. He's Edge's first son.

November

Early in the month, Bono visits the US Congress to promote Jubilee 2000. He does an interview with Fox News.

Issue 30 of *Propaganda* magazine is published around this time. In it, Adam talks about the new material U2 has been working on for the past year: "The principle we're working with this time is that the most unique music we make as U2 is with the four of us playing instruments in a room together."

Bono is in the studio with Daniel Lanois and others working on the

soundtrack to *The Million Dollar Hotel*, so U2 takes a break from working on its own new album.

While in Dublin this month, Anton Corbijn conducts a photo shoot with all four members of U2 and their dads. The eight men dress in similar suits and ties and make a stunning collection of photographs that don't see the light of day until Corbijn issues a retrospective book of his U2 photography in 2005.

November 1

The Dublin City Council votes unanimously to grant U2 the Freedom of Dublin. The keys of Dublin City are only presented to those who have made great contributions to peace and humanity or to people who have brought honour to Dublin or Ireland. "Despite their international success they continue to live, record and plan their world-class campaigns here," says Dublin's Lord Mayor Mary Freehill. "The band are always quick to support the city's charities and cultural initiatives." An official ceremony is planned for next spring.

Also today, Bono appears in an RTE TV documentary, *Luke*, about the life of The Dubliners' singer Luke Kelly.

November 10

Bono is photographed in Dublin tonight with Naomi Campbell.

November 11

Bono is given the Free Your Mind

Right: Bono and R.E.M.'s Michael Stipe at NetAid, October 9.

Above: Bono on stage
at NetAid, October 9.

Award at the 1999 MTV Europe Music Awards in Dublin for his work on behalf of Jubilee 2000 and at NetAid. Edge is also at the ceremony to present the award for Best Video (which Blur wins). After the ceremony, Bono joins Iggy Pop and Marilyn Manson for an impromptu jam at a post-event private party; they cover 'Johnny B. Goode' and 'TV Eye'.

November 27
Bono and Larry attend the funeral of Jean Corr, the 57-year-old mother of The Corrs, in Dundalk, Ireland.

December
Bono creates an original cover sleeve for a repackaged release of John Lennon's 'Imagine'. The release is a fund raiser organised by Yoko Ono for Shelter, a homeless charity.

December 3
Edge presents the Best Dance Track award at the Irish Dance Club Awards.

December 6
Bono's laptop computer is taken from his car tonight in Dublin. Principle Management offers a £2,000 reward for its return.

December 9
Bono gets his laptop back thanks to *The Star* newspaper and a Dublin man named Paul who had purchased it for £300 from what he thought was a reputable source. Bono is grateful to get the machine back, and offers to buy the young man a new laptop. "Everything I've written since August was on this and I hadn't backed up any of it – so I would really have been a goner," Bono says. "This is like my portable brain – unfortunately I've got a smaller one so this stores all my information. Now the album is back on track. Thanks so much."

December 31
Bono attends America's Millennium Gala in Washington, DC, at the invitation of event co-producer Quincy Jones. He performs 'One' with Daniel Lanois on guitar and a full orchestra. Prior to the outdoor show, Bono, Ali and the Hewson children go through a reception line to greet President Clinton and his family. The White House speaker introduces him as "Mr. Bono".

2000

Still smarting from the mistakes of the *Pop* era, U2 gear up to regain lost ground this year. Ongoing work on a new album in Dublin occupies the first part of the year. Bono takes care of obligations related to *The Million Dollar Hotel*, and his debt relief work keeps him away from the studio, too.

But as the year goes along, the U2 machine moves into what they call "war footing". The new single, 'Beautiful Day', is out in September, with the new album, *All That You Can't Leave Behind*, out a month later.

Believing that large-scale success requires new promotional tactics, U2 hatch a plan that involves the type of public appearances they haven't made in a couple decades. They perform live on *Top Of The Pops*, *MTV*, *Saturday Night Live*, and several awards shows. There's even a trip to Brazil. The plan works, as 'Beautiful Day' and *All That You Can't Leave Behind* are immediate smashes with both fans and critics. U2 ends 2000 as popular, perhaps more popular than they've ever been.

January

With Bono's work on *The Million Dollar Hotel* soundtrack finished, U2 continue working on their next album in Dublin. They also shoot a music video for 'The Ground Beneath Her Feet' in the Sandyford mountains near Dublin. Wim Wenders directs, and Salman Rushdie appears in the video. The song, however, won't see the light of day as a commercial release.

Marc Marot: "It will cause you embarrassment"

Island Records' Marc Marot recalls explaining to Bono why they shouldn't release 'The Ground Beneath Her Feet' as a single.

"I had the really difficult duty of sitting in a viewing theatre next to Bono in Dublin, *cringing... thinking, This film isn't very good. Bono's written it. He's sitting next to me. And he wants me to put out a single and have a hit record with it.* And I had to say to him, 'I'm really sorry, Bono, but I don't think you should release a single. You can release the soundtrack album, but I don't think strategically you should release a single because it draws too much attention to a film that isn't gonna do very well. And it will cause you embarrassment.'"

January 4

PopMart Live From Mexico City is nominated for a Grammy Award in the Best Long Form Music Video category (The video does not win when awards are announced in February).

January 6

Bono writes an article for the French newspaper, *Le Monde*, urging the country to cancel the debt owed to it by developing nations.

Despite a previous statement by Dublin's Lord Mayor, U2 announce that they will not perform a free concert in Dublin when city leaders give the band the Freedom of Dublin award on March 19. The announcement is met with criticism in and around Dublin.

January 22

Bono receives the Man of the Year award at the NRJ Awards in Cannes, France for his work on behalf of Jubilee 2000. "This award is not for me," Bono says while accepting the award. "It's not about the Man of the Year, but it's about an idea, the idea of the year. It's about Jubilee 2000." He attends the festivities with Ali and their five-month-old son, Eli.

February 5

Bono appears on RTE's *Saturday Night Live* TV program, which is hosted this week by longtime friend Dave Fanning. During the interview, Bono tells Fanning that U2 is ready to make the best record of their lives, and fires jabs at some of the band's rock competition: "Oasis? Radiohead? They are good. They're the boys. But we're the men."

February 7

Edge visits Londonderry in Northern Ireland on the invitation of John Hume. His visit prompts speculation that U2 will perform at a major outdoor concert city officials are organising. Paul McGuinness contacts the press to quash the rumours.

February 9

Bono attends the Berlin Film Festival for the world premiere of *The Million Dollar Hotel*. The film, written by Nicholas Klein and based on Bono's original story, wins the Silver Bear award. Bono is credited as a co-producer and makes a very brief cameo in the movie.

The day begins with a news conference in the morning with Bono, director Wim Wenders, stars Jeremy Davies and Milla Jovovich and others. The movie is premiered for the press immediately after the

Right: Bono with Nelson Mandela and Naomi Campbell at the Laureus Sports Awards, Monaco, May 25.
Above: Bono and Milla Jovovich on the *Million Dollar Hotel* set.

news conference, and then has its public premiere in the evening.

While in Berlin, Bono meets Adam Dorn, who records under the name Mocean Worker. Bono gives Dorn permission to use one of the film's songs that was left off the soundtrack on Dorn's next album.

February 10

Bono arrives back in Dublin and is photographed being wheeled through Dublin Airport by Gavin Friday.

February 11

Larry takes to the catwalk as a model at tonight's Brown Thomas Fashion Show at the Point Theatre in Dublin.

February 14

Songs from *The Million Dollar Hotel* soundtrack are leaked on the Internet.

February 17

Citing a lack of time, Paul McGuinness resigns his 11-year position on the Arts Council of Ireland.

February 22

Bono is a co-winner (with Sting) of Rock the Vote's Patrick Lipper Award. Due to other commitments, he's unable to attend the ceremony in Los Angeles.

February 23

In Rome, Bono and Italian rap star Lorenzo Jovanotti visit Italian Prime Minister Massimo D'Alema

Bono: "I have written some straight love songs" March

"I don't wanna write a song that reddens my face when I hear it on the radio. And I have written some straight love songs only to have them put aside because they might elicit projectile vomiting from the great outdoors! I like love songs that are bittersweet, and I like women to be more complex in songs because that's my experience of them in life."

and persuade him to support more Third World debt relief.

February 26
Bono and Edge perform together on the last day of Italy's Festival of San Remo. They play acoustic versions of 'All I Want Is You' and 'The Ground Beneath Her Feet' – the latter song receiving its first live performance. Speaking in Italian, Bono thanks the Pope and Prime Minister D"Alema for supporting debt relief.

February 29
Bono attends a birthday celebration in Rossiniere, Switzerland, for his friend, the painter Balthus. He also appears tonight in *From a Whisper To A Scream*, a new documentary about Irish music premiering on RTE TV.

March
As part of the publicity for *The Million Dollar Hotel*, Bono does an interview early this month in Paris with Peter Murphy of *Hot Press*. Reflecting on the theme of the movie and the songs Bono wrote for the soundtrack, Murphy asks Bono about his dislike for writing traditional love songs.

March 12
To help promote *The Million Dollar Hotel*, Bono does an online chat hosted by Yahoo!. The chat takes place while U2 is at a birthday party for Adam.

March 13/14
The Million Dollar Hotel soundtrack album is released, and features three U2 tracks: 'The Ground Beneath Her Feet', 'Stateless', and 'The First Time'. Bono also sings on four other songs, Larry plays on four songs, and Adam plays on one. 'Stateless' and 'The Ground Beneath Her Feet' were both candidates for the next U2 album, but the band decides to give them to Bono for the film soundtrack instead.

Edge explains why U2 let go of two new tracks for the MDH soundtrack
"It seemed like the perfect thing to do with them, because they weren't going to make the U2 album. The only one that was in any doubt was 'The Ground Beneath Her Feet,' but we already had so many great ballads that it seemed like we really didn't need another one."

Though the movie is getting mixed reviews, the soundtrack album fares better critically. John Walshe rates the album 10 out of 12 in *Hot Press*, saying it "manages to maintain a core humanity and warmth that makes you want to check in, order a penthouse suite and enjoy its manifold charms again and again."

March 17
Bono and Edge appear on the *TFI Friday* TV programme in Dublin with host Chris Evans. After a short interview, they perform a live acoustic version of 'The Ground Beneath Her Feet'.

March 18
Smithfield Civic Plaza, Dublin. U2 and Paul McGuinness receive the Freedom of Dublin, the highest honour the city can give. Mayor Mary Freehill praises the band and presents each with Waterford Crystal replicas of a Joshua tree. "I'd have thought people would be sick of U2 by now," Bono tells the thousands in attendance. "It's still moving to come home and see the amount of goodwill toward us." After the ceremony, U2 performs a four-song set that includes the first live performance of 'The Sweetest Thing'.

Also honoured with the Freedom of Dublin is Burmese political prisoner Aung San Suu Kyi. U2 doesn't know much about her, but after they learn her story, they're inspired to do a song in her honour, 'Walk On'.

March 19
Taking advantage of their newfound Freedom of Dublin, Bono and Edge graze lambs in Dublin's St. Stephen's Green. Alerted in advance of the photo opportunity, Irish media flock (no pun intended) to the Green to capture the moment. The sheep Bono is carrying answers nature's call while in Bono's arms. Grazing sheep on the Green is one of the many unique privileges afforded to Freemen of Dublin.

April
U2 and Anton Corbijn begin shooting photographs to be used for their upcoming album. An unproductive shoot in Dublin is passed over in favour of photos taken later this summer at Charles de Gaulle airport in Paris and in Nice.

April 8
Bono speaks at the opening of an exhibition of the photography of Anton Corbijn in Groningen, The Netherlands.

April 27
Campaigners fighting to stop a garbage dump from being built in Joshua Tree National Park attack U2 for not doing enough to help

Left: Bono with
U2's photographer
of choice, Anton
Corbijn, Groningen,
April 8.

their cause. They call U2 "the most exploitative band ever" for using the park for *The Joshua Tree* album, but refusing to get involved in the battle against the dump. A U2 spokesperson says the band was invited to take part in a concert to support the cause, but couldn't make it. The campaigners retract their criticism of U2 days later.

May 10
To celebrate Bono's 40th birthday, Ali takes Bono and a couple dozen friends on a tour of Europe, traveling from place to place in a vintage airplane for a couple of days.

May 25
Bono attends the Laureus Sports Awards in Monaco where he finally meets Nelson Mandela. As a longtime supporter of the former South African President, Bono had hoped to meet Mandela when U2 took the PopMart tour to South Africa in March, 1998, a meeting which never happened.

June
Bono writes an introduction to the *God* CD, which is part of a new, three-disc Johnny Cash anthology.

June 8
U2's *PopMart Live From Mexico City* concert is webcast by Internet media company Burst.com, using their Burstware technology, which claims to offer faster-than-real-time streaming. The concert remains available as a showcase for Burst.com for three weeks. U2 are minority owners in the company, which makes $500,000 in server sales and $12 million in investments from the increased attention and exposure. (U2 will sell its stake in the company in 2005.)

June 23
Thousands of U2 fans worldwide get an e-mail from Bono, urging them to sign Jubilee 2000's latest petition supporting debt relief for developing nations.

July 18
U2's opens a beta version of its first official web site at U2.com. The site features live studio webcams in its early incarnation. An official launch of the full site is still a few months away.

July 28
Germany's public broadcaster, ZDF, announces today that it will use 'Beautiful Day' as the theme song for its coverage of the Sydney Olympic Games.

August
Volume 2, Issue 1 of *Propaganda* magazine is published around this time. It arrives in a new, smaller format and includes a fanclub-only CD, *Hasta La Vista, Baby!*, featuring 14 tracks from U2's December, 1997, PopMart concerts in Mexico City. Tracks: 'Pop Muzik', 'Mofo', 'I Will Follow', 'Gone', 'New Year's Day', 'Staring At The Sun', 'Bullet The Blue Sky', 'Please, Where The Streets Have No Name', 'Lemon', 'Discotheque', 'With Or Without You', 'Hold Me', 'Thrill Me, Kiss Me, Kill Me', 'One'

The magazine also features an interview with Edge talking about U2's upcoming album.

August 9
Around this time, U2 shoots a music video in Paris for their new single, 'Beautiful Day', with director Jonas Akerlund. The band is filmed performing the song on a runway at Charles de Gaulle Airport. Anton Corbijn shoots still photos in and around the airport, including the photos that will eventually grace the covers of both the 'Beautiful Day' single and the new album.

August 20
U2 announces *All That You Can't Leave Behind* as the title of their next album on the band's official web site. They also confirm a late autumn release date and the full track listing for the album.

August 25
Bono and family arrive in Sarajevo

Edge previews the next U2 album in *Propaganda*, August

"It is very much a band record. It's us playing together, very simple, perhaps back to like our first few records with guitar, bass, drums, maybe some keyboards but not that much.... For the moment, we are interested in exploring what actually it is to be in a band."

for the final two days of the Sarajevo Film Festival, where Bono will present *The Million Dollar Hotel*.

August 26
While in Sarajevo, Bono spends 2,200 French francs at an auction to purchase a minefield in Bosnia-Herzegovina that will be demined.

August 31
U2 releases 'Beautiful Day' to radio stations. The commercial single won't be released for more than a month.

September 7
Bono appears with Nigerian President Olusegun Obasanjo at the United Nations Millennium Summit to present a petition with more than 21 million signatures from people in 155 countries calling for global debt relief. "It's madness that a pop star has to be standing here... somebody else should be doing this, somebody else more qualified," Bono tells reporters outside the UN headquarters. "But you know what? They don't have time. They're not bad guys in Washington, they're just busy guys."

Later, Bono and Larry introduce Rage Against The Machine at the 2000 MTV Video Music Awards.

September 8
The 'Beautiful Day' video premieres during a special broadcast on VH1 in the US.

September 10
Bono plays himself in a short film called *Sightings Of Bono*, which is filmed in Dublin today. Paul McGuinness' wife, Kathy Gilfillan, writes the film. The film tells the story of a Dublin girl who sees Bono everywhere and finally meets him in the shop where she works.

September 13
Adam is in attendance tonight as Bob Dylan plays an intimate gig at Dublin's Vicar Street.

September 15
U2 offer 30-second clips of its new songs, two songs at a time, starting today on U2.com.

September 21
Paul McGuinness tells BBC's Radio 1 that the next U2 tour will begin in Miami in March, 2001.

Bono appears in Washington, DC, at a news conference urging the US Congress to authorize payment of the US proposed share of funds to erase Third World debt. While in the capital, Bono meets ultra-conservative Senator Jesse Helms for the first time.

September 23
Bono sings Willie Nelson's 'Blue Skies' at the funeral of Paula Yates in Kent, England.

September 25
Bono appears in Prague at a joint meeting of the World Bank/IMF to urge international cancellation of Third World debts.

September 26
Bono sings on the track 'Air Suspension' from the Mocean Worker album, *Aural And Hearty*, out today in North America. The track was dropped from *The Million Dollar Hotel* soundtrack. The album will be released February 19, 2001, outside North America.

September 27
Clarence Hotel, Dublin. U2 performs on the roof of the Clarence Hotel in Dublin for BBC's *Top Of The Pops* program. It's their first live performance for the venerable programme in 17 years. A crowd of several thousand fans gathers for the performance, though most can only hear the music from the street below. The band does multiple takes of 'Beautiful Day' and 'Elevation', with Bono singing live over a backing track on both songs. The performance airs on *Top of the Pops* on October 6.

October
Bono contributes an essay about Bob Dylan for a Q magazine special edition dedicated to the legendary singer.

October 2
Bono joins a diverse group of people at the White House urging Congress to approve $435 million in debt relief. Bono sits with President Clinton and conservative Christian spokesman Pat Robertson, among others.

October 4
Mark Neale's documentary about William Gibson, *No Maps For These Territories*, premieres at the Vancouver International Film Festival. Bono and Edge both appear in the film with speaking roles. Edge also performs a song called 'Chiba City Blues' (which is the name of the first chapter of Gibson's landmark book, *Neuromancer*).

October 9/10
U2 releases 'Beautiful Day' in a variety of formats, which also include the tracks 'Summer Rain', 'Always', 'Discotheque (Live from Mexico City)', 'If You Wear That Velvet Dress (Live from Mexico City)', and 'Last Night On Earth (Live from Mexico City)'. The single hits number one in Ireland, the UK, The Netherlands, Australia, Norway, and Canada. There's no commercial release in the US, but the song still reaches number 21 on the *Billboard* Hot 100.

October 12
The full set of tracks from U2's forthcoming album, *All That You Can't Leave Behind*, becomes available for free download via Napster and various web sites. The album is not due for official release for another 18 days.

October 15
'Beautiful Day' debuts at number one on the charts in the UK, Ireland, Holland, and Australia. With no commercially available single, the track only debuts at number 75 in the US.

October 17
It's meet the press day at U2's Hanover Studios. The band does interviews with MTV, BBC, RTE and *Hot Press*, among others.

October 19
ManRay, Paris. U2 plays a promotional gig in front of a small audience in a Paris nightclub. They

debut four tracks from *All That You Can't Leave Behind*.

Top: Adam on stage at the *FarmClub.com* TV show, October 27. Below: Bono with Wynona Rider and Kevin Spacey.

October 20

U2 record an interview with Irish DJ Dave Fanning for airing on 2FM on October 29.

Around this time, Bono sends a letter and a copy of *All That You Can't Leave Behind* to Stanley McCombe, whose wife Ann died in the Omagh bombing and is mentioned by name in the new song, 'Peace On Earth'. "Bono said he used Ann's name in the song and he hoped I didn't mind. I was very honoured and I know Ann would have been too," McCombe says. (It's presumable, but unknown if Bono sent similar letters to the families of the other Omagh victims mentioned in the song.)

October 23

BBC Maida Vale Studio, London. U2 performs a short session for the BBC and does an interview with Radio 1 hosts Simon Mayo and Jo Whiley. Ten U2 fans who won a Radio 1 competition are at the gig. Bono visits with the fans up on the balcony where they're sitting before U2's set. Afterward, he invites them downstairs for a champagne celebration and group photo.

Also today, U2 fans online confirm a rumor that had started earlier in the month – the Joshua tree depicted on *The Joshua Tree* album has fallen over. The tree had become a landmark of sorts for U2 fans over the years, many of whom spent days searching through the California desert for the tree's location. Those who discovered it kept the location secret in an attempt to make sure the casual fan, or U2 basher, didn't find the tree and try to damage it in some way.

October 26

Universal Studios, Los Angeles. U2 appears on KROQ-FM's *Kevin & Bean* show, and performs four songs live.

Continuing a bad week for U2-related trees, the famous lone pine tree at New Zealand's One Tree Hill site is destroyed today after being deemed unsafe. The tree had been attacked in 1994 and 1999 and suffered enough damage to cause it to lean heavily to one side.

October 27

Universal Studios, Los Angeles. U2 performs and does an interview on the *FarmClub.com* TV show. When the programme airs on October 30, the interview is not shown. Celebrities who come out for the show include Dr. Dre, Winona Ryder, Sheryl Crow, and Kevin Spacey.

'Beautiful Day' is certified Silver by the BPI, with UK sales exceeding 200,000.

October 30

MTV Studios, New York. On the day its new album hits stores, U2 perform a short set on the outdoor balcony of MTV's New York studios for the *TRL* programme. Afterward, the whole band does a live chat on AOL/CompuServe to help promote the album.

U2's 10th studio album, *All That You Can't Leave Behind*, is released worldwide. It's U2's first studio album since *Pop* more than three-and-a-half years ago. U2 makes a dramatic change of direction on the new album, opting for a simpler, more stripped-down sound that many say is reminiscent of earlier records like *The Joshua Tree*.

The album debuts at number one in 32 countries, but not in the US, where it debuts at number three despite having the largest first-week record sales for any U2 release in the US. The top US album is Jay-Z's *Roc La Familia 2000*, another Universal Music release. "It was extremely annoying that U2 didn't go to number one," Paul McGuinness says later. "It was particularly annoying that it was dislodged by another artist from the same company."

Critics overwhelmingly love the album, though a few identify it as a retreat. In *Rolling Stone*, James Hunter says *All That You Can't Leave Behind* is U2's "third masterpiece" after *The Joshua Tree* and *Achtung Baby*: "U2 distill two decades of music-making into the illusion of effortlessness usually only possible from veterans. The album represents the most uninterrupted collection of strong melodies U2 have ever mounted." Writing in the *New Zealand Herald*, Russell Baillie says, "They're back and seem to be saying with this album, there's actually nothing better to do if you're U2 than to be U2 – and a grand, swaggering, heroic, heartfelt, soaring, stop-the-traffic, shout-it-from-the-rooftops U2 at that." The *Irish Times*' Kevin Courtney is less enthusiastic, saying the album is too safe: "What's lacking, however, is the sense of danger. After 20 years of swashbuckling and globetrotting, U2 have come home, and *All That You Can't Leave Behind* is the crackling of the hearth fire: warm, tender, laughing, forgiving, but not very exciting."

Reflecting the music's simplicity, the album cover is a

Adam & Larry describe *All That You Can't Leave Behind*, October 30

Adam: "To some extent, the term 'back to basics' is misleading. It's a minimalist U2 record with the things that we all took for granted as players. There's a maturity to realising that actually, we do one or two things very well.... I think it is a record where we've had a look at what's out there, and we've gone 'maybe we still have something to offer which we're not hearing in anyone else.' If not maturity, it's a kind of self-confidence." Larry: "Pop was an attempt to deconstruct U2 and this album was us saying, 'Oh shit, we've gotta put this back together again.'"

black-and-white photo of the four band members standing together in Charles de Gaulle Airport in Paris. Shortly before printing, at Bono's request, an airport departure sign is edited to show J33-3, a Biblical reference to the book of Jeremiah, Chapter 33, Verse 3. The passage, which Christians refer to as "God's phone number," reads: "Call to me and I will answer you and will tell you great and hidden things which you have not known."

On learning that the track 'Walk On' is dedicated to activist Aung San Suu Kyi, the Burmese government bans the album. Tracks: 'Beautiful Day', 'Stuck In A Moment You Can't Get Out Of', 'Elevation', 'Walk On', 'Kite', 'In A Little While', 'Wild Honey', 'Peace On Earth', 'When I Look At The World', 'New York', 'Grace'. Bonus tracks on various releases include 'The Ground Beneath Her Feet', 'Always', 'Summer Rain', and 'Big Girls Are Best'.

Coinciding with the album's release, U2.com re-launches with a new design and more content. And U2's heavy promotion continues with a live appearance today on MTV's teen-skewing program, *TRL*.

Adam on U2's new marketing tactics
"With this record, we took the attitude that the business had changed an awful lot and we knew we couldn't just do the things that we relied on 15 or 20 years ago. So we did TV, we did TRL, and we enjoyed doing it."

November 2
BBC Television, London. U2 records three songs live in the studio for the BBC's *Top Of The Pops* programme. 'Elevation' airs a day later, while the other performances are held for future broadcast.

November 3
ITV Television, London. U2 records three songs live in the studio for the British TV show *CD:UK*. The performance airs November 11.

November 6
President Bill Clinton praises Bono while signing legislation that cancels all US bilateral debt owed by the world's poorest countries. Though Bono is not at the signing ceremony, Clinton says Bono's "passionate devotion" brought together Democrats and Republicans to make the debt cancellation possible.

November 11
Bono, Adam and other friends help Bono's dad, Bob, celebrate his 75th birthday (which is two days away) with a surprise party at the Clarence Hotel.

All That You Can't Leave Behind debuts at number one on the UK album chart. It's the band's eighth number one album in the UK.

November 12
U2 rehearses at the Palacio de Congresos in Madrid for their performance at tomorrow's Amigo Awards.

November 13
Palacio de Congresos, Madrid. U2 performs 'Beautiful Day' at the Amigo Awards, but only Bono's vocals are live; the band's performance is played back from yesterday's rehearsal. Earlier in the day, the band does a photo shoot and press conference.

November 14
U2 leave Madrid for Stockholm, where the MTV Europe Music Awards will take place in two days.

November 16
Globe Arena, Stockholm. U2 performs 'Beautiful Day' at the MTV Europe Music Awards.

November 17
A panel of music experts put together by MTV and *Rolling Stone* magazine vote 'With Or Without You' as the number eight song in the Top 100 Pop Songs Since 1963.

November 23
Globo Studios, Rio de Janeiro. U2 performs a six-song set in front of a small TV audience. 'Beautiful Day' and 'Elevation' are shown three days later on Brazilian TV.

Director Jonas Akerlund starts shooting a new video for 'Walk On' this morning in Brazil. It's a rush job – Akerlund got the call to come to Rio de Janeiro only two days ago. He and U2 shoot the video in and around Rio for three days. During a break in the live performance filming, Edge and Larry start jamming on a cover of The Who's 'Won't Get Fooled Again', planting an idea in the band's collective mind to consider playing the song live.

November 27
U2 spends two days shooting a music video for 'Stuck In A Moment You Can't Get Out Of' this week in Los Angeles with director Kevin Godley.

November 30
Shrine Auditorium, Los Angeles. U2 performs 'Beautiful Day' at the inaugural My VH-1 Awards show.

The Million Dollar Hotel premieres in Australia.

December
Early in the month, U2 tapes an interview from their New York City hotel room with Chris Douridas for the *New Ground* show on Los Angeles-area radio station KCRW. The interview airs December 9.

December 4
U2 rehearse for tomorrow's gig in New York. During soundcheck, they stop to listen to The Who's 'Won't Get Fooled Again', trying to figure out how to play the song. As Edge works out the song, Bono speaks up: "I just want to warn you, Lenny Kravitz will be out there, and he'll know all the chords." The soundcheck also includes a

Above: Bono at the MTV Awards, November 16.

few covers that won't be played tomorrow, such as Thin Lizzy's 'Dancing In The Moonlight' and 'Rock & Roll Part 1' by Gary Glitter.

December 5
Irving Plaza, New York, with The Chemical Brothers. U2 does a free concert as part of their promotional tour for *All That You Can't Leave Behind*. Tickets are given out to contest winners. The show, which lasts a little more than an hour, is broadcast live on radio stations across the US. The last song of the gig is a cover of of The Who's 'Won't Get Fooled Again', realising an idea that was planted a couple weeks ago in Brazil.

December 8
U2 rehearses at NBC Studios for their performance tomorrow on *Saturday Night Live*. It's the 20th anniversary of John Lennon's death, and Bono gives thought to

leaving flowers at The Dakota (the building where Lennon was killed), but decides against it.

While in New York, *Rolling Stone*'s Chris Heath interviews U2 for an upcoming feature.

December 9
NBC Studios, New York. U2 makes its first appearance on the long-running US variety show, *Saturday Night Live*. The band performs 'Beautiful Day' and 'Elevation'. Joey Ramone comes to the NBC studios to hang out with U2.

December 15
All That You Can't Leave Behind is certified Double Platinum by the BPI, with UK sales surpassing the 600,000 mark.

December 18
All That You Can't Leave Behind is certified Platinum, with US sales eclipsing the one million level.

It's a year of incredible highs and deep lows for U2, most of which are played out in public as U2 takes the Elevation Tour across North American and Europe.

The year begins with 'Beautiful Day' sweeping three Grammy Awards, a validation of what the music-buying public considers U2's "return to form". Bono tells the Grammy audience that U2 are "reapplying for the job" of best band in the world, and when the Elevation Tour launches to rave reviews from fans and critics, that application is accepted. The tour is a big success and U2 are once again the "it" band.

Bono continues to make a very public push for debt and AIDS relief in the Third World, and his growing stature as a humanitarian leads to a prestigious speaking gig at Harvard University. But as the summer goes along, Bono has personal problems to deal with: his dad is ill and has little time left to live. Bono shares this with fans during U2's concerts, dedicating songs to his dad and flying back to Dublin afterward to be at his side. Bob Hewson dies in August, just days before two historic U2 shows at Slane Castle that turn into a public memorial service.

Personal tragedy turns to international tragedy with the terrorist attacks of 9/11. U2 decides to tour the US despite safety concerns. The songs from *All That You Can't Leave Behind* take on new resonance after 9/11, and each night the tour becomes a public catharsis, a time for the band and fans alike to share their grief and, more importantly, *release* it in some of the most uplifting and emotional shows U2 has ever played.

January
Volume 2, Issue 2 of *Propaganda* magazine is published around this time.

January 3
'Beautiful Day' earns three Grammy Award nominations: Song of the Year, Record of the Year, and Best Rock Performance by a Duo or Group with Vocal.

January 9
U2 announce details of the first leg of the Elevation World Tour. The North American tour will begin in late March in Miami/Ft. Lauderdale and send the band across the continent and back before winding up in mid-June in the New York area. Some industry watchers are concerned about the band's plan to use general admission ticketing – there will be no seats on the floor – but fans are excited by the idea, not to mention the fact that floor tickets, the best in the house, will be the least expensive at $45 each. Reserved seats will cost $45, $85, and $130.

Bono appears on MTV's *TRL* programme to promote the tour announcement, and explains the band's decision to use general admission: "There's no seats in front of the stage. The best seats are actually the cheapest seats in the house, and that's right in front of us. And we are gonna elevate our

Left: Elevation Tour, Chicago, May.

mind, elevate our soul, elevate your heart, maybe. I hope so."

January 13
Tickets for six Elevation Tour shows go on sale today and each one sells out immediately. Six additional shows are added, go on sale immediately, and those six also sell out. This same scenario will be repeated several times in coming weeks as additional shows go on sale.

January 17
Though rumours have hinted at it for a couple months, RTE confirms today that U2 will play the annual Slane Festival outside Dublin this summer, an event which will attract over 150,000 fans.

January 23
All That You Can't Leave Behind is certified Multi-Platinum, with US sales of more than two million.

January 26

U2 announces a "secret" show on February 7 at the Astoria in London.

January 29

'Stuck In A Moment You Can't Get Out Of' is released in the UK, with varying formats including the tracks 'Big Girls Are Best', 'Beautiful Day (Quincey & Sonance remix)', 'Beautiful Day (live)', and 'New York (live)'. The single reaches number two in the UK.

February 1

Bono speaks at the opening of the *Beckett on Film* project at Dublin Castle, in honour of Irish author Samuel Beckett.

February 2

Nearly a year after its premiere in Europe, *The Million Dollar Hotel* makes its US premiere in limited distribution at theaters in New York and Los Angeles. Bono takes this as an opportunity to start a war of words with the film's lead actor, Mel Gibson, who months ago told Australian media that the movie was "as boring as a dog's arse" and then said he was only joking.

February 6

U2 earn two awards at the Brats, sponsored by *NME*/Carling in London. They pick up hardware in the Best Rock Act category, and in the creatively titled God-like Geniuses category. Readers of the UK rock magazine *NME* vote for the awards, prompting Bono to say this group of rock fans has "impeccable taste".

February 7

Astoria Theatre, London, with Jon Carter (DJ). U2 continue to warm-up for the Elevation Tour by playing the Astoria, a small venue that holds about 2,000. Tickets are given away to competition winners, who come from all over Europe for the gig. On the streets, touts are selling their tickets for as much as £1,000. They're joined in the crowd by dozens of celebrities including Mick Jagger, Salman Rushdie, Queen's Roger Taylor, Liam Gallagher, and half of Radiohead.

Above: Bono at the Brit Awards, London, February 26. Opposite page: Bono with Andrea Corr and Steven Tyler of Aerosmith at the Brits.

The show includes a few hints of what's to come on the Elevation Tour, such as Bono taking a break to introduce each member of the band to rapturous applause.

During the show, Bono announces to the crowd that Larry Mullen and his longtime partner Ann Acheson are parents for the third time. Days later, Dublin media report that the child is a boy called Ezra, Larry and Ann's second son.

February 12

'Stuck In A Moment You Can't Get Out Of' is released in Australia on two CDs including the tracks 'Big Girls Are Best', 'Beautiful Day (Quincey & Sonance remix)', 'Beautiful Day (live)', 'New York (live)', and two remixes of 'Beautiful Day'. It reaches number three on the charts.

February 18

French painter Balthus, a friend of Bono's, dies today.

February 20

Adam wins Best Male Bassist at the annual Gibson Guitar Awards in Los Angeles.

'Walk On' is released in Canada on two CDs including the same additional tracks that are appearing on the 'Stuck In A Moment' release elsewhere in the world: 'Big Girls Are Best', 'Beautiful Day (Quincey & Sonance remix)', 'Beautiful Day (live)', and 'New York (live)'. It reaches number one on the Canadian charts.

February 21

Staples Center, Los Angeles. 'Beautiful Day' wins all three Grammy Awards for which it's nominated: Song of the Year, Record of the Year, and Best Performance by a Rock Group or Duo with Vocal. Bono accepts the awards by saying U2 has gone "back to scratch" and is "re-applying for the job. What job? Best band in the world." With tonight's awards, U2 now has 10 career Grammys. The band also performs the song, the first time U2 has ever performed at the Grammy Awards.

Larry on the impact of winning three Grammy Awards

"After Pop, America kind of lost interest in U2 and felt we had pushed the boat out too far. We felt vulnerable and slightly shaken by what had happened. So when *All That You Can't Leave Behind* did so well and 'Beautiful Day' won all those Grammies, it felt like a real endorsement. For the first time in ages, I remember feeling grateful for the gongs. I was embarrassed that I hadn't appreciated

Larry on the *The Million Dollar Hotel*

"I don't think (Mel) likes himself in [the film] much and, as a result, I think he kind of wishes it would go away. I think Mel maybe wanted to be involved in an independent project... but that he actually doesn't like independent films. Deep down, maybe he likes the explosions and the car chases."

them before. Since then, I value awards and I value people's applause in a very different way."

Bono hangs out after the awards with B.B. King, Eminem, Dr. Dre and others at a Universal Music Group party.

February 23
Bono arrives in Switzerland for tomorrow's funeral of the French artist Balthus. He reaches the artist's home and visits with his family. Balthus' wife, Setsuko, tells Bono she wants to convert from Buddhism to Catholicism and asks Bono to be her godfather. He accepts.

February 24
Bono attends and sings at Balthus' funeral in the Swiss village of Rossiniere.

February 26
Earl's Court, London. U2 receives the Outstanding Contribution to Music award at the Brit Awards, an award usually reserved for British artists. The Brits committee is willing to overlook that U2 are Irish, and points out that they

signed their first record contract in London. The band also wins Best International Group and performs four songs.

Earlier today, U2 shoots a music video for 'Walk On' with director Liz Friedlander.

February 28
U2 confirms long-standing rumours with the announcement of a concert at Slane Castle on August 25. The Slane Festival lineup will include Red Hot Chili Peppers, Coldplay, and others. Tickets will go on sale March 10.

March 6
U2's tour crew arrives in Florida and begins loading and building the stage at the empty Miami Arena. The tour will start in 18 days at the nearby National Car Rental Center.

U2 releases plans for its summer tour in Europe. Only 16 shows are announced at first, but the number eventually doubles as shows sell out and extra shows are added. Tickets for some shows will go on sale later in the week.

March 9
Tickets for U2's summer concerts in the UK and The Netherlands sell

out at record paces.

With U2's popularity soaring, seven albums land in the UK's Top 100 albums chart: *All That You Can't Leave Behind* at number three, *The Joshua Tree* at number 24, *The Best Of 1980-1990* at number 25, *Achtung Baby* at number 37, *Rattle And Hum* at number 53, *Zooropa* at number 93 and *Pop* at number 97.

March 10
Tickets for the Slane Festival sell out in 45 minutes, leading to hostile scenes at Irish ticket outlets. U2 and concert promoter MCD begin an effort to get Irish planning laws changed to allow two shows at Slane instead of one each year.

March 16
Bono is in Washington, DC, where he visits with Bush Administration officials, including Secretary of State Colin Powell, to discuss Third World debt relief and other issues. "The younger people were really going gaga," says one State Department official about Bono's visit. Bono flies from Washington to Miami where U2 begins rehearsals tonight for the upcoming Elevation Tour.

In Dublin, U2 win three times at the Meteor Irish Music Awards: Best Irish Band, Best Selling Irish Rock Album (*All That You Can't Leave Behind*), and Best Irish Songwriter (Bono).

Achtung Baby and *The Best of*

1980-1990 are certified Multi-Platinum by the BPI, with UK sales of more than 1.2 million each.

March 17
U2 rehearses again tonight at Miami Arena.

March 18
U2 plays a full set during tonight's rehearsals.

March 19
Bono inducts Island Records founder Chris Blackwell into the Rock and Roll Hall of Fame at a ceremony in New York. During the traditional jam session at the end of the show, he sings Bob Marley's 'Could You Be Loved' with Mary J. Blige.

March 20
U2 does a dress rehearsal, running through their full two-hour set.

March 21
U2 does another dress rehearsal tonight.

March 22
U2 does its final dress rehearsal before the tour opener in two days. The band is still uncertain how to start the show; Willie Williams argues in favour of the band taking the stage with the house lights on. Before everyone leaves for the night, U2's travelling tour chaplain, Father Jack Heaslip, leads a prayer

Edge: "We want to get out of the way of the music"
March 24-26

"As a live band, we're always looking for a magic that occurs when we play with our audience present. That's why people come back to U2 shows time and again. We want to get out of the way of the music on this tour. Let it just be, and speak, and connect with the audience."

Above: Edge on stage at Fort Lauderdale, March 26.

asking for blessings on the tour.

March 23
There's no rehearsal today because the stage is being moved from Miami Arena to the National Car Rental Center.

March 24-26
National Car Rental Center, Sunrise, with The Corrs. U2 open the Elevation Tour in front of a packed house in southern Florida. For the first time in the US, the tour features general admission on the floor of the arena, a decision that generates a mild amount of controversy leading up to opening night. The stage includes a heart-shaped catwalk that extends more than halfway out onto the floor of the arena. The first 300 fans with general admission tickets are allowed inside the heart. PJ Harvey is scheduled to open, but she falls ill and misses the first four shows of the tour.

U2 take the stage casually while the house lights are still on. They're wearing common t-shirts and pants except for Bono, who is dressed in his customary black leather jacket and black pants. There's no gigantic video wall, but four small screens hang above the stage, each one showing a black-and-white camera feed of one band member. The entrance and overall presentation is a far cry from the spectacle of U2's last two tours.

Early in the show, Bono falls off the catwalk while walking backwards. He quickly climbs back on stage and continues the show. The band performs seven tracks from *All That You Can't Leave Behind* and a collection of their biggest back catalog hits and concert favourites. The show is universally praised by fans and critics alike.

While the Elevation Tour sees U2 skipping the high-tech approach of the past two tours, technology changes the tour experience for U2 fans online. In 1997-98, Internet fans often rushed home after shows to post the setlist and their concert reviews on mailing lists and message boards. Now, thanks to the widespread use of mobile phones and text messaging, waiting until after the show is passé. Fans in the arena tonight text the setlist as it happens, and fan sites report each song online as soon as it begins to a hungry audience of U2 fans around the world who want to know what they're missing.

After the show, the celebration is on. The backstage party includes Lenny Kravitz, Elvis Costello and The Corrs, along with supermodels Helena Christensen and Christy Turlington. Even Lord Henry Mountcharles, the owner of Slane Castle, is there. Paul McGuinness speaks with photographer Diana Scrimgeour, who began shooting U2 shows for the band on the PopMart Tour, and they agree to do a book about U2's tours (*U2 Show* will be released in 2004).

The second show is similar to the first night, but includes a video before 'Bullet The Blue Sky' of Charlton Heston, president of the National Rifle Association, defending gun rights. Tacked onto the end of the Heston clip is a home video of a small girl picking up a pistol she finds in her house. The clip will be used for the remainder of the first leg.

March 27
'Stuck In A Moment You Can't Get Out Of' is released in France in a limited edition CD with unique packaging. Extra tracks include 'Big Girls Are Best', 'All I Want is You (Live in Paris)', and 'Even Better Than the Real Thing (Live in Paris)'.

March 29
Charlotte Coliseum, Charlotte, with Nelly Furtado.

March 30
Philips Arena, Atlanta, with Nelly Furtado. R.E.M.'s Michael Stipe and Mike Mills are at the show.

April 2
Compaq Center, Houston, with PJ Harvey.

April 3
Reunion Arena, Dallas, with PJ Harvey. After the show, U2 fly to Los Angeles, their headquarters for the next five days.

April 6
Pepsi Center, Denver, with PJ Harvey.

April 7-8
During a two-day break in the tour, U2 shoot a video for 'Elevation', which will be featured prominently in the upcoming blockbuster film, *Tomb Raider*. The shoot runs overtime, keeping U2 occupied into the early hours of the morning April 9. Around this time, they're also working in a music studio with former Nine Inch Nails drummer Chris Vrenna, who's doing the 'Elevation' remix that will appear on the movie soundtrack.

Chris Vrenna on working with U2
"What we did was to book two days at a studio in Los Angeles, 'cause they were there getting ready... they were gonna be filming the video and everything else. So anyway, U2 brings in all their gear and I spent one day with the band, everybody but Bono, going through the parts that we

Below: Bono on stage at Portland, April 15, remebering Joey Ramone.

had added and then The Edge coming out: 'We really like the heavy guitar, I wanna play it like you're hearing, but I wanna do it my way'. This guy Edge in the room, playing five different huge guitar riffs and saying, 'How about this one? Is it heavy enough?', and I was 'Oh, my God, you're asking me?'"

April 9-10
Pengrowth Saddledome, Calgary, with PJ Harvey. U2 arrive in Calgary just minutes before PJ Harvey takes the stage.

April 12
Tacoma Dome, Tacoma, with PJ Harvey. Edge's family and parents are at the show.

April 13
G.M. Place, Vancouver, with PJ Harvey.

April 15
Rose Garden, Portland, with PJ Harvey. Microsoft co-founder Paul Allen, a big music fan who plays guitar and started the Experience Music Project in Seattle, gets a tour of the stage before the show. He spends time standing at Edge's guitar rack and talking with guitar tech Dallas Schoo. Bono and Edge perform a cover of The Ramones' 'I Remember You' to pay tribute to Joey Ramone, who died earlier in the day.

April 17
Sports Arena, San Diego, with PJ Harvey.

April 19-20
San Jose Arena, San Jose, with PJ Harvey. At the second show, U2 play 'Kite' for the first time. Fans had taken to bringing signs to every recent show asking to hear it. It brings the house down, and U2 surprise again by playing 'Stay' – the first time a *Zooropa* song has been played in North America. For these

reasons and many others, it's a magical show that both Bono and Willie Williams will later rank among U2's best. Bono even calls it the best show of his life.

Above: On stage at San Diego, April 17, the smallest arena on the Elevation Tour.

April 23-24-26
Arrowhead Pond, Anaheim, with PJ Harvey. Before the first show, U2 meets with Ned O'Hanlon, Hamish Hamilton, and others to discuss doing a video shoot later in the tour. Before the third show, Bono, Ali and their kids visit Disneyland. They walk through the park escorted by a Disneyland employee, but go unnoticed as crowds flock instead to Buzz Lightyear, Mickey Mouse and the park's regular cast of

characters. Bono sings 'Stay' for Wim Wenders, who's at the show. Bono's friend Bobby Shriver is there, too, as are Anton Corbijn, Queen Noor of Jordan, Neil Diamond, Cher and many other music and movie stars.

April 28
America West Arena, Phoenix, with PJ Harvey. After tonight's show in Phoenix, the band plan to fly back to Los Angeles, but Bono has made a secret plan to fly everyone to Las Vegas to celebrate the birthdays of several staff and crew members. The band and crew pile into two buses and tour Vegas into the wee hours of the morning. They stop at a bar, where Bono gets on stage for a duet with that evening's entertainment.

May 1
Target Center, Minneapolis, with PJ Harvey. U2's flight into Minneapolis is delayed by bad weather and the band arrive at the arena just as PJ Harvey is going on.

May 3
Gund Arena, Cleveland, with PJ Harvey.

May 4
Rupp Arena, Lexington, with PJ Harvey.

May 5
On a day off, U2 visit the Rock and Roll Hall of Fame in Cleveland where Bono uses the Alan Freed radio studio to record his voiceovers for the 'Elevation' music video ("This is Evil Bono. I have the Edge..."). The band sees tonight's Bon Jovi concert at Gund Arena.

May 6
Mellon Arena, Pittsburgh, with PJ Harvey.

May 7
Nationwide Arena, Columbus, with PJ Harvey. Bono acknowledges his friend, Republican Senator John Kasich, who's in the crowd.

May 8
Bono sings with Gavin Friday on the *Moulin Rouge* soundtrack, which is

released today. They do a cover of the T-Rex track, 'Children Of The Revolution'.

May 9
Bradley Center, Milwaukee, with PJ Harvey.

May 10
Conseco Fieldhouse, Indianapolis, with PJ Harvey. The show is like one big party for Bono's birthday. A couple dozen girls get on stage during 'Mysterious Ways' and follow him around the stage.

May 12-13-15-16
United Center, Chicago, with PJ Harvey. U2 praise their Chicago fans at each show for being so "hip" to the *Pop* album and PopMart Tour. At the third show, U2 treat the crowd to rare performances of 'Out Of Control' and '11 O'Clock Tick Tock'. After the last show, Bono flies to Dublin to be with Ali, who's expecting a child any day.

May 20
Bono and Ali give birth to their fourth child, a son, John Abraham.

May 24-25
Air Canada Centre, Toronto, with PJ Harvey. Before the second show, Canada's MuchMusic follows the band in the hallways, with George Stroumboulopoulos trying to do an interview, but mainly just being a nuisance. 'Stay' is recorded and shown on June 3 at the Secret Policeman's Ball in London. The whole band does a 75-minute live interview at the MuchMusic studios after the show.

May 27-28
Molson Centre, Montreal, with PJ Harvey.

May 30
Palace of Auburn Hills, Detroit, with PJ Harvey.

May 31
HSBC Arena, Buffalo, with PJ Harvey.

June 2
Pepsi Arena, Albany, with PJ Harvey. Bono has been struggling with a bug

since the tour resumed in Toronto more than a week ago, but tonight he's in bad shape. He ends 'Elevation', the first song of the show, by asking the crowd to help him sing, and later tells them he feels "really shitty".

June 3
Civic Center, Hartford, with PJ Harvey.

U2 are on the cover of today's *Sunday Times* magazine, which also includes a free CD with five songs and two videos.
Songs: 'Beautiful Day', 'The Ground Beneath Her Feet', 'I Remember You (Live from Irving Plaza)', 'New York (Live from Irving Plaza)', 'I Will Follow (Live from Irving Plaza)'. Videos: 'Beautiful Day', 'Don't Take Your Guns to Town'. The CD also promotes the new Windows XP operating system.

Below: Edge at Albany, June 2.

Bono: "There was a mutiny", June 6

"Some of our most ardent fans were following from gig to gig. So whatever city we'd turn up in there would be the same people in front of us, which was a little disorienting. And when we tried to make sure that locals got in the heart, there was a mutiny.... They thought they weren't telegenic enough and that's why we were trying to keep them out. It was just that we wanted to play in front of a fresh audience."

June 5
Fleet Center, Boston, with PJ Harvey. Ned O'Hanlon, Maurice Linnane, Hamish Hamilton, and a large video crew record tonight's show – and tomorrow's – for a future video release. U2 does a full rehearsal in the afternoon to help the crew prepare for the real show.

June 6
Fleet Center, Boston, with PJ Harvey. Bono speaks to the graduating seniors at Harvard University's annual Class Day ceremony. With students, friends, family members, and other onlookers, the crowd numbers 15,000 according to one media report. He introduces himself by saying, "My name is Bono, and I am a rock star. I say that not as a boast, but more as a confession." His 20-minute speech is focused on Third World debt relief, and the University gives him an honorary degree during the ceremony.

There's controversy before the show even begins involving fans in the General Admission line. Shortly before the doors open, U2's security crew goes through the line and handpicks a group of fans to be let in early – ahead of fans who've been in line for almost 24 hours. Some fans in line feel the most attractive fans are being picked to be up front so that the home video U2 is shooting tonight will look better. As the show begins, the disgruntled fans let their anger be known by sitting down in the heart, a protest that's clearly visible when the video is released.

NBC-TV airs 'Where the Streets Have No Name' live during halftime of its coverage of Game 1 of the NBA Finals between Los Angeles and Philadelphia. They also show 'Elevation' on tape from earlier in the show. Most of the footage in U2's *Elevation 2001 – Live From Boston* home video is taken from this show.

June 8-9

Fleet Center, Boston, with PJ Harvey. U2 wraps up a string of four concerts in five nights at the Fleet Center in Boston, Massachusetts. The setlist is mixed up for the final show, with 'Pride' being played second and several songs from *Achtung Baby* early in the set. 'Party Girl' is played for the first time since June 6, 1993. A fan gets on stage during 'Walk On', lifts and cradles Bono, then runs a lap around the heart. Portions of the show are recorded and will later appear on the *U2 Elevation 2001 – Live From Boston* video release. U2 has also been in talks with HBO to air the concert, but the cable network passes at the last minute.

June 11-12

First Union Center, Philadelphia, with PJ Harvey. At the first show, Bono weaves in the execution of Timothy McVeigh earlier in the day into U2's concert. At the end of 'Bullet The Blue Sky', Bono changes the lyrics to "On a closed-circuit TV, before an invitation audience only, we watch as Timothy ... runs into the arms of America." McVeigh was executed for the deaths of 168 people in the 1995 bombing of the Oklahoma City federal building.

June 13

Bono is in Washington, DC, for a full day of meetings with politicians and government officials about third world debt and the AIDS crisis. His day begins with a news conference with Senator Bill Frist and includes meetings with Treasury Secretary Paul O'Neill, Health & Human Services Secretary Tommy Thompson, World Bank President Jim Wolfensohn, and various members of Congress and the Bush administration. His meeting with O'Neill is scheduled to last a half-hour, but the two talk for 90 minutes. They agree to travel to Africa together in late September to see the situation there up close.

Perhaps the most notable event of the day is a Capitol Hill lunch hosted by Republican Senator Jesse Helms of North Carolina, whom Bono first met last fall. Bono praises Helms as a "bold and brave man" for inviting him to lunch, and says he's impressed that Helms – who's been notoriously opposed to AIDS relief efforts in the past – "cares deeply about what is happening in Africa right now." Helms returns the praise, telling Bono, "You'll never be an outsider. You'll always be a friend here." Several other senators from both sides of the political aisle are also at the lunch.

Bono explains his affection for Jesse Helms
"He did an incredible thing: he publicly repented for the way he had thought about HIV/AIDS. Politicians rarely do that. He really changed the way people on the right thought about this disease. People said to me: this is the devil himself you're going to meet, and his politics are just right of Attila the Hun.... But I found him to be a beautiful man with convictions that I wouldn't all agree with, but had to accept that he believed in them passionately."

June 14-15

MCI Center, Washington, DC, with PJ Harvey. Prior to the first concert at the MCI Center, Edge takes part in a live chat on U2.com.

The first show is filled with guests from the DC beltway, including Senate Majority Leader Tom Daschle and Senator Jesse Helms. Bono invites Helms to meet the band backstage before the concert begins. Helms later calls the concert "the noisiest thing I ever heard," but says he was "fascinated" by his first rock concert. "It was filled to the gills, and people were moving back and forth like corn in the breeze,"

Above: Bono and Edge take a break from the Elevation Tour during their stay in Boston.

Helms says. "They had that crowd going wild. When Bono shook his hips, that crowd shook their hips."

June 16

U2 and friends celebrate Paul McGuinness' 50th birthday with a party at their New York hotel.

June 17-19

Madison Square Garden, New York, with PJ Harvey. At the second show, Daniel Lanois comes on stage to play guitar and sing 'Stuck In A Moment'. Tiger Woods, Chris Blackwell, Robert De Niro, Chris Rock and Christy Turlington are just some of the celebrities at the show.

While the band is in New York, Bono and Edge do interviews with Gary Jermyn for an upcoming RTE TV special, *New York Tumble* (also known as *Made In Manhattan*). It's a documentary about two Irish events happening almost simultaneously in New York this week: U2's shows at Madison Square Garden, and Guggi's art exhibit at the Tony Shafrazi Gallery. Edge and Jermyn spend a few hours one afternoon visiting guitar shops in Manhattan, while Bono and Jermyn walk around Central Park and visit the John Lennon memorial. The show will air in September. (Jermyn is an old friend of U2's, who helped Bono translate the Latin lyrics he sang in the song 'Gloria'.) The programme airs August 28 on RTE.

Also around this time, Bono tapes an interview with Charlie Rose for his nightly PBS-TV program. The interview airs on June 21.

June 21

Continental Airlines Arena, E. Rutherford, with PJ Harvey.

Blues legend John Lee Hooker dies today at age 83. When asked to comment on Hooker's passing, Bono reveals that the song 'Daddy's Gonna Pay For Your Crashed Car' was written for Hooker to record. "It sounds kind of electronic the way it was recorded, but originally it was a blues number," Bono says. "But Daddy never recorded. Daddy never got into the studio for that one. So, I'm very sad. A genius. I think he was told that before he died, so I think that makes it a little less of a tragedy." Says Edge, who met Hooker at the San Francisco Blues Festival in 1988: "He was one of the two or three most influential blues artists that have ever been. They created a whole genre of music. A lot of bands from the Sixties and Seventies borrowed a lot of his ideas."

June 22

Continental Airlines Arena, E. Rutherford, with PJ Harvey. U2 wraps up the first leg of the Elevation Tour. Prior to the show,

Bono and Edge attend the opening of an art exhibit in New York featuring the works of their longtime friend, Guggi. Bono gives a speech praising Guggi, and does an interview with VH1. When the interview gets to the subject of John Lee Hooker's death, Bono sings a bit of 'Daddy's Gonna Pay For Your Crashed Car' on camera.

Bill Clinton and daughter Chelsea are at the show, and watch some of the show from inside the heart. Michael Stipe and The Beastie Boys are there, too. Daniel Lanois comes on stage to perform 'Wild Honey' and 'The Ground Beneath Her Feet'.

June 25

Although permission has yet to be granted for U2 to play a second show at Slane Castle this summer, *NME* reports that staff are being hired to work a second show on September 1.

'Elevation (Tomb Raider Mix)' is released in Australia on two CDs, with additional tracks including 'I Remember You (Live from Irving Plaza)', 'New York (Live from Irving Plaza)', 'Don't Take Your Guns to Town' and four remixes of the main track. The song is an edit of the original album version and is being used in the Hollywood blockbuster, *Tomb Raider*.

June 30

Bono appears at Frock and Roll in Barcelona. It's a combination concert and fashion show organised by Naomi Campbell to benefit the Nelson Mandela Foundation. Bono sings a solo acoustic version of 'I Shall Be Released' before performing 'One' and 'Sunday, Bloody Sunday' with Wyclef Jean and his band. Later in the show, Bono and Jean duet on 'Redemption Song'. Though 16,000 are expected to attend, only about 4,000 show up – likely due to the late cancellations by many performers.

July 2

'Elevation (Tomb Raider Mix)' is released in Europe on multiple formats, with additional tracks including 'I Remember You (Live

from Irving Plaza)', 'New York (Live from Irving Plaza)', 'Don't Take Your Guns To Town', three remixes of 'Beautiful Day', and five remixes of the main track. The single reaches number three in the UK charts.

July 6-7

Forum, Copenhagen, with Stereophonics (July 6); with JJ72 (July 7). U2 opens the European leg of the Elevation Tour at the 10,000-seat Forum in Copenhagen. It's unusually hot in Denmark, and the windowless arena hits temperatures of 110-120 degrees Fahrenheit during the show. Larry's dad is in the audience for the second show.

July 8

Ned O'Hanlon and Hamish Hamilton visit Bono and Willie Williams in Copenhagen and show them a rough cut of the video footage shot a month ago in Boston.

July 9-10

Globe, Stockholm, with

Bono: They held Mandela back, June 30

"People, right up to the last day, were just pulling out. At seven o'clock, there were about 500 people in the 20,000-seat arena. At eight o'clock there was about 2,000. Mandela was supposed to walk on at eight o'clock. So they held him back. There had been confusion. People thought the gig was cancelled or whatever. So we waited until eight-thirty."

Stereophonics.

On July 9, Irish authorities give U2 permission to add a second concert at Slane Castle. Tickets for the September 1 show go on sale immediately, and sell out in 94 minutes.

July 10

'Elevation (Tomb Raider Mix)' is released in Canada on two CDs, with additional tracks including 'Last Night On Earth (Live from Mexico)', 'Don't Take Your Guns To Town' and four remixes of the main track. It reaches number one on the Canadian charts.

July 12-13

Arena, Cologne, with Sohne Mannheims. At the first show, 'Stuck In A Moment' is dedicated to Dutch artist Herman Brood, a friend of Bono's who committed suicide a day earlier. Before the second show, Bono records vocals in his hotel room for 'Joy', a song on Mick Jagger's upcoming solo album.

Back in Dublin, Bono's father's health is getting progressively worse. Though the band is willing to cancel shows so Bono can be with his dad, Bono decides to continue the tour, using the nightly shows to let his grief out in the songs. After the second concert, Bono flies home to Dublin to be with his dad in the hospital. Bono's brother Norman tells the *Irish Mirror* their 75-old father "is not in great shape". Bono is able to spend much of the weekend in Dublin before a Sunday concert in Munich.

July 15

Olympiahalle, Munich, with Sohne Mannheims.

July 17-18

Palais Omnisports De Paris Bercy, Paris, with Stereophonics. Bono flies back to Dublin after the first show in Paris. French rocker Johnny Hallyday is in the audience for the second show. After the show, U2 and crew head to the ManRay club for a party. Bono visits with Michka Assayas and suggests the two do a book together.

Above: Paris, July 17.

July 20-21

Bono attends the G8 Summit in Genoa, Italy. He's there with Bob Geldof to continue pressing for Third World debt relief, and meets with UK Prime Minister Tony Blair, Russian President Vladimir Putin, and Canadian Prime Minister Jean Chretien. The summit is marked by violent protests, which Bono decries as an attempt to "ruin this dialogue" on debt relief. "I don't think violence is ever right, but anger is understandable when facing the obscenity of the ever widening gap of inequality on the planet between the haves and the have nots," Bono tells reporters.

On July 20, the single-disc version of *The Best Of 1980-1990* is certified Platinum by the RIAA, with sales of more than one million.

July 21

Stadio Delle Alpi, Turin, with Timoria, Verdena, Fun Lovin' Criminals. U2 plays an outdoor show and use it as a test run for the Slane Castle gigs coming up.

July 23-24

Hallenstadion, Zurich, with Kelis. U2 soundcheck 'The Playboy Mansion' before the first show, but the song isn't played.

Also before the first show, U2 picks up five nominations for the MTV Video Music Awards: 'Beautiful Day' is nominated in the Best Video Of The Year category, while 'Elevation' is nominated in the following categories: Best Group Video, Best Video From A Film, Best Editing In A Video, Best Special Effects. U2 is also announced as a performer for the awards, scheduled for September 6 in New York.

July 26-27

Stadthalle, Vienna, with Kelis. While in Vienna, Bono records a poem that he's contributing to Andrea Bocelli's upcoming album. Bono and Edge also record an acoustic version of 'Stuck In A Moment' that will be a B-side on upcoming releases.

July 28
In Berlin, U2 shoots part of a new video for 'Stuck In A Moment You Can't Get Out Of' over the next several days. The song is soon to be released in the US. (It had been released elsewhere in the world earlier in the year.)

July 29
Waldbuehne, Berlin, with Michael Mittermeier. Sohne Mannheims are due to open the show, but poor weather at this outdoor amphitheatre leaves their equipment unusable. Michael Mittermeier, a German comedian and U2 fan, replaces him.

July 30
Edge takes a balloon ride over Berlin in the morning; Adam is spotted shopping in the city. They resume shooting the new 'Stuck In A Moment' in the afternoon.

July 31, August 1 & 3
Gelredome, Arnhem, with Kelis. While in the Netherlands, Anton Corbijn conducts a photo shoot in Amsterdam for *GQ* magazine. The photos show U2 on bicycles. Before the second show, Bono visits with a small group of fans outside their hotel in Amsterdam, and listens as one fan plays an acoustic guitar.

On August 2, a day off, Bono visits the studio of artist Herman Brood.

During the third show, Bono brings almost a dozen photographers on stage during 'Until The End Of The World' and walks around the heart with them as they shoot photos.

August 5-6
Sportpaleis, Antwerp, with Stereophonics. Before the second show, Bono views an exhibition by Walter Van Beirendonck at the Museum of Contemporary Art (MUKHA). Van Beirendonck designed the clothes for the PopMart tour. U2 debuts a new song at the second show. The song seems to be unfinished, at least lyrically. It has Bono singing "I love you" as part of the chorus.

Below: Arnhem.

August 8
Palau St. Jordi, Barcelona, with Stereophonics. U2 does a rare performance of 'Spanish Eyes', with Bono singing to Ali, who's at the show. The band celebrates Edge's birthday with champagne during 'Party Girl', but Adam passes on the drink. After the show, U2 and friends fly to Ibiza for more birthday partying.

August 11-12
MEN Arena, Manchester, with Kelis. During the first show, Bono tells the crowd that Larry's 22-month-old son, Aaron Elvis, is attending hs first U2 show. Bono makes another announcement before 'Kite', saying

his father Bob only has "a few days left in this world".

August 14-15
NEC Arena, Birmingham, with Kelis.

August 17
U2 announces that the Elevation Tour will return to North America in the fall.

August 18
ITV's new football show, *The Premiereship*, debuts tonight with a shortened version of 'Beautiful Day' as the theme song.

August 18-19-21-22
Earl's Court, London, with Kelis (August 18); with P.J. Harvey (August 19); with Nelly Furtado (August 21); with JJ72 (August 22). Bono's father, Bob Hewson, dies at 4 a.m. on August 21 in Dublin after a bout with cancer. He had been hospitalized for several weeks and Bono has been flying to see his dad after recent Elevation concerts.

Despite his father's passing, Bono and U2 take the stage that night in London. In an emotional performance, Bono speaks at length about his dad prior to performing 'Kite': "I want to thank my old man, my father, for giving me this voice. He was a fine tenor and he always said if I had his voice, who knows what might have happened. He had been ill for one week and has gone now. He's free of all that now. This is a song I wrote for him. This is 'Kite'." In the dressing room after the show, Edge tells writer Neil McCormick, "That was a tough one. I don't know how he [Bono] got through that."

August 23
U2 announces plans to play two shows next week in Glasgow. Tickets go on sale at midday and sell out in less than two hours.

August 24
Bono's father is laid to rest today at Old Balgriffin Cemetery in County Dublin, the same cemetery where Bono's mom, Iris, was buried in 1974. During the funeral at Church of the Assumption, Howth, Bono tells the congregation that his dad

had "more rock and roll than most of my friends". All four members of U2 are on hand, as is Paul McGuinness and a host of well-known well wishers. Bono, Larry, and Edge serve as pallbearers. Bono and Edge sing a song called 'Sometimes You Can't Make It On Your Own'.

August 25
Slane Castle, Dublin. U2 brings the Elevation Tour to Slane Castle north of Dublin, site of the annual Slane Festival since 1981. It's U2's first performance at Slane since that first festival 20 years ago, when they were on the support bill for Thin Lizzy. Tonight, U2 takes the stage as Thin Lizzy's 'The Boys Are Back In Town' plays over the speakers. 80,000 fans are on hand as U2 plays 'A Sort of Homecoming' – one of the songs recorded at Slane Castle for 1984's *The Unforgettable Fire* – live for the first time since

Above: U2 on stage at Earls Court – shows that Bono turned into memorials for his father who died on August 21.

1987. Bono speaks to the crowd about the recent death of his father, and dedicates 'Kite' to him. He also introduces his older brother Norman to the crowd, and those around Norman lift him up on their shoulders. During 'One', images of Bob Hewson are shown on the video screens above the stage. Bono chokes up while trying to sing 'When Will I See You Again'. After U2 exit the stage, the crowd is treated to a brief fireworks show as 'The Unforgettable Fire' plays over the speakers.

August 27-28
SECC, Glasgow, with Cosmic Rough Riders.

September 1
Slane Castle, Dublin. U2 performs a landmark second show at Slane Castle. The concert is only possible thanks to special approval from County Meath planners and

residents. It's the first time any band has been allowed to play two concerts at Slane Castle in the same year. The show is more upbeat and joyous than last week's Slane gig, though there are plenty of serious moments, too. Bono recites the names of 29 Omagh bombing victims at the end of 'Sunday, Bloody Sunday', and Bob Hewson's image is again shown on the video screens. The *U2 Go Home – Live From Slane Castle* video comes from this show. Larry attends the Ireland-Holland World Cup qualifying match at Lansdowne Road stadium before taking a helicopter to Slane Castle.

September 5
With many of music's biggest names converging on New York City for the MTV Video Music Awards, Bono calls on some of them to help record a charity record for AIDS victims in Africa. More than

20 artists, including Britney Spears, Jennifer Lopez, Destiny's Child, 'N Sync and more, record Marvin Gaye's 'What's Going On?' at Revolution Studios. The artists work together for three days. Bono and other organisers say they hope the record will surpass previous fund raising efforts such as Band Aid and USA for Africa.

September 6
Metropolitan Opera House, New York. Despite having two videos nominated for a total of five awards, U2 doesn't pick up any hardware for the 'Beautiful Day' or 'Elevation' videos at the MTV Video Music Awards. But they don't go home empty-handed – MTV honours the band with its Michael Jackson Video Vanguard Award. Bono pays tribute to the remaining members of The Ramones during his acceptance speech. U2 also perform tonight, doing a medley of 'Elevation' and 'Stuck In a Moment You Can't Get Out Of'.

Less than a week after U2's second hugely successful homecoming concert at Slane Castle, the band's entire 12-album catalog appears within the top 60 spots of the Irish album sales chart:
1. *All That You Can't Leave Behind*
5. *The Joshua Tree*
10. *The Best Of 1980-1990*
11. *Achtung Baby*
17. *Rattle and Hum*
33. *The Unforgettable Fire*
35. *Zooropa*
37. *Pop*
40. *War*
43. *Under A Blood Red Sky*
45. *Boy*
60. *October*

September 7
With their commitments over, U2 plan time off before more tour dates later in the year. Bono heads to Venice where he meets with Martin Scorcese at the Venice Film Festival. He also attends an exhibition of Balthus' paintings with the painter's daughter, Harumi.

September 10
Clear Channel/SFX announces details of the third leg of the

Bono and Adam on *All That You Can't Leave Behind* and 9/11, September 17

Bono: "These songs that we wrote about mortality and fate vs. fear and all of the various themes on *All That You Can't Leave Behind* have suddenly come into focus after September the 11th for people."

Adam: "Somehow the events in New York and D.C. have actually focused people on that aspect of the record that is about loss, which is amazing."

Elevation Tour. The tour includes an initial 15 shows in North America, and tickets will go on sale on September 15.

September 11
Bono is walking in Venice with his son, Elijah, and Elijah's nanny when he hears the news that terrorists have attacked New York City and Washington, DC.

Bono talks about hearing the news of 9/11
"I got lost in this sort of labyrinth of little roads and laneways in Venice and canals obviously. And I found – I just saw a sign up saying, *The American Hotel*, and I thought, well, they'll speak English. So, I went in there, and that's when it was on the TV, and there were a lot of Americans sort of just

---

shell-shocked.... I couldn't believe what I was seeing."

As the gravity of the attacks becomes apparent, Clear Channel/SFX makes the following announcement about ticket sales: "Out of respect for the tragedies of Tuesday, 9/11/01, all U2 on-sales scheduled for this weekend have been cancelled. Please stay tuned for details."

The attacks also force Bono and US Treasury Secretary Paul O'Neill to postpone their late September tour of Africa until next spring.

September 17
Under the headline, "Elevation Tour Still a Go!," Clear Channel/SFX announces new ticket on-sale dates for the third leg of the Elevation Tour. Three shows will go on sale September 21, six on September 22, and the rest will go on sale between September 24 and October 1.

As the US continues to struggle with the events of 9/11, songs from *All That You Can't Leave Behind* are popular choices to help with the healing process. The album had been as low as number 108 on the *Billboard* album chart, but it begins to climb higher as new fans are drawn to the album's themes. Songs such as 'Walk On' and 'Peace On Earth' are played frequently on US radio, including a haunting version of the latter in which a DJ has edited sound clips from news coverage of the terrorist attacks.

September 21
BBC Studios, London. U2 performs live at 2:15 am in London for *A Tribute To Heroes*, a televised fundraiser for victims of the terrorist attacks in the US ten days earlier. U2 perform a medley of 'Peace On Earth' and 'Walk On' in front of millions who watch on TV and listen on radio around the world. The event raises some $150 million for attack victims.

September 22
Ten of the 11 Elevation concerts that go on sale today are logged as sellouts. In the wake of the

September 11 attacks, U2 had delayed ticket sales by a week and industry watchers speculated the tour might not fare as well in light of those events.

Above: Bono on stage with Michael Stipe, New York, October 29.

Late September/Early October
Before the tour re-starts, Bono spends six days in Bali to allow himself time to grieve his father's death. While there, he also starts writing songs such as 'One Step Closer' and 'Electrical Storm'. Two others are 'You Can't Give Your Heart Away' and 'A Man's A Man', which Bono says is for Martin Scorsese's film, *Gangs Of New York*. (The song could've turned into 'The Hands That Built America', or could be an entirely different song.)

October 10
Joyce Center, South Bend, with Garbage. U2 open the third leg of its Elevation Tour 2001 at the University of Notre Dame in Indiana – home of the "Fighting Irish". This is the band's first concert since the September 11 attacks and the show serves as a tribute to those who lost their lives and the rescuers in New York City and Washington, DC. Bono changes lyrics to a couple of songs to reflect what happened on 9/11. In 'New York', he sings "Religious nuts, political fanatics don't belong..." More than a dozen New York City police and firemen are brought on

stage at the end of the concert for a walk around the heart. The show is webcast live on the Internet to an estimated audience of five million people.

Earlier in the day, Bono borrows a bicycle and tours the Notre Dame campus.

October 12
Molson Centre, Montreal, with Garbage. Before today's show in Montreal, Bono meets with Canadian Prime Minister Jean Chretien and attends the Montreal International Film Festival with Wim Wenders.

October 13
Copps Coliseum, Hamilton, with Garbage. The names of passengers who died on September 11 on the four hijacked flights are scrolled on the video screens during 'One'. This list of victims is soon expanded to include New York City firefighters and police officers who lost their lives, and is shown for the remainder of the third leg of the tour.

October 15-16
United Center, Chicago, with Garbage. While in Chicago, U2 does a photo shoot for an upcoming issue of *Spin* magazine.

Andrea Bocelli's *Cieli Di Toscana* album is released. Bono recites a poem at the beginning of the song 'L'Incontro'.

October 19
Baltimore Arena, Baltimore, with Graham Parker & the Figgs. U2 plays the city of Baltimore for the first time. Opening act Garbage is forced to cancel at the last minute when their drummer Butch Vig falls ill. Veteran Graham Parker opens the show with a brief set before heading to a local club for his band's planned gig that night.

October 20
U2 is forced to cancel an appearance at the all-star *Concert for New York City* tonight. A band spokesperson later reveals that the cancellation was due to "family matters". Some reports eventually suggest the cancellation was related

to an Anthrax scare at the school that Bono's daughter, Jordan, attends in the Dublin area.

October 24
Madison Square Garden, New York, with Garbage. Tonight's concert is U2's first in New York City since the terrorist attacks of September 11. It's also a star-studded event, with Trent Reznor, Moby, Christy Turlington, Salma Hayekl, Gina Gershon and many other stars in attendance. During 'One', the names of NYPD and FDNY victims scroll on the screen along with names of the hijack victims. The audience is in tears and the show turns into an emotional catharsis.

U2 remembers playing post-9/11 New York City
Bono: "That was one of the most extraordinary moments of our lives. New York had let us into a very private moment. We did not feel in any way like visitors or tourists. We were the same people.... I felt it was important to [show the victims' names] because these people weren't statistics. They were real people.

"[9/11] completely changed everything. The mood at the shows was very different. People were holding on much tighter to our band – as I do myself when things are going on in my life."

October 25
Madison Square Garden, New York, with No Doubt.

All That You Can't Leave Behind is certified Multi-Platinum, with US sales of more than three million.

October 27
Madison Square Garden, New York, with Stereophonics. U2 brings Bruce Brody – whose career includes stints with Patti Smith, Rickie Lee Jones, and others – on stage to play piano during an emotional version of 'Please'.

A couple dozen New York firefighters and emergency medical workers are brought on stage during 'Walk On'. They stay on stage the rest of the night, even after the band has left, and many take the mic for spoken tributes to their friends and family.

October 28
Continental Airlines Arena, E. Rutherford, with Stereophonics. Prior to tonight's concert, U2 visits Ground Zero in New York City – the site of the World Trade Center attacks of September 11.

October 29
Ed Sullivan Theatre, New York. U2 performs for the first time on *The Late Show with David Letterman*. Although the show limits musical guests to one song of five minutes or less, they let U2 perform full versions of 'New York' and 'Stuck In A Moment'. Bono is interviewed briefly at the end of U2's performance.
Hammerstein Ballroom, New York. After the *Letterman* appearance, Bono joins Michael Stipe and Moby on stage to sing a couple songs at the second annual New York Against Violence concert.
U2 also earns the People's Choice Award at the Q Awards in London.

October 30
'Stuck In A Moment You Can't Get Out Of' is released in North America, but only Canada gets a

Above: Baltimore, October 19.

commercially available CD single. It features three additional tracks: 'Stuck in A Moment (Acoustic)', 'Stay (Live from Toronto)', 'Elevation (Vandit Club Remix)'. It reaches number one in Canada and number 52 on the *Billboard* Hot 100.

Also out today is the 'What's Going On?' charity single, which Bono organized in September. Bono and Edge appear on several tracks. The project was originally intended to raise funds for African AIDS relief, but funds will also be used for 9/11 victims.

October 30-31
Dunkin Donuts Center, Providence, with Stereophonics. At the second concert in Providence, Bono leads the crowd in singing 'Happy Birthday' to Larry, who's 40 years old today. A cake and champagne are brought on stage. Larry thanks the crowd from Bono's mic while Bono briefly sits at Larry's drums.

November 2
First Union Center, Philadelphia, with Stereophonics. Prior to the show, Bono attends the US-Africa Business Summit to discuss Third World Debt issues with African dignitaries, including leaders from Algeria, Senegal and Ivory Coast.

November 5
Frank Erwin Center, Austin, with No Doubt.

November 6
Still in Austin, U2 eat dinner at a well-known local joint, the Salt Lick BBQ in Driftwood, Texas. A few patrons recognize them and approach the band. Bono ends up sitting at a table of U2 fans and having coffee with them for a half-hour. Their conversation includes last night's show, gun control in Texas and education.
U2 announce another eight shows that are added to the end of the tour. Rather than ending in Los Angeles on November 19, they'll now finish in Miami on December 2.

November 7
Pepsi Center, Denver, with No Doubt.

November 9
Delta Center, Salt Lake City, with No Doubt.

November 12-13
Staples Center, Los Angeles, with No Doubt. Gwen Stefani of No Doubt duets with Bono on 'What's Going

U2 remembers playing post-9/11 New York City, October 24

Edge: "The level of emotion in the building was unbelievable. I don't think there was a dry eye in the house, including the band. It was an unbelievably moving thing to be part of it.

"We were just the soundtrack to a city that was going through mourning and coming to terms with great loss. And somehow the music was a salve of some kind."

On' at both shows, and at each show that No Doubt opens the rest of the tour.

November 15-16

The Arena in Oakland, Oakland, with No Doubt. Though U2 have brought fans on stage to play during several shows this tour, the second Oakland show is unique because the fan, Scott Perretta, begins playing 'A Sort Of Homecoming' before U2 has a clue what's going on. The band eventually follows Scott's lead, plays an almost full version of the rarity, and the crowd roars with approval.

November 18

Thomas and Mack Center, Las Vegas, with No Doubt. Before the show,

Below: Philadelphia, November 2.

Bono visits via conference call with Don Van Vliet, aka Captain Beefheart, for a brief chat about music and painting, Van Vliet's current pastime. Anton Corbijn arranges the call, and contributes a transcript to a special Christmas edition of the Dutch magazine, *Oor*. Representatives from the NFL are at the show tonight, and decide they want U2 to perform at halftime of the Super Bowl in early February.

November 19

Staples Center, Los Angeles, with No Doubt.

'Walk On' is released as a single in Europe on varying formats also including the tracks 'Where The Streets Have No Name (Live

from Boston)', 'Stay (Live from Toronto)', and 'Stuck In A Moment (Acoustic)'. The single reaches number five in the UK charts.

Bono appears on *Goddess In The Doorway*, a new solo album from Mick Jagger. Bono sings with Jagger on a track called 'Joy'.

November 20

Arco Arena, Sacramento, with No Doubt.

U2's *Elevation 2001 – U2 Live From Boston* home video is released today in the US through an exclusive partnership with the national Best Buy chain.

November 21

U2's *The Joshua Tree* is named the

best album ever in a VH1 poll of more than a quarter of a million music fans, ousting The Beatles from their usual spot as creators of the greatest album of all time.

November 22
NBC Studios, Burbank. U2 performs for the first time on NBC's *The Tonight Show.* Host Jay Leno interviews Bono after the band finishes 'Walk On'. The show is a special Thanksgiving night broadcast in honour of the US military: the live audience is made up entirely of military personnel and the show is aired live around the world on Armed Forces TV.

November 23
America West Arena, Phoenix, with No Doubt. U2 play an acoustic version of 'In God's Country', the first time the song's been played since October 9, 1989, in Melbourne. Arizona Diamondbacks pitcher Randy Johnson is invited on stage during 'Walk On'. He walks around the heart carrying the World Series trophy that his team recently won in a seven-game series over the New York Yankees.

Meanwhile, this is "Black Friday" in the US, the unofficial start of the holiday shopping season when stores open in the wee hours of the morning and lure customers with one-time only sales. Shoppers at the Best Buy chain are also given a free U2 CD, *Three Live Tracks From Boston*. The CD helps promote the *Live From Boston* video that was released earlier in the week. Tracks: 'Beautiful Day', 'Gone', 'I Will Follow'

November 25
Reunion Arena, Dallas, with No Doubt.

November 26
'Walk On' is released as a single in Australia on two CDs with the additional tracks 'Where The Streets Have No Name (Live from Boston)', 'Stay (Live from Toronto)', 'Gone (Live from Boston)', 'Stuck In A Moment (Acoustic)', and 'Elevation (The Vandit Club Mix)'.

U2 wins two awards at the second Italian Music Awards: Best Album (*All That You Can't Leave Behind*) and Best International Group.

November 27
Kemper Arena, Kansas City, with Garbage.

November 28
Savvis Center, St. Louis, with Garbage.

November 29
Atlanta newspapers report that Bono and Edge are seen tonight at Cheetah, a nude club. Bono also hangs out at the Leopard Lounge later in the evening.

November 30
Philips Arena, Atlanta, with Garbage. U2 sings 'My Sweet Lord' in tribute to ex-Beatle George Harrison, who died yesterday of cancer at age 58.

December 1
Ice Palace, Tampa, with Garbage. Elvis Costello is at the show.

December 2
American Airlines Arena, Miami, with Garbage. The Elevation Tour ends in Miami, just down the road from where it began (in Sunrise, Florida) back in March. Larry plays drums on 'Only Happy When It Rains', the last song of Garbage's opening set. Bono thanks several people before 'One', including Sheila Roche, Paul McGuinness, U2's road crew, and Chris Blackwell. Bono ends the show by leading the crowd in the '40' chorus and singing "Honey, I'm coming home!"

Within days after the tour, U2 are working on new material in the basement of an unused Monte Carlo nightclub. 'Electrical Storm' and 'The Hands That Built America' are two tracks the band works on in Monaco. There's also an early version of 'All Because Of You'. After Monte Carlo, they continue working in a London studio.

The National Football League announces that U2 will perform at halftime of Super Bowl XXXVI on February 3, 2002, in New Orleans.

December 4
Beating a host of political figures and industry leaders, Bono is named European of the Year by *European Voice* magazine.

Spin magazine announces that U2 has been named its Band of the Year for 2001. The honour is to be announced in the January, 2002, issue of the magazine.

America: A Tribute To Heroes is released on CD, featuring U2's September 21 performance of 'Peace On Earth/Walk On'.

December 10
U2 work this week in a London studio. Tonight, Bono has dinner with actor Will Smith in London.

December 13
Bono and Ali attend a lecture by Bill Clinton at the Institute of Education in London. Then it's dinner with Clinton, his daughter Chelsea, and pop star Ronan Keating. The night ends at the Groucho Club, where Bono sings a song on the piano for Chelsea Clinton.

December 15
Bono attends the opening of the London branch of the Ibizan nightclub Pacha.

December 17
Bono meets with Prime Minister Tony Blair and a UN adviser to discuss famine and debt in Africa.

December 19
In a statement on U2.com, Edge pays tribute to Stuart Adamson, who died three days ago: "He was a great inspiration to me when U2 were starting out. His first band The Skids made such a big noise and with songs like 'Into The Valley' and 'The Saints Are Coming' made most of the other music of the time seem mundane and insignificant."

December 20
Bono resumes his role as a campaigner for Third World issues. He appears at a World Health Organization press conference and speaks about the relationship between economic development and health in poor countries.

2002

U2 head into what's supposed to be a quiet year still on a high from the Elevation Tour. And the early part of the year only elevates them more. U2 play at halftime of the Super Bowl, getting rave reviews for what many say is the best halftime performance ever. *All That You Can't Leave Behind* picks up four more Grammy Awards, and U2 collect several other awards around the world.

Bono continues his tireless campaign for the sick and poor in Third World countries. His efforts are formalized early in the year with the creation of DATA. He tours Africa with US Treasury Secretary Paul O'Neill in the spring, and tours the "Heart of America" in December, bringing DATA's message to churches, diners and anyone who'll listen. *Time* magazine puts Bono on the cover and asks, "Can Bono Save the World?" It may not be a rhetorical question.

January
Though it's barely a month since the third leg of the Elevation Tour has ended, reports surface that the band is already in the studio working on new material for another album. "The band is so tight, coming straight off the tour. We've hit form," Bono tells *Hot Press* magazine. U2 is working on three projects: the *Gangs of New York* soundtrack, new material for the upcoming *Best of 1990-2000* collection, and new material for the next studio album.

January 4
U2 gets eight nominations for the 2002 Grammy Awards, including two nominations in one category with 'Elevation' and 'Walk On' nominated for Best Rock Song. They also earn nominations in the key categories Album Of The Year, Song Of The Year, and Record Of The Year. Paul McGuinness tells reporters the band is "thrilled and really excited". He also confirms U2 will perform at the Grammys, and is considering a summer tour of Europe.

January 8
U2 dominates the annual *Rolling Stone* magazine polls, winning three categories in the Critics' Poll and eight categories in the Readers' Poll.

January 9
U2 is named Internet Artist of the Year at the American Music Awards.

January 11
The Edge – proving that Bono was right to introduce him as "the scientist in the band" during the Elevation Tour – is in attendance at a lecture today by star physicist Stephen Hawking at Cambridge University. Edge explains his presence, saying, "I was there to learn something about quantum physics."

January 14
Bono attends the opening of the Extraordinary Summit of the Southern African Development Community (SADC) in Malawi. Professor Jeffrey Sachs of Harvard University joins Bono to present a World Health Organization (WHO) report on global health needs.

January 17
U2 win eight categories in the 2001 *Hot Press* Readers' Poll, including Best Group, Best Live Act and Best Polling Act.

January 21
Around this time, production crews begin using Tad Gormley Stadium at the University of New Orleans to prepare for U2's upcoming performance at Super Bowl XXXVI. They work mostly on the logistical side of creating and striking U2's heart-shaped stage within the strict time limits established by the NFL. Volunteers are also used to simulate the crowd that will be on the field while U2 performs.

January 22
U2 release a seven-track EP titled *7*, which is sold only through the Target department store chain in the US. The EP includes songs from various *All That You Can't Leave Behind* singles that were never released in the US. An estimated 100 CDs are distributed to each of Target's 1,055 stores. The CD is also available through the Target.com web site, but only to US residents. Tracks: 'Summer Rain', 'Always', 'Big

Girls Are Best', 'Beautiful Day (Quincey & Sonance remix)', 'Elevation – (Influx remix)', 'Walk On (single version)', S'tuck In A Moment You Can't Get Out Of (acoustic)'

January 25
Bono performs two songs with the Corrs, who are taping a live TV special for the US in a studio outside Dublin. He duets with Andrea Corr on Ryan Adams's 'When The Stars Go Blue' and on 'Summer Wine', originally made famous by Lee Hazelwood and Nancy Sinatra.

January 28
Bono speaks on Third World debt relief and AIDS in Africa at a three-day retreat for US Republican lawmakers.

January 29
U2 offer formal objections to a plan to demolish its Hanover Quay recording studio at a hearing of Dublin's planning commission, An Bord Pleanala. The band's lawyer calls the studio a "landmark" during the hearing and argues that the studio where it has recorded four albums and has started recording new material this year should not be demolished. The Dublin Docklands Development Authority (DDDA) has issued a compulsory purchase order on the building as part of a development plan in this area of the city.

January 30
U2 arrive in New Orleans, the site of Super Bowl XXXVI in four days, to begin rehearsals for their halftime performance. They rehearse inside the Superdome and debate whether to raise or drop a large scrim that hangs behind them

during their set. The band also conduct a 20-minute press conference about their upcoming performance. They crack a few jokes about the game itself: "There's been a lot written about the whole Brady-versus-Bledsoe issue over the past few days," Edge tells reporters. "We are not here to add to that topic today. So we're not going to be fielding any questions on that issue. That will be up to coach Belichick, what he wants to do. However, it does have to be said that Drew Bledsoe has a superior long pass, and Tom Brady's sore ankle is a bit of a problem. I had a sore ankle once and it lasted for a good deal longer than one week. But we are not here to talk about Brady and Bledsoe."

January 31

Bono attends the opening of the annual World Economic Forum, held this year in New York City. Bono sits on a panel with UN Secretary General Kofi Annan, Archbishop Desmond Tutu, Nobel Peace Prize winner Elie Weisel, Queen Rania of Jordan, as well as leaders and diplomats from Afghanistan, the Philippines, and others. Bono surprises delegates by announcing he will tour Africa in March with US Treasury Secretary Paul O'Neill. Bono also appears – but doesn't perform – at tonight's Unity in Diversity concert in New York City.

February 1

Still at the World Economic Forum, Bono meets with Canadian Prime Minister Jean Chretien, who promises that Africa will be the main topic of discussion at the upcoming G8 Summit in Canada. Later, Bono offers comments to delegates gathered for an evening concert. There are reports that Bono also sings during the concert, but these reports are never confirmed.

Meanwhile, U2 lose some of its musical gear when a pipe bursts, causing an eight-foot tidal wave to rage through the Crosbie Business Centre in Dublin. U2 and the Corrs both use the facility for storage. Fortunately, much of U2's most important equipment is with them in New Orleans.

February 2

On day three of the World Economic Forum in New York, Bono sits on a panel and debates foreign aid with US Treasury Secretary Paul O'Neill. Many summit participants crowd the stage afterward to get Bono's autograph.

Later in the day he joins Microsoft Chairman Bill Gates to announce the creation of a new organization, DATA, whose focus will be on eliminating extreme poverty and AIDS in Africa. The name is an acronym for "Debt AIDS Trade Africa." Gates announces

Edge Counts His Blessings After the Dublin Flood, February 1

"We lost an awful lot of instruments.... The storage area where we had all our equipment was completely flooded. But luckily my main guitars were with us in New Orleans ... the Gibson Explorer that I've had since I was 17-years-old, and the amplifier I've used on every album for every show since we got a record deal."

that the Bill and Melinda Gates Foundation will pledge $50 million to support the DATA agenda. The formation of DATA shifts the burden of scheduling and promoting Bono's humanitarian activities away from Principle Management.

Meanwhile, the rest of the band attend a Super Bowl party at the House of Blues in New Orleans.

February 3

Superdome, New Orleans. U2 performs at halftime of Super Bowl XXXVI. Bono walks through the crowd to take the stage as 'Beautiful Day' begins. A larger version of the Elevation Tour's heart is used for the stage, surrounded by people on the field and in the heart. As 'MLK' starts, a screen rises from the back of the stage, which scrolls the names of the people who lost their lives on 9/11. The scrolling continues through most of 'Where The Streets Have No Name', before dropping to the ground. As the band's performance comes to an end, Bono reveals the US flag-like lining of his jacket. Unconfirmed

Left: Bono and Bill Gates at the DATA launch news conference, February 2.

reports later say that only Bono and Edge perform live and Adam and Larry are pre-recorded.

An Almost-Super Disaster

Bono explains how U2's Super Bowl performance almost ended before it began.

"Our idea was to have a music crowd on the pitch and then walk through that crowd to get up on the stage. I had on these earphones that were wireless. The band are walking through the crowd [sic; only Bono walked through the crowd] and there's a camera right in front of me, and the punters start slapping me on the back. I realise that the tiny wires of my earplugs are vulnerable. All one person has to do is pull the wire, and I'm off air. I would hear nothing. Off the air in front of a billion people! And this is going out live, and there's nothing you could do. So because this wire had been left exposed, I just started to quietly panic. But if you look at the film of that, you'll see me swaggering with the most annoying smirk ever seen. You just think: That guy is such a prat!"

U2's performance is well received by both football fans and the media, as well as by other musicians who performed prior to the game including Paul McCartney and Mariah Carey. Many call it the best Super Bowl halftime performance ever. *All That You Can't Leave Behind* reaches number 25 on the charts after the Super Bowl. As for the game, the New England Patriots beat the St. Louis Rams 20-17 on a field goal on the game's last play.

After the game, U2 and friends enjoy a celebratory dinner in the French Quarter. Though he's allergic to red wine, Bono has a glass and later passes out on the floor in the restaurant's bathroom.

February 9
U2 earns three awards at the 13th annual Pollstar Concert Industry Awards in Los Angeles: Major Tour of the Year, Most Creative Stage Production and Personal Manager of the Year – Paul McGuinness. In addition, Clear Channel Entertainment's UK division – which promoted U2 – wins the award for Best International Promoter.

February 13
Rumours begin to spread that U2 will tour across Europe in the summer of 2002 with Oasis on the bill as a supporting act.

February 14
Bono is honoured by stars from TV, music, and movies at the first annual Love Rocks tribute in Los Angeles. Comedian Drew Carey, actor Tom Cruise, former President Bill Clinton, Mick Jagger, and a host of others pay tribute to Bono for his philanthropy, humanitarian concern, and social activism. The event is sponsored by the Entertainment Industry Foundation, which presents Bono with the Heart of Entertainment award. Performers include No Doubt, who perform a cover of U2's 'Sweetest Thing', as well as Lauryn Hill and R.E.M. Bono closes the show by joining R.E.M. on stage to sing U2's 'One'.

While in Los Angeles, Bono calls a meeting with DATA's Jamie Drummond, Bobby Shriver, Quincy Jones and Michael Stipe. They brainstorm ideas to raise awareness of DATA's platform. Says Jones: "I think you've got too many issues. That's how we blew it before. You have to particularise the drama. You've got to have a melody line."

February 23
Edge attends a gig by guitarist Kelly Joe Phelps at Whelan's in Dublin.

February 24
Bono is on the cover of *Time* magazine's newest issue, which arrives on newsstands today. The

Above: Bono and Ali at Love Rocks, February 14. Below: Souvenir Super Bowl guitar pick, February 3.

cover headline asks, "Can Bono Save the World?" and he is profiled in two articles that discuss his recent efforts to get industrial countries to forgive the debts of Third World nations and his advocacy for AIDS relief on the African continent. The issue is dated March 4, 2002. It's the second time Bono has appeared on the cover of *Time*; he and the rest of U2 were pictured on the magazine's April 29, 1987, issue at the height of their worldwide popularity during *The Joshua Tree* era.

February 25
U2 is named Best Live Act at the 2002 Brat Awards (more formally known as the *NME* Carling Awards) in London. Part of their videotaped

acceptance is a performance of The Ramones' 'Beat On The Brat' recorded at Hanover Quay. Adam is missing from the taped performance, so bass tech Stuart Morgan plays behind a cardboard cutout of Adam.

February 26
At the annual Gibson Guitar Awards, U2 wins in three categories: Best Guitar Band, Best Rock Guitarist (The Edge) and Best Bassist (Adam). It's the second straight year Adam has won the Best Bassist award.

February 27
Staples Center, Los Angeles. U2 open the Grammy Awards with a live performance of 'Walk On'. They're nominated eight times, and win four Grammys: Record Of The Year ('Walk On'); Pop Performance By A Duo Or Group With Vocal ('Stuck In A Moment You Can't Get Out Of'); Rock Performance By A Duo Or Group With Vocal ('Elevation'); and Rock Album (*All That You Can't Leave Behind*). Combined with the

three awards last year for 'Beautiful Day', this makes seven Grammy Awards for one album. U2's career total now stands at 14 Grammys.

March
U2 returns to Dublin and continues working on new material at Hanover Quay.

March 1
Bono spends the day in Washington, DC, where his meetings include lunch with US National Security Adviser Condoleeze Rice.

March 4
U2 wins seven times at the second annual Meteor Irish Music Awards in Dublin. The band's awards include Best Irish Pop/Rock Group, Best Irish Pop/Rock Male Singer (Bono), Best Irish Pop/Rock Single ('Walk On'), Best Irish Pop/Rock Album (*All That You Can't Leave Behind*), Best Irish Video ('Elevation'), and Best Irish Live Artist. In addition, manager Paul McGuinness is presented with an

Above: New Orleans, February 3.

award for contributions to the Irish music industry.

March 6
Flush off the success of winning four Grammy Awards, U2's *All That You Can't Leave Behind* climbs up the album sales charts in countries including Australia, Canada, and the US. It moves from number 46 to number 19 in Australia and from number 28 to number 10 in the US

The single-disc version of *The Best of 1980-1990* is certified Multi-Platinum, with US sales of more than two million.

March 11
U2's plans to tour Europe are scotched suddenly, just weeks before an official release of the itinerary is due. While the tour was never formally announced, the band has signed contracts for shows across Europe. Several sources have reported that the tour would begin July 19 in Amsterdam, and the Amsterdam Arena posted on its web site that they were holding the venue on that date (and the 20th) for a major rock concert. A concert promoter in Portugal tells media there that U2 cancelled the tour for "personal reasons". U2's official web site, U2.com, posts the following message: "Stories have been swirling round the net for some time about possible dates in 2002 but contrary to current rumours there'll be no U2 dates this summer." Meanwhile, U2's official fan club, Propaganda, stops accepting new members and representatives tell fans via e-mail the decision has been made "at U2's request". The timing of these events leaves fans wondering about the band's future.

Bono joins Bruce Springsteen and others at the annual Nordoff Robbins charity dinner in New York to pay tribute to Premier Talent's Frank Barsalona. Barsalona is recognised in the music industry as the first booking agent to realise the enormous potential of rock music, and was responsible for booking U2's first tour across the US before he had even seen the band perform.

March 12

Bono appears on the Corrs' new album, *Live In Dublin*. He sings on two tracks: 'When The Stars Go Blue' and 'Summer Wine'.

March 13

U2 wins the Best Concert by a Touring Band award at the Austin Music Awards, an event that kicks off the annual SXSW Festival in Austin, Texas.

March 14

Wrapping up several days in Washington, Bono appears with President George Bush at the Inter-American Development Bank, where Bush announces a US pledge of $5 billion to help fight poverty in Africa. In his speech, Bush praises Bono: "As you can see, I'm traveling in some pretty good company today: Bono. [*laughter and applause*] We just had a great visit in the Oval Office. Here's what I know about him: first, he's a good musician; secondly, he is willing to use his position in a responsible way. He is willing to lead to achieve what his heart tells him, and that is nobody – nobody – should be living in poverty and hopelessness in the world. Bono, I appreciate your heart and to tell you what an influence you've had, Dick Cheney walked in the Oval Office, he said, 'Jesse Helms wants us to listen to Bono's ideas.'" [*laughter and applause*]

After the speech, photographers capture the pair arriving at the White House. Bono waves and Bush flashes the peace sign; the photo makes news all over the world.

Bono: Bush calls it "Irish rock star with the Toxic Texan"

"It is an amusing photograph. I had just got back from accompanying the president as he announced [the US pledge] at the Inter-American Bank. I kept my face straight as we passed the press corps, but the peace sign was pretty funny. He thought so too. Keeping his face straight, he whispered under his breath, 'There goes a front page somewhere: Irish rock star with the Toxic Texan.'"

March 20

With rumours continuing to fly about U2's future after the recent cancellation of a summer tour, manager Paul McGuinness releases a brief statement on U2.com about the band's plans for 2002: "U2 would like to clarify that, contrary to certain speculation in the press, they will be neither touring Europe this summer, nor splitting up. Instead, they are spending time in the studio working on new material for a possible release later this year."

While leaving a fashion show in Dublin with Bono, Edge finds his vintage green Mercedes missing. He learns that the car has been towed away by police because he parked it illegally in front of the Clarence Hotel.

March 25

Bono makes a surprise appearance at the London trial of R.E.M. guitarist Peter Buck, who is facing "air rage" charges related to an incident on board a British Airways flight from Seattle to London in April, 2001. Bono tells the court that Buck "is actually famously known for being a peaceable person. Of all the people in the music business, I couldn't believe my eyes when I read about this." Buck is later acquitted of all charges against him.

Bono is announced as a member of the advisory board for DMZ Records, a new label formed by T-Bone Burnett and filmmakers Joel and Ethan Coen.

March 31

Bono spends Easter morning in the church near his home in France and finally releases the emotions that have been building up inside since the death of his father last year.

April

Bono draws a "joker" card for a new deck of playing cards called Art:Pack, which will be sold as a fund raiser for the Irish Hospice Foundation. Christie's will auction his original artwork this month.

April 2

Edge visits Daniel Lanois at home in Los Angeles to discuss U2's plans for the upcoming *Best of 1990-2000* compilation.

Bono: "An emotional volcano had gone off...", March 31

"I just felt this was the moment that I had to let it go. An emotional volcano had gone off during the week before Easter, and I just wanted to find out. I wanted to deal with the source of whatever it was. In this little church, on Easter morning, I just got down on my knees, and I let go of whatever anger I had against my father. And I thanked God for him being my father, and for the gifts that I have been given through him. And I let go of that. I wept, and I felt rid of it."

April 6
Officials at U2's Clarence Hotel confirm that The Kitchen nightclub, housed in the basement of the Dublin hotel, will close its doors on May 4th. Falling attendance and new licensing laws – which allow pubs to remain open later – are blamed for the decision.

April 13
U2 appears in a pre-recorded video tribute to Daniel Lanois at Canada's Juno Awards. While Bono talks, the rest of U2 sing 'Danny Boy' in the background.

April 15/16
Bono appears on Craig Armstrong's album, *As If To Nothing*. He sings a new vocal on Armstrong's cover of U2's 'Stay (Faraway, So Close!)'.

April 19
Edge and Bono perform at a special retirement party for SDLP politicians John Hume and Seamus Mallon. Singing 'Stand By Me', the pair have guests at Dublin's Burlington Hotel on their feet to mark the retirement of two key players in the Northern Ireland peace process. Bono pays tribute to Hume and Mallon, calling them "giants of peace making in Ireland".

April 25
U2 picks up three awards at the *Hot Press* Irish Music Awards in Belfast: Best Irish Band, Best Live Act for last summer's Slane gig, and the Best Male Singer award for Bono.

May
Around this time, Bono writes the foreword for *They've Hijacked God*, a new book by Adam Harbinson that takes an unfavourable look at organised religion.

May 1
Bono and Ali show up at the opening of a new office complex in Dublin to support Guggi, one of the building's designers.

May 9
U2 shoot a live performance video for a new song, 'The Hands That Built America', which will be included on the soundtrack to Martin Scorsese's upcoming film *Gangs Of New York*. Maurice Linnance directs the shoot in U2's Dublin rehearsal studios.

May 10
'The Hands That Built America' music video debuts at the Tribeca Film Festival in New York. It airs during an MTV comedy and music special shot on location during the film festival.

May 11
Bono sings the praises of Kylie Minogue in a documentary, *Kylie: Spinning Around*, which airs on Channel 5 in the UK.

May 12
Bono appears on an episode of the British TV programme *South Bank Show* that's dedicated to R.E.M. Bono talks about the "strong sense of fuck off" that Peter Buck brings to R.E.M.'s stage performances, a counterbalance to Michael Stipe, whom Bono calls "the butterfly".

May 20
Bono meets up in Frankfurt with US Treasury Secretary Paul O'Neill. They fly to Accra, Ghana, to begin a four-nation, 11-day tour across Africa. The trip is a chance for Bono to show O'Neill examples where US aid is succeeding in improving the lives of Africans. For O'Neill, the trip is chance to promote private-sector initiatives.

May 22
On the third day of his African tour with US Treasury Secretary Paul O'Neill, Bono obliges the request of a 12-year-old girl in Accra, Ghana, who had never heard of him by singing a few lines of 'I Still Haven't Found What I'm Looking For'. Later, Bono and O'Neill travel north to the Tamale region. After touring medical facilities there, their return trip to Accra is delayed by a few hours when a violent storm makes flying impossible.

U2's 'Elevation' music video wins the Best Soundtrack Video award at the Music Video Production Association (MVPA) Awards in Hollywood.

May 23
'Walk On' beats David Gray's 'Sail Away' and Travis's 'Side' to win the Best Song Musically and Lyrically award at the Ivor Novello Awards. Edge attends the award ceremony in London.

May 24
On day five of their tour of Africa, Bono and US Treasury Secretary Paul O'Neill visit Chris Hani Baragwanath hospital – a 2,888-bed hospital listed in the *Guinness Book of Records* as the world's biggest hospital. There, hospital staff and donor agency officials tell them that although $50 million comes in yearly for AIDS, most of the 2,000 HIV positive mothers at the unit, who would need just $2 million for treatment, remained untreated. Bono and O'Neill are shocked by what they are told and see. Bono says, "I am speechless," while Secretary O'Neill – whose voice is described as "quivering" by reporters in attendance – says: "This whole business about having so much money...and it not going primarily to treatment is just a stunning revelation. Before we ask for more money, for God's sake what are we doing with what we've got?". Later, the pair travel to a housing project in Soweto, where Bono is greeted by schoolchildren singing along to U2's 'I Still Haven't Found What I'm Looking For'. When their tape player breaks, Bono steps in to finish the song.

May 25
Bono visits with Nelson Mandela at Mandela's home in the Johannesburg suburb of Houghton.

May 27
A week into their tour of Africa, Bono and US Treasury Secretary Paul O'Neill openly speak of their differences over African aid. After visiting a poorly equipped school and a village water well in Uganda, O'Neill questions how agencies spent the $300 million they received in aid last year and why many Ugandans don't have clean water when new wells could be built for all residents for roughly $25 million. Bono disagrees, telling

reporters the school and water well issues are examples of why more aid is needed. "If the secretary can't see that," he says, "we're going to have to get him a pair of glasses and a new set of ears."

May 29
Bono puts on a suit and tie to address the African Development Bank's (ADB) annual conference in Addis Ababa, Ethiopia. Bono uses his speech to call on more aid from the US and Europe to help eradicate poverty across Africa.

May 30
Bono and US Treasury Secretary Paul O'Neill wrap up their tour of Africa today. While the two continue to have differences over the amount of foreign aid that the US and Europe should send to Africa, O'Neill calls for an all-out effort to solve some of the developing world's most critical problems. "Programs are working. Aid is helping. And standards of living are improving. But more needs to be done. And it needs to be done right. And it needs to be done right now," O'Neill says.

May 31
The *New York Times* reports that U2 has turned down an invitation to play at a concert next week in honour of Queen Elizabeth's 50-year reign.

June 5
Former US president Bill Clinton joins U2 to watch the Ireland-Germany World Cup match at the Spy club in Dublin. Clinton later attends a party at Bono's house and stays the night.

June 6
Bono and Bill Clinton are inducted into the Washington-based Academy of Achievement's hall of fame at the Four Seasons Hotel in Dublin.

June 11
Bono attends the wedding of Paul McCartney and Heather Mills today at Castle Leslie in County Monaghan, Ireland.

June 17
Edge and Morleigh marry today in a civil service at a Dublin registry office. Bono serves as Edge's best man. Edge and Morleigh will have a public ceremony in France in a few days.

Also today, Dublin's planning board rules against U2's appeal to stop the demolition of the band's Hanover Quay recording studio. The docklands area will be redeveloped, and the project includes 1,200 new homes and the creation of 20,000 jobs in a development of shops, restaurants, bars and an open-air amphitheatre for concerts. Shortly after the planning board's ruling, U2 announce it has an agreement with the Dublin Docklands Development Authority (DDDA) for a replacement studio building, which will enable them to remain in the docklands area. U2 has invested heavily in the development of the Hanover studios over the past seven years and recorded four albums there: *Passengers*, *Pop*, the soundtrack for *The Million Dollar Hotel* and *All That You Can't Leave Behind*.

June 20
Bono meets with French President Jacques Chirac at the presidential Elysee Palace to talk about AIDS and debt relief in developing nations. Chirac promises Bono that French aid will increase in coming years.

June 22
Edge and Morleigh Steinberg have a public wedding ceremony today at the Garden of Eze in southern France. Edge wears his trademark hat with a white/cream-colored jacket over a dark shirt. Morleigh, of course, wears white. The ceremony takes place at the ruins of a medieval castle near the village where Bono and Edge also share a home. The whole band is on hand for the festivities, and Bono serves as best man. Among the 100+ guests are Michael Stipe, Dave Stewart, Dennis Hopper and models Helena Christensen and Christy Turlington.

June 29
Bono attends the live finale of David Bowie's Meltdown Festival at London's Royal Albert Hall.

July 17
Bono appears on RTE radio's *Today With Vincent Browne* programme. He tells Browne and co-host Brenda Fricker that the band is getting along fine without him in the studio.

July 25
Bono pays a visit to the home of Dublin Archbishop Walton Empey, who is days away from retiring. The

Bono: "They've gone from strength to strength" July 17

"It does disturb me a little bit that the less time I spend in the studio, the better we seem to be getting. Cause I'm doing all this extracurricular stuff – I thought the band would collapse, but sadly they've gone from strength to strength!"

Archbishop has expressed his admiration for Bono in recent interviews and said he'd like to talk about world issues together.

July 26
Bono tells fans outside the band's Dublin studio that they finished working on the upcoming *Best of 1990-2000* compilation at 6:00 am this morning.

July 27
Edge makes a surprise appearance for a number of inner city children during their music graduations in Dublin. He speaks and sings with the students, and poses for pictures.

August 14
Bono and Ali visit with Prince Albert of Monaco on his luxury yacht off St. Tropez. They later join Edge at a birthday party for the son of French singer Johnny Hallyday.

August 21
U2 shoots the music video for 'Electrical Storm' on the beach in Eze, France, near Bono's seaside home. They start at about 6:00 a.m., and don't finish until 3:00 a.m. the following day. The song is the band's next single, to be included on the upcoming *Best of 1990-2000* album due later in the year. Anton Corbijn directs the video, with a storyline that involves Larry and a mermaid. Actress Samantha Morton, who co-starred with Tom Cruise and Colin Farrell in the film *Minority Report*, plays the mermaid.

August 22
Bono, Edge, and Larry are in attendance as Caroline Corr, drummer with the Corrs, marries Frank Woods on the Spanish island of Majorca.

August 22
Elevation 2001 – Live From Boston picks up the Best Music Release DVD award at the DVD Awards in Hollywood.

August 25
BBC Radio 1 DJ Sarah HB airs 'Electrical Storm', and within hours, the song is available from

Below: The Irish Rock Legends stamp series featuring U2, Phil Lynott, Van Morrison and Rory Gallagher.

many U2 fan sites as a downloadable MP3. All this happens some three weeks before the song is supposed to be released to radio stations. A notice on U2.com says DJ Sarah received the song on CD as a wedding present from Bono and that she aired an unfinished demo version. Meanwhile, with radio stations around the world beginning to play the demo version obtained on the Internet, Interscope Records rushes to release a finished version of the song for radio play.

August 28
Radio stations in North America receive 'Electrical Storm' three days after BBC Radio 1 aired an unfinished demo of the new single. The promo CD-R has two tracks – both different from the version aired by the BBC. In Ireland, Dave Fanning gives the song its official premiere on 2FM.

September 1
U2 announces that *The Best of 1990-2000* will be released on November 4/5. An accompanying DVD will come out in December.

September 3
Bono performs with Patti LaBelle at the fifth annual Vincent Longo benefit concert for amfAR/Sabera in

Cannes. Before headliner Sting takes the stage, Bono pokes fun at his anatomy: "He plays a mean bass guitar. He's good-looking. He's fit. He has a beautiful wife, Trudy. But God is fair... Let's just say he has no visible means for procreation."

September 4
Bono attends a star-studded charity dinner for amfAR and Sabera in Cannes.

September 13
Volume 3, Issue 3 of *Propaganda* magazine begins to arrive in subscribers' mailboxes. It's the first issue in about 18 months, and will also be the last: the band's fanclub will switch to an online version through U2.com.

September 14
Larry sees Irish boxer Wayne McCullough defeat Johannes Maisa at York Hall Bethnal Green in London.

September 16
Bono joins the Rolling Stones on stage during their concert at the Aragon Ballroom in Chicago. He duets with Mick Jagger on 'It's Only Rock And Roll'.

September 17
Bono tapes an interview with Oprah Winfrey. It'll air on her wildly popular daytime chat show later in the week.

September 19-20
Bono is in New York for the annual Fashion Week shows and parties. On the 19th, he attends Christy Turlington's book launch for *Living Yoga* at the Hudson Hotel and sees the Rosa Cha show. On the 20th, he's at the grand opening of Stella McCartney's new store.

September 20
Bono appears on *The Oprah Winfrey Show*. He answers questions and talks about his debt relief and AIDS prevention efforts in Africa. Movie star Chris Tucker and US Treasury Secretary Paul O'Neill – who traveled with Bono last May during a tour of Africa – appear on the programme via satellite to share

their thoughts on the effort and on Bono.

September 24
Bono gives a speech at a private conference about international economics at Waddesdon Manor in Buckinghamshire, England. Warren Buffet hosts the event.

October 1
Six U2 albums are included in a *Rolling Stone* magazine readers' poll of the Top 100 albums of all-time. *The Joshua Tree* rates highest at number four, followed by *Achtung Baby* at number 10 and *All That You Can't Leave Behind* at number 15.

October 3
Q magazine names Bono the Most Powerful Man in Music, based on a poll of top music industry executives. Bono is tapped for the honour not only for U2's continuing success, but also for his "high profile pronouncements on political issues ranging from Third World debt to the enlargement of the European Union". Coming in second in the survey is Universal Music Group chairman and CEO Doug Morris. Universal is the label that distributes U2 worldwide.

October 7
Bono and Edge attend the opening of a new exhibition of Guggi's art in Dublin's Solomon Gallery.

October 10
Bono and Edge attend a Prince concert at The Point in Dublin. *Hot Press* quotes Edge today saying that U2 are planning to have a new album out by next summer. The article says three tracks are already done: 'Sometimes You Can't Make It On Your Own', 'Original Of The Species' and 'All Because Of You'.

October 17
U2 appears on an official Irish stamp for the first time when An Post, Ireland's Post Office, issues a set of stamps commemorating Irish Rock Legends. The set includes a U2 stamp, and stamps for Van Morrison, Phil Lynott and Rory Gallagher.

Above: Promoting *The Best of 1990-2000*, **with a projection on London's Marble Arch.**

October 18
Bono meets with Professor Richard Feachem, executive director of the UN-backed Global Fund to Fight AIDS, TB and Malaria, in Dublin.

October 21/22
The William Orbit mix of 'Electrical Storm' is released as a single in varying formats with extra tracks including 'New York (Nice Mix)', 'New York (Nasty Mix)', 'Electrical Storm (Band Version)', and 'Bad – 40 – Where The Streets Have No Name (Live from Boston)'. The song hits number one in Canada and some European countries, number four in the UK, number five in Australia, and number 77 in the US, where there's no commercial CD available.

October 24
Bono attends Africare's annual dinner in Washington, DC, which honours Harry Belafonte tonight. Bono tells the crowd, "I learned from Harry Belafonte that as ridiculous as celebrity is, it can be currency, so spend it wisely." The event raises almost $1 million to fight AIDS in Africa.

November 4/5
U2 releases *The Best of 1990-2000* in what's advertised as a "limited edition" three-disc set: the main CD album, an extra CD of B-sides, and a bonus DVD. Just as they did with *The Best of 1980-1990* four years earlier, a single CD version will be released a week later. The compilation features two versions of the new single, 'Electrical Storm', as well as new versions of all three *Pop* tracks chosen for the album: 'Discotheque', 'Staring At The Sun', and 'Gone'.

The album tops the charts in several countries (Australia, New Zealand, Canada, and others), and reaches number two in the UK and number three in the US. In *Salon*, critic Annie Zaleski says the songs chosen for the compilation aren't an accurate reflection of U2's journey in the 1990s: "U2 is trying to rewrite that story.... *1990-2000* is the band's version of themselves as they want to be remembered." Stuart Derdeyn of the Vancouver Province gives the album 3.5 stars (out of five), and sums it up thus: "What makes U2 great isn't just the hits. This collection proves the band is all about its albums."

Tracks, Disc 1: 'Even Better Than The Real Thing', 'Mysterious Ways', 'Beautiful Day', 'Electrical Storm – (William Orbit mix)', 'One', 'Miss Sarajevo', 'Stay (Faraway, So Close!)', 'Stuck In A Moment You Can't Get Out Of', 'Gone (New Mix)', 'Until The End Of The World', 'The Hands That Built America', 'Discotheque (New Mix)', 'Hold Me, Thrill Me, Kiss Me, Kill Me', 'Staring At The Sun (New Mix)', 'Numb', 'The First Time'. 'The Fly' appears as a bonus track in some regions.

Tracks, Disc 2: 'Lady With The Spinning Head – (Extended Dance mix)', 'Dirty Day – (Junk Day mix)', 'Summer Rain', 'Electrical Storm', 'North And South Of The River', 'Your Blue Room', 'Happiness Is A Warm Gun – (Gun mix)', 'Salome – (Zooromancer mix)', 'Even Better Than The Real Thing – (Perfecto mix)', 'Numb – (Gimme Some More Dignity mix)', 'Mysterious Ways – (Solar Plexus Club mix)', 'If God Will Send His Angels – (Big Yam mix)', 'Lemon – (Jeep mix)', 'Discotheque – (Hexidecimal mix)'

To promote the compilation, all four members of U2 take part in an online chat with an estimated three million fans. The chat is hosted by BBC personality Jo Whiley who asks questions submitted previously by fans, as well as some of her own questions. Larry also does an interview with Larry Gogan on 2FM.

Also on November 4, U2 appears on the compilation album, *The Very Best of The Tube*, a 20th anniversary tribute to the British music programme. U2 contributes both the album version of 'New Year's Day' and their live TV performance of the song that was recorded on March 18, 1983.

November 7
At a banquet in New York City, Bono is honoured as the 2002 Gold Medal recipient of the American Irish Historical Society. In choosing Bono for the award, the AIHS cites his "unwavering commitment to many important worldwide humanitarian causes".

November 8
The Best of 1990-2000 is certified

Above: The Simon Wiesenthal Center honors Bono, November 18.

Platinum by the BPI, with UK sales surpassing the 300,000 mark. *The Best of 1980-1990* is certified Multi-Platinum, with sales of more than 1.5 million.

November 10
The Best of 1990-2000 debuts at number two on the UK album charts, behind *One Love* by the group Blue.

November 11/12
U2 releases the single-CD, cassette, and vinyl versions of *The Best of 1990-2000*.

November 12
The Dublin Docklands Development Authority and U2 announce plans to build a new high-rise tower in Dublin that will house a new penthouse recording studio for U2. The new building

will replace U2's Hanover Quay studio, which the DDDA plans to tear down as part of a redevelopment project. Bono attends and speaks to reporters at the news conference.

November 14
Bono spends the day at home with writer Michka Assayas. They're beginning a series of conversations that will lead to a 2005 book, *Bono: In Conversation with Michka Assayas*. Tonight, they watch the MTV European Music Awards on TV. U2 doesn't win any of the four categories in which the band is nominated.

Elevation 2001: Live From Boston is certified Multi-Platinum, with US video sales surpassing two million.

November 17
The Edge joins Wyclef Jean on stage tonight during Jean's concert at the Ambassador Theatre in Dublin. The two play an instrumental version of 'With Or Without You', and some reports suggest they also do a medley of other U2 songs. Edge returns to the stage a second time later in the show to join in on a cover of 'Knockin' On Heaven's Door'.

November 18
Bono becomes the first rock and roll personality to receive the Humanitarian Laureate Award from the Simon Wiesenthal Center. He's honoured for his international campaign to raise awareness of the AIDS epidemic in Africa and forgive the crushing monetary debt of poverty-stricken Third World countries. "When the center started its award process this year, only one name came to mind – Bono," says Wiesenthal Center Eastern director Rhonda Barad. "Not only does he address issues, he creates concrete viable plans to make the world a more equitable place."

Jools Holland's new album, *More Friends, Small World, Big Band Vol. 2*, is released today in the UK. Bono sings on a new version of U2's 'If God Will Send His Angels'. The album will be released in 2003 outside the UK.

November 19

Bono is in Los Angeles for an interview with CNN's Larry King. The interview will air on December 1.

After Los Angeles, Bono heads to Seattle to visit with Trevor Neilson, one of DATA's founding board members.

November 23

Bono makes a guest appearance at Bruce Springsteen's concert tonight in Miami. Bono and Dave Stewart join The Boss and the E Street Band to perform 'Because The Night'.

November 28

Bono appears on an NBC special, *Elvis Lives*. As the hour-long programme ends, Bono recites a shortened version of 'American David', the poem he wrote about Elvis in 1995.

November 29

CBS television airs the one-hour concert special *U2's Beautiful Day* in its 10:00 p.m. time slot tonight, the day after Thanksgiving. The show manages just a 1.5 rating and a 5 share. It's by far the lowest-rated concert special of the week on any network, and is beaten by specials from Faith Hill, Tim McGraw, Paul McCartney and an Elvis retrospective earlier in the week.

November 30

Bono arrives in Lincoln, Nebraska, for the start of the Heart of America tour, which is being coordinated by Bono's DATA organization. He does phone interviews with reporters from the cities the tour will visit over the next eight days. Though Bono is the leader of this caravan, he's not alone on the road. He'll get help during the seven-state tour from the likes of financier Warren Buffet, cycling star Lance Armstrong, actors Ashley Judd and Chris Tucker, Ugandan nurse Agnes Nyamayarwo, a young Ghanaian choir called the Gateway Ambassadors, and doctors and others familiar with the fight against AIDS. Together, their goal is to spread the news about the AIDS crisis in Africa to the heartland of America and help start a grassroots movement of churchgoers, local politicians, soccer moms and the like.

December

Interscope Records and Miramax Pictures distribute a CD featuring 'The Hands That Built America' to members of the Oscar Awards Nominees Committee. The front of the CD says, "For Your Consideration: BEST ORIGINAL SONG."

December 1

The Heart of America Tour opens in Lincoln, Nebraska, on World AIDS Day.

Bono's day begins at Sunday services at United Methodist Church where he speaks to a thousand people about his story and being called to help Africa. From there, the group heads to the University of Nebraska-Lincoln, where Bono and Ashley Judd climb a 20-foot ladder and place a panel on an AIDS Memorial Quilt.

Speaking tonight to about 2,300 people at the university, Bono says, "There's a sense here of community and family. We came to the heartland to get at the hearts and minds of America." At the end of the evening's presentation, Bono sings a song, reported by local press to be a U2 track called 'American Prayer'. He also leads the crowd in 'God Bless America'.

While in Nebraska, Bono does an interview with Cathleen Falsani of the *Chicago Sun-Times*, who is following the tour, and calls Chicago's WGN radio to do another interview. Also today, Bono appears on CNN's *Larry King Weekend* program, doing an hour-long interview that had been pre-taped in Los Angeles.

December 2

The Heart of America tour arrives by bus in Iowa today. They make a pre-arranged stop at a diner in Greenfield, where Bono sits with local residents and a state legislator while video cameras capture the discussion. Bono and friends later visit the editorial board of the *Des Moines Register*, and then do a

presentation at the University of Iowa in Iowa City tonight. "We're here largely because politicians have told us people in the Midwest don't care about issues outside of the US," Bono tells the Iowans. "We believe there's kind of a moral compass that lives here."

December 3

The day begins early in Iowa City, where Bono meets with local government officials. Then it's back on the road, eastbound, for a stop in Walcott at the largest truck stop in the country. Bono talks to a group of truck drivers, who are shocked to learn that 50% of truck drivers in Africa will die of AIDS. The tour continues on to Central High School in Davenport, where Bono honks the bus's horn repeatedly as they arrive for what was supposed to be a surprise visit. From there, the group makes another stop in Dubuque.

Then it's into Illinois for a meeting with Bill Hybels, pastor of the Willow Creek Community Church, to talk about the Heart of America tour and how to get the message out to churches. The long day ends with a late arrival in Chicago.

December 4

Edge is spotted at Lillie's Bordello in Dublin, where many top supermodels have a party following a fashion show.

Meanwhile, Bono and friends speak at the Apostolic Faith Church in Chicago, where actors Ashley Judd and Chris Tucker both break into tears while listening to Agnes Nyamayarwo of Uganda, who is HIV positive and has already lost her husband and a son to AIDS.

The group also visits today with the *Chicago Tribune* and *Chicago Sun-Times* editorial boards. Their meeting with the latter gets heated when someone from the paper asks why Americans should try to solve the African problem when AIDS is also a problem in the US. "Don't give me that 'poor man' for the United States, please!" Bono says. "I hate the idea that somehow the masses are just consumed with self-interest and don't give a shit...

I don't care how you do it. It has to be done. And if you don't, you will reap an ill will." By the end of the meeting, actor Chris Tucker manages to get the *Sun-Times* board members to pray together about AIDS in Africa.

The group moves on to Wheaton College tonight where Bono receives and reads a telegram from the Reverend Billy Graham, the school's most well known alumnus. Bono encourages students at the Christian school to fulfill their "moral obligation" to fight the battle against AIDS in Africa.

December 5

Bono and Ashley Judd do an interview with NBC's *The Today Show*. The Heart of America Tour travels to Indianapolis. On the way, they make an unannounced stop at a travel rest stop about an hour outside of the city. Bono eats lunch and talks with other travelers about the situation in Africa. Once in Indianapolis, Bono meets with the *Indianapolis Star*'s editorial board.

The tour makes a presentation at the Madame Walker Theatre Centre.

December 6

In Cincinnati today, Bono and friends visit the Caracol HIV Consortium and meet with the *Cincinnati Enquirer*'s editorial board. Later, they do a press conference and reception with the National Underground Railroad Freedom Center. While in the city, Bono bumps into Peter Frampton and tells him that his song 'Show Me The Way' taught Bono how to sing.

After dinner tonight, Bono and Chris Tucker dance with other guests in the hotel ballroom and Bono sings 'Lady Marmalade' with the hotel band.

December 7

The Heart of America Tour stops in Louisville, Kentucky, where Bono and his traveling group visit the Presbyterian Church national headquarters. Tonight's programme takes places at Northeast Christian Church. Bono sees an old friend: Steve Reynolds,

the man who organized Bono's and Ali's visit to Ethopia in 1985. It's the first time they've seen each other in 17 years.

December 8

Still in Louisville, Bono, Chris Tucker, and others do interviews with CNN's Daryn Kagan. Bono also meets with Archbishop Thomas Kelly and speaks to about 100 Presbyterian preachers.

December 9

Early in the day, Bono leads a meeting of about 50 Christian music artists at what has become known as the "Nashville Summit". Members of Third Day, Switchfoot, Sixpence None the Richer, and Jars of Clay have come to Nashville for the meeting, along with Michael W. Smith and others. All have shown some interest in Africa already, but Bono wants more from them. Over the course of a couple hours, Bono encourages the artists to become

Below: Edge, Bono and Ali at the *Gangs Of New York* premiere, December 9.

more publicly supportive of the DATA initiative and to get their fellow Christian artists involved. In doing so, Bono hopes the message will spread to churchgoers across the US. When he finishes speaking, Bono picks up a guitar and leads the group in 'They Will Know We Are Christians By Our Love'.

"I came to see Bono..."
Switchfoot's Jon Foreman wrote the following in his journal after meeting Bono at the Nashville Summit.
"There was a strange feeling in my stomach today watching Bono. I recall feeling the same way when I saw the remains of the world trade towers this past year. This feeling is hard to put into words but could be compared to that of a tourist sightseeing at a funeral. I came to see Bono... I would not have dropped everything and booked a ticket at the last minute to hear a social worker discuss the problems in Africa. I probably wouldn't have attended the same sort of meeting in my hometown.

"I am a selfish, star-struck, rich, American, Anglo-Saxon fan of Bono. Bono came to work. He took a couple hours to talk to a bunch of fans to tell them to use their clout to change the world... To feed the poor, to clothe the homeless, to heal the sick, to preach the good news of the kingdom of heaven. Sounds like an odd headline: 'Bono Comes to Nashville to Convert the Christian Music Industry.' I was convicted. Guilty. This was my chance to meet my hero; Bono came to work.

"Give us Grace, oh God, to finish the task at hand."

**Above: Bono at JFK
Airport, New York,
for Operation
Christmas Child,
December 10.**

After the meeting, Bono speaks at an AIDS-related conference in downtown Nashville. The Heart of America tour wraps up with one more event in Nashville this evening, but Bono has flown to New York for other commitments.

In New York, Bono and Edge sing 'The Hands That Built America' live for the first time at a party after the world premiere of Martin Scorsese's film, *Gangs Of New York*.

December 10
Bono joins US Senator Bill Frist, the Reverend Franklin Graham, and others in airlifting 83,000 Christmas gifts to HIV-positive children in Africa. The group does a news conference at Kennedy Airport in New York, where a cargo plane is loaded with the gifts. The airlift is part of Operation

Christmas Child, a relief effort headed by Graham, the son of evangelist Billy Graham.

After the event, Bono heads to a recording studio in Manhattan. Later, he and Ali have lunch with Rupert Murdoch.

December 17
'The Hands That Built America' appears on the *Gangs Of New York* soundtrack, which is released today. It's a slightly different version of the song than has already appeared on *The Best of 1990-2000*.

December 19
'The Hands That Built America' is nominated for a Golden Globe award for Best Original Song in a Motion Picture.

December 20
Principle Management throw a

Christmas party tonight at the Clarence Hotel. The whole band, minus Larry, show up for the festivities.

December 23
Joe Strummer, frontman of The Clash, dies of a heart attack at his home in England at the age of 50. Bono pays tribute by saying, "The Clash was the greatest rock band. They wrote the rule book for U2." At the time of his death, Strummer is working with Bono and Dave Stewart on a song titled '46664' for a Nelson Mandela charity concert two months away.

December 30
The Las Vegas Film Critics Society honors 'The Hands That Built America' as Best Original Song during its annual awards ceremony.

2003

U2 spend much of 2003 in the studio, and plan to have a new album out by the end of the year. There are a few minor distractions along the way, including several awards shows and guest appearances at other artists' concerts. Bono and Edge spend a fair amount of time early in the year promoting 'The Hands That Built America'.

Distractions or not, U2's studio sessions this year aren't working out. The decision to work with a new producer, Chris Thomas, doesn't generate the sparks U2 hoped for; it "didn't change the room temperature", as Bono puts it. After eight months of work with Thomas, U2 ends the year back at the drawing board, without a new album, and with a lot of work still to come.

January 7
'Walk On' is nominated for a Grammy Award in the Best Rock Performance By A Duo Or Group With Vocal category. The song nominated is the live version that U2 performed September 21, 2001, which appeared on the *America: A Tribute to Heroes* album for victims of the September 11 attacks ('The album version of 'Walk On' from *All That You Can't Leave Behind* won the coveted Record Of The Year Grammy at last year's awards).

January 9
As tensions continue to mount in Iraq, a U2 spokesperson denies recent London media reports that Bono is planning to visit Iraq to protest the looming war there. "There is no truth whatsoever to this story," the statement says.

January 9
Bono and Edge attend the Dublin premiere of Martin Scorsese's film, *Gangs Of New York* at the Savoy Cinema. Later, they perform their soundtrack contribution, 'The Hands That Built America', as well as 'All I Want Is You' at the party.

January 10
Gangs Of New York festivities continue with a fund raising auction at Dublin's Burlington Hotel, where Edge bids €85,000 to send a four-year-old Dublin girl to Disneyland as part of the Make-A-Wish program. "We're just happy to be able to help out at these events," Edge says. "The magnificent work Make-A-Wish carries out is invaluable to the children and their parents."

January 18
Bono attends a DATA board meeting at Indian Harbour Beach in Florida.

January 19
The Hands That Built America' wins a Golden Globe Award for Best Original Song. Bono and Edge are U2's representatives at the awards ceremony. Bono causes a stir when he says "fucking brilliant!" while accepting the award. His slip of the tongue starts a long-running battle in the US over televised obscenities.

January 22
Bono hangs out in Dublin with Helena Christensen, who's in town for a fashion show tomorrow.

January 23
The Edge struts his stuff on the catwalk as a model at the Brown-Thomas International Fashion Show in Dublin. Bono is one of many celebrities watching in the audience. The event at Dublin's Point Theatre benefits charities including the Chernobyl Children's Project, ISPCC, and The Christina Noble Foundation.

January 27
A day before President Bush's State of the Union address, Bono pens a letter to the President in today's *Washington Post*. Under the headline, "Mr. President, Africa Needs Us," Bono says at least $2.5 billion in US funding is needed this year to fight AIDS in Africa.

January 28
In his State of the Union address, President Bush calls for $15 billion over five years to be used in the battle against AIDS in Africa. Bono praises the President's proposal: "If we can turn the president's bold long term vision into near term results, we're excited."

January 30
U2 pick up four honors in the 2002 *Hot Press* Readers' Poll: Best Irish Singer (Bono), Best Irish Musician (Edge), Best Irish Single and Best Irish Music Video (both 'Electrical Storm').

February
U2 regroups at Hanover Quay studios to begin work on a new album with producer Chris Thomas. It's the first time the band has worked with Thomas, whose previous production credits include Roxy Music and The Sex Pistols. The plan is to have an album out by the end of the year.

February 8
In The Name Of Love: Two Decades Of U2, an exhibit of artifacts and memorabilia from U2's career, opens at the Rock and Roll Hall of Fame and Museum in Cleveland. The exhibit, which features early artifacts never seen before by the public at large, as well as handwritten notes and lyrics, the band's instruments and tour fashions, and much more, will remain open through September.

February 10/11
We're A Happy Family, a Ramones tribute album is released, with U2's cover of 'Beat On The Brat'.

February 11
'The Hands That Built America' earns an Oscar nomination for Best Original Song.

February 14
Edge attends the Dublin premiere of Salma Hayek's new movie, *Frida*. Bono is reportedly unable to be there due to back pain.

'The Hands That Built America'.

February 24
Bono writes a letter to readers of the UK tabloid, *The Sun*, urging them to help fight AIDS in Africa.

February 26
NBC's popular morning program, *Today*, airs its recent interview with Bono and Edge, and their in-studio performance of 'The Hands That Built America'.

February 28
French President Jacques Chirac awards Bono with the Chevalier of Legion of Honour during a visit to Paris. Ali accompanies Bono to the ceremony, as do Paul McGuinness and his wife, Kathy. After receiving the award, Bono makes a rare public comment on the tensions and pending war in Iraq: "Tony Blair is not going to war for oil. Tony Blair is sincere in his convictions about Iraq. In my opinion he is sincerely wrong."

Following the ceremony, Bono and friends have a celebratory lunch at the Hotel de Crillon. Though no one is prepared, the group decides to stay in Paris overnight.

February 18
Bono is unable to attend the Dublin premiere of Neil Jordan's *The Good Thief*, his second cancelled appearance in the past week. Dublin media learn that Bono has a slipped disc in his back.

February 20
Bono and Edge tape an interview and a performance of 'The Hands That Built America' at NBC Studios in New York. It airs on the *Today* show six days later.

Later, Bono and Edge spend a couple hours rehearsing prior to tomorrow's performance at the MusiCares event honoring Bono.

February 21
The Recording Academy honours Bono as the MusiCares 2003 Person of the Year, recognising his musical and humanitarian achievements. Bono and Edge arrive early at the Marriott Marquis Hotel to wrap up rehearsals for their performance tonight. Bono decides against doing the traditional honouree's news conference, saying he doesn't want to look like he's tooting his own horn. He does, though, meet with fans outside the hotel and talk

briefly with reporters there. "MusiCares is about looking after our own kind so that's pretty good," he says. "I'm hanging with a lot of un-hip company trying to do the political work that I do, business people, congressmen and politicians. But this is my own tribe. I feel, in truth, more comfortable here."

Tonight's event attracts stars from music, fashion, television, sports, movies and politics. Bono, Ali, and their daughters sit at a table with President Bill Clinton, Robert De Niro and Salman Rushdie. Clinton presents Bono with his award, praising Bono for his work on debt relief, AIDS and poverty. The tribute includes a concert featuring other artists performing U2 songs. Among the performances: Mary J. Blige sings 'One', B.B. King and Wynonna sing 'When Love Comes To Town', and Elvis Costello sings 'Kite'. After his performance, Costello calls Bono to the stage and tells the crowd to "give him the fucking Nobel Peace Prize *now*!" The evening ends with Bono and Edge taking the stage for a three-song set of their own: 'That's Life', 'Night And Day', and

Above: Edge and Bono rehearse for the MusiCares event, February 20.
Below: Bono and Bill Clinton, February 21.

March 3
U2 wins for Best Group and Bono collects a Humanitarian Award at the Meteor Irish Music Awards in Dublin.

March 9
Reports surface that Bono's back pain is so bad, he has to lie down in the studio while working on U2's new album.

Larry attends the Dublin premiere of Colin Farrell's new movie, *The Recruit*.

March 10
Subbing for Bono, whose back is in too much pain, Edge and Tom Morello (of Audioslave) induct The Clash into the Rock and Roll Hall of Fame. "There's no doubt in my mind that 'Sunday, Bloody Sunday' wouldn't and couldn't have been written if it wasn't for the Clash," Edge says at the New York ceremony.

Bono sings a cover of Frank Sinatra's 'That's Life' on *The Good Thief* soundtrack. The album is released today in Europe, and will be issued April 8 in North America.

March 16
Bono speaks at the Times Talks lecture series hosted by the *New York Times*. He jokes with the crowd about his bad back, and talks about debt relief and AIDS in Africa.

March 17
Bono receives a Humanitarian Award at the 11th annual American Ireland Fund National Gala in Washington, DC.

March 18
Bono meets with US lawmakers on Capitol Hill to talk about AIDS funding for Africa.

March 20
With war underway in Iraq, MTV Europe puts 'Miss Sarajevo' on a list of videos their programmers should avoid playing. Bono and Edge appear on MTV's *TRL* program.

March 22
Bono and Ali, Larry and Ann attend the Miramax 2003 MAX Awards in Los Angeles.

March 23
Kodak Theatre, Los Angeles. U2 performs 'The Hands That Built America' at the Oscar Awards ceremony, but the song fails to win Best Original Song (Eminem's 'Lose Yourself' takes the honour). U2 and friends attend a party hosted by *Vanity Fair* magazine after the awards.

While in Los Angeles, U2 meets with Apple Computer representatives at Jimmy Iovine's home. The Apple staffers show U2 a demo of their new online music store, which is due to launch in about a month. The band want to know if Apple's small market share will hurt the store's chances of success; Apple assures them the store will eventually be available to PC users, too.

Edge stays in Los Angeles a while longer and works on new material alone. He comes up with

Above: Edge and Tom Morello with Topper Headon, Mick Jones and Paul Simenon at The Clash's induction into The Rock and Roll Hall of Fame, New York, March 10.

the guitar riff for 'Vertigo' and an early version of 'Yahweh' during this period, and several other song ideas to play for the band when they reconvene in Dublin soon.

Late March
During an online chat, pop star Jennifer Lopez reveals that she's recorded a duet with Bono. She doesn't say what song they sung, and doesn't know if or when it will be released.

March 31
The single disc version of *The Best Of 1990-2000* is certified Platinum, with US sales of more than one million.

April 8
The UN confirms that Bono and Luciano Pavarotti will perform together at the Italian tenor's annual charity concert near his hometown of Modena, Italy. This year's concert, to be held on May 27, is slated to benefit Iraq war refugees. Bono and Pavarotti sang together in 1995 to aid children in Bosnia.

April 15
In an interview with *Hot Press* magazine, Daniel Lanois reveals that he and Brian Eno are not working with U2 on the band's new album. He says the band is working with veteran rock producer Chris Thomas. It's the first time Thomas' involvement has been publicised.

April 17
The Earth Institute at Columbia University announces that Bono has joined its first external advisory board. The Institute is headed by Bono's friend, Jeffrey Sachs.

April 22
Organisers of the 2003 World Special Olympics Summer Games announce that U2 will be one of the performers at the event's opening ceremonies in Dublin on June 21.

April 28
Apple Computer launches the iTunes Music Store. During the announcement, Bono appears on a video praising the service. One

Paul McGuinness on why U2 supported the iTunes Music Store, March 23

"In the end we felt there was no decision to take but to go with it. Other major artists like Madonna and the Beatles have declined – partly I think because they don't like the idea of individual tunes being downloaded. We took the view that when an industry is sick, and penicillin is available, they should start taking it as soon as possible."

breakfast at 10 Downing Street to discuss ongoing efforts to combat the AIDS crisis in Africa. The meeting comes two weeks ahead of the G8 Summit in France.

Tonight, U2 collect an award for Outstanding Song Collection at the annual Ivor Novello songwriting awards in London, but Avril Lavigne's 'Complicated' beats 'Electrical Storm' for International Hit of the Year. The whole band is in attendance at the awards ceremony.

May 23
Larry, Ann and Ali attend the first Tooth Fairy Ball at Royal Hospital in Dublin. Ali is one of the organisers of this new charity event, which aims to raise money to start a dental clinic in Mongolia that will specialise in cleft palate surgery.

May 24
Bono attends a birthday party for Naomi Campbell at Nikki Beach in St. Tropez.

May 25
Bono arrives in Italy in advance of a performance with Luciano Pavarotti in Modena. Today, they rehearse 'One' with a full orchestra, and then practice a new version of Schubert's 'Ave Maria'. They do a news conference after rehearsal, and then Bono and others have dinner at a restaurant that Pavarotti owns in the country. There, Bono joins the house band to sing a bit of 'Unchain My Heart'. While in Italy, Bono realizes he left his favourite hat back in London, so he spends an estimated £1,000 to have the hat flown in before this week's performance.

May 26
Bono has lunch in Bologna with Michka Assayas, who's continuing to interview Bono for an upcoming book.

May 27
Bono makes a solo appearance at the Pavarotti and Friends concert in Modena, Italy. His performances include 'One' with an orchestra backing, 'Miserere' with Zucchero

of the store's early exclusives is a U2 EP that features an acoustic version of 'Stuck In A Moment' and two tracks that appeared in 2001 on *Three Live Tracks From Boston*: 'I Will Follow' and 'Beautiful Day'. It's U2's first exclusive arrangement with Apple.

May 5
Bono and Robert DeNiro are spotted together in Dublin. They also watch the horse races in Naas.

May 6
A day after hanging out in Dublin with Robert DeNiro, Bono is in New York for the opening of the second annual Tribeca Film Festival... which is co-founded by Robert DeNiro. Bono speaks during the Ceremony of Remembrance and Commemoration, and then attends the premiere of *Down With Love*.

May 11
Bono, Ali, Edge, and Morleigh attend a Neil Young concert in Dublin.

May 17
Edge sees Radiohead play the

Olympia Theatre in Dublin.

May 18
Another Radiohead show at the Olympia, and Bono and Edge are both in the crowd this time.

May 19
Bono is in Turin, Italy, for the launch of the World Political Forum – an event organised in part by Mikhail Gorbachev with the aim of promoting diplomacy as the path to solving global issues. While in Italy, Bono interviews the former Soviet president as part of a project called *What's so hard about peace?* Plans are in place to sell the interview to international TV news networks with the money going to charity.

May 21
Bono attends a *Time* magazine award ceremony at the Royal Opera House in London and is honoured as one of the European Heroes featured in a recent issue of *Time Europe*.

May 22
Bono and Bob Geldof meet British Prime Minister Tony Blair for

Above: Bono with Renee Zellweger and Ewan McGregor at the Tribeca Film Festival, May 6.

and Pavarotti, and a duet with Pavarotti on 'Ave Maria'. Bono has written new lyrics for the song that reflect the ongoing situation in the Middle East:

Ave Maria
Where is the justice in this world?
The wicked make so much noise, mother
The righteous stay oddly still
With no wisdom, all of the riches in the world leave us poor tonight
And strength is not without humility
It's weakness, an untreatable disease
And war is always the choice
Of the chosen who will not have to fight

The concert raises an estimated £1 million pounds for Iraqi war refugees. It's Bono's second performance at Pavarotti's concert – he performed with Edge and Brian Eno in September, 1995.

May 30
Bono writes an essay titled "It Takes Only a Dollar a Day to Stop an African Dying of AIDS" for the *Daily Telegraph*.

June 1
Bono attends the Formula 1 Monaco Grand Prix today, presumably as the guest of fellow Irishman and F1 racer Eddie Jordan, who is also his neighbour in Killiney.

June 2
Larry is one of three Irish music stars who design a t-shirt to raise money for the Down Syndrome Ireland association. With Ireland set to host the Special Olympics this month, Larry's design features a medal-winning athlete, a star and a replica of the Olympic torch. Andrea Corr and Samantha Mumba also contribute designs.

June 4/5/6
Bono is spotted in Seattle. On the 4th, he's seen at dinner with Microsoft co-founder Paul Allen, members of R.E.M., and Ann and Nancy Wilson of Heart. On the 6th, Bono and some DATA board members visit the Bill and Melinda Gates Foundation. Bono also meets with the *Seattle Post-Intelligencer*'s editorial board.

June 5
Edge is a guest performer at Daniel Lanois' concert at the Fonda Theater in Los Angeles. They perform three songs together: 'Falling At Your Feet', 'Still Water', and 'I Still Haven't Found What I'm Looking For'.

June 7
Bono gives away the bride at the wedding of supermodel Christy Turlington and actor Ed Burns in San Francisco. Turlington is a longtime friend of Bono and Ali.

June 9
Bono continues his crusade for Africa with a speech to editors of the world's newspapers at a conference in Dublin. He gives the 56th World Newspaper Congress a familiar message – the war on terrorism is bound together with the war on poverty – and urges the editors to support his appeal to help AIDS victims in Africa.

June 12
Bono and Edge attend the opening of a Charlie Whisker art exhibit at Solomon Gallery in Dublin.

June 13
The Best Of 1990-2000 is certified Double Platinum by the BPI, with UK sales surpassing the 600,000 mark.

June 14
The Rock and Roll Hall of Fame and the atu2.com Web site host a "U2 Fan Celebration" in Cleveland to coincide with the opening of a new part of the Hall's ongoing U2 exhibit featuring the artwork of graphic designers Four5One. Steve Averill and Shaughn McGrath from Four5One, along with Hall curator Jim Henke, host an evening presentation for a small group of fans and discuss their history of working with U2 from the band's beginning to today. Averill and McGrath also tell fans that U2's new songs sound like "it's time to have revenge on The Strokes and The Hives."

June 21
Croke Park, Dublin. U2 performs

'One' and 'Pride' at the Opening Ceremonies of the Special Olympics World Summer Games. 'One' included backing from a full orchestra. During 'Pride', Bono changes lyrics to reference the day's events and the presence of former South African president Nelson Mandela. Toward the end of the song, Bono goes backstage and returns with Mandela, calling him "the president of everyone, everywhere who loves and fights for freedom". After the ceremony, Bono hangs out with Jon Bon Jovi and Nelson Mandela at the Four Seasons Hotel, and then goes to a party at The Clarence.

June 22
British Royal Mail officials confirm that they're investigating death threats against Bono that began two years ago. An officer says they've intercepted two dozens threatening letters that originated in London, and that others probably made it through to U2's Dublin offices.

July 8
Bono makes an appearance in Dublin with Irish Taoiseach Bertie Ahern to launch the Human Development Report 2003. The UN report warns that international programmes to help poor nations out of poverty are failing in many countries. "I am ready to march with my activist friends in campaigns of civil disobedience," Bono tells reporters. "We are about to get very noisy, we are about to bang a lot of dustbin lids. This issue is the defining issue of our time and some of us are ready to really work on it."

Later, Bono and Ali attend the world premiere of *Veronica Guerin* at the Savoy Cinema in Dublin.

July 11
Dublin's Trinity College confers Bono with an honorary degree today. He's named a Doctor in Laws, and is cited for his humanitarian work and for his rock and roll success.

July 15
In today's *Frankfurter Rundschau* newspaper, Bono writes an open

letter to German Chancellor Gerhard Schroeder criticizing Germany for blocking creation of a global fund to fight AIDS in Africa.

July 16
Bono and Ali attend R.E.M.'s concert in Dublin, and Bono is later spotted at an exclusive after-show party.

July 19
Bono joins The Corrs to sing 'When The Stars Go Blue' at a birthday celebration in Johannesburg, South Africa, for Nelson Mandela.

August 8
The Dublin Docklands Development Authority reveals the winning design in its competition to build a new tower in Dublin that will house, among other things, U2's new recording studio. The winning architect – Burdon Dunne/Craig Henry of Blackrock in Co Dublin – is partially owned by Felim Dunne, brother-in-law of U2 manager Paul McGuinness. The DDDA says development should begin in the next 1-2 years.

August 27
Bono attends a Rolling Stones concert at the Astoria Theatre in London.

September 12
Bono praises music legend Johnny Cash, who dies today in Nashville at the age of 71. "I considered myself a friend, he considered me a fan – he indulged me. He was more than wise. In a garden full of weeds – the oak tree," Bono says.

Also today, Bono appears in *The Clinton Presidential Center Cookbook*, contributing his simple recipe for a Black Velvet. "Half-fill champagne flute with Guinness. Top with champagne and stir," Bono's recipe says. "The whole is not greater than the sum of the parts, but the hangover is."

September 15
The Turin, Italy, City Council confers Honorary Citizenship on Bono, its highest award for a non-citizen.

September 16
Bono meets President Bush at the White House, urging him to spend $1 billion more in the first year of Bush's five-year plan to fight AIDS in Africa and the Caribbean. The US Congress is considering spending $2 billion on that programme, not the $3 billion the President originally proposed.

September 17
Universal Music announces the November release of *U2 Go Home – Live from Slane Castle, Ireland*, the band's first home video recorded in their native country. The release features U2's September 1, 2001, concert at the castle north of Dublin.

September 21
An article in the *Sunday Times*

reports that the announced winner of the architectural contest to design a new "landmark tower" in Dublin with recording studios for U2 was not the original winner selected by the Dublin Docklands Development Authority (DDDA). The article suggests that procedural errors and administrative mistakes led the original winner of the contest to be set aside because the jury could not identify the creators of the entry. In the article, the DDDA denies any mistakes were made and says no entries were lost.

September 23
Larry and Paul McGuinness attend Gavin Friday's music and poetry show on the opening night of the Dublin Fringe Festival.

October 1
Sony Music hosts a listening party in Los Angeles for the upcoming Bruce Springsteen *Essentials* album. The party includes a Springsteen and Bono duet titled 'Break Of Dawn', which is said to be on a bonus CD of rarities that will be included with the *Essentials* album. But when the final track list is announced for the compilation, the song is nowhere to be found.

October 3
Bono launches an exhibition of art that he's drawn with his daughters for a new version of the children's classic, *Peter & The Wolf*. The book will include Bono's artwork, and an accompanying CD with voiceovers

Above: Bono at the UN Leadership Awards, October 8.

and music by Gavin Friday and Maurice Seezer. Proceeds from the project willl benefit the Irish Hospice Foundation, which took care of Bono's dad, Bob, in his last days. After the launch, Bono, Ali, Edge and others attend a party at The Clarence hotel. The art exhibit will move to London next, and then to the US where Bono's paintings will be auctioned at Christie's in New York.

October 6
Bono is on hand at Christie's in London as the auction house hosts a temporary exhibition of his paintings for *Peter & The Wolf*. With him are Gavin Friday, The Edge and Morleigh, as well as Paul McGuinness.

Also today, U2 begin a two-day photo shoot with Anton Corbijn. The photos are for the band's upcoming album in early 2004, but the shoot is unproductive. No matter, as the album will be delayed until late 2004, buying U2 and Corbijn more time to shoot photos.

In Washington, the Federal Communications Commission rules that Bono's use of the F-word on this year's Golden Globes telecast did not violate indecency laws because the word didn't describe sexual activities.

October 8
Bono is one of the featured speakers at the 2003 Global Leadership and Humanitarian Action Awards, presented in New York by the United Nations Association of the USA and the Business Council for the UN. Bono speaks to the attendees about DATA and the situation in Africa, and presents the night's big award to Dr. Alex Godwin Coutinho, Executive Director of the AIDS Support Organization (TASO).

October 9
Bono attends the International Crisis Group Awards Dinner in New York, which honours philanthropist George Soros and Morton Abramowitz, a former US ambassador to Turkey.

While in New York, Bono reportedly meets with producers of the upcoming blockbuster, *Spiderman 2*, who want U2 to do a song for the soundtrack. They show Bono an early version of the film at Sony headquarters, and Bono reportedly sings a few lines of a song he thinks will fit as the movie's theme. Ultimately, U2's struggles on its own album will prevent the band from contributing to the movie soundtrack.

October 12
Bono appears in a pre-recorded interview on Virgin Radio. He tells host Dominic Mohan that U2's new album will be a "dragon".

October 14
'The Hands That Built America' wins the Best Original Song prize at the World Soundtrack Awards in Belgium.

October 20
Bono is in attendance as the National Gallery of Ireland unveils a new painting by Louis le Brocquy called *Image of Bono*.

Late October
U2 spend a week at Air Studios in London with producer Chris Thomas. They bring in a 50-piece orchestra to perform on a few songs. But the session is a disaster; Thomas reportedly tells the band it's the worst day he's ever spent in a studio. The orchestra is sent home.

Adam explains what went wrong in London
"We could read the room. And they were not going, 'Wow, guys, this is really happening!'"

Also during the same week, writer Michka Assayas arrives in London to continue the ongoing conversations with Bono for his upcoming book.

October 28
Bono joins Daniel Lanois on stage at Shepherd's Bush in London. They sing 'Falling At Your Feet'.

October 31
Bono and Edge appear on RTE TV's *The Late Late Show* during a special tribute to Irish film director Jim Sheridan. During the show, they perform 'Falling At Your Feet' with Daniel Lanois. While being

interviewed, Bono tells host Pat Kenny that the band had recently been in the studio working on three songs with a 50-piece orchestra, but that the band didn't like how the songs turned out.

November 1
Bono and Ali, along with Paul McGuinness and his wife, Kathy, attend the 2003 Irish Film and TV Awards in Dublin.

November 3
A sign of struggles in the studio: Daniel Lanois arrives in Dublin to listen to U2's new album, which is supposed to be nearing completion with producer Chris Thomas. Before he arrives, Lanois talks to RTE radio: "I haven't heard a note. I'm looking forward to it, it's gonna be exciting. I can be a friend and give them an objective opinion. They're at the tail-end [of the project], so they're not gonna want to be buttered-up or anything."

While Lanois is in the studio, he plays pedal steel guitar on 'One Step Closer'.

November 4
Edge appears on the new Wyclef Jean album, *The Preacher's Son*. He plays guitar on the track, 'Class Reunion'.

November 10
Bono appears on videotape during a tribute concert for the late Johnny Cash. In his message, Bono raises a pint of Guinness and says of Cash: "He was an oak tree in a garden of weeds. He's not in a garden of weeds now. He's in heaven where all the saints are."

Also today, *Hot Press* reports that Sheila Roche has resigned as Managing Director at Principle Management after 18 years on staff. She'll stay on board until April, 2004. Steve Matthews, an Island Records executive, will come on board in January to take over for Roche.

November 14
Bono speaks tonight at the Liberal Party convention in Toronto for incoming Canadian Prime Minister Paul Martin. He begins his 25-

Above: Edge, Bono, Beyoncé Knowles, and Dave Stewart, at the Nelson Mandela concert, November 29.

minute speech by telling the gathered crowd, "I'm not a supporter of any political party." And the focus of his speech is not on one party or another, but on the need to relieve Third World debt and raise money to fight the AIDS crisis in Africa. To the incoming Prime Minister, Bono promises, "I'm going to become the biggest pain of his life! Paul Martin thinks he likes me. He doesn't know what he signed on for – more lobbying about debt, begging for letters, petitions for unfair trade, phone calls about money for the global health fund."

November 17/18
U2 Go Home – Live from Slane Castle is released worldwide. The release is the first DVD-only release of U2's career, and is taken from the September 1, 2001, performance at the historic Slane Castle north of Dublin. It's the second Elevation Tour concert to be released as a home video, following the release of *Elevation 2001 – U2 Live From Boston* two years ago. To help

promote the DVD, U2 releases 'Beautiful Day (Live From Slane)' as an exclusive single on iTunes on November 18.

Rolling Stone publishes its list of the Top 500 Albums of All-Time, which includes five from U2:

26. *The Joshua Tree*
62. *Achtung Baby*
139. *All That You Can't Leave Behind*
221. *War*
417. *Boy*

November 21

An auction of 16 paintings by Bono and his daughters Jordan and Eve for the *Peter & The Wolf* charity project raises $368,000 for the Irish Hospice Foundation. Bono and Ali are on hand at Christie's in New York, along with *Peter & The Wolf* co-collaborators Gavin Friday and Maurice Seezer.

An audio CD called *Voices And Poetry Of Ireland* is released today. Bono recites the Brendan Kennelly poem, 'God's Laughter', and Paul McGuinness recites 'Shapes And Shadows' by Derek Mahon. The project is a fund raiser for Focus Ireland, a group that helps the homeless in Ireland.

November 24

Bono attends the premiere of Jim Sheridan's new film, *In America*, in New York City. Bono co-writes the theme song for the film, 'Time Enough For Tears', which is released today.

November 27

Bono and Edge are in Cape Town, South Africa, for this week's 46664 concert. They have dinner tonight with Nelson Mandela.

Peter & The Wolf is released. The package includes a book with illustrations by Bono and his daughters and a CD narrated by Gavin Friday. Proceeds benefit the Irish Hospice Foundation.

November 28

Bono and Edge rehearse for tomorrow's 46664 concert in Cape Town, South Africa. Bono gets a laugh when he approaches the podium to do an impression of the former South African president.

Below: Edge, Morleigh, Ali, and Bono, at the wedding of Luciano Pavarotti, December 13.

November 29

Bono and the Edge perform at the 46664 concert at Greenpoint Stadium in Cape Town. The concert is designed to raise awareness and funds for the fight against AIDS in Africa. Bono and Edge appear early in the show to perform 'American Prayer' with Beyonce and David Stewart, and '46664' with David Stewart and others. At the end of '46664', Bono introduces Nelson Mandela:

"Not just a president for South Africa
Not just a president for Africa
This is a president for anyone, anywhere
Who knows freedom ... Nelson Mandela!"

Bono and Edge return to the stage late in the show to perform a 'One / Unchained Melody' combo. Anastasia, Queen, David Stewart and Beyonce then join them on stage for a new song called 'Amandla'.

Earlier in the day, Bono and Beyonce visit a day clinic and an orphanage that treats women and children infected with HIV and AIDS.

November 30

Bono and Edge spend time visiting local townships in and around Cape Town, talking with residents and visiting an AIDS Days rally. They also pay a visit to Nelson Mandela at his home. Bono does an interview with Oprah Winfrey for an upcoming issue of her O magazine at the Cape Grace Hotel.

December 1

Bono and Edge visit Anglican Archbishop Njongonkulu Ndungane in Cape Town to discuss AIDS, debt, and trade issues.

New York media report that Bono recently purchased the restaurant Le Zoo and will reopen it early next year.

December 3

Bono is the guest today at a Kaiser Health Conversations event in Washington, DC. He's interviewed by Kaiser Family Foundation Senior Visiting Fellow Jackie Judd, a former correspondent with ABC News, about the spread of AIDS in Africa. Bono also takes questions from the audience and individuals around the world who watch a live webcast.

December 4

'The Hands That Built America' is nominated for a Grammy Award in the Song Written for a Motion Picture, Television or other Visual Media category.

December 5

Bono takes part at the Peace Concert at the Library of Congress in Washington, DC. He uses the stage to appeal for peace and to read a William Butler Yeats piece ('September 1913') accompanied by 24 musicians, including World Bank President James D. Wolfensohn on cello.

December 13

Bono and Edge, with their wives Ali and Morleigh, are on hand for the wedding of Luciano Pavarotti to Nicoletta Mantovani in Modena, Italy. At the reception, Bono sings 'All I Want Is You' for the newlyweds, changing the lyrics to something more topical: "When the pasta has run dry/And the wine no longer gets you high/All I want is you."

December 20

Edge, Bono, Ali and one of their daughters are in attendance for a VIP-only concert in Dublin by pop singer Justin Timberlake.

U2 are back at square one as the year begins. Their work last year with Chris Thomas doesn't produce the material U2 had expected. They turn to a familiar friend, Steve Lillywhite, to fill the empty producer's chair as they begin again on a new album. Bono continues to make appearances related to his humanitarian causes, but not as frequently as in 2000. With the band so far behind schedule, he's needed in the studio as much as possible.

He does get out of the studio to launch the ONE Campaign in May. It's the grassroots arm of DATA, the activist side that aims to mobilize citizens to support DATA's goals. It's not named after U2's song, 'One', but Bono admits the connection will help.

After seven months of work, U2 finishes its new album in the summer. *How To Dismantle An Atomic Bomb* is released in October, and U2 hits the promotional trail hard. There's the regular run of TV appearances and a few live gigs. Then there's a historic partnership with Apple Computer, which includes the creation of a U2-branded iPod, a TV commercial promoting iTunes (and U2's new single), and more. *U2 partnering with a commercial entity? A U2 song in a TV commercial?* Some U2 fans cry, "sell out", but U2 recognises that new times call for new tactics.

In any case, it works. The album is an instant smash, winning some of the best reviews U2's ever had. As the year ends, U2 is scheduling another world tour when Edge receives personal news that throws the band's plans into disarray.

January
Unknown to anyone outside U2's immediate circle, Steve Lillywhite arrives in Dublin this month to take over album production duties from Chris Thomas. The news won't reach the public until early February. Also not widely reported until later is that Steve brings Garrett "Jacknife" Lee with him to help out.

Early in the month, the NFL rejects Bono's idea to focus on the AIDS epidemic during halftime of the upcoming Super Bowl. Bono wants to perform 'American Prayer' with Jennifer Lopez, reprising an unreleased duet they recorded last year. The NFL says the Super Bowl halftime show is meant for entertainment, not to promote causes.

January 8
Edge makes an appearance at the Consumer Electronics Show in Las Vegas, speaking out against music piracy along with Sheryl Crow and actor Ben Affleck. They're joined on stage by country artist Toby Keith, Dr. Dre, and Jimmy Iovine among others.

January 17
Bono is honored for his humanitarian efforts at the annual "Salute to Greatness" Awards Dinner hosted by The King Center in Atlanta. The event is part of the Center's celebration of what would have been Martin Luther King, Jr.'s, 75th birthday.

Coretta Scott King honours Bono
"This young man we are honouring tonight provides the shining example of a 21st century artist/humanitarian. Bono, on behalf of the King Center, I salute you for your outstanding contributions as an eloquent and passionate advocate of the teachings of MLK Jr., and for your energetic and dedicated work for numerous human rights campaigns."

Before the awards ceremony, Bono visits King's grave to pay his respects. He also drops in on the Hands On Atlanta Service Summit at a local church, and joins actor Chris Tucker for a meeting with area AIDS officials at the King Center.

Bono's appearance helps the annual event record its largest crowd ever, and raises more than $600,000, also an event record.

While Bono is in the US this week, the rest of the band is in the studio with Steve Lillywhite and Jacknife Lee. They quickly come up with four new songs: 'Vertigo', 'All Because Of You', 'Crumbs From Your Table', and 'Original Of The Species'.

January 18
Universal Music Italy announces that U2's new album will be released in May.

January 22
Bono attends the American Film Institute Awards in Los Angeles with director Jim Sheridan. Sheridan's film, *In America*, is honored as one of the AFI's 10 best movies of 2003. Bono wrote the lyrics to the movie's theme, 'Time Enough for Tears'.

February 2
Even without a new album since 2000, U2 still scores well in the *Hot Press* Readers Poll. U2 comes in fourth in the Irish Group category; Bono takes number three for Irish Male and number two for Irish Songwriter; and Edge is voted the number two Irish Musician. The band is also rated number four for Live Irish Act.

February 3
Irish media report today that Paul McGuinness has agreed to manage a new band, The Rapture. *The Irish Voice* describes the New York-based quartet as a "dance rock" band. "These people are a dynamite live act, and that's kind of what I like best about rock 'n' roll," McGuinness says.

Bono gets to be the opening act tonight in Dublin as he helps open an exhibition by Italian artist Francesco Clemente at the Irish Museum of Modern Art. Bono also presents Clemente with a book of his own artwork from the *Peter & The Wolf* project.

Above: U2 play live from their Hanover Quay Studio for the BBC, November 16.

February 6

Bono is in attendance as Hothouse Flowers launch their new album, *Into Your Heart*, at Lillie's Bordello in Dublin.

Broadcasting & Cable magazine reports that Edge will do the theme music for a new animated children's cartoon series called *The Batman*, which will air this fall in the US.

February 10

The news finally hits: *Billboard* reports that U2 has called on the familiar talents of Steve Lillywhite to produce the band's new album. Lillywhite produced U2's first three albums, and helped during sessions for *The Joshua Tree*, *Achtung Baby*, and *All That You Can't Leave Behind*. The news comes nearly a year after reports that U2 had been working with veteran rock producer Chris Thomas, and fans are left to speculate why Lillywhite would replace Thomas after reports months ago that they were in the "final stages" of recording.

Paul McGuinness issues a statement via U2.com: "There are various producers involved in this album," he writes. "Chris Thomas has done some great work. It's good to work with Steve again but it's not as if we're starting from scratch." Lillywhite's comments in the *Billboard* article, though, suggest otherwise: "It's the first time I'll have gone in to actually start a record with them in 20 years."

Edge explains what happened with Chris Thomas

"We were on the final lap of finishing an album with [Thomas].... The record felt finished one day and then, suddenly, it wasn't finished. So that's when we asked Steve Lillywhite to come in and help us figure it all out…. Near what we thought was the end of the record, we had a substantial amount of rethinking to do – and re-recording. Going back to the drawing board in such an extreme way felt a little odd at first. You tell yourself, 'Nothing like a fresh start.' You have internal pep talks and all that jazz. But it's hard not to feel a little defeated, like you're going around in circles."

Also today, U2 donates 'Beautiful Day' to the Nebraska Organ and Tissue Donor Coalition for use in radio and TV ads promoting organ donation.

February 12
All That You Can't Leave Behind is certified Multi-Platinum, with US sales of more than four million.

Mid-February
Bono writes an essay about Elvis Presley for an upcoming issue of *Rolling Stone* magazine. Later the same day, he speaks on the phone with writer Michka Assayas for his upcoming book.

February 16
Bono speaks via satellite at a globalisation conference in London.

February 26
Larry makes an appearance to help promote motorcycle safety in Ireland. He helps launch a booklet, *This Is Your Bike*, by the National Safety Council and the Irish Motorcyclists' Action Group. During the event, Larry admits that he's never had formal motorcycle training and says he'll go back to driving school for lessons. "I went into town, bought a bike and just got on it," he says. "When I think back now, I wonder how I could have been so stupid. People just don't have the basic training. Anyone can buy a bike and ride away with it without any sort of training."

February 27
The Edge presents Irish folk legend Christy Moore with a lifetime achievement award at an industry party at the Burlington Hotel in Dublin. "There is no one like Christy Moore," Edge says. "It's only when you hear Christy that you really get it because the man is totally unique."

March 1
Larry does an interview with Gerry Ryan on RTE radio, talking about motorcycle safety. Larry shares a scary story about accidently running a red light last summer after a long recording session and nearly getting hit by a car.
  Later, at the Meteor Irish Music Awards ceremony in Dublin, Larry presents a lifetime achievement award to Dave Fanning. U2 contribute a video tribute to Fanning, changing the title of the Kinks' song 'David Watts' to 'Dave Fanning' and singing the remade song for him.

March 4
U2 and many other industry heavyweights pay tribute to Paul McGuinness as he receives the Strat Award at the Music Week Awards in London.

March 10
Edge is in New York to record the theme song to the new animated series, *The Batman*.

March 18
Overruling its own previous decision, the Federal Communications Commission announces that Bono's use of the F-word on NBC last year is indecent and profane. The FCC won't fine NBC or Bono, but proposes harsh punishments for future indecencies.

March 25
Rolling Stone includes U2 on its cover as one of its "immortals" of rock, along with The Beatles, Elvis Presley, Bob Dylan and other all-time greats.

March 26
A collection of rare U2 memorabilia – including a reel-to-reel copy of U2's very first recording session – is offered for auction on eBay with an opening bid of $18,000 (USD) and a "Buy It Now" price of $35,000. The collection also includes Bono's handwritten lyrics for one of the three songs ('Shadows And Tall Trees') and typed lyric sheets for the other two two tracks ('Street Missions' and 'The Fool'), along with proof sheets from early photo sessions with all four band members. The auction causes a stir amongst U2 fans online, as they debate whether it's real. Paul McGuiness answers that question in the *Irish Times*: "I've seen it on the site and it's clearly genuine. Someone can buy the tape but they can't release anything from it without the band's permission." McGuinness adds that permission will not be granted to the owner because the tracks are "pretty rough". The auction ends on April 4 with no bids.

March 27
After shopping around the rights to an official book, tentatively titled *In the Name of Love: U2 by U2*, the band finds a buyer. Publishing industry news sources report that the book's rights have been sold to Harper Entertainment UK with an estimated price tag of $3 million. Publication is planned for 2005.

April 3
Bono and Edge appear on the 46664 concert compilaton album. The three-disc set includes each of their performances from the November 29, 2003, concert in South Africa.

April 10
Bono speaks on the phone with writer Michka Assayas for his upcoming book.

April 15
Rolling Stone publishes "Elvis Ate America Before America Ate Him", an essay Bono writes about Elvis Presley. It's part of a special issue of the magazine.

Bono remembers Elvis Presley, April 15

"I was barely conscious when I saw the '68 comeback special, at eight years old – which was probably an advantage. I hadn't the critical faculties to divide the different Elvises into different categories or sort through the contradictions. Pretty much everything I want from guitar, bass and drums was present: a performer annoyed by the distance from his audience; a persona that made a prism of fame's wide-angle lens; a sexuality matched only by a thirst for God's instruction."

April 18

Time magazine lists Bono as one of the 100 Most Influential People in the World in its new issue, dated April 26. Bono appears in the Heroes and Icons segment of the list, alongside the likes of Nelson Mandela and Aung San Suu Kyi. A small image of Bono also appears in the collage on the magazine's cover, making it Bono's third appearance on the cover of *Time*.

April 21

Bono is in Germany to speak during the Awards for Business Excellence Dinner in Berlin, an event put on by the Global Business Coalition on HIV/AIDS. His day begins in private meetings with German AIDS and poverty relief organizations, and then more private meetings with German government officials. He does a news conference with German singer/activist Herbert Gronemeyer and attends a demonstration outside the awards hall at Potsdamer Platz. After the awards ceremony, Bono and Gronemeyer share dinner at Schwarzenraben restaurant in Berlin.

April 28

U2 arrive in Portugal with photographer Anton Corbijn and a video crew to shoot images that are planned for use in promoting the band's new album. Portuguese newspapers report the band's arrival and activities in Lisbon, and publish photos that show Corbijn taking pictures while U2 stand in an empty swimming pool. Newspapers also report that video footage from the visit to Portugal will be used on a DVD that will accompany the upcoming album.

Also today, Bono makes a videotaped appearance at the Dove Awards, the Christian Music industry's Grammy awards. Bono is introduced by Amy Grant, and speaks to the audience about the AIDS situation in Africa and the work of Jars of Clay and other Christian artists. Bono goes on to introduce a Jars of Clay performance: "As a fan, I don't think anyone has had a bigger voice than the activists in Jars of Clay. I've had their version of the song, 'Jesus Blood Never Failed Me Yet' in my car for a year now, and you know what, it never has failed me yet. God Bless You."

April 29

U2 continue to shoot video and still photos in Portugal, using a local beach, shipyards, a nightclub, and other locations.

April 30

U2 leave Portugal after three days of work with Anton Corbijn. The band sign autographs with fans at the airport on their way home.

May 1

Bono and British Prime Minister Tony Blair have lunch at Bono's house in Killiney.

May 6

Edge joins Yoko Ono to launch a

Right: Bono and Herbert Gronemeyer in Berlin, April 21.

new art exhibit called *In the time of shaking* at the Irish Museum of Modern Art. The exhibit is a fund raiser for Amnesty International. Later, Edge brings Yoko to U2's studio to visit with the rest of the band.

Also around this time, well known US pastor Bill Hybels visits U2's studio and hears some new songs. The band ask him to bless them, their families and the upcoming album.

Paul McGuinness speaks at Oxford University's famous Oxford Union annual debate. The topic is "This House believes that Reality TV is killing Real Music." McGuinness is one of three speakers on the "pro" side of the argument and makes the case against programs like *Pop Idol*, *American Idol* and the rest. After the debate, McGuinness tells BBC radio that U2's next album will be released in November, and a tour will start in Miami in March, 2005.

May 8
Bono is in New York City for an appearance at a free concert at the annual Tribeca Film Festival. Africa and AIDS are the main topics of what turns into a fairly lengthy speech to the crowd gathered at New York's Battery Park.

May 10
Bono calls Michka Assayas in the morning to continue their conversations for Assayas' upcoming book. Bono reveals that he and friend Simon Carmody have written a song for Tom Jones called 'Sugar Daddy'.

It's Bono's 44th birthday, and he's in New York with his family. To celebrate, Bono, Ali and daughter Jordan – who's celebrating her 15th birthday today – see the New York premiere of the Hollywood blockbuster *Troy* and attend a party afterward.

May 12
Bono visits Canadian Prime Minister Paul Martin in Ottawa, and praises Martin for doubling Canada's contribution to fight AIDS. They both do an interview with CNN.

May 16
Bono helps launch DATA's newest initiative today outside Independence Hall in Philadelphia. Called "The ONE Campaign", the initiative aims to rally Americans to fight global AIDS and extreme poverty. A crowd of about 4,000 hears music, dance, prayer and speeches by a diverse group of activists, including NBA star Dikembe Mutombo and Grammy-winning Christian musician Michael W. Smith. Near the end of the event, Bono recalls the Zoo TV era by calling Pennsylvania Senator Arlen Specter from the podium, but he only gets through to the Senator's answering machine. "Hello, Senator Specter? This is Bono, and I'm here with a few thousand friends and we need to talk to you." Similar events are held in Nashville, Louisville, Cedar Rapids, Iowa, and Tucson, Arizona. The campaign is not named for U2's song, 'One', but Bono admits, "that'll come in handy."

May 17
A day after launching The ONE Campaign, Bono is the opening speaker for the University of Pennsylvania's graduation ceremony. The prestigious Ivy League school also gives Bono an honorary Doctor of Laws degree. His nearly 30-minute speech is well received by the students and crowd at Franklin Field, the football stadium where U2 played in 1997 during the PopMart Tour. He speaks about the need for action to fight AIDS and poverty in Africa, and tells the graduates, "The world is more malleable than you think, and it's waiting for you to hammer it into shape."

May 18
Bono heads to Washington, DC, where he speaks to the Senate Appropriations Committee about AIDS funding. The hearing is not without incident; several protestors calling for increased availability of generic AIDS medicines disrupt the hearing and are kicked out of the room.

Above: Bono is awarded an honorary degree from the University of Pennsylvania, May 17.

May 21
Universal Music and Interscope Records officials are in Dublin this weekend, and are spotted around town with Bono.

May 23
Bono is on hand at the Monaco Grand Prix in Monte Carlo today as a guest of Irish driver Eddie Jordan. It's the second year in a row Bono attends the race and visits with the Jordan racing team. Edge is also spotted in Monte Carlo.

May 27
Irish media spot U2 at a party in the Temple Bar section of Dublin, and later see Bono and Larry riding in horse-drawn carriages to Lillie's Bordello.

June

Writer Michka Assayas visits Bono this month at home in Killiney, where the two have another conversation for Assayas' upcoming book. Bono plays him a couple of songs from the forthcoming U2 album, including 'Sometimes You Can't Make It On Your Own' and 'City Of Blinding Lights'.

June 1

On his way into a speech to EU ministers in Dublin, Bono denies a recent report that he's organizing a "Live Aid 2" concert to raise money for African AIDS and poverty relief. "It's always there in the background but right now, no," he tells reporters. "Right now we're after billions (of dollars) not millions. A Live Aid 2 would help, but it wouldn't fix the problem."

During the meeting, Bono condemns the continent's leaders for failing to follow through on promises to increase aid to Africa. "There are promises being broken and that's unacceptable," he tells the group. "You can't make promises and not keep them. People have pledged 14 billion dollars to the EU but the EU haven't found a way of spending it. At a time when 6,500 Africans are dying every day of AIDS that's not the Europe I want to be in."

June 9-10

U2 videotapes several live-in-studio performances of new material at Hanover Quay. The videos will be used on a special edition release of their new album later this year.

June 12

Edge sees the Red Hot Chili Peppers gig at Phoenix Park in Dublin.

June 13

Bono is seen smoking a cigarette while hanging out at the Clarence Hotel with members of the Red Hot Chili Peppers. In doing so, Bono is in violation of Ireland's new ban on all public smoking. Hotel staffers are reportedly upset by the incident because they've been warned that smoking in the hotel could lead to being fired. Bono later apologizes:

"It was the wee small hours. I was in the company of people from out of town who didn't know about the ban and for a moment nor did I. I was quickly reminded by the staff and a few friends. I apologised then and I apologise now."

June 14

The Wall Street Journal reports today that Bono has joined a Silicon Valley venture capital fund named, appropriately, Elevation Partners. Bono's title will be managing director, and he'll reportedly help the firm with investments and buyouts of media and entertainment companies.

Also today, *The Casino* premieres on Fox TV in the US The show's theme song is a cover of U2's 'Two Shots Of Happy, One Shot Of Sad', sung by newcomer Matt Dusk.

June 27

Bono sees Alicia Keys perform at the Olympia Theatre in Dublin.

July 3-4

U2 wraps up recording on its new album. One of the final songs they record is 'Fast Cars', which includes the lyric that will give the album its title: *How To Dismantle An Atomic Bomb*.

Also this weekend, a 53-second clip of the new song, 'All Because Of You', is posted online. The clip is of fairly low quality, and sounds like it was recorded outside the band's Dublin studios. Online fans aren't bothered by the quality, and most like what they hear.

July 8

Variety reports that Bono and Edge will write the score for an upcoming Broadway musical production of Spider-Man.

July 13

The band is in Nice, France, for a variety of business today. One is a meeting with Willie Williams to begin discussing general staging concepts for U2's next tour.

Willie Williams discusses early ideas for the Vertigo Tour

"We started with an end

Bono: "I don't want to be a casualty" June 14

"I want U2 to be a part of the future, and a part in shaping the future. This opportunity with Elevation Partners is for me a chance to involve myself in the business that runs my life. I don't want to be a casualty."

Below: Bono at the launch of The One Campaign, Philadelphia, May 16.

stage – with no B-stage, no frills, and then looked at center stages, round stages, modular stages, pod stages, trucks that drove on to the pitch, spherical stages that opened up, and everything you could imagine. I wanted them to grasp that the placement of a stage isn't necessarily an aesthetic choice. Edge initially wanted to contain the energy to a single end stage, which was really interesting for me. I also showed an idea to Bono which was a bomb that would just sit there throughout the show in the middle of the arena, completely unexplained, and people could graffiti on it. Then maybe it would have open up and become a B stage. Obviously it's a metaphor for the fact that we're on the brink of destruction, and no one seems to be particularly fussed about it.

"Bono really liked it but Edge didn't get it at all and said, dead seriously, 'So are you telling me that you think the album title refers to an actual atomic bomb?' And there was a pregnant pause. I realised, very crucially, that the album title is entirely metaphorical, because actually, all the songs are about relationships. The bomb could be Bono's relationship with his dad, or it could be a dysfunctional marriage, or any of the atomic bombs that we have to deal with in our personal lives.

"Understanding this was a real turning point for me and it sowed the seeds for them realising that using the title literally or changing the shape of the stage just for the sake of it would be shooting themselves in the foot."

There's also a photo shoot at the Victorine studios, where a CD containing songs from the upcoming album goes missing. French authorities launch an immediate investigation by interviewing about 20 people who were at the photo shoot, but no one is sure if the CD is lost or was stolen. Edge tells U2.com: "A large slice of two years' work lifted via a piece of round plastic. It doesn't seem credible but that's what's just happened to us... and it was my CD."

Paul McGuinness voices his concern that the songs may reach the Internet: "The recording of this album has been going so well. The band is so excited about its release. It would be a shame if unfinished work fell into the wrong hands." The album isn't due for release for more than four months, although there's speculation that timetable will change if the songs are leaked online.

July 25
As the Democratic Party National Convention begins in Boston, Bono writes an op-ed piece for today's *Boston Globe* newspaper. He promises to attend both party conventions (the Republican convention is a month away) to make sure the AIDS crisis in Africa

Above: Bono and Ali at the Democratic National Convention, July 27.

is on the agenda for both parties. He writes that he plans to listen and to talk: "Because when I last looked I couldn't find the biggest global challenge, AIDS and the extreme poverty in which it thrives, on the schedules."

July 27
With the Democratic Party National Convention underway, Bono makes several appearances in and around Boston today. His day begins with a rally to speak out in support of AIDS relief at the Boston launch of the ONE Campaign, where Bono says he's a fan of America. "That is the kind of America I love – face out. It is concerned about what is going on in the rest of the world, and not just about its interests." Bono later appears on the floor of the Democratic Convention with Ali, where he mingles with other convention attendees and does a live interview with CNN's Anderson Cooper. His evening ends at a tribute for Senator Ted Kennedy, where Bono sings 'Pride (In The Name of Love)' with the Boston Pops orchestra providing support. Bono changes several key lyrics to personalize them for Kennedy, most notably the refrain about Martin Luther King, Jr., instead making references to John F. Kennedy, Robert Kennedy and John F. Kennedy Jr. He also sings 'The Hands That Built America' with backing from Yo-Yo Ma and the Boston Pops. As he walks backstage, Bono says, "It's a long way from CBGB's" – a reference to the legendary small club in New York (which U2 actually never played).

After the event, Bono, Ali, Paul McGuinness and others hang out at the Fairmont Hotel. While there, Lisa Robinson interviews Bono.

August
In France this month, Bono and Michka Assayas get together to review the manuscript of Assayas' book and have one final conversation. Bono has U2's new album playing loudly inside his villa, and the two are fully aware that fans outside are hearing

everything – they hear the fans' applause in between each track.

Also around this time, U2 meets in France with directors Alex Courtes and Martin Fougerole. They listen to 'Vertigo', and the band asks Martin and Alex to come up with ideas for a music video. They return a few days later with an original treatment whose storyline includes two monsters – one representing good; the other, evil – that will battle as the band performs "somewhere in the middle of the desert."

August 2
Bono attends and sings two songs at the funeral of Susan Buffett in Omaha, Nebraska: 'Forever Young' and 'All I Want Is You'. Susan is the wife of well-known investor Warren Buffett. Bono knows them from past participation in economic conferences and meetings, and Susan Buffett was also a champion of AIDS awareness and prevention causes, much like Bono. Their daughter, also named Susan, is a DATA board member.

August 17
For the second time this summer, a portion of what's thought to be one of U2's new tracks is made available by fans online. This time it's a 90-second clip of 'Vertigo'. This track has been recorded by fans outside Bono's house in the south of France, and the voices of those fans are the most prominent sound heard. But just like the 'All Because Of You' clip in early July, online fans are generally pleased with what they hear in the new clip.

August 28
Madonna's first concert in Ireland is at the historic Slane Festival. Media reports about the show say that "members of U2" are in attendance.

September
Photographer Kevin Davies does a shoot this month in the south of France with the whole band. Several of the photos appear in a November feature in the *Sunday Times Magazine*.

September 1

As he promised to do a month ago, Bono attends the Republican National Convention in New York. He appears on Fox News Channel's popular *The O'Reilly Factor* program, sitting down for a lengthy interview with Bill O'Reilly about politics, the AIDS crisis in Africa and related issues. Bono tells O'Reilly – who's noted for his confrontational style – that he's not "rooting" for either US presidential candidate, and says "America is taking the lead" in funding aid programmes for Africa. Before the end of the interview, O'Reilly compliments Bono for his work: "You're certainly doing God's work. I mean, I admire you very much for what you're doing. We need people like you to command a worldwide audience and to get people at least thinking about this. And then we need the politicians out here in the convention, in both conventions to come up with a strategy. I do agree that if America could take the lead, it would turn public opinion around and help us in the war on terror." After the interview, Bono tells reporters that he thought the interview went well. "I asked [O'Reilly] to take the gloves off, if he ever had them on."

September 2

U2 Show by Diana Scrimgeour is released. It's the first official book about U2's touring history.

September 4

The Edge takes the stage with Paul McCartney at a fund raiser for the children's charity Barretstown in Co. Kildare, Ireland. They perform Buddy Holly's 'Peggy Sue', and McCartney's guitar is later auctioned to the highest bidder.

September 13

Thought it's already been widely rumored and reported on the Internet, U2 confirms that the upcoming album will be called *How To Dismantle An Atomic Bomb*.

September 14-15

U2 is in Spain for a two-day shoot for the 'Vertigo' music video with directors Alex and Martin. The

Bono's challenge to the Labour Party, September 29

"There's no way we can look at Africa – a continent bursting into flames – and if we're honest conclude that it would ever be allowed to happen anywhere else. Certainly not here. In Europe. Or America. Or Australia, or Canada. There's just no chance."

shoot takes place in a desert-like area of Spain's eastern coast called "Punta del Fangar (Delta de L'Ebre)." The band does about 40 playbacks of the tune in high winds and occasional rain.

September 17

U2 begins an official countdown toward the release of *How To Dismantle An Atomic Bomb* with the launch of two web sites – htdaab.com and howtodismantle anatomicbomb.com. Both sites show the same thing: a real-time, red LED timer counting down the days, hours, minutes, and seconds until November 22, the album's release date.

September 18-19

U2 does two days of shooting for a new 'Vertigo' video, but this one won't premiere on MTV. It's for Apple Computer's iTunes Music Store and iPod digital music player. The video is edited to match the look and feel of previous iPod/iTunes commercials – the band appears in black silhouette against a variety of brightly colored backgrounds. The video is shot at a West London soundstage, and is directed by Mark Romanek.

September 23

Bono picks up the Pablo Neruda

Medal of Honour from Alberto Yoacham, the Chilean Ambassador to Ireland, at a ceremony at the Chilean embassy in Dublin. The award is presented to the 100 most outstanding figures in public life for their contribution to arts and culture all over the world.

Dave Fanning does his traditional "official" world premiere of U2's new single, playing 'Vertigo' on Ireland's 2FM radio. Four U2 fans around the world are invited on-air to provide instant reviews of the song, and the comments are, as expected, very favourable.

September 24

A 7-inch vinyl single of 'Vertigo' is released in limited quantities in the US. It'll be more widely available when the single is released worldwide in early November.

September 27

Hot Press confirms that U2 are planning at least two concerts next June at Croke Park.

September 28

Nancy Sinatra's self-titled album is released in the US, and includes an appearance by Adam and Larry on her cover of U2's 'Two Shots Of Happy, One Shot Of Sad'. The album will be released October 4 in the UK.

September 29

Bono speaks today at the Labour Party Conference in Brighton, England. He praises Labour party leaders Tony Blair and Gordon Brown for their efforts to help Africa deal with the ongoing AIDS crisis, but tells the party to "get real" and finish what they started.

October

Bono visits writer Richard Curtis at his home in the Notting Hill area of London to discuss the upcoming launch of the Make Poverty History campaign. They both agree that the G8 Summit next July in Scotland – which will be led by British Prime Minister Tony Blair, a known supporter of anti-poverty efforts – will offer an unprecedented opportunity for change. Believing that only an enormous show of public support will create such change, Bono suggests a Live Aid-style concert. Curtis reminds Bono that Bob Geldof is against the idea, and instead proposes an "Intellectual Live8" debate about the issues.

October 2
Edge attends a Dublin screening of *Chernobyl Heart*, a film that documents the effects of the 1986 nuclear accident at the Chernobyl nuclear power plant in Ukraine.

October 3
Bono attends a birthday party in Paris for Jean Roch, founder of the VIP Room nightclubs in St. Tropez and other locations.

October 4
U2 attends the annual Q Awards in London. U2 doesn't win for Best Act in the World Today, but the magazine gives them a special Q Icon Award, instead. Bono sings his presentation of the Merit Award to Shane MacGowan of The Pogues. During a photo session, MacGowan puts his arm around Bono while holding a cigarette, and almost sets Bono's hair on fire.

October 12
Apple Computer premieres two versions of a new commercial promoting its iTunes Music Store and iPod digital music player that feature U2 performing 'Vertigo'. A 30-second spot gets instant exposure during TV broadcasts of the baseball playoffs and other programmes in the US. A two-minute version of the commercial is also made available for viewing at the iTunes Music Store. The commercials spark an instant debate among U2 fans about the band's ties to Apple, with some suggesting U2 has sold out. Media even pick up on the discussion, and U2 eventually announces they received no money for appearing in the TV spots.

October 15
BBC Television, London. U2 record a handful of tracks live for the BBC's *Top Of The Pops*. They perform in the rain on a stage outside the BBC studio building. 'Vertigo' is the only track that airs live, and only Bono's vocals are actually performed live (because of BBC timing requirements). The band also tapes a performance of other songs in the BBC studio for future airing on *Top Of The Pops*.

October 16
Riverside Studios, London. U2 are about three hours late for a four-song taping for the British music show, *CD:UK*. The live performances will air separately in future weeks and months to support U2's single releases, but today's *CD:UK* programme includes a Cat Deeley interview with U2 taped recently in France. After today's taping, U2 invites the US band Kings Of Leon – another *CD:UK* guest – to their dressing room where everyone has a few drinks and gets to know each other. A few weeks later, U2 invite the band to be their opening act for next year's Vertigo Tour.

October 18
Bono receives the 2004 Freedom Award in a ceremony at the National Civil Rights Museum in Memphis. The day begins with a public forum where Bono and US Representative John Lewis speak with hundreds of students. "We've got a whole lot of marching to do," Bono says. "This is the generation. This is the time. Memphis, I believe in you." Later, Bono and Lewis tour the Lorraine Motel, which is attached to the museum and is the site of Dr. Martin Luther King's assassination in 1968. It was then on to a press conference before the day concludes with the banquet and awards ceremony.

October 19
The Neville Brothers release *Walkin' In The Shadow Of Life*, which includes the track 'Kingdom Come' – a song Bono wrote for them in 1989.

Bono is named as one of the winners of the inaugural TED prizes, an award given by the Technology, Entertainment, and Design community. Bono will receive his prize in February.

October 20
Bono speaks at the World Affairs Council's International Speaker Series at the Rose Garden in Portland. The main topics are AIDS, debt and Third World poverty, but Bono begins his speech by telling the crowd of more than 4,000 that earlier in the day two females returned to him the contents of a briefcase that went missing when U2 first played Portland in 1981 (see March 1981). Bono doesn't get the actual briefcase back, but the girls do return numerous personal items such as photos, letters to and from Ali, a passport, and – perhaps most importantly in terms of the band – his unfinished lyrics for the *October* album. During the speech, Bono says what the girls did was "an act of grace", and adds, "You will never know how much that means to me."

Although the story told over the years is that two girls had stolen Bono's belongings, the truth is that they'd been stored by a local crew member who found them after the March 22, 1981, show. The crew member sold his house, but left Bono's belongings in the attic where the new owners – Dave and Cindy Harris – discovered them and shared them in 2003 with U2 fan Danielle Rheaume. Rheaume and Harris returned the material to Bono before tonight's speech, a meeting that was helped along by the U2 fan site U2log.com.

October 21
The day after a speaking engagement in Portland, Bono is in Seattle where his itinerary includes a meeting with Howard Schultz, the chairman of Starbucks.

Bono appears via pre-recorded video at the start of the 2004 Latin American MTV Awards, which are taped tonight in Miami.

October 24
A blog that covers news from Silicon Valley reports today that computer chipmaker Intel will pay $20 million to sponsor U2's upcoming world tour. No other news outlets pick up on the story, and it never becomes reality.

Edge explains U2's relationship with Apple, October 26

"Our position on sponsorship hasn't changed, it's always been that we do not sell our reputation or our fans' regard for our work to anybody. But this is a different thing; this is a technology partnership. We're selling U2 branded iPods – the U2 iPod. And we're selling our music on iTunes. We just get a share of the revenues earned by these two releases. That's it, plain and simple. We're also in an iTunes ad, because iTunes as a music distribution system is promoting our music. It's really simple."

Above: The U2 iPod.

October 26
California Theatre, San Jose. Bono and Edge join Apple Computer chairman Steve Jobs to introduce two new results of the U2-Apple partnership. The first is what Jobs calls a historical moment in music: the introduction of the first "digital box set". Called *The Complete U2*, it's a collection of more than 400 U2 songs that will be sold exclusively on Apple's iTunes Music Store at a cost of $149. The second announcement is the creation of a U2-themed iPod, the first time

Apple has produced a branded version of its super-popular digital music player. The unit is colored black with a red Click Wheel to match the branding of U2's upcoming album, *How To Dismantle An Atomic Bomb*. The signatures of each band member are engraved on the back. The unit has 20GB of storage and comes with an exclusive U2 poster. It's priced at $349 and will be available to ship in November. Bono and Edge speak during the event, and also perform two new songs: 'Original Of The Species' and 'All Because Of You'. Bono, Edge and Jobs also appear live on CNBC-TV after the event where they're interviewed about today's announcements.

October 28
Bono attends an Eminem concert in New York City.

October 29
'Vertigo' reaches the top spot on *Billboard*'s Modern Rock Tracks chart. It's the band's first Modern Rock number one since 'Staring At The Sun' did it in 1997, and the band's eighth overall Modern Rock number one.

October 31
A British tabloid reports that Adam recently spent a week taking cooking classes with celebrity chef Jamie Oliver.

November
Bono is one of several entertainers to appear in a series of posters promoting the Make Trade Fair movement. Bono is photographed with sugar being poured on his head and piling up around him.

November 6
All 11 songs from U2's upcoming album, *How To Dismantle An Atomic Bomb*, are leaked online more than two weeks before the November 22 release date. U2 gives thought to releasing the album sooner, but decides to leave it alone.

November 8/9
'Vertigo' is released commercially in multiple formats with extra tracks including 'Are You Gonna Wait Forever?', 'Neon Lights', and six remixes of the main track. The single hits number one in Ireland, Italy, the UK, and several other countries.

November 10
Rather than move up the release of its new album, U2 and Interscope Records come up with a different plan to fight back against the illegal sharing of *How To Dismantle An Atomic Bomb*: They invite radio stations to play the album in its entirety. Many stations jump at the opportunity, including Chicago's WXRT-FM, which plays the album non-stop for 12 hours.

In London, the Adam Clayton Collection of Carpets sells at a Christie's auction for £82,000.

November 11
U2 is inducted as one of the original five members of the new UK Music Hall of Fame at a London ceremony. Bono, however, tells reporters that he's not thrilled by the honor.

Bono: "We don't want to be in any Hall of Fame"
"I really didn't want to come. Only respect for the

people who were running the show has me here. I hate the idea of being in the UK Hall of Fame to be honest with you ... We don't want to be in any Hall of Fame until we're retired or dead."

November 14

'Vertigo' enters the UK singles chart at number one this week, knocking Eminem's 'Just Lose It' out of the top spot.

Under the watchful eyes of Bob Geldof and Midge Ure, some of today's hottest British artists re-record 'Do They Know It's Christmas?' Justin Hawkins of The Darkness sings Bono's line from the original version. Tabloids report that Principle Management demands Bono sing the line. Bono will reportedly re-sing the line in the coming days, and if it doesn't work, they'll re-use his vocal from 1984.

November 16

Hanover Quay Studio, Dublin. U2 play a five-song set that airs live on BBC Radio 1. Bono introduces 'Miracle Drug' by telling the story of a former Mount Temple student named Christopher Nolan who overcame cerebral palsy, used medical and scientific advancements to be able to write, and is now a published poet and novelist. A small crowd of about 20 fans is in the room after winning tickets from Radio 1.

November 18

Clinton Presidential Center and Library, Little Rock. Bono and Edge perform at the dedication of the Clinton Presidential Center and Library. It's the first time U2 (or half of U2) have performed in Arkansas. They begin with a cover of The Beatles' 'Rain', since they're performing under a steady rainfall. Bono changes the lyrics to fit the occasion in both 'Rain' and 'Sunday, Bloody Sunday'. They finish with 'The Hands That Built America'.

November 20

NBC Studios, New York. U2 makes

Above: U2 perform under New York's Brooklyn Bridge, November 22.
Right: Shooting the 'All Because Of You' video, November 22.

its second appearance on the long-running NBC variety show *Saturday Night Live*. Bono is late for the afternoon soundcheck, but the rest of the band rehearses without him. Enthralled, the *Saturday Night Live* crew stops what they're doing to listen and applauds at the end. Unlike most acts that perform on SNL, U2 are allowed to do three full songs (rather than the usual two) and the end credits of the show roll as the band does 'I Will Follow'. They go on to play 'All Because of You' and an encore of 'Vertigo' after the broadcast ends. Also today, *Rolling Stone*'s David Fricke interviews the band for an upcoming feature.

November 22/23

U2 releases its 11th studio album and 14th overall, *How To Dismantle An Atomic Bomb*. Some countries, including Ireland, have actually had the album on store shelves for four days now. The album is released in four formats: a single CD, a CD with bonus DVD, a box set with an additional hardbound book, and vinyl. The album cover is an Anton Corbijn black-and-white photo, but is set inside a frame similarly to the two *Best Of* album covers. The red, white, and black color scheme harkens back to U2's earliest days.

After a long and difficult recording process, eight different producers are credited in the liner notes. The album sounds like a natural follow-up to *All That You Can't Leave Behind*, a very band-based record with little of the effects and experimentation that characterized U2 in the 1990s. Though the title sounds political, and there are a few tracks that capture what's happening in the world at this moment, Bono reveals that the "bomb" referred to in the title is actually his father, Bob.

The album reaches number one in 30 countries, and draws mostly rave reviews from critics. In the *Boston Globe*, Steve Morse calls it a "great album". USA Today's Edna Gundersen gushes, "*Atomic Bomb* is U2's best album, eclipsing not only *Achtung Baby* and *The Joshua Tree*, but a good many 20th-century holy grails and prematurely anointed classics of the new millennium."

Russell Baillie writes in the New *Zealand Herald*, "*Atomic Bomb* goes from being just another think-big U2 album to something great –it's got a bruised soul and musical grit beneath all the grandeur and global vision." Far from those critics is John Waters, author of the U2 tome *Race Of Angels*, who reviews the album for *The Guardian*: "*How To Dismantle An Atomic Bomb* is ... a nondescript collection by a band nearly two decades at the top and desperate not to slip.... They are prisoners of success. They know whom they have to beat now, and how to do it. But they have lost the collective recklessness that made them great."

Tracks: 'Vertigo', 'Miracle Drug', 'Sometimes You Can't Make It On Your Own', 'Love And Peace Or Else', 'City Of Blinding Lights', 'All Because Of You', 'A Man And A Woman', 'Crumbs From Your Table', 'One Step Closer', 'Original Of The Species', 'Yahweh'. 'Fast Cars' is a bonus track in some regions and appears on the box set.

Also released today is *The Complete U2*, a digital box set available only via Apple's iTunes Music Store.

Empire Fulton Ferry State Park, New York. To promote the album, U2 takes to the streets of New York, shooting a video for 'All Because Of You', which is slated to be the second US single from *How To Dismantle An Atomic Bomb*. The video shoot is directed by Phil Joanou, and sees U2 performing the song repeatedly on the back of a flatbed truck as it drives through the streets of the Big Apple. Thousands of fans chase the truck as far as they can through the city, some bringing the band food and drinks. U2 invite a fan onboard to play drums as they perform 'I Will Follow'. In between takes of 'All Because Of You', U2 do a rendition of 'Santa Claus Is Coming Town Town.' Although U2's video shoot is against the law, New York authorities let the band off the hook as a way of saying thanks for the shows U2 did in New York right after 9/11.

While all of this is happening, word is spreading online and on

Edge on the personal themes of *Atomic Bomb*, November 22/23

"When we make a record, it's not a contrived process. It's not like we sit down and say, 'We're going to write about this.' I don't think any of us thought, 'Let's make it a political record.' But we certainly thought that was going to be part of it. I am a little bit surprised that it's so personal. I was expecting it to be a little more political, but it hasn't gone that way."

New York radio that U2 is planning a free concert later in a park near the Brooklyn Bridge. By the time the gig is officially announced in the afternoon, thousands of fans have already scoped out the location and are waiting to be let in. With the New York skyline as its backdrop, U2 plays a nearly hour-long free concert featuring several songs from the new album. The concert is taped for later showing on MTV.

November 23
Bono does an interview in his Manhattan apartment with David Fricke of *Rolling Stone*.

November 26
How To Dismantle An Atomic Bomb is certified Platinum by the BPI, with sales of more than 300,000 in the UK.

U2 fans around the world begin receiving letters in their mailboxes announcing the formal end of *Propaganda*, the band's nearly 20-year-old fan club. In its place will be a membership option at the official web site, U2.com. The letter includes a temporary membership card with a unique ID number on the back; use of that ID number will give *Propaganda* members a $20 discount off the $40 yearly membership fee.

November 29
Bono sings a line on the new

iTunes. It includes four tracks that were recorded just a couple weeks ago in New York: 'All Because Of You', 'Sometimes You Can't Make It On Your Own', 'I Will Follow', and 'Vertigo'.

December 13

U2 shoot the video for 'Sometimes You Can't Make It On Your Own' at the Gaiety Theatre in Dublin.

U2 are set to announce their world tour and put tickets on sale over the Christmas holiday, but Edge gets news today that his daughter, Sian, is seriously ill. Their plans are put on hold while Edge and Morleigh take care of their daughter. The band decides to keep the news quiet as long as they can.

December 14

An early photo of U2 taken by Anton Corbijn sells tonight at a Dublin auction for $12,000 (EU).

December 17

How To Dismantle An Atomic Bomb is certified Multi-Platinum, with US sales of more than three million.

December 26

An earthquake with a magnitude estimated between 9.1 and 9.3 strikes the Indian Ocean off the coast of Indonesia, causing tsunamis that kill more than 200,000 people in 11 countries. Rumours circulate quickly that Adam is in southern Asia. Two days later, *The Belfast Telegraph* confirms those rumours, but the paper says he's not in the affected areas and is safe. A source tells the *Telegraph* that Clayton was on vacation in Thailand when the disaster happened. "He is enjoying a break before the new tour gets under way but has not been close to the affected areas and hasn't been in any danger at any time."

December 28

Bono is the guest producer today on BBC Radio Four's *Today* news show. Poverty is the theme of Bono's news coverage, which includes interviews with UK Chancellor Gordon Brown and former President Bill Clinton.

version of 'Do They Know It's Christmas?', which features some of today's biggest UK music stars.

December 1

How To Dismantle An Atomic Bomb debuts at number one on the US album charts. It's U2's sixth number one album in the US, and with first-week sales of nearly 840,000 units, it nearly doubles the first-week sales of *All That You Can't Leave Behind*.

Edge, Adam and Bono appear at the opening night of Guggi's first London exhibition.

December 2

BBC Television, London. U2 make their first appearance on the BBC's *Friday Night with Jonathan Ross* programme. They show is taped for airing tomorrow. U2 performs four songs (counting two versions of 'Vertigo') and are interviewed during the programme.

December 3

How To Dismantle An Atomic Bomb goes Double Platinum in the UK, with sales surpassing the 600,000 mark.

December 4

How To Dismantle An Atomic Bomb begins a three-week run at number one on the UK album chart.

December 7

'Vertigo' earns three Grammy nominations today: Best Rock Performance By A Duo Or Group With Vocal, Best Rock Song (songwriters award), and Best Short Form Music Video. The awards are scheduled for mid-February in Los Angeles.

December 9

U2 release the *Live From Under The Brooklyn Bridge* EP exclusively on

Above and below: The free concert in New York, November 22.

As the year starts, U2 fans are anxious to learn the band's plans to tour. Rumours are already spreading about an opening date in early March in Los Angeles. But less than a week into the year, *Rolling Stone* delivers news that stuns fans worldwide: U2 has postponed its tour due to a "family illness".

After a difficult internal debate, U2 decide to go ahead with the tour, but ticket sales are a mess. 25 years after its first album, U2 is a bigger draw than ever, and no one's happy with either the fan club or traditional ticket sales. By the time the tour begins, all that is forgotten and U2 plays some of the best shows of their career with an unashamed mix of music and message that fans haven't seen since *The Joshua Tree* tour, or perhaps the Amnesty International Conspiracy of Hope tour.

Away from the stage, U2 continue to collect awards – including three more Grammys – and earn a home in the Rock and Roll Hall of Fame. Bono's humanitarian efforts continue during the year, leading ultimately to his selection as one of *Time* magazine's Persons of the Year. Edge joins him on the front lines of charity work, forming a movement called Music Rising in the aftermath of Hurricane Katrina.

On the business side, Harry Crosbie sells his stake in the Clarence Hotel to Derek Quinlan and Paddy McKillen. The pair holds a 50% stake in the hotel, with Bono and Edge holding the other half.

As the year ends, fans in Australia, South America, and Mexico celebrate the news that the Vertigo Tour is coming their way in 2006.

January 4
U2's new video for 'All Because Of You' – shot six weeks ago on the streets of New York – makes its world premiere tonight on ABC-TV when an edited version of the video airs at halftime of the Orange Bowl, college football's championship game. The full version airs later in the evening on ESPN's *Sportscenter* programmme. In both cases, the clip has highlights from the football game edited into it. The full video without football highlights is made available for viewing on ESPN.com.

January 5
Rolling Stone magazine reports on its web site that U2 has postponed its upcoming tour due to a "family illness". The magazine reports that the tour was due to be announced and tickets would go on sale later this month, but those plans are also delayed. As the news spreads online, fans use mailing lists and message boards to post messages of prayers and support for Edge and his family, though they don't specifically know what's going on.

January 6
U2.com posts an update to U2's tour plans with a quote from Paul McGuinness saying, "The routing is still being worked on". The news item is online briefly before being removed.

Below: Edge, his younger self, and Bono at an Anton Corbijn photo exhibit, October 9.

January 7
Hot Press confirms what several Irish newspapers reported today: U2's tour has been delayed because a member of Edge's family is ill. Attorneys representing Edge contact a number of media outlets to ask they respect the family's privacy and not report any additional details.

How To Dismantle An Atomic Bomb is certified Multi-Platinum by the BPI, with UK sales surpassing the 900,000 mark.

January 8
Edge's attorneys contact *The Sunday World* – which was not contacted yesterday – just as the paper is going to press with a story detailing who in Edge's family is ill and with what condition. The paper

refuses to withdraw its article, which appears in tomorrow's paper with a pixelated image of the family member.

January 9
A Dublin judge issues an injunction against *The Sunday World* after today's article revealing details about the member of Edge's family who is ill.

U2 is not in attendance as the band is named Favourite Group at the People's Choice Awards in Los Angeles.

January 12
Bono is the guest speaker tonight at a meeting in Rotterdam of top officials from the Dutch postal group, TPG. Bono, who has praised the company in the past for its work with the World Food Bank, speaks about African famine relief.

January 16
U2 scores big in the 2004 *Rolling Stone* magazine readers' poll, taking the number one spot for Best Single ('Vertigo'), Best Album (*How To Dismantle An Atomic Bomb*), Artist of the Year, Best Band, and Best Video ('Vertigo'). They don't do quite so well in the critics' poll, with 'Vertigo' ranking seventh for Best Single and *Bomb* seventh for Best Album.

January 18
Bono and Ali attend the opening of *Uncertain Sins*, a new exhibition by Charlie Whisker at the Solomon Gallery in Dublin.

January 22
Bono is honoured with a Special Achievement Award at tonight's NRJ Awards in France. As he accepts the award from presenter Naomi Campbell, Bono tells the audience (in French), "I'm not from this country, but I'll make a little confession to you. It's at the Côte d'Azur I feel at home." U2 had been expected to perform, but Bono tells reporters one of his band mates is attending to a sick child. After the awards show, Bono attends an aftershow party where Alicia Keys, Usher, and Prince Albert of Monaco are also on the guest list.

January 24
U2 announce details of their Vertigo 2005 world tour, which will begin March 28 at the Sports Arena in San Diego. The first leg of the tour, delayed nearly a month from the planned March 1 start date, will visit only 13 cities in North American before crossing the Atlantic for European shows this summer.

Edge explains the behind-the-scenes decision to tour
U2 remained understandably tight-lipped about what was happening at home as Edge and Morleigh cared for Sian, and the band struggled to determine if it would be able to tour at all in 2005. The band finally revealed what was happening in this period in 2006 in its own book, U2 by U2, though no details about Sian's illness were shared.
"A new tour schedule was drawn up, built around Sian's needs, and in a strange way I think it honoured her. It was as if we were saying, 'We're not going to lie down and just roll over, we're going to meet this head on and continue with our lives and make it work for everybody.' But it was a very tough decision for me to make and in the end it was Sian who gave me the strength to go ahead with the tour."

Fans have no idea why the announcement and tour is delayed, but they're excited and ready to begin buying tickets so quickly. General ticket sales will begin January 29. U2.com members will be able to purchase tickets beginning tomorrow.

January 25
The online presale of Vertigo Tour tickets for paid U2.com members is a flop. Tens of thousands of fans try to buy tickets, but websites crash and ticketing systems fail, leaving most fans unable to even get a chance at buying tickets. The few U2.com members who are able to get past technical problems find that what were marketed as "some of the best seats in the house" are most commonly tickets in the upper levels of arenas, or far away seats at stadiums. Making matters worse is that thousands of General Admission tickets – the actual "best seats in the house" – are immediately listed for sale on auction and ticket broker web sites.

Almost immediately, Internet mailing lists and message boards are filled with postings from angry fans. U2.com has sold memberships with a promise of "guaranteed priority booking" of concert tickets, and has told members of the now-defunct Propaganda offline fan club that they'd "go to the front of the line" during today's presale. U2.com remains largely mum on the issue, at first brushing off the problems as the result of incredible demand for U2 tickets. The uproar continues for about a week, as U2 fan websites continue to report on all the developments and push for the band to rectify the situation.

January 27
Bono attends the World Economic Forum in Davos, Switzerland. He takes part in the "G8 and Africa" panel discussion with former US President Bill Clinton, Bill Gates, Thabo Mbeki, President of South Africa, Britain's Prime Minister Tony Blair and Nigerian President Olusegun Obasanjo.

January 28
U2.com issues an apology for the bungled ticket pre-sale earlier this week, blaming "new technology" for the problems and saying they'll try to identify scalpers who are selling fan club tickets at prices often exceeding $1,000.

February 3
As the Vertigo Tour presale problems continue to be reported by worldwide media, Larry Mullen

awards, Bono joins an all-star chorus to sing The Beatles' 'Across The Universe' as a fund raiser for victims of the Asian tsunami in late December.

Although the song won't be available in stores for one more day, 'Sometimes You Can't Make It On Your Own' debuts at number one today on the UK singles chart, barely edging Elvis Presley's 'Wooden Heart'. It's U2's sixth number one single in the UK.

February 14

'Sometimes You Can't Make It On Your Own' is released worldwide, except in North America (where 'All Because Of You' was just released instead). The single comes in multiple formats with additional tracks 'Fast Cars (Jacknife Lee Mix)', 'Ave Maria (Jacknife Lee Mix)', 'Vertigo (Redanka Remix)', and 'Vertigo (Trent Reznor Remix)'.

February 16

U2 begins ten days of tour rehearsals at the Fox Baja Studios in Rosarito, Mexico.

February 24

Bono is honoured as one of three recipients of the TED prize, so named by the Technology, Entertainment and Design conference that created it. The conference brings together many of the world's "movers and shakers" in these industries. Bono's prize includes an opportunity to make three wishes, and $100,000 from TED to help grant those wishes. His wishes are all aimed at furthering the plight of the African continent. He asks TED to
1) help build a social movement of more than one million American activists for Africa,
2) tell people one billion times about ONE, with as much of this as possible before the G8 Africa Summit in July 2005, and
3) connect every hospital, health clinic, and school in one African country, Ethiopia, to the Internet. Bono accepts the award via video hookup from an undisclosed location outside the US (likely Mexico). The members of TED are able to grant Bono's first two

---

Jr. speaks out on U2.com, offering an apology – and some choice words – for U2 fans. In the "open letter," Larry says he is speaking on behalf of the band: "There was a mess up in the way the tickets were distributed through U2.com for the Vertigo pre-sale. Some of it was beyond our control, but some of it wasn't." He goes on to promise that he will personally be involved in finding a solution to avoid similar problems when U2 returns to North America in the fall, saying that former Propaganda members will have priority when tickets are sold. Larry's letter ends with a verbal jab at U2 fans: "By the way, a note to those so-called U2 fans who are quick to accuse U2 of unseemly behaviour, I've only got two words for you..."

February 4

U2 set records today when two shows at Croke Park in Dublin sell out in less than an hour. Concert promoters MCD say about 160,000 tickets are sold in only 50 minutes.

February 8

'All Because Of You' is released in North America. The commercial CD sold in Canada includes one additional track, 'Fast Cars (Jacknife Lee Mix)', and reaches number one in the charts.

February 13

Staples Center, Los Angeles. 'Vertigo' sweeps all three categories in which it is nominated at tonight's Grammy Awards: Best Rock Performance By a Duo or Group With Vocal; Best Rock Song (songwriters award); and Best Short Form Music Video. With 17 Grammy Awards, U2 is now tied for eighth on the all-time list of Grammy winners. Only one of the awards is given during the TV broadcast, and U2 makes the most of the brief time allowed for acceptance speeches. Edge speaks first, holding up his Grammy and dedicating the award to his daughter, Sian. After Bono says he's "genuinely surprised" by the award, Larry talks about the uncertainty that U2 would be able to perform tonight, and the uncertainty they'd be able to tour at all this year. He also apologises for the recent ticket sales problem. U2 perform 'Sometimes You Can't Make It On Your Own', and near the end of the

Above: U2 at the Grammy Awards, February 13.

wishes, but not the third. Political instability and poor tele-communications infrastructure in Ethiopia make it impossible.

February 25

In an editorial today, *The Los Angeles Times* suggests Bono "should be named the next president of the World Bank". The paper cites Bono's familiarity and concern for the issues that affect the world's poorest nations.

March

Bono and Richard Curtis continue to plead with Bob Geldof to sanction another Live Aid-style concert to coincide with this summer's G8 Summit in Scotland. Geldof tells them it won't happen. Bono, though, starts to change Geldof's mind during one phone call when he suggests that U2 and Paul McCartney start the concert with a rendition of 'Sgt. Pepper's Lonely Hearts Club Band'.

Bono travels to Acapulco this month where he visits with the well-known Camil family. Actor Jaime Camil tells Bono about U2's role in a Mexican film called *7 Dias*, and shows him the movie. *7 Dias* tells the story of a man who tries to bring a U2 concert to Monterrey, Mexico, within a seven-day, mob-enforced deadline. Bono promptly calls director Fernando Kalife to compliment him on the film. Larry sees the film a couple weeks later and agrees to let Kalife use a live version of 'Miracle Drug' and other U2 concert footage for free.

March 6

U2 surprises many fans with their announcement today of dates and cities for the third leg of the Vertigo Tour – which won't begin for more than six months. The announcement lists 33 initial dates beginning in Toronto in mid-September and continuing almost until Christmas with a final show in Portland. Since the first leg is shorter than originally planned, U2 makes sure to hit many of the missed North American cities on the third leg. This forces the band to cancel plans to play Japan and Australia at the end of the year.

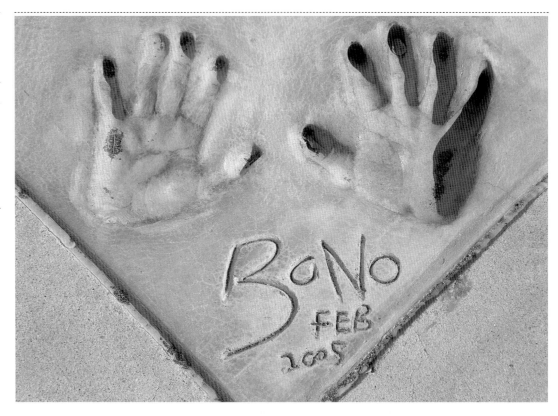

Above: Bono's cement handprint at Fox Baja Studios, Mexico.

March 7

Rolling Stone publishes its first mainland Chinese edition. While the cover shows an image of Chinese rocker Cui Jian, a U2 feature is advertised on the cover.

March 8

Internet presales for the third leg of U2's Vertigo Tour begin today, and unlike the pre-sale debacle of six weeks earlier, today's is an overwhelming success. As Larry had promised a month ago, the system is overhauled for today's pre-sale. U2.com members who were also members of the Propaganda fan club are the only ones able to order tickets today, and fans are thrilled with the experience. Other U2.com members are able to order tickets later in the week, and again those presales are an overall success. The new system appears to include more tickets for U2.com members to choose from, as well as higher quality seats. Unlike the earlier presale, there are few complaints, if any, from fans that the only tickets available are in the upper levels or far away from the stage.

March 11

The Irish Recorded Music Association (IRMA) honours veteran DJ Larry Gogan tonight with the IRMA Honours Award at a ceremony in Dublin. Larry appears on a videotaped tribute to Gogan, saying, "In the early eighties when there was no-one playing rock music in the afternoons you were the exception. You still are an exception."

In New York, Bono and Ali launch their Edun clothing line today at Saks Fifth Avenue. The fashion line will be produced in Third World countries and reflects "a marriage of social activism and aesthetic innovation". Edun will be available in the spring at Saks Fifth Avenue stores and additional stores later in the year.

Bono and Ali do an interview with Katie Couric that will air on NBC's *Today* show on March 15.

March 14

U2 are inducted into the Rock and Roll Hall of Fame during ceremonies at the Waldorf-Astoria Hotel in New York. Inducting the band is Bruce Springsteen, whom

Bono had inducted into the Hall six years earlier. Springsteen praises U2 for staying together for so long with no break-ups and no line-up changes: "... Bands get formed by accident, but they don't survive by accident. It takes will, intent, a sense of shared purpose, and a tolerance for your friends' fallibilities... and they of yours. And that only evens the odds. U2 has not only evened the odds but they've beaten them by continuing to do their finest work and remaining at the top of their game and the charts for 25 years. I feel a great affinity for these guys as people as well as musicians." U2 go on to play a four-song set, which includes a duet with Springsteen on 'I Still Haven't Found What I'm Looking For'. Also inducted tonight are The Pretenders, The O'Jays, Buddy Guy and Percy Sledge. Non-performers inducted are Frank Barsalona and Seymour Stein.

Earlier in the day, Bono does an interview with filmmaker John Wilson, who's working on a documentary about Jesse Helms.

March 17
Bono speaks twice via phone with Paul Wolfowitz, the recent nominee to lead the World Bank.

March 23
U2 arrives in Los Angeles for tour rehearsals.

March 25
Bono and Ali appear at Saks Fifth Avenue in Beverly Hills for that store's launch of their Edun clothing line.

March 26
Sports Arena, Los Angeles. Two nights before opening night of the Vertigo Tour, U2 do a dress rehearsal in front of 200-300 radio contest winners from across the country. At the last minute, the band lets in another 200 or so fans that had gathered outside the arena. Security is very strict tonight, and no cameras, cellphones or similar devices are allowed into the building. Possibly the two biggest surprises the small crowd sees are the inclusion of three *Boy* songs early in the set – 'Electric Co.', 'An Cat Dubh', and 'Into The Heart' – and a new look for 'Where The Streets Have No Name', which has always had a red backdrop but tonight is played while the flags of African countries appear on LED screens behind the band.

March 28-30
iPayOne Center, San Diego, with Kings Of Leon. U2's Vertigo Tour 2005 begins in San Diego. Unlike the casual, lights-on beginning of the Elevation Tour, U2 take the stage in the dark to the opening strains of 'City Of Blinding Lights'. Confetti falls from above onto fans inside the "ellipse", which is this tour's version of the Elevation "heart". The opening song shows off a custom lighting system that uses curtains of LED lights hanging down from various spots behind and to the sides of the stage. The

Edge explains the mix of music and message on the Vertigo Tour, March 28-30

"The issues of the moment are folded into our work. The biggest difference is that, now, instead of standing outside a meeting with a placard, Bono is actually *inside* the meeting, beating everybody up with his statistics and knowledge of the issues. As a person, he's in a much different place than he was years ago, and what we do is we draw that back into the band and give it a rock and roll context."

stage itself is shaped in concentric circles that mirror imagery from the recent 'Vertigo' music video.

Seven songs from *How To Dismantle An Atomic Bomb* are featured, including a rousing version of 'Love And Peace Or Else' that ends with Bono slamming a tom drum at the tip of the ellipse. The show also features a few oldies that haven't been played live in two decades: 'Electric Co.' is played for the first time since 1987, while 'An Cat Dubh / Into the Heart' hasn't been played since 1984. 'One' and 'Where The Streets Have No Name', two familiar U2 concert songs, take on a new direction tonight as Bono uses them to advance his efforts for African aid. "We are more extraordinary and more powerful when we act as one," Bono says, and he encourages fans to send a text message showing their support of the ONE Campaign. The show as a whole is much more political than the

SAN DIEGO SPORTS ARENA

U2 IN CONCERT

MARCH 28 & 30 @ 7:30 PM

Above: Opening night of the Vertigo Tour, San Diego, March 28.

Elevation Tour four years ago, and reflects many of the themes and messages of Bono's humanitarian activity.

While the concert has a few opening night mistakes, it's widely praised by both fans and critics. After the opening night gig, Paul McGuinness does a live interview with Gerry Ryan on 2FM, where it's already morning. At different times during the call, both Bono and Edge "crash" the interview to talk about the gig and tell jokes. It's clear the band is pleased with how things went.

Eddie Vedder is in attendance at the second show, which includes the first performance of 'Gloria' since the end of the Lovetown Tour in 1990.

On March 29, supposedly an off day, U2 spends several hours at the arena doing more rehearsals.

March 31

Bono appears in a new public service video for the ONE Campaign. He's one of many celebrities who are shown snapping their fingers at three-second intervals to emphasise how often a child dies from extreme poverty. The video can be watched online, and is part of the ONE Campaign's television ad campaign, too.

April 1-2

Arrowhead Pond, Anaheim, with Kings Of Leon. U2 mix up the setlist for both shows, opening with 'Love And Peace Or Else' as each band member walks around the ellipse shinging a spotlight on the crowd. The first show has an unusual structure: U2 play 13 songs, take a five-minute intermission, and then plays another nine-song set. Fans leave the arena feeling there was no encore. At the second show, Bono dedicates 'Miracle Drug' to Pope John Paul II, who died earlier in the day. He retells the story of meeting the Pope in 1999, when Bono famously gave John Paul a pair of sunglasses to wear, and later called him "the first funky pontiff".

3ality Digital, a company that's developing new technology to shoot live action in 3D, does a single-camera test while U2 plays Anaheim. The company works with Catherine Owens to make a short film clip that impresses the band.

April 5-6

Staples Center, Los Angeles, with Kings Of Leon. Brad Pitt attends the first show. At the second show, U2 plays 'The Ocean' for the first time since 1982.

On April 6, Bono appears with actors Brad Pitt and Djimon Hounsou at a news conference in Beverly Hills announcing a new, 60-second ONE Campaign PSA that will begin airing soon on network and cable television. The PSA features an unlikely assortment of Hollywood stars and religious leaders encouraging Americans to join the ONE Campaign.

April 9-10

HP Pavilion, San Jose, with Kings Of Leon. Bono has a busy day in San Francisco before U2's second concert in San Jose. He begins the day by attending Sunday services at Glide Memorial Church with Ali and their kids. During the sermon, Reverend Cecil Williams acknowledges Bono and calls him up to the front of the church. Bono speaks briefly to the congregation about Pope John Paul II and tells them how much he appreciates Glide Memorial. At the end of the service, he leads the choir and congregation in singing 'Stand By Me'. From there, it's on to a meeting with US Representative Nancy Pelosi. Bono also has time to launch the Edun clothing line with wife Ali at the San Francisco Saks Fifth Avenue store. After the second show, Steve Jobs is one of the guests at a small party at the band's hotel.

April 14-15

Glendale Arena, Glendale, with Kings Of Leon. With a few days off after the second show in Phoenix, U2 flies to Cabo San Lucas for a short break.

On the 15th, publisher Harper Collins announces that the highly anticipated official book, *U2 By U2*, will be delayed a full year from the original publishing date. According to today's *Publisher's Lunch* newsletter, "the bookseller says 'the band cited the punishing schedule of their current world tour as the reason for the delay.'" Harper

Collins says the book will be out in September, 2006.

April 20-21

Pepsi Center, Denver, with Kings Of Leon. Video directors Alex and Martin arrive for the Denver shows to prepare for a live shoot in Vancouver next week. Just before they take the stage for the second show, U2 stop to meet and shoot a photo with Elsha Stockseth, a 21-year-old fan with muscular dystrophy whom Bono had invited backstage.

April 22

U2 announce a third concert this summer at Dublin's Croke Park. The show is set for June 27. No ticket sale information is announced.

How To Dismantle An Atomic Bomb is certified Multi-Platinum by the BPI, with UK sales surpassing the 1.2 million mark.

Below: 'Beautiful Day' in Seattle, April 24.

April 24-25

Key Arena, Seattle, with Kings Of Leon. The crowd applauds before the show as Microsoft co-founder Bill Gates and his wife Melinda arrive at their prime, stage-side seats. (Bono stays at the Gates' residence while the band is in town this week.) Eddie Vedder and William Gibson are also at the show. 'One' is dedicated to Steve Reynolds of World Vision – the man who set up Bono's and Ali's visit to Ethiopia in 1985. Bono and Reynolds visit after the show.

At the second show, Bono brings a young boy named Jason on stage during 'Sometimes You Can't Make It On Your Own'. They're arm-in-arm as Bono sings the song to Jason, who is also mouthing the words back to Bono. It's an incredibly emotional moment, and tears stream down Bono's face as he sings the song like he's singing to his own son. Reminiscent of U2's

earliest shows, 'Vertigo' is played a second time to close the show.

April 27

GM Place, Vancouver. It's an off day for the Vertigo Tour, but you'd never know by the scene inside Vancouver's General Motor Place. U2 and their crew are shooting a live performance video for 'City Of Blinding Lights', which will be the next single from *How To Dismantle An Atomic Bomb*. A last-minute announcement on local radio and the Internet helps round up about 3,000 fans who are needed for the video shoot. They sit through a half-dozen performances of the song while cameras shoot a variety of different angles and scenes. It's a long process, and at one point the band kills time between takes by performing the 'Hokey Pokey'. To reward the crowd for its patience and help, U2 ends the night with a brief set.

April 28-29
GM Place, Vancouver, with Kings Of Leon. Both shows are filmed as a dry run for the real video shoot coming up in Chicago. The first show begins (and ends) late due to last-minute work preparing for the shoot.

With about a week off before the next show, U2 reportedly go to the Bahamas for a short vacation.

Late April
Bono continues to press Bob Geldof to put together a massive concert to coincide with the G8 Summit in Scotland, which is a little more than two months away. Bono also calls Chris Martin of Coldplay and Paul McCartney, both of whom say they'd be interested in performing at a concert that Bono refers to as "Live 8."

May
Bob Geldof continues to reject the idea of another Live Aid-style concert, but he finally gives in when Bono tells him the concert will go on whether Geldof is involved or not. Together, they canvass for bands and artists to perform at the concert, which is tentatively schedule for July 2 – the Saturday before the G8 Summit in Scotland.

May 7
United Center, Chicago, with Kings Of Leon. Hamish Hamilton and crew do a dry-run video shoot, in preparation for the formal effort in two days. After some time off, U2 struggle to get back into the groove of playing live. Technical problems plague Bono and Edge, especially early in the show, and some fans are left unsatisfied with tonight's performance. Perhaps worse, Chicago critics reviewing tonight's show spare no words, calling the show "tired nostalgia" (*Chicago Tribune*) and "pointlessly pretentious and preachy" (*Chicago Sun-Times*). The band is about to film the next two shows for a home video release; today, film crews interview U2 fans in the GA line for possible inclusion on the DVD. Coldplay is in attendance. The whole band does interviews a couple hours after the show for

a Dutch TV programme.

Tickets for U2's 3rd concert this summer at Croke Park in Dublin go on sale without a pre-announcement, as U2 and the concert promoters go out of their way to thwart scalpers from getting most of the tickets. They also try to make sure Irish U2 fans have the best chance to get tickets. A majority of tickets for the show are only available through local ticket outlets in Ireland. Says Paul McGuinness: "It's very important to the band that these tickets get to the fans. Playing at home is always something special, these gigs will be no exception."

May 8
On a day off, U2 and crew have a screening party at their hotel to review the video footage Hamish Hamilton shot at last night's show.

May 9
United Center, Chicago, with Kings Of Leon. Tonight's show is the first of a two-night video shoot for a planned DVD release. The show is, by almost all accounts, better than two nights ago. Bono brings a female fan on stage to play 'Party Girl', a song that hasn't been performed yet this tour.

May 10
United Center, Chicago, with Kings Of Leon. The video shoot wraps up and "continuity" is the theme, as U2 wears the same clothes and plays nearly the same setlist as last night. The same fan comes on stage to do 'Party Girl' again, but with a new twist: Bono ends the song by spraying a bottle of champagne on her, the band, and the crowd. It's Bono's birthday, and the crowd sings 'Happy Birthday' to him after 'Mysterious Ways'. The band and crew throw Bono a birthday party after the show, and guests include Chris Martin and Gwyneth Paltrow.

May 11
On an off day, Bono watches The Killers play a small theatre in the Windy City. The Killers are one of the bands scheduled to open for U2 during the European leg of the Vertigo Tour this summer.

May 12
United Center, Chicago, with Kings Of Leon.

May 14
Wachovia Center, Philadelphia, with Kings Of Leon. Actor Jim Carrey is at the show.

May 17-18
Continental Airlines Arena, E. Rutherford, with Kings Of Leon. While signing autographs outside the venue before the first show, Bono meets a local three-piece band called The Bank Robbers. He calls out their name during 'The Fly'. He sees them again before the second show and asks them if they want to play a song with U2. Duh. Of course! Bono gives the band and his security instructions on where to stand, and calls them up near the end of the show. The Bank Robbers choose to play 'I Still Haven't Found', borrowing some of U2's gear while U2 plays along, too. ABC's Diane Sawyer interviews U2 before the second show. It'll air on *Good Morning America* on May 20.

While in New York, Bono has dinner one night at *Time* magazine's offices with managing editor Jim Kelly and president Eileen Naughton. He spots an autographed U2 album on the wall, tells his hosts that the autograph is a fake, and signs his name over it, adding a message: "Even better than the real thing."

May 19
U2 shoot a music video for the Leonard Cohen track 'Tower Of Song' this afternoon at the Slipper Room in New York. The shoot is for an upcoming documentary about Cohen. The band has been heard rehearsing the song prior to recent Vertigo Tour concerts.

In London, U2's European tour coordinators deny reports that the band are planning to add a fourth show at Croke Park.

The *New York Daily News* reports that Bono has seen a back specialist while in the area this week. The paper says Bono saw Dr. Vijay Vad, a physician who specialises in non-surgical treatment of the spine, at the Hospital for Special Surgery.

May 19-20
On one of these days, Edge does an interview and photo shoot with *Guitar World* magazine at M Studio in Manhattan.

May 21
Madison Square Garden, New York, with Kings Of Leon. After rescheduling the spring tour dates, U2 play their only show at Madison Square Garden. They'll make up for it on the third leg this fall. David Bowie, Patti Smith, Julie Roberts, and Kofi Annan are just a few of the big names at the show.

May 22
Wachovia Center, Philadelphia, with Kings Of Leon. Before the show,

Bono appears at the Edun Fall 2005 trunk show at Barney's in New York City.

May 24
FleetCenter, Boston, with Kings Of Leon. Bono namechecks former J. Geils Band singer Peter Wolf during 'Beautiful Day', and '40' is dedicated to Teresa Earnhardt, the widow of racing legend Dale Earnhardt, who is presumably at the show. After the show, Bono flies to Washington, DC, arriving at 2:00 a.m.

May 25
On an off day in between concerts in Boston, Bono has a full day of politicking in Washington, DC. His schedule includes lunch with US Secretary of State Condoleezza Rice, where they talk about the upcoming G8 meeting and aid to Africa. It's not their first meeting, but it is the first since Rice was promoted to Secretary of State from her previous role as National Security Adviser. Bono also visits Capitol Hill to speak with several lawmakers about increasing assistance for the poor.

May 26
FleetCenter, Boston, with Kings Of Leon. Before the show, Adam Clayton confirms to Steve Morse of the *Boston Globe* that U2 will perform July 2 at the Live 8 concert in London. Just before the show begins, a noticeable security detail leads former Vice President Al Gore and wife Tipper to their seats in a prime spot to the side of the stage. Bono sings bits of two Aerosmith songs because Steven Tyler and his band mates are at the show.

'Vertigo' is named International Hit of the Year during the Ivor Novello Awards tonight in London.

May 28
FleetCenter, Boston, with Kings Of Leon. It's the last show of the first leg, and considering all that U2 has been through in the past six months, Bono is in the mood to reminisce. Before 'Miracle Drug', he talks about the uncertainty of touring and says it was faith in each other and in their fans that made it possible. After the show, Bono and

Adam fly to The Netherlands.

May 29
Bono and Adam show up at a 50th birthday/housewarming party for Anton Corbijn in The Hague. Bono helps celebrate by singing the Golden Earring song 'Radar Love'.

May 31
Twenty years after the Live Aid concerts for African famine relief, organisers Bob Geldof and Midge Ure announce they'll do it again this year. The concerts will be called Live 8, and are scheduled to take place July 2, shortly before world leaders gather for the G8 Summit in Scotland (July 6-8). Some things will be different this time: Rather than two concerts, five are announced (and more are added later); and rather than raising money, Live 8 is designed to raise awareness of extreme poverty in developing nations.

U2 is confirmed as one of the artists who will perform at London's Hyde Park, even though they're scheduled to perform a Vertigo Tour concert that night in Vienna. The rumored plan is for U2 to perform early at Live 8, and then fly to Austria for their regular show that night.

Meanwhile, the start of the European Vertigo Tour is just 10 days away. U2's crew begins construction of the stage today at Roi Baudouin Stadium in Brussels. The stage will be completely new, since these are the first outdoor stadium shows of the year. Because U2 will take the stage while it's still light outside, new video screen technology is being used and the band are keen to get the screens installed and test them. U2, however, are back in Dublin rehearsing and won't arrive in Brussels for several more days.

June 5
With days to go before the Vertigo Tour resumes, Bono is spotted in St. Tropez, France.

June 6
'City Of Blinding Lights' is released on multiple formats with extra tracks 'The Fly (Live at Stop

U2's letter to the people of Brussels, June 8

"The show on Friday night is very important to us," the letter reads. "We are using brand new screens, Belgian technology in fact, that have never been used before. It is imperative for this tour that we test these in real concert and real time conditions, so that we get the best effect from them. This means that on Thursday evening, we will be rehearsing the full show from 21:15 until 23:30. We thank you very much for your understanding!"

Above: Roi Baudouin Stadium, Brussels – opening night of Vertigo in Europe, June 10.

Sellafield concert)', 'Even Better Than The Real Thing (Live at Stop Sellafield concert)', 'Out Of Control (Live at Brooklyn Bridge)', and 'All Because Of You (Killahurtz Fly Mix)'. The single hits number one in Chile, Spain, and Portugal, and number two in the UK, Canada, and Denmark. The song is also released as an exclusive download only on the UK iTunes Music Store.

June 7
Bono is a topic of conversation as US President George Bush and UK Prime Minister Tony Blair talk to reporters at the White House. President Bush, responding to a question about poverty and whether the Make Poverty History campaign is just "rhetoric from rock stars", says: "... do I believe in my gut we can eradicate poverty?

I do believe we can eradicate poverty. And, by the way, Bono has come to see me. I admire him. He is a man of depth and a great heart who cares deeply about the impoverished folks on the continent of Africa, and I admire hisleadership on the issue. And so I do believe – I don't view – I can't remember how you characterised the rock stars, but I don't characterise them that way, having met the man."

June 8
With some elements of the stage still being built, U2 begin rehearsals at Roi Baudouin Stadium in Brussels for the start of the European Vertigo Tour. Edge remains back in Dublin longer than the rest of the band, missing the first rehearsal today but arriving in

time for the evening session. Fans outside the stadium hear the band practice 'Crumbs From Your Table' and 'Electrical Storm', two songs that have never been played live.

Meanwhile, U2 distribute a letter addressed to "the neighbours of the Stadium King Baudoin", letting them know about a full dress rehearsal planned for tomorrow and apologising for the "inconvenience" associated with Friday's concert in their neighbourhood.

June 9
U2 performs a full dress rehearsal on the eve of their European Tour's opening night.

Earlier, Bono visits the European Commission headquarters in Brussels to speak with EC President Jose Manuel Barroso about aid for

Africa and developing nations. They meet privately for a half-hour before speaking during a joint news conference.

June 10

Roi Baudouin Stadium, Brussels, with the Thrills, Snow Patrol. U2 launches the European Vertigo tour in front of 60,000 fans in Brussels. The show features a brand new stage design that includes a large LED video wall behind the band, and two b-stages that extend out into the crowd. The setlist is largely similar to the first leg, but 'Vertigo' opens and closes the show (replacing '40'), 'Until The End Of The World' is played second, and 'Running To Stand Still' is done acoustically. U2 dedicates a song to former Irish president Mary Robinson, who is in attendance.

June 11

Bono and Edge do an interview in Brussels with Dave Fanning of 2FM. The audio will air on Fanning's radio programme, and a video version will be distributed to international TV outlets.

Led by UK Prime Minister Tony Blair and US President George Bush, the G8 nations announce an agreement to cancel more than $40 billion of African debt. Bono issues a statement after today's debt agreement which mirrors a message he's been talking about on the road with U2 during the Vertigo Tour: "The journey of equality took another step today, and broke free millions of people in some of the poorest countries from the bondage of immoral and unjust debts. The leadership of the jubilee campaigners is bearing fruit once

Below: Bono and Larry, Manchester, June 14.

more, we really owe those people, from church basements to national treasuries who have worked so long and so hard for this day."

June 12

Schalke Arena, Gelsenkirchen, with the Thrills, Feeder.

'City Of Blinding Lights' debuts at number two on the UK charts, falling short of Crazy Frog's version of 'Axel F', a mobile ring tone which tops the singles chart for the third week in a row.

June 13

Brainpool TV Studios, Cologne. U2 appear on the German late night programme *TV Total.* Host Stefan Raab interviews the band between live performances of 'City Of Blinding Lights' and 'Vertigo'. Earlier in the day, a team of German doctors visits Bono in his hotel room and administers about two-dozen injections to alleviate pain in his back.

June 14-15

Manchester Stadium, Manchester, with Snow Patrol, the Bravery (June 14); with Athlete, Idlewild (June 15). Former Joy Division bassist Peter Hook is at the first show, and hears Bono sings snippets of two of his band's songs during 'With Or Without You'.

June 16

Bono appears on BBC2's *Newsnight* programme. The topic is Africa, and host Jeremy Paxman conducts a spirited debate with Bono on issues including trade, debt cancellation and more.

Edge presents a *Mojo* Icon Award to Siouxsie Sioux at tonight's *Mojo* Awards in London.

June 17

U2 receives a Lifetime Achievement Award at the Nordoff-Robbins Silver Clef Awards in London. The entire band is on hand to accept the honour. Never at a loss for words, Bono thanks the band and gives a plug for the upcoming Live 8 concerts, too.

June 18-19

Twickenham Stadium, London, with the Doves, Athlete (June 18); with Idlewild, Ash (June 19). The final 80-90 minutes of the first show airs live on BBC2 radio. Former Alarm singer Mike Peters is at the second show, as is Chelsea Clinton.

Around this time, various media report that Bono and Barry Devlin are teaming up to produce a film titled *A Version Of Las Vegas.*

June 21

Hampden Park, Glasgow, with Interpol, Black Rebel Motorcycle Club.

June 24

Croke Park, Dublin, with the Radiators, Snow Patrol. U2 returns to Croke Park almost 20 years to the date after their first gig in the historic Dublin stadium. U2 gets a police escort to the stadium, and helicopters are on standby in case they can't get through heavy traffic. Rain falls for much of the day and night, but it doesn't bother the band or the 80,000-strong audience. Before today's show, Bono visits with Taoiseach Bertie Ahern.

June 25

Croke Park, Dublin, with Paddy Casey, the Thrills. The highlight of the show comes when Bono pulls a fan on stage to play 'Party Girl'. The fan has just arrived from

Canada earlier in the day and has a sign that says, "I flew from Canada to play 'Party Girl'." He nails the performance and draws roars from the crowd. Taoiseach Bertie Ahern attends the show. Bono addresses him from the stage, saying Ahern needs to "stand up for Africa". The mention of Ahern's name draws boos from some in the crowd. Tonight's show is filmed.

Above: Twickenham Stadium, June. Right: Cardiff, June 29.

June 26

Bono appears on NBC's *Meet The Press* news programme for an interview with host Tim Russert. They discuss issues related to Third World poverty and the upcoming Live 8 concerts. The interview is done by satellite with Bono sitting in a studio in Dublin, though it's unclear if the interview is live or on tape.

June 27

Croke Park, Dublin, with Ash, the Bravery. All bets are off for the last show in Dublin, which sees U2 take a stroll down memory lane with the inclusion of 'Gloria', 'An Cat Dubh-Into The Heart', 'Bad', and '40' – all played for the first time on the European tour. 'Miracle Drug' is played for Christopher Nolan, who is at the show. Tonight's show is filmed.

Earlier in the day, U2 make plans for their upcoming performance at Live 8. Bono floats an idea: Can we release doves into the sky during 'Beautiful Day'? (Yes, they can and will).

June 28

Bono, Larry and Paul McGuinness are in Dublin Circuit Civil Court trying to get back items valued at £3,500 that are in the possession of Lola Cashman, a stylist who worked for U2 in the 1980s. The material includes pants, a Stetson hat, earrings and other material from her work with the band during *The Joshua Tree* tour. Cashman claims the band gave the items to her as a gift, but the band accuses her of stealing them.

Cashman's problems began when she tried to sell the goods at Christie's in London. When the auctioneers contacted U2 to authenticate the items, they were told the items were not Cashman's property, setting the stage for today's court case.

The scene in the civil court is a bit chaotic as Bono cracks jokes while being questioned. Even the barristers line up for autographs from Bono and Larry.

June 29

Millennium Stadium, Cardiff, with Starsailor, the Killers.

July 1

U2 and Paul McCartney rehearse for tomorrow's Live 8 concert in London. McCartney brings his band along in case U2 need help learning 'Sgt. Pepper's Lonely Hearts Club Band'. But U2 have been good students, practicing on their own, and have no problem picking up the song.

July 2

Hyde Park, London. U2 and Paul McCartney take the stage together to open the flagship concert of today's Live 8 events around the world. But before the show begins, they have to sort out a fashion faux pas: inside U2's trailer, McCartney notices that Bono is planning to wear the same designer jacket McCartney will be wearing later in the show. Bono ends up taking the stage in a simple denim jacket instead. On stage, they perform 'Sgt. Pepper's Lonely Hearts Club Band' together. The opening line – "It was 20 years ago today…" – harkens back to the Live Aid concerts of 1985. A four-piece horn section joins them on stage, wearing replicas of the colourful Sgt. Pepper's uniforms the Beatles wore on the original album.

Within 45 minutes, the U2-McCartney collaboration is available for download on iTunes. Days later, it's available on more than 200 online music stores in 30 countries.

After the opening song, U2 remain on stage to perform its own three-song set: 'Beautiful Day', 'Vertigo', and 'One'. Before 'One', Bono delivers a concise speech about the day's events and what Live 8 aims to accomplish. He addresses the G8 leaders, telling them to "make history, by making poverty history". The song concludes with a brief version of 'Unchained Melody', in which Bono sings, "God, speed your love to Africa."

The Hyde Park concert is one of nine shows happening worldwide today. A tenth concert is scheduled days later in Scotland, where the G8 leaders are to meet beginning on July 6. Unlike Live Aid in 1985, Live 8 is not a fund raising concert. The goal is raising awareness and putting pressure on world leaders to increase aid and eliminate poverty in the developing world. U2 open the show because they have a Vertigo concert later in the

Bono talks about working with Paul McCartney, July 2

"We had a very easy kind of repartee between him and the band. He was probably waiting for us to have a lot of attitude, but we played students to the professor, not big rock band, which is correct pecking order."

day in Vienna.

Happel Stadium, Vienna, with the Magic Numbers, the Thrills. U2 arrive late and take the stage nearly an hour past the scheduled time.

July 5

Slaski Stadium, Katowice, with the Magic Numbers, the Killers. U2 fans put on a show themselves tonight: when the band begins 'New Year's Day', the stadium holds up red and white shirts and scarves to form an image of the Polish flag. The display refers to the song's inspiration – the Polish Solidarity movement of the early 1980s. The band are surprised and visibly moved by the moment, and Bono joins in by turning his jacket inside out to wear it with the red inner lining showing. The coordinated effort is the work of online fans and local radio stations that helped spread the instructions to concertgoers.

Willie Williams: "My mouth must have fallen open"

In his U2.com Tour Diary, Willie Williams writes about the red and white display put on by U2 fans at Slaski Stadium.
"I have never seen an audience do anything like it before – getting it together to surprise and delight us. I think my mouth must have fallen open. Who organized this? The fact that it was premeditated made it all the more extraordinary; an audience consciously plotting to put on a show for the performers. It was absolutely wonderful, humbling, thrilling all at the same time. A great, great crowd, and a unique atmosphere."

Piotr Mlodozeniec, the original creator of the COEXIST image that has been a central part of the Vertigo Tour, is at the show. Since he's in the homeland of Pope John Paul II, Bono wants to tell fans about meeting the pontiff in 1999. He asks a fan to come on stage and translate the story into Polish, but when she should be translating Bono's words, she tells the crowd in Polish that she can't speak English.

In Dublin, Judge Matthew Deery rules in favour of U2 in a Circuit Civil Court lawsuit against their former stylist, Lola Cashman. The judge orders Cashman to return to U2 personal belongings she had claimed were given to her. U2 issues a statement that reads in part, "This case was brought very reluctantly, in the context of a larger dispute which we never invited. The point of principle involved was of much greater significance to us than any item of memorabilia." Cashman says she will appeal the decision.

July 6

Bono is in Scotland for the opening day of the G8 Summit at Gleneagles. With the momentum of the Live 8 concerts still strong, he and Bob Geldof are there to meet and talk to as many leaders, politicians, and even press as possible. Here's a recap of Bono's day:
– meets with UK Prime Minister Tony Blair
– meets with German Chancellor Gerhard Schroeder
– speaks at a news conference
– meets with Canadian Prime Minister Paul Martin
– meets with US President George W. Bush and his wife, Laura
– takes a box of CDs with 38 million electronic signatures of the "Live 8 List" to a news conference and to tonight's "Final Push" concert at

Murrayfield Stadium – sings 'When The Stars Go Blue' at Murrayfield Stadium with the Corrs

In Berlin tonight, Adam attends the opening of a photo exhibit showing some of Anton Corbijn's photos from his *U2 & I* book and then goes to see a concert by the Killers.

July 7

Olympic Stadium, Berlin, the Kaiser Chiefs, Snow Patrol. There's an odd moment early in the show: during 'I Will Follow', Bono sings "these shoes, well they hurt me ... excuse me, I have a problem here" and a stage assistant brings out a new pair of shoes. Bono sits on the front of the stage and changes shoes while singing the song. Despite the levity of that moment, there's heaviness in the air after today's bombings in London. The mood inspires the band, Bono especially, to an energetic performance. 'Running To Stand Still' is dedicated to those affected by the London attacks.

July 8

Back in Scotland for the final day of the G8 Summit, Bono has separate meetings with French President Jacques Chirac and UN Secretary-General Kofi Annan. In all, Bono meets with five of the eight heads of state at the summit.

Bono also conducts a press conference with Bob Geldof, where the pair praise today's agreement to fight poverty in Africa. The G8 leaders commit to spend about $25 billion more a year on Africa and also pledge, with other donors, to roughly double total aid for all developing countries, boosting it by about $50 billion a year by 2010.

Willie Williams, Ned O'Hanlon, Hamish Hamilton and others on the crew fly to Milan to scout the San Siro Stadium and make plans for an upcoming video shoot there.

July 9-10

Stade de France, Paris, with Starsailor, Snow Patrol (July 9); with the Music, Snow Patrol (July 10). The first show includes another coordinated fan event: as the human rights video plays, thousands of fans hold up white balloons as a statement of peace. The French fan site U2achtung.com organises the display. At the second show, Bono leads the crowd in singing 'Happy Birthday' for Edge's daughter, Hollie, who's at the show and recently turned 21.

Bono on the success of the G8 Summit, July 8

"Six hundred thousand people will be alive to remember this G8 in Gleneagles who would have lost their lives to a mosquito bite. If an Irish rock star can quote Churchill, this is not the end of extreme poverty, but it is the beginning of the end."

July 12

Fresh off the success of their recent three-night stand at Dublin's Croke Park, U2 place almost their entire album catalog in the Irish Top 75, as tracked by the Irish Recorded Music Association (IRMA):

4. *How To Dismantle An Atomic Bomb*
12. *The Joshua Tree*
13. *The Best of 1980-1990*
19. *The Best of 1990-2000*
32. *All That You Can't Leave Behind*
35. *Achtung Baby*
43. *Rattle And Hum*
48. *Under A Blood Red Sky*
53. *The Unforgettable Fire*
63. *Boy*
67. *War*

A similar phenomenon happened in 2001, when all 12 of U2's albums reached the Top 60 the week after the band's two gigs at Slane Castle.

July 13-15-16

Arena, Amsterdam, with the Kaiser Chiefs, the Killers (July 13); with the Music, Snow Patrol (July 15); with Athlete, Snow Patrol (July 16). During the first show, Bono leads the crowd in singing 'Happy Birthday' to Anton Corbijn, who is at the show, even though his birthday was in late May. At the final show, U2 surprise the crowd by performing 'Miss Sarajevo' for the first time since 1997. Bono sings the operatic verses that were handled in the studio by Luciano

Above: Bono playfully accepts honorary citizenship of Turin, July 20.
Left: Bono changing his shoes during the concert in Berlin, July 7.

Pavarotti, and draws loud cheers as he hits every note. U2's usually unseen keyboard player, Terry Lawless, joins U2 on stage for 'Original Of The Species'.

While in Amsterdam, Bono and Edge work on a new song called 'Don't Come Knocking', which they're doing for Wim Wenders' upcoming movie of the same name. The song features Bono and Andrea Corr on vocals.

While in The Netherlands, U2 works with producer Jacknife Lee on a new version of 'Original Of The Species'. They bring in an orchestra and use two studios at Wisseloord Studios in Hilversum.

July 14
Solely on the strength of online downloads, the U2 & Paul McCartney version of 'Sgt. Pepper's Lonely Hearts Club Band' from Live 8 debuts at number 48 on *Billboard*'s Hot 100 Singles chart. It's the top debut song this week, and is also number 12 on the Hot Digital Songs list.

July 18
Letzigrund Stadium, Zurich, with Feeder, Ash. U2 attend the funeral of Gavin Friday's father, Robert, at St. Canice's Church in Dublin, then fly to Zurich for tonight's show.

July 20-21
San Siro Stadium, Milan, with Feeder, Ash. Both shows are filmed with Hamish Hamilton directing. 'Original Of The Species' is played with members of the Symphony Orchestra of Theatre Carlo Coccia de Novara, along with Terry Lawless on keyboards. The orchestra is seated at the end of the b-stage ramps. R.E.M.'s Michael Stipe and Mike Mills attend both shows. On the first night, the video production truck loses power for about 30 minutes, putting more pressure on the crew to get everything right on the second night of the shoot. Prior to the first show, Bono meets with representatives of the Turin City Council, who present him with Honorary Citizenship, the highest dignity a non-resident can have in Turin. The honour was bestowed in September, 2003, but Turin officials were unable to meet up with Bono until today.

U2 is back in the Guinness Book of World Records, thanks to the Live 8 performance of 'Sgt. Pepper's Lonely Hearts Club Band' with Paul McCartney. The song will be listed for being the "quickest single put on sale" – it was available on iTunes and other digital stores within 45 minutes after the performance.

July 23
Olympic Stadium, Rome, with Feeder, Ash. 'Miss Sarajevo' is dedicated to the victims and all those affected by the terrorist attack in Egypt today.

July 25
'Vertigo picks up five nominations for the 2005 MTV Video Music Awards: Best Group Video; Breakthrough Video; Best Direction in a Video (Alex & Martin); Best Special Effects in a Video; and Best Cinematography in a Video. The awards are scheduled later this summer in Miami.

July 27
Valle Hovin, Oslo, with Paddy Casey, Razorlight. Prior to the show, Bono meets privately with Norway's Prime Minister Kjell Magne Bondevik. They discuss anti-poverty efforts, as well as problems of the developing world, including the famine in Niger and the situation for democracy in Burma. The concert is U2's first in Norway since 1997, and the country responds enthusiastically. Within a week, nine U2 albums are included in the Norway's Top 40 sales chart.

July 28
On a day off in Gothenburg, U2 takes a tour along the Gota River in a yacht. A reporter spots Bono outside a restaurant and shows him a copy of today's IRA disarmament announcement. "This requires great courage and compromise," Bono says. "This has been a long struggle and many people have suffered great losses. This is a great day for Northern Ireland."

July 29
Ullevi Stadium, Gothenburg, with the Soundtrack of Our Lives, Razorlight. Fans organise another display during tonight's show. This time, it's a "white wave" as the band takes the stage; it's organised by the U2.se fan site. Thousands of fans wave shirts, towels, anything white above their heads as the concert starts, prompting Bono to ask, "Oh my God, what do we have here?"

July 31
Parken, Copenhagen, with the Soundtrack of Our Lives, Razorlight.

August 3
Olympic Stadium, Munich, with the Zutons, Keane. Prior to tonight's concert, Bono meets German Foreign Minister Joschka Fischer to discuss aid for Africa.

August 5
Charles Ehrmann Park, Nice, with the Zutons, Keane.

August 7
Camp Nou, Barcelona, with the Kaiser Chiefs, Keane.

August 9
Anoeta Stadium, San Sebastian, with the Kaiser Chiefs, Franz Ferdinand.

Pat Boone releases *Glory Train: The Lost Sessions*. Bono does an introduction to the track, 'Thank You, Billy Graham'. The appearance was first discussed when Boone met U2 at the 2001 Grammy Awards.

August 11

Estadio Vicente Calderon, Madrid, with the Kaiser Chiefs, Franz Ferdinand. On the way to the show, Bono does a phone interview with Sean O'Hagan of *The Guardian* about John Lennon. Says Bono: "Though he [Lennon] was a hero to many, his whole point was not heroic. He hadn't always been the man he wanted to be, yet he kept struggling to redefine himself and to find himself. His real strength was his raw honesty and vulnerability. This was the guy who sang 'Help', don't forget. He dared to bare his soul, and he dared to fail. That takes real courage."

August 14

Estadio Jose Alvalade, Lisbon, with the Kaiser Chiefs. U2 receive Portugal's Order of Liberty, one of the country's highest honours, at a formal ceremony before the concert. President Jorge Sampaio presents the medals to U2 in recognition of their work for humanitarian causes over the last 25 years, including heightening awareness on the debt issues facing developing countries.

August 15

Bono appears on the cover of *Information Week* magazine. The feature article is about the growth of online video and discusses the live webcast of the recent Live 8 concert.

August 31

U2 wins the award for the World's Best-Selling Rock Artist at the World Music Awards in Hollywood tonight, but they're not present to accept the honour. The World Music Awards are based on record sales, which are certified by the International Federation of the Phonographic Industry.

September

Around this time, Bono meets with Muhammad Yunus, founder of Grameen Bank in Bangladesh, and a champion of micro-loans to solve Third World poverty.

September 9

Air Canada Center, Toronto. U2

Above: Bono And Lian Lunson At The Toronto International Film Festival, September 10.

arrive in Toronto to get ready for the third leg of the Vertigo Tour, but their first order of business is to tape two performances that will raise money for Hurricane Katrina relief efforts. First they tape a somber performance of 'One', on which Mary J. Blige provides guest vocals. During rehearsals, Bono tells Blige and the band, "Perfection. We need nothing but perfection." The song airs tonight during the *Shelter From The Storm* telethon on the six major US broadcast networks and other outlets around the world.

The second performance is 'Love And Peace Or Else', which includes the full Vertigo Tour light show and visuals. This airs a day later on the MTV/VH-1 telethon *React Now*. The song will be made available download via Sony Music Connect on September 11.

Edge tells the Toronto Sun about the impact of Hurricane Katrina

"The story's just seemed to have gotten worse and worse and worse. For the first few days I couldn't [help] but watch it.... To know that it's mainland USA is jaw-dropping and bewildering because you couldn't ever have imagined that a natural disaster could have presented so many problems for such a powerful country. I think that's the thing that's hit everybody."

September 10

Bono appears at the Toronto International Film Festival where he sees the screening of Neil Jordan's new film, *Breakfast On Pluto*, which co-stars Gavin Friday.

September 11

Bono makes two appearances tonight in Toronto. First, he attends and speaks before the screening Of *Leonard Cohen – I'm Your Man*, a documentary about the legendary singer, at the Toronto Film Festival. U2 also makes an appearance in the

film, singing 'Tower Of Song' with Cohen.

Later, he attends the One X One charity dinner and auction, a fund raiser for African debt relief and cancer-patient care in Canada. Bono only stays for the cocktail reception, but that's long enough to do an impromptu a *cappella* performance with the African Children's Choir.

September 12

Air Canada Center, Toronto, with Dashboard Confessional. U2 open the third leg of Vertigo 2005. Bono makes several references to the Gulf Coast and Hurricane Katrina during the show. Before 'One', he compares the devastation there to the images of extreme poverty in Africa. 'Fast Cars' is played live for the first time. Daniel Lanois and Leonard Cohen are among the celebrities at the show.

September 14

Air Canada Center, Toronto, with Dashboard Confessional. Daniel Lanois joins U2 on stage, playing guitar during 'Bad'.

September 15

Bono participates in the inaugural Clinton Global Initiative, a three-day forum in New York. The event brings together leaders to discuss poverty and other world issues.

September 16

Air Canada Center, Toronto, with Dashboard Confessional. Daniel Lanois makes another appearance, joining the band for an extended version of 'One'. Director Lian Lunson (of the Leonard Cohen documentary *I'm Your Man*) is on stage with a film crew, taping 'All Because Of You' and 'Fast Cars'. After 'Fast Cars', Bono calls B.B. King at home to wish him a happy 80th birthday, and leads the crowd in singing 'Happy Birthday'. A local band, Menew, comes on stage and uses U2's instruments to play the first half of 'Out Of Control'. U2 come back to reclaim their gear and finish the song.

September 17

Air Canada Center, Toronto, with

Dashboard Confessional. Daniel Lanois joins U2 for the third straight show, again playing guitar on an extended version of 'One'. Eddie Vedder joins them on stage as the song segues into 'Ol' Man River'. Bono dedicates 'Yahweh' to the departing Willie Williams, who is stepping away for the rest of the year.

September 18
The *New York Times* puts Bono on the cover of its Sunday magazine and runs a lengthy profile headlined "The Statesman". Author James Traub writes a largely glowing profile based on time spent with Bono at a number of events (U2 and non-U2) over the past year. Says Traub: "He's a kind of one-man state who fills his treasury with the global currency of fame. He is also, of course, an emanation of the celebrity culture. But it is Bono's willingness to invest his fame, and to do so with a steady sense of purpose and a tolerance for detail, that has made him the most politically effective figure in the recent history of popular culture."

September 19
Just two days after Eddie Vedder appeared at a U2 concert in Toronto, Bono returns the favour tonight at a Pearl Jam concert in the same city. He sings 'Rockin' In The Free World' while Edge and Larry watch from the side of the stage.

September 20-21
United Center, Chicago, with Dashboard Confessional. While in Chicago, U2 have their heads "scanned" for use in an upcoming music video for 'Original Of The Species'. During the first show, Bono forgets the words at the end of an acoustic version of 'Walk On', so a crew member brings out a binder full of lyrics while Edge continues to play. Bono finds what he's looking for, cracks a joke about the situation, and finishes the song.

September 23
Target Center, Minneapolis, with Dashboard Confessional. U2 plays 'Crumbs From Your Table' for the first time.

Below: Bono and Adam, Boston, October 3.

September 25
Bradley Center, Milwaukee, with Dashboard Confessional. Prior to tonight's concert, Bono meets with US Representative Mark Green of Wisconsin, a Republican who is sympathetic to AIDS and debt issues affecting Africa. Immediately after the show, Bono and Larry fly to Cancun on Mexico's Carribean coast, where they'll spend a week off with their families before the next show in Boston.

October 1-2
While Bono and Larry are still in Cancun with their families, *Rolling Stone* editor Jann S. Wenner arrives to interview Bono for an upcoming cover story/interview. Bono tells Wenner he's writing a poem called 'The Pilgrim and His Lack of Progress'.

October 3-4
TD Banknorth Garden, Boston, with Keane. John Kerry and football star Tom Brady are at the first show. Bono tells the crowd that Brady has recently become the two millionth member of the ONE Campaign. Before the second encore, U2 tape a short acceptance speech for the upcoming Q Awards.

October 5
Bono is the opening act for economist Jeffrey Sachs tonight at an event on the campus of New York University. It's the inaugural Daniel Patrick Moynihan Memorial Lecture, and Bono introduces his friend and collaborator of many years – the man who helped Bono learn the ins and outs of the economics of debt and poverty. Paul McGuinness and The Edge also attend the lecture.

October 6
NBC Studios, New York. U2 is the sole guest on the hour-long *Late Night With Conan O'Brien* show on NBC. It's the first time the 12-year-old programme has ever dedicated a show to one musical guest. In addition to interview segments, U2 perform four songs throughout the show. They also take part in a comedy sketch that airs during the show, and tape another skit that will air on tomorrow's *Late Night* show.

October 7
Madison Square Garden, New York, with Keane.

October 8
Madison Square Garden, New York, with Keane. Mary J. Blige joins U2 to sing 'One'. Bono calls Gavin Friday during the show and gets the whole crowd to sing 'Happy Birthday' to him. Jon Bon Jovi and Salman Rushdie are among many notable names in the audience. Also tonight, the Vertigo Tour wins the Best Tour Sound Production award at the Technical Excellence and Creativity Awards, an important audio industry event held in New York City.

During the band's lengthy stay in New York, they shoot performance scenes backstage at Madison Square Garden for a new music video for 'Original Of The Species'.

Below: Edge at the Anton Corbijn exhibit, October 9.

October 9
Anton Corbijn opens an exhibit of his U2 photographs at Stellan Holm Gallery in New York. The exhibit complements Corbijn's successful book, *U2 And I: The Photographs 1982-2004*. Edge, Bono and Ali are in attendance.

October 10
Madison Square Garden, New York, with Keane. Patti Smith, Michael Stipe and Alicia Keys are among the many celebrities at the show. Earlier in the day, U2 have a variety of commitments: Bono does a photo shoot with Anton Corbijn

and is interviewed by *Rolling Stone*'s Jann Wenner. Edge speaks with a UK magazine. Larry and Adam are interviewed for an upcoming piece on the CBS news magazine, *60 Minutes*.

U2 is named Best Live Act at the Q Awards.

'All Because Of You (Live From Chicago)' is released as an exclusive single on the UK iTunes Music Store.

October 11
Madison Square Garden, New York, with Keane.

'All Because Of You' is released worldwide, except in North America where it was already issued earlier in the year. Additional tracks include 'She's A Mystery To Me (Live from Brooklyn)', 'Miss Sarajevo (Live from Milan)', and 'A Man And A Woman (acoustic)'.

October 12
Jann Wenner hosts a star-studded dinner for U2 at his home in New York City. Guests include the Beastie Boys, the Strokes, Lou Reed, Jon Bon Jovi, Robert DeNiro, Charlize Theron, Scarlett Johannson, Conan O'Brien, Christy Turlington, Michael Stipe, Lenny Kravitz and others.

U2's new music video – a live performance of 'Original of the Species' taken from the upcoming *Live from Chicago* DVD – debuts today on the iTunes Music Store. It's timed to coincide with Apple's launch today of a video iPod, and the 30-second TV commercial for the launch also uses U2's new video.

October 13
Bono and Edge are on hand for a charity auction in New York to benefit hunger relief organisations. They've created lunch box designs to raise money for the Lunch Box Fund and the Food Bank of New York. Edge wins the bidding on a lunchbox designed by former President Bill Clinton. Bono also pays a visit to Jann Wenner at his office today to clarify some of the things they've discussed in the past two weeks for Rolling Stone's upcoming cover interview.

October 14
Madison Square Garden, New York, with Keane. U2 finish up five consecutive shows at Madison Square Garden. Backstage, Bono gets a visit from Kal Khalique, the then-15-year-old girl he pulled from the crowd and danced with during the Live Aid concert twenty years earlier. It's the first time they've met since that day. Also at tonight's show: Jay-Z and Beyoncé, Patti Smith, Chris Martin and Gwyneth Paltrow, Moby and many other celebrities.

October 15
A photo many thought would never see the light of day – that of Pope John Paul II wearing Bono's shades when they met in 1999 – is published today in the book *Do Zobaczenia w Raju*, which translates as "See You in Paradise." Polish newspaper *Gazeta Wyborcza* issues the book as a remembrance by Arturo Mari – the pope's longtime photographer.

October 16
Wachovia Center, Philadelphia, with Damian Marley. Bono and his family attend church this morning in Harlem. Bono also spends time in New York today with Michael O'Dell, who's writing a Q magazine "Man of the Year" feature for publication in a couple months. Shortly before he's due to catch the band's flight to Philadelphia for tonight's concert, Bono and O'Dell visit the John Lennon memorial at Strawberry Fields in Central Park. The unexpected jaunt throws everyone's schedule off-kilter and when the pair don't return quickly, U2 staff head into the park to look for them. Everyone regroups and O'Dell continues to interview Bono on the flight to Philadelphia. Damian Marley – Bob's son – makes his first appearance opening for U2, and Bono marks the occasion by singing a bit of 'Exodus' during 'I Still Haven't Found'. After the show, the band fly back to New York without Bono. He gets on a different plane and flies to Phoenix.

'All Because of You' debuts at number four on the UK singles chart.

Above: Bruce Springsteen joins U2 on stage, Philadalphia, October 17.

October 17
Wachovia Center, Philadelphia, with Damian Marley. Bono begins the day in Phoenix, Arizona, meeting with executives from Viacom – which owns MTV and other media outlets – to get their support for various anti-poverty projects. Immediately afterward, he flies back to Philadelphia for another concert at the Wachovia Center in Philadelphia. During the show, Bono tells the crowd he wants to play 'People Get Ready', but they need an extra guitarist to help. Rather than invite someone up from the crowd, though, Bruce Springsteen strolls on stage and the audience goes nuts. Bono also calls Bruce's wife, Patti Scialfa, on stage to sing a few verses. They play an extended version of the song with mostly made-up lyrics, eventually leaving only Bruce (playing Bono's Irish Falcon guitar) and Larry on stage to close out the first encore. It's a reprise of the collaboration that first happened September 25, 1987, in Philadelphia's now-demolished JFK Stadium.

October 18
Bono meets with House and Senate Democrats on Capitol Hill today, urging them to fund the US's commitments to poverty, AIDS and Africa. He has a private lunch with prominent Democrats including Nancy Pelosi, John Kerry, and Barack Obama.

October 19-20
MCI Center, Washington, DC, with Damian Marley. Prior to the first concert, Bono has lunch with President George W. Bush in the White House. The White House invited Bono to the lunch meeting, giving Bono a chance to cover both sides of the political aisle a day after meeting with Democratic leaders on Capitol Hill. Bono uses today's meeting to press the Bush Administration to fully fund its recent commitments to poverty and AIDS relief. A number of politicians attend the first show, prompting Bono to give a longer speech at the start of 'One' – so long that Larry puts down his drum sticks and seems to be timing Bono. US Secretary of State Condoleeza

Rice is in the audience for the second show.

October 21
Bono travels from Washington, DC, to Philadelphia to speak at an event hosted by the World Affairs Council of Philadelphia. When the helicopter he had planned to take becomes unavailable, Bono hops on an Amtrak train for the trip north. During the evening, the council gives Bono its International Statesman Award.

October 22
Mellon Arena, Pittsburgh, with Damian Marley. 'One' is dedicated to former Treasury Secretary Paul O'Neill, who went to Africa with Bono on a 10-day trip in 2002. O'Neill is at the show tonight.

October 24-25
Palace of Auburn Hills, Detroit, with Institute. During the second show, U2 pays homage to civil rights pioneer Rosa Parks, who had died earlier in the day. Bono mentions Parks by name on a couple occasions during the show, and dedicates 'One' to her.

October 26
U2 wins all four awards for which they are nominated at the *Billboard* Roadwork '05 Touring Awards: Top Tour, Top Draw, Top Boxscore, and Top Manager (for Principle Management). The band is on the road and not in attendance at the ceremony in New York.

October 28
Toyota Center, Houston, with Damian Marley. Before the show, a couple fans present Bono with a proclamation from the Houston Mayor's Office proclaiming today "U2 Day" in the city. Bono thanks Houston Rockets basketball player Dikembe Mutombo, who is at the show, for his work with the ONE Campaign. Other local celebrities at the show are Houston Astros Craig Biggio and Roger Clemens.

October 29
American Airlines Center, Dallas, with Damian Marley.

November 1

Bono writes an essay titled "This Generation's Moon Shot" for *Time* magazine. "Beating AIDS and extreme, stupid poverty, this is our moon shot," he writes. "This is our civil rights struggle, our anti-apartheid movement. This is what the history books will remember our generation for – or blame us for, if we fail."

November 1-2

Staples Center, Los Angeles, with Damian Marley. The first show becomes a belated 44th birthday party for Larry. Bono leads the crowd in singing 'Happy Birthday' to Larry during the first encore. The entire band is wearing *The Larry Mullen Band* t-shirts when they come out for the second encore. After 'All Because Of You', Bono invites Exit, a four-piece, all-girl, former U2 tribute band to come on stage and they play 'Out Of Control' to great applause from the crowd. At the end of the show, Larry approaches the mic and thanks the crowd for coming to his party, then thanks Bono, Edge, and Adam for being in his band.

Prior to the second show, U2 soundchecks 'The Wanderer', a song they've never played before in concert, and may still not: it's expected that the soundcheck performance is recorded for inclusion in an upcoming TV special about Johnny Cash. It was Cash, not Bono, who sang the song on the *Zooropa* album in 1993. Earlier in the day, Bono records a video segment talking about AIDS and health issues in Africa that will be shown via satellite tomorrow at the *Time* magazine 2005 Global Health Summit in New York.

November 3

Another day, another satellite appearance for Bono. Today, it's the annual Black Ball Concert in New York City, a fundraiser for Alicia Keys' Keep A Child Alive Foundation. Keys sits at the piano in the Lincoln Center while Bono appears on an overhead screen from Los Angeles. They sing Peter Gabriel's 'Don't Give Up'.

November 4-5

MGM Grand Arena, Las Vegas, with Damian Marley. At the first show, a fan dressed as Elvis dances at the tip of the ellipse while Bono sings 'Can't Help Falling In Love'. Bono dedicates '40' to Irish boxer Wayne McCullough, who's in the audience. McCullough is a longtime friend of the band, and he visits with them backstage before and after the show. Two guest vocalists highlight the second show: Mary J. Blige sings 'One' with Bono, and Brandon Flowers of the Killers joins U2 for 'In A Little While'. Bono brings tour manager Dennis Sheehan on stage between encores to wish him happy birthday with cake and a crowd sing-a-long.

November 6

Edge and Morleigh have dinner in Beverly Hills with Lance Armstrong. After dinner, they see the Rolling Stones perform at the Hollywood Bowl.

November 7

The Edge lands a cover interview in the December issue of the UK magazine, *The Word*, which is published today.

November 8-9

Oakland Arena, Oakland, with Damian Marley. Prior to the first show, Bono meets with the editorial

Above: Bono welcomes Mary J. Blige on stage, Las Vegas, November 5.

board of the *San Francisco Chronicle* and the paper's rock critic, Joel Selvin. He's at their offices to discuss poverty and AIDS in Africa, DATA and even rock and roll. At the arena, Bono and Edge visit with U2 fan Jack Grandcolas, whose wife Lauren – also a U2 fan – was one of the victims who died on United Airlines flight 93 when it crashed in Pennsylvania on 9/11. Jack tells Bono and Edge that 'One Tree Hill' was Lauren's favourite song. In her honour, Bono and Edge add a bit of the song to the end of 'One', saying, "This is for Lauren." After the show, U2 reserves the bar at the Four Seasons Hotel for a small party that includes the likes of Metallica's Lars Ulrich, actors Sean Penn, Robin Williams and Winona Ryder and champion cyclist Lance Armstrong.

Before the second show, Bono visits the campuses of both Google and Yahoo!, speaking with their staffers about debt relief projects and trying to organise an online community for the ONE Campaign.

Also on November 9, U2 announces that the Vertigo Tour will continue into 2006 with planned visits to Mexico, South America, Australia, New Zealand, and Japan. Bono, Edge, and Adam do interviews in the afternoon with Australian media about the upcoming tour dates there.

November 10

'Original Of The Species' arrives at radio stations in North America today as the fifth single from *How To Dismantle An Atomic Bomb*. It's a special edit of the album track, which was recorded with a string section in The Netherlands in July.

November 13-14

American Airlines Arena, Miami, with Institute. Before the second show, Bono and Edge videotape a movie called *A Day In The Life Of Edge*. They begin shooting inside their rooms at The Setai hotel and later head out to South Beach with the camera rolling. They visit a lifeguard tower and surprise the guard and a small crowd with impromptu acoustic renditions of 'In A Little While' and 'The First Time'.

Videotaping continues when the two arrive at American Airlines Arena in the late afternoon. Bono plays cameraman, asking U2 fans for their comments about The Edge... all the while another camera is taping Bono as he does his interviews. The fun even continues during the concert: Bono is still holding a videocamera as the show begins, and shoots video of Edge and U2 fans during 'City Of Blinding Lights'.

November 15

U2.com members are invited to renew their memberships. After the Vertigo Tour ticket presale mess early in the year, the most notable thing about membership renewals is the lack of any ticket presale guarantees: "There will not be any ticket guarantees as part of the re-subscription package... We continue to look for fair ways in which we can distribute tickets to our fans on future tours but any solution will not be tied to this re-subscription."

Below: Oakland, November 9.

November 16

St. Pete Times Forum, Tampa, with Institute. U2 appear on a CBS-TV special honouring Johnny Cash with a live performance of 'The Wanderer'. It's the first time U2 has performed the song live. The performance was taped two weeks ago, November 2, during a soundcheck at Staples Center in Los Angeles.

November 17

Edge tours the hurricane-ravaged city of New Orleans on foot and by helicopter. He's there to announce Music Rising, a campaign he's organised with veteran record producer Bob Ezrin. The goal is to replace instruments that were lost after hurricanes Katrina and Rita struck the area, providing up to 3,000 instruments for musicians, plus gear for churches, schools, repair shops and music academies. Edge spends time with musicians who live in the city, touring several neighbourhoods and struggling music venues. At one stop, he jams with local icon Walter "Wolfman" Washington. "Anyone who has earned money from music owes a huge debt to New Orleans," Edge says. "It's the birthplace of jazz, it has origins of rock'n'roll, and it's spawned some amazing hip-hop. The music culture is so rich and unique that it's absolutely crucial to support it. You'd see and hear things you'd get nowhere else. We all need New Orleans. We can't let that culture vanish in the flood."

Tonight, Edge has dinner at the recently reopened Restaurant August with New Orleans Jazz Festival organiser Quint Davis and Louisiana Lt. Gov. Mitch Landrieu.

Edge Talks About His First Visit to Post-Katrina New Orleans

"I was there a few months after the disaster, so I was there really when many areas of the city were still closed. I had a contact in the police force down there, so I was actually able to go down and see some of the areas, and it was quite overwhelming, the level of destruction. I'm used to seeing areas that have been hit with smaller-scale problems – I've seen firsthand bomb sites and all that – but this was on a totally different scale. This was not just a block or a few buildings. This was square kilometers of suburban development that were totally annihilated. I found it quite overwhelming to see just the scale of it. I saw things very few people would have seen. I got to see the dump where the authorities had been piling up the detritus of lives – the ruined cars, the ruined ovens and refrigerators and air-conditioning units, all these things. Acres and acres of ruined family possessions. When you see that, it's on just this unbelievable scale. It's hard to explain, really, if you haven't seen it."

November 18-19

Philips Arena, Atlanta, with Institute. During the first concert in Atlanta, Bono tells the crowd he wants to tape a TV message to be sent to Canada as part of a tribute to Daniel Lanois. Bono offers a brief tribute and then dedicates 'All Because Of You' to him. The clip will be played two days later when Lanois receives a lifetime achievement award in his hometown of Hamilton, Ontario. R.E.M. and Rick Wright of Pink Floyd are at the show. At the second show Bono sings 'MLK' for members of the King family who are in the crowd.

On November 19, U2 confirm a set of Vertigo Tour dates for Australia and New Zealand. The fourth leg of the Vertigo Tour will begin in Auckland on March 17, 2006, and continue for two weeks in Australia. Additional dates in other countries are still to be announced.

November 20

Bono is in New York for the filming of a new movie, *Across The Universe*, with director Julie Taymor. Bono's role in the film includes a performance of the Beatles' classic, 'I Am The Walrus'.

Edge is in the front row for an Echo & The Bunnymen gig at Irving Plaza.

Meanwhile, U2 is featured for the first time on the long running American news magazine, *60 Minutes*.

November 21

Madison Square Garden, New York, with Patti Smith. Smith joins U2 on stage to perform a cover of John Lennon's 'Instant Karma'.

Earlier in the day, Edge shoots a Music Rising public service announcement in a quiet alley in Manhattan. The alley is made to look like New Orleans, with trash and debris on the ground, including a broken acoustic guitar that Edge picks up as the cameras roll. Bono sits down for an interview in his Manhattan apartment with *Time* magazine's Josh Tyrangiel. The interview is for a special issue coming up in which Bono, along with Bill and Melinda Gates, will be named the magazine's "Persons of the Year". The interview is interrupted by Bono's participation in a videoconference to discuss the yet-to-be-launched Product (RED) campaign, which will aim to raise money to fight AIDS via sales of popular products. Bono also appears via pre-recorded video tonight at a tribute event in London to former British cabinet minister Mo Mowlam.

November 22

Madison Square Garden, New York, with Patti Smith. Smith joins U2 on stage again, just as she did last night, to sing 'Instant Karma' during U2's encore. But the concert comes to an abrupt end at the end of the song. Bono leads Smith off-stage, Edge follows while still playing the song, and then Adam leaves. They come back out and sing another chorus before everyone leaves again. The lights come on and the show is over, even though two more songs are on the printed set list.

While in New York, U2 show up at a birthday party for MTV chief Tom Freston at the Spotted Pig restaurant.

November 23

Concert promoter DG Medios & Espectaculos issues a news release announcing a handful of Vertigo Tour concerts in South America in 2006. Shows mentioned are in Sao Paulo, Santiago, and Buenos Aires, but U2 doesn't confirm the dates.

November 25

Corel Centre, Ottawa, with Arcade Fire. Prior to tonight's show in the Canadian capital of Ottawa, Bono conducts a news conference on Parliament Hill to discuss his ongoing disagreement about African aid with Prime Minister Paul Martin. Bono tells reporters he's "crushed" that the Canadian government hasn't committed 0.7 percent of GDP to eliminating global poverty. Mayor Bob Chiarelli declares today "U2 Day" in Ottawa, where the band is playing its first concert in 20 years. *Time*'s Josh Tyrangiel is tagging along with Bono today and tomorrow for the magazine's upcoming feature.

A new video – the second version – for 'Original Of The Species' premieres today. It features a futuristic animation of a woman that morphs into images of each band member. Says director Catherine Owens: "[Bono] said to me he wanted to be in a video with her, he wanted to be in her world and could I make that happen?"

Right: Edge shoots the Music Rising TV spot, November 21.

November 26-28
Bell Centre, Montreal, with Arcade Fire. At the first show, Daniel Lanois joins U2 on stage to perform 'Bad'. At the second show, hometown favourites Arcade Fire join U2 on stage to perform a rowdy cover of Joy Division's 'Love Will Tear Us Apart'. Bono spends most of the song crouching over in front of a teleprompter to see the lyrics. Tonight is the last of Arcade Fire's three-night opening slots in Canada, and they are warmly received by the U2 audience.

November 29
With almost a week off between shows, U2 arrive in Acapulco today for some rest and relaxation. But it won't be all fun for Bono, who travels to Guadalajara for two days to scout stadiums and see a performance of Cirque du Soleil. When he gets to Acapulco, Bono stays with the well-known Camil family.

December 1
Bono, Nelson Mandela and Coldplay's Chris Martin join forces for a World AIDS Day podcast made available on The ONE Campaign's web site.

December 3
Bono takes part in Mexico's ninth national telethon by speaking via telephone with Isabella Camil. Bono praises Mexico and recites in Spanish a few lines of the poem 'Instants' by Jorge Luis Borges. Before hanging up, Bono says he's looking forward to returning to Mexico next year with U2. The annual telethon is a fundraiser for the construction of two children's rehabilitation centers in Mexico.

December 4
TD Banknorth Garden, Boston, with Institute. Bono brings about a dozen fans on stage with different national flags tied together and they stand behind Larry during 'One' holding the flags up as a backdrop. U2 surprises the audience by returning for a third, unplanned encore. Many in the crowd have left – including some fans who went outside to get in line for

tomorrow's show – and miss a surprise performance of 'All Because Of You' and 'Fast Cars'.

While in Boston, Bono sits down for another interview with *Time*'s Josh Tyrangiel in preparation for the "Persons of the Year" issue.

December 5

TD Banknorth Garden, Boston, with Institute. U2's final concert of the year in its adopted hometown of Boston is special, with several Christmas-themed moments throughout the show. Bono tells the crowd what's on his Christmas list – "Five million people for the Make Poverty History campaign, a fire engine, more time with my kids" – and says that Edge wants a train set. During 'Mysterious Ways', he invites a fan dressed as Santa to dance on stage, and another fan dressed as Elvis soon joins the fun. After the show, Bono and Paul McGuinness join a private party at J.J. Foley's bar, where friends are saying goodbye to Steve Morse, the longtime rock critic of the *Boston Globe* newspaper. At one point, Bono stands on a table to wish Morse well. Former J. Geils front man Peter Wolf is also there and leads a raucous version of 'For He's A Jolly Good Fellow' in Morse's honour. Shortly before the show, the band had given Morse an autographed copy of *U2 & I: The Photographs 1982-2004*.

Tickets for an initial round of stadium shows in Australia and New Zealand go on sale this morning. A show in Auckland sells out in 90 minutes. A concert in Melbourne sells out 70,000 tickets in two hours; promoters say it's the fastest-selling concert in the Telstra Dome's history. And a concert in Sydney, also about 70,000 tickets, sells out in less than 50 minutes. Shows in Adelaide and Brisbane sell out, too, though not as briskly as the others. The quick sales prompt the addition of three extra shows – one each in Auckland, Melbourne, and Sydney.

December 6

Bono and DATA officials visit two of the most prestigious universities in the world: Harvard and the

Massachusetts Institute of Technology (MIT).

At Harvard, University President Larry Summers – a longtime supporter of Bono's debt relief campaign – hosts a question-and-answer session with students at the school's John F. Kennedy School of Government. Bono encourages the students to become active in fighting AIDS and supporting global development. He also tells the students about a possible future collaboration with the university, but doesn't reveal any details. About 80 students attend the 40-minute private event.

Later, at MIT, Bono's group meets with members of the school's Poverty Action Lab to learn about the group's research. Bono's thrilled with what he learns. "Do you know we've been chased down hallways with the words 'measurable results'?," he says. "What you have here is the stuff that can change the world!"

Tonight, the entire band plus Paul McGuinness have dinner at Boston's Radius Restaurant with singer Peter Wolf and investment manager/philanthropist James Palotta.

Also today, 'Don't Give Up (Africa)', the new charity single featuring Bono's duet with Alicia Keys, goes on sale via Apple's iTunes Music Store. The song was recorded last month for Keys' Black Ball fundraiser in New York.

December 7

Civic Center, Hartford, with Institute. While in Hartford, Paul McGuinness visits ESPN's campus to see and discuss a new cross-promotional partnership. The sports network wants to use 'City Of Blinding Lights' as a theme song for its coverage of next year's World Cup. McGuinness is impressed with ESPN's plans and makes the deal. The first step will involve ESPN shooting special concert footage next week when U2 plays in Charlotte.

Bono appears via videotape at a *Sports Illustrated* reception honouring Tom Brady as the magazine's Sportsman of the Year. Brady is a big U2 fan, and the two have met before. Bono praised Brady during a U2 gig in Boston in October for being the two millionth person to join the One Campaign. Bono's segment is taped a day or two earlier while the band was in Boston.

December 8

U2 are nominated for five Grammy Awards: Album of the Year and Best Rock Album for *How To Dismantle An Atomic Bomb*, Song of the Year and Best Rock Performance By a Duo or Group With Vocal for 'Sometimes You Can't Make It on Your Own', and Best Rock Song for 'City of Blinding Lights'.

Bono is in New York today, and calls writer Michka Assayas to have one final conversation for the paperback version of his book, *Bono: In Conversation with Michka Assayas*. Bono reveals that he has started working on a song, 'If I Could Live My Life Again', and says it's inspired by the poet Jorge Luis Borges.

December 9

HSBC Arena, Buffalo, with Institute. Bono does an interview in Boston this morning with PBS-TV for their upcoming program, *Frontline: The Age of AIDS*. A snow and icestorm delays U2's flight to Buffalo by three hours. Though the band arrive late, the show goes on and Bono makes several references to yesterday's 25th anniversary of John Lennon's death.

U2 formally announces a pair of concerts in Mexico next year. The 2006 leg of the Vertigo Tour will begin February 12 in Monterrey, and will be followed by a show in Mexico City on the February 15. The shows will be U2's first in Mexico since 1997, when a post-concert incident involving the sons of then-President Zedillo left U2's longtime security chief Jerry Mele seriously injured.

December 10
Quicken Loans Arena, Cleveland, with Institute. Amnesty International honours U2 with its 2005 Ambassador of Conscience Award for their "21 years of commitment" to equality.

December 12
New Charlotte Arena, Charlotte, with Institute. Prior to tonight's show, Bono has dinner at the arena with former Senator Jesse Helms. They eat in the cafeteria and discuss the campaign's progress, but the 84-year-old Helms doesn't stay for the concert. A Helms' spokesman says Bono called a couple weeks ago and requested the meeting.

Six ESPN videocameras shoot tonight's gig as part of the agreement reached last week in Hartford. Before the show, U2's crew works with ESPN as the network shoots the pixel panels with a video display showing the flags of countries taking part in the World Cup.

Tickets for a second U2 show in Auckland, New Zealand, next year sell out in less than two hours.

December 14
Savvis Center, St. Louis, with Kanye West. Kanye West begins a brief, four-show stint as U2's opening act. Bono takes the unusual step of personally introducing the controversial rapper to the crowd before West takes the stage, but many in the crowd voice their displeasure during U2's set by booing when Bono thanks West for opening tonight's show.

December 15
Qwest Center, Omaha, with Kanye West. Tonight's concert is the first

time U2 has played a show in Nebraska.

December 16
Bono remains in Omaha and has a busy day planned away from the band, which includes attending a DATA board meeting at the Joslyn Art Museum. *Time*'s Josh Tyrangiel interviews Bono and Bill and Melinda Gates, and the three also do a photo shoot for the magazine.

Billboard magazine declares the Vertigo Tour the top-grossing tour of the year. The magazine says U2 sold $260 million worth of tickets and drew more than three million people to 90 concerts, all of which were sell-outs. The Eagles, who grossed $117 million from 77 shows, are second, followed by Neil Diamond, who earned more than $71 million. The results don't include the Rolling Stones' A Bigger Bang tour because their promoter doesn't submit financial figures until the tour is over.

December 17
Delta Center, Salt Lake City, with Kanye West.

December 18
Time magazine names Bono and Bill and Melinda Gates its "Persons of the Year" for 2005. The magazine explains the choice by saying they were selected "for being shrewd about doing good, for rewiring politics and re-engineering justice, for making mercy smarter and hope strategic and then daring the rest of us to follow." The three will appear together on the cover of the magazine, which hits store shelves tomorrow. It's Bono's fourth time on the cover, having appeared with U2 in 1987, alone in 2002, and earlier this year when *Time*'s cover story about Apple Computer showed his image on a video iPod.

December 19
Rose Garden, Portland, with Kanye West. U2 plays its final show of the year, a show filled with thank you's all around – from fans, from the band, and from the U2 crew. As U2 begins 'Elevation', thousands of fans hold up white THANK YOU signs which had been distributed

Above: Fans display their 'Thank You' signs at the final Vertigo concert, Portland, December 19.

and promoted by members of the atu2.com, interference.com, and U2.com web sites. Bono is taken aback by the fans' gesture, and says "No, thank YOU!" before asking Edge and Adam for help saying "thank you" in other languages. Bono gives his thanks to the crew, mentioning dozens of people by name during several songs throughout the show. The crew returns the favour before the second encore, as each person lines the ellipse wearing single-lettered t-shirts that spell out THE U2 CREW WOULD LIKE TO THANK EDGE BONO LARRY AND ADAM FOR A GREAT 2005.

Also today, U2 announces it will return to South America for a show in Buenos Aires on March 1. Additional South American dates will be announced later.

December 26
Bono and Ali spend the day at the Leopardstown horse races in south Dublin.

Late December
Bono is interviewed by Queen Noor of Jordan, who's a "guest editor" on BBC's *Today* programme. They talk about the situation in Africa, but media pick up instead on Bono's comments about tension in the band caused by his humanitarian work. "There was one point when I thought 'I'm going to be thrown out of the band for this stuff'," says Bono. The phone conversation will air on December 31.

2006

After navigating some rough waters and making 2005 one of their most successful years, U2 hope to continue the momentum in 2006. And they do, with a sweep of five awards at the Grammys and rapturous response as the Vertigo Tour plays Central and South America – where fans haven't seen U2 in eight years.

But the band hit rough waters again with just ten concerts to go; those dates are postponed indefinitely due to an illness in one of the band member's families. Although there are several reports that new dates are about to be released, fans in Australia, New Zealand, and Japan wait more than four months to find out that U2 will finish the tour at the end of the year.

During the time off, Bono goes into overdrive with his work on AIDS and poverty, including a 10-day visit to Africa. U2 also work on new material and collaborate with Green Day on a benefit single and live performance for Edge's Music Rising organisation. U2 release an official biography in which Edge reveals that his daughter Sian's illness is what has led to tour-related delays. The biography is complemented by the release of another U2 compilation, *U2 18 Singles*. Some fans look at the release as a money grab on the part of U2 and its record company, but by the end of the year, most of that's forgotten and the focus is back on the astonishing success of the now-complete Vertigo Tour.

January 4
U2's relationship with ABC/ESPN continues tonight when ABC uses 'Vertigo' as background music for a highlight segment at half time of the college football championship game between the University of Texas and USC. The short video clip mixes U2 performing 'Vertigo' from the recently released *Live In Chicago* DVD with first-half highlights of the game.

January 5
Bono and Willie Williams talk on the phone to plan for U2's upcoming performance at the Grammy Awards, and about the fourth leg of the Vertigo Tour, which is a little more than a month away.

January 10
The Vertigo Tour wins the People's Choice Award for Best Tour. U2 are not in attendance to collect the honour.

January 11
A new version – the third overall – of the 'Original Of The Species' video premieres on AOL Music today. This version is a re-edit of the second video, the Catherine Owens version that features CGI-animated humans, including computerised versions of each U2 band member. The computer effects are mostly gone from this new version of the video. The first video was the *Live From Chicago* version that helped promote

Apple's video iPod.
Bono and Ali, along with Paul McGuinness and his family, enjoy a night on the town tonight, taking in the Irish premiere of Neil Jordan's film *Breakfast On Pluto* at the Savoy Cinema on O' Connell Street in Dublin. The film's stars include, among others, Gavin Friday acting the role of Billy Hatchet. The fun continues after the film as Bono and Ali join parties at the Clarence Hotel and Lillie's Bordello, where Irish media report that Bono hands a €100 dollar bill to a homeless man.

January 12
An article on RollingStone.com causes a small stir over the future of U2. In an interview with Evan Serpick, Edge talks about the upcoming end of the Vertigo Tour: "From a really great start, it's just built and built and built. I'm happy to say bye-bye, because I don't think we could ever top it." Other media outlets pick up only on the second half of Edge's statement, interpreting it to mean that U2 plans to stop touring altogether.

January 16
Ticket sales for U2's upcoming concert in Sao Paulo, Brazil, quickly turn chaotic as demand far outweighs supply, and the system setup to sell tickets is a complete failure. Concert organisers sell only a tiny percentage of tickets online, and the rest are sold only through the Pao de Acucar supermarket

Left: Bono and Eddie Vedder, Hawaii, December 9.
Above: Bono signs for a fan in Baden-Baden, January 23.

chain, which has just 10 stores in Sao Paulo and two in Rio de Janeiro. There isn't enough staff to handle the long lines, and the supermarket's equipment breaks down. Organisers quickly issue an apology and promise a second concert will be added.

January 23
Bono is in Copenhagen for meetings with Danish politicians about AIDS and poverty. He also delivers a speech to the Borsen Executive Club. He flies to Baden-Baden, Germany, and signs autographs for fans in the evening.
Meanwhile, Edge is in Park City, Utah, as Lian Lunson's guest at the Sundance Film Festival. Lunson is there to screen her film, *Leonard Cohen – I'm Your Man*, which includes a performance by U2.

Above: COEXIST in Spanish, Mexico City, February 15.

Edge tells MTV about U2's progress in the studio, January 23

"We haven't really got to the point where we're thinking seriously about the next record. We're at that wonderful place where we're just experimenting, and trying things, just really letting our imaginations go. It's my favourite phase of making an album because there are no constraints, you just write and explore possibilities. That's where I am now: loads of possibilities, but nothing concrete."

During the day, Edge does some shopping at the small town's shops and takes part in a variety of interviews and photo shoots. One of the interviews is with Benjamin Wagner, who's representing MTV News.

January 24
Bono receives the German Media Award for his efforts on debt relief at a ceremony in Baden-Baden.

January 25
Bono's week of travel finds him in Davos, Switzerland, for the start of the annual World Economic Conference. Bono meets with new German Chancellor Angela Merkel, and the two promise to meet later in the year to talk about AIDS and poverty in Africa. Bono tells reporters he's "delighted" with the speech Merkel delivered today, and that he was honoured she approached him immediately afterward, even before seeking out other world leaders.

Edge is one of the judges of a create-a-ringtone competition sponsored by MIT and h-lounge.com. He spends about 90 minutes on a conference call with fellow judges, listening to the competition's finalists in a variety of categories. In the official press announcement of winners two days later, Edge explains his reasons for taking part as a judge: "Ringtones are a legitimate branch of pop music and this is a great opportunity for up-and-coming songwriters to create something designed specifically for the medium."

January 26
Bono uses the spotlight of the World Economic Forum to announce Product (RED), a campaign aimed at using commerce to beat AIDS in Africa. Several major companies are announced as participants, including Gap, Armani, and Converse. American Express introduces a new credit card – the Red Card – as part of the campaign. "Red is a 21st century idea," Bono says. "I think doing the Red thing, doing good, will turn out to be good business for them." The

idea is simple: Buy or use the red products and a portion of the money goes to fight AIDS. The money from Red will go to the Global Fund, a public-private partnership that has committed $4.5 billion for AIDS, tuberculosis and malaria programmes since it was created in 2002. According to today's announcement, Bono is the owner of Product (RED), and Bobby Shriver is its chief executive.

January 27

Still in Davos, Bono speaks during the Next Steps for Africa session at the World Economic Forum. He also meets with World Bank President Paul Wolfowitz, along with actors and fellow campaigners Angelina Jolie and Brad Pitt.

Meanwhile, Edge makes an appearance with a few New Orleans-based musicians at the Guitar Center in Los Angeles today. He's there to promote the Music Rising campaign, of which the Guitar Center is a major sponsor. Edge autographs a specially designed Gibson guitar and takes part in a photo shoot and interviews, while the musicians from New Orleans are there to pick up new instruments given to them by Music Rising.

January 29

For his work on the Vertigo Tour, Willie Williams is named Lighting Designer of the Year at the *Total Production* International Awards 2006 in London.

February 2

Bono is the keynote speaker today at the annual National Prayer Breakfast in Washington, DC, an event hosted by Democratic and Republican members of Congress. During his 20-minute speech, Bono quotes the Old Testament, New Testament, and the Koran. He uses a faith-based argument to encourage the US to give "an additional one percent of the federal budget" to the poor. President George W. Bush speaks shortly after Bono, about Bono: "He's a doer. The thing about this good citizen of the world is he's used his position to get things done.

You're an amazing guy, Bono. God bless you."

Shortly after the breakfast, Bono spends about 45 minutes at the Washington Hilton Hotel in a meeting with a small group of religion reporters who were invited to cover the event. They discuss his speech, the ONE Campaign, and Bono's own spiritual walk.

Later in the day, Bono speaks at an annual retreat of House Democrats in Kingsmill, Virginia, again touching on themes of fighting AIDS and promoting debt relief in Africa. The event is not open to press or the public.

U2 wins all three categories in which they are nominated at the annual Meteor Irish Music Awards in Dublin. Adam is the lone band member on hand to accept trophies for Best Irish Band, Best Irish Album (*How To Dismantle An Atomic Bomb*), and Best Live Performance (Croke Park concerts).

February 5

It's Fashion Week in New York, and Bono and Ali attend a party presenting fall fashions from their Edun clothing line. Also on hand are musicians Michael Stipe, Lou Reed, and Laurie Anderson.

February 7

U2 rehearses at the Staples Center in Los Angeles for a performance at tomorrow's Grammy Awards. Edge also rehearses with Bruce Springsteen, Elvis Costello and others for their New Orleans tribute. Backstage, Bono does an interview with talk show host Ellen Degeneres for a segment that will air on her show in a couple days.

Later, Bono makes a surprise appearance the Wilshire Ebell Theatre, where he and Recording Academy President Neil Portnow present the Trustees Award to Island Records founder Chris Blackwell. Bono praises Blackwell's willingness to let musicians take risks without corporate interference or fear of getting dropped. "If U2 arrived right now, in the current climate, we would not have gotten past our second album, and I think that's kinda sad. I especially think it's very sad,

because we're doing very well now," he says, to laughter. Blackwell replies that his only contribution to U2's success was that he "pretty much stood out of the way".

February 8

Staples Center, Los Angeles. U2 sweeps all five awards for which it's nominated at the Grammy Awards. *How To Dismantle An Atomic Bomb* wins for Album of the Year and Best Rock Album; 'Sometimes You Can't Make It On Your Own' wins Song of the Year and Best Rock Performance By A Duo Or Group With Vocal; and 'City of Blinding Lights' is named Best Rock Song. Steve Lillywhite also picks up the Grammy for Producer of the Year, Non-Classical, for his work on *How To Dismantle An Atomic Bomb* and Jason Mraz's album, Mr. A-Z.

U2 performs 'Vertigo' and 'One' – the latter with Mary J. Blige guesting as she has several times in recent months. At the end of the night, Edge performs in an all-star tribute to the music and sounds of New Orleans. Along with the likes of Allen Toussaint, Dr. John, Bonnie Raitt, Bruce Springsteen, and Elvis Costello, the group performs 'Yes We Can' and 'In The Midnight Hour'.

After the ceremony, U2 heads to the Tom Tom Club in Santa Monica for a party hosted by Interscope chief Jimmy Iovine, which includes guests Bruce Springsteen, Green Day, Arcade Fire, members of Coldplay and others. They also call 2FM's Gerry Ryan, who's on-air in Dublin, and share the news of U2's big night.

In the week following U2's Grammy sweep, *How To Dismantle An Atomic Bomb* returns to the *Billboard* chart at number 49 with sales of 27,000 copies, a 512% jump.

February 10

With much of the crew already in Mexico, U2 fly from Los Angeles to Monterrey to prepare for the fourth leg of the Vertigo Tour. During the flight, the band review the scripts for a series of World Cup commercials ESPN wants to air later this year. The scripts call for each band member to provide voice-overs for a set of five commercials.

February 11
U2 rehearse at Tecnológico Stadium.

February 12
Tecnológico Stadium, Monterrey, with the Secret Machines. U2 open the fourth leg of the Vertigo Tour with their first show in Mexico since 1997. At the start of 'I Still Haven't Found What I'm Looking For', Bono apologises for being gone so long. The band skipped Mexico after an incident that left longtime security chief Jerry Mele injured at the hands of bodyguards of the son of the Mexican president at the time. Salma Hayek is at the show. In the afternoon, U2 record a video with Tour Production Manager Jake Berry, who's about to be honoured with a concert industry award in three days.

Before the show, police seize counterfeit merchandise outside the stadium, leading to a confrontation with merchants. One officer shoots his gun into the air to maintain control of the situation. Days later, federal agents announce the seizure of 1,375 pirated U2 items, including 1,100 t-shirts, 70 hats, 60 DVDs, 60 CDs, 50 magazines and 35 coffee mugs featuring U2.

February 15-16
Azteca Stadium, Mexico City, with the Secret Machines.

On February 15 U2 wins the Major Tour of the Year and Most Creative Stage Production awards at the Pollstar Concert Industry Awards in Las Vegas. Jake Berry is named Road Warrior of the Year.

On the following day U2's 2005 concert in Munich receives an award at the Live Entertainment Awards in Hamburg.

February 17
U2 shoots a music video with Mary J. Blige at the Teatro Ferrocarrilero (Railroad Theatre) in Mexico City. They're doing a performance video for Blige's cover of 'One', which will be a single from her current album, *The Breakthrough*.

February 19
U2, minus Edge, arrive in Sao Paolo in preparation for two shows at Morumbi Stadium. Bono hops a plane for Brasilia to meet with President Luiz Inacio Lula da Silva and Culture Minister Gilberto Gil. Bono has strong praise for da Silva's work fighting poverty. Bono and da Silva meet at the Granja do Torto presidential resort outside the capital city, where they talk about reducing hunger and developing renewable energy sources. Bono agrees to donate a guitar to be auctioned after U2's concerts this week as a fund raiser for the country's Zero Hunger programme. Da Silva and Bono are not strangers – they met a year ago during the World Economic Forum in Davos, Switzerland.

Also today, Bono and Larry sit down for a interview on the TV programme *Fantastico*.

The Sunday Times runs a recent interview Bono has done with Michka Assayas. Bono hits back against critics who have attacked the work he's doing and the people he's working with.

February 20-21
Morumbi Stadium, Sao Paulo, with Franz Ferdinand. The first show airs live on Brazilian TV. Quincy Jones and Gilberto Gil, Brazil's Culture Minister, are at the second show.

February 22
At a formal dinner in the city of Salvador with Culture Minister Gilberto Gil, the Brazilian government gives Bono a packet of condoms and anti-AIDS information.

February 23
Bono appears via videotape at the *NME* Awards in London, where he introduces Bob Geldof, who wins the Hero of the Year award. The taped segment is a shocker, as Bono uses the F-word 14 times. "Bob Geldof has told me to fuck off perhaps hundreds, maybe thousands of times ... Thank you very much for this award and to my friend who is picking it up in all our honour – fuck off."

Bono, Edge, and Larry join in the opening night of Carnaval in the city of Salvador, Brazil. They watch the festivities from Culture Minister Gilberto Gil's private box above the parade. When Brazilian pop star Ivete Sangalo sings 'Vertigo' from atop a sound truck in front of them, Bono and Edge help her finish the song. Later, they join another singer who covers Bob Marley's 'No Woman, No Cry'.

February 25
U2 arrive in Chile in preparation for tomorrow's concert. Adam is first to land, traveling by himself and getting in almost two hours before the rest of the band. Hundreds of fans are waiting for U2 at the airport and outside the Hyatt Hotel.

Bono is named Most Inspired Artist at the fourth annual MTV TRL Awards in New York.

February 26
Estadio Nacional, Santiago, with Franz Ferdinand. It's show day in Santiago, but there's other business going on before the show. During the day, Bono visits the La Moneda presidential palace, where President Ricardo Lagos gives Bono the Pablo Neruda Merit Award – the country's highest award for the arts. Bono says he admired the late Chilean Nobel Prize laureate, who died in 1973. "It is an extraordinary thing to be here, after eight years, and to see how Chile has changed. It is a different country," Bono says. Lagos also presents Bono with a traditional Andean instrument known as the charango, and suggests Bono should learn to play it before U2's next concert in Chile.

Bono rails against his critics, February 19

"We get hits from the left, we get hits from the right, but in the end, every year, the world's poor are better off for our presence."

Later in the day, U2 receives Amnesty International's 2005 Ambassador of Conscience award during a ceremony at the National Stadium. U2 chooses to get the honour there as a reminder of those killed under General Augusto Pinochet – during his rule, the stadium was turned into a place of detention, torture and death. Chile's President-elect, Michelle Bachelet, praises U2 for its good works. "You are a reminder to all of us that the world is not changed only by politicians and governments," she tells them. "The world is changed by all of us." After the ceremony, Bono meets with relatives of political dissidents who disappeared during the dictatorship of General Pinochet.

During the show, Bono and Edge sing 'Mothers Of The Disappeared', and Edge plays the charango given to Bono earlier in the day. Both Lagos and Bachelet are at tonight's show.

February 28
As huge crowds of fans wait outside, U2 finally comes out to wave from a balcony at their hotel in Buenos Aires, Argentina. Later in the evening, they perform about a dozen songs at River Plate Stadium while 3D film crews shoot close-ups and other shots that will be impossible to get during a real show with a full stadium.

March 1-2
River Plate Stadium, Buenos Aires, with Franz Ferdinand. Hours before the first show, Bono visits Argentine President Nestor Kirchner at the Government House. The first show ends with 'Love Is Blindness', performed for the first time since the end of the Zoo TV Tour in 1993. Before the second show, U2 meets with five members of the Mothers of the Plaza De Mayo. The mothers stay for the concert, and U2 sings 'Mothers Of The Disappeared' in their honour. Bono also acknowledges them at the end of 'Miss Sarajevo'. After the show, the band visit with Brazilian football legend Diego Maradona, whose presence causes quite a stir among the many football fans on the U2

Above: U2 greets fans from their Buenos Aires hotel, February 28.

crew. Both shows are filmed with eight high-definition 3D camera rigs for an expected IMAX film release.

March 4
Bono and his family arrive in Australia early for a short vacation before the Vertigo tour is due to resume. Australian media report that the family has rented out Altona, an exclusive harbourside mansion in Sydney.

March 8
The Hewsons spend the day cruising Sydney Harbor in a speedboat and visiting the Taronga Zoo. Australian photographers catch the Hewsons relaxing on the boat, and photos appear in tomorrow's morning papers.

March 9
Citing the "illness of an immediate family member of one of the band", U2 announce the postponement of the final ten dates of the Vertigo 2006 Tour. Affected are dates in New Zealand, Australia, Japan, and Hawaii.

Ticketmaster Australia tells fans, "Please retain your tickets until further announcements are made." Airlines take the unusual step of allowing cancellations and rescheduling of flights without charge, and keep their rules loose for months while fans wait for a new tour itinerary. Rumours spread on the Internet as fans wonder who's ill and how serious the situation is. Australian media report the story aggressively, naming the immediate family member rumored to be ill.

March 11
Australian concert promoter Michael Coppel meets with Bono and later tells reporters the future of the Vertigo Tour will be announced during the coming week.

U2's Vertigo Tour is named Least Painful Tour at the International Live Music Conference's "Arthur" Awards in London.

March 13
Bono appears on the Australian

programme *Enough Rope*, telling host Andrew Denton that the band expects to reschedule the postponed Vertigo Tour shows in November. He says exact dates may be announced within 24 hours, but it doesn't happen. The interview takes place at the Park Hyatt Hotel in Sydney.

March 14
While on the way to the airport for a flight home to Ireland, Bono chats on-air with New Zealand radio station, The Rock. He reiterates the band's tentative plans to return in November, and thanks fans for their patience.

March 29
Bono sings the praises of Irish writer Samuel Beckett at the launch of the Beckett Centenary Festival in Dublin Castle. "I've read most of his works, I'm a fan. I don't know what he's on about half the time but I have enjoyed not knowing," Bono says. Bono also recites a poem he wrote for the occasion called 'Waiting for Colgan'.

March 31
Bono and Ali are on hand as Bob Geldof receives the annual IRMA Honour in Dublin. It's the highest honour given out by the Irish music industry. Bono says a few words in Geldof's honor.

Late March
At Westland Studio in Dublin, Bono records a solo version of the sea shanty, 'A Dying Sailor To His Shipmates'. Maurice Seezer accompanies him on the accordion, and Hal Willner produces the track for an upcoming album of pirate songs collected by actor Johnny Depp, star of the *Pirates Of The Caribbean* film series.

April 2
Bono writes an open letter to Italian Prime Minister Silvio Berlusconi, which is published on the front page of *Corriere della Sera*, Italy's biggest-selling newspaper. In the letter, Bono challenges the prime minister's use of a photo of Bono in an election campaign brochure promoting Berlusconi's

Bono on U2 and dealing with crisis, March 13

"Our music does come out of community. It's a very tight community and so if one of us is going through it, we're all going through it. He will be out the other side of it. They will be out the other side of it. And God willing it will be a very positive outcome and we work through it. We've all been through diffcrent ups and downs and you've got to give yourself freedom within a band to get out of each other's way as well as to get in somebody's face at the right time. Sometimes you have to know when not to. This is one of those moments."

candidacy. The photo is used to promote Italy's aid to poor nations. "Mr. Berlusconi, regardless of how flattered I may feel to be included in your brochure, I also feel a bit exploited," Bono writes. "Tragically, in the past years under this government, Italy has become the last among the 22 richest nations in terms of spending toward aid to the Third World."

April 10
U2.com confirms today that Adam Clayton is engaged to Susie Smith, his girlfriend of ten years. The pair became engaged on Valentine's

Day. The couple plans to marry later this year, according to the announcement.

April 16
Music fans in Britain vote the line, "One life, with each other, sisters, brothers" (from 'One', of course) as their favourite lyric, according to a poll released by VH1. More than 13,000 music fans vote in the survey, choosing from a list of 100 lyrics. Coming in second is the lyric, "So you go and you stand on your own, and you leave on your own, and you go home, and you cry, and you want to die" from The Smiths' track 'How Soon Is Now'.

April 19
Paul McGuinness receives the Peter Grant Lifetime Achievement / Manager of the Year Award in London. Bono and Adam are in attendance as Chris Blackwell presents Paul with the prestigious award. Well-known music industry names such as Doug Morris, Louis Walsh, Jann Wenner and Jimmy Iovine send video tributes.

April 21
Edge attends a fund raising event in Beverly Hills for Senator Hillary Clinton. The event raises almost $1 million for Clinton's Senate re-election campaign.

April 27
Edge arrives in New Orleans in anticipation of the annual Jazz Festival – in this case, the first festival since Hurricane Katrina. He meets up with Music Rising co-founder Bob Ezrin for a news conference at the historic Preservation Hall jazz club. Edge also sits in on the Preservation Hall band's afternoon rehearsal, and doubles over when he first hears their unique arrangement of 'Vertigo'. The Hall's official re-opening happens in the evening with an invitation-only party, and Edge plays guitar as the Hall band again performs 'Vertigo'. Edge later attends a party at the Masquerade Lounge in Harrah's New Orleans Casino hosted by the Memphis chapter of the Recording Academy, then wraps up the night by catching

most of a show by local band Galactic at Tipitina, a night club.

April 29
Edge's day in New Orleans begins with a CNN interview at Preservation Hall. From there, he heads to the New Orleans Jazz Festival for a guest vocal performance with the New Birth Brass Band, singing 'Stand By Me' in tribute to New Orleans. He also watches other performances, including one by the Mahogany Brass Band, before taking the stage again, guesting on guitar with the Dave Matthews Band on their song, 'Smooth Rider'. Finally, with a CNN crew in tow, Edge visits a couple of New Orleans bars on Saturday night – playing 'Stand By Me' and two other songs with local musicians at the Bank Street Bar, then jamming with Trombone Shorty at the Maple Leaf.

May 2
A U2 fan bumps into Edge in Los Angeles and asks about the rescheduled Vertigo Tour dates. "They're still working out some kinks in the scheduling, but it should be up soon," Edge says.

Up the coast, Bono attends a birthday party for his friend and Elevation Partners co-founder, Roger McNamee, at the San Francisco Zoo. He takes photos with fans while walking around the zoo grounds.

May 4
Bono's day begins in Washington, DC, where he meets with various members of Congress to continue pushing for funding to fight poverty and AIDS in Third World nations. From there, he heads to Michigan for a 40-minute speech at the annual dinner of the Economic Club of Grand Rapids, again to call for more assistance for developing nations.

May 5
Bono's speaking tour moves on to Dallas, where he appears before an audience of 3,500 at Fair Park Music Hall. Africa, poverty, and AIDS are again the main topics at the event, which is presented by the World

Affairs Council of Dallas/Fort Worth. Earlier in the day, Bono meets with local faith and spiritual leaders to encourage their involvement with the ONE Campaign. Bono also meets today with Karen Hughes, George Bush's Under Secretary of State for Public Diplomacy and Public Affairs.

May 6
ESPN begins airing a series of commercials promoting its coverage of the upcoming World Cup football/soccer tournament. Four of the commercials feature U2 heavily. Bono does the voiceover on two spots: One is a montage of kids playing soccer around the world with 'City Of Blinding Lights' as

theme music; the other is about the military truce in Ivory Coast when the nation's soccer team qualified for the World Cup with 'Where The Streets Have No Name' as backing music. Adam Clayton voices the humorous third spot, which uses 'I Will Follow' and shows Scottish fans dancing in the streets. Edge voices the fourth spot, which uses 'Beautiful Day' and jokes about the extensive absenteeism that takes places during the World Cup. The ONE Campaign gets a brief but noticeable mention at the end of one of the U2-themed commercials. Paul McGuinness tells the *New York Times* that U2's compensation is "nothing extraordinary, but we did get paid".

Paul McGuinness on U2's deal with ESPN
"There's something wonderfully democratic about soccer. It's the cheapest game in the world. All you need is a ball, and boys and girls can play it. Not that we're zealots, but we feel that soccer is a good thing, so our association with it is a good one.

"With record companies decreasingly able to spend money on paid advertising, these kinds of hookups are more attractive."

May 11
Bono celebrates his birthday with a low-key evening at Lillie's Bordello in Dublin, hanging out with longtime friends Guggi and Gavin Friday.

May 15
In London today, Bono introduces the newest addition to the Product (RED) line: Motorola cellular phones. Motorola and several mobile service providers are teaming up to raise money for Global Fund-financed programs that help fight AIDS in Africa. A percentage of all sales of the new phone, as well as a percentage of user's phone bills, will be included

Below: Bono and Bobby Shriver introduce the (RED) cellphone, May 15.

Above: Bono and Ali in Lesotho, May 17.

in the Product (RED) initiative. "I think doing the Red thing, doing good, will turn out to be good business for them," Bono says at today's launch.

Later, Bono heads to the offices of the UK newspaper, *The Independent*, where he'll be the guest editor for tomorrow's newspaper. His work actually began weeks earlier with lining up writers, articles, and interviews on the subjects he wants featured in the paper. His tasks today include an interview of Tony Blair and Gordon Brown, and final editing of the rest of the day's news.

Tomorrow's paper features a stunning front page design by artist Damien Hirst, showing the headline NO NEWS TODAY, followed in tiny print by "Just 6,500 Africans died today as a result of a preventable, treatable disease. (HIV/AIDS)" Inside the paper, Bono interviews comedian Eddie Izzard, writes an editorial about the situation in Africa, and shares his horse racing picks in the sports section. A separate article focuses on Edge's work with Music Rising in New Orleans. Half the revenue from the day's paper is donated to the Global Fund to Fight Aids.

May 16
Four years after his first tour of the African continent, Bono is back to start a six-nation, 10-day tour to assess progress and identify needs.

He's traveling with executives from GAP and Motorola, two companies involved in the Product (RED) initiative, as well as others from the Product (RED) organisation. Bono arrives today in South Africa, but is refused entry to the country because his passport is full. A call to Nelson Mandela solves that problem, and Bono heads on to the country of Lesotho, where the tour begins.

May 17
A *New York Post* article today reports that Bono and Ali's Edun clothing line is "floundering" with lower-than-expected sales and several specialty stores dropping the line altogether. An Edun spokesperson admits they've "experienced bumps in the road".

May 18
Bono is in Rwanda to take part in a memorial service for victims of the 1994 genocide in the country. He places an arrangement of white lilies on a vault housing the remains of mainly minority Tutsis who were killed by extremists.

Adam catches tonight's Radiohead gig at the Hammersmith Apollo in London.

May 19
Bono meets in Kigali with Rwandan President Paul Kagame.

May 20
In Tanzania, Bono visits a local factory making nets to help protect against malaria.

May 22
Bono is in Mali to meet with cotton farmers who are struggling to earn a living because of agriculture subsidies and trade barriers. He also visits with Oxfam policy advisors to discuss the Make Trade Fair campaign. Tonight, Bono listens to the Samaquera band perform at a local bar and restaurant. The band is playing songs that are more than 1,000 years old. During the last song, Bono stands up, takes a microphone and joins in for about 10 minutes in an African chant, adding words as he goes along.

May 25
Larry makes a surprise appearance behind the drum kit during a party at the Summit Inn in Howth. It's a going away party for Stephen Galligan, the Summit Inn's manager. Larry plays on 'One' and 'New Year's Day' with Diablo, a local cover band with a strong U2 repertoire.

May 26
Bono and Edge attend the Cannes Film Festival in France. Paparazzi photograph Edge at a Dolce & Gabbana party.

May 27
Bono is in Monte Carlo for the Monaco Grand Prix Formula One race this weekend. During the day, Bono and Jay-Z party on a yacht owned by Renault boss Flavio Briatore, where Bono even sings a few songs. In the evening, it's on to the La Dolce Vita Ball, where Bono sings 'Redemption Song' with Wyclef Jean. The fundraising event benefits Jean's efforts to help Haitians raise themselves out of poverty.

June 6
Apple introduces an updated version of the U2 iPod. Unlike its 2004 predecessor's 20GB audio-only storage, the new model can store 30GB of music and video. The back continues to have the band's signatures, but is now on black stainless steel, not silver. The new version also includes a coupon for a 30-minute U2 video at the iTunes Music Store with U2 music and interviews.

June 9
Newspaper reports tell of U2's plans to develop a €36 million apartment complex in Dublin. The band's application to city officials calls for three eight-story buildings with a total of 90 apartment units.

June 9
U2.com thanks fans for patience with the rescheduling of Vertigo Tour dates and says, "We hope to have the situation resolved soon."

June 15

Bono and Paul McGuinness visit the historic Castlecoote House in Roscommon, Ireland, the site of a former medieval castle. While in the area, Bono is also heard singing 'Four Wheels On My Wagon' in a local pub. Their visit sparks immediate speculation that Bono is interested in buying the mansion, but newspaper reports quickly put a damper on the rumours.

June 16

The Edge helps unveil a guitar sculpture in honour of legendary guitarist Rory Gallagher in Dublin. More than a thousand fans are in the Temple Bar section of Dublin for the event. Edge tells the crowd about Gallagher's influence: "I just want to say Rory was an incredible influence on me as a guitar player. He laid the road on which we followed."

June 23

U2.com confirms the upcoming DVD release of 1993's *Zoo TV Live From Sydney* concert video. Along with the digitally remastered live show, the new release will include a bonus DVD of live tracks, mini-documentaries and more. A September release is planned.

June 29

Bono appears on CNN's *American Morning* programme via satellite from Monaco. The interview is timed to coincide closely with the anniversary of Live 8, and Bono talks about the progress made since the historic concert.

July 1

Dublin officials give another go-ahead to redevelopment plans in the Dublin Docklands area, which includes the construction of a 100-meter tower with new recording studios for U2's use.

July 4

A U2.com member email confirms that U2 are back at work in the studio: "U2 are off the road and spending some time working on

Daily Mail, Wednesday, June 21, 2006   Page 3

Bono views home where the streets have no name

Country retreat: Locals in Roscommon claim Bono has an interest in purchasing historic Castlecoote House, which dates back to the 17th century

U2 frontman may be seeking some privacy in deepest Co. Roscommon

By Helen Bruce

Family home? It is not known if Bono and Ali Hewson will move in

Part of history: Some of the ruins from the original castle

Above: The Irish press follow Bono's every move, June 15.

new songs in the recording studio, so it's a chance for us to mail you one of our occasional U2.Com updates."

July 7

Bono makes a virtual appearance on the popular Yahoo! Answers service, asking readers for a reply to the question, "What can we do to make poverty history?" It's part of Yahoo's "Ask the World" promotion, which involves a different celebrity asking a new question each day.

July 10

With anticipation continuing to build, especially in Australia, New Zealand, and Japan, U2.com announces that the revamped fourth leg of the Vertigo Tour will be announced "within a week".

July 13

Bono calls RTE Radio 1 from France to pay tribute to DJ John Kelly during the final edition of Kelly's *Mystery Train* programme. Bono and Edge both call Kelly again later in the show – but not on-air – to request Kelly play 'Death Is Not the End' by Bob Dylan.

July 20

Ending months of fan nervousness and speculation, U2 announce new dates for the Vertigo Tour that make up for dates postponed earlier in the year. All cities and shows that missed out in the spring get new dates, with the exception of Yokohama, Japan. In place of that show, U2 announces three dates in Tokyo. The fifth leg of the tour will begin on November 7 in Brisbane and end December 9 in Hawaii. Kanye West is announced as the opening act for all dates in Australia and New Zealand. In Hawaii, fellow rock legends Pearl Jam will open the show.

July 25

The *Leonard Cohen – I'm Your Man* soundtrack is released with the U2/Cohen collaboration, 'Tower Of Song'.

July 25-29

Around this time, Bono sees French rock icon Johnny Hallyday perform in Monaco. After the show, Bono says he wants to write a song for Hallyday. The French singer later reveals Bono has given him a song called 'I Am The Blues'.

July 31

A survey of 4,000 MTV viewers crowns Bono as the most influential pop star of the past 25 years. The survey coincides with MTV's 25th anniversary – the network began programming on August 1, 1981. Michael Jackson and Madonna come second and third in the poll, respectively.

August 1

In an article in today's *Independent*, reporter Allan Hall reports that U2 moved control of their publishing royalties out of Ireland to the Netherlands on June 1 in order to avoid paying substantial taxes under a new Irish law. There is no direct tax on royalties in the Netherlands. Hall reports that U2's royalties are now in the control of Dutchman Jan Favie, who shares the same duties for the Rolling Stones.

As other media spread the news, reaction to U2's decision is swift and harsh. Pundits say it's hypocritical for U2 to take potential tax money out of Ireland while Bono calls on the Irish government to give more of its tax revenue to Africa. Writing in the *Sunday Times*, Matt Cooper asks: "How can [Bono] be taken seriously on issues like the government's contribution to overseas aid, when he himself is reducing the pool of income from which that funding comes? If he does try it on then, in classic Irish fashion, he is likely to be told to 'shut up and sing'."

Also around this time, there's media backlash against Bono's involvement with the Elevation Partners venture fund for buying a stake in *Forbes* magazine, which is owned by conservative Steve Forbes.

August 2
U2 adds a third concert in Sydney on November 13. Meanwhile, 'Original Of The Species' picks up two MTV Video Music Award nominations: Best Special Effects In A Video and Best Editing In A Video. The video goes winless when awards are handed out later this month.

August 11
Bono appears in a pre-recorded interview with Bill Hybels at the Willow Creek Association Leadership Summit, a gathering of hundreds of church leaders from across North America. As he's been doing for some time now, Bono encourages the church leaders to take the initiative on campaigning for more support for AIDS and poverty victims in Africa. The interview is thought to have taken place about a month earlier in a Dublin hotel.

August 18
Hot Press reports that Jacknife Lee will handle production duties on U2's new studio album, with confirmation coming from Lee's management company. The company says Lee and U2 will get together in September for a month of recording.

August 19
News arrives that Edge has written the foreword for Andy Summers' upcoming autobiography, *One Train Later*. The former Police guitarist's book is due in stores on October 3, but U2 fans don't have to wait to read it – Edge's foreword is already available on *AndySummers.com*.

August 20
Bono and Ali arrive in Sarajevo for the annual Sarajevo Film Festival. It's Bono's second visit to the festival. While in town, he does an interview with Bosnian TV, and announces that U2 will have a new album out in 2007. He also sounds an all-too-familiar refrain: "Edge, right now, is on fire. He's really rockin'. He's playing guitar like I've never seen him playing guitar."

August 21
Bono visits Luciano Pavarotti at the tenor's home in Italy. Pavarotti is recovering from surgery for pancreatic cancer in July.

August 27
Time magazine features U2's longtime tour designer, Willie Williams, in a brief feature called "Innovators: Forging The Future" about visual and aural artists who are "showing us new ways to see and hear."

August 29
The Joshua Tree is ranked third in a BBC Radio 2 poll of the Top 100 Albums, coming in behind The Beatles' *Sgt. Pepper's Lonely Hearts Club Band* and *Thriller* by Michael Jackson. More than 220,000 people vote in the nation-wide survey designed to commemorate the 50th anniversary of the official British album charts.

Also today, *Rogue's Gallery* is released. The album features

Bono's solo version of 'A Dying Sailor To His Shipmates', which was recorded in the spring.

August 30
Bono visits German Chancellor Angela Merkel in Berlin to discuss Germany's upcoming G8 presidency in 2007.

September 2
A report in the *Chicago Tribune* says Bono has appealed to the Sudanese government for the release of imprisoned journalist Paul Salopek.

September 5
U2 arrive at Abbey Road studios in London to begin work on new material with producer Rick Rubin. Much of today's work is spent on a cover of The Skids' song, 'The Saints Are Coming', which will be recorded with Green Day – although that collaboration has yet to be announced publicly. U2 is in the studio past midnight.

September 6
U2 gets a visit from Paul McCartney and Beatles producer George Martin at Abbey Road in the afternoon. Today's work is on new U2 material.

September 7
It's another day of work on U2 material at Abbey Road.

September 8
An announcement on Green Day's official web site says the band will soon join U2 in the studio to record a cover of 'The Saints Are Coming'. The track will be a benefit single for Music Rising.

Meanwhile, U2 continue to work on new material at Abbey Road with Rick Rubin.

September 13
U2 and Green Day recreate the famous photo of The Beatles walking across the street outside Abbey Road studios. Seeing two of the biggest bands in the world out and about prompts many passers-by to stop and shoot photos. The bands sign autographs for some of the onlookers. Capturing it all on camera is photographer Anton

Corbijn, while videographer Chris Milk has his cameras rolling, too.

September 15
Bono and Ali are at the Hudson Hotel in New York for the launch of a new Edun-ONE Campaign t-shirt. The $40 t-shirts are made in Africa with African cotton, and $10 from every shirt goes to a fund to fight AIDS. The party/fashion show includes a speech by economist Jeffrey Sachs and a brief performance by Irish vocalist Damien Rice. Upset by the talking during Rice's performance, Bono grabs a microphone and tells the fashion VIPs to "take your fucking finger food and fuck off".

September 16
Bono and Ali visit the Chicago Nordstrom store for the Edun-ONE Campaign t-shirt launch.

Edge appears in a new TV public service announcement for The Food Bank For New York City. The spot is reminiscent of recent ONE Campaign PSAs, and features celebrities including Charlize Theron and Mike Myers, among others.

September 17
The Edun-ONE Campaign t-shirt launch tour continues at a Los Angeles-area Nordstrom. Bono and Ali visit The Grove mall, where 200 fans are waiting to see them.

Edge is this week's interviewee in *Time* magazine's regular feature, "10 Questions with...".

September 18
Bono rejoins the band at Abbey Road Studios in London.

September 19
Coldplay frontman Chris Martin visits U2 at Abbey Road.

September 20
U2 wrap up about two weeks of recording at Abbey Road. The whole band signs autographs for fans as they leave at around 11:00 p.m.

A Day In The Life of Edge premieres on the launch of Yahoo! Current, a new online video venture between the search engine

and Al Gore's Current TV network. The home movie was filmed and directed by Bono while the band was in Miami last November for Vertigo Tour shows. Part one premieres today, with parts two and three premiering each of the next two days. The clips run about 12-15 minutes in all, but include none of the footage shot with fans outside the American Airlines Arena in Miami.

September 21
In an interview hitting newsstands today, U2 manager Paul McGuinness tells *Hot Press* magazine why U2 recently moved some of its business to The Netherlands to avoid paying new Irish taxes: "The reality is that U2's business is 90% conducted around the world. 90% of our tickets and 98% of our records are sold outside of Ireland. It's where we live and where we work and where we employ a lot of people. But we pay taxes all over the world – of many different kinds. And like any other business, we are perfectly entitled to minimise the tax we pay."

Bono speaks tonight at a fashion event in London's Earls Court arena hosted by Giorgio Armani. It's part fashion show, part concert and part party – and Bono gives a speech about the Product (RED) campaign, to which Armani is contributing a portion of the profits from his Emporio Armani line. "You buy a Red product here," Bono says, "the Red company will buy lifesaving medicine over there. And you will be a good-looking Samaritan." During the night, Bono talks to RTE News about the situation in Darfur, saying the Sudanese government's refusal to allow UN troops into Darfur has "broken every shred of dignity possible in a government".

September 22
U2 is in London for the first of three book signings to launch their first autobiography, *U2 By U2*. The event takes place at Waterstone's in Piccadilly, central London, and only 200 fans are able to get in to buy the book and have the band sign it individually. The book is a massive

Bono signs autographs and chats with fans outside Abbey Road Studios, September 20.

345 pages and weighs almost six pounds. HarperCollins prints more than half a million copies in ten languages. In the book, Edge reveals that his daughter, Sian, got sick in late 2005 and her illness is why the Vertigo Tour was delayed. He keeps the details of her illness private.

Critical reaction to the book is mixed. Some critics praise the depth of U2's involvement and their willingness to talk about even the most unexciting moments of their career. Some critics recognize that die-hard U2 fans will love the book and its collection of never-before-seen photos – and those critics are right. U2 fans love the book, instantly declaring in online surveys that it's the best U2-related book of all. Other critics aren't so generous. Says Mark Beech of *Bloomberg News*: "For all their achievements, the Irish band's first stab at literary posterity is decidedly mundane." Irish author John Waters, who wrote a scathing review of *How To Dismantle An Atomic Bomb*, has it out for U2 again in his article for *The Irish Book Review*: "This book, indeed, ultimately makes you wonder about even U2's ability to understand what is happening to itself. What comes across most strongly is a degree of self-obsession that becomes tedious and dismaying...."

September 23
U2 sign copies of *U2 By U2* at Eason's on O'Connell Street in Dublin. The bookstore decides to close down for the day on the advice of local police, even though Saturday is their biggest sales day of the week. 250 fans show up to have their books signed.

September 24
U2 are in New Orleans to rehearse with Green Day in advance of tomorrow's live performance of 'The Saints Are Coming' on *Monday Night Football*. The bands are performing a short set before the football game between Atlanta and New Orleans – the first football game at the Superdome since Hurricane Katrina. Before this afternoon's rehearsal, Edge and Billie Joe Armstrong do interviews

with CNN and ABC, sitting on chairs in the Superdome end zone.

September 25

Superdome, New Orleans. U2 and Green Day do a 10-minute set before a *Monday Night Football* game at the Superdome. The performance opens with Edge joining Green Day for 'Wake Me Up When September Ends'. The rest of U2 come on stage for a three-song medley: 'House Of The Rising Sun', 'The Saints Are Coming', and 'Beautiful Day'. 'The Saints Are Coming' is immediately made available for download in the US on the Rhapsody music service, with proceeds benefiting Music Rising.

Earlier in the day, U2 and Green Day visit the Lower Ninth Ward, one of the most heavily damaged areas of New Orleans.

September 26

U2's book signing tour for *U2 by U2* moves to a Barnes and Noble in New York City. The band talks to the press before signing books for 200 fans. Later, Bono and Edge attend the New York premiere of Martin Scorsese's new film, *The Departed*. They head to the popular Marquee nightclub afterward.

Bono appears on Tony Bennett's album, *Duets: An American Classic*. Bono and Bennett sing 'I Wanna Be Around'.

September 27

Interscope issues a studio version of the U2/Green Day collaboration, 'The Saints Are Coming', which arrives today at US radio stations. It's the first U2 release with Rick Rubin getting production credits.

Edge is spotted tonight at the Rolling Stones' concert at Giants Stadium in E. Rutherford, New Jersey.

September 30

Edge, Morleigh and Ali attend a special advance screening in Dublin of Lian Lunson's film, *Leonard Cohen – I'm Your Man*.

October 2

With the uproar over U2's tax situation continuing, Edge addresses the issue on Dublin's

Below: U2 at the New York launch of the book U2 by U2, September 26.

radio station, Newstalk: "Our business is a very complex business. Of course we're trying to be tax-efficient. Who doesn't want to be tax-efficient?"

October 3

U2 announce plans to release a "definitive" compilation on November 20. The album will contain sixteen previously released tracks and two new releases, one of which is the U2/Green Day collaboration, 'The Saints Are Coming'. No title is given for the new release. On the web, many fans react negatively to the idea, suggesting the album is nothing but a money-grab during the upcoming holiday season.

October 5

Bono and Edge are in New York City today to tape an interview with their friend, and former Eurhythmic, Dave Stewart. The interview is for Stewart's new HBO program, *Off The Record*. U2.com gives away 50 tickets to paid members. The programme will premiere November 24.

October 7

Reports circulate that U2 is leaving Island Records after 27 years with the label. The BBC reports that Mercury Records will issue the band's upcoming hits collection. While there's no official comment yet, industry watchers believe U2 want to continue working with Jason Iley, who switched from Island to Mercury earlier this year.

Tonight, Bono and Penelope Cruz attend the New York Film Festival premiere of Cruz's film, *Volver*.

October 11

Bono is in Carefree, Arizona, for meetings with his Elevation Partners investment group at The Boulders resort.

U2 is named Best International Live Act at the Vodafone Live Music Awards in London.

October 12

Bono and Oprah Winfrey go shopping on Chicago's Magnificent Mile, buying products left and right while video cameras (and fans) follow their every move. The

shopping spree is taped for tomorrow's *Oprah* show, on which Bono will launch Product (RED) in the US. Bono and Oprah shop at the Gap – where Christy Turlington and Penelope Cruz model some of the (RED) clothing line – at the Apple Store, at Giorgio Armani, and at the Motorola store, where Kanye West helps them promote the new red RAZR cell phone. Back at the studio, they tape tomorrow's programme, which includes Bono and Alicia Keys performing 'Don't Give Up (Africa)'.

As Bono tries to leave Chicago in the evening, his plane is delayed because President George Bush is on Air Force One, also at O'Hare. Bono takes the opportunity to pay the president a visit, going on Air Force One for a 10-minute visit with Bobby Shriver and Christy Turlington in tow.

October 13
Bono and Bobby Shriver continue to promote the US launch of Product (RED), with live visits and interviews on Fox News Channel, CNN (on the *Larry King Live* program), and NBC Nightly News.

October 15
Today's *Sunday Star Times* newspaper includes a letter from Bono to the people of New Zealand, encouraging them to join the Make Poverty History movement and pressure their government to "keep their promises to the weak".

October 17
Bono testifies in Dublin's High Court in a case brought by U2's former stylist Lola Cashman, who is appealing an earlier court decision that demanded she return items belonging to the band.

October 18
Bono is back in Dublin's High Court again, continuing to testify against former stylist Lola Cashman. In his two days of testimony, Bono is in the witness box for more than three hours.

After his court appearance in Dublin, Bono heads to London to join wife Ali for the launch of the Edun-ONE Campaign t-shirts at

Above: Bono in Melbourne, November 18.

Harvey Nichols store. Adam and Susie Smith are also on hand for the launch party, along with actors Heath Ledger, Pierce Brosnan and Kim Cattrall.

October 19
Bono, Edge, Willie Williams and Steve Matthews (Principle Management) have a conference call to discuss plans for the upcoming tour dates. They talk about set list ideas, and Willie suggests adding some Australian Aboriginal video pieces.

October 25
Bono appears via video at the Center for Communication's award luncheon honoring MTV honcho Tom Freston.

October 28
Bono and Ali attend the 40th birthday celebration of Monaco AMADE in Monte Carlo. Founded by Princess Grace of Monaco, AMADE-Monaco is a charity association that helps children in need all over the world. The event raises more than 165,000 Euros for the construction of a new school in Giuniée, Africa.

October 29
Construction of the Vertigo Tour outdoor stage begins at the Queensland Sports & Athletics Centre. U2's Vertigo Tour resumes there in just over a week.

Meanwhile, Bono makes a pre-taped appearance at the Aria Awards in Australia, paying tribute to legendary Aussie rockers Midnight Oil, who are being inducted into the Aria Hall of Fame.

October 30
U2 enjoy a good night at the annual Q Awards in London. Larry presents an award for Track of the Year to Gnarls Barkley for the hit song, 'Crazy'. Edge collects a Q Innovation in Sound award. And the night culminates with U2 receiving a special Q Award of Awards: Band of Bands honor.

October 31/November 1
Larry's birthday is a travel day as U2 arrives in Australia to prepare for

the upcoming fifth leg of the Vertigo Tour. The band lands in Sydney, then takes a private jet to the Gold Coast to make camp at the six-star Palazzo Versace hotel with its $2,000-a-night luxury condominiums.

November 2
About 100 fans wait for U2 outside their Gold Coast hotel, and are rewarded when the band comes out in the afternoon to sign autographs and take pictures. When that's done, they travel by Careflight helicopter for a rehearsal at the Queensland Sport and Athletics Centre in Brisbane (U2 makes what's reported as a "sizable donation" to Careflight in exchange for use of the helicopter). Adam tells local reporters that U2 won't have much time for sightseeing before the tour resumes: "We have been to Queensland many, many times and always enjoyed it, but we will be busy with rehearsals while we are here." After tonight's rehearsal, Bono and Edge spend time outside the stadium with a group of about a dozen fans.

November 3
U2 continues to rehearse at the Queensland Sport and Athletics Centre in Brisbane.

November 4
During rehearsals, U2 put on wigs and 1970s-style clothes and play a short medley of Led Zeppelin songs (with Iggy Pop's 'Lust For Life' thrown in as a bonus). It's part of a surprise for tour manager and former Zeppelin employee Dennis Sheehan, who has a birthday tomorrow.

After rehearsals, U2 and some of the crew visit the Dreamworld theme park. The band has the park to themselves, and they spend time trying thrill rides such as the Giant Drop, Wipeout and Tower of Terror. They also have a close encounter with a 12-year-old Bengal tiger on the theme park's Tiger Island.

November 5
U2 rehearse in Brisbane. Fans gathered outside the stadium hear

most of the band's practice set.

'The Saints Are Coming' debuts at number six on the UK singles chart solely on the strength of digital downloads. The commercial CD isn't available until tomorrow.

November 6

'The Saints Are Coming' is released today. The single includes the studio/single version and the live version performed in New Orleans on September 25 as an extra track. U2 do an interview with Australian TV host Rove McManus inside the Queensland Sports & Athletics Centre in Brisbane. The interview airs on *Rove Live* tomorrow night. U2 does a full rehearsal tonight.

November 7

Queensland Sports & Athletics Centre, Brisbane, with Kanye West. More than eight months since being postponed, the Vertigo Tour resumes in Brisbane. 45,000 fans fill the Queensland Sports & Athletics Centre, and see a show that resembles earlier legs of the tour, but has a few new additions. Since the Elevation Tour never reached these shores, U2 adds 'Walk On' and 'Kite' to the setlist as

a taste of what fans missed in 2001. 'Kite' closes the show, and is turned into an epic experience unlike the Elevation Tour version. The song begins with a cluster of balloons and a single kite hovering above the B-stage. Larry plays a tambourine and a local musician, Tim Moriarty, plays a didgeridoo. Edge and Adam join in later in the song, which climaxes when Bono uses a lighter to break the string and send the balloons and kite into the Australian night sky.

Before the show, the band and some of the crew get together in Bono's hotel room to watch the Melbourne Cup horse race.

November 8

Bono and Australian Prime Minister John Howard continue their verbal sparring. Howard tells reporters he'd like to meet with Bono, but not with the conditions Bono has placed on such a meeting. On arrival last week in Australia, Bono told reporters he wanted to meet with the prime minister, but only if Howard is serious about committing 0.7 per cent of Australia's gross domestic product to foreign aid. Howard tells the

Below: Opening night of Vertigo Down Under, Brisbane, November 7.

press today, "I don't accept preconditions from anybody. I don't commit in advance to businessmen in this country and I certainly don't do it to – much in all as he's high grade – Irish entertainers." Ultimately, the two never meet. Bono does meet, however, with Treasurer Peter Costello later this month.

Interscope sends a digital version of U2's new single, 'Window In the Skies', to radio stations in North America today. A proper promo CD will arrive tomorrow.

November 9

Bono joins the members of Pearl Jam at Sydney nightclub Hemmesphere, where they watch US election returns on cable TV.

'The Saints Are Coming' debuts at number one on the Irish singles chart.

November 10-11-13

Telstra Stadium, Sydney, with Kanye West. Bono mentions that Edge's family is in attendance for the second show. The third show is a party, and a historic one, as Bono tells the crowd no band has ever played three gigs at Telstra Staium. "They said it's never been done before, and it will never be done again. Do they not think we're coming back?" he asks.

November 12

Bono hosts a small barbecue party at the house where he's staying while in Sydney. Later, he joins Kylie Minogue at her show in Sydney for a duet on the hit song, 'Kids'. She's wearing a tight-fitting leopard print bodysuit, while Bono appears in a black suit and sunglasses. They dance and sing together, with Bono telling Minogue, "You're perfect." The entire band and some of U2's crew is at the show. Minogue is supposed to return the favour by appearing at U2's show the next day, but she cites exhaustion and cancels the appearance.

November 14

Bono attends the Sydney premiere of *Catch A Fire*, a new film starring

Gary Koepke on putting U2 in a crowd of U2 fans, November 20

"Once the song started and people went crazy to make it look like a concert, they [U2] were actually in a concert hearing their song and feeling the way people feel in their concerts. And I remember we got back to the blue [waiting] room, and it's like, '*Man, that was the best thing that happened in 15 years!*' – I think is what Bono said. And he couldn't believe it. They couldn't believe that energy, because they're always up on stage."

Tim Robbins that is set in apartheid-era South Africa.

Above: Bono in the rain, Sydney, November 10.

November 15
Dublin's High Court rules in favour of U2 in its lengthy legal battle with former stylist Lola Cashman over clothing and souvenirs Cashman claimed were a gift from the band. The band told the court that Cashman had taken the items without permission. In a statement, U2 say they're "relieved" the court battle is over and that they will not pursue legal costs from Cashman, despite being permitted to. "Proceedings were issued in Ireland very much as a last resort and with great reluctance," the band says.

Also today, U2 shoot a "TV Ident" spot (TV identification) for Channel 4 at Fox Studios in Sydney.

November 16
AAMI Stadium, Adelaide, with Kanye West. Odd, this: During 'Elevation', a fan throws a pillow on stage near Bono, so he lies down on it at the front of the stage. Odd, this, too: As the kite begins to fly away at the end of the show, a fan grabs the string and reels it in, spoiling the effect.

November 17
Bono and Edge join Pearl Jam for a rousing version of 'Rockin' In the Free World' to open tonight's Make Poverty History concert at the Sidney Myer Music Bowl in Melbourne. During the song, Bono calls the collaboration "U-Jam". The performance is a shock to concertgoers, as neither U2 nor Pearl Jam was expected to perform. The concert takes place on the eve of the G20 finance summit in Melbourne.

November 18-19
Telstra Dome, Melbourne, with Kanye West. A couple of hundred fans are stranded outside the stadium before the first show because their tickets couldn't be scanned for entry. Midnight Oil's Peter Garrett is on hand for the second show in Melbourne, the last show of the tour in Australia. Tim Moriarty makes his final guest appearance playing the didgeridoo during 'Kite'. At the end of the show, Adam and Edge both say goodbye to Australia, but Edge mistakenly gives thanks to the city of Sydney. As some fans boo his mistake, Edge quickly corrects himself, giving thanks to fans in Sydney, Brisbane, *and* Melbourne.

November 20
After a meeting with Australian Treasurer Peter Costello in Canberra, Bono joins the rest of the

band at the Corner Hotel in Melbourne to shoot a music video for 'Window In The Skies'. About 300 extras are involved in the shoot, which includes U2 standing in a crowd of music fans while the song plays. Director Gary Koepke shoots it to look like U2 and the crowd are at a rock concert watching the song being performed.

U2 head back to their hotel after the video shoot, and then to the hip restaurant/bar Gingerboy, where they stay until the wee hours of the morning.

November 21

Bono meets and signs autographs for fans outside the Park Hyatt Hotel in Melbourne.

November 22

U2 arrive in New Zealand for two upcoming concerts, and manager Paul McGuinness meets local reporters on the field at Mt. Smart Stadium in Auckland. He talks about the cost of bringing a big production to New Zealand: "I hope we'll be back pretty soon. It is difficult to include New Zealand on big productions for obvious reasons. Bringing something as big as this in and out of the country by air costs the earth, I have to tell

you." McGuinness also refutes rumours that U2 will play a secret club show while they're in the country.

November 24-25

Mt Smart Stadium, Auckland, with Kanye West. U2 play New Zealand for the first time since the Zoo TV tour in 1993. In honour of former tour crew member and New Zealander Greg Carroll, the first show includes a full-band version of 'One Tree Hill' for the first time since 1990. As the band plays, Maori koru designs fill the video screen. Bono talks about attending Carroll's funeral in 1986 after the song, and relates it to his father's funeral in 2001 as a prelude to 'Sometimes You Can't Make It On Your Own'. At the second show, Bono dedicates 'One Tree Hill' to the family of Greg Carroll, who are at the show.

November 29-30

Saitama Super Arena, Tokyo. Prior to the first show in Tokyo, Bono visits Japanese Prime Minister Shinzo Abe to discuss relief money to fight poverty and AIDS in Africa. Abe restates Japan's promise to fulfill the funding promise it made at last year's G8 Summit in Scotland. In a

lighter moment, the prime minister puts on a pair of Product (RED) sunglasses that Bono gives him as cameras snap away. During the first show, U2 play 'Window In The Skies' live for the first time. It replaces 'Love And Peace Or Else', leaving just three songs from *How To Dismantle An Atomic Bomb* in the setlist.

On November 29, *Zoo TV – Live From Sydney* is certified Platinum, with US sales of more than one million.

December

U2 appear on Mary J. Blige's cover of 'One', which is released this month.

December 1

TV Asahi Studio, Tokyo. U2 perform 'Vertigo' and 'Window In The Skies' on TV Asahi's music program, *Music Station*. They perform on the roof of the TV station, with the Tokyo night skyline as a backdrop.

December 4

Saitama Super Arena, Tokyo. At the final show in Tokyo, Bono tells the crowd of a recent visit to the Church of Light in Kyoto. During 'Mysterious Ways', three geishas from Kyoto join U2 on stage to dance, with help from Morleigh Steinberg, who's guiding them from the main floor below. Japanese architect Tadao Ando is at the show. While in Japan, Adam Clayton spends time with guitar legend Eric Clapton, who is also on tour here and is staying at the same hotel as U2.

'Window In The Skies' reaches number one on the *Radio and Records* Triple-A chart in the US

December 7

Two of U2's recent collaborations earn Grammy nominations: Best Pop Collaboration with Vocals for 'One', their duet with Mary J. Blige, and Best Rock Performance by a Duo or Group Vocal for 'The Saints Are Coming', their duet with Green Day.

December 8

Paparazzi shoot photos today of Larry playing with his children on a Hawaii beach. Bono is having dinner at Aaron's Atop Ala Moana tonight when Bill Gates walks in. When Bono and Gates leave, they autograph a bottle of wine for the restaurant staff.

U218 Singles is certified Platinum by the BPI, with UK sales surpassing the 300,000 mark.

December 9
Aloha Stadium, Honolulu, with Rocko and the Devils, Pearl Jam. The stars come out in force to help U2 close out the fifth and final leg of the Vertigo Tour. Green Day's Billie Joe Armstrong joins the band for 'The Saints Are Coming', and that's followed immediately by a cover of 'Rockin' In The Free World' with Pearl Jam's Eddie Vedder and Mike McCready. But it's a U2 fan who steals the show: Bono brings a fan on stage during 'Angel Of Harlem', but the guy wants to play 'Who's Gonna Ride Your Wild Horses' on piano, instead. U2 stop the show in its tracks, the fan takes his spot at Edge's keyboards, and together they go through a rough but fun version of the rarely played song. Celebrities at the show include Kid Rock, Anthrax's Scott Ian, Jeremy Piven, Mira Sorvino, Alyssa Milano and several cast members of the hit ABC show *LOST*. After the show, U2 celebrate on board the Battleship Missouri Memorial, which is docked at Pearl Harbor. Bill Gates hosts the 300-person party, which includes actor Pierce Brosnan and philanthropist Warren Buffett.

The Vertigo Tour ends as the second-highest grossing tour in music history, bringing in $389 million from 4,619,021 tickets sold. Only the Rolling Stones' A Bigger Bang tour, which ran from August 2005 to August 2007, earned more ($558 million).

December 10
U2 stay in Hawaii for some rest and relaxation. They're spotted at the Kahala resort's Veranda and Plumeria Beach House. Larry is spotted dining at Duke's in Waikiki.

December 14
Bono is in Washington, DC, to discuss funding for AIDS and poverty relief with incoming Democratic leaders Nancy Pelosi, Harry Reid and others. Bono has a verbal scrap with Democrat Harry Obey, who tells Bono "To hell with you" after hearing Bono's "lecture" about AIDS funding. The day leaves Bono in a foul mood, and DATA issues a statement from him saying, "I'm alarmed we could not get a commitment from the Democratic leadership to prevent the loss of $1 billion in the continuing resolution to fight AIDS, malaria and extreme poverty."

December 15
U2 premiere the new video for 'Window In The Skies' on the YouTube video-sharing site. The video, which features rock and music legends appearing to lip-synch the words of U2's song, is an instant sensation with fans. For days, fans go frame-by-frame through the video, trying to list all the stars who appear – and hoping U2 will publish an official list.

December 23
U2 premiere a second video for 'Window In The Skies', this time making the clip available to subscribers on U2.com. While the first video offers a stroll through the history of popular music, this version looks back at U2's history with stills and clips from the band's 25-plus-years career.

The British Embassy prematurely announces that Bono will soon be granted an honorary knighthood by the Queen for "his services to the music industry and for his humanitarian work". The honour will be conferred early in 2007 in Dublin. Bono issues a statement on U2.com saying he's "very flattered" for the recognition, and that he hopes it will open doors for his anti-poverty campaign. Since Bono's not a British national, he won't be able to use the title "Sir". The news causes a stir in British government, where some MPs say that announcing Bono's knighthood a week before other similar honours are made public is a "political ploy" by Tony Blair and the ruling party.

Bono predicts U2's future, December 25

"Our band has certainly reached the end of where we've been at for the last couple of albums. I want to see what else we can do with it, take it to the next level; I think that's what we've got to do. We're gonna continue to be a band, but maybe the rock will have to go; maybe the rock has to get a lot harder. But whatever it is, it's not gonna stay where it is."

December 25
BBC Radio 1 airs a new, pre-recorded Jo Whiley interview with Bono. The interview appears to have been conducted within the past week, as Bono refers to getting back home to Dublin on "Sunday night". They cover a wide range of topics, with Bono saying he'd like to tour in China and India in the future. He also talks about U2's future in terms reminiscent of the famous "dream it all up again" speech from 1989.

December 26
Continuing an ongoing tradition, Bono and Ali plus Edge and Morleigh attend the annual Leopardstown Races in Dublin.

December 28
Bono, Ali and Paul McGuinness attend the funeral of Maureen Ryan at St. John the Baptist Church in Dublin. Maureen is the mother of 2FM presenter Gerry Ryan, a longtime friend of the band.

2007

With the Vertigo Tour over and the *Atomic Bomb* campaign at an end, U2 take a break early in the year. Well, everyone but Bono, who dives headfirst into his campaigns for AIDS and poverty relief in Africa. That work occupies much of the year for Bono. He guest edits *Vanity Fair* magazine, meets various US presidential candidates and other politicians, attends the G8 Summit in Germany, and picks up several awards along the way – including the prestigious Liberty Medal in Philadelphia.

U2 make an appearance at the Cannes Film Festival in May, doing a brief live set before watching the premiere of their new film, *U2 3D*. They leave Cannes and go straight to Morocco to record new songs with Brian Eno and Daniel Lanois in a co-writing capacity.

By year's end, one of U2's associates reveals that the band is actually working on two separate album projects. Word on the street is that at least one of those albums will surface in 2008, but U2 are tight-lipped about their plans. The only new U2 material to come out this year is a handful of outtakes that appear on a remastered release of *The Joshua Tree* to mark the album's 20th anniversary.

January

Bono visits Conde Nast headquarters in New York to begin work as guest editor of the July issue of *Vanity Fair* magazine. Bono arrives with some sketches of the magazine cover, showing the name changed to "Fair Vanity". Editor Graydon Carter isn't impressed, and jokingly says he'll allow it only if Bono changes the band's name to 2U.

Also this month, Bono meets with New Jersey Senator Frank Lautenberg in Washington, DC.

January 1

'Window In The Skies' is released in Europe on varying formats, also including the tracks 'Zoo Station (Live from Buenos Aires)', 'Kite (Live from Sydney)', and 'Tower Of Song (featuring Leonard Cohen)'.

January 7

'Window In The Skies' debuts at number four on the UK singles chart, the highest new entry of the week, but climbs no higher.

January 16

'Window In The Skies' is released in Canada on two CDs, also including the tracks 'Zoo Station (Live from Buenos Aires)' and 'Kite (Live from Sydney)'. It reaches number one in the charts.

January 21

Writing for today's *Observer* newspaper, Bono lists a 1977 gig in Dublin by The Clash as his favourite concert: "It wasn't so much a musical event. It was more like the Red Army had arrived, on a cold October night, to force-feed a new cultural revolution, punk rock. Marching boots and the smell of sulphur."

January 22

Bono attends the Sundance Film Festival in Utah to support the new film, *Joe Strummer: The Future Is Unwritten*. Bono appears in the documentary about The Clash's lead singer. He and director Julien Temple speak with the media, and later Bono attends the premiere of *Son Of Rambow*.

January 23

After tonight's State of the Union address by President Bush, Bono calls Senator Orrin Hatch from the senator's home state of Utah. The two talk about funding for AIDS treatment in Africa, one of the issues Bush mentioned in his speech.

January 26

Bono returns to Davos, Switzerland, to speak to the World Economic Forum. With Tony Blair, he urges political and business leaders to keep their promises to aid Africa.

U218 Singles is certified Multi-Platinum by the BPI, with UK sales surpassing the 600,000 mark.

February 1

Bono appears on video at the 2007 Meteor Ireland Music Awards, helping to honour Clannad with a Lifetime Achievement Award. He reads a tribute to Clannad off his laptop computer while sitting in what appears to be his home.

The video was likely recorded sometime in January.

February 4

Bono and Ali are in New York for the launch of their Edun clothing line's fall collection. Rather than using the traditional models-on-runway approach, a variety of actors and dancers perform song and dance routines while wearing Edun clothes.

February 10

Bono and Edge attend the launch of *Consilience*, an exhibition of paintings by their old friend, Charlie Whisker, at the Solomon Gallery in Dublin.

February 15

Bono is known in the halls of government all over the world, he can get a meeting with anyone he wants, and he's been named *Time*'s Person of the Year – but he's not a hit in North Dakota. The state's House of Representatives votes 58 to 35 to reject a resolution honouring Bono for his humanitarian work. Opponents of the bill say Bono doesn't have any connection to North Dakota. Other legislators say they don't know who Bono is, including one who thinks the resolution is about Sonny Bono, the late husband of the singer Cher.

Meanwhile, Bono praises US Senator Harry Reid of Nevada for helping secure a $1.3 billion boost in federal funding for global AIDS programs this week. "Sen. Reid and his colleagues came through. His leadership and their resolve deserve the respect of all who work on these issues, and the countless souls, literally hundreds and thousands, who will now owe the United States their lives."

February 21
Bono attends the Dublin Film Festival to see the Irish premiere of *The Groomsmen*, a film set among an Irish American community in suburban New York. The film is the work of Ed Burns, a friend of Bono's who's married to supermodel Christy Turlington. Bono hosts a party in town for Burns and Turlington.

Meanwhile, Edge helps launch the Celeb-Am Golf Classic in Dublin, a charity golf event to raise money for research into childhood leukemia. The golf tournament will take place at Druid's Glen on May 2.

February 24
Bono, Ali and Paul McGuinness help local nightclub king Robbie Fox celebrate his 50th birthday at a party at Barracuda restaurant in Bray, County Wicklow.

February 27
While making the rounds in Washington, DC, Bono visits Democratic presidential hopeful Barack Obama to discuss the fight against AIDS and poverty in Third World countries. Tonight, Bono is in New York for a "Conversation with Bono" hosted by Jim Kelly of *Time* magazine. The audience includes dozens of movie stars, musicians, and politicians.

February 28
A day after meeting with Democratic presidential hopeful Barack Obama, Bono visits with Republican candidate Rudy Giuliani in New York. Bono begins his day by doing a radio interview with NAACP Chairman Julian Bond. He caps the day by taking good friend Helena Christensen to see the new film, *Zodiac*.

March 1
Bono has dinner with Bill Clinton, Jay-Z and Clinton's close friend Ron Burkle at The Spotted Pig in New York City. He flies to Oakland afterward.

March 2
Bono's day begins at 9:00 a.m. in a meeting with Oakland officials to discuss the inner-city AIDS situation. He's there on the invite of Democratic Representative Barbara Lee, who introduces Bono to her pastor. The three conduct a short news conference before Bono has to leave for Southern California.

Tonight, Bono is in Los Angeles where the NAACP gives him its Chairman's Award in honour of Bono's work for the poor, especially in Africa. In a speech that would've made Martin Luther King, Jr., smile with pride, Bono tells the crowd about growing up in Dublin and the religious strife there, and how he was "parched for ideas from the pulpits of black America, the ideas of a preacher from Atlanta who refused to hate because he knew love could do better." The spirit of MLK is in the house as Bono's speech climaxes with a King-style litany of declarations, each one beginning with "God is...", and Bono shouting louder with each one. As he talks, the crowd rises to its feet, almost row by row, clapping and shouting him along.

March 4
Irish media report that Adam and fiancée Susie Smith have split on amicable terms. They were engaged last year on Valentine's Day.

March 5
Edge and Larry see Arcade Fire perform at Dublin's Olympia Theatre.

March 6
U2 places three albums on "The Definitive 200", a list of the best albums ever that's compiled by the Rock and Roll Hall of Fame and the National Association of Recording Merchandisers. *The Joshua Tree* comes in at number five, *Achtung Baby* at number 45, and *All That You Can't Leave Behind* at number 197.

March 15
Visitors to the ShoWest conference in Las Vegas see a sneak peek of *U2 3D*. Audiences are shown the movie's trailer and a performance of 'Sunday Bloody Sunday'.

Above: Bono with Ali after receiving his honorary British knighthood, March 29.

March 17
Italian media report that Bono and Larry have been in Rome for two days and will attend today's Six Nations Rugby Final between Ireland and Italy at Stadio Flaminio.

March 23
For the 50th anniversary of the Treaty of Rome – which established what we now know as the European Community – Bono writes an essay called "A Time For Miracles", which appears today in the new issue of *Time* magazine, as well as major

European newspapers such as *Süddeutsche Zeitung* (Germany), *Corriere della Sera* (Italy), and *Le Monde* (France). The essay calls on European leaders to reach out to help Africa.

March 25

Bono picks up an Echo Award in Berlin from the German Phonographic Academy. The award honors Bono's work against AIDS and poverty in the Third World. Bono urges the audience to get involved when the G8 Summit takes place in Germany this summer. During the awards, the German version of Make Poverty History premieres a new TV commercial which includes Bono and other celebrities speaking German.

March 26

Still in Berlin, Bono meets with German NGOs at the DATA office and does an interview with the weekly newspaper *Die Zeit*.

March 29

British Ambassador to Ireland David Reddaway confers on Bono an honorary British knighthood in recognition of his services to the music industry and for his humanitarian work. The ceremony takes places at the British embassy in Dublin. "I couldn't be more proud," Bono says. "I would like to thank Her Majesty's Ambassador for pinning this award on me in my home town, and the band for not bursting my balloon." Bono is now a Knight Commander of the Most Excellent Order of the British Empire, or KBE. But as an Irish citizen, he will not be able to use the title "Sir".

Mid-April

Bono meets with record producer Rick Rubin in Morocco.

April 17

Bono visits in Germany with Chancellor Angela Merkel, who promises him that Africa will play "an outstanding role" at the G-8 Summit in June. Germany is hosting this year's meeting.

April 18

Adam reportedly attends Patti Smith's show at the Hiro Ballroom in New York City.

April 21

Several U2 artifacts are auctioned off at the Icons of Music fundraiser in New York that raises $2.4 million for Music Rising. Edge's Gibson Les Paul guitar, which he's been using since 1985, is one of the big sellers, going for $240,000. One of Bono's autographed Gretsch guitars goes for $180,000. One of Adam's bass guitars is auctioned for $22,000 and a tom-tom drum used by Larry and Bono on the Vertigo Tour – during 'Love and Peace or Else' – goes for $19,000. Other U2 items are included in the auction, as well.

April 22

The *Los Angeles Times* reports that Edge (and Morleigh) have purchased a 120-acre property in Malibu for about $15 million. The canyon property is said to include a cottage and creek.

Bono is in Los Angeles this weekend to tape an appearance for the super-popular *American Idol* TV show, which is doing a special charity edition this week to benefit the ONE Campaign and other relief efforts. Bono spends time with the six Idol finalists, talking with them about the situation in Africa. He also coaches them on a group performance of 'American Prayer', a song written several years earlier about Africa. His visit with the Idol contestants is taped for airing later in the week.

April 23

The New York Food Bank honours Edge at the 2007 Can-Do Awards on Pier 60 in New York. With the likes of David Bowie, Michael Stipe, Patti Smith and other big names from the fashion and movie industries in attendance, President Clinton presents Edge with his award, the "Orange Plate". The event raises more than $1.3 million to fight hunger in New York City. Elvis Costello closes the night by performing an acoustic version of 'Where The Streets Have No Name'.

In Los Angeles, Bono attends the Ambassadors for Humanity Gala Dinner hosted by USC's Shoah Foundation Institute. Steven Spielberg presents the award to Wallis Annenberg. The Shoah Foundation has completed its original task of interviewing all survivors of the Holocaust, and tonight announces its plans to videotape genocide and apartheid victims in several African nations.

April 25

Bono's recent visit with the *American Idol* finalists airs during tonight's "Idol Gives Back" charity programme. The programme is a huge success, raising an estimated $70 million for African and US relief projects. The ONE Campaign, which is profiled during the show, gets an estimated 70,000 new members in the days after the show.

April 26

Bono has a busy day in New York today, starting with a visit to *Vanity Fair* headquarters where he does an interview with Cynthia McFadden of ABC News. The interview will appear on the long-running *Nightline* news programme in early June. Later, Bono joins Alicia Keys for a screening of *We Are Together* at the Tribeca Film Festival. The film is a documentary about an orphanage in Africa and the stories of the children living there.

After the film, Bono attends a Syracuse University event in New York City honouring alumnus Lou Reed with the George Arents Pioneer Medal, the school's highest alumni award. When asked why he's there, Bono tells *New York* magazine: "Because I am in a state of genuflection. I would carry Lou Reed's luggage; I probably have carried his luggage! There are about nine or ten U2 songs that he deserves royalties for that I don't think he's ever received."

April 30

Edge does a photo shoot at U2's Dublin studio for an upcoming issue of Q magazine.

May 1

In Dublin, Bono attends a City Hall

ceremony where he presents a Front Line Award to sexual violence campaigner Gege Katana Bukuru from the Democratic Republic of Congo. Bukuru is president of the Solidarity Movement of Women Human Rights Activists, and has dedicated her life to research and campaigns against sexual violence. Bono honours her by reciting a poem during the ceremony.

Later, Bono takes part in a telephone conference call with US Senator Hillary Rodham Clinton and US Representatives Nita Lowey and Spencer Bachus to push legislation that would add $10 billion to a global fund providing education to millions of children in Africa and elsewhere.

May 8
U2 is at work today at Hanover Quay. After about 10 hours in the studio, Larry and Adam speak briefly with fans waiting outside. Adam confirms the band is working on new songs, but says a new album won't be ready until 2008.

May 11
Edge is in Boston for the annual commencement concert put on by the graduating class of the Berklee College of Music. He watches a variety of student performances, including covers of U2 songs 'Pride (In The Name of Love)', 'Vertigo', 'I Still Haven't Found What I'm Looking For' and 'Van Diemen's Land'. Edge will receive an honorary degree from the college tomorrow, joining such musical legends as B.B. King, Duke Ellington and David Bowie.

May 12
The Berklee College of Music in Boston bestows an honorary degree on Edge during its graduation ceremony at Boston University. With Morleigh looking on, Edge tells the graduates of this esteemed music school to "find your own voice", but stresses that working with others is the path to greatness.

Edge ends his remarks with a quote from AC/DC: "For those about to rock, we salute you!"

Edge's secret to success in the music industry, May 12

"The thing I want to say is collaborate. Collaborating with talented people is not easy, but it's the way to really shine – you shine brighter if you are working with really great people. The important thing in the end is not that you are proved right every time, the important thing is that the music is the best that it can be."

May 14
Bono is back in Germany for the third time this year. He meets with Kurt Beck, chairman of the Social Democratic political party to talk about debt relief and Africa.

May 15
Still in Germany, Bono, Bob Geldof, and others present a DATA progress report showing that G8 nations have fallen behind on meeting their promises to increase aid to Africa.

"The G8 are sleepwalking into a crisis of credibility. I know the DATA report will feel like a cold shower, but I hope it will wake us all up," Bono says. He does an interview with CNN after the news conference.

Later, Bono heads to Brussels for a meeting with European Commission President Jose Manuel Barroso. The two hold a news conference discussing today's DATA report.

May 16
The *New York Times* reports that Bono is in a dispute with Eighties rocker Billy Squier over chimney smoke at the San Remo, where both have apartments. The argument is over whether smoke from chimneys below is drifting into the penthouse duplex where Bono and his family often spend time.

May 18
An abbreviated version of *U2 3D* is screened at 8:30 a.m. for journalists covering the Cannes Film Festival. Reaction to the 55-minute preview is overwhelmingly positive. Peter Howell of the *Toronto Star* says, "This is the future of concert films. It's going to be hard for conventional 2D rock films to make a splash after people get a look at this." Tom Brook of the BBC says, "I liked it because it was more than just a gimmick – it made it very intimate at times." And Charles Ealy, writing for the *Austin American-Statesman*, says "It was

Right: U2 live in Cannes before the premiere of *U2 3D*, May 20.

phenomenon. That's been going on there for centuries, the drumming and the groove would keep going, sending everyone into a kind of trance state. And for musicians like ourselves, whose exposure is to mostly UK and American music, it is incredibly inspiring to hear this totally fresh and different set of roots and influences."

May 30
Bono does a phone interview from Fez with *USA Today*, praising President George Bush for a new proposal to spend an additional $30 billion over five years to fight AIDS worldwide. Tomorrow's paper includes Bono's quotes about the AIDS proposal, and also breaks the previously unreported news that U2 is working on new material in Morocco.

June 1
French President Nicolas Sarkozy calls Bono to discuss aid for Africa and the upcoming G8 Summit in Germany. Bob Geldof is the guest editor of today's edition of *Bild*, a German newspaper. Bono's contribution is a hand-drawn sketch of the COEXIST logo with this message below it: "We have no future without this thought."

June 2
U2 attend the Festival of World Sacred Music in Fez. They listen to a performance by Parissa, a popular traditional Iranian singer who's performing with the five-piece Dastan Ensemble. Their two-song set lasts 70 minutes. After the festival, Bono does an interview with *TelQuel*, a weekly Moroccan newspaper.

U2.com confirms today that the band is working in Fez with Brian Eno and Daniel Lanois. "It's the first time we've worked with Brian and Dan in a purely songwriting capacity," Larry says. "So it's very different, quite experimental and kind of liberating because of that." While U2 work on new material,

like having the best seat in the house at a U2 concert. Quite amazing."

May 20
Grand Lumiere Theater, Cannes.
U2 arrive in Cannes about an hour too late to take part in a news conference about *U2 3D*. Instead, they attend a party being hosted by *Vanity Fair* magazine. At about 12:30 a.m. local time (May 21), U2 play a two-song set on the steps of the Grand Lumiere Theatre, immediately before the world premiere of *U2 3D*. They perform 'Vertigo' and 'Where The Streets Have No Name', with Bono singing several lyrics in French as a huge crowd sings and dances along. After their performance, they head inside the theater to watch the film. When it's over, they celebrate at a local club until about 6:00 a.m.

May 21
While in Cannes, Bono reportedly jams with James Blunt and Kid Rock at a party on the latter's yacht.

Ireland's Aid Minister Conor Lenihan announces that Bono has joined the Hunger Task Force, an international group tasked with developing ideas to reduce world hunger. The task force includes experts from Nigeria, Peru, Britain, Ireland and the United States.

May 22
U2 are spotted leaving the Nice, France, airport for Morocco. They set up in the city of Fez, the same city where they shot the video for 'Mysterious Ways' in 1991. Brian Eno and Daniel Lanois join the band, but not as producers this time; they're working with U2 as co-writers.

Why Morocco? Edge tells all
"When you go to Morocco, it's a whole different set of beats and rhythms and ideas. I mean, they could really lay claim to the whole trance music

Above: U2 and director Catherine Owens on the red carpet, Cannes, May 20.

Bono: "It's never been this easy to write" June 3

"We had an oud player in, and some Gnawa and Sufi musicians. These guys were great masters. It was a very special atmosphere. Now, we don't really know what's going to come of all that. We wrote about ten songs here in two weeks. They're not completely finished, but I feel as if it's never been this easy to write, so many things were just flowing by themselves."

Lanois works on his own movie, *Here Is What Is*. Lanois films some of the recording sessions for inclusion in the movie.

June 3

U2 wrap up about two weeks of writing and recording in Fez, and have about ten songs in progress. They do some recording with an oud player as well as local percussionists.

The band, minus Bono, head back to Dublin. Bono is reportedly picked up by Google co-founder Larry Page in the "Google jet" on the way to Tanzania.

June 4-5

Bono attends the TEDGlobal 2007 conference in Tanzania. While listening to conference delegate Andrew Mwenda speak, Bono begins to heckle him with what one witness calls "expletive-laden interruptions". Mwenda, a Ugandan journalist and social worker argues that aid to Africa is ineffective and only contributes to African poverty. "Bollocks!" Bono shouts. "That's bullshit."

When it's his turn to speak, Bono begins with a video message from German Chancellor Angela Merkel tying this event to the upcoming G8 Summit. Bono takes a couple questions after his speech. One question is about African culture, and prompts Bono to sing

briefly during his reply while explaining that Irish melodies can be traced to Morocco.

In New York, the Council of Fashion Designers bestows an honorary award on Bono and Ali for their charity work through the Edun fashion label. Bono and Ali appear via a pre-taped video.

On June 5, Bono makes a brief, pre-recorded appearance on *The Oprah Winfrey Show*, updating Oprah and her viewers on what's happening with the fight against AIDS and poverty.

June 6

Bono is in Heiligendamm, Germany, for the start of the G8 Summit. Along with Bob Geldof and Youssou N'Dour, he visits with President George Bush shortly before the summit begins. Later meetings happen with German Chancellor Angela Merkel, Prime Minister Tony Blair of Britain, France's President Nicolas Sarkozy and Italian Prime Minister Romano Prodi. Canadian Prime Minister Stephen Harper, however, refuses to meet with Bono, Geldof, and N'Dour, sparking a debate in the media over Canada's commitment to aid. Within a week, a poll shows that Canadians believe Bono's side more than Harper's by a 48% to 28% margin.

ABC's *Nightline* airs its interview with Bono taped in late April.

June 7

Bono appears at the "Deine Stimme gegen Armut" (Your Voice for Poverty) concert in Rostock, Germany, which is timed to coincide with the nearby G8 Summit. He sings 'Redemption Song' and 'Get Up Stand Up' with Youssou N'Dour and Bob Geldof; Campino, from the German band Die Toten Hosen, joins them for 'You Never Give Me Your Money'. Later in the show, Bono makes a guest appearance and sings in German on Herbert Gronemeyer's song, 'Mensch'.

June 8

As the G8 Summit concludes in Germany, Bono rips into world leaders at a news conference over a $60 billion pledge to fight AIDS that has no timetable and doesn't specifically apply to Africa. "It is not real in any language. We are looking for accountable language and numbers," he says. Bono is also interviewed today about the G8 Summit on NPR's *Morning Edition* program.

Vanity Fair magazine publishes its July issue, "The Africa Issue", which guest editor Bono has put together over the past several months. The issue features 20 different covers – two of which include Bono – with various celebrities and statesmen posing together. Says Editor Graydon Carter about Bono's aptitude for becoming a magazine editor: "He [Bono] has the instincts of a great journalist, but I am not sure if he'd have the patience. He'd be a much better editor of a daily newspaper actually. He's, like, standing up all the time and jumping around."

June 11

Bono attends the funeral of Deirdre Drew, wife of Irish folk legend Ronnie Drew of The Dubliners, at Greystones Church, County Wicklow.

June 13

Bono pays tribute to William Butler Yeats by reading poetry during the Josephine Hart Poetry Hour at the National Library of Ireland in Dublin. He reads three poems –

'The Host Of The Air', 'When You Are Old', and 'He Wishes For The Clothes For Heaven'. The event airs on RTE TV's arts show *The Eleventh Hour*. The Poetry Hour is a birthday tribute to Yeats, who was born June 13, 1865.

June 14

Following up on last night's poetry event, Bono does an interview this morning about the event on BBC Radio Four's *Today* program.

June 25

U2 contributes a cover of John Lennon's 'Instant Karma' to *Instant Karma: The Amnesty International Campaign To Save Darfur*, an all-star fund raising album released today in the UK. It'll be released on various dates in other countries.

June 27

Bono shares his admiration for outgoing UK Prime Minister Tony Blair in today's edition of *The Sun*. "What I admire the most about Tony Blair is that despite all accusations of a slick PR machine, spin doctoring and the like, he has almost all of the time exposed himself to bad press and outcry for doing the things he believed in," Bono writes. Today is Blair's final day in office.

June 30

Bono, Ali, Edge and Morleigh are in the crowd as R.E.M. plays a "working rehearsal" gig at Dublin's Olympia Theatre. They meet and sign autographs for a couple U2 fans after the show.

July 5

Bono and Edge are spotted at a Broadway performance of the musical, *Spring Awakening*.

July 6

Today's Bono and Edge sighting happens during lunch at the trendy Pastis restaurant in New York City.

July 7

Bono and Edge are spotted again in New York City, this time entering the Julian Schnabel building with what appear to be a couple real estate agents.

July 9

Bono is spotted hanging out with friends in Montauk on Long Island, New York City.

July 25

Bono is spotted partying at a St. Tropez nightclub with actress Penelope Cruz and model Helena Christensen. Bono meets 19-year-old British Princess Beatrice, who cautiously approaches him to say hello, and hip-hop mogul P. Diddy (Sean Combs), who asks for a photo with Bono and then keeps retaking it until he gets one he likes. But the media are more interested in paparazzi photos of Bono and Cruz holding hands as they leave the club at about 4 a.m.

July 26

Bono and Cruz are seen again this morning in St. Tropez, this time with Ali and the Hewson kids. But Bono and Cruz are again caught holding hands in photos at the Club 55 harbour beach. The pictures immediately spark rumours that Bono and Cruz are romantically involved and that Bono's 25-year-marriage is on the rocks. The reality, though, is quite different, as Cruz explains later:

Penelope Cruz lashes out at the press, July 26

"I went on holiday to Bono's house with his wife and kids. We were walking along, holding hands because we're very good friends, and do you know what the paparazzi did to us? They took photos and cropped out Bono's wife and children. So they made up a story about us being together."

July 27

Bono and Ali fly from Nice to Arteixo, Spain, where they spend a couple hours visiting the Inditex Group factory and its owner, Amancio Ortega. Bono and Ali reportedly ask about the working conditions at Inditex, and the countries where Inditex does business. The press speculates about a future collaboration between Inditex and Ali's Edun clothing line.

July 30

Bono and Ali attend a Wyclef Jean party in St. Tropez.

August 1

Bono appears in *Respect Yourself: The Stax Records Story* on PBS, a documentary about the legendary soul record labels' performers.

August 7

Bono helps Edge celebrate his 46th birthday a day early at a party in St. Tropez.

August 10

Newspapers report that Larry has teamed with actor Colin Farrell to purchase a new apartment building in Bolton, England.

August 23

Bono and family are on vacation in Italy. Having already visited the Aeolian Islands and the island of Ortigia, Bono is seen tonight at the St. Catherine Hotel in Amalfi, Italy.

August 25

Bono, Ali and the Hewson family are spotted on a yacht off Naples, Italy.

August 30

Edge attends a fund raising golf outing and dinner put on by the Children's Leukemia Research Project in Dublin.

September 2

Bono attends a charity event honouring Nelson Mandela at the Hotel de Paris in Monaco. Meanwhile, Edge is the celebrity guest at the Mencap Northern Ireland "Race Day" fund raiser at Curragh Racecourse outside

Dublin. The event raises money to help people with learning disabilities.

September 3
Bono helps to dedicate a "Coexist" peace fountain in St Jean Cap Ferrat, France. He spends time with former UK Prime Minister Tony Blair and his wife, Cherie, as guests on board a yacht owned by billionaire Bernard Arnault.

September 4
Edge attends the GQ Men of the Year Awards in London. Bono is ranked number 10 in *USA Today*'s list of the Top 25 Most Influential People of the last 25 years.

September 6
Opera star Luciano Pavarotti dies this morning at home in Italy after a fight with pancreatic cancer. He was 71. Bono does interviews with BBC Radio in the UK and ABC-TV in the US, among others, sharing his thoughts and memories about his work and friendship with the tenor. Bono reveals that he spoke with Pavarotti last week, and had planned to visit him this week. But Pavarotti's wife, Nicoletta, says visiting isn't a good idea. On the night before her husband's death, Nicoletta texts a message to Bono asking for prayers, saying Pavarotti is in his final hours.

September 8
Bono and Ali, Edge and Morleigh, and Paul McGuinness attend the

Above: Edge and his cousin, Ciara Evans (fourth from left), with friends at the races, September 2.

funeral of Luciano Pavarotti in Modena, Italy.

September 12
Bono is named Celebrity of the Year by the Malaria Foundation International for his efforts to raise awareness of the disease.

September 14
The soundtrack to *Across The Universe* is released today in North America. Bono sings 'I Am The Walrus' with the band Secret Machines, and 'Lucy In The Sky With Diamonds'. The album will be released in other countries over the next few weeks.

London's *Daily Mail* reports that Adam has outbid model Kate Moss for a seven-bedroom home in northwest London. The paper says Adam's offer of £12.5 million is more than double the asking price. His neighbours on the exclusive street include Chrissie Hynde, Annie Lennox and Sir Richard Branson.

September 15
Bono and Ali are seen attending a polo match at Phoenix Park in Dublin.

September 23
Bono introduces Japanese architect Tadao Ando during a public lecture on architecture at the Royal Dublin Showgrounds in Dublin. "Tadao Ando didn't just find a voice, he found a language," Bono tells the

crowd. "Awe is a word to describe Ando's work – he's simply awesome."

September 26
Bono and Edge make a surprise appearance at the London premiere of *Across The Universe*, a Beatles-inspired musical set in the Sixties. Bono acts and sings in the film, playing the psychedelic Dr. Robert character.

September 27
Bono and DATA are honoured with the prestigious 2007 Liberty Medal at the National Constitution Center in Philadelphia. In a 15-minute acceptance speech, Bono encourages the crowd to use "our science, your technology, your creativity. America has so many great answers to offer. We can't fix all the world's problems. But the ones we can, we must." Former President George H.W. Bush presents Bono's award, prompting Bono to remind him of the phone calls the President never answered when Bono called during the Zoo TV tour. The Liberty Medal honour includes a $100,000 prize, which Bono says will be donated to DATA.

Before tonight's ceremony, Bono spends an hour speaking with the editorial boards of the *Philadelphia Inquirer* and *Philadelphia Daily News* newspapers.

September 28
Bono is in New York to meet with

Bono Remembers Luciano Pavarotti, September 6

"Some can sing opera, Luciano Pavarotti was an opera. No one could inhabit those acrobatic melodies and words like him. He lived the songs, his opera was a great mash of joy and sadness; surreal and earthy at the same time; a great volcano of a man who sang fire but spilled over with a love of life in all its complexity, a great and generous friend."

the *New York Times* editorial board and other editorial staff.

September 29

Bono and Edge attend the premiere of Julian Schnabel's film, *The Diving Bell And The Butterfly*, at the New York Film Festival. Later tonight, Bono is one of the speakers at "Giving – Live at the Apollo", a roundtable discussion at the Apollo Theatre on the state of youth activism hosted by former President Bill Clinton. Edge watches from the front row.

During a cocktail party before the Apollo event, Bono meets with Israel's Foreign Affairs Minister, Tzipi Livni. They discuss the Israeli-Palestinian conflict, and Livni invites Bono to visit Jerusalem.

U2's European Album Sales as of September 30, 2007
While the Recording Industry Association of America (RIAA) and the British Phonographic Industry (BPI) provide fairly detailed records on album sale milestones going back to the early 1980s, there's no such comparable detail on U2's European album sales. The International Federation of the Phonographic Industry (IFPI) began assigning Platinum Europe awards in 1996 for albums selling more than one million copies in Europe. Here are the IFPI sales figures for U2's post-1996 albums as of September 30, 2007.
Pop – 2,000,000+
The Best of 1980-1990 – 7,000,000+
All That You Can't Leave Behind – 4,000,000+
The Best of 1990-2000 – 2,000,000+
How To Dismantle An Atomic Bomb – 3,000,000+
U218 Singles – 2,000,000+

October 3

Bono makes the rounds on Capitol Hill. He's a guest at the weekly meeting of Democratic representatives and later meets with members of the Senate Foreign Relations Committee. While in Washington, Bono hosts a dinner party with a bipartisan guest list representing the White House, Capitol Hill and other Washington insiders. He gives a speech encouraging everyone to continue their support for AIDS and poverty relief.

October 5

Bono does an interview at his New York apartment with Anthony DeCurtis, who's working on a feature for the upcoming third 40th anniversary issue of *Rolling Stone*.

October 6

Bono returns to the New York Film Festival to see the film, *No Country For Old Men*.

In Dublin, the Four5One design team presents *Stealing Hearts at a Traveling Show*, its exhibition of U2 artwork over the years that was first presented in 2003 at the Rock and Roll Hall of Fame and Museum. During a Q&A session with U2 fans, Steve Averill says U2 is working on two separate album projects right now: a Passengers-style album with Brian Eno and Daniel Lanois, and a separate U2 album.

October 8

Paul McGuinness denies recent tabloid rumours that Bono has written a song for the Spice Girls to sing on their upcoming greatest hits album.

October 10

Bono attends the Elevation Partners annual meeting at St. Regis Resort south of Los Angeles.

U2 fans online receive survey invitations from Live Nation, a spin-off company that was formerly the concert promotion arm of Clear Channel Communications. In the e-mail, Live Nation says: "We want to hear your thoughts and experiences about U2. Your feedback helps us to create unforgettable live music

experiences for you, the fan." Questions address the cost of U2 concert tickets, as well as seating preferences and the stadium/arena debate.

October 15/16

Larry plays drums on 'Boy, Boy, Boy', a track on the new Underworld album released today, *Oblivion With Bells*.

October 16

Bono gives a speech at the annual convention of the Mortgage Bankers Association in Boston.

October 17

Bono is on hand to see Bruce Springsteen & the E Street Band play Madison Square Garden.

October 19

U2.com confirms recent reports that U2 will release a remastered, 20th anniversary edition of *The Joshua Tree* later this year. The album will be released in four formats, including a box set with DVD that will include the never-before-seen promo video for 'Red Hill Mining Town'.

October 23

Edge offers an exclusive video and ringtone during the annual meeting of the Cellular Telecommunications Industry Association in San Francisco. He's helping the CTIA promote the availability of video content on mobile phones.

In New York, Bono is spotted with artist Damien Hirst. They're planning a Product (RED) charity art auction that Hirst is helping organise for early 2008.

October 25

Bono and Ali attend the annual Black Ball Concert in New York organised by Alicia Keys' Keep A Child Alive foundation. The foundation honours Bono for his humanitarian efforts in Africa. Bono gives an acceptance speech and sings 'Don't Give Up' with Keys.

October 26

Bono hosts a private screening of *Control*, Anton Corbijn's film about

Joy Division, for a small group of friends and associates in New York.

October 27
Bono dons an ape mask at a Halloween party in the TriBeCa area of New York City. Paparazzi catch him playing with Ed Burns' and Christy Turlington's son, Finn.

October 29
Edge sees Bruce Springsteen & the E Street Band play at the L.A. Sports Arena.

DATA and the ONE Campaign announce plans to merge into a single organization fighting against AIDS and extreme poverty, especially in Africa. Bono explains the merger: "ONE and DATA are two organisations with the same outrage: extreme, stupid poverty in the 21st century makes no sense when the resources and technology exist to do something about it. What makes sense is to harness these two forces into a single organisation and redouble our efforts. One goal, One team."

October 30
Bono gives a speech at the Claremont Colleges near Los Angeles.

November
Early in the month, Bono records a new vocal for an old song, 'Wave Of Sorrow (Birdland)', which will appear soon on the 20th anniversary release of *The Joshua Tree*. The song is an outtake from the *Joshua Tree* recording sessions that U2 felt was too good to use as a B-side (see January 1987).

After the song is complete, Bono sings and explains the lyric in a video clip posted on U2.com on November 9.

November 1
Bono visits New York Mayor Michael Bloomberg at City Hall – at the mayor's invitation – to discuss humanitarian issues and philanthropy. "What I'm interested in is not just his cash, but his intellect, and how his business acumen could be used to work for the world's poor," Bono tells reporters afterward. He also visits

NBC Studios to tape an interview with Brian Williams about progress in Africa. The interview will air a day later on the NBC Nightly News. While at NBC, Bono also tapes a few lines that will be used on *Saturday Night Live* this weekend.

November 2
Bono attends the annual YouthAIDS benefit gala in McLean, Virginia. He's there to talk about the fight against AIDS in Africa, and to present US Representative Nancy Pelosi with the YouthAIDS Outstanding Achievement Award. Bono's friend, actress Ashley Judd, works with YouthAIDS and hosts the event.

November 3/4
Bono and Edge are guests at a birthday party in London for Irish property mogul Derek Quinlan, who's one of the investors in the Clarence Hotel.

On November 3, Bono makes a brief appearance on NBC's *Saturday Night Live*, speaking a couple pre-recorded lines during a segment with NBC news anchor Brian Williams.

Edge appears in *Amazing Journey: The Story Of The Who*, a new documentary that premieres on VH1.

November 8
Edge appears on Zane Lowe's BBC

Edge on Led Zeppelin

"At the time that punk rock happened, they were at the top of the list of bands that had to be seen off. But the dust has settled on their legacy, and listening back at this point it's clear that they've made an immense impact."

Radio 1 show, singing the praises of Led Zeppelin during a tribute to their *Led Zeppelin IV* album.

November 12
U2 spend this week in their Dublin studios working on new material with Brian Eno and Daniel Lanois. By the end of the week, fans see studio staff removing much of the band's gear. Adam tells the fans this is U2's last week of recording for the year.

French rocker Johnny Hallyday's new album out today, *Le Couer d'Un Homme*, features a song with lyrics written by Bono: 'I Am The Blues'.

Another release available today, the XO laptop computer, features a contribution from Edge: he's created a custom start-up sound for the unique computer, which is part of the One Laptop Per Child effort to increase educational opportunities in developing countries.

November 13
U2 share their video of Bono explaining the *Joshua Tree* outtake, 'Wave Of Sorrow (Birdland)' with the online music service, iLike, which in turn distributes the clip via the ultra-popular social networking site, Facebook. Within days, more than 2,000 fans comment on the Facebook video page. Some industry watchers wonder why U2 would partner with iLike, while others point out one possible connection: Marc Bodnick, a co-founder with Bono of Elevation Partners, is a board member at iLike.

November 14
Another day, another social networking/Web 2.0 outreach by U2. Today, the band shares the never-before-seen 'Red Hill Mining Town' music video on YouTube. The video will also be included on the upcoming special edition re-issue of *The Joshua Tree*.

November 16
Bono attends a Hunger Task Force meeting in Cork, and praises his country's contributions toward fighting hunger and famine in the Third World. Speaking to the press,

he also defends U2's decision to move part of the band's business out of Ireland to lower their tax bill.

November 17
Bono and Edge are given permission to demolish four historical buildings next to the Clarence Hotel to make way for a (EU)150 million revamp of the hotel into what Bono says will be "the most spectacular hotel in Europe". Conservationists and environmentalists are outraged by the Dublin City Council's decision and promise to challenge it in court.

November 20
The Joshua Tree is re-released in the US in several formats: a single CD, a double CD with rarities and outtakes, and a deluxe box set that includes a DVD. In Canada, many stores hold off on selling the album because they haven't received all three versions. A vinyl version is expected in early December, which is also when the full release will happen in most European countries.

November 21
Edge joins Ron Wood at the Euro 2008 qualifying football match between England and Croatia at Wembley Stadium. Afterward, Edge attends a private screening of Wood's upcoming DVD, *The First Barbarians: Live From Kilburn*.

November 22
U2 denies reports that they're planning to play a 14-show "residency" at London's O2 Arena in June, 2008.

November 23
Union Chapel, London. Bono and Edge make a surprise appearance in London, playing a four-song set as part of Mencap's Little Noise sessions. Their set includes the first live performance of 'Wave Of Sorrow (Birdland)', a 1986 track that U2 recently completed for *The Joshua Tree*'s re-release. Adam watches it all from the balcony.

November 27
Bono appears on the soundtrack album from the film, *Darfur Now*,

Above: Union Chapel, London, November 23.

which is released today. He duets with Stevie Wonder on a remake of Wonder's song, 'Love's In Need Of Love Today'.

November 30
Bono and Edge appear in a pre-taped interview during *My Night At The Grammys*, a CBS-TV special that counts down the best moments in the awards' 50-year history.

December 1
Bono and Larry make separate appearances to mark World AIDS Day. Larry is one of several celebrities appearing in TV commercials for Stamp Out Stigma, an Irish group aiming to fight the stigma against those living with HIV and AIDS. The TV spots were filmed in October at Hannay Studios in Dublin. Meanwhile, Bono appears on video today at the Youth Summit on AIDS hosted by Saddleback Church in southern California.

In Dublin, Bono appears in the flesh at a global warming speech given by former US Vice-President Al Gore.

December 2
A rare Ducati motorcycle that both Bono and Adam have owned is auctioned for £11,500 at the International Motorcycle and Scooter Show in Birmingham. The money benefits the Riders for Health organisation, which provides vehicles to healthcare

personnel in Africa and trains the workers how to ride safely.

December 6
U2 pick up two Grammy nominations: Best Pop Performance By A Duo Or Group With Vocals ('Window In The Skies') and Best Rock Performance By A Duo Or Group With Vocals ('Instant Karma'). The awards ceremony will take place February 10, 2008.

December 9
Bono attends the wedding of Google co-founder Larry Page on Necker Island in the Caribbean. Bono recites a poem for the newlyweds and does an impromptu performance with members of The Wailers, Bob Marley's former band.

December 10
Edge attends the Led Zeppelin reunion concert at O2 Arena in London.

December 16
Bono is in Omaha, where he visits with DATA board member Susie Buffett. Around this time, Bono also visits Hallmark headquarters in Kansas City – one of the newest companies taking part in Product (RED).

December 19
Time magazine names Al Gore one of the runners-up in its Person of the Year issue, which is published today. Bono pens a lengthy essay, saying Gore "is like an Old Testament prophet amped up with PowerPoint and an army of the world's scientists at his disposal".

December 22
Bono is spotted dining with Bill Gates in Seattle.

December 24
U2, Paul McGuinness and the Principle Management staff get together for a Christmas lunch party at Lock's Restaurant in Dublin.

December 26
Bono and Ali attend the annual Leopardstown Races in Dublin.

Acknowledgments

In some ways, I'm the last person who should be writing this book. I've never met U2. I don't wait before or after concerts to get their autographs. I don't hang around in front of the hotel when they're on tour. I'm completely uncomfortable with the typical band-fan relationship, and have no desire to meet them on that level. I blame them: I became a fan in the early 1980s, when U2 repeatedly told interviewers that the music was special, but the people making it were ordinary. I believed them.

On the other hand, this is probably the perfect book for me to write. I've been a U2 fan since 1981, and have seen every tour since *The Unforgettable Fire*. In 1995, I created one of the first U2-related web sites: @U2 (www.atu2.com), an award winning site which remains today the oldest, continually updated U2 site online. @U2 began with the goal of chronicling the band's history. It gave me a place to store all the U2-related newspaper and magazine clippings I'd saved up since the 1980s. I started a U2 history timeline on the site, and that came in handy when it was time to write *U2, A Diary*. The timeline gave me about 25% of the material in the book. The other 75% came from more than a year of late night and all-weekend research and writing sessions.

With that in mind, I have to first thank my wife, Cari, for pretty much running the house while I worked on this book, and my two, wonderful children for letting me disappear into my office when I probably should've been helping with homework or baths and things like that. (I promise to make it up by reading this book to you before bed.)

There are more than two dozen U2 fans who work on @U2, and I want to thank them for running the site while I went on hiatus to write. (I think the site was better in my absence!) Many of them also helped directly with this book. They're an amazing group of people, and I'm glad to count them as friends.

It's no exaggeration to say that this book wouldn't have been possible without the great response and contributions from the online U2 fan community. Donal Murphy in Ireland warrants a particular shout-out, for regularly doing research locally that I could never have hoped to do on my own. Thank you, Donal! Bjorn Lampe, Hans-Jurgen Becker, and Didi Reicht were very helpful throughout my research. Thanks also to my fellow U2 webmasters for helping spread the word about the book and encouraging their readers to help out: Caroline van Oosten de Boer, Matthias Muehlbradt, Cara Vox, Claudia Espinosa, Marie Kristensson, Kevin Dolph and others I may have missed.

I'd like to thank all of the fans who followed my progress and answered my questions on U2diary.com, including those who helped without leaving a full name. In the almost two years I spent writing *U2, A Diary*, I tried to keep a list of everyone who helped in some way with the book. Thank you to the following, and apologies to those whose names I'm missing: Marina Aira, Carter Alan, Barry Ankers, Ayaz Asif, Meiert Avis, Xavi Balart, Kathleen Barnes, Dennis Bell, Stuart Blessman, Bibien1, Deanna Blazejewski, John Boland, Steve Borgovini, Tincek Bradac Sam Boutros, Denise Burgess, Scott Calhoun, John Cheek, Mary Cipriani, Martha Class, Scott Cleaver, James Combs, Teresa Cook, Chris Coppin, Michele Coppola, David Cowan, Tim Cunningham, Derek D., John Daly, Morgan Daniel, Kevin Davies, Michiel de Boever, Michele De Masi, Chas de Whalley, Anthony DeCurtis, Michael DeWitt, Claudio Dirani, Kevin Dolph, Helen Donlon, Jean Dowling, Lynn Edelstein, Steve Eagles, Deirdre Elder, Jason Engel, Ciara Evans, Iqbal Faizer, Zory Falto, Sue Fell, Bob Ferrell, Erika Finch McCaffrey, Shane Fontayne, Brian Freeman, Tommaso Gastaldi, Amanda Gilligan, Olivier Giovanoli, Dana Graffeo, Miranda Greer, Julian Hall, Mike Hanrahan, David Greg Harth, Steve Harvey, Tamara Hawkinson, Jack Healey, Jamie Henderson, Joe Hebert, Ahmed Hernandez, Salvador Hernandez, Carmen Hernandez-Lara, Dr. Susan Hood, Harold Hoyle, Orest Hrywnak, Catherina Hurlburt, Ermanno Iannacci, Mick and Ellie James, Kaisa Kantalainen, Richard Kearney, Nigel Keough, Firas Khatib, Liz Kloepping, Tassoula Kokkoris, Richard Lamberti, Andreas Landstrom, Kent Langdon, Sherry Lawrence, Jacob Lee, Lisa Lee, Michelle Llewellyn, Raul Lufinha, Brian Madl, Marc Marot, Leticia Marote, Steve Matthews, Karine Maucourt, Beth Maynard, Declan McConville, Neil McCormick, Declan McNally, Liseth Meijer, Jerry Mele, Dina Wilson Mensing, Cédric Métrat, Kristina Morago, Niall Moran, Emmett Murphy, Eamon Murray, Eric Naulaerts, Nico, Elysia Nicolas, Valerie Nielsen, Tom Nolan, Frederic "Fredo" Noyon, Sean O'Connor, Sean O'Kane, Aidan O'Rourke, Angela Pancella, Gary Paterson, Scott Perretta, Rob Perry, Markku Pesonen, Jason Peterson, Virginia Pratt, Rarry, Todd Richards, Eric Risdon, Jaime Rodriguez, Phil Romans, Mike Rusiniak, Aaron Sams, Joe Sands, Jakob Sekse, Stacey Silliman, Fran Solomon, Susan Soshinsky, Erika Sparby, Jeff Springut, John Stark, Mark Stevens, Elsha Stockseth, Jon Stram, Maryann Stump, Jay Swartzendruber, Maria Teresa, Joe Tracey, Nonata Trevia, Christopher Trimm, John Tuohy, Josh Tyrangiel, Rajiv Udani, Astrid van der Vleut, Danielle Virgin, Derek Walmsley, Rob Wanenchak, Brian White, Willie Williams, Chris Wolf, Martin Wroe, Zbyszko Zalewski, and Jean (an angel on earth).

Thanks also to Chris Charlesworth for commissioning the book and editing me, Sarah Bacon for photo research and Stephen Coates and Henrietta Molinaro for the beautiful design. Thanks to Euan Thorneycroft for explaining all the details.

My research involved reading nearly every U2 book I could find, and well over a thousand print articles about the band. I visited more than 150 web sites while researching the book, including almost 30 U2-related sites. The following is a list of the books and web sites consulted for *U2, A Diary*.

Web sites

U2 WEB SITES

– @U2: www.atu2.com
– Achtung Baby Working Tapes Compendium: home.comcast.net/~sira/u2.htm
– Scatter o'Light: scatterolight.blogspot.com
– Three Chords and the Truth: www.threechordsandthetruth.net
– U2 FAQS: www.u2faqs.com
– U2tours.com: www.u2tours.com
– U2Wanderer: www.u2wanderer.org
– U2 New Zooland: www.u2newzooland.com
– U2tour.de: www.u2tour.de
– U2world.com: www.u2world.com
– U2log: www.u2log.com
– U2.com: www.u2.com
– U2town.com: www.u2town.com
– U2Place: www.u2place.com
– Interference: www.interference.com
– U2france.com: www.u2france.com
– Macphisto.net: www.macphisto.net
– U2 Setlists: www.u2setlists.com
– U2 Star: www.u2star.com
– U2 Station: www.u2station.com
– U2Achtung.com: www.u2achtung.com
– U2 PopMart South Africa: home.intekom.com/vasago/popmart/main.htm
– Aussie U2 News Log: www.lyptonvillage.org/u2/
– U2 Vertigo Tour: www.u2-vertigo-tour.com
– U2info.com: www.u2info.com
– Zootopia.de: www.zootopia.de
– U2 Interviews: u2_interviews.tripod.com
– U2.se: www.u2.se

MUSIC WEB SITES

– AllMusic: www.allmusic.com
– BBC Top of the Pops: www.bbc.co.uk/totp2/
– Billboard: www.billboard.com
– Black Market Clash: www.blackmarketclash.com
– Bob (Dylan) Dates: my.execpc.com/~billp61/dates15.html
– BP Fallon: www.bpfallon.com
– Brit Awards: brits.co.uk
– British Phonographic Industry: www.bpi.co.uk
– Bruce Setlists:
www.brucesetlists.com
– Captain Beefheart Radar Station: www.beefheart.com
– CrackedActor.com: www.crackedactor.com
– David Bowie Wonderworld: www.bowiewonderworld.com
– Dry County: www.drycounty.com
– Duran Duran Slovakia: www.duranduran.sk
– Every Hit: www.everyhit.co.uk
– Exclaim!: www.exclaim.ca
– Fresh-Lyrics.com: www.fresh-lyrics.com
– Gavin Friday: www.gavinfriday.com
– Gibson Guitars: www.gibson.com
– Gil Scott-Heron: www.gilscottheron.com
– Horslips: www.horslips.ie
– Hot Press: www.hotpress.com
– Hot Source: www.hotsource.com.au
– International Live Music Conference: www.ilmc.com
– The Intruder (Peter Gabriel fan site): users.libero.it/the.intruder/
– Irish Punk and New Wave Discography: www.irishrock.org
– James: www.wearejames.com
– Kelly Joe Phelps: www.kellyjoephelps.com
– Little Steven: www.littlesteven.com
– Lizard King's Duran Duran site: www.lizardkingduran.com/
– Meteor Irish Music Awards: www.meteor.ie
– Method Studios: www.methodstudios.com
– Michael Jackson Trader: www.michael-jackson-trader.com
– Moonalice Band: www.moonaliceband.com
– Music & Cinema Memorabilia: www.vinylandfilmposters.co.uk
– National Assn. of Record Industry Professionals: www.narip.com
– Neck and Neck: www.neck-and-neck.com
– Official UK Charts Company: www.theofficialcharts.com
– Pollstar: www.pollstaronline.com
– Prince.org: www.prince.org
– Radiohead At East: www.ateaseweb.com
– RamoneStory.it: www.ramonestory.it
– Recording Industry Association of America: www.riaa.com
– R.E.M. Timeline:
www.remtimeline.com
– Rock and Roll Hall of Fame: www.rockhall.com
– Rock On the Net: www.rockonthenet.com
– RockCritics.com: www.rockcritics.com
– RockList.net: www.rocklist.net
– Rolling Stones: www.rollingstones.com
– Rory Gallagher: www.reurie.nl
– Scatheweb: www.scathe.demon.co.uk
– Shane Fontayne: www.shanefontayne.com
– ShowBiz Ireland: www.showbizireland.com
– Simple Minds Live: www.simplemindslive.com
– Solsbury Hill: www.solsburyhill.org
– UKMusic.com: www.ukmusic.com
– Virgin Prunes: www.virginprunes.com
– Wire Train: www.wiretrain.co.uk
– World Violation: www.worldviolation.de
– WXRT-FM: www.93xrt.com

OTHER WEB SITES

– Access My Library: www.accessmylibrary.com
– AllExperts.com: www.allexperts.com
– Amazon: www.amazon.com
– Answers.com: www.answers.com
– Ask.com: www.ask.com
– Basketball Reference: www.basketball-reference.com
– Bepress Legal Repository: law.bepress.com
– Berklee College of Music: www.berklee.edu
– BFI: www.bfi.org.uk
– Bloomberg News: www.bloomberg.com
– Boards.ie: www.boards.ie
– BoxRec: www.boxrec.com
– Brush With Fame: www.brushwithfame.com
– Celebrity Mound: www.celebritymound.com
– Central Park Conservancy: www.centralparknyc.org
– CNN: www.cnn.com
– Curbed: www.curbed.com
– DATA: www.data.org
– Dotspotter: www.dotspotter.com
– Douglas Yaney Gallery: www.douglasyaney.com
– Eircom: www.eircom.net
– Emigrant Online: www.emigrant.ie
– EPGuides.com: www.epguides.com
– Farm Aid: www.farmaid.org
– FAQS.org: www.faqs.org
– Find Articles: www.findarticles.com
– Flickr: www.flickr.com
– Gawker: www.gawker.com
– GlobalSecurity.org: www.globalsecurity.org
– Google: www.google.com
– Google Maps: maps.google.com
– Greenpeace: www.greenpeace.org
– HighBeam Research: www.highbeam.com
– Images of El Salvador: mikeoso.homestead.com
– Internet Movie Database: www.imdb.com
– IP Law and Business: www.iplawandbusiness.com
– Joblo.com: www.joblo.com
– Just Jared: justjared.buzznet.com
– Massachusetts Institute of Technology: www.mit.edu
– Metroactive: www.metroactive.com
– Monaco Tourism: www.monaco-tourisme.com
– MVDBase.com: www.mvdbase.com
– MySpace: www.myspace.com
– Newscom: www.newscom.com
– No Maps For These Territories: www.nomaps.com
– Oxfam America: www.oxfamamerica.org
– The Pitch: www.pitch.com
– Planet World Cup: www.planetworldcup.com
– PBS: www.pbs.org
– Portfolio magazine: www.portfolio.com
– Rathfarnham Community Web Site: student.dcu.ie/~brennd22/
– Rec.Sport.Soccer Statistics Foundation: www.rsssf.com
– ReliefWeb: www.reliefweb.int
– The Simpsons Archive: www.snpp.com
– Stumped Magazine: stumpedmagazine.com
– Technology Review: www.technologyreview.com
– The Telegraph (India): www.telegraphindia.com
– Tour Egypt!: www.touregypt.net
– TV Barn: www.tvbarn.com
– The View from Fez: riadzany.blogspot.com

Books

USC Shoah Foundation Institute: www.usc.edu/schools/college/vhi/
– Valleywag: www.valleywag.com
– Wikipedia: www.wikipedia.org
– William Morris Lives Here: williammorrisliveshere.wordpress.com
– Wire Image: www.wireimage.com
– World Sites Atlas: www.sitesatlas.com
– World Vision: www.worldvision.org
– Worldwide Faith News: www.wfn.org
– Yahoo!: www.yahoo.com
– Ynetnews: www.ynetnews.com
– YouTube: www.youtube.com

I would be grateful for any additional information and/or corrections that can be used in future editions of this book. I can be reached via www.u2diary.com or www.atu2.com.

Matt McGee, January 2008

Stokes, Niall: *U2 In The Name of Love* (New York, Harmony Books, 1985)

Dunphy, Eamon: *Unforgettable Fire* (New York, Warner Books, 1987)

Parkyn, Geoff: *U2 – Touch the Flame* (London, Omnibus Press, 1987)

Williams, Peter and Turner, Steve: *U2 Rattle and Hum – The Official Book of the U2 Movie* (New York, Harmony Books, 1988)

Stokes, Niall: *U2 – Three Chords and the Truth* (New York, Harmony Books, 1989)

Graham, Bill: *U2, The Early Days* (New York, Delta, 1990)

Van Oosten de Boer, Caroline: *Gavin Friday – The Light and Dark* (Utrecht, Von B Press, 1991)

Alan, Carter: *Outside is America – U2 in the U.S.* (Boston, Faber and Faber, 1992)

Bowler, Dave and Dray, Bryan: *U2 – A Conspiracy of Hope* (London, Pan Books, 1993)

U2 – The Rolling Stone Files (New York, Hyperion, 1994)

Waters, John: *Race of Angels – The Genesis of U2* (London, Fourth Estate, 1994)

De la Parra, Pimm Jal and Van Oosten de Boer, Caroline: *U2 Live – A Concert Documentary* (London, Omnibus Press, 1994, 1997 & 2003)

Fallon, BP: *U2 – Faraway So Close* (New York, Little, Brown, 1994)

Taylor, Mark: *U2* (London, Carlton, 1994)

Flanagan, Bill: *U2 At the End of the World* (London, Bantam Press, 1995)

Graham, Bill: *The Complete Guide to the Music of U2* (London, Omnibus Press, 1995)

Negativland: *Fair Use – The Story of the Letter U and the Numeral 2* (Concord, CA, Seeland, 1995)

U2 – The Complete Songs (London, Wise Publications, 1999)

U2 – The Best of Propaganda (New York, Thunder's Mouth Press, 2003)

Chatterton, Mark: *U2 – The Ultimate Encyclopedia* (London, Firefly, 2004)

McCormick, Neil: *Killing Bono* (New York, Pocket Books, 2004)

Scrimgeour, Diana: *U2 Show* (New York, Riverhead Books, 2004)

Corbijn, Anton: *U2 & I: The Photographs 1982-2004* (Munich, Schirmer/Mosel, 2005)

Assayas, Michka: *Bono: In Conversation with Michka Assayas* (New York, Riverhead Books, 2005)

Gimarc, George: *Punk Diary: The Ultimate Trainspotter's Guide to Underground Rock, 1970-1982* (London, Backbeat, 2005)

U2 by U2 (London, HarperCollins, 2006)

Visconti, Tony: *Tony Visconti: Bowie, Bolan, and the Brooklyn Boy* (London, HarperCollins, 2007)